BY THE EDITORS OF

CONSUMER GUIDE®

1000s of PRACTICAL HINTS & TIPS

CONTRIBUTING WRITER AND EDITOR:
LYNN ORR MILLER

ILLUSTRATORS:
LANE GREGORY AND TERRY PRESNALL

FRONT AND BACK COVER ILLUSTRATIONS:
LANE GREGORY

Publications International, Ltd.

Louis Weber, C.E.O.
Publications International, Ltd.
7373 North Cicero Avenue
Lincolnwood, Illinois 60646

Manufactured in USA.

8 7 6 5 4 3 2 1

ISBN 1-56173-735-6

Library of Congress Catalog Card Number
93-84367

Lynn Orr Miller is a freelance writer and editor
who has served as a regular contributor to the "Know-How"
section of the *Chicago Tribune*. She is the author of *How to Retire with
More Money* and was contributing writer to *You and the Law,*
an American Bar Association publication.

CONTENTS

CARS
6

• New Cars • Used Cars • Selling Your Car
• Maintaining Your Car • Cleaning Your Car

CLEANING
40
• Your Cleaning Closet • Bathrooms • Bedding • Carpeting
• Fireplaces • Floors • Furnishings • The Kitchen • Windows

CLOTHES CARE
102

• Knowing Your Materials • The Basics of Laundry
• Ironing Timesavers • Eight Ways to Beat Stains • Caring
for Your Clothes

FOOD
154
• Stocking the Kitchen • Storage Tips • Dietary Guidelines for
Americans Age 2 and Over • Limiting Fat and Cholesterol • Handling
Foods Safely • Dairy Products • Fruit • Grains • Meat • Nuts • Poultry
• Seasonings • Seafood • Vegetables • All About Baking

MAINTENANCE & REPAIR
238
• Basic Tools and Supplies • Gates and Fences • Roofs • Walls and
Surfaces • Electricity • Heating and Cooling • Plumbing
• Drywall • Windows and Screens • Outdoor Gardens
• Pest Control

Owning a car involves a lot of work. You have to do research on what type of car to buy, and then find the best deal for your needs and the amount of money you can and are willing to spend. When you finally buy an auto, you then have to spend more time, effort, and money maintaining and cleaning it to keep it running smoothly and comfortably.

Few people have all of the necessary information to do this at their fingertips, and often feel overwhelmed when the subject of cars comes up. While all of this may seem very complicated, breaking it down into segments and dealing with separate questions as they come along can make it quite manageable.

NEW CARS

Car shoppers face dozens of decisions, including what type and size of car to buy. Keep in mind that small cars are generally cheaper to buy and to run, yet large ones tend to protect occupants better in collisions. Young drivers crave sporty cars, but not their high insurance premiums. Choosing a model with a good reputation for reliability and a low incidence of theft and accident claims will save money on operating costs and insurance.

Be flexible when deciding which makes and models are satisfactory. Having an alternate choice in mind can keep you from jumping into a decision that you may later regret. And always visit as many dealerships as possible before you put down your hard-earned money on a new set of wheels. Planning ahead can save time, effort, and money.

Shopping for a Loan

If you need to borrow money to buy a new car, you need to figure out how much car you can afford. This means that the first step in shopping for a car is shopping for a loan. Do

you have your eyes on a $20,000 car? A 20-minute session with a loan officer at your bank may convince you that you can only afford a $15,000 car. It's best to find this out at the bank, rather than in a dealer's showroom, where they can juggle numbers faster than you can count.

The typical new-car loan runs four years, and an increasing number go for five. Many dealers even write six-year loans on new cars. Banks tend to be conservative in lending money; they want to be sure you'll pay it back. Car dealers tend to be more liberal; they'll do whatever it takes to sell you a car. The following guidelines should help you in financing your purchase:

▶ Borrow as little as possible, and pay it back as soon as you can. Most people want a monthly payment that won't strain their budget. You may be attracted to a longer-term loan because it means smaller monthly payments than a short-term loan. But remember that the longer the loan, the higher the interest rate—and the more you'll pay in the end.

▶ A shorter loan—say, 36 months instead of 48—makes for higher monthly payments but a lower interest rate. Your car will be paid off sooner and you'll pay less in total.

▶ Now that the interest on car loans is no longer deductible from your federal income taxes, it makes even better sense to borrow as little as possible and pay it back as soon is feasible.

▶ Shop for the lowest price on a loan, just as you shop for the lowest price on your new car. Get a quote from at least one bank, credit union, or other lending institution. The "price" of a loan is the interest rate, expressed as an annual percentage rate, or APR. Besides the APR, you should also know the exact amount of your monthly payments and the total amount you will have to pay over the life of the loan. To compare quotes on loans, get all three figures in writing.

▶ Have loan quotes in hand when you go car shopping. That way, when a dealer offers to finance your purchase, you'll have a basis for comparison.

▶ See how dealer financing affects your total price. Although many manufacturers and dealers offer low-rate financing, their lowest rates are always on the shortest loans (two or three years). While that can save you money, make sure the dealer isn't making up the low interest rate by padding the price of your new

TAKE THE CAR-BUYING PROCESS IN STEPS

▶ Choose a model and options that suit your family's needs.

▶ Decide how much you can afford—or are willing—to pay. Most people must borrow money to buy a new car, which requires shopping for a loan. Be sure to include the annual cost of insurance in your budget. This can vary dramatically, depending on what kind of car you buy.

▶ Once you've settled on a car, shop at least three dealers to compare prices on the same model with the same equipment. Get written price quotes that spell out what options are on the car. Be on the lookout for dealers who appear to give the best service after the sale.

▶ Learn the value of your old car; then decide whether to trade it in or to sell it yourself.

vehicle. Compare your total price with and without the dealer's financing to see which is cheaper in the long run—the dealer's loan or the one from your bank.

▶ Don't shop for a monthly payment. If you tell dealers you can afford no more than $250 a month, they will write a loan to fit that amount—with a higher interest rate, more monthly payments, and more money in total.

▶ Investigate other ways to borrow. You might be able to get a loan from your auto-insurance company or on a life-insurance policy. Homeowners may be able to arrange a home-equity loan, although that is a more involved transaction. However, interest on a home-equity loan is generally fully tax deductible.

THE LONGER THE LOAN, THE MORE YOU PAY

Monthly payments and total paid for a $15,000 loan at various interest rates and loan periods:

Interest Rate	No. of Months	Monthly Payment	Total Amount	Interest
2.9	24	$644.05	$15,457.20	$ 457.20
2.9	36	435.56	15,680.16	680.16
5.9	36	455.64	16,403.04	1,403.04
5.9	48	351.59	16,876.32	1,876.32
8.9	48	372.56	17,882.88	2,882.88
8.9	60	310.65	18,639.00	3,639.00
12.0	48	395.00	18,960.00	3,960.00
12.0	60	333.66	20,019.60	5,019.60
14.0	48	382.56	18,362.88	3,362.88

▶ Think twice about credit life insurance, which guarantees that your loan will be paid off should you die. It's an option, like an extended service contract for your car, so don't let a salesperson or banker talk you into taking it. If you die before your car is paid for, it can be sold to cover the balance of the loan.

Dealing with Dealers

Once you've figured out how much car you can buy, you'll want to shop for a dealer. A car salesperson's job is to make as much money as he or she can on each car sold. Your objective as a consumer is to get the lowest possible price on the car you want. Car salespeople aren't on your side. They're working for an owner or manager who is pressuring them to generate as much profit as possible. It's your responsibility to make sure you aren't being taken advantage of or paying more than you need to. How can you spot the good guys? A businesslike attitude and willingness to cooperate are two valuable clues. Here are some others:

▶ Beware of advertising that screams "No Money Down!" and "Instant Credit!" Some dealers appear to be mainly in the credit business and may stock a large number of repossessed cars.

▶ Both dealers and manufacturers are promoting the importance of customer satisfaction. Nothing beats buying a car with a track record of reliability from a dealer with a good reputation for service. Pick a dealer as carefully as you choose a car—by investigation.

▶ Ask your friends and neighbors for recommendations: Did a particular dealer treat them fairly and courteously? If a problem occurred, was the staff helpful or indifferent? A quick, concerned response can be as important as what's actually done to resolve the problem. Was the car ready when promised, with the repair made correctly? Were they ever overcharged, or expected to pay for a part or service they didn't ask for? Would they buy from this dealer again?

▶ Ask your local Better Business Bureau about each dealer you plan to visit.

The BBB can't recommend a particular dealer, but it can tell you how many complaints have been lodged against a given dealer, the nature of those complaints, and how the dealer responded. BBB reports cover advertising, selling, and service practices. Your state's Attorney General's office or other government agency may also be able to tell you if a dealer is under investigation for violation of the Consumer Fraud Act or for odometer tampering.

▶ You should try to get dealers to "bid" for your business through lower prices. This works best in a very competitive market. Let them know you're interested in buying one of their cars, but also let them know you'll go elsewhere, or buy a different car, to get a better price or better treatment. If three or four dealers in your area sell the same brand of car, what else can they do to win your business except offer you a better price or better service? Caution: If you're after a popular model and only one dealer is selling that car in your area, he's in the driver's seat on price—not you.

▶ For a good deal, find a good dealer. While price is certainly important, it shouldn't be your only buying consideration. A dealer on the other side of town may sell you a car for $200 less than the dealer down the street, but may not give you the best service in the long run. A dealership with a reputation for good service and giving its customers the benefit of the doubt may deserve to charge a slightly higher price.

Smart Shopping

Even in a buyer's market, consumers have to be smart to get the best deal. Here are some tips:

▶ Arm yourself with as much information as possible about the car you want and how much it costs. An informed shopper is much less likely to get ripped off than one who buys without doing any research.

▶ Know what you want, but be flexible. That's not conflicting advice. Narrow your list down

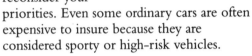

to two or three models that best suit your needs and your bank account, and then start to shop.

▶ If you're interested in a sporty or high-performance car, you may want to check with your insurance agent before buying. Some are subject to sizable surcharges that might make you reconsider your priorities. Even some ordinary cars are often expensive to insure because they are considered sporty or high-risk vehicles.

▶ Shop several competing dealers to compare prices on the same car with the same equipment. Get written price quotes that are good next week, not just today. Don't put a deposit on a car just to get a price quote. Instead, go to another dealer.

▶ Size up supply and demand for the cars you want. A good deal on a slow-selling car might be close to dealer invoice, while a good deal on a popular model might be close to full suggested retail price. There are no formulas for figuring this out. It all depends on the market conditions for that model in your area and how much competition there is among dealers. The only way you'll know if you're getting a good deal is to get prices from three or more dealers.

▶ Test-drive the car you finally decide to buy before you buy it. Think you want a 5-speed manual and a firm sport suspension? A 15-minute test drive might convince you to go with automatic transmission and a softer suspension. It's okay to change your color choice at the last minute, but don't choose engines, transmissions, or other major features until you've experienced them on the road.

▶ In addition to financing, dealers make money by selling extra-cost options such as rustproofing, "protection packages," and extended service contracts. Dealers pay very little for these and mark them up considerably.

LEASE VERSUS BUY

Leasing has become a popular alternative to buying, particularly since interest on car loans is no longer deductible from your federal income tax. The major advantage of leasing is that a large down payment isn't required, although some leases require a substantial initial payment. (These are sometimes couched in terms like "capital cost reduction.") Also, monthly lease payments are often lower than the monthly loan payment for an equivalent car.

Leasing, however, is usually cheaper than buying in the long run only if you can deduct automobile costs as a business expense. Consult an accountant or the Internal Revenue Service for advice. Leasing usually benefits those who drive less than 15,000 miles a year, trade for a new model every three years or so, and maintain their cars well.

Here are some common lease terms and conditions:

▶ Open vs. closed-end leases: A closed-end lease, also called a walk-away lease, simply lets you walk away from the deal at the end of the lease period. No additional payments are required unless the vehicle has serious damage or excessive wear. Nearly all leases written today are closed-end.

▶ With an open-end lease, you and the lessor (the agency that leases the car to you) estimate what the car will be worth at the end of the period. If the car winds up worth less than the estimate, you're responsible for the difference.

▶ In most cases, the amount for which you are responsible is no more than the equivalent of three monthly payments. Monthly payments are usually lower with an open-end lease, but the risks are greater. Best bet: Pick a car likely to hold its value.

▶ Monthly payments: Be certain of both the monthly payment and the total amount to be paid over the lease term.

▶ Mileage limits: Most leases specify a limit of around 15,000 miles per year. Beyond that, you have to pay extra (usually ten or more cents per mile). A lower mileage charge might be negotiable at the start of the lease.

▶ Security deposit: Find out how much must be put down at the start of the lease, and whether you have to pay the first and/or last monthly payment in advance. Ask who pays for state sales tax, license, and title fees.

▶ Insurance and maintenance: The lease must specify who provides insurance coverage and pays for maintenance.

▶ Early termination and purchase options: Before signing, learn whether you can terminate the lease early, and how much penalty must be paid. Find out if you can buy the car after the lease ends. The purchase price or method of calculating it should be specified.

▶ End-of-lease costs: You might have to pay for excessive wear or have the car prepped for resale.

▶ Shopping for a lease is no different than shopping for a car. Compare price quotes from leasing agents for the same car and terms. First negotiate a price as if you were going to buy the car. Then negotiate the terms of the lease. A 16-page booklet called "A Consumer Guide to Vehicle Leasing" is available from the Federal Trade Commission for 50 cents. Write:

Consumer Information Center
Department 406V
Pueblo, CO 81009

You can usually buy them elsewhere for less money. With most cars, you don't need to buy rustproofing because the manufacturer has provided ample corrosion protection.

▶ Keep your trade-in out of the new-car price. If you're thinking about trading in your old vehicle, get a written trade-in value after you get a price on the new car. Some dealers will try to lure you with the offer of a high trade-in allowance and then inflate the price of the new vehicle.

▶ Take your time. Don't rush to buy anything until you feel you're ready.

▶ Special-ordering the exact car and equipment you want is usually available only on domestic models. Import dealers can search other dealers for the model you want and can sometimes install or delete options once the car arrives, but seldom can they order a car from the factory. Even domestic dealers might be reluctant to order a car for you, which usually takes a minimum of six weeks. Even though they require a deposit, they have no guarantee you won't back out of the deal, leaving them with a car they might have troubling unloading. Dealers have a financial interest in getting you to buy a car that's in stock. They want to retire the loan they took out to buy the car. Storing the car is costing them money. In addition, rebates and other incentives generally apply only to vehicles "in dealer stock."

▶ If you're in the market for a minivan or larger car, you might want to first check to see if it will fit in your garage. Some larger cars may be too long, while some minivans may be too tall to clear the door opening.

Trading In Your Old Car

Most new-car buyers trade in their old car. It's fast and easy, and it also usually covers all or most of the down payment on the new vehicle. Because the new-car market is so competitive, dealers often make more profit on the resale of used cars than on the sale of new ones. So dealers have a strong incentive to offer you as little as possible for your car.

Try to avoid trading a car before it's paid for. The dealer will gladly pay off your old loan, use any residual value as a down payment, and write another loan for the new car—all at your expense and with ample profit.

Selling the old car yourself is likely to bring you more money. A dealer is going to give you wholesale value—or less—while you might be able to get actual retail value for your car, or close to it, by finding a private buyer. (See the section titled "Selling Your Car.") Additionally, keep two things in mind:

▶ If a dealer offers you an extremely low trade-in value for your old car, what should you do? You can argue that it's worth more, but it's not likely to be effective. You'll probably have to go somewhere else, try again to sell your car, or take the dealer's price. If you don't need the money for the old car as a down payment, then you're better off trying to sell it yourself.

▶ If a dealer offers you an extremely high trade-in value, then something's fishy. Car dealers seldom make mistakes like that. It's likely that they're picking it up somewhere else in the deal—the price of the new car, financing, or dealer-installed options. Check it out.

REBATES AND INCENTIVES

Cash rebates are sales tools designed to get the buyer's attention, but there's a lot of confusion about how they work. In most cases, a cash rebate *isn't* a present from the dealer. That $500 or $1000 rebate comes from the manufacturer. Now, what has the dealer done for you as far as cutting the price? Probably nothing—unless you point out that you want more of a discount beyond the manufacturer's rebate.

If there is a cash rebate, should you get the cash up front and use it as part of your down payment, or should you have the manufacturer mail you a check later? It's up to you, because there's no real advantage to either way.

When dealers suggest that you sign the rebate check over to them, that doesn't mean they're trying to steal your money. As long as you're satisfied the rebate is reducing the selling price, there's nothing wrong with letting a dealer get the money. In some states, if you sign a rebate over to the dealer, then you may not have to pay sales tax on that amount. Check your local tax laws.

An incentive is like a rebate in that it comes from the manufacturer, but it goes to the *dealer,* not to you. How much of that goes toward reducing the selling price is up to your negotiating skills. Keep in mind, however, that while rebates are usually advertised, incentives are not.

Closing the Deal

You probably thought you'd never get to the point of signing a contract, after all that haggling over price and getting a loan to fit your budget. Don't relax now, however. You still have to be on your toes.

BEFORE YOU SIGN

First and foremost, read the entire contract and be sure you understand what you're actually buying. The dealership isn't the best place to do this. The salesperson will likely pressure you to sign so he or she can guarantee a contract, a legally binding document that sets the terms of your purchase. Worse, you may be in a hurry because you're eager to drive off in your new car. But once you sign that document, it's difficult, if not impossible, to get it changed. Take the contract home, where you can go over it at your own pace. And don't be afraid to call the dealer if you have questions. If a dealer doesn't want you to take the contract home, get a written purchase agreement that spells out all the details. Once you're satisfied with the purchase agreement, it can be written into a contract.

The contract should spell out the following:

▶ Sale price: This is the amount you've agreed to pay for the car and optional equipment, plus any dealer-installed accessories.

▶ Dealer prep charge: Dealers are supposed to clean the car, install options and necessary fluids in some cases, and make sure everything works properly. On domestic models, dealer prep is included in the dealer invoice price; don't let them charge you for it. If you're buying an import where a preparation charge is listed, try to negotiate it out of the deal. In every case, inspect the car before you drive it off the lot to be sure that it actually was "prepped" and not just washed.

▶ Down payment: How much you have to pay up front in cash and/or your trade-in.

▶ Trade-in value: This is the amount you're getting for your old car if you're trading it in.

This often covers most or all of the down payment. Trade-ins give dealers plenty of room for manipulation, so know how much you're getting and whether it's an equitable amount.

▶ Destination charge: Sometimes called freight, this is the cost of shipping the car to the dealer. It's listed as a separate item on the window sticker (the official Monroney sticker, not the dealer's). There is no discount to dealers; they pay the same amount listed on the factory price sticker. Don't pay this charge twice; some dealers hide the destination charge in the sale price and then add it again as a separate item, pocketing the money. Beware!

▶ Sales tax: Sales-tax rates vary with locality. In some states they are calculated on the net

WINDOW STICKER SMARTS

Federal law requires that all cars sold in the U.S. have what is officially called a Monroney sticker, but is commonly referred to as the "window sticker." It's required to show:

▶ The manufacturer's suggested retail price for the vehicle and all its factory-installed options.

▶ A destination charge for shipping from final assembly point (or port of importation) to the dealer.

▶ EPA fuel economy estimates.

This law does not apply to light trucks, which include passenger vans and most 4-wheel-drive vehicles.

Most dealers add a second window sticker that lists accessories installed at the dealership, as well as various other charges. Many are bogus, typically including:

▶ Rustproofing: Most manufacturers advise against additional rustproofing. A car backed by a 6-year/100,000-mile corrosion warranty

doesn't need extra-cost treatment.

▶ Protection packages: These usually consist of dealer-applied paint sealers and fabric protectors, often in addition to rustproofing. They are of little or no value or duplicate substances applied at the factory or those you can apply for a fraction of this cost.

▶ Burglar alarms: Useful, but investigate whether you can buy a better alarm for less somewhere else.

▶ Dealer prep charge: Domestic manufacturers include this expense in the price of the car; some imports—but not all—also include prep in the price.

▶ Documentary fees: These ostensibly cover the cost of the dealer's paperwork and getting the title transferred into your name. Except for normal state title and license fees, these expenses are part of the dealer's cost of doing business

and should not be borne by the consumer. Some states now limit documentary fees dealers can charge because of past abuses.

▶ Ocean freight; currency valuation fee; import tariff; market value adjustment: We aren't making these up. Dealers have invented such fees and similar-sounding charges. None are legitimate.

▶ Challenge everything you see on a dealer's window sticker that doesn't look proper or you don't want—before you sign the contract. The dealer won't take them off? Then don't sign the contract.

price after your trade-in value has been deducted. Most states levy sales tax on the full purchase price of the new vehicle. Check with your state or local governments to determine how sales tax is assessed in your area.

▶ Total cost: Be sure the all-important "bottom line" is filled in, so you know your total price including options, accessories, destination charge, dealer prep, and taxes. Don't let a dealer leave this blank, because you can end up paying a lot more than you bargained for.

▶ Loans: Federal regulations require lenders to disclose all charges to borrowers. Be sure you know how much you're actually borrowing, the interest rate (expressed as Annual Percentage Rate, or APR), what your monthly payment will be, the length of the loan (48 months, for example), and the total amount of money you will pay over the course of the loan.

BEFORE YOU DRIVE AWAY

Don't succumb to new-car fever. Inspect the vehicle thoroughly. Cars can be damaged in transit, and dealer prep work isn't always perfect. Here are some suggestions:

▶ Take delivery in daylight. Artificial light can hide scratches or blemishes.

▶ Make sure it's the car you paid for. Compare the Vehicle Identification Number (VIN) and the information on the window sticker to the title and all other documents.

▶ Is every option you've purchased listed on the window sticker? Are they all on the car and in working order?

▶ Inspect paint, trim, and body panels. Look for evidence of body repair, such as a color mismatch; glass fragments on the floor; and loose or missing pieces.

▶ See that doors, hood, and trunk lid open and close easily.

▶ Check for such items as the spare tire and jack, cigar lighter, and (most important) the owner's manual.

Before you drive your new car away from the dealer, make sure it is the car you paid for.

▶ Examine upholstery and interior trim.

▶ Be sure you know how to start the engine properly and operate all features.

▶ Do you have copies of all documents, including the bill of sale, warranty papers, licensing materials, etc.?

▶ Do you know where to go and whom to contact if service is needed?

▶ Do you have a copy of the recommended maintenance schedule?

▶ The contract should include details of any known problems, in case a minor flaw leads to something more serious.

▶ If a dealer-installed option isn't available at the time of delivery, get installation details in writing.

▶ ALWAYS test-drive the car before taking final delivery.

USED CARS

There are three primary sources for used cars: used-car departments of new-car dealerships, independent used-car dealerships, and private parties. Which is best? That depends on what you're looking for, how much time you have, and what you're willing to pay. As with a new car, you'll want to figure out what type of car you want, shop for a loan if you need to borrow money, and check out the dealers. But you'll also want to investigate the individual car more closely.

Checking Out a Used Car

While used cars are always a gamble, many people find that they get more for their money with a previously owned car. This is because, with rare exceptions, every vehicle loses value as it ages. Buying a used car can be more difficult, but the following tips should help make the job easier:

▶ Inspect in daylight. Artificial lights (and rainy days) hide too many defects in body metal. Faded paint looks glossy when wet.

▶ Allow enough time to make a thorough inspection, and take a test drive that's more than just a spin around the block.

▶ Bring a friend along. He or she may notice problems that escape your attention.

▶ Concentrate. Take your time, take notes, use checklists. Ask plenty of questions.

▶ Dress for the occasion. You need to poke around the engine compartment and get down on the ground. Bring a flashlight.

▶ Don't rule out a car because of minor problems that aren't difficult or costly to fix— or that you can live with. Concentrate on big defects.

▶ Be thorough, but discreet. Neither dealers nor private sellers appreciate shoppers who spend hours probing every little detail.

▶ Deciding what you want from a car will help you determine what size and model to purchase. If you're looking for economy, buy the smallest car that meets your major driving needs. Keep in mind that the more accessories a car has, the more likely it is to require expensive repairs.

▶ Check for body damage: dents, dings, scratches, rust spots. Also look for less obvious evidence that the car has been in an accident or is deteriorating. Stand back. Inspect each side, from front and rear. Wavy or rippled metal, uneven contours, crooked moldings, mismatched paint, and poorly fitted panels suggest body repairs.

▶ The fenders, doors, and other body parts of a car are often aligned through the use of shims. At the factory, these shims are painted the same color as the car. However, body repairpeople often use shiny, new, cadmium-plated shims, which should alert you to the fact that a used car has been in a collision.

▶ Corrosion usually first attacks the most vulnerable lower portions of the body: rocker panels, lower fenders, door bottoms. Bubbles along a molding suggest rust beneath.

▶ Get on your hands and knees 10 or 15 feet from the car at several angles. Does the car sit level? A corner lower than the others suggests a bad spring or other chassis/suspension woes.

▶ Examine the exhaust system. Peek underneath, but *never* crawl under a car that's held up by a jack. Surface rust is permissible; tin cans or tape wrapped around the exhaust pipe or muffler are not. If in doubt, tap with a metal instrument. A clear, ringing sound signals metal in good shape.

▶ Virtually all cars made in the past decade are supposed to have a catalytic converter. Make sure it's still there. (It's in the exhaust system between the muffler and engine and looks like an oblong roasting pan.) Converters are expensive, and a previous owner may have installed a bypass pipe that lets pollutants escape. In many areas, you must make certain the car will pass local emissions tests.

▶ Listen for loud, rumbling noises or hissing that may indicate leaks. If you smell exhaust in the car, something's wrong. While replacing a muffler is relatively cheap, the whole exhaust system can run $400 or more.

▶ Nearly all modern cars require unleaded fuel. Check the filler neck to see if the restricting plate has been punched out so a larger, leaded-fuel nozzle can fit. Leaded gas can quickly ruin the catalytic converter and oxygen sensor. If you see a locking gas cap, make sure you get the key if you buy the car.

▶ Although dealers must declare in writing that the odometer reading is correct, check for misaligned numbers—one sign of tampering. Worn or recently replaced pedal pads suggest high mileage; obvious signs of wear on the steering wheel, seats, or armrests do, too. Check lubrication stickers on the door jamb or under the hood to see that the mileage indicated is in line with the odometer reading.

THE FTC BUYER'S GUIDE

Federal law requires that every used car sold by a dealer must display a filled-in copy of a sticker called the Buyer's Guide. The Federal Trade Commission produces the window sticker, which states whether a warranty is included with the car, what type of warranty it is, and other information required under the FTC's Used Car Rule.

▶ Try to inspect the car when the engine is cold. If the engine is warm when you arrive, the seller may have been running it to hide starting difficulties or other problems.

▶ After the engine is warm, stomp on the gas pedal once or twice and look out the back for smoke coming from the tailpipe. Better yet, bring a friend along to watch. Blue smoke signals oil burning that could mean an imminent engine overhaul. Black smoke is unburned gasoline and reveals fuel-system problems that might be expensive to fix. White smoke that disappears after warm-up is normal condensation; if it persists, there could be internal coolant leakage—another costly repair.

▶ Never buy a car without driving it extensively first. No exceptions! If the owner or dealer balks, walk away. Get a license plate or other authorization for your test drive, but sign no paper; it could be a sales contract.

▶ If the engine didn't run well or it made suspicious noises during the test drive, don't fall for the old line that "it just needs a tune-up." Modern cars seldom improve magically with a quick fix. Maladies that seem tune-up related are often caused by major (and expensive) problems with the fuel injection system or valvetrain. Although it may indeed be something simple, who would try to sell a poor-running car when, for the price of a good tune-up ($50-$100), they could offer a smooth specimen? Tell the seller that you won't consider the vehicle until your mechanic takes a look at it. If he balks, you can walk away or you can gamble—but the odds won't be in your favor.

▶ Any car worth more than a few hundred dollars deserves analysis by a professional mechanic if at all feasible; the more expensive the car, the more you should try to make it "feasible." Unfortunately, getting professional help isn't always practical. Most private owners, and even dealerships, may have legitimate concerns about you taking their car to have it "checked out." After all, they are responsible for any damage done to or by the car while it is in your (or the mechanic's) possession.

▶ Ask to see any service documents (to verify maintenance). If none are available, find out the reason.

▶ If the dealer claims the vehicle was a new-car trade-in (especially if "bought and serviced here"), ask for the name and phone number of the car's former owner. If they give it to you (no dealer is obligated to reveal information about the prior owner), call and ask about the car's history and problems.

▶ Find out about the recall history of the model that interests you.

▶ Watch out for bandits in private sales. A few pose as private sellers but are really dealers without a license or lot.

▶ Auctions, estate sales, and government sales are for the knowledgeable buyer. You will rarely have the opportunity to give the car a thorough checkout before bidding or buying, and competition is keen.

USED CAR WORKSHEET

Use a copy of this blank worksheet to calculate costs for each car you're considering. Insist that the dealer explain any additional fees, and make sure the fees are legitimate before agreeing to pay them. Dealers and financing institutions must disclose complete interest-rate information and the total amount to be paid in interest.

Vehicle Make: _____

Body Style: _____ Model: _____

Selling price _____ Year: 19 _____

+ State and/or local taxes $ _____

+ License fees $ _____

+ Additional fees $ _____

Total purchase price $ _____

- Trade-in allowance $ _____

Total amount due $ _____

- Down payment $ _____

Amount to be financed $ _____

Interest: _____

_____ months at _____ percent annual percentage rate (APR)

Total amount to be paid $ _____

(_____ monthly payments of $ _____ each)

HANDLING SERVICE PROBLEMS

Service advisors need complete information to successfully fix a problem. Be sure the advisor writes down a complete and correct description of each problem you've noticed. Mechanics rely on that written service order. Later, don't leave until you're satisfied that all the work has been done correctly.

Ordering parts is a pain. Dealers can't stock everything, but many can be obtained overnight. Parts for low-volume makes and models often take longer—something to ponder when choosing a car.

Letting the dealer handle routine servicing, such as oil changes, may be wise. Regular customers tend to get more careful attention when a real problem appears. Your car will also be up-to-date in the dealer's records—a point in your favor if a serious flaw develops. Keep a detailed record of service visits, including all receipts. Always be prepared to:

► Provide full vehicle data (mileage, date of purchase, and Vehicle Identification Number).

► Describe the problem and what's been done to correct it.

► Explain exactly why you're displeased, and what solution you're seeking.

SELLING YOUR CAR

It's very likely that you can get more money for your car by selling it yourself than by trading it in. But most likely, it will take more time and may cause you aggravation. You'll have to determine your car's value, advertise it, and negotiate with prospective buyers. If you're still prepared to try it, the following tips should help:

► Determine your car's value. There are several ways to find how much your car is worth. 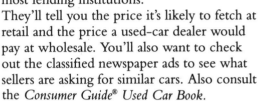 Used-car price guides (often called "blue books") are available at public libraries and at most lending institutions. They'll tell you the price it's likely to fetch at retail and the price a used-car dealer would pay at wholesale. You'll also want to check out the classified newspaper ads to see what sellers are asking for similar cars. Also consult the *Consumer Guide® Used Car Book.*

► Give your car a thorough cleaning—don't forget the trunk—and a wax job. A dirty car, like a dirty house, turns off many buyers.

► Make sure your car is in good working condition if you want top price.

► Write a history of your car for prospective buyers. Include: purchase date; number of owners; why you are selling it; repair history; whether it's been in an accident; whether the body has been repainted or if it's had any rust; where it was driven (highway versus short trips); and where regular maintenance was done. Your prospective buyer will be impressed with your diligence, and you'll

HOW TO READ THE ADS

Both private sellers and dealers advertise in newspapers and in free "shopper" publications. Ads are also posted in laundromats, supermarkets, and workplaces. An ad without an asking price typically suggests the seller has a high figure in mind. Here's a look at the most common terms and abbreviations:

A/C, air—air conditioning.

AT, auto—automatic transmission.

Cherry—excellent condition.

Clean—usually a well-kept car in very good condition, although one person's "good" is another's mediocre.

Fac.—factory-installed accessory.

Ext. warr.—extended warranty (actually an insurance policy).

Fact. warr.—factory warranty, which might be transferrable to the next owner.

Firm—stated price not open to bargaining. Many sellers turn out to be flexible, however.

Full pwr., Loaded—equipped with all common power accessories including power steering, brakes, and windows. Probably pricey.

Gar. kept—garage kept; if true, generally means that a car is in above-average condition. But a heated garage can actually accelerate rust because road salt suspended in snow and slush eats into a car's finish faster when subjected to frequent temperature changes.

Gd. transp.—good transportation; may be in acceptable running condition but otherwise dilapidated.

Lo mi—low mileage; generally good news, but a car that's spent most of its life making short trips may have exhausted more of its useful miles than one driven frequently on the highway.

Mechanic's dream, Handyman's special—euphemisms for a car sure to need much attention.

Mint—like-new condition; if accurate, the car will likely be priced high.

Must see to appreciate—suggests either a price far out of line or a truly superior example.

Must sell, Sacrifice—examine carefully; the owner may really be moving out of town, but could be trying to unload a lemon.

Needs work—look only if you're mechanically adept.

New paint—how much body work does it cover up, and why would it be needed on a late-model vehicle?

No rust—remember that the most serious rusting could be on the car's underside.

OBO—or best offer; owner has little hope of getting the asking price.

One owner, Orig. owner—as a rule, the best car to get, provided the sole owner has been a careful one.

PB, PS—power brakes and steering.

PDL, PL—power door locks.

Private—private seller. Remember, some shady professional dealers represent themselves as private in classified ads.

Rblt.—usually, a rebuilt engine or transmission.

Runs good—probably doesn't look too good.

Tilt—equipped with tilt steering column.

20K—20,000 miles on odometer.

CAR EVALUATION CHECKLISTS

These simple checklists will help you organize your evaluation. Why not take copies along when you go shopping?

On the Lot

☐ **Body:** Look for dents, rust, ripples, wavy metal.

☐ **Paint:** Check for scratches, chips, blisters, mismatched colors, fading.

☐ **Glass (windshield, windows):** Look for cracks and scratches; roll windows up and down to check for proper operation.

☐ **Trim (bumpers, moldings):** Look for dents, paint overspray, rust, cracks.

☐ **Hood:** Check for proper alignment.

☐ **Trunk/hatch:** Check proper alignment of lid or tailgate; look for signs of rust; make sure spare tire, jack, and lug wrench are present and in good shape.

☐ **Underside:** Look for cracks, welds, rust-through, spring sag; check CV-joint boots.

☐ **Doors:** Should open and close easily, and be properly aligned.

☐ **Shock absorbers:** Perform the bounce test; look for seeping fluid.

☐ **Exhaust system:** Check for makeshift patches, serious rust, loose parts, catalytic converter in place.

☐ **Tires:** Inspect for minimum tread depth, uneven wear, matched brands, cracked wheels, and locking lug nuts.

☐ **Leaks:** Oil, coolant, transmission fluid, brake fluid, fuel.

☐ **Gauges and controls:** All present and working.

☐ **Hoses and belts:** Inspect for wear, cracks. Make sure they're all in place.

☐ **Filters:** Check cleanliness of air filter. Oil and fuel filters shouldn't look old.

☐ **Fluids:** Check condition, level.

☐ **Interior:** Upholstery, carpets, lights. No dangling wires under dash.

☐ **Odometer:** Look for misaligned numbers. Compare mileage reading to wearing surfaces (brake pedal, seats) and any oil-change stickers.

☐ **Lights and accessories:** All operate properly?

☐ **Engine:** Should start easily and run smoothly; check for odd noises; turn engine off and see if it's hard to restart.

☐ **Warning lights:** Should glow when ignition is first turned on, and go off once engine is running. Gauges should give proper readings.

☐ **Gearshift:** Operation should be smooth, positive.

☐ **Wiring:** Should be complete, unfrayed, with tight connections.

☐ **Smoke:** Blue smoke suggests internal engine problems; black smoke means carburetor needs adjustment, injectors clogged, or more serious fuel system woes; white smoke after warm-up suggests a blown head gasket.

Test Drive

☐ **Steering:** Car shouldn't wander or feel unstable; action should be smooth, without pulling to side; if power-assisted, turn wheels with vehicle at rest and listen for squeals from pump.

☐ **Brakes:** Should stop the car quickly without grabbing or feeling spongy; no pulling to side. Some brakes squeal when cold, but the noise should go away once the brakes warm up.

☐ **Automatic transmission:** Should shift smoothly and work properly in each gear, forward and reverse.

☐ **Clutch:** Action should be smooth; no slip or chatter.

☐ **Manual gearbox:** Should shift easily, without grinding.

☐ **Driveline:** Check for clunks, especially when changing gears or making tight turns; also for rattles, whine, and vibration.

☐ **Acceleration:** Should be smooth, responsive; no hesitation.

☐ **Engine temperature:** Be alert to overheating.

☐ **Ride:** Excessive bounce or sway suggests suspension problems, as do ominous noises over bumps.

☐ **Oil pressure/charging:** Indicator lights should stay off at idle.

become a better salesperson if you have the answers to their questions.

▶ Be wary. Weigh the extra money you might get against the chance you might be inviting strangers to your home to see the car. Also, there's the time you'll spend showing the car and negotiating price. There's no guarantee you'll even get any calls about your car. Even if people are interested, they might not be able to afford your price.

▶ Never accept a personal check for the car, unless the buyer is willing to let you keep possession until the check clears. It's easier to ask for a certified check.

▶ Avoid selling to friends or relatives, unless both parties specifically agree to not comment on the future performance of the car. You don't want to be reminded about how the car needed a new battery one week after you sold it at every family gathering for the next ten years.

▶ Have a bill of sale on hand, which must be signed by both parties, and witnessed, if at all possible.

▶ No luck? Be ready to trade in your car and get less money for it. However, don't tell the new-car dealer you're going to trade until you have a firm price on the new one.

MAINTAINING YOUR CAR

To successfully maintain your car you need to prevent premature wear and the problems caused by wear. This can be done through periodic inspections and replacement of wear-prone components, including the motor oil, automatic transmission fluid, coolant, filters, and various engine, suspension, and brake components that are subjected to rubbing, sliding, turning, pounding, heat, corrosion, or extreme pressure.

Your car's maintenance items should be checked and/or replaced according to the mileage and time recommendations in your owner's manual. You can also do some of these things quite easily yourself. If you're a typical car owner, you're probably spending hundreds of dollars annually on maintenance and repairs if you're paying someone else to do all the work for you. Many owners find, however, that they can save themselves money by doing at least minimal maintenance and repairs. Doing your own work saves you 100 percent of the labor costs and at least 40 percent of the cost of parts. Over the life of your car, these savings can add up to hundreds of dollars. In addition, you'll have the satisfaction of knowing you did the work—

and learned a little more about how your car works.

HANDLING THE BASICS
Setting Up a Shop

If you do not have a workbench, set up a makeshift work area near your car with a picnic table or a sturdy plywood panel supported on two trash cans. If you work outdoors, be sure there's an outlet where you can plug in a trouble lamp if your chores continue after dark. The following should help you set up your workbench:

▶ Keep a good flashlight in your auto repair toolbox. It is often easier, quicker, and more effective to use a flashlight to spot an area than a standard trouble light.

▶ You can save a lot of time and trouble by including a selection of popular-size nuts, bolts, washers, and lock washers, plus sheet metal screws, plastic and electrical tape,

penetrating oil, sealers, and other commonly used materials in your "shop" inventory.

▶ If you're making your first venture into do-it-yourself car maintenance, look for sales of

SIX STEPS TO SATISFACTION

Some cars just don't stay fixed. Some problems defy the experts. These are the steps to take when a long-term or recurrent problem develops:

1. After two fruitless visits to the dealer's service department, speak to someone in authority. Go up the management ladder one step at a time, all the way to the owner, if necessary.

2. The service manager should contact the manufacturer's service representative in case of any recurring problem. Other cars may suffer from the same malady, and the corporate headquarters might have details on an appropriate fix.

3. Consider trying another dealer's service. A fresh approach might help; however, some dealers may be reluctant to tackle something another dealer couldn't fix.

4. After all the mechanics run out of tricks, contact a customer-service or technical-support representative at the manufacturer's zone office. Their number—frequently a toll-free hotline—should be in your owner's manual. Jot down the names and phone numbers of all people with whom you speak.

5. Contact a third-party dispute-resolution program for mediation and, if necessary, arbitration.

6. Only as a last resort, consult a lawyer about possible legal action.

complete sets of tools. You can buy a basic set that includes most common sockets, open-end wrenches, hex keys (for hex head bolts), and other miscellaneous necessities for about $50. This way you can save about 30 to 40 percent as compared to buying individual pieces. Make sure you know whether you need standard or metric wrenches and sockets in order to fit the nuts and bolts on your car.

► If you are tuning your car and a fastener is difficult to remove, apply a little penetrating oil and allow it time to work. When you remove parts, arrange them in the order of removal and place them in a tray or other container so they won't get lost. This also eases reassembly.

► When checking the gap on a spark plug, use a round-wire gap gauge. A flat gauge can give you an inaccurate reading.

Tires and Tire Pressure

► To extend the life of your tires, make sure you rotate them periodically. You can choose whether to have the spare tire included in the rotation. Space-saver spare tires, however, should not be included in the rotation; they are designed only for emergency use.

► Never deflate tires because they indicate an overinflated condition when hot. When they cool, they will return to their normal inflation pressure.

BILL OF SALE

A bill of sale, whether typed or handwritten, is essential when buying from a private party. Keep the wording simple; include only the essential details. Make two copies—both the buyer and seller should sign them, and each keep a copy. Here's a sample:

Bill of Sale

I, _____
(seller's name)

(living at) _____
(address)

(hereby sell to) _____
(buyer's name)

(of) _____
(address)

one_____
(year, make)   (model)

automobile, Vehicle Identification Number _____

As Is and As Shown, with clear title to same, for the sum of $ ____
(dollars)

Signed _____ Date _____,
199_____
(seller)

Signed _____ Date _____,
199_____
(buyer)

▶ An accurate tire pressure gauge is a good investment that costs only a few dollars. Do not rely on the accuracy of a gauge mounted on a hose at the service station. Such gauges are frequently inaccurate.

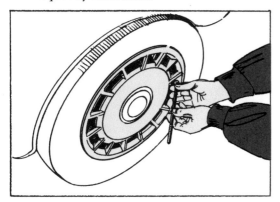

▶ Repair of a puncture should be performed with the tire dismounted from the rim. Any on-the-wheel repair should be considered only an emergency measure and should be corrected properly as soon as possible.

▶ If your car is carrying a heavy load or pulling a trailer, check the manufacturer's recommendations for increasing tire pressures for maximum load.

Painting and Body Work

▶ Rubbing alcohol on a clean rag works well for cleaning a sanded metal surface before priming.

▶ When applying primer to an area of metal before painting, do not attempt to cover the area completely with a heavy coat of primer. Best results are obtained by applying several fine, misty coats. The same applies to the first coat of paint used over the primer; after the first coat, you should still be able to see plenty of the primer through the paint. Subsequent fine, misty coats will complete the job.

▶ When applying primer from a spray can, hold the nozzle at least 12 inches away from the object being sprayed. If it's closer, you're likely to get runs. If you find that the primer runs, allow it to dry thoroughly, then sand the run with #400 sandpaper, wipe the area clean, and apply another coat of primer.

▶ After touching up the paint on your car, allow it to dry for at least two days. Then apply a little rubbing compound with a clean, soft cloth to rub the paint out. This will result in a more professional-looking job. Rubbing compound applied according to the directions on the product adds luster to the paint and helps it blend in with the older paint.

▶ If the nozzle on a spray can is clogged with paint, pull the nozzle off the can and soak it in paint thinner or another petroleum-based solvent to clear the passage. When the nozzle is clean again, replace it on the can.

▶ A shallow scratch on your car can be removed with rubbing compound on a soft, slightly damp rag. Using the tip of one finger, gently rub the compound back and forth—never in a circular motion—along the scratch until the scratch vanishes. Remember that rubbing compound is an abrasive that can remove paint and primer, so stop as soon as the scratch disappears.

▶ To make it easier to apply primer or paint to a chipped spot on the paint, cut a small hole about twice the size of the chipped area in a piece of thin cardboard and hold the cardboard with the hole a few inches away from the chipped area; then spray.

▶ An ordinary wax crayon can cover scratches on your car's finish. Match the color of the crayon to your car and rub it over the scratches. Buff the area with a cloth.

▶ Weather-strip cement can be used to resecure glued molding that has come loose

MAINTENANCE AND SAFETY INSPECTION CHECKLIST

Maintenance and Lubrication Recommendations

☐ **Weekly:**
- Check engine oil level.
- Check coolant level.
- Check tire pressure.
- Check washer fluid.
- Check headlights, taillights, brake lights, and other running lights.
- Check turn signals.

☐ **Monthly:**
- Check levels of automatic transmission fluid, brake fluid, and power steering fluid.
- Check battery water level (or charge indicator on maintenance-free batteries).
- Inspect drive belts, radiator hoses, and heater hoses.

☐ **Twice a Year:**
- Change engine oil and filter (every six months or 3,000 miles, whichever comes first).
- Lubricate chassis, door hinges, locks, and hood and trunk latches.
- Inspect suspension (ball joints, tie-rod ends, control arm bushings, etc.)

- Check differential and manual transmission/transaxle fluid levels.
- Inspect U-joints and CV joints.
- Inspect exhaust system.
- Check coolant concentration and appearance.
- Check air pressure in spare tire.
- Check operation of emergency brake.
- Check emergency flashers.
- Touch up paint nicks and minor rust damage.
- Wax car body.

☐ **Yearly:**
- Replace air filter and fuel filter.
- Check PCV valve.
- Inspect vacuum hoses.
- Inspect brake linings.

☐ **Every Two Years:**
- Replace spark plugs (30,000 miles average recommendation).
- Replace automatic transmission fluid and filter.
- Replace coolant.
- Replace PCV breather filter.

☐ **Every Three Years:**
- Replace drive belts.

from your car. Apply a thin line of weather-strip cement along the middle of the back of the molding and press into position. Make sure you position the molding correctly.

► Those decals and stickers some cities and communities require you to display on your car windshield can be a real problem to remove once they've expired. Make the task easier by using a sharp, single-edged razor blade held in a pair of pliers.

► Getting a bumper sticker off your chrome bumper will be easier if you soak the sticker with a petroleum-based solvent and use a plastic ice scraper to scrape the softened sticker from the chrome.

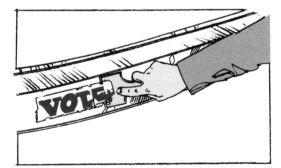

CHANGING YOUR OIL

There is probably nothing you can do on your car that can save you more dollars per hour than a simple oil and oil filter change. Changing your motor oil regularly is particularly important, because the protective additives in it are mostly depleted after 3000 to 4000 miles of driving. Once they're gone, wear accelerates quickly. Once you've become accustomed to the job, it can be done in about 15 minutes, which will save you $10 or more in labor costs. By shopping sales, you can also save money on the oil and oil filters.

Before you begin, however, make sure you know where to take the used crankcase oil. Recycling centers, service stations, and quick-lube centers often accept old oil. Call to make sure.

Tools and materials you'll need are:
▸ Oil filter wrench.
▸ Oil filter.
▸ Motor oil.
▸ Jack and safety stands or ramps.
▸ Wheel chocks.
▸ Oil drain pan.
▸ Wrenches.

Steps to Take

1. Start the car and bring the engine up to its normal operating temperature by driving it for 15–20 minutes. This gets all the contaminants suspended in the oil.

2. Slide an oil drain pan under the oil pan drain plug. The plug is located in the oil pan, which is directly under the engine block.

3. With the proper-size box wrench, loosen—do not remove—the oil pan drain plug by turning it counterclockwise.

4. Move out of the way so the hot oil will not drip on you or run down your arm as the plug is removed. Then, remove the oil pan drain plug all the way.

5. Allow the oil to drain completely out of the oil pan.

6. Replace and tighten the oil pan drain plug with the wrench.

7. Find the oil filter. It looks like a quart-sized canister. It can be located on either side of the engine, depending on your car. On four- or six-cylinder engines, the oil filter is often accessible from the top. But on most American-made eight-cylinder engines, it will be necessary for you to remove it from under the car.

8. Slide the oil drain pan under the oil filter.

9. To loosen the filter, you will need an oil filter wrench. Filters in use on today's cars are the spin-off type—that is, they go on and come off just like a nut. Remove the oil filter by slipping the oil filter wrench around the body of the oil filter and twisting it off counterclockwise. It will be full of oil, so carefully tip it over into the pan.

10. Place a light coating of clean motor oil on the rubber gasket on top of the new oil filter. Make sure you have the right filter for your specific car model, and the correct amount and type of motor oil as specified in your owner's manual. If the filter is mounted in a fairly upright position, pour some clean oil into the filter until it is about ¾ full. This will help

build oil pressure faster when the engine is started. Then screw the oil filter onto its mounting. It should not be necessary to use the oil filter wrench to tighten the oil filter. Oil filters should be hand-tightened only.

11. Raise the hood of your car and locate the oil filler cap. It is usually mounted on a valve cover or on a round tube coming from the engine block.

12. Remove the oil filler cap and refill the engine with the correct amount and type of motor oil as specified in your owner's manual. Remember, because you changed the filter, you also have to replace the oil it contained.

13. Replace the oil filler cap and start the engine. Watch for the oil pressure warning light to go off in about 10 or 15 seconds. Do not race the engine. Caution:

If the light does not go off, shut off the engine and make sure you have remembered to put the oil pan drain plug, oil, and oil filter back in the engine.

14. Look under the car for signs of leakage from the oil pan drain plug and oil filter. Retighten, if necessary.

15. After the engine has run for a few minutes, shut it off. After five minutes, check the oil level on your dipstick. Note: Do not overfill. Using more oil than is recommended can cause just as much damage as not having enough oil.

16. Dispose of the used crankcase oil in a sealable container by taking it to a recycling center, service station, or quick-lube center. Caution: Do not pour it down the drain or into a storm sewer, because used motor oil can seep into groundwater supplies.

(Left) Slip the oil filter wrench around the body of the filter and twist it off counterclockwise. (Middle) Coat the gasket on the new oil filter with clean motor oil before threading the filter onto its mounting. (Right) Tighten the oil pan drain plug securely.

HOW TO SAVE GAS

When you save gas, you save yourself money, as well as do less damage to the environment. Try to incorporate the following into your routine:

Off the Road

▶ Get yourself ready to drive before you start the engine. Adjust the mirrors and seat and put on your seat belt and glasses before you switch on the ignition.

▶ Avoid warming up your car excessively. After 30 seconds of idling, even in the coldest weather, your car should be ready to go.

▶ Keep the fuel level above the "empty" zone, to avoid dredging up sediment that collects at the bottom of the gas tank. This can lead to inefficient engine operation because of a clogged fuel filter and gas line.

▶ Remove snow tires when warm weather approaches. The tread pattern and weight of snow tires make the engine work harder.

▶ Clear your trunk of unnecessary ballast—tire chains, sandbags, golf clubs, etc. A heavy car uses more gasoline than a light car.

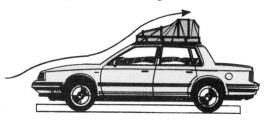

▶ Reserve your air conditioner for extremely warm weather. Use your air vents instead.

On the Road

Gas guzzling isn't restricted to big engines—some people manage to erase the savings of a fuel-conscious model by the way they drive. Here are some methods that can help you lessen the pain at the pump:

▶ Whenever possible, increase and decrease speed gradually. Gas is wasted when you suddenly floor the accelerator or slam on the brakes.

▶ When coasting down a hill or toward a stop light, keep the engine running but take advantage of gravity and ease up on the accelerator.

▶ Experiment with alternative routes to routine destinations. The shortest—and most economical—route isn't necessarily a straight line when stop lights and traffic jams interfere.

▶ Remove old spark plugs on schedule. If one plug out of eight is misfiring, you're losing an eighth of the engine's output.

HOMEMADE CLEANER FOR CHROME

Dip a moistened sponge into baking soda and rub it on the chrome. Let it sit for a minute, then rinse, and buff the chrome dry with a soft cloth. Use a synthetic scouring pad with the baking soda for particularly stubborn spots.

HOMEMADE CAR UPHOLSTERY CLEANER

Make a stiff foam by mixing $1/4$ cup white liquid dishwashing detergent in 1 cup warm water and beating the mixture with an eggbeater. Spread the foam over the upholstery with a sponge, using circular, overlapping strokes. Let it dry, then vacuum the soil away.

SAFETY FIRST

Accident Prevention

The word "accident" means both misfortune and collision. While no one can completely ensure that they won't have an accident, there are steps to take to minimize risks:

▶ Install reflector tape strips on the inside of your car doors. If you have to pull over to the side of the road or highway at night, these will alert motorists approaching you from behind in the dark.

▶ Always keep an emergency box in your car. It should contain a blanket, flares, small shovel, cat litter or sand, water in a plastic bottle, and a flashlight.

▶ Keep plastic gloves and rubber bands in your car to protect your hands if you have to tinker under the hood. Slip the gloves over your hands and sleeves and hold in place with the rubber bands.

▶ If your car door locks are frozen, hold a flame under the key for a few seconds and insert the key into the lock. The heat from the key should loosen the locks.

▶ If you don't have an ice scraper at hand, use a credit card.

▶ Keep a blackboard eraser in the glove compartment for cleaning off steamy windows.

▶ If you find yourself on the side of the road with a rusted jack and no oil can, take the dipstick from your engine and let a little of the oil drip onto the jack.

▶ Keep an old window shade in your trunk. If you have to change a tire, unroll the shade on the ground to protect your clothes from the dirty roadway.

▶ Don't smoke when working under the hood of a car. There are too many flammable liquids and gases around the engine.

▶ When cleaning engine parts, only use cleaners designed for the job. Never use gasoline or lacquer thinner, which emit toxic fumes. Both of these substances also have such low flash points that no spark is needed to cause them to burst into flame.

▶ Never carry a spare can of gasoline in your car—it could explode. An empty, clean can, however, could come in handy if you run out of gas and must walk to a station. A siphon pump might also come in handy.

▶ Keep change for an emergency phone call under the floor mat or in some other handy hiding place.

▶ Never crawl under a car that isn't adequately supported and never rely on the jack alone to hold it up.

▶ When purchasing a set of jumper cables, be sure they're equipped with a good electrical conductor, such as copper. Copper carries electrical current much better than aluminum and most other metals.

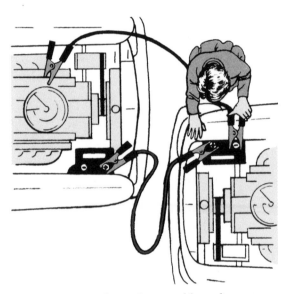

▶ Don't do anything that would produce a spark or flame near a leaky gas tank or fuel line. This includes using electric power tools, grinding, welding, or using a propane torch to loosen rusted fasteners. Fix the leak first, then do the other work.

▶ Wear protective eye gear when working under the car, when using a chisel and hammer, when drilling or grinding, and when working on the air-conditioning system.

▶ Avoid breathing the dust from brake linings and clutches. It may contain asbestos dust. Use a liquid cleaner, a vacuum cleaner, or an old paint brush to remove dust from brake parts.

▶ Never run an engine inside a closed garage. The buildup of carbon monoxide fumes, which are odorless and colorless, can be lethal.

▶ Don't open the radiator cap when the engine is hot. Pressure can spray hot water out of the radiator.

▶ Store antifreeze where children or pets cannot get it. It is poisonous. The same goes for brake fluid, gasoline, engine oil, transmission fluid, power steering fluid, and windshield washer fluid. If possible, store these items in a cabinet that can be locked and store the key on a ring high on the garage wall. This type of storage may be the easiest way to safeguard these items.

▶ Be careful to avoid touching spark plug wires or the ignition coil high voltage lead while the engine is running. Although the ignition system doesn't carry enough voltage to kill you, it could give you a nasty shock.

▶ Disconnect the battery ground cable first when doing any kind of electrical work, such as replacing a starter, ignition switch, alternator, voltage regulator, radio, etc. This eliminates the possibility of accidentally grounding the circuit and starting a fire or damaging some component in the electrical system.

Deterring Theft

More than 1.3 million cars were stolen in 1990, and that number continues to rise. Little can be done to stop a determined thief, but you can reduce the risk by choosing a car that thieves don't often target. While it goes without saying that you should lock your car when it is parked, there are other ways to protect your car from theft:

▶ An expensive radio in any kind of car invites break-ins. On the positive side, some recent models are equipped with factory-installed alarms, and some radios feature antitheft circuitry. If removed from the car, they won't play until a secret code is punched in.

▶ Avoid the removable roof panels found on some sporty coupes and luxury cars. Even with factory-fitted locks, they are relatively easy for thieves to remove and are often stolen.

▶ Try to park in a busy, well-lit area to deter thieves.

▶ Consider replacing the mushroom locks on your car door with tapered ones. They're more difficult for a thief to open.

▶ To prove ownership of your car in the event of theft, drop your business card or an index card listing your name and address into the window slot.

CLEANING YOUR CAR

Cleaning and maintaining the original appearance of your car may not be high on your list of favorite ways to spend your weekend, but it is time well spent. You can expect to receive at least several hundred dollars more at trade-in time or when you sell your car to a private individual if you've taken the time to preserve its good looks. Your car is a very big investment, and keeping it looking as new as possible protects that investment.

Exteriors

Salt, grime, sand, tar, and even residues from trees and leaves can ruin your car's finish, which protects the metal underneath. Think of the finish as your car's skin, and you'll realize why it's important to keep that finish intact to prevent corrosion. Keeping your car in a garage, particularly in cold climates, helps preserve your finish, but you also need to clean it regularly. In fact, your cleaning schedule will depend on how much you drive the car, how long it is exposed to the elements, and whether your car is exposed to salt spray. Regular cleaning also consumes far less time in the long run, because you can avoid lengthy car-cleaning stints caused by hardened soil. Because your car is composed of different elements, you'll want to clean these separately, as the following sections demonstrate.

Chrome

▶ Regular cleaning and polishing prevent rust and corrosion on chrome trim.

▶ Polish chrome after the car has been washed.

▶ Remove rust spots with a steel-wool pad or a piece of crumpled aluminum foil.

▶ Wax chrome trim when you wax the car's body. Use different cloths for the body and the chrome.

▶ Salt residues will pit chrome. Have your car washed frequently during the winter when the roads have been salted, and hose off any salt residues when the temperature is above freezing.

▶ After cleaning large areas of chrome, protect them with a coat of durable clear acrylic. This can be purchased in spray cans in auto-supply stores.

▶ Many commercial chrome cleaners and polishes are available. If you use one, follow the manufacturer's instructions for the best results.

Finish

Drive-through car washes are convenient, and many use the proper equipment and techniques to clean and protect a car's finish. Some, however, use strong detergents that can eventually ruin the finish. Washing your car yourself is a safe alternative to high-priced car washes. You can achieve professional results by washing, drying, and waxing your car by hand with the right equipment and techniques.

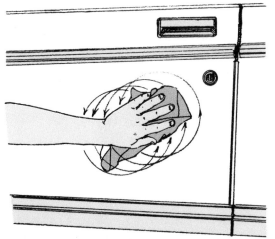

▶ Wash your car on a cloudy day or move your car to a shady spot. Washing or waxing a car in the hot sun or when the surface is hot may cause streaking and may damage the finish.

▶ Close all the car windows tightly before starting to wash the car. Thoroughly hose off the dust and loose dirt; brushing it off with a cloth or even your hand may scratch the finish. Use a garden nozzle on the hose that provides strong water pressure. Spray the wheels, hubcaps, undersurface of the fenders (avoid wetting the engine compartment), bumpers, and as far under the chassis as possible with a hard stream of water to remove dirt, mud, and salt.

▶ Use mild dishwashing liquid or professional car shampoo to clean your car. Remember that you are using cold water and will need to use plenty of detergent. Apply the cleaning solution with a clean, soft sponge, mitt, or cloth, scrubbing lightly where necessary. Work from the top down. Wash one area at a time, but keep water running over the entire car so that the dirt slides off rather than being scrubbed in.

▶ Use a cleaner, automotive polishing compound, or cleaner/wax on older cars to help rejuvenate dull paint.

▶ Rinse the car before the suds dry. You may have to work quickly to do this on hot days and in dry climates.

SPECIAL CAR-CLEANING HINTS

▶ Keep your car-cleaning supplies together in a storage box near the garage to make it easier to get started.

▶ To remove odors from your trunk, fill an empty coffee can with kitty litter and leave it in the trunk overnight.

▶ Remove tar deposits with a special tar remover. You can also remove tar, as well as bird droppings and insects, with a cloth saturated with vegetable oil. Hold the cloth on the dirty area until the material lifts off with gentle rubbing.

▶ Make it your habit to roll up your car windows whenever you park your car outside. If rain or water from the neighbor's lawn sprinkler leaks into your car and soaks the carpet, it is difficult to dry it out, and mildew can set in quickly.

▶ Most interior and exterior woodgrain trim is actually plastic. Clean these surfaces with a mild solution of dishwashing liquid and water. Rub the chrome trim that surrounds the wood grain with baking soda to bring up the shine.

▶ A child's crayon can be used to camouflage small scratches if you can match the color on your car's paint job.

▶ Carpet scraps make good car scrubbers and polishing pads.

▶ A vegetable brush makes a good tool for cleaning the grillework on your car.

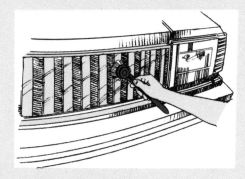

▶ When polishing your car, a soft-bristled brush will remove dried polish around trim work better than cloth.

▶ Dry the car with a soft, absorbent terry-cloth towel or a chamois to prevent water spots. Paper towels can scratch automobile finishes, and they should not be used to dry the exterior parts of the car except the windows.

▶ When water no longer beads up on the car's surface, apply a wax or polish, following the manufacturer's instructions. If dried wax remains around the chrome trim, remove it with a soft-bristled brush—an old toothbrush works well, too.

▶ If you've applied wax too thickly or let it set too long after drying, the residue will be difficult to remove. If this happens, apply a light dusting of cornstarch, which absorbs the dried residue without removing the wax finish. Then wipe it away.

Tires

Keeping tires clean can be a problem, particularly because various restrictions on the use of phosphates in commercial cleaners have resulted in some products that do not do a very good job. Regular cleaning can help you as much as the choice of product.

▶ Wash tires and hubcaps after the rest of the car has been washed. Hose them with a hard stream of water to remove loose dirt before scrubbing. Use a special tire brush or a large sponge to remove soil and pebbles from the tires and the spokes of the hubcaps.

▶ Tires can be cleaned with all-purpose cleaners, steel-wool soap pads, and special whitewall cleaners. A synthetic scouring pad should be used to remove black scuff marks from whitewalls. Alloy hubcaps must be treated especially gently.

▶ Trisodium phosphate will remove any stain from a whitewall tire, but if phosphates are banned in your area, or if you prefer not to use them, substitute an abrasive household cleaner. Apply it with a damp cloth and use a scrub brush to work it into discolored areas of the whitewall. Rinse with clean water.

▶ Coat the cleaned tires with a special rubber protectant to help maintain a shiny appearance and to minimize rubber deterioration. Self-polishing floor wax will also make tires shine.

Vinyl Car Tops

Some cars have decorative vinyl tops, which require special cleaning products to keep them looking good for a long time. Here's how you can do it:

▶ Scrub the vinyl top with a soft-bristled brush and a mild cleaner to get soil out of the grain. Many commercial products are available to clean and protect vinyl car tops. If you use one of these products, read and follow the manufacturer's instructions. Do not use ordinary car wax.

Windows and Windshields

Clean windows can save your life, as well as the life of your car. To ensure good visibility, keep your car windows clean and your windshield wipers in good operating condition.

▶ Clean all exterior glass and plastic windows each time you refuel your car. Use a synthetic scouring pad to remove stubborn street grime and bugs.

▶ Make sure that the cloth with which you wipe the windows is free of grit that can scratch the surface. Ideally, you should use only a full-skin, clean chamois; it will not streak and will not scratch the windows of your car.

▶ Each time you wash the car, clean the glass and plastic windows inside and out with a glass-cleaning product or windshield-washer fluid. Clean the inside of the windows with strokes in one direction and the outside with strokes in another direction; this makes it easy to find and correct streaks.

▶ To properly care for your windshield, always use specially formulated windshield-washer fluid and keep the washer jets clear and adjusted so that they spray onto the windshield correctly. Replace windshield-wiper blades when they begin to smear or skip on the windshield. The blades will last longer if you always wet the windshield before using the wipers.

Interiors

Carpets

It's almost impossible to keep your car's carpet as clean as your home carpet, because you rarely have a place to clean your shoes—or boots—before stepping into your car. By installing mats as soon as possible and replacing them when they become worn, you can provide some protection from dirt and grime. Still, soil inevitably accumulates in the carpet fibers. To extend the life of your car's carpets, try the following:

▶ Frequent vacuuming of the carpeting removes the grit and soil that can break down carpet fibers and cause unnecessary wear. Each time you vacuum the car, remove the mats, shake them thoroughly, and vacuum them.

▶ Spills in the car are not like spills in the house. When you turn a corner too fast and spill your morning coffee, you can't stop in the middle of traffic and clean up the mess.

But you should try to wipe up spills soon after they occur. Keep paper towels and a whisk broom in the car for emergency cleanups.

▶ When the carpeting in your car needs to be cleaned, use a spray or spray-foam carpet cleaner. Some manufacturers make carpet-cleaning products especially for cars. Read and follow the instructions for the best results. Vacuum the carpet after cleaning only when it is completely dry.

Floor Mats

Rubber mats give your automobile's carpet essential protection from excessive wear. Clean the mats each time you wash your car. Even though it may take a bit of extra effort, you should clean car mats frequently in the winter, because they accumulate salt and sand when it's snowy.

▶ Use a stiff-bristled brush and scrub them with a detergent solution. Do not use harsh chemicals, solvents, or steel wool to clean the mats; these cleaners will damage the rubber. After washing the mats, apply a rubber protectant or liquid-wax shoe polish.

Cloth Upholstery

Care should be taken to avoid spots and spills on cloth upholstery because it is not easy to clean. Still, there are ways to make the job easier:

▶ Mop up all spills as soon as possible, and spot-treat them to avoid stains. Always carry paper towels in your car to absorb spills.

▶ Vacuum cloth upholstery, using your vacuum cleaner with an upholstery brush or a cordless vacuum. Use a crevice tool to pick up dirt from hard-to-reach places and crevices.

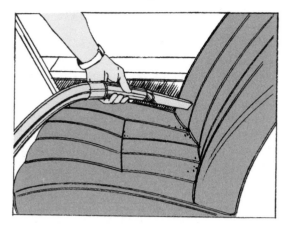

▶ Any commercial upholstery shampoo can be used to clean automobile upholstery. Follow the manufacturer's instructions, and vacuum the upholstery thoroughly when the product is completely dry.

Vinyl and Leather Upholstery

Vinyl upholstery is cold in winter and hot in summer, but it's durable and easy to care for. Leather upholstery is a luxury-car option, but the care for both kinds of upholstery is the same:

▶ Vacuum the creases and crevices of the upholstery as part of routine, general car cleaning, but avoid scratching the upholstery with sharp-edged attachments. Use a leather or vinyl conditioner to prevent cracking, drying out, and fading. If you use a commercial product, follow the manufacturer's instructions.

MIRACULOUS BAKING SODA

▶ A half-inch of baking soda in car ashtrays helps eliminate stale tobacco odors and also makes it easier to extinguish cigarettes.

▶ Use a baking soda solution to remove salt deposits.

▶ Rub baking soda into fresh stains on car upholstery. When completely dry, brush or vacuum off.

▶ Dip a wet sponge in baking soda to remove insects without scratching the car finish.

▶ A baking soda paste (three parts baking soda to one part water) is useful for removing corrosion buildup from your car's battery terminals.

CAR BUYER'S GLOSSARY

If you're venturing into a new-car showroom for the first time in several years, your automotive vocabulary may be out of date. Such terms as antilock brakes, 4-wheel steering, fuel injection, and multi-valve engines await you. The unprepared face an avalanche of high-tech double-talk. The following glossary explains automotive features and recent technical innovations.

Air bag

A fabric bag that inflates in frontal collisions of about 12 mph or higher to prevent front-seat occupants from hitting the steering wheel, dashboard, or windshield. Air bags are designed to inflate within fractions of a second, then immediately deflate so the driver's ability to control the car isn't impeded. Most cars equipped with air bags have one only for the driver, which is located in the steering-wheel hub.

All-season tires

Tread designs that allow water and snow to escape from under the tire for better traction. Ordinary tread designs tend to trap water, causing "hydroplaning," in which the tire rides on a thin film of water. Most all-season tires are designed for a soft ride rather than good handling, though some tire companies now offer all-season radials that have a high-performance tread.

Antilock braking system (ABS)

A computer-controlled braking system that operates to prevent the wheels from locking in a panic stop. This safety feature is designed to dramatically reduce stopping distances and improve steering control, especially in rain, snow, or on icy pavement. Locked brakes result in skids, in which the driver can neither stop nor steer the car. When ABS brakes are applied, the computer senses when a wheel is about to lock up and then "pumps" the brakes many times per second. The driver simply continues to apply steady force to the brake pedal, but the computer allows the wheels to continue to rotate while slowing the car.

Automatic seatbelts

Front seatbelts that engage automatically upon entering a car or turning on the ignition. There are two basic types currently made. Motorized shoulder belts anchored to the door frame pivot around front-seat occupants when the front doors are closed and the ignition is on (separate lap belts usually have to be buckled manually). Nonmotorized automatic belts can be left buckled, but will automatically extend or retract when the front doors are opened or closed. Automatic seatbelts are part of a passive-restraint system.

Curb weight

The weight of the vehicle when ready for the road, including fuel and other fluids.

Direct ignition

System designed to eliminate the ignition distributor and ignition wires to the plugs. Ignition coils, which supply the spark that ignites the air/fuel mixture inside the engine, are mounted directly on top of the spark plugs.

Disc brakes

A brake design in which a caliper squeezes two friction pads against a disc that's attached to the wheel. Considered more efficient than a drum brake, in which a drum-shaped iron casting is attached to the wheel, and curved brake shoes press against the inside of the drum to provide braking action.

Double overhead camshafts

Two camshafts per cylinder bank, with one operating the intake valves and the other the exhaust valves. Double-overhead-cam engines usually have four valves—two intake and two exhaust—per cylinder. A V-type engine with one overhead camshaft per cylinder bank is still a single-cam engine.

Electronically controlled suspension

A suspension system that changes the ride quality to suit road or driving conditions, usually by altering shock-absorber damping or air-spring rates. Some electronically controlled suspensions are designed to enhance ride comfort by softening settings for rough roads. Others stiffen settings to improve handling at the expense of ride quality. Some systems are automatic, with microprocessors sensing inputs from the steering, brakes, throttle, and other sources to determine the suspension setting. Others are adjustable by the driver from the cockpit.

Four-wheel drive (4WD)

(Sometimes called all-wheel drive.) System to deliver engine power to all four wheels. The chief advantage is added traction on slippery surfaces. Disadvantages include a higher purchase price, extra weight, and reduced fuel economy. The most common system is part-time, on-demand 4WD, which allows the driver to shift from 2WD into 4WD via a transfer-case lever or an electric switch in the interior. This system is meant for use only on slippery pavement. Full-time 4WD can be used on any surface and is of two types: on-demand or permanent (it's always engaged). The most sophisticated full-time systems engage automatically, using a viscous, or fluid, coupling to sense which wheels need traction and then deliver engine power accordingly. The driver does nothing to engage or disengage the system. Some on-demand 4WD systems lack shift-on-the-fly capability—they require that the vehicle be stopped and the front-wheel hubs be locked by hand before 4WD can be engaged.

Four-wheel steering (4WS)
Allows rear wheels to steer the vehicle in tandem with the front wheels. With 4WS, the rear wheels turn in the same direction as the front ones at higher speeds to enhance cornering and stability. On some systems, the rear wheels steer opposite the front ones a few degrees at slow speeds to decrease the turning radius and increase maneuverability.

Front-wheel drive (FWD)
System designed to transmit engine power to the front wheels. The effect is to pull the car by the front wheels, rather than push it by the rear wheels. Because FWD eliminates the drive shaft extending from the transmission to the rear-mounted differential, engineers can design the vehicle with more passenger and cargo room.

Fuel injection
Replaces the carburetor to supply fuel for combustion. Fuel injection is of two basic designs, both of which meter fuel more efficiently than a carburetor. One design is called port (or multi-point) fuel injection, in which fuel is squirted directly into each cylinder at its intake port. The other is throttle-body (or single-point) fuel injection, in which fuel is squirted from one or two injectors into an intake manifold on top of the engine and then distributed to the cylinders. Multi-point injection is more expensive, but also more precise; it provides more efficient combustion, more power, better mileage, and lower emissions. Computers turn the fuel injectors on and off based on signals from sensors that measure oxygen in the exhaust, coolant temperature, engine speed, and other operating conditions.

Hatchback
Sedan or coupe body with a rear liftgate that opens to a cargo area. Cars with two passenger doors and a liftgate are called 3-door hatchbacks; four passenger doors and a liftgate make it a 5-door hatchback.

Head-up display (HUD)
Use of vacuum fluorescent displays to project information—such as vehicle speed—from the main instrument cluster to the windshield or to the driver's field of view so that this information can be read without glancing away from the road.

Horsepower
A measurement of an engine's ability to perform work measured by a dynamometer and expressed as brake horsepower (bhp). Engines that produce most of their horsepower at low rpms—such as 3000 rpm (revolutions-per-minute of the crankshaft)—often provide better low-speed pickup than engines that develop more horsepower at higher rpm—5000 rpm, for example. Horsepower is not the only measurement of an engine's overall strength. Its ability to produce torque—turning or twisting force—is also a key factor.

Intercooler
Acts as a radiator to cool air before it enters the combustion chamber. It is found on some turbocharged and supercharged cars. Cooling makes the air denser and increases the power of the ignited fuel-air mixture.

Lockup torque converter
A fuel-saving device found on some automatic transmissions. Power is sent from the engine to the transmission through a viscous, or fluid, coupling. A lockup torque converter locks the engine crankshaft to the transmission input shaft so the two turn as one, eliminating the slippage, or power loss, of the viscous coupling. It is usually activated at highway speeds. In most cars, the lockup torque converter can be felt engaging and disengaging.

Multi-valve engines
Engines with three or four valves per cylinder instead of the customary two. Multiple-valve cylinder heads move more air and fuel through the engine quickly, letting the engine "breathe" better. In all engines, separate valves open in sequence to allow air-fuel mixture into the combustion chambers and to expel the spent exhaust gases. Instead of simply enlarging one intake valve and one exhaust valve, the use of three or four valves of smaller size and lighter weight allows better airflow for higher engine speeds, more

power, and more efficient combustion.

Naturally aspirated engines
Engines that draw air/fuel mixture into their cylinders without aid of a supercharger or turbocharger.

Notchback
Sedan or coupe with a separate trunk.

Overdrive
Fuel-saving transmission gear that lowers engine speed to save fuel and reduce noise. It is usually the fourth gear of an automatic transmission and the fifth gear of a manual transmission. Overdrive transmissions allow the drive shafts to spin at a faster speed than the engine; those without overdrive have a less-efficient direct-drive top gear, in which the engine and drive shafts turn at the same speed.

Overhead-camshaft (ohc) and overhead-valve (ohv) engines
Distinguishing feature of camshaft placement. The camshaft in either design activates the valves. In an overhead-valve engine (ohv), the camshaft is located in the engine block below the valves. It activates the valves by means of pushrods and other components. In an overhead-cam (ohc) engine, the camshaft is located in the cylinder head, with the valves mounted below. The ohc design is more expensive to manufacture, but acts more directly on the valves, thus allowing the engine to run more efficiently and at higher speeds. Some engines use double overhead cams (dohc) for still more efficiency.

Passive restraints
Safety features designed to protect occupants in crashes without being actively engaged. The two kinds are automatic seatbelts and air bags. Associated components may include under-dashboard knee bolsters. Federal regulations require passive

restraints on all passenger cars sold in the U.S.

Performance
An overall evaluation of how a car accelerates, holds the road, corners, and brakes. Good performance enables a driver to merge easily with expressway traffic, pass quickly on 2-lane roads, negotiate turns and bumpy roads with good control, and stop safely. A car can have good performance without being a high-performance or sports car.

Powertrain
All of the items that are necessary to transmit power to the wheels: engine, transmission or transaxle, clutch (on manual-transmission cars), torque converter (on automatic-transmission cars), and drive shafts.

Rear-wheel drive
Only the rear wheels receive power. The most common configuration has the engine mounted in front. Advantages are simplicity and better front-rear weight balance than front-drive cars. Disadvantages include reduced wet-weather traction compared to front-wheel drive and less efficient use of space. Passenger room is reduced because the drive shaft that links the transmission with the rear-mounted differential runs the length of the interior, taking up passenger and cargo space.

Redline
An engine's maximum recommended speed in revolutions per minute (rpm). Tachometers indicate this maximum engine speed with a small red line at the appropriate rpm.

RPM (revolutions per minute)
A measurement of engine speed based on how fast the crankshaft is rotating. Rpm is displayed on a tachometer.

Stabilizer (antiroll) bar
A bar used to link the left and right sides of a suspension system. Can be used at the front, rear, or both ends of a car. It reduces body roll by helping the suspension system resist the weight shift that occurs when a car changes direction.

Supercharger
Forces additional air/fuel mixture into the combustion chamber to produce more power like a turbocharger. An important difference is that a turbocharger is driven by spent exhaust gases; a supercharger is driven by the engine's crankshaft and thus reacts more directly to the throttle and without the lag in response found on many turbochargers.

Suspension
The components that support the weight of the car, keep the tread of the tires on the road, absorb bumps and road shocks, and control forces produced during acceleration, braking, and cornering. Suspensions vary in design and components, but typical parts include springs, shock absorbers (or struts), control arms, and stabilizer bars. An independent suspension means each wheel operates independently of the others, so that when one tire hits a pothole, the spring and shock absorber at that corner absorb the bump without affecting the rest of the suspension.

Tachometer
Dashboard gauge that displays engine speed in revolutions per minute (rpm) of the crankshaft.

Tire sizes
A series of numerals and letters stamped into the sidewall to denote the tire's intended use, tread width, profile, construction, and wheel diameter. An example is a P185/70R14 tire. "P" stands for passenger car tire; "185" is the tread width in millimeters; "70" is the

tire's profile, meaning the height of the sidewall is 70 percent of the width of the tread; "R" stands for radial; and "14" is the wheel diameter in inches. Tire widths generally increase and decrease in increments of 10 millimeters (185, 195, 205). Tires with a 70-series profile or less (60, 50, 45) are called low-profile tires and are designed for better handling. Tires with a 75-series profile or taller (80, 85) are designed for ride comfort. Some tires have an "H," "V," or another letter as part of the size description, such as P185/70HR14. Those letters denote maximum speed ratings: "S" for up to 112 mph; "H" for up to 130 mph; "V" for up to 149 mph; and "Z" for over 149 mph.

Torque

The amount of twisting force generated by an engine measured at the crankshaft and expressed in pounds/feet. This is different from horsepower. The amount of torque an engine produces affects ability to accelerate and move heavy loads. As with horsepower, engine speed is a factor with torque. An engine that develops 250 pounds/feet at 2000 rpm can accelerate well from low speeds. It also tends to work well with automatic transmission. An engine that produces 150 pounds/feet of torque at 4000 rpm will have to be revved much higher to accelerate well from low speeds and will have a harder time hauling heavy loads. An engine with poor low-end torque is probably better suited for use with a manual transmission, which gives the driver more control over engine speed. Engines that produce maximum horsepower at high rpm often have little torque at low rpm.

Turbocharger

An air compressor that delivers more air to an engine than it could draw in naturally, thus increasing engine power. Exhaust gas rotates a turbine, which in turn drives the compressor to force more air into the engine. The amount of pressure generated is described as boost and measured in terms of pounds per square inch. Turbos enable engineers to increase horsepower without increasing engine size. A major disadvantage is the lag between the time that the throttle pedal is depressed and when the turbo generates boost.

VIN (vehicle identification number)

A series of letters and numbers stamped onto a metal plate attached to the front top-left side of the dashboard and visible from the outside of a car through the windshield. The VIN contains such coded information as the vehicle's model year, production series, and place of manufacture.

Wheelbase

The distance between the center of a car's front wheels and the center of its rear wheels.

Even though cleaning is not much fun, most of us take the time to do it. To minimize the drudgery while maximizing your cleaning power, you'll need the right tools, reliable cleaning products, and an efficient cleaning strategy that accommodates your personal and household needs. Your cleaning schedule for both regular and seasonal care should be comfortable for you. You may want to clean for an hour every morning, two hours after work, or all Saturday morning. As long as you have a schedule that leaves room for the occassional change of plans, you'll stay ahead of housework.

Basic day-to-day chores, such as beds, dishes, bathrooms, laundry, and floor care, require a firm routine and should be shared by the family. Major tasks, such as closets, ovens, and silverware, often require a flexible plan. And, as in most major chores, cleaning will go much faster if you have help. To tackle a big project—such as cleaning the garage or the basement—divide the labor among all the members of the household, including the children, or invite friends to help out. You can reciprocate when their garages need cleaning.

Remember that your cleaning tasks will get done much faster if there are no interruptions. So turn on the answering machine and concentrate on the task at hand.

YOUR CLEANING CLOSET

Creating a Cleaning Center

A well-stocked cleaning center is the house cleaner's best friend. You will be more likely to start your cleaning chores and to finish the task if you have everything you need on hand and in one place. A cleaning center that saves you time and steps is the efficient beginning to quick and easy cleaning methods.

To determine whether you need all the tools listed, think about the cleaning tasks you perform regularly and stock your cleaning closet with the tools that will help you accomplish them most efficiently. Before you supply your cleaning closet, consider the following:

▶ Make sure the closet is equipped to store all the cleaning tools and products you buy or make. If you can't fit them all into one orderly place, you'll waste time digging around under the sink for the cleanser and going out to the garage for the mop.

▶ Put up a pegboard or hooks to hang brushes and mops. They'll not only be easier to find, but they'll last longer if they are hung.

▶ Install plenty of shelves to hold bottles and cartons. This will get dangerous cleaning products out of the reach of children and give you space to store a complete array of cleaning supplies.

▶ If possible, put a lock on the door of the cleaning closet to secure these tools and solutions from children. Otherwise, be sure to store cleaning solutions and any tools that could harm young children on high shelves.

▶ If you need to make room in your closet, store bathroom cleaning supplies in a secure storage area in the bathroom. If you have more than one bathroom, duplicate your supplies so you don't have to carry them around. You may want to refer to the "Creating Storage" section to get some tips on how to expand storage space in the bathroom to store cleaning supplies.

▶ If you're absolutely cramped for space, consider dividing a closet in half. Much of the space in a regular two-foot deep closet is wasted, because it's difficult to see what's in back. That's why many pantries are built with a 12- to 15-inch depth. By putting a divider down the middle and doors on each side, you increase the amount of efficient space and create two separate closets. This solution works only if the closet can open into two different rooms or areas.

Tools of the Trade

You'll want to make sure you stock your cleaning closet with most of the following items:

▶ Baskets for carrying supplies from one room to another and to collect dirty ashtrays, collectibles you want to polish, magazines you want to recycle, and/or the toys the children left in the family room.

▶ Broom, dustpan, and dust mop for quick cleanups.

▶ Brushes in an assortment of sizes: a hard-bristled scrub brush, toilet brushes (one for each bathroom), a radiator brush, and other soft- and medium-bristled brushes for scrubbing and dusting.

▶ Buckets with double compartments to hold both your cleaning solution and rinse water. To avoid guessing when trying to mix correct solutions of cleaning compounds, use red fingernail polish to plainly mark pint, quart, and gallon levels inside a bucket.

▶ Chamois are expensive, but they will last almost indefinitely when properly handled. Nothing absorbs water better than soft leather, so a chamois is perfect for drying washed cars and windows. After you use it, wash your chamois in detergent and water, rinse thoroughly, squeeze out the water, stretch it to full size, and place it on a flat surface to dry. Don't wash a chamois with soap.

▶ Cleaning agents. Whether you make your own or purchase commercial products, make sure you know how to use them.

▶ Cleaning cloths can be made from worn-out clothes, sheets, and towels. Cotton or linen, white, or light-colored fabrics are best. Synthetic fabrics do not make good cleaning cloths, because they are not absorbent. They also create static electricity.

▶ Long-handled dust mop for cleaning ceilings and cobwebs.

▶ Mops with detachable heads.

▶ Rubber gloves protect your hands whenever you work with cleaning solutions. Don't forget to put them on.

▶ Scouring pads, made of both synthetics and steel wool.

▶ Sponges in various sizes. These should be tossed out as soon as they start to shred. Have plenty on hand.

▶ Stepladder. Those that are at least three feet tall are a safe substitute for the unsteady chair or stack of boxes you may have been standing on to clean out-of-reach places.

▶ Squeegees speed window washing, but if you don't have one, an old windshield wiper is a good stand-in for a commercial squeegee.

▶ Vacuum cleaner. Uprights are especially good for wall-to-wall carpets and large rugs,

GLOSSARY OF CLEANING AGENTS

▶ All-purpose cleaners remove grease and grimy dirt.

▶ Ammonia is available in clear or sudsy form. It is an excellent cleaner or cleaning booster for many household surfaces, because it is a good grease cutter, wax stripper, window cleaner, and general soil remover. If you object to the strong odor of ammonia, buy a scented product. Neither scented ammonia nor sudsy ammonia is suitable for stain removal.

▶ Baking soda is one of the most versatile cleaning products available. Used by itself in dry form, it acts as a very mild scouring powder that will not scratch even the most delicate surfaces. Add water to make a paste, and use it to scour dirty surfaces. Combined with other ingredients, it makes a very good cleaning/deodorizing solution.

▶ Bleach helps remove stains and whiten laundry; it's also good for cleaning toilets.

▶ Dishwashing liquid detergents are used for many cleaning tasks in addition to doing dishes.

carpeted areas with heavy traffic, and deep-pile carpeting. Because of their portability and their design, canisters are superior to uprights for cleaning walls, woodwork, shelves, and furniture. Canisters are especially good for homes with varied floor surfaces; apartments, dorm rooms, and small homes; stairways and second stories; hard floors and above-floor surfaces; upholstery and furniture; and households needing a second all-purpose vacuum cleaner.

▸ Waxes, polishes, and oils for wood, leather, brass, chrome, silver, glass, and all the other surfaces that you'll want to shine.

BATHROOMS

The average person can tolerate a growing collection of dust balls under the bed or a drawer full of tarnished flatware in the sideboard. But a grimy bathroom is another story. The bathroom should be cleaned once a week, and even more frequently if it gets heavy use from a large family. Fortunately, most bathrooms are made of materials that are easy to keep clean. Tile and porcelain surfaces are stain-resistant if dirt and scum are not allowed to build up on them. Make it a firm rule in your home to rinse out the tub or shower stall immediately after you use it. Spray water from the shower head on all interior surfaces, then lather soap onto a damp sponge, swish it around the tub or stall, and rinse.

Keeping tile and porcelain surfaces clean so that they never need to be scoured not only saves time, it also protects these surfaces from unnecessary wear and keeps them looking their best. Most scouring powders and nonabrasive cleaners will safely rid tile and porcelain surfaces of dirt, but if stains have to be removed with harsh abrasives, the porcelain or ceramic tile will be scratched. These tiny scratches invite more dirt buildup, and your cleaning problems increase. The following specifically addresses the various materials encountered in the bathroom.

Countertops and Basins

Bathroom countertops are sloshed, splotched, and splattered with everything from hair spray to shoe polish. In most homes, countertops are made of materials that can stand up to the assault: ceramic tile, plastic laminate, and cultured marble. Because these materials are durable, they are easy to clean.

SUBSTITUTE TOOLS

Just as in carpentry, the right tools can make the job much easier. Try a few of the following:

▸ An automobile snow brush is perfect for cleaning under a refrigerator.

▸ Old toothbrushes work well to clean combs, silverware, and typewriter keys.

▸ Use an old shaving brush or baby's hairbrush to avoid snagging or harming delicate fabric or pleated lampshades when dusting.

▸ Paintbrushes make excellent dusters for small or hard-to-reach areas. Flick them along door jambs, around windows, and into corners where dust cloths won't fit.

▸ Instead of buying dust cloths chemically treated to "attract" dust, make your own from cheesecloth. Dip the cloth in a solution of 2 cups of water and 1/4 cup of lemon oil and allow it to dry before using.

▸ An old nylon stocking rolled into a ball becomes a nonscratch scrub pad for cleaning the sink and tub.

▸ A typewriter eraser from the stationery store is an excellent tool for cleaning the grout between bathroom tiles.

▸ Dust and other debris often collect in hard-to-reach corners, such as behind large appliances. Clean out these corners by making a yardstick "duster"—just cover the end with a sock, secured with rubber bands, or fasten a small sponge to the end of the yardstick with staples or rubber bands.

Cultured Marble

Cultured marble resembles real marble, but it is a lot more versatile and much easier to care for. Avoid using abrasive cleaners and steel-wool pads, because they will scratch the surface, making it difficult to keep clean.

Plastic Laminate

This is very durable if you don't scratch it, chip it, knock off its edges, burn it, scrub it, let water seep under it, stain it, or otherwise mistreat it. In other words, its durability is limited. Plastic laminate is made of thin layers of plastic superimposed on craft paper and overlaid on particle board or plywood. The color of most plastic laminate is only in the top layer. The glossy, matte, or textured surface is also laid on. This is the reason plastic laminate cannot be restored if it is damaged— all of its beauty is on the surface. A light application of an appliance wax or light furniture wax will protect and brighten plastic laminate surfaces.

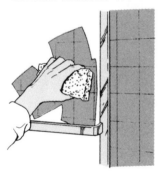 ▶ To clean plastic laminate, use a two-sided scrubbing pad with fiber on one side and a sponge on the other. Moistened slightly with water, the fiber side is just abrasive enough to loosen greasy smears and other soil. Turning the scrubber over, use the sponge side to wipe the surface damp-dry.

▶ When a spot or stain persists, first sprinkle baking soda on the spot and scrub gently. If this doesn't take care of the problem, apply a polishing cleanser with a wet sponge.

Mirrors

To clean mirrors, use a clean, dry cloth and one of the following solutions:

(1) Mix ⅓ cup clear ammonia in 1 gallon warm water. Apply it with a sponge/squeegee or pour the solution into a spray container and spray it directly on the mirror. Buff with a lint-free cloth, chamois, or paper toweling. Vinegar may be substituted for ammonia.

(2) Pour vinegar into a shallow bowl or pan, then crumple a sheet of newspaper, dip it in the vinegar, and apply to the mirror. Wipe the glass several times with the same newspaper until the mirror is almost dry. Then shine it with a clean, soft cloth or dry newspaper.

(3) Mix 2 cups isopropyl rubbing alcohol (70-percent solution), 2 tablespoons liquid dishwashing detergent, and 2 cups water. Stir until thoroughly mixed and then pour into a spray bottle. Spray directly on the mirror. Buff with a lint-free cloth, chamois, or paper towel.

Shower Stalls

Shower enclosures are a chore to keep clean—but they can be less of a problem if you follow these suggestions:

▶ Keep mildew from taking hold by wiping shower walls with a towel after each shower, while you're still in the tub.

▶ If the shower area is subject to mildew, periodically spray it with a mildew inhibitor and disinfectant.

▶ Leave the shower door slightly open to allow air to circulate; this will discourage the growth of mildew.

▶ If possible, install a venting fan, which greatly reduces the moisture that causes mildew.

▶ Remove hard-water deposits on shower enclosures with a solution of white vinegar and water.

▶ Glass shower doors will sparkle when you clean them with a sponge dipped in white vinegar.

▶ Remove water spots on the metal frames around shower doors and enclosures with lemon oil.

▸ If the grout or caulking in your shower breaks away where the walls join the tub or shower floor, recaulk immediately to prevent water damage.

▸ When tile walls need a thorough cleaning, run the shower water at its hottest temperature so the steam will loosen the dirt. Then, using a sponge mop, clean with a mixture of ½ cup vinegar, 1 cup clear ammonia, and ¼ cup baking soda in 1 gallon of warm water. After cleaning, rinse with clear water. Note: Never use harsh abrasive powders or steel-wool pads.

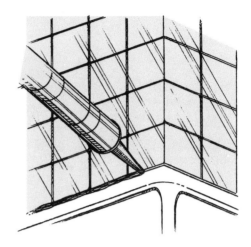

CLEANING SCHEDULE

Every Day

Remove surface litter from carpets and bare floors with a canister vacuum cleaner or broom.

Wash dishes, wipe countertops and cooking appliances.

Empty wastebaskets and kitchen garbage.

Wipe basins and bathtubs.

Make beds, straighten rooms.

Every Week or Two

Vacuum carpets and bare floors thoroughly with your vacuum cleaner.

Vacuum upholstery and drapes with the upholstery tool, using the crevice tool in the seams of furniture coverings.

Dust and/or polish furniture.

Clean the range and wipe out the refrigerator.

Wash kitchen and bathroom floors.

Clean toilets, fixtures, and bathroom mirrors.

Change bed linens.

Seasonal or As Needed

Surface-clean rugs and carpets using a carpet-cleaning solution or an absorbent powder.

Remove old wax, apply new wax, and buff bare floors.

Shampoo upholstered furniture.

Wash lamp shades, walls, and woodwork.

Dust books, pictures, and lamps.

Clean mirrors, TVs, picture frames, and art objects.

Clean ovens, microwave, refrigerator, freezer, and other appliances.

Wash bathroom carpeting and shower curtain.

Organize closets.

Turn mattresses, wash pads and pillow covers, and air or wash pillows.

Yearly

Vacuum rug pads and the backs of rugs.

Shampoo carpets and clean rugs. Turn rugs to equalize wear.

Wash windows, curtains, blinds, and shades. Clean draperies.

Wash or dry-clean bedspreads, blankets, and slipcovers.

Emergencies

Remove spots and stains while they are fresh.

SHOWER STALL CLEANER

Mix ½ cup vinegar, 1 cup ammonia, ¼ cup baking soda, and 1 gallon hot water. Caution: Wear rubber gloves and work in a well-ventilated area when using this powerful solution. Apply it to the walls of the shower with a sponge, scrubbing with a brush, if necessary, to remove all the scum. Rinse well with clear water and wipe dry.

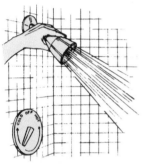

▶ Clean mineral deposits from a shower head by removing the head, taking it apart, and soaking it in vinegar. Then brush deposits loose with an old toothbrush. Clean the holes by poking them with a wire, pin, toothpick, or ice pick.

Tubs and Basins

Most bathtubs and basins are made of porcelain. If the fixtures are older, chances are the material is porcelain on cast iron. These fixtures may not be as acid- and alkaline-resistant as newer porcelain-on-steel tubs and basins. Cultured marble is also used for one-piece basin/countertops. Fiberglass and acrylic tubs, which are lighter and easier to install than steel tubs, are used in new-home construction and remodeling, but they are not as durable as porcelain-coated steel. If you have a fiberglass tub, you will have to be especially careful when you clean it to avoid scratching the surface.

▶ Porcelain basins and tubs should be cleaned with powdered cleanser or nonabrasive liquid cleanser. Sprinkle a mild abrasive powder on a damp sponge and apply it to the porcelain surface of the tub or basin. Use a synthetic scouring pad on stubborn soil. Rinse with clear water.

▶ When you clean the bathtub and basin, also remove hair from the traps in the drains to prevent clogging.

▶ Cultured marble or fiberglass tubs and basins should be cleaned with a commercial fiberglass-cleaning product or nonabrasive liquid cleanser. Apply either product with a damp sponge and rinse with clear water.

▶ Commercial rust removers are very effective in removing rust stains. Caution: Wear rubber gloves when you work with these products because they contain acid. You can also clean discolored porcelain fixtures with a paste made of cream of tartar moistened with hydrogen peroxide or a paste made of borax moistened with lemon juice. Scrub the paste into lightly stained areas with a brush and rinse well.

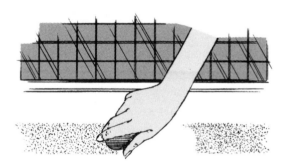

▶ A ring around the tub can be rubbed away without cleaners with a nylon net ball or pad.

▶ Cover a stubborn ring with a paste of cream of tartar and hydrogen peroxide. When the paste dries, wipe it off—along with the ring.

▶ To remove discoloration from a yellowed bathtub, rub the tub with a solution of salt and turpentine. Caution: Wear rubber gloves when you work with this solution and rinse well.

Shower Curtains and Bath Mats

Like tubs and enclosures, shower curtains and bath mats are subject to mildew. Fortunately, they're much easier to clean than grout. The

TIMESAVERS

▶ Each week, give special attention to one room in the house. This will save you time on fall and spring cleaning, because you've been cleaning more thoroughly throughout the year.

▶ Make an efficient cleaning apron from a compartmented shoe bag by attaching strings and filling the pockets with rags, polishes, brushes, and other objects.

▶ Gather together all the cleaning supplies you will need. This will save extra steps between your cleaning closet and your work site. Then take everything out of the room that does not belong in it.

▶ Put small decorative items into a basket and out of harm's way, and put the dirty items that you want to clean separately, such as ashtrays and metal objects that need polishing, in a box or basket and take them to the kitchen. Don't redistribute anything until you have finished cleaning the room.

▶ Pull all furniture away from the walls. Turn back rugs at the edges and take up small scatter rugs to make vacuuming the floor easier. Choose a starting point and work your way around the room.

▶ Dust settles downward, so avoid dirtying what you have just cleaned by working from top to bottom. Clean floors last.

▶ If you don't have a bucket with two compartments, carry two buckets when you are washing items that also need rinsing so that you don't need to continually return to the sink.

▶ Sweep, vacuum, and/or dust before cleaning with a liquid cleaning solution to avoid making mud.

▶ Go easy on cleaners. Soap or wax used sparingly cleans and beautifies surfaces. If you use too much, you will have to spend time removing the buildup.

▶ When you are cleaning something up high, don't stand on tiptoe. Grab a stepladder. If you are cleaning down low, sit on the floor. Straining up or down is tiring, inefficient, and bad for your back.

▶ Concentrate on one room at a time; don't run all over your house or apartment pushing dirt around.

▶ To clean your radiators, hang a damp cloth or damp newspapers behind the radiator. Blow on the radiator with a hair dryer to force hidden dirt and dust onto the damp cloth.

▶ To clean a dust mop without mess, slip a large paper bag over the head of the mop, secure the top, and shake so the dust falls into the bag.

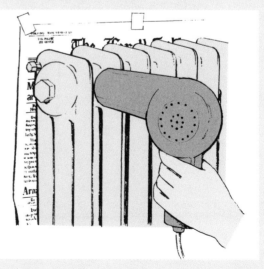

following tips should help make this chore a breeze:

▶ Hand-washing works better than machine-washing for plastic shower curtains. You get fewer wrinkles.

▶ Keep a new shower curtain looking fresh by using the old shower curtain as a liner. Hang the new curtain on the same hooks in front of the old curtain. The old curtain will take the beating from water and soap scum while the new one stays clean.

▶ To prevent machine-washed shower curtains from wrinkling, put them in the washing machine with ½ cup of detergent and ½ cup of baking soda, along with two large bath towels. Add a cup of vinegar to the rinse cycle; hang the curtains up immediately after washing and let them air-dry.

▶ When you clean a plastic shower curtain, keep it soft and flexible by adding a few drops of mineral oil to the rinse water. Maintain its softness by wiping it occasionally with a solution of warm water and mineral oil.

▶ Eliminate mildew by spraying newly washed shower curtains with a disinfectant.

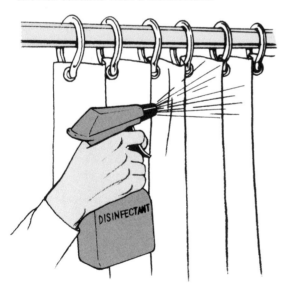

▶ Clean a rubber or vinyl bathtub mat by tossing it into the washer with bath towels. The terry cloth scrubs the mat, and everything comes out clean.

Toilets

Cleaning the toilet is one of those chores that you want to get through as quickly as possible. Many toilet-bowl cleaners and deodorizers claim that they'll help you do this. Some products are truly helpful, some are not. Most cleaners that are placed in the tank and are dispensed each time the toilet is flushed do little more than color the water. Some clean the bowl a little better than plain water, but in-tank cleaners are not a substitute for a regular scrubbing that includes the seat and the rim. Toilet bowls and tanks are usually made of vitreous china, which is nonporous and easy to clean. Before you clean your toilet, read the label on your cleaning product to learn its exact chemical makeup and how it should be used. Be especially careful never to mix products that contain chlorine bleach

CLOGGED DRAIN OPENER

Moderately clogged drains sometimes can be opened by pouring ½ cup baking soda, followed by ½ cup vinegar down the drain. Caution: The interaction of these two ingredients creates foaming and fumes, so replace the drain cover loosely. Flush the drain with clear water after about three hours.

with ammonia-based products. Always wear rubber gloves when you work with toilet cleaners. They contain strong chemicals and should be flushed immediately after the bowl has been cleaned. Be careful not to allow cleaners to remain in the toilet or to touch other bathroom surfaces.

Toilet-Bowl Cleaners

Clean and disinfect your toilet bowl with ½ cup chlorine bleach. Pour it into the bowl and let it stand for ten minutes. Then scrub with the toilet brush and flush. Caution: Wear rubber gloves and do not mix chlorine bleach with any other cleaner.

▶ Keep a long-handled brush for cleaning toilet bowls.

▶ Clean the exterior of a toilet with the same products you use for tubs and basins.

▶ A ¼ cup of sodium bisulfate (sodium acid sulfate) can be sprinkled into a wet toilet bowl for a single scrubbing and flushing. (Wear rubber gloves.) Let it stand for 15 minutes and then scrub and flush as usual. Caution: Never combine bleach with toilet-bowl cleaners; the mix can release toxic gases.

▶ Rust stains under a toilet-bowl rim sometimes yield to laundry bleach—be sure to protect your hands with plastic or rubber gloves. Rub off truly stubborn stains with

extra-fine steel wool or with wet-dry sandpaper (available at hardware stores).

▶ Chemical toilet-bowl cleaners should never be used to clean the bathtub or sink; the chemical will ruin the finish.

BEDDING

All bedding should be cleaned on a regular basis. The key to successful cleaning is to do it before the soil is heavy and to know the fabrics involved in order to use the right cleaning procedures. Keep a file of manufacturers' care labels and follow their directions when cleaning is necessary.

Bedspreads

Bedspreads are made from many different kinds of fabric, many of which are washable. Bedspreads should be washed before they become heavily soiled. Treat spots and stains with a spray prewash product or a liquid detergent. Before you clean your bedspread, dip a corner of the bedspread in the detergent solution to check for colorfastness. If the color bleeds, have your bedspread dry-cleaned.

UNCLOGGING DRAINS

In many homes, the bathroom sink doubles as a dressing table, and everyone in the family shampoos in the shower. Hair and soap are washed into bathroom drains day and night, and the cruddy mess can quickly jam up the plumbing. All that is needed to clean some clogged drains is to clear the trap of hair and soap curds. Regular clearing of the traps saves your plumbing, and it also cuts down on cleaning time—water that flows out of the basin and tub quickly doesn't allow dirt to settle on these surfaces.

If clearing the trap doesn't clear the drain, you'll have to take stronger measures. First plunge the drain with a plumber's helper. Before you use the

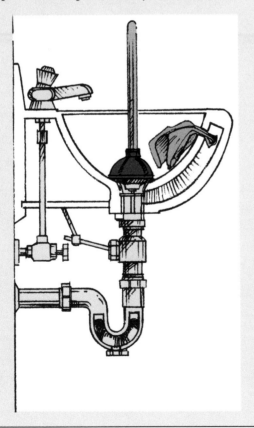

plunger in the bathroom basin, plug the overflow opening. This allows the plunger to exercise its maximum suction effect on the clogged drain.

If plunging does not open the drain, use a chemical drain opener. These products must be handled with special care because they are caustic and harmful to skin and eyes. Use them in a well-ventilated area and follow the manufacturer's instructions. Commercial drain openers are sold in granular, liquid, and pressurized forms. Granular products utilize lye to do their work, liquid drain openers use lye and other chemicals, and pressurized products work by chloro-fluorocarbon propellant and pressure. If you use a granular drain opener, you must first remove standing water from the sink; this is not necessary for liquid and pressurized products. Chemical drain openers will damage porcelain enamel and should not be allowed to remain on the surface of your fixtures for any length of time.

If the first type of chemical drain opener you use does not work, do not use a different chemical drain cleaner unless the initial cleaner has been totally flushed away. Never use a plunger or a pressurized drain opener after using a chemical cleaner; it may cause dangerous chemicals to splash back on you. Also, be sure to tell your plumber what you have put into the drain before he or she starts to work. The combination of ammonia and other household cleaners with chemical drain openers produces hazardous gases.

▶ Use a large, commercial washing machine for oversized bedspreads. An overcrowded washer won't clean very well, and the wet weight can be hard on your washer.

▶ Dry bedspreads on a clothesline or in a large, commercial dryer.

Blankets

Although blankets are made of many different fibers and blends, most of them are washable by hand or machine. Even some wool blankets can be machine-washed.

▶ Vacuum blankets occasionally to remove dust and lint.

▶ Air blankets on a clothesline periodically to freshen them.

▶ Before you wash a blanket, mend or replace bindings and treat spots and stains.

▶ Use a large commercial washer to wash large blankets. Fill the washer with water and put in the detergent so it can completely dissolve before you add the blanket. Use a gentle, or delicate, wash cycle; long periods of agitation will mat blanket fibers. Also avoid overcrowding the machine.

▶ A fabric softener will increase a blanket's fluffiness and reduce static electricity.

▶ Electric blankets should always be washed, not dry-cleaned, since cleaning solvents can damage the wiring. Mothproofing is harmful to the wiring, too.

Down-Filled Comforters and Quilts

The down filling in comforters and quilts is held in place by tufts of yarn or by stitched-through patterns. Most down-filled comforters and quilts are washable, but some older ones are too fragile to be cleaned at home. Test older comforters and quilts for colorfastness by wetting an inconspicuous spot with the detergent solution you plan to use and blotting the area with a white blotter.

▶ If comforters or quilts are in good condition, machine-wash and dry them. Use cold wash and rinse water and an all-purpose detergent.

▶ Fragile down comforters and quilts should be hand-washed in the bathtub or a deep laundry tub.

▶ Drape the wet comforter or quilt over several clotheslines to allow excess moisture to drip out; reposition periodically.

▶ If the comforter or quilt is strong enough to be dried in a clothes dryer, preheat the dryer to a low temperature and include a pair of clean, dry sneakers to help fluff the down. The dryer can also be set on air-dry (no heat) to dry the quilt.

Comforters and Quilts

Padded bed coverings may be filled with wool, cotton batting, or polyester fiber. The filling is held in place by tufts of yarn or by stitched-through patterns. Most cotton- or polyester-filled comforters and quilts are washable, but some older ones are too delicate to be cleaned at home. While some newer wool-filled or wool-covered comforters and quilts can be washed at home, others should be dry-cleaned; check the manufacturer's instructions.

▶ Test old quilts and comforters for colorfastness before attempting to wash them by wetting a small area with the detergent solution and blotting it with a white blotter.

▶ Clean patchwork quilts with the method that is appropriate for the most delicate fabric in the quilt.

▶ Never attempt to wash silk- or velvet-covered quilts and comforters. Unless a wool batting or covering is marked washable, do not wash it.

▶ For large quilts, use a commercial washer. Let quilts and comforters soak in the machine for about ten minutes before starting them through a short, gentle washing cycle.

▶ Hand-wash and line-dry old or fragile quilts and all quilts with cotton batting. Machine-washing is too harsh and can cause the batting to bunch up. Use a bathtub or deep laundry tub and allow the soap or detergent to dissolve in the wash water before adding the quilt.

Mattresses and Box Springs

Mattresses are usually made from foam or springs and casing; some older mattresses were made of hair, and futon mattresses are filled with cotton. All mattresses benefit from routine care.

▶ Every month, vacuum mattresses and box springs; turn the mattress over and around end to end to ensure even wear.

▶ Use an upholstery attachment and work around buttons carefully. Remove dust and blanket fluff from the edges of the box spring with a brush attachment.

▶ Cover mattresses with quilted or rubberized covers to prevent soiling.

▶ Remove spots and stains promptly, but do not allow the mattress to become excessively wet when you spot-treat or clean it. Do not make the bed until the mattress is fully dry.

Pillows

Pillowcases are routinely replaced when soiled bed linens are changed, but the pillow itself also requires regular cleaning. Know the pillow's filling—down, feather, foam, polyester, or kapok—so that you use the appropriate cleaning method. For polyester-filled pillows, read the care instruction tags; some polyester-filled pillows are washable, while others are not. Kapok is the silky covering of seeds from the ceiba tree; pillows with this stuffing need frequent airing but cannot be washed.

▶ Protect each pillow with a zip-on cotton or polyester cover, which you can wash regularly.

▶ Refresh pillows once a month by airing them near an open window or hanging them on a clothesline.

▶ Fluff feather and down pillows daily to get rid of dust and to redistribute the filling.

▶ Before you wash feather or down pillows, make sure there are no holes or ripped seams. Machine- or hand-wash feather and down pillows in cool water with a cold-water, light-duty detergent. Wash two pillows at a time or add a couple of bath towels to balance the load. If the fabric is worn or the pillow is heavily stuffed, wash feathers and ticking separately. Secure the feathers in a large muslin bag and stitch the opening closed.

▶ Dry down and feather pillows in the dryer on the low-heat setting. Including a pair of tennis shoes in the dryer will help distribute the down as it dries.

▶ Hand-wash and line-dry foam pillows. Change the hanging position hourly to dry the filling evenly. Never put a foam pillow in the dryer.

▶ Machine- or hand-wash polyester-filled pillows in warm water with an all-purpose detergent. A front-loading tumble washer rather than a top-loading machine works best for polyester pillows. Dry the pillows in the dryer on a moderate heat setting.

Sleeping Bags

Sleeping bags are practical not only for camping—they also serve as excellent beds for overnight visitors. The most common fillings are polyester or down. Both will have a long life if given proper care. Wash your sleeping bag after each outdoor use.

▶ Pretreat spots and stains on the bag cover with liquid detergent.

▶ Wash down-filled sleeping bags in cool water with a cold-water, mild detergent.

▶ Wash polyester-filled sleeping bags in warm water with an all-purpose detergent.

▶ If your sleeping bag can be machine-dried, tumble it with a clean, dry tennis shoe to prevent matting and a clean, dry bath towel to absorb excess moisture.

▶ If you line-dry the sleeping bag, unzip it before air-drying.

CARPETING

Routine Carpet Cleaning

Carpets need to be vacuumed once a week and more often in areas of heavy traffic. Frequent vacuuming prolongs the life of your carpet because it prevents a buildup of gritty particles that can cut carpet fibers. Every few weeks, take a little extra time and use your crevice tool for in-depth cleaning around baseboards and radiators and in other hard-to-reach places.

A surefire way to cut your cleaning time in half is to put thick mats or throw rugs at all the entrances to your home, both inside and outside the doors. These mats intercept and trap loose dirt, keeping it from being tracked through your house. Compared with cleaning a whole room, throwing a washable rug into the washing machine or vacuuming a doormat takes practically no time at all.

▶ To vacuum wall-to-wall carpeting, divide the floor into quadrants and vacuum an entire quadrant before moving on to the next.

▶ Take your time when you vacuum a carpet, especially a thick, plush carpet in which dirt is sure to be deeply embedded. One pass with even a high-powered upright is not enough. Go over each section of carpeting several times and work slowly to allow the suction to remove all the ground-in dust and dirt.

▶ Pay special attention to the carpet in front of chairs and couches and under desks where people sit and move their feet. Vacuum these areas of heavy traffic with a crisscross pattern of overlapping strokes.

TREATING SPECIFIC STAINS

► Acid stains: Acid spills, such as toilet-bowl cleaner, drain cleaner, and vinegar, demand especially quick action. Dilute them immediately with baking soda and water or with club soda. Then apply a solution of ammonia (1 part) and water (10 parts). Rinse with cold water, let dry, and vacuum gently.

► Alcoholic beverages: Quickly dilute the spot with cold water so that the alcohol does not have time to attack the dyes. Absorb the excess liquid. Then mix 1 teaspoon mild detergent, 1 teaspoon white vinegar, and 1 quart warm water. Apply the solution to the spot and let the carpet dry. Vacuum gently.

► Blood: Absorb as much of the blood as you can. Then mix 1 teaspoon mild detergent, 1 teaspoon white vinegar, and 1 quart warm water. Apply the solution to the spot. Let the carpet dry. Apply dry-cleaning fluid and let the carpet dry completely. Vacuum gently.

► Butter: Scrape up as much solid or melted butter as you can. Apply dry-cleaning fluid and let the carpet dry. If the spot remains, repeat the procedure. Vacuum gently.

► Candle wax: The easiest way to remove candle wax from your carpet is to press an ice cube against the drip. The wax will harden and can then be pulled off. Treat any remaining traces of wax with dry-cleaning fluid. Let the carpet dry and vacuum. Another way to remove candle wax on carpeting is to place a blotter over the spilled wax and press with a warm iron until the blotter absorbs the wax. Let dry and vacuum.

► Candy: Candy that contains no chocolate is usually easily removed from carpet. Scrape up as much of the candy as you can. Mix 1 teaspoon mild detergent, 1 teaspoon white vinegar, and 1 quart warm water. Apply the solution to the spot. Let the carpet dry. Vacuum gently.

► Chewing gum: Chewing gum can be a sticky mess, so harden it by pressing an ice cube against the blob of gum. The gum will harden and can then be pulled off. Treat any remaining traces of the chewing gum with dry-cleaning fluid. Let the carpet dry and vacuum.

► Chocolate: The longer chocolate is allowed to stay on your carpet, the more difficult it is to remove. Scrape the chocolate from the carpet. Mix 1 teaspoon mild detergent, 1 teaspoon white vinegar, and 1 quart warm water. Apply the solution to the spot. Rinse well. Vacuum gently.

► Coffee: Blot spilled coffee immediately. Then mix 1 teaspoon mild detergent, 1 teaspoon white vinegar, and 1 quart warm water. Apply the solution to the spot. Allow the carpet to dry. Apply dry-cleaning fluid and let the carpet dry again. Vacuum gently.

► Crayon: Scrape away excess crayon or remove it by placing a blotter over the crayon stain and pressing it with a warm iron until the blotter absorbs the melted crayon. Move the blotter frequently so that it doesn't get oversaturated. Apply dry-cleaning fluid and let the carpet dry. Vacuum gently.

► Egg: Scrape up as much cooked egg as possible or mop up raw egg. Mix 1 teaspoon mild detergent, 1 teaspoon white vinegar, and 1 quart warm water. Apply the solution to the spot and let the carpet dry. If the spot remains, repeat the procedure. Vacuum.

► Fruit: Fruit stains can be very hard to remove if they are allowed to set, but if you act quickly this method usually prevents a permanent stain. Scrape up spilled fruit and absorb fruit juice. Mix 1 teaspoon mild detergent, 1 teaspoon white vinegar, and 1 quart warm water. Apply the solution to the spot and let the carpet dry. If the spot remains, repeat the procedure. Vacuum gently.

► Gravy: Wipe up as much of the spilled gravy as possible. Mix 1 teaspoon mild detergent, 1 teaspoon white vinegar, and 1 quart warm water. Apply the solution to the spot. Let the carpet dry. Apply dry-cleaning fluid and let the carpet dry. Vacuum.

► Hand cream: Wipe up the spill immediately. Apply a dry-cleaning fluid and let the carpet dry. If the spot remains, repeat the procedure. Vacuum.

► Ink: Fast action is essential when you spill ink on carpet. Immediately apply dry-cleaning fluid and let the carpet dry. If the spot remains, reapply the dry-cleaning fluid. Let the carpet dry thoroughly and vacuum.

► Mildew: The first step in removing mildew stains is to kill the fungus. To do this, mix 1 teaspoon disinfectant cleaner and 1 cup water. Apply the solution to the mildewed carpet and blot. To remove the stain, apply a solution of 1 part ammonia to 10 parts water. Blot, rinse, and let dry. Vacuum.

► Mud: Allow the mud tracked on to carpeting to dry completely and then brush or scrape off as much as possible. Mix 1 teaspoon mild detergent, 1 teaspoon white vinegar, and 1 quart warm water. Apply the solution to the spot. Let the carpet dry. If the stain remains, apply dry-cleaning fluid and blot dry. When the spot is completely dry, vacuum gently.

► Nail polish: Apply dry-cleaning fluid or amyl acetate, acetone, or nail-polish remover to the spilled polish. Test the solvent you plan to use on an inconspicuous part of the carpet. Never apply acetate, acetone, or nail-polish remover to acetate carpet fibers. If the stain remains, mix 1 teaspoon mild detergent, 1 teaspoon white vinegar, and 1 quart warm water. Apply the solution to the spot. Let the carpet dry. Vacuum gently.

► Salad dressing: Absorb as much salad dressing as you can. Mix 1 teaspoon mild detergent, 1 teaspoon white vinegar, and 1 quart warm water. Apply the solution to the spot. Let the carpet dry. If the spot remains, repeat the procedure. Vacuum gently.

► Soft drinks: The carbonation in soft drinks will help you clean spilled drinks quickly, but act fast because some of the dyes in the drinks can permanently stain your carpet. Blot up the spilled drink. Mix 1 teaspoon mild detergent, 1 teaspoon white vinegar, and 1 quart warm water. Apply the solution to the spot. Let the carpet dry. If the spot remains, repeat the procedure. Vacuum gently.

► Urine: Mix 1 teaspoon mild detergent, 1 teaspoon white vinegar, and 1 quart warm water. Apply the solution to the spot. Let the carpet dry. If the spot remains, repeat the procedure. Vacuum gently.

► Vomit: Treat vomit quickly. Blot up as much as possible, then dilute immediately with baking soda and water or with club soda. Apply a solution of 1 part ammonia and 10 parts water. Rinse with cold water, let dry, and then vacuum.

► Wine: When red wine is spilled on your carpet, dilute it with white wine, then clean the spot with cold water and cover with table salt. Wait ten minutes, then vacuum up the salt.

▶ Soil retardants can be applied to new carpets or to newly cleaned carpets. Follow manufacturers' advice. Apply soil retardants only with professional equipment using the recommended application techniques.

▶ Carpet odor can be eliminated without resorting to deep-cleaning. Sprinkle baking soda on the carpet before vacuuming. If you prefer, you can use 1 cup of borax mixed with 2 cups of cornmeal, but you must let this mixture stand on the carpet for at least an hour before vacuuming. Remember that these fine particles may stop the airflow through your disposable dust bag sooner than larger dust particles, and a bag that appears to be only partially filled may need to be changed. Don't forget to check the filter on your canister as well.

Cleaning Spots and Spills

Clean spots and spills immediately. If you catch the spill when it's fresh, before it has become a stain, you've got a three out of four chance of removing it totally. So when something spills, immediately move into action and follow this procedure:

▶ Carefully blot or scrape the entire stained area before applying any cleaning solution. Remove as much of the spill as possible. If you just start cleaning, you'll make an even bigger mess because the cleaning solutions you pour on will only spread the stain over more of the carpet.

▶ Before using any cleaning solution, test your carpet in an inconspicuous area to make sure the cleaner won't damage or discolor it. Since you want to move fast once a spill occurs, test the cleaning agents that you keep on hand before you have to use them to make sure that they will not harm your carpeting.

▶ Do not rub the spill because rubbing might spread the problem to a larger area of the rug.

▶ When you apply spot cleaner, work from the outside of the stain toward the inside to avoid spreading the stain. Most of us want to start cleaning the worst part of the stain first,

but most substances stain as they dry. Cleaning the stain from the outside edges in toward the center gathers up the spill in order to get rid of it completely. After an application of a cleaning solution, blot up all the moisture.

▶ A clean, white bath towel is unsurpassed for drying carpet and brushing the nap back up to a standing position.

▶ If you feel that there is still too much moisture after blotting the carpet, place a 3/4-inch-thick stack of white cloth towels over the spot and weigh them down with a heavy object.

Deep-Cleaning Carpets

There comes a time in the life of every carpet when vacuuming can no longer restore its clean appearance. There are four major indicators of the need for a deep-cleaning job: the carpet is matted and feels sticky to bare feet; the carpet is no longer the same color as the remnant you saved when the carpet was new; the carpet has grimy circles around the chairs where people sit to read or watch TV; and the carpet releases a dust storm when you run across the room to answer the phone.

If any of these descriptions fit your carpet, then it is time to deep-clean it. Unless you have the time and strength to do a thorough cleaning job, it's time to call in the professionals. One of the reasons that many people believe that carpets soil faster after they have been shampooed is that many people clean only the surface of their carpeting when they think they are deep-cleaning it. The only method to clean carpeting down to the backing is to agitate it with a shampooer and rinse with an extractor.

Should you decide to rent carpet-cleaning equipment and shampoo your carpets yourself, allow plenty of uninterrupted time for the task. This is a very big job and rushing it will mean disappointing results. To speed drying, you should also plan to shampoo rugs during dry periods of the year or when the heating system is operating. The following steps are required to deep-clean a carpet:

▶ Before cleaning your carpeting, test for colorfastness. Moisten a white towel with the cleaning solution that you are going to be using and apply it to an inconspicuous area. If the towel does not pick up any color from the carpet, it is probably safe to use the solution on the entire carpet.

▶ Remove as much furniture from the room as possible and place foil or plastic film under the legs and bases of the remaining furniture to prevent stains. (The foil or plastic should be left in place until the carpet is completely dry.)

▶ Vacuum the carpet thoroughly, then spot-clean and pretreat stains before shampooing the carpet.

▶ Follow the instructions printed on the carpet cleaner you rent.

▶ Use single strokes over the carpet surface.

▶ Do not apply heavy pressure with the machine.

▶ Wipe cleaner solutions and foam from furniture legs and woodwork immediately to prevent damage to the wood or upholstery.

▶ Fluff damp fibers against the nap after shampooing to aid drying and prevent matting.

▶ Make sure the room is well-ventilated after cleaning to speed drying.

▶ Try not to walk on carpets until they are completely dry.

FIREPLACES

Whether you have a small fireplace set into the corner of your den or one that spans the entire length of a wall, a fireplace needs regular care and cleaning to assure a safe and efficient fire. Creosote, a flammable, tarlike substance that accumulates in the chimney and flue, should be removed by a professional, eliminating the worry of at least one potential fire hazard. Give your fireplace and its accessories routine cleaning throughout the wood-burning season to eliminate an end-of-the-year accumulation of soot, ashes, and creosote tars.

▶ Vacuum or dust the hearth area weekly to prevent dust and soot buildup, but do not sweep or vacuum until all the embers have been extinguished for at least 12 hours.

▶ Burn only seasoned, well-dried wood to minimize dangerous creosote buildup.

▶ Inspect the firebox, flue, and chimney annually for creosote accumulation.

▶ Do not use water to drown a fire unless there is an absolute emergency. It will make a paste of the ashes that is difficult to remove.

SPECIAL CARPET PROBLEMS

When your carpet is burned, stained, or discolored, you could simply move a big chair over the spot and forget about it. Or you can use one of the following simple methods to restore your carpet to its original good looks.

▶ If the spot remover you use alters the color of your carpet, try touching up small places with artists' acrylic paint. If acrylic paint doesn't work, try using a felt-tip marker or a permanent-ink marker of the appropriate color. Go slowly and blend the color into the fibers.

▶ To raise depressions left in a carpet by heavy furniture, try steaming. Hold a steam iron close enough for steam to reach the carpet, but don't let the iron touch the fibers, especially if they are synthetic, because they could melt. Lift the fibers by scraping them with the edge of a coin or spoon.

▶ If a carpet thread is loose, snip it level with the pile. If you try to pull out the thread, you risk unraveling part of the carpet.

▶ To repair a large burned area in a carpet, cut out the damaged area and substitute a patch of identical size and shape. Secure the new piece of carpeting with double-faced carpet tape or a latex adhesive.

▶ To repair a small area burned down to the carpet backing, snip off the charred fibers and put white glue in the opening. Then snip fibers from a scrap of carpet or an inconspicuous part of the carpet (perhaps in a closet). When the glue gets tacky, poke the fibers into place. If the burn isn't all the way down to the backing, just snip off the charred tips of the fibers with scissors. The slightly shorter length of a few carpet fibers will never be noticed.

Depressions in carpets can be raised by steaming (center) and by scraping the fibers with the edge of a spoon (right).

▸ Never use an abrasive cleanser inside the fireplace. Many leave a flammable residue, and they can wear away firebrick.

Firebox

The firebox is the area that contains the fire; it is commonly constructed of either metal sheeting or firebrick. Since the heat of the fire keeps the firebox clean (in much the same way a self-cleaning oven works), very little upkeep is required.

▸ Gently scrub the walls of the firebox opening with a stiff-bristled brush (not a wire brush) only to the height of the lintel (the heavy steel brace that supports the masonry above the fireplace opening).

▸ Be gentle with firebrick because it crumbles easily. Be careful not to bend any edges on a metal firebox where it joins the flue. Bent edges leave openings to the wall stud or supports where fire could spread.

HOME RECIPE FOR CLEANING PAINTED WOOD

Mix 2 tablespoons of gentle dishwashing detergent in 1 gallon of warm water. Wipe with a cloth or sponge. Don't let any excess run off. Clean from the bottom up to avoid streaking.

HOME RECIPE FOR CLEANING MASONRY TILE

Sprinkle dry baking soda on the tile. Rub it with a bristle brush to absorb most stains and clean the tile. Vacuum the dry powder.

▸ If your fireplace does not have an ash pit, shovel the bulk of the ashes into a bag and vacuum the remaining lightweight ashes.

Fire Screen

Most fire screens are black painted metal, but if your screen is brass-plated, clean it as you would other brass objects.

Glass Enclosure

Glass enclosures for the fireplace present a special cleaning problem. They are constructed of a heat-resistant, tempered glass. To clean the glass and metal edging facing the room, see "Windows." Clean the glass facing the fire after every other fire to remove the residue of soot. For baked-on soot, scrape the glass very carefully with a glass scraper to avoid scratching the surface.

Grate and Cast-Iron Tools

Like the chimney, the grate is usually made from cast iron and can accumulate a buildup of creosote tars or sap from burning green wood. Cast-iron tools may be cleaned in the same way as grates. To remove the buildup that is not baked on, take the grate or tool outside and hose it down. Sprinkle an abrasive cleanser on the surface and scrub with a stiff-bristled brush or use steel-wool soap pads. Ordinarily, no precautions need to be taken, but wearing rubber gloves will protect your hands from abrasion.

Mantel and Hearth

The trim surrounding a fireplace is usually made from wood or masonry tile. Brick, marble, or ceramic tile are also used.

Andirons and Brass or Brass-Plated Tools

There are many products that can restore brass fireplace tools to their original beauty with a little time and effort. To make your own, use the following:

HOME RECIPE FOR CLEANING GLASS FIREPLACE ENCLOSURES

To remove smoke stains, mix ½ cup vinegar with 1 gallon clear, warm water. Add 1 tablespoon clear ammonia. Either spray this solution on the glass or wipe it on with a cloth dipped in the solution. Rinse with clear, warm water and dry with a clean cloth. Repeat several times if the enclosure is really dirty.

HOME RECIPE FOR CLEANING PAINTED FIRE SCREENS

Mix ½ cup vinegar and 1 gallon warm water. Add 1 teaspoon ammonia. Dip a cloth into the solution and wipe down both sides of the screen. Rinse with a cloth dipped in clear, warm water.

HOME RECIPE FOR CLEANING FIREPLACE TOOLS

Clean andirons by dipping fine-grade (000) steel wool in cooking oil and rubbing gently. Apply a polish to bring up the shine.

FLOORS

Dirt from the street collects on feet and gets walked into your house a dozen times a day, and the little dumps, spills, and heel marks of daily living accumulate with

startling speed. And unless your home has only one kind of floor throughout, you will have to deal with cleaning several different kinds of hard-surface floors. Unfortunately, weekly vacuuming is not all it takes to keep a hard-surface floor looking its best. The first step toward efficient floor cleaning is to know what your floor is made of. The cleaning method that works for one surface may ruin another. Whenever you go to the grocery or hardware store, you will find an array of specialized cleaning products. Many commercial products are very good at cleaning what they are designed to clean. Which product you use to clean your floors is entirely up to you.

Asphalt Tile

Asphalt tile floor won't retain the footprints when you replace your favorite old TV chair in the family room with a new one. But even though asphalt tile recovers well from indentations, use plastic, not rubber, casters and cups on furniture legs to minimize scratches and indentations. Although asphalt is resilient, you should know that grease; oil; solvents, such as kerosene, gasoline, naphtha, and turpentine; harsh cleaning preparations; strong soaps; and scouring can damage the surface. If you take the time to damp-mop your asphalt floor every week, you will not have to wash it and apply polish as often as if you allow dirt to build up. But make sure that the cleaner/polish you use can withstand damp-mopping. If it can't,

ASPHALT FLOOR CLEANER

Mix 1/4 cup low-sudsing, all-purpose cleaner; 1 cup ammonia; and 1/2 gallon cool or cold water. Caution: Wear rubber gloves and work in a well-ventilated area when using this powerful solution. Apply to the floor with a sponge mop, using pressure for heavily soiled areas. Rinse with cool, clear water for spotless results. Apply two thin coats of a water-based, self-polishing floor finish, allowing the floor to dry between coats. Apply the polish with a long-handled wax applicator with a washable chenille pad.

you will have to reapply it anyway. Adding a cup of fabric softener to 1/2 pail of water will prevent damp-mopping from dulling the shine on your floor.

▶ Don't flood the floor with water; excess water can seep into the seams and loosen adhesives that hold down the flooring.

▶ Remove heel marks by dipping fine-grade (000) steel wool in liquid floor wax and rubbing the spot gently. Wipe with a damp cloth.

▶ For a fast cleaning job, use a one-step cleaner/polish. If you use a commercial water-based polish, don't shake it before use.

Brick

A brick floor may appear to be very durable because of its hard, fired surface, but brick is porous and stains easily. Caring for a porous brick floor is a lot of work no matter what you do. If you use a solvent-based wax on the floor, you have to seal it. If you use a water-based polish, you'll occasionally have to strip the wax buildup. The best way to care for your brick floor is to keep it sealed and waxed. You'll need to use a commercial sealer for brick; neither varnish nor lacquer will do.

▶ Damp-mopping with a sponge mop or string mop after vacuuming will prevent dirt

QUICK CARE FOR A BRICK FLOOR

While the following method of caring for a brick floor is not as effective as treatment with a stripper, sealer, and paste wax, it is quick and inexpensive. Since this homemade solution contains ammonia, you strip the floor every time you wash it, eliminating wax buildup. Most acrylic liquid waxes are self-sealing, allowing you to skip the application of a sealer. Clean and strip the floor with a solution of 1/4 cup low-sudsing, all-purpose cleaner; 1 cup clear ammonia; and 1/2 gallon cool or cold water. Caution: Wear rubber gloves and work in a well-ventilated area when using this powerful solution. Apply the solution to the floor with a sponge mop, using pressure for heavily soiled areas; rinse with cool, clear water for spotless results. Then apply two thin coats of an acrylic floor wax.

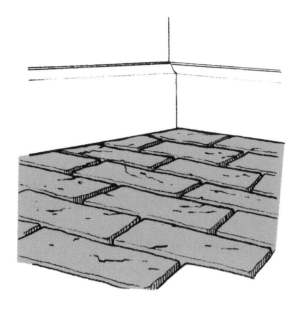

from building up on your brick floor, so you can put off washing and/or stripping the floor. Try putting a cup of vinegar in the water; the floor will glisten without being polished—a real timesaver.

▶ If you use a water-based, self-polishing liquid wax, you'll occasionally have to strip the wax buildup before you rewax. Use a solvent-based wax, so that you don't have to strip your floor. A solvent-based polish can be applied over a water-based polish, but a water-based polish cannot be applied over a solvent-based polish. The solvents in the wax dissolve the layer of wax that is on the floor every time solvent-based wax is applied, so there is no wax buildup.

▶ Remove wax buildup by applying a wax-stripping product with a scrub brush or floor-scrubbing machine that has a brush attachment. Rinse the floor thoroughly with clear water after applying the stripper. Do not clean your brick floor with acids, strong soaps, or abrasives.

Ceramic Tile

It's easy to tell the difference between glazed and unglazed ceramic tile: glazed tile is very shiny. Glazed ceramic tile is virtually

stainproof, but unglazed ceramic tile is porous and must be sealed to resist stains. A new unglazed ceramic-tile floor needs to be sealed with a commercial sealer and a water-based wax. Both types of tile are installed with grout, which is porous and soft and presents a real cleaning challenge.

▶ Never use harsh abrasive cleaners that might scratch the glaze.

▶ Do not clean an unglazed ceramic-tile floor with acids, strong soaps, or abrasives.

▶ Damp-mop ceramic tile with an all-purpose cleaner, using a synthetic scouring pad and nonabrasive cleaner for stubborn spots. Then dry the floor with a soft cloth to avoid streaks. If the freshly mopped floor dries with a luster-dulling film, mop it again with water containing a cup of white vinegar, and the floor will glisten.

▶ Sparkle your ceramic tile walls and countertops by rubbing the tile with car wax. Buff after ten minutes.

▶ About once a year strip the wax buildup on your unglazed ceramic tile floor or counter and rewax. A floor-scrubbing machine that has a brush attachment really saves time on this job, but if you don't have or can't rent a machine, a scrub brush can be used to apply the wax-stripping product. Rinse the floor thoroughly with clear water after applying the stripper.

CLEANER FOR GLAZED CERAMIC TILE

Mix ¼ cup low-sudsing, all-purpose cleaner; 1 cup ammonia; and ½ gallon cool or cold water. Caution: Wear rubber gloves and work in a well-ventilated area when using this powerful solution. Apply the solution to the floor with a sponge mop, using pressure for heavily soiled areas; rinse with cool, clear water for spotless results. Dry with a soft cloth.

QUICK CLEANUP FOR UNGLAZED TILE

Either a water-based, self-polishing wax or a paste wax can be used to rewax unglazed ceramic tile. Use the following homemade solution in conjunction with a water-based, acrylic self-polishing wax. This method is not as effective as a treatment with stripper, sealer, and paste wax, but it works nearly as well and is quick and inexpensive.

Clean and strip the floor with a solution of ¼ cup low-sudsing, all-purpose cleaner; 1 cup clear ammonia; and ½ gallon cool or cold water. Caution: Wear rubber gloves and work in a well-ventilated area when using this powerful solution. Apply the solution to the floor with a sponge mop, using pressure for heavily soiled areas; rinse with cool, clear water for spotless results. Then apply two thin coats of an acrylic floor wax.

purpose cleaning solution or the following homemade cleaning solution. (It works as well as a commercial heavy-duty cleaner, and it's much less expensive.)

Cork

A cork floor recovers quickly from the pressure of chair legs and the wear and tear of heavy foot traffic, but water will do it in every time. Even the small amount of water in water-based cleaners is too wet for a cork floor. Use only solvent-based cleaners and polishes to maintain cork-tile flooring.

Concrete

If you're like most people, you probably put off dealing with the concrete floors in your unfinished basement or garage for as long as possible. The result is that your concrete floor really gets dirty because concrete is very porous and soaks up stains quickly. While few of us are so fastidious that we seal or paint our garage floors, the time you take to seal a basement floor, especially if it is new, will save time in the long run, because the sealed floor will require little more cleaning than vacuuming.

For an unsealed concrete floor, sweep up the loose surface dirt and then wash it with either a strong, all-

CLEANER FOR CONCRETE

Mix ¼ cup low-sudsing, all-purpose cleaner; 1 cup clear ammonia; and ½ gallon cool or cold water. Caution: Wear rubber gloves and work in a well-ventilated area when using this powerful solution. If you can't open your basement windows or a basement door, you'll want to divide the basement into sections and do it on separate days to avoid too much contact at one time with this solution. Apply the solution to the concrete floor with a sponge mop, using pressure for heavily soiled areas; rinse with cool, clear water for spotless results. Let the floor dry.

The fastest way to clean a cork floor is with a one-step product specifically formulated to clean and polish cork floors. Unfortunately, the fastest way is not the best way to care for cork. If your floor is new or a focal point of your home, you should take the time twice a year to clean the floor with a liquid wood-floor cleaning product and to rewax. Use a liquid cleaner/wax that soaks into the floor. Wipe up the excess liquid and allow the floor to dry, then buff it with a floor polisher.

The second step of this process is to apply a liquid or paste solvent-based wax. No stripping will ever be necessary because the solvents in the new wax will strip off the old wax. Shake solvent-based liquid polishes vigorously before use. To renew the shine between cleanings, buff the floor when it appears dull.

▶ Seal a new cork floor with varnish, shellac, or lacquer; paint or lacquer thinner, alcohol, and other chemicals will damage these sealers, so try not to use them near the floor.

▶ Remove heel marks from a cork floor by applying a solvent-based wax, polish, or cleaner to a rag and rubbing the mark.

Flagstone and Slate

These natural-stone flooring materials are similar; they have rough, porous surfaces and are set into grout. This type of flooring wears like rock, but it will look as if it should have

been left in nature if it is not cared for properly. Flagstone and slate floors must be sealed with a commercial sealer, not lacquer or varnish.

▶ The best way to seal a flagstone or slate floor is with a commercial sealer for terrazzo and slate. After the sealer dries, apply two thin coats of an acrylic floor finish with a long-handled wax applicator fitted with a lamb's wool pad, or apply paste wax with a floor-polishing machine. To do this, use a spatula to spread a small amount of paste wax directly on the brushes of the polisher. Slowly operate the polisher back and forth to apply an even, thin coat of wax. When dry, buff the floor.

▶ A self-polishing liquid will build up on your floor, and you'll occasionally have to strip the wax buildup and rewax. Applying a wax-stripping product with a floor-scrubbing machine that has a brush attachment will keep you off your knees, but if you don't have a machine, a scrub brush will work. After applying the stripper according to the manufacturer's directions, rinse the floor thoroughly with clear water. Then apply wax.

▶ To keep ahead of dirt, damp-mop flagstone or slate floors with a sponge mop or string mop, using either clear water, an all-purpose cleaning solution in warm water, or water to which fabric softener has been added. Wring the mop until it doesn't drip and apply it to the floor in slow, even strokes with just

HOMEMADE CLEANER FOR FLAGSTONE AND SLATE FLOORS

Mix ¼ cup low-sudsing, all-purpose cleaner; 1 cup clear ammonia; and ½ gallon cool or cold water. Caution: Wear rubber gloves and work in a well-ventilated area when using this powerful solution. Apply to the floor with a sponge mop, using pressure for heavily soiled areas. Rinse the floor thoroughly with clean water. Apply sealer, then buff.

enough pressure to loosen and pick up dirt. If the freshly mopped floor dries with a luster-dulling film, you can mop it again with water containing a cup of white vinegar; the floor will glisten.

Linoleum

To shine and resist foot traffic, linoleum must be waxed. But once it is waxed, the only regular maintenance linoleum floors need is vacuuming and an occasional swipe with a damp mop.

▶ A cup of vinegar in the mop water will bring up the shine on the floor, so you can delay rewaxing until it's really necessary.

▶ Remove heel marks from linoleum by dipping fine-grade (000) steel wool in liquid floor wax. Rub the spot gently and wipe with a damp cloth.

▶ A water-based cleaner/polish or an all-purpose cleaning solution is best for the routine care of a linoleum floor. Solvent-based products can soften and damage linoleum. Scouring the floor, flooding it with water, or using very hot water or strong soaps are also bad for linoleum floors.

▶ The fastest way to clean a linoleum floor is with a one-step cleaner/polish, but the best way to clean the floor is to mop it with an all-purpose cleaner. Dissolve the cleaner in very warm water, rinse, and apply two thin coats (let dry between coats) of a water-based, self-polishing liquid. Use a long-handled wax applicator fitted with a washable, reusable chenille pad.

▶ Use an all-purpose cleaner or stripper to remove wax buildup. Test a corner of the floor before stripping the whole thing to make sure the product you're using won't permanently damage the flooring. This is particularly true of older linoleum.

HOMEMADE LINOLEUM FLOOR CLEANER/POLISH

Mix ½ cup vinegar, 2 tablespoons furniture polish, and 1 gallon of warm water. Caution: Wear rubber gloves. Mop the floor with this mixture using a sponge or string mop.

Marble

Marble is showing up throughout the house—on floors, countertops, and even bathroom walls. It is available in a variety of colors, with a polished or nonpolished finish, and in an array of new thicknesses and shapes. Nonpolished marble is very porous, stains easily, and must be sealed with a commercial sealer. Do not use varnish or lacquer to seal marble; it quickly peels off. Polished marble is less porous but can still be stained; a commercial marble sealer is also recommended for this finish.

▶ Marble floors look great after being damp-mopped with a sponge mop or string mop, using either clear water, an all-purpose cleaning solution in warm water, or a mixture of 1 cup fabric softener and ½ gallon water. Wring the mop until it doesn't drip and apply it to the floor in slow, even strokes with just enough pressure to loosen and pick up dirt. If the mopped floor dries with a luster-dulling film, mop it again with water containing a cup of white vinegar.

▶ Water-based, self-polishing liquid wax is a fast, shiny finish for marble. There's only one problem (and it's a big one); occasionally, you'll have to strip the wax buildup and rewax. Applying a wax-stripping product with a floor-scrubbing machine with a brush attachment makes the job easier. After applying the stripper according to the manufacturer's directions, rinse the floor thoroughly with clear water. Then apply wax to the floor.

▶ Use either a water-based, self-polishing wax or a paste wax. If you use a water-based polish, don't shake it before use. A solvent-based polish can be applied over a water-based polish, but a water-based polish cannot be applied over a solvent-based polish. If you use a paste wax, test it in a corner to see if it will discolor the flooring. If a solvent-based paste wax is used, rewax to strip the old wax and to renew the shine.

Quarry Tile

Like brick, quarry tile looks durable, but this unglazed clay tile is very porous and readily soaks up stains. Quarry-tile floors have to be sealed with as many as three coats of sealer and further protected by a high-quality wax. While there is no easy way to seal a quarry-tile floor, if you do it right, you won't have to do it very often.

▶ Seal a quarry-tile floor with a commercial sealer for terrazzo and slate. After the sealer dries, apply two thin coats of an acrylic floor finish. Use a long-handled wax applicator fitted with a lamb's wool pad or apply paste wax with a floor-polishing machine. To do this, use a spatula to spread a small amount of paste wax directly on the brushes of the polisher. Slowly operate the polisher back and forth to apply an even, thin coat of wax. When the wax is dry, buff the floor.

▶ To keep your sealed and waxed quarry-tile floor looking new, all you have to do is to damp-mop it occasionally after you vacuum. If the mopped floor dries with a luster-dulling film, restore the shine by mopping it again with water containing a cup of white vinegar.

▶ To strip the wax buildup and rewax, apply a commercial wax-stripping product with a floor-scrubbing machine that has a brush attachment. After applying the stripper according to the manufacturer's directions, rinse the floor thoroughly with clear water. Use a nonabrasive powder and a synthetic scouring pad for stubborn spots.

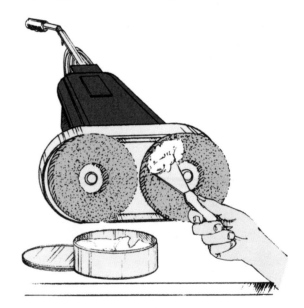

▶ If you use a paste wax, such as those used on wood floors, you will never have to strip the wax. Test the wax in a corner to see if it will discolor the tile. Rewaxing will strip the old wax and renew the shine if you use a solvent-based product.

Rubber Tile

Rubber tile is delicate; it can be damaged by exposure to direct sunlight and is easily wrecked by strong cleaners. You'll have to be careful with its care.

▶ Make a rubber-tile floor look freshly waxed by adding a cup of fabric softener to ½ pail of water. This prevents damp-mopping from dulling the shine on your floor.

▶ Be sure that you use a cleaner/polish that can withstand damp-mopping; if it can't, you'll have to reapply the cleaner/polish every time you mop.

▶ The quickest way to clean a rubber-tile floor is to use a water-based cleaner/polish or an all-purpose cleaning solution. Read the product label for precautionary measures and test any cleaner in a corner before using it on the entire floor.

▶ Occasionally, remove wax buildup with a cleaner or wax stripper. Follow stripping with two thin coats of self-polishing wax; allow to dry between coats. Two thin coats make a much more durable, long-lasting finish than one thick coat, which may dry slowly and leave a gummy, dust-collecting mess on your floor.

▶ Remove heel marks from rubber tile by dipping fine-grade (000) steel wool in liquid floor wax. Rub the spot gently and wipe with a damp cloth.

▶ Solvent-based products can soften and damage a rubber-tile floor. Also, keep scouring pads, strong soaps, and hot water away from rubber tile. Flooding the floor with water will also cause big problems; excess water can seep into the seams and loosen the adhesives that hold down the flooring.

HOMEMADE FLOOR CLEANER/POLISH

Mix 1/2 cup vinegar, 2 tablespoons furniture polish, and 1 gallon of warm water. Caution: Wear rubber gloves. Mop the floor with this mixture, using a sponge or string mop.

Terrazzo

Terrazzo is a very durable floor that used to be used only in schools and other public buildings, but is now showing up in bathrooms and entrance halls in homes. This flooring is made of marble chips set in cement. After it cures, terrazzo is ground and polished. As durable as it seems, terrazzo stains easily and must be sealed with a commercial sealer, not with varnish or lacquer.

▶ The best way to seal a terrazzo floor is with a commercial sealer for terrazzo and slate. After the sealer dries, apply two thin coats of an acrylic floor finish. Use a long-handled wax applicator fitted with a lamb's wool pad or apply paste wax with a floor-polishing machine. To do this, use a spatula to spread a small amount of paste wax directly on the brushes of the polisher. Slowly operate the polisher back and forth to apply an even, thin coat of wax. When the wax is dry, buff the floor.

▶ All a terrazzo floor needs to keep it looking good is a quick going over with a damp mop, using either clear water, an all-purpose cleaner in warm water, or a mixture of 1 cup fabric softener and 1/2 gallon water. If your mopped floor dries with a luster-dulling film, mop it again with water containing a cup of white vinegar, and the floor will glisten.

▶ To strip the wax buildup on your floor and rewax, use a water-based, self-polishing liquid. Apply a commercial wax-stripping product with a floor-scrubbing machine that has a brush attachment. After applying the stripper according to the manufacturer's directions, rinse the floor thoroughly with clear water. A nonabrasive powder and a synthetic scouring pad will remove stubborn spots without scratching the floor.

Vinyl

A no-wax vinyl floor is a breeze to maintain. All you have to do is keep it clean.

▶ Wipe up spills with a sponge dipped in dishwashing liquid.

▸ Scrub off heel marks with a synthetic scouring pad.

▸ To wash the floor, use an all-purpose cleaning solution. Be sure to read the product label for precautionary measures and instructions. It pays to test any cleaner in a corner before using it on the entire floor.

▸ Sometimes a no-wax floor dries with a luster-dulling film. Don't panic; just mop it again with water containing a cup of white vinegar, and the floor will glisten like new.

▸ If your no-wax floor loses its shine in high-traffic areas, use a gloss-renewing product

CLEANING THE GARAGE FLOOR

The garage floor is the biggest cleaning challenge, because it is not easily maintained. Cement floors soak up oil and grease stains, gather piles of litter, and collect road dirt. But not many people spend much time in the garage, so you don't need to attack the mess very often. As strange as it seems, kitty litter can be a big help in the garage. Spread some around to absorb oil and grease. Also, keep the garage door closed so that leaves and other windblown debris don't collect in your garage.

When it comes time to clean the garage floor, sweep out the dirt, dust, and spread kitty litter with a stiff broom, working from the back of the garage to the front. Then get out the garden hose and flush the floor with clear water. You can scour tough globs of dirt with your stiff broom or blast them with a jet of water.

After you have gotten rid of the loose surface dirt, use the following homemade cleaning solution. It works as well as a commercial heavy-duty cleaner, and it's much less expensive. Mix $1/4$ cup low-sudsing, all-purpose cleaner; 1 cup clear ammonia; and $1/2$ gallon cool or cold water. Caution: Wear rubber gloves and work in a well-ventilated area when using this powerful solution. Apply to the concrete floor with a sponge mop, using pressure for heavily soiled areas; rinse with cool, clear water for spotless results. Let the floor dry.

available from the manufacturer of your floor or another commercial product designed for this purpose. Never throw just anything you have around the house on the dull floor: Solvent-based products or cleaners that contain pine oil can soften and permanently damage a vinyl-tile floor.

▶ Do not scour the tile, use strong soaps and hot water, or flood the floor with water. Excess water can seep into the seams and loosen the adhesives that hold it down.

▶ If your vinyl floor is old or not a no-wax variety, clean it with an all-purpose cleaner

CARING FOR A WOOD FLOOR

There is almost nothing as elegant as a glimmering wood floor. The sight of such a floor speaks to us of glamour, good living, and a lot of very hard work on somebody's part (preferably not yours). It's true that you have to take care of a wood floor, but you don't have to break your back to do it if you take care of it on a regular basis.

The product used to seal a wood floor determines how it can be cared for. Varnish, shellac, polyurethane, or lacquer are used to finish floors, but only polyurethane requires no further treatment—not even waxing. The integrity and beauty of wood floors, not finished with polyurethane, can be maintained only by using solvent-based cleaners and polishes. Water should never be used on wood floors, except those treated with polyurethane. They can be damp-mopped.

The fastest way to clean a lacquered, varnished, or shellacked floor is with a one-step cleaner/polish. After vacuuming the floor, pour the solvent-based liquid on a small area and rub lightly with a clean, dry wax applicator. Working on a small section at a time, stroke the floor in the direction of the grain. Blot up any excess liquid with a clean cloth.

The best way to clean a wood floor is not the fastest, so if you want a long-lasting shine on your wood floor, you will have to spend more time and follow this method. After vacuuming the floor, apply a liquid wood-floor cleaner with a dry wax applicator or a cloth on a small area at a time. Let it soak for three minutes and wipe up the excess. When the floor is dry, buff with a floor polisher. Caution: This is a combustible mixture; use in a well-ventilated area. Apply a liquid or paste solvent-based wax to your wood floor about twice a year. No stripping is necessary because the solvents in the new wax will strip off the old wax. Make sure the room is well ventilated.

dissolved in water. After you have cleaned the floor, rinse the tile with clear water to make sure no film remains to dull the finish. When the floor is dry, apply two thin coats of a water-based, self-polishing floor finish, allowing the floor to dry between coats. Apply the wax with a long-handled wax applicator fitted with a washable chenille pad.

▶ To damp-mop after vacuuming, add a cup of fabric softener to ½ pail of water to prevent damp-mopping from dulling the shine on vinyl floors.

FURNISHINGS

Books and Records

Books and records rarely require heavy-duty cleaning, but they appreciate a dusting now and then.

▶ If you arrange books at the front of shelves, air will be able to circulate around the books to prevent mustiness.

▶ Protect books from direct sunlight, which will fade the bindings and cause them to deteriorate.

▶ Clean books with the small brush attachment on your vacuum cleaner. Tilt each book back and then forward, one at a time, on the shelf so you can remove the dust from the binding and the book's edges.

▶ To keep vinyl and imitation-leather book bindings looking new, wipe the covers with a mild detergent solution and then treat them with a light coat of petroleum jelly or a vinyl dressing.

▶ Leather-bound books should be treated periodically with a light oil so that the leather won't dry out and crack.

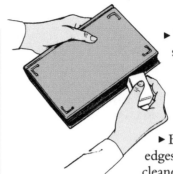

▶ To remove grease stains from books, rub the affected areas with soft white bread crumbs.

▶ Badly soiled paper edges of books can be cleaned with an art gum eraser. Hold the book firmly by the covers so it won't accidentally open and cause damage to the pages.

▶ If a book is damp, sprinkle the pages with cornstarch until the moisture has been absorbed; then vacuum the powder away.

▶ Vacuum your record, compact disc, audio cassette collection, and stereo equipment regularly.

▶ If dust accumulates around the stylus, or needle, of your turntable, remove it with an artist's brush dipped in isopropyl alcohol.

▶ Clean lightly soiled records on the turntable. Gently hold a clean dust cloth on a record and allow the disc to turn at least three revolutions under the cloth. Since you are cleaning with the grooves, not across them, there is less chance of damaging the record.

Lamp Shades

Lamp shades are made of many different materials; some are washable and some are not. Keep all the care information from the manufacturer so you know the proper cleaning procedure.

▶ Vacuum lamp shades regularly with the brush attachment.

▶ Dry-clean shades that are glued to their frames. Remove spots from nonwashable fabric shades with a spot remover.

▶ Wash silk, nylon, and rayon shades only if they are sewn to the frame.

▶ Plastic and fiberglass shades only need to be wiped occasionally with a cloth to remove soil.

CLEANING CHANDELIERS

A chandelier can be cleaned without taking it down. Vacuum chandeliers thoroughly on a regular basis and before cleaning. In a drinking glass, mix a solution of ¼ cup denatured alcohol and ¾ cup water. Cover the floor or table under the chandelier with newspaper or plastic and set up a ladder so that you can reach the pendants. Submerge the crystals in the glass for a few seconds, swishing them back and forth, and then let them air-dry.

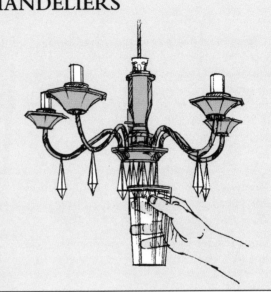

HOME RECIPES FOR WASHING LAMP SHADES

Using the bathtub or a large laundry sink, make a sudsy warm-water solution with liquid dishwashing detergent. Dip the shade in and out of the solution, making sure that the shade is completely covered, and then rinse it in lukewarm water, following the same dipping procedure. Rinse until the water is clear. Take the shade outside and swing it vigorously in a circle to get rid of excess moisture, and then dry it quickly in the sun or with an electric fan or hair dryer.

If the lamp shade is washable but has a glued-on trim that prevents immersing it in water, use the following method for cleaning. Mix ¼ cup dishwashing liquid with 1 cup warm water and whip the mixture with an eggbeater until it makes a stiff foam. Apply the foam to the shade with a sponge, being careful not to wet the trim. Rinse by going over the shade with a clean cloth wrung out in clear water. Allow the shade to dry.

Metals

BRASS

Strip cracked and peeling lacquer from coated brass and brass-plated objects with a solution of baking soda and boiling water (1 cup soda to 2 gallons water). Let the article stand in the water until it cools, then peel off the lacquer. You can either have the piece relacquered or clean and polish it.

PEWTER

▶ Pewter can be cleaned with the outer leaves from a head of cabbage. Rub a leaf over the surface and then buff it with a soft cloth.

▶ Since pewter stains easily, wash pewter food containers and flatware immediately after use.

HOME RECIPES FOR CLEANING COPPER

(1) Make a paste of 1 tablespoon salt, 1 tablespoon flour, and 1 tablespoon vinegar. Rub it over the surface, then wash the copper object in hot soapy water. Rinse and buff for a shiny finish.

(2) Mix 2 tablespoons vinegar and 1 tablespoon salt to make a copper cleaner. Wash, rinse, and dry the item after this treatment. A cut lemon dipped in salt will also clean copper.

HOME RECIPE FOR CLEANING GOLD

Mix 1 teaspoon of cigarette ash with enough water to form a paste. Rub the paste on the surface of the gold with a soft cloth, rinse, and buff-dry with a chamois. Baking soda can be substituted for ash.

HOME RECIPES FOR CLEANING BRASS

Make a paste from 1 tablespoon salt, 1 tablespoon flour, and 1 tablespoon vinegar. Apply the paste with a soft cloth and rub. You may also dip a cut lemon in salt and rub it on the brass. Wash the object in warm soapsuds and buff it dry to bring up the shine.

HOME RECIPES FOR POLISHING SILVER

(1) Place tarnished silver in a glass dish, add a piece of aluminum foil, and cover with 1 quart of hot water mixed with 1 tablespoon baking soda. A reaction between the foil and the silver will remove any tarnish. Don't use this process on raised designs; you will lose the dark accents of the pattern.

(2) Make a paste of 3 parts baking soda to 1 part water. Using a soft cloth, rub the paste gently on the silver. Tarnish will disappear rapidly. After rinsing, buff the silver with a soft cloth.

(3) Make a paste by mixing powdered white chalk with just enough ammonia to moisten. Rub the paste gently on the silver with a soft cloth. Rinse and buff to bring up the shine.

Acid foods, salt, and salad dressing are likely to blacken pewter.

▸ Pewter objects will need less polishing if you use them regularly.

Pianos

A piano should be treated with respect and care. Whether or not it is being played regularly, have it tuned by a licensed piano tuner approximately four times the first year for a new piano, semiannually for an older model, and whenever the piano is moved from one location to another. Also, keep your piano out of direct sunlight or cover it. To clean:

▸ Dust the piano case regularly with a soft cloth and vacuum the interior occasionally using the brush attachment and crevice tool of your vacuum.

▸ Use a nonsilicone furniture polish or wax on the case of a piano that has a varnish or lacquer finish.

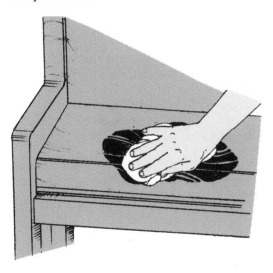

▸ A piano that has a high-gloss, polyester epoxy finish can be cleaned with a cloth or chamois and buff-dried; it should never be waxed or rubbed with furniture polish.

▸ Remove stubborn stains from ivory or plastic keys with a cloth dipped in baking soda, being careful not to let the soda fall

between the keys. Wipe the keys with another cloth and buff-dry.

▸ To brighten ivory keys, rub them with very fine (400 or 600) sandpaper along the length of each key with the grain and then buff. This treatment mars plastic keys, so be sure your piano has ivory keys before you start sanding.

Pictures and Decorative Objects

FABRIC FLOWERS

Delicate fabric blossoms collect dust and eventually look dingy unless you clean them regularly. Read and follow the manufacturer's instructions for the care of fabric flowers; some are washable, many are not.

▸ Remove dust with a vacuum cleaner set at low suction.

▸ Remove stubborn dust by gently wiping each petal with a soft toothbrush.

▸ Wipe silk flowers with a sponge; don't wash them.

▸ Dip washable flowers into a mild solution of dishwashing detergent only when other

CLEANING DELICATE DECORATIVE OBJECTS

Objects of art add visual interest to a room and often become treasured family heirlooms. Some things can be safely cleaned at home, especially if frequent dusting has kept dirt from building up on the surface. To avoid breakage, pad the bottom of the sink with a towel and wrap another towel around the faucet whenever you wash a fragile object. Never use abrasives or steel-wool pads on delicate objects and do not wash them in the dishwasher.

cleaning methods have failed. Hang the flowers by the stems to dry or use a hair dryer.

▶ Perk up slightly wilted flowers with steam from a tea kettle or a steam iron.

▶ Some sturdy fabric flowers may be freshened when shaken in a paper bag with dry cut oats, cornmeal, or salt.

PAINTINGS

Paintings, whether oil, acrylic, or watercolor, require a minimum amount of care. If the painting becomes damaged, it should not be repaired or cleaned at home.

▶ Vacuum the painting, frame, and glass regularly using the brush attachment.

▶ When you clean the glass over a painting, be careful not to allow any moisture to get behind the glass.

▶ Do not spray furniture polish directly on picture frames. Spray it on a cloth and then carefully apply the polish to the frame, making sure that it does not get on the painting.

▶ To make a tarnished gilt frame gleam again, wipe it with a rag dampened with turpentine.

ALABASTER

Alabaster looks like marble and is made into vases, statues, lamp bases, and other ornamental

HOME RECIPE FOR REMOVING WAX FROM CANDLESTICKS

One problem common to all candlesticks is caused by dripped wax. Remove a hardened wax drip by gently pushing it off the candlestick with the balls of your fingers or by using a fingernail that has been covered with a thin cloth to prevent scratching the surface. If the wax resists these methods, dip the candlestick in warm water to soften the wax for removal, or if the candlestick cannot be immersed, the wax can be softened with warm air from a hair dryer. Silver candlesticks that have wax dripped on them can be cleaned unharmed if you put them in the freezer first. After the wax freezes, it will peel off easily.

objects. Although it comes in several colors and sometimes has a dark streak or band of color, pure white and translucent ivory is the best quality. It is fine grained, but soft enough to be scratched with a fingernail. Alabaster is easily broken, soiled, and weathered and must be handled with care. The best ways to clean alabaster:

▶ Dust alabaster frequently with a soft, untreated cloth or the brush attachment of your vacuum cleaner; you may also gently blow dust away from intricate carving with the vacuum's blower.

▶ An oil polish or soft wax will probably discolor alabaster, and abrasive or caustic cleaners will scratch it. It can be cleaned with commercial products that clean marble. Caution: Work in a well-ventilated area to avoid breathing fumes from these products; do not smoke while using them or work near an open flame because some marble-cleaning products are flammable.

HOME RECIPE FOR BRIGHTENING YELLOWED IVORY

When ivory begins to yellow, treat it with a lemon and salt mixture. Cut a lemon in half, dip it in salt, and rub it over the ivory surface. Let it dry, wipe the object with a cloth, and buff it dry for a bright finish.

HOME RECIPE FOR CLEANING ALABASTER

Clean alabaster with borax; it is mild enough not to scratch the surface. Dip a moistened cloth into a small amount of dry borax and rub it on the alabaster. Rinse with warm water and buff-dry with a soft cloth. This process will brighten alabaster.

BONE AND IVORY

Bone is made into many useful and decorative objects, including sword and knife handles and miniature carvings. Like ivory, it is an animal product and must be treated with special care. Ivory, an animal dentine taken from elephants, hippopotamuses, walruses, and other sea creatures, is used for ornamental objects and piano keys. Most "ivory" objects manufactured today are synthetic, because most countries ban the importation of ivory to protect endangered elephants. To clean bone and real ivory:

▶ Dust frequently with a soft, untreated cloth or the brush attachment of your vacuum cleaner or gently blow dust away from intricate carving with the vacuum's blower.

▶ Occasionally wash bone and ivory objects in mild soapsuds; rinse and buff-dry.

▶ Do not allow bone or ivory pieces that are cemented together to soak in water; the adhesive will loosen.

▶ Never wash bone- or ivory-handled knives in the dishwasher.

▶ Keep ivory objects where light will reach them; continual darkness causes ivory to yellow.

JADE

Jade is a beautiful stone that is used to make lamp bases, vases, carved ornaments, and jewelry. It is hard, heavy, and fine grained. The color of jade ranges from white to dark green with occasional tints of brown, mauve, blue, yellow, red, gray, or black. Because jade is hard and not porous, very little care is required. Dust it regularly and buff it with a soft cloth or chamois when it begins to look dull. If a jade piece becomes soiled or sticky, wipe it with a cloth and buff with a dry cloth to restore it.

MARBLE

Marble is a beautiful, polished form of limestone that is used for tabletops, floors, countertops, walls, steps, fireplace facings, window and door sills, other building materials, and statuary. It comes in a variety of colors and has either a shiny or a matte finish. Marble used for floors, tabletops, countertops, steps, and window- and doorsills should be sealed with a special stone sealer to reduce its porosity.

▶ Protect marble tabletops with coasters to prevent staining and wipe up wine, fruit juice, and other acid food spills immediately to prevent permanent surface etching.

▶ Wipe marble surfaces with a sponge to remove light soil and buff-dry. Do not use an abrasive or caustic cleaner on marble. It will mar the surface. Do not use oil polish or soft wax, because they will discolor the marble.

HOME RECIPE FOR CLEANING MARBLE

Borax is an effective, inexpensive way to clean marble. It is mild enough not to scratch the surface. Dip a moistened cloth into a small amount of dry borax and rub it on the marble. Rinse with warm water and buff-dry with a soft cloth. This technique brightens light-colored marble.

▶ Commercial polishes, some of which are flammable, are available for cleaning marble. Read and follow the manufacturer's directions.

PORCELAIN

Porcelain and other types of clay are fashioned into many kinds of art objects, including vases, lamp bases, candlesticks, and statuary.

▶ Dust porcelain regularly with the brush attachment of your vacuum cleaner or a soft cloth.

▶ If a porcelain object becomes dirty, wash it in mild soapsuds, using warm water.

Wood

Whether your wood furniture is oiled, painted, polished—or even rattan or wicker—

affects how it is cleaned. It's obvious when wood is painted, but be sure that you know the surface before you tackle it. For example, some wood furniture is lightly lacquered and will not absorb oil, while other woods, particularly teak and rosewood, have no finish and benefit from a yearly application of furniture oil.

OILED WOOD

Oiled-wood surfaces have a warm, soft glow and require only an occasional application of furniture oil to keep them looking nice.

▶ Be careful never to wax an oil finish. Wax blocks the pores of the wood, and it will dry out and become brittle.

▶ There are several ways to remove white spots on oil-finished furniture, such as those left by wet drinking glasses. You can rub them with toothpaste on a cloth. (Try this on other

HOME RECIPE FOR OIL FINISH FOR WOOD

Pour equal parts of turpentine and boiled linseed oil into a jar, tighten the lid, and shake the liquid to blend it thoroughly. Caution: Wear rubber gloves. Pour a small amount of the mixture on a soft cloth and rub the surface of the furniture following the grain of the wood. The wood will appear oily, but within an hour the polish will be completely absorbed, leaving a lovely soft sheen.

surface stains as well.) Or rub the white spots with a mild abrasive and oil. Appropriate abrasives are ashes, salt, soda, or pumice; suitable oils are olive oil, petroleum jelly, cooking oil, or lemon-oil furniture polish.

PAINTED WOOD

For painted-wood furniture, the best care is probably the least since some polishes and waxes can damage the color and decoration.

▶ Vacuum the furniture regularly with a brush attachment; wipe occasionally with a sponge to remove smudges and finger marks.

▶ If you feel you must wax, use a hard paste wax only once a year.

POLISHED WOOD

This kind of furniture is finished with varnish, lacquer, or wax. Any commercial aerosol polishing/waxing product will clean and polish wood surfaces quickly. Choose a product that is appropriate for the high-gloss or satin finish of your furniture. Paste wax gives a harder, longer-lasting finish than spray or liquid polish and is recommended for antiques. Although paste wax takes a bit of "elbow grease," the beautiful results are worth the effort.

▶ If you wear cotton gloves while you wax furniture, you will not leave fingerprints.

▶ Sprinkle cornstarch over the surface of recently polished furniture and rub it to a high gloss. Cornstarch absorbs excess oil or wax and leaves a glistening surface that is free of fingerprints.

▶ Wipe polished wood furniture with a cloth dipped in tea. Buff-dry.

SPECIALTY WOODS

The specialty woods used for furniture are wicker, rattan, bamboo, cane, and rush. They usually have a natural finish, but some pieces may have a varnish or shellac coating.

▶ Vacuum specialty-wood furniture regularly with the brush attachment.

▶ With the exception of rush chair seats that are damaged by moisture, occasionally wet-down specialty woods outdoors with a garden hose or in the shower to restore moisture to the fibers to keep them soft.

▶ Wetting cane seats tightens them; spray the unvarnished side with water and allow it to dry naturally.

▶ If specialty-wood furniture is especially dirty, clean it with an all-purpose cleaner. Rinse well and allow it to air-dry before using it again.

Upholstery

The vast majority of furniture is upholstered in a fabric, leather, or vinyl. Most furniture upholstered in fabric can be shampooed safely at home; the exception to this is fabric marked "Dry-clean only." You can spot-clean this kind of fabric with a solvent-based cleaner or try this recipe:

Leather must be cleaned with pure soap products (no detergents) and benefits from applying conditioner occasionally to restore moisture and bring up the sheen.

Vinyl upholstery can be cleaned in the same way as leather or with a commercial cleaner developed especially for cleaning vinyl. Never use oil; it will harden the upholstery.

HOME RECIPE FOR LEATHER-UPHOLSTERY CLEANER

A sudsy solution of soap flakes and warm water is one of the best ways to clean leather upholstery. Apply the suds only, scrubbing gently with a soft-bristled brush; wipe clean with a sponge.

HOME RECIPE FOR CLEANING VINYL UPHOLSTERY

The best way to clean vinyl upholstery is with baking soda on a cloth, followed by a light washing with dishwashing liquid.

HOME RECIPE FOR UPHOLSTERY SHAMPOO

Mix ¼ cup of dishwashing liquid with 1 cup of warm water and whip the solution with an eggbeater. Apply the foam to the upholstery, a small section at a time, with a clean, soft-bristled brush. Shake off any excess water. Rinse the upholstery by gently rubbing the fabric with a moist, clean cloth; rinse the cloth as necessary.

INTERIOR SURFACES

Light, routine cleaning of your walls and ceilings will keep them looking fresh and delay the need for a major cleaning. Generally, walls and ceilings are painted with either latex or alkyd paint. Latex, a water-based paint, is easy to wash after it has "cured" or set for a period of time. Alkyd, or oil-base paint, is durable and washable. Both types come in three finishes: flat (for walls and ceiling), semigloss (for walls), and gloss (for kitchen and bathroom walls and woodwork throughout the house). You can clean painted walls with all-purpose cleaners.

Ceilings

Most painted ceiling surfaces are washable, but some ceilings, especially the acoustical type, need special treatment. Remove cobwebs from all ceilings monthly, or as needed, with a vacuum brush attachment or a long-handled mop; be careful not to crush cobwebs on the ceiling—they will leave marks. Wash or clean ceilings first if you are cleaning the whole room. Do not allow drips to run down walls. Protect furniture and floors with drop cloths or newspaper while you clean. Use a sponge mop to clean ceilings so you won't need a ladder.

ACOUSTICAL TILE

Acoustical tile absorbs noise, because it is made of porous material, which is also vulnerable to dirt. Vinyl-coated acoustical tiles can be washed with an all-purpose cleaning solution applied with a sponge. Noncoated tiles generally are not washable but can be spot-cleaned using special products available at hardware stores. When an overall cleaning is needed, an application of acoustical tile paint is recommended.

HOME RECIPE FOR CLEANING PAINTED WALLS AND CEILINGS

Mix ½ cup vinegar, 1 cup clear ammonia, ¼ cup baking soda, and 1 gallon warm water. Caution: Wear rubber gloves and work in a well-ventilated area when using this powerful solution. Apply to the wall with a sponge and rinse with clear water. If your walls have a rough texture, use old nylon stockings or socks rather than a sponge because they won't tear and leave difficult-to-remove bits on the surface.

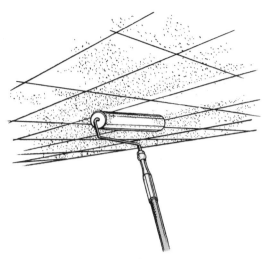

CEILING TILE

Vinyl-coated ceiling tile can be cleaned with an all-purpose cleaning solution. Nonwashable tiles can be spot-cleaned with special products available at hardware stores. When an overall cleaning is needed, the tiles may be painted. There's no need for special paint.

PLASTER

Decorative plaster ceilings, as opposed to flat, painted plastered ceilings, are really not cleanable because of the unpainted surface and deep texture. When a plaster ceiling becomes dirty, the best treatment is to vacuum it, using a brush attachment, and then to respray it.

SPRAY-ON ACOUSTICAL FINISH

This rough, sound-absorbing finish is often used in new construction and remodeling. While it is relatively cheap and quick to apply, spray-on acoustical finishes cannot be cleaned. When the ceiling becomes dirty, the best thing to do is to vacuum it, using a brush attachment, and then respray it.

Painted Walls

Walls require more routine cleaning than ceilings, mainly because it's a lot easier for fingerprints, crayon marks, and scuff marks to land on them. Most paints today are very durable, but be sure not to scrub too hard or use abrasive cleaners that will remove the paint. Using a floor/wall brush, vacuum walls when you clean the room. Go behind pictures and mirrors with the small brush attachment. Remove cobwebs monthly, or as needed. When you vacuum, be careful not to press cobwebs against the wall. When you're ready to wash the entire wall, you'll want to use an all-purpose cleaner for cleaning washable walls. Test the product to make sure it does not harm your wall covering by washing an inconspicuous place.

▶ Wash walls from the bottom to the top, overlapping the cleaned areas to prevent streaks.

▶ To prevent water from running down your arm when washing walls, make a bracelet from a sponge or washcloth held in place with a thick rubber band.

▶ Lift crayon marks off a painted wall by rubbing them carefully with a cloth or sponge dampened with mineral spirits or lighter fluid. Remove any shine by sponging it lightly with hot water.

▶ To remove transparent tape from a wall without marring the paint or wallpaper, use a warm iron. Through a protective cloth, press the tape to soften and loosen its adhesive backing.

CLEANING A BRICK WALL

A brick wall requires little attention. A solution of hot water and all-purpose cleaner can be used to clean accumulated dirt and stains from the surface. If the mortar between the bricks is especially dirty, add chlorine bleach to the cleaning solution.

▶ Remove finger smudges while they are fresh, but do not scrub with excessive pressure or use synthetic scouring pads or abrasive cleansers.

▶ To clean rough-textured walls, old nylon stockings or socks are better than sponges or cloths because they won't tear and leave difficult-to-remove bits and pieces on the surface.

▶ Wet the areas below a smoke stain before you wash it; this will prevent runoffs from setting on a lower tier of bricks.

▶ Slight smoke stains above a fireplace opening are quickly removed with abrasive cleanser. Scrub the powder into the moistened brick and then rinse well with clear water to make sure that no white residue remains.

▶ If spot-cleaning changes the color of the brick, even out the color by rubbing another brick of the same color over the discolored surface.

▶ If the brick wall is especially dirty, use a commercial brick cleaner and a stiff brush. Rinse with clean, hot water and wipe dry. Caution: Wear rubber gloves when using a strong solution and keep this and other dangerous chemicals out of the reach of children.

Wall Coverings

Wall coverings range from paper to vinyl to grass cloth. Paper wall coverings are considered nonwashable and require special cleaning techniques. Many wall coverings are vinyl-coated or made of washable vinyl. Some manufacturers caution against using ammonia-based cleaners on these products, so be sure to check the instructions for cleaning your vinyl wall covering or test the cleaning product you plan to use on your wall covering in an inconspicuous area or on a leftover piece. Follow the manufacturer's instructions for the best results.

▶ Sponge washable wall coverings and some vinyl coverings with a mild detergent. To find out how much elbow grease your paper can take, first work on a scrap.

CLEANING SPECIAL WALL TILES

Decorator Tile

Self-sticking decorator tiles, which are often vinyl-coated, are grease- and stain-resistant. A quick wipe with a sponge dipped in an all-purpose cleaning solution is usually all that is needed to keep them fresh and bright. Excessive moisture should be avoided, because it might seep between the seams and loosen the backing.

Metal Tile

Metal tile can be wiped clean with a cloth dampened in an all-purpose cleaner and then buff-dried with a soft cloth to avoid streaking.

Mirror Tile

These wall tiles, whether clear, smoked, or with a design, are cleaned in the same way as wall mirrors. Quickly remove spots and spatters with a facial tissue and polish with a dry one. Do not use soap on mirror tile; it will streak and leave a film. Also be careful not to use too much liquid that could seep into the grooves and loosen the backing.

HOME RECIPES FOR CLEANING MIRROR TILES

Mix ⅓ cup clear ammonia in 1 gallon of warm water. Apply with a sponge/squeegee or pour the solution into a spray container and spray directly on the mirror tiles. Caution: Wear rubber gloves. Buff with a lint-free cloth, chamois, or paper toweling. Vinegar may be substituted for ammonia.

Pour vinegar into a shallow bowl or pan, crumple a sheet of newspaper, dip it in the vinegar, and apply to the tile. Wipe the glass several times with the same newspaper until the mirror tile is almost dry, then shine the tile with a clean, soft cloth or dry newspaper.

Mix 2 cups isopropyl rubbing alcohol (70 percent), 2 tablespoons liquid dishwashing detergent, and 2 cups water. Stir until thoroughly mixed and then pour into a spray bottle. Spray directly on the mirror tiles. Buff with a lint-free cloth, chamois, or paper towel.

▶ Lift grease stains from washable wallpaper with a paste made of cornstarch and water. Alternatively, rub dry borax over stains.

▶ Remove ordinary soil marks from wallpaper by rubbing them with an art gum eraser.

▶ To remove crayon marks on wallpaper, rub carefully with a dry soap-filled, fine-grade steel-wool pad; or use a wad of white paper toweling moistened with dry-cleaning solvent and delicately sponge the surface. Carefully blot small areas to prevent the solvent from spreading and discoloring the paper.

▶ Remove transparent tape from a wall without marring the paint or wallpaper if you press the tape—through a protective cloth—with a warm iron to soften and loosen the tape's adhesive backing.

▶ Smudges, finger marks, and pencil marks can be removed from the surface of papered walls by very gently rubbing the spots with an art gum eraser.

▶ To clean a grease spot, blot it with paper toweling and sprinkle cornstarch on the stain. After the cornstarch absorbs the grease, rub it off gently and vacuum. You can also place a white blotter over the spot and press it with a moderately hot iron. The blotter will soak up the grease. Repeat as required.

▶ To remove crayon marks on wallpaper, rub carefully with a dry, soap-filled, fine-grade

HOME RECIPES FOR CLEANING VINYL WALL COVERINGS

(1) Mix ½ cup vinegar and 1 quart water and gently apply to the surface with a sponge. Caution: Wear rubber gloves. Don't use too much moisture; it could seep under the seams and loosen the backing.

(2) Make a dry detergent to clean vinyl wall covering with a minimum of moisture. Mix ¼ cup dishwashing liquid with 1 cup warm water in a mixing bowl and beat the mixture to a stiff foam with an egg beater. Working in a small area, dip a sponge into the foam and apply it to the wall to loosen dirt. Rinse the detergent with a sponge dipped in clear water and squeezed dry.

HOME RECIPE FOR AN OIL FINISH

This make-it-yourself polish is one of the best products for restoring the beauty of wood paneling with an oil finish. Pour equal parts of turpentine and boiled linseed oil into a jar, tighten the lid, and shake the liquid to blend it thoroughly. Caution: Wear rubber gloves. Pour a small amount of the mixture on a soft cloth and rub up and down the paneling following the grain of the wood. The wood will appear oily, but within an hour the polish will be completely absorbed, leaving a lovely soft sheen.

Wood Paneling

Wood paneling can have a natural, stained, oil, or waxed finish. Routine care requires occasional vacuuming with a brush attachment. Never use water to clean wood paneling. Many commercial oil and wax finishes are available. For best results follow the manufacturer's instructions.

To remove white water marks from wood paneling, rub mayonnaise into them. Wipe off the mayonnaise 12 hours later. The marks will have vanished.

Woodwork

Woodwork is either painted, stained, or left natural with an oil or varnish finish. Like walls, it benefits from a regular cleaning routine.

▶ Vacuum or dust woodwork regularly. Don't forget the tops of doorjambs, window frames, cornices, ledges, and baseboards.

▶ Keep a small container of matching paint or stain handy to touch up nicks and scratches.

▶ Wash door and window frames from the bottom up.

steel-wool pad. A wad of white paper toweling moistened with dry-cleaning solvent can also be used to delicately sponge the surface. Carefully blot small areas to prevent the solvent from spreading and discoloring the wallpaper.

▶ To remove grease stains from a grass-cloth wall or ceiling covering, apply an aerosol dry cleaner. Follow instructions carefully.

▶ To remove a grease spot from nonwashable wallpaper, place a blotter over the spot and press it with a moderately hot iron. The blotter will soak up the grease. Repeat, as required. You can also use talcum powder to remove a grease spot on nonwashable wallpaper. Dust on the talc with a powder puff, leave it for an hour, and then brush it off. Repeat, if necessary.

▶ Clean nonwashable wallpaper with rye bread. Make a fist-sized wad of bread and rub it across discolorations and dirt.

► Clean stained and natural woodwork with a wood cleaner/polish. Do not use water or water-based cleaners on stained or natural woodwork except for light touch-ups that you buff-dry quickly. Spray the cleaner on a cloth instead of directly on the woodwork to prevent staining adjoining surfaces.

► Many commercial oil and wax finishes are available. For best results follow the manufacturer's instructions.

THE KITCHEN

Cooking is a messy task, but it is easily controlled with quick, daily cleanups. One way to lighten this daily load is to divide chores between cooks and eaters. Cooks take responsibility for blotting spills when they occur and getting dirty cooking utensils into the sink or dishwasher. After dinner, the cleanup crew washes dishes, wipes countertops and appliances, cleans the sink, and sweeps the floor.

Next to maid service, a kitchen cleaner's best friend is an exhaust fan. Smoke and grease are the major culprits behind the grime that accumulates in the kitchen, despite the daily cleanups. An exhaust fan vented to the outside minimizes the buildup of grime. But while keeping the kitchen fairly clean beats having to spend regular long stretches of time cleaning it, plenty of unavoidable kitchen

chores will eventually have to be done. Refer to the following when you want to get these jobs done fast.

Cooktops

Most cooktops are sheathed in ceramic (glass cooktops), porcelain, or stainless steel. While all of these surfaces make for fairly easy cleanup, they require individualized care.

Ceramic Cooktops

The ceramic cooktop is a glass cooktop with electric heating elements under the glass. While smooth tops may appear to be easy to clean, special care must be taken to avoid damaging or discoloring the ceramic surface. The best way to clean a ceramic cooktop is to sprinkle a nonabrasive cleanser or baking soda over the surface and rub with a synthetic scouring pad or sponge. Rinse well with clear water and buff-dry with a soft cloth for a clean finish. Additionally, you'll want to keep the following in mind:

► Wait until the top cools to wipe up spills.

► Never use a wet sponge or cloth on a hot panel.

► Don't set soiled pots or pans on the surface; they can mar it permanently.

► Abrasive cleaning products will scratch the surface, discoloring it and making it difficult to keep clean.

Gas and Electric Stovetops and Range Exteriors

The exteriors of most gas and electric ranges are baked-on porcelain enamel; the trim is usually chrome; and the control knobs are plastic. The easiest way to keep these clean is to wipe the surface around the heating elements after each use. While you can use a synthetic scouring pad for stubborn soil, avoid harsh abrasives or steel wool, which will damage the stove's enamel finish.

▶ Wash reflector bowls, or drip pans, and grids in warm soapsuds whenever food or grease is spilled on them. Clean reflector bowls make your stove more efficient, because blackened and dull reflector bowls absorb heat rather than reflecting it to the cooking pot.

▶ Gas burners should be washed occasionally. Clear the holes with a fine wire or a pipe cleaner. Don't clean the holes with a toothpick; it could break off and clog a hole. Quickly dry the gas burners in a warm oven after they have been washed.

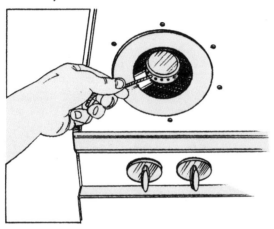

▶ Electric heating elements are self cleaning and should never be submerged in water. If you need to clean an element, turn off the power to your electric range first.

▶ Remove all the control knobs when you clean the exterior of the range to make the job easier. Soak the knobs in sudsy warm water and dry them with a soft towel before putting them back in place.

Stainless Steel

Stainless steel can take a lot of abuse before it needs a commercial stainless steel cleaner to eliminate tarnish or water spots. For tough stains, try a little baking soda on a cloth.

Cookware and Serving Ware

Basic care for all cookware and serving ware starts with reading the manufacturer's care instructions. Wash all pots and pans thoroughly inside and out soon after use. Clean seasoned omelet pans with a paper towel. If baked-on food requires washing the pan in soapsuds, dry it thoroughly over a warm burner and rub vegetable oil into the warm pan with a pad of folded paper towel.

Prevent heat stains on the outside of pans by keeping gas flames low so that they cannot lick up the side of the pot. Do not subject cookware to sudden temperature changes and allow all cookware to cool before washing or soaking. The following addresses specific materials:

ALUMINUM

The only way to protect aluminum cookware from discoloration is never to wash it in an automatic dishwasher or let it soak in soapy water for long periods of time. Don't allow food to stand in aluminum cookware and don't use it to store food; some kinds of food can discolor or pit the metal. Use a steel-wool soap pad to remove burned-on food on cast-aluminum cookware. Liquid nonabrasive bathroom cleanser or a paste of baking soda and water used with a synthetic scouring pad will polish both cast and sheet aluminum.

CAST IRON

Cast-iron cookware has a tendency to rust if it is not kept properly seasoned. Some new cast-iron cooking utensils come from the

HOME REMEDY FOR DISCOLORED ALUMINUM COOKWARE

To remove interior discoloration, fill the pan with water, add 1 tablespoon cream of tartar or 1 tablespoon lemon juice per quart of water, and simmer until the discoloration is gone. Complete the cleaning process by scouring the pan with a steel-wool soap pad. Caution: Wear rubber gloves.

factory already sealed, but most will have to be seasoned before their first use. Season cast-iron cookware in the traditional way: Scour cast-iron pots with a steel-wool soap pad, then wipe the inside of the pot with vegetable oil, place it in a warm oven for two hours, and wipe off the excess oil. To maintain your cookware's seasoning, repeat this procedure periodically and whenever rust spots appear.

Wash cast-iron cookware in hot, sudsy water, then dry it thoroughly, and store in a dry cupboard without its lid in place. Never wash cast-iron cookware in the dishwasher; it will remove the seasoning and cause rust.

CLAY

Soak new clay cookware in water for about ½ hour before using it for the first time. Be sure to soak both the top and the bottom, then scrub them well with a stiff brush to

remove any clay dust. Line the cooker with parchment paper to prevent the porous surface from absorbing food stains and strong flavors. If your clay pot becomes stained or takes on pungent odors, fill the cooker with water, add 1 to 4 tablespoons baking soda, and let it stand.

▶ Never put a hot clay cooker on a cold surface—the cooker might crack.

▶ Wash clay cookware immediately after it cools to prevent food from drying and crusting, but never wash clay cookware in the dishwasher or scrub it with a steel-wool soap pad.

▶ Carefully dry the cooker before storing it to prevent mold. Storing clay cookware with its lid off will also discourage mold.

▶ If mold spots appear on a clay cooker, brush the surface with a paste made of equal parts baking soda and water. Let stand 30 minutes, preferably in strong sunlight; brush the paste away, rinse well in clear water, and dry thoroughly in a well-ventilated location.

COPPER

Copper darkens with use and exposure to air. If you prefer shiny copper, you can clean and polish it easily with commercial copper cleaner. Copper cookware is lined with some other metal, usually tin or steel, to prevent harmful chemical reactions with food. Although a copper pan can be retinned when the lining begins to wear thin, this is an expensive procedure and easily avoided by using wood, nylon, or nonstick-coated spoons for stirring to prevent scratching the lining.

▶ Avoid sharp metal cooking utensils that could scratch the tin.

▶ Some copper cookware comes with a protective lacquer coating that must be removed before the utensil is heated. Follow the manufacturer's instructions or place the utensil in a solution of 1 cup baking soda and 2 gallons boiling water. Let it stand until the water is cool, peel off the lacquer, wash, rinse, and dry.

▶ Protect copper pans from scorching by making sure there is always liquid or fat in the pan before it is placed on the heat.

▶ When melting butter, swirl it around in the bottom of the pan and up the sides. Lower the heat as soon as the contents of the pot reach the boiling point.

HOMEMADE COPPER POLISH

To clean a discolored copper pot, use a paste of 1 tablespoon salt, 1 tablespoon white vinegar, and 1 tablespoon flour. Caution: Wear rubber gloves. Because the vinegar is acid, wash the pot in hot soapy water and rinse it before vigorously buffing for shiny results. You'll have the same success with a paste made of 2 tablespoons lemon juice and 1 tablespoon salt.

DINNERWARE

To make short work of dinnerware, remove food residue as quickly as possible. Scrape dishes with a rubber scraper or plastic brush to prevent scratches. Never scrape plates with knives or other sharp objects.

▶ Rinse out coffee cups and tea cups before residues have a chance to stain the cups.

▶ Leftover egg and cheese should be soaked in cool water.

▶ Acid foods, such as tomatoes, vinegar, and wine, allowed to remain on glazed dinnerware can pit the surface.

▶ To protect glass and china from chipping or breaking while you are hand-washing it, use a plastic dishpan or rubber sink mat. You can also pad the bottom of the sink with a towel.

▶ Avoid abrupt changes of temperature when you wash china.

▶ Do not wash delicate, hand-painted, gold- or silver-trimmed, or antique dinnerware in the dishwasher. Metal-trimmed dinnerware should also not be soaked in soapy water for long periods of time; this will damage the trim.

▶ High temperatures may also damage dishes. Do not warm plates in the oven unless they are heat-proof. Do not rinse glazed dinnerware with very hot or boiling water; this may cause the glaze to craze or develop minute cracks.

ENAMELWARE

Always let enamel cookware cool before washing. Rapid changes in temperature can crack the enamel coating. If necessary, soak a dirty pot to loosen cooked-on foods. Use a synthetic scouring pad—never abrasive cleansers or steel wool—to scrub stubborn soil. Enamelware can be washed safely in the dishwasher. Dishwashing detergent will clean enamel cookware quickly. Encrusted food or stains can be removed with a liquid nonabrasive bathroom cleanser.

FLATWARE AND CUTLERY

Most people wash knives, forks, and spoons along with other dishes. If washing by hand, wash flatware after the glasses and before the plates.

Cutlery (knives and other cutting instruments) can be cleaned in the same way as flatware, but observe the manufacturer's instructions to be sure that the cutlery is dishwasher-safe. Here are some other methods for cleaning and polishing flatware and cutlery.

▶ Always wash pewter and gold-plated flatware by hand and buff-dry to bring up the shine and prevent water spots.

▶ Sterling-silver and silver-plate flatware may be washed in the dishwasher, but they will need to be polished less often if they are washed by hand.

▶ Rinse salt and acid food off flatware as soon as possible to avoid stains.

▶ Do not soak any flatware or cutlery with bone, ivory, or wood handles, and do not wash them in the dishwasher.

▶ Use silver often; it tarnishes less and grows more beautiful with use.

▶ Store silver and gold flatware in rolls, bags, or cases made with special tarnish-resistant cloth.

▶ Do not allow stainless-steel flatware to touch anything made of silver in the dishwasher. It will set up an electrolytic action that pits the stainless steel and leaves black spots on the silver.

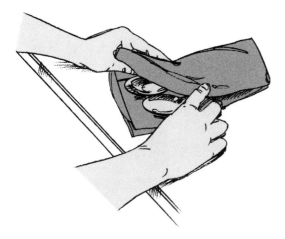

▶ Never use an abrasive cleaner, steel-wool pad, or synthetic scouring pad on flatware.

▶ Avoid overcrowding the sink to prevent scratching your flatware.

GLASSWARE

Most glassware can be safely washed in the dishwasher, but gilt- and silver-trimmed glass, delicate crystal, milk glass, and ornamental glass must be washed by hand. If you have soft water in your area, wash all glassware by hand because the combination of soft water and dishwasher detergent will etch and permanently dull glassware.

▶ Before you wash glassware, cushion the bottom of the sink with a towel or rubber mat.

▶ Add vinegar to the wash water or rinse water for more sparkle; ammonia in the wash water will cut grease on glassware.

▶ Wash glasses first, before cutlery or dinnerware. Slowly slide stemware into the

wash water, holding the glass by the base; if you push a glass into the water bottom first, it is likely to crack.

▶ Remove dirt from crevices with a soft brush; remove stains by rubbing with a cut lemon or washing in a vinegar solution.

▶ Allow glassware to drip-dry upside down or polish with a soft, lint-free cloth.

▶ Clean stained decanters by filling them with water and adding 1 cup ammonia or vinegar. Soak overnight. If this solution does not clean the decanter, use two packs of powdered denture cleaner dissolved in water.

GLASS AND CERAMIC-GLASS

Most heat-resistant glass and ceramic-glass cookware is designed for oven use only, but some can be used on stovetops. Read the manufacturer's instructions carefully to make sure that you use your cookware appropriately. All glass and ceramic-glass cookware is dishwasher-safe.

▶ Glass cookware that is allowed to boil dry is likely to shatter. If a pot boils dry, the safest way for you to handle this potentially explosive situation is to turn off the heat and leave the pot where it is until it has cooled.

▶ Remove mineral deposits from glass coffeepots and teapots by boiling full-strength cider vinegar in the container for 15 minutes.

NONSTICK FINISHES

Nonstick finishes or coatings are relatively thin and easily damaged. Use wood, nylon, or specially coated spoons and spatulas to prevent surface damage. Most nonstick-coated cookware can be safely washed in the dishwasher. Wash new pans before using them and lightly coat the inside with vegetable oil. Apply vegetable oil again after each washing in the dishwasher and after treating for stains, following the procedure described below. Do not soak pans in soapy water; the coating can retain a soap flavor.

PLASTIC AND RUBBER

Plastic utensils and containers—such as orange-juice pitchers, covered storage bowls, and spatulas—and rubber food-preparation tools—such as scrapers, drain boards, and sink mats—should never be exposed to high heat, because some plastics will melt and warp, and heat and sunlight can cause rubber products to crack.

Check the manufacturer's instructions to see if an item is dishwasher-safe. Do not use solvents, harsh abrasives, or scouring pads to remove stains from plastic or rubber.

▶ A paste made of baking soda and water is very effective for removing stubborn soils and stains from plastic and rubber utensils. It deodorizes as it cleans. Apply the paste to plastic with a sponge or soft cloth; a synthetic scouring pad can be used on rubber. Caution: Wear rubber gloves.

▶ Remove odor from a plastic container by crumpling a piece of newspaper into the container. Secure the lid tightly, and leave it until morning. The paper will absorb the odor.

STAINLESS STEEL

Stainless steel requires practically no special care. It is dishwasher-safe, but if you wash it by hand, dry it promptly to prevent water spots. Letting a pot boil over high heat for a long period of time or allowing a gas flame to lick up the sides of a pan will discolor stainless steel. Storing the cookware stacked with other pots and pans may cause surface scratches. Many commercial products will shine stainless steel.

HOMEMADE STAINLESS-STEEL POLISH

Sprinkle baking soda on the wet surface of a pan and scrub the metal with a synthetic scouring pad. Caution: Wear rubber gloves. After rinsing and drying, the pan will be as bright as new.

HOMEMADE CLEANER FOR NONSTICK COOKWARE

When you want to remove stains from nonstick-coated cookware, mix 2 tablespoons baking soda with 1 cup water and ½ cup liquid bleach. Boil the solution in the pan for several minutes until the stains disappear. After washing the pan, wipe the inner surface with cooking oil to season it.

WOODENWARE

Wood food-preparation equipment, such as bowls, trays, rolling pins, spoons, salad utensils, and cutting boards, need special care to prevent warping and cracking. Because wood is porous, it absorbs moisture. When it dries out, the wood may be rough because the water may have raised the grain. Periodically clean and oil cutting boards to restore their smooth surfaces and to protect them from moisture. Some salad bowls are finished with a waterproof varnish, but many people prefer to keep their bowls untreated to absorb seasonings and enhance the flavor of the salad.

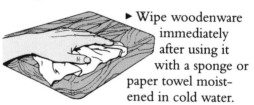

▶ Wipe woodenware immediately after using it with a sponge or paper towel moistened in cold water.

▶ If the item needs to be washed, don't let it soak in water and never put it in the dishwasher.

▶ Remove stains from woodenware with a solution of ¼ cup chlorine bleach and 1 quart warm water. Rinse and dry, then coat with vegetable oil.

▶ Eliminate odors by rubbing the surface with a slice of lemon.

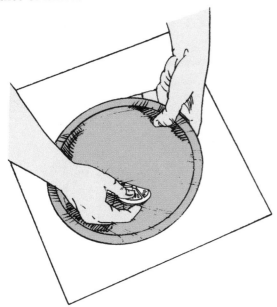

HOMEMADE WOODENWARE CLEANER

Baking soda cleans and deodorizes wood. Mix ½ cup baking soda with 1 quart warm water and rub it on the wood surface. Caution: Wear rubber gloves. Use a synthetic scouring pad to clean a cutting board. Scour the gummy residue on the edges of the board. Rinse with clear water, blot the moisture with a towel, and air-dry completely. Bring back the natural wood finish by giving woodenware a coat of boiled linseed oil, salad-bowl finishing oil, or vegetable oil, rubbed in with a synthetic scouring pad. Apply two thin coats 24 hours apart, wiping off the excess ½ hour after each application.

Countertops

Kitchen countertops have to be ready for anything—a slice from a paring knife that goes off course or a slosh of grape juice intent on staining the surface. Acrylic, ceramic tile, cultured marble, marble, plastic laminate, and wood countertops can take the abuse of our cooking if we make it up to them with regular, gentle cleaning and care. These surfaces are all easy to clean.

ACRYLIC

You have to go out of your way to harm an acrylic countertop. A very hot pan or lighted cigarette will leave a permanent burn mark on the surface, but scouring powder or steel wool will remove stains and scratches. For routine cleaning, use a mildly abrasive liquid or powdered cleansers applied directly to the wet surface to dissolve dirt. Rinse well and buff-dry with a soft cloth.

CERAMIC TILE

Both glazed and unglazed ceramic tile are used for countertops in the kitchen. Unlike most other kitchen surfaces, ceramic-tile counters can take the heat; you don't have to fumble around searching for a trivet whenever you need to find a spot to set a hot pot. Ceramic tile itself is extremely durable, but the grout between the tiles is soft, porous, and prone to cracks.

▶ Use a toothbrush or nailbrush to scrub grout clean.

▶ To remove mildew, dip the brush in laundry bleach.

▶ When you clean grout, don't use harsh abrasive cleaners, which might scratch the glaze on ceramic tile.

▶ Many aerosol-foam and spray tile-and-grout cleaners are available. Follow the manufacturer's instructions and rinse with clear water to finish

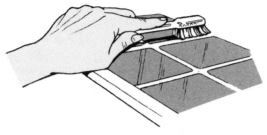

the job. Caution: Wear rubber gloves to avoid skin contact with these powerful cleaners and take care not to breathe the mist from spray cleaners.

CULTURED MARBLE

Cultured marble is an acrylic material that resembles real marble, but it's easier to care for because it is less porous and does not have to be sealed. Avoid abrasive cleaners and steel-wool soap pads; they will scratch the surface. Mildly abrasive liquid and powdered cleansers should be applied directly to the wet surface to dissolve dirt and soap film. Rinse well and buff-dry with a soft cloth. Note that hot pots and lighted cigarettes will leave permanent burn marks on cultured marble.

MARBLE

Marble countertops are porous and susceptible to stains, but they are not affected by heat. Seal marble with a special stone sealer to reduce its porousness and wipe up wine, fruit juice, and other acid food spills immediately to prevent permanent surface

HOMEMADE ACRYLIC CLEANER

Mix ½ cup vinegar, 1 cup ammonia, and ¼ cup baking soda in 1 gallon hot water. Caution: Wear rubber gloves and work in a well-ventilated area when using this powerful solution. Apply it to the acrylic countertop with a sponge, rinse with clear water, and buff-dry. Dirt and soap film are quickly and inexpensively removed with this mixture.

HOMEMADE GROUT CLEANER

To make this heavy-duty cleaner, put 3 cups baking soda in a medium-size bowl and add 1 cup warm water. Caution: Wear rubber gloves. Mix to form a smooth paste; scrub into the grout with a sponge or toothbrush and rinse thoroughly after cleaning. Mix a fresh batch for each cleaning.

HOMEMADE CERAMIC-TILE CLEANER

Mix ½ cup vinegar, 1 cup clear ammonia, ¼ cup baking soda, and 1 gallon warm water. Caution: Wear rubber gloves and work in a well-ventilated area when using this powerful solution. Apply the solution to the countertop with a sponge and rinse with clear water. Wipe dry to prevent dull water spots. Mix a fresh batch of this cleaner for each cleaning.

etching. Abrasive and caustic cleaners will mar the surface of marble, and oil polish and soft waxes may discolor it. While many appropriate commercial cleaners are available, borax rubbed into the surface with a moistened

HOMEMADE CULTURED-MARBLE CLEANER

Dirt and soap film are quickly and inexpensively removed with this mixture. Mix ½ cup vinegar, 1 cup ammonia, and ¼ cup baking soda in 1 gallon hot water. Caution: Wear rubber gloves and work in a well-ventilated area when using this powerful solution. Apply it to the cultured marble with a sponge, rinse with clear water, and buff-dry.

cloth will also clean marble. Rinse with warm water and buff-dry with a soft cloth.

PLASTIC LAMINATE

Most kitchens have plastic-laminate countertops. They're practically seamless, giving cooks a smooth, waterproof work surface that is easy to clean. Unfortunately, moisture is not the only difficulty we must expect our kitchen countertops to overcome. Plastic laminate burns, scratches, and stains fairly easily, so you'll have to be considerate of your countertops to keep them looking good.

▶ Regular applications of an appliance wax or light furniture wax will help plastic-laminate surfaces to resist stains and scratching.

▶ Never use abrasive cleansers or steel wool on laminate countertops.

HOMEMADE PLASTIC-LAMINATE CLEANER

Using baking soda is the cheapest way to rid countertops of stains. Caution: Wear rubber gloves when working with this cleaner. Just sprinkle the soda on the stain, rub in with a cloth or sponge, and rinse with clear water.

PRESERVING A WOOD COUNTERTOP

Butcher-block and other wood countertops require more care than you might expect, if you don't want them to look like they belong in the workroom of a butcher shop. You can restore a scratched and/or stained wood countertop by sanding it and applying a wood-preservative product, but that's a lot of work. You'll save time in the long run by preserving your wood countertop's good looks.

Always use a cutting board on a wood countertop, just as you would with any other surface. Wipe up stains and keep your wood countertops as dry as you possibly can. Periodically, rub oil into wood countertops to protect them from moisture. Use boiled linseed oil or salad oil and follow the procedure described below.

▶ Remove stains with a solution of ¼ cup chlorine bleach in 1 quart warm water. Rinse, dry, and coat with oil.

▶ To get rid of odors that are absorbed by wood countertops, rub the surface with a slice of lemon.

▶ To clean and deodorize wood countertops, mix ½ cup baking soda in 1 quart warm water. Caution: Wear rubber gloves. Rub the paste into the wood countertop using a synthetic scouring pad. Rinse well with clear water and pat-dry to remove excess moisture. When completely dry, restore the finish by using boiled linseed oil or salad oil rubbed in with a fine steel-wool pad. Treat the countertop with two coats of oil, applied 24 hours apart, blotting up the excess after each application.

▶ For general cleaning, a two-sided scrubbing pad with fiber on one side and a sponge on the other works particularly well. Moistened slightly with water, the fiber side is just abrasive enough to loosen greasy smears and other soil. Turning the scrubber over, use the sponge side to wipe the surface dry.

▶ When a spot or stain persists, apply a polishing cleanser with a wet sponge. Then rinse and dry the countertop.

Large Appliances

Large appliances range from big, enamel-coated metal boxes that clean up with the swipe of a wet cloth to ranges that have at least four depressions to trap and hold spilled food. If you keep up appearances by regularly wiping sticky fingerprints off the refrigerator door and drips off the front of the dishwasher, you can put off cleaning the messes that lurk within your large appliances until you have time to deal with them thoroughly. When you do find the time to tackle the inside of your large appliances, follow these time-tested hints to speed you through your work:

DISHWASHERS

▶ Baking soda comes in handy when the dishwasher needs cleaning inside and out. Dip a cloth into the soda and use it to clean smudges and fingerprints from the exterior; the same method will also remove stains from the liner. Use a synthetic scouring pad to clean stubborn soil.

▶ If the interior of your dishwasher retains odors, sprinkle three tablespoons of baking soda in the bottom of the machine and allow it to sit overnight. The odors will be washed away with the baking soda during the next wash cycle. To prevent the liner from retaining odors, occasionally leave the dishwasher door open to air.

MICROWAVES

One reason we all probably like the microwave oven so much is that it's so easy to clean. Use a mild dishwashing detergent, baking soda, or glass cleaner to clean the inside of the microwave and wash the glass tray in the sink or the dishwasher when it is soiled. Never use a commercial oven cleaner in a microwave oven.

RANGE HOODS

Many ranges have separate or built-in range hoods above their cooking surfaces. Range hoods are usually vented to the outside and remove grease, steam, and cooking odors from the kitchen. Some hoods do not have outside vents and rely on replaceable charcoal filters to clean smoke and odors from the air. Both vented and nonvented hoods have fans to draw up air and smoke from the cooking area, and both need to be cleaned to keep them free from grease buildup and working effectively.

▶ Wipe the exterior and interior of the range hood regularly. When you need to give it a thorough scrub, use a solution of hot water, dishwashing detergent, and ammonia to cut the grease; wear rubber gloves.

▶ Remove the filter cover and wash it in soapy hot water. Allow it to dry completely before replacing. Wipe the blades of the fan with an ammonia solution.

▶ Clean metal mesh filters when they are dirty and replace the filters on nonvented range hoods every six to nine months or as often as the manufacturer recommends.

▶ Avoid washing charcoal filters; washing will reduce their effectiveness.

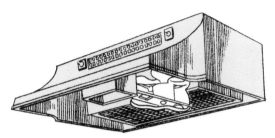

OVENS

There are many strong cleaning products designed to clean standard ovens. Caution: Many oven cleaners are dangerous when they come in contact with your skin or eyes. Wear rubber gloves and protect your eyes while cleaning. Don't breathe the spray mist or the fumes. Avoid dripping the cleaner on any surfaces other than those it is intended to clean. Carefully read and follow the manufacturer's instructions when you use a commercial oven cleaner.

When you clean a traditional oven, protect the heating elements, oven wiring, and thermostat from commercial oven cleaners with strips of aluminum foil.

Many stoves are equipped with self-cleaning or continuous-cleaning ovens. A self-cleaning oven uses a pyrolytic, or high heat, system to incinerate oven grime, creating a powdery ash. A continuous-cleaning, or catalytic, system eliminates small spatters through the porous porcelain-enamel finish on the oven liner, which absorbs and spreads soil to promote cleaning at normal temperature settings. Large spills must be wiped up; they will burn and may permanently stain the oven surface. Dust continuous-cleaning ovens weekly and self-cleaning ovens after the cleaning cycle, using the dusting attachment of your vacuum to remove dried food particles and/or ash.

Follow the manufacturer's instructions when using the cleaning cycle of a self-cleaning oven and follow the manufacturer's recommendations for caring for a continuous-cleaning oven. Neither kind of oven should be cleaned with commercial oven cleaners. Continuous-cleaning ovens should never be scrubbed with abrasives or powdered cleansers; these products will damage the surface.

REFRIGERATORS

A frost-free refrigerator should be cleaned when it's dirty or about every four to six months. Clean a manual-defrost refrigerator when you defrost the freezer compartment.

▶ Wash the drip pan whenever you defrost and/or clean your refrigerator.

▶ Defrost the freezer section of your refrigerator when the frost gets to be $1/2$-inch thick. Turn off the freezer controls and remove all the food. Put the food in an ice chest or wrap it in layers of newspaper. Remove all shelves, bins, racks, and trays and wash them in a mild soap solution. Dry thoroughly.

▶ Do not put food back into the freezer until you have wiped off any condensation that develops, and the freezer has been running for at least $1/2$ hour. Wipe the interior of the refrigerator to prevent puddles from remaining in the bottom when you replace the bins.

HOMEMADE OVEN CLEANER

Pour 1 cup ammonia in a glass or ceramic bowl, place it in a cold oven, and allow it to sit in the closed oven overnight. The next morning, pour the ammonia into a pail of warm water and use this solution and a sponge to wipe away the loosened soil. Caution: Wear rubber gloves whenever you work with an ammonia solution. The fumes are strong at first, but they soon dissipate.

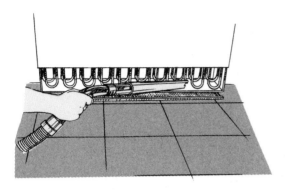

▶ Vacuum the dust from the area behind the bottom grille of your refrigerator at least once every six months. Clean the condenser coils with the crevice tool about once a month.

▶ Control refrigerator odors with a box of baking soda placed at the back of a shelf. Replace the box every other month. Also, place a box in the freezer if odors are a problem there.

▶ Do not wash ice trays in a detergent solution; this can remove the special nonstick coating that some of them have.

▶ Commercial kitchen wax/cleaners will remove smudges and dirt and leave a protective wax coating on the exterior of the refrigerator, but baking soda will also clean and shine your refrigerator. Rub the exterior with a cloth dipped in baking soda, rinse well, and wipe dry with a soft cloth.

TRASH COMPACTORS

Follow the manufacturer's cleaning instructions for the interior of your trash compactor. Clean it when necessary, watching out for small glass particles that may be left from the trash.

▶ Generally, the bags made especially for a particular trash compactor will give you the best results.

▶ Remember that no compactor is designed to handle wet garbage.

▶ Emptying the trash compactor frequently and using a deodorant spray will discourage bad odors from collecting in the compactor.

▶ Routinely wipe the exterior of your trash compactor to remove smudges and fingerprints. Use a commercial kitchen-appliance cleaner or baking soda.

Small Appliances

The little machines that line up along our kitchen countertops or park themselves in appliance garages save us time and effort when we cook. But they sometimes seem to use up the time they've saved us in the amount of time they take to clean. Food sloshes out of blenders and spins out of food processors. Blades and cutters hide food in their intricate designs and can cut our fingers when we try to clean them. Most small appliances are designed to be easy to clean, but it still requires some work.

BLENDERS AND FOOD PROCESSORS

Most plastic work bowls and blender jars can be washed in your dishwasher; some cannot. Some blades are dulled by repeated exposure to the dishwasher detergents; some are not. Always read and follow the manufacturer's cleaning instructions. If you wipe the bases of food-preparation appliances after each use, you will rarely have to scrub them.

▶ To clean the blender jar, fill it with a warm detergent solution and run the blender for about 15 seconds at high speed. Rinse well and dry.

▶ To retain the sharpness of the blades, do not wash the blender's assembly in the dishwasher.

▶ Wash the food processor's work bowl, cover, pusher, blade, and discs in warm, soapy water or in the dishwasher. Because the blade is razor sharp, carefully wash it by hand. Left in the rack of the dishwasher, the blade might cut your hand when you are loading or unloading other items.

▶ A glass cleaner is excellent for cleaning stainless-steel blender bases and trim. Simply spray it on and immediately buff-dry with a soft cloth.

▶ An all-purpose cleaner or a solution of baking soda and water cleans plastic blender and food-processor bases.

HOMEMADE CLEANERS FOR PERCOLATORS

Aluminum: Sprinkle baking soda on the wet surface to make a paste and use a synthetic scouring pad to spread it. Caution: Wear rubber gloves. Wipe with a cloth and buff for a bright finish.

Chromium: Pour baking soda in a saucer, dip a dry cloth in the soda, and rub the chrome surface. This will remove fingerprints, smudges, and even sticky residue with no further rinsing or wiping. Kitchen flour rubbed on the surface with a dry cloth will also remove greasy film and smudges.

Stainless Steel: Sprinkle baking soda on the wet surface and scrub with a synthetic scouring pad. Caution: Wear rubber gloves. Wipe with a cloth and buff with a soft, dry cloth.

COFFEE MAKERS

Drip coffee makers are easy to clean—all you have to do is change the filter; wash the pot, lid, and basket in a detergent solution; and quickly wipe the base with a cloth. Percolators need a thorough, occasional cleaning to get rid of oil buildup that can affect the taste of the coffee.

▶ Allow a heated percolator to cool before cleaning.

▶ Clean the spout and tubes of a percolator with a special percolator brush and a warm dishwashing-detergent solution.

▶ Wash all percolator parts in a warm detergent solution after each use.

▶ If your percolator is not immersible, wipe the exterior with a cloth and buff-dry.

▶ Use a synthetic scouring pad—never harsh abrasives or steel wool—to remove stubborn soil from percolator parts. If the surface becomes scratched, oil and other coffee residues will accumulate in the scratches.

▶ While commercial products designed especially to clean percolators are very effective, the following methods work equally well: With the stem and basket in place, fill the percolator completely full with cold water and add 6 tablespoons baking soda. Plug in the machine and allow the percolator to run through its complete cycle. Wait for 15 minutes, unplug the machine, and empty the solution. Wash in a mild detergent, rinse, and dry. Adding ¼ cup white vinegar to a potful of water and running it through the brewing cycle will also clean the percolator.

ELECTRIC CAN OPENERS

Your can opener needs light but regular care. Always remember to unplug a can opener before cleaning it; do not immerse the case in water. Wipe the can opener after each use to remove food spills or drips. Use a sponge dampened in a warm soapsuds solution made from liquid dishwashing detergent. Buff-dry. Periodically, remove the cutting wheel and lid holder and soak them in hot sudsy water. Scrub caked-on food with a toothbrush; rinse, dry, and replace the parts.

ELECTRIC IRONS

The obvious problem with a clogged steam iron is that it doesn't deliver enough steam. An even worse problem is the tendency of clogged irons to become suddenly unclogged and spew white mineral globs all over your best black suit. A clean iron speeds your pressing and protects your clothes.

▸ Follow the manufacturer's instructions to keep the steam vents from becoming clogged with mineral deposits. Some irons use tap water; others require distilled water.

▸ When you clean the soleplate of your iron, be sure to remove cleaning-product residue from the vents with a cotton swab or pipe cleaner. A sharp knife or other tool may scratch the soleplate.

▸ Commercial products are available to clean hot irons, but if you don't have one of these products, you can use a cloth dipped in baking soda to clean the soleplate of a slightly warm iron. Scrub starch buildup or other soil. Rinse well with another cloth, taking particular care to clear the vents.

▸ Even if your steam iron is designed to be used with tap water, you should use distilled water if you live in a part of the country that has hard water. Melted frost from the freezer is a good substitute for distilled water.

Cleaning Water Reservoirs

Remove mineral deposits from the water reservoir when the steam action begins to decrease. Pour a solution of $1/3$ cup white vinegar and $1/3$ cup water into the water reservoir. Heat the iron and let it steam for

about three minutes. Unplug the iron and position it, soleplate down, on a small glass dish that has been placed in a larger shallow pan. Allow the water to drain from the vents for about an hour. Drain away any remaining solution and flush the reservoir with clear water before using the iron.

GARBAGE DISPOSERS

Garbage disposers are self-cleaning, but they can get smelly, especially if you let food sit in them for any length of time. To keep your disposer odorless and running smoothly, operate it with a full stream of running cold water. Flush the disposer for a few seconds after turning it off to ensure that all debris is washed away. Keep the following materials out of the disposer: metal, wood, glass, paper, or plastic objects; fibrous organic waste, such as artichoke leaves and corn husks; and caustic drain cleaners. If an unpleasant odor begins to come from your disposer, eliminate it by tearing up the peels of citrus fruit and putting them into the disposer. Grind them with a stream of cold running water and enjoy the fresh smell. Or sprinkle baking soda over several ice cubes and grind them in the disposer.

HOT TRAYS

A quick wipe with a sponge is usually sufficient to clean a hot tray, but if spilled food is baked on, stronger measures are needed. Remember never to immerse a hot tray in water. To remove baked-on food from a hot tray, use a commercial oven cleaner. Heat the tray to a warm temperature and carefully spray the cleaner on the tray. Cover the outer perimeter of the tray and all plastic and wood parts with aluminum foil to prevent oven cleaner from touching these surfaces. Do not let oven cleaner seep into the crevice between the frame and the surface of the tray. You'll need to allow the oven cleaner to stand on the tray for ten minutes and then remove it with a clean, wet sponge. Caution: Follow the manufacturer's warnings for proper use of oven cleaners. Wear rubber gloves, protect your eyes, and do not breathe the spray or fumes.

TOASTER OVENS/BROILERS

When the puddle of cheese from last night's nachos meets the butter crumbs from this morning's toast in the bottom of your toaster oven, you have a major mess, not to mention a fire hazard. Cleaning your toaster oven/broiler after you use it prevents a squalid buildup of food spatters and crumbs that is likely to become a permanent condition because baked-on messes are very difficult to remove from toaster ovens.

▶ Wipe the exterior of the oven and the crumb tray regularly; wipe the interior of the oven with a warm dishwashing solution after cooking greasy foods. A synthetic scouring pad will remove stubborn soil from the tray and racks. The plastic parts are best cleaned with a warm detergent solution; buff the surfaces dry.

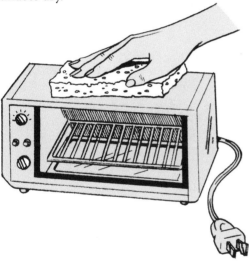

▶ Clean a toaster oven only when it is cool and has been disconnected.

▶ Never immerse the oven in water and don't use harsh abrasives, steel wool, or commercial oven cleaner to clean a toaster oven.

TOASTERS

Toasters are crumb catchers and smudge collectors; they need regular attention to keep them clean, shiny, and crumb-free.

▶ Remember to unplug the toaster and let it cool before cleaning it.

▶ Wipe the exterior of the toaster regularly. Remove the crumb tray at the base of the toaster and shake out accumulated crumbs; wash the tray in warm soapsuds.

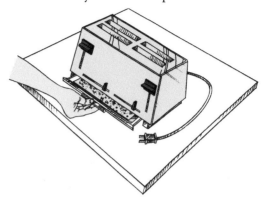

▶ If your toaster does not have a crumb tray, turn the toaster upside down and shake it over the sink or a large garbage can.

▶ Use a thin, soft brush to remove crumbs from the interior.

▶ Never wash the inside of the toaster with water or immerse the whole unit.

▶ Metal utensils should not be used to clean the inside of the toaster.

▶ Polish the exterior of your toaster with baking soda or flour, using the same method as for toaster ovens/broilers.

WAFFLE IRONS

Waffle irons need little care. The grids are made from seasoned cast iron or a nonstick

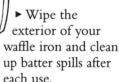

surface and generally do not require washing after ordinary use.

▶ Wipe the exterior of your waffle iron and clean up batter spills after each use.

▶ Wipe the grids with a paper towel that has been dampened with vegetable oil.

▶ If waffles stick to the grids and burn, you'll have to remove the grids and wash them in warm soapsuds, using a plastic brush to remove the burned-waffle debris.

▶ Season the surface with a light brushing of vegetable oil.

▶ Never clean a waffle iron until it is cool and has been unplugged. Do not immerse a waffle iron in water.

WINDOWS AND WINDOW COVERINGS

Windows look best if they are cleaned on a regular basis, at least twice a year on the inside and outside. Home recipes work just as well as commercial products for washing windows, and you'll save money. But remember that window cleaners pose a threat to woodwork. Don't let them drip on the windowsill where they can harm the paint or varnish.

Most windows respond well to several different cleaners, as long as they don't contain soap, which will leave smudges on windowpanes. Also, avoid abrasive cleansers or steel wool that will scratch the glass.

Window Coverings

BLINDS

Blinds are made from narrow slats of wood,  metal, or plastic held in place by tapes, cords, or colored yarns and ribbons. All blinds can be adjusted up and down; venetian blinds can also have the angle of their slats adjusted for light control. Blinds are made with horizontally or vertically placed slats. To clean:

▶ Vacuum blinds regularly with the brush attachment of your vacuum. Close adjustable slats when vacuuming so you can reach more of their surface.

▶ Remove finger marks with a sponge.

▶ When blinds require a thorough cleaning, immerse plastic, metal, and painted blinds in water. Wash them in the bathtub or outdoors by hanging them on the clothesline for scrubbing.

▶ Natural wood blinds with decorative yarn tapes should not be immersed.

▶ Touch up dingy white tapes on venetian blinds with white shoe polish.

CURTAINS

Carefully read all the care labels attached to new curtains and follow the manufacturer's instructions for cleaning.

▶ Using the upholstery attachment on your vacuum, regularly go over curtain panels for quick cleaning. This is almost all the cleaning fiberglass curtains ever need.

▶ Vacuum curtains to remove excess dust before washing. Remove curtain rings and clips unless they are permanently attached.

▶ Fiberglass curtains should always be washed and never dry-cleaned, but you must wear rubber gloves when hand-washing them to protect your hands from glass filaments.

TECHNIQUES FOR CLEANING WINDOWS

▶ Washing one side of a window with horizontal strokes and the other side with vertical strokes will pinpoint which side of the window has a streak.

▶ Use a squeegee on a long handle or a sponge/squeegee combination to prevent streaks on large windows. An old windshield-wiper blade makes a good squeegee.

▶ Rubbing a clean blackboard eraser over a freshly washed (and dried) window gives it a diamond-bright shine.

▶ Eliminate tiny scratches on glass by polishing the affected areas with toothpaste.

▶ Wash windows on a cloudy day, because direct sunlight dries cleaning solutions before you can polish the glass properly.

▶ Use a soft toothbrush or cotton swab to clean corners.

▶ To give an extra shine to window glass, polish it with well-washed cotton T-shirts or old diapers.

▶ If you wash windows on a hot or sunny day, the glass is more likely to streak.

▶ Polish windows to a sparkling shine with crumpled-up newspaper.

▶ Wash windows from the top down to prevent drips.

HOME RECIPE FOR CLEANING BLINDS

Pour a low-sudsing, all-purpose cleaner into a bathtub filled with warm water or mix a solution of ½ cup cleaner in 1 gallon warm water for outdoor cleaning and apply with a brush. If you wear cotton gloves when you wash venetian blinds, you can use your fingers to rub the slats. Rinse the blinds with clean water; allow them to drip-dry either on a clothesline or on a shower-curtain rod, placing towels underneath them to catch the drips. Rehang the blinds on the window when the dripping has stopped; stretch the tapes or cords to full length to prevent shrinking. Leave the slats in the open position until the blinds are completely dry.

HOME RECIPE FOR WASHABLE WINDOW SHADES

Make a mild soapsuds solution using a liquid dishwashing detergent and apply it to a rolled-out shade with a sponge. Rinse with a clean sponge dipped in clear water and allow it to dry before rerolling.

HOME RECIPE FOR CLEANING NONWASHABLE WINDOW SHADES

Thoroughly rub the surface with a rough, absorbent cloth dipped in cornmeal. The secret of this treatment is that the abrasiveness and absorption of the cloth and cornmeal pick up soil and grease. Terry cloth is good for this job, but an old sweatshirt turned inside out is even better. Dry kitchen flour can be substituted for cornmeal.

▶ Thoroughly rinse the washing machine after washing fiberglass to ensure that no fine glass fragments remain in the tub.

▶ Handle cotton curtains gently if they have been hanging in a sunny window; sunlight may have weakened the fabric.

▶ Machine-wash sheers, open weave, and other delicate fabrics in a mesh bag or hand-wash so that the fabric does not stretch or tear.

▶ Use curtain stretchers for drying lace or net curtains; if they need to be pressed, iron curtains before they are completely dry.

DRAPERIES

Draperies are often lined and are usually made of fabrics that are much heavier than those used for curtains. It is usually best to dry-clean draperies. Some drapery fabric is washable; check the care label for this

information. You can prolong trips to the cleaners by dusting draperies with the upholstery attachment on your vacuum weekly and before you wash them or send them out to be cleaned. Don't forget to dust the tops of the drapes, valances, and drapery hardware. Occasionally, air draperies on a clothesline on a breezy day to refresh them between cleanings.

▶ Remove all hooks and pins unless they are permanently attached before washing or dry-cleaning.

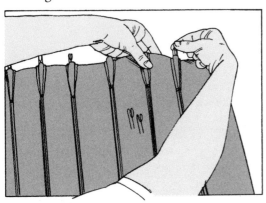

▶ If you plan to wash your draperies, test a corner of the fabric in a bowl of warm water and detergent to see if it bleeds. Use only the gentle cycle to wash draperies.

SHADES

Light-diffusing or opaque shades are usually made of fabric that is washable, and some shades have a protective vinyl coating that makes them easy to clean. Other shades are not washable and must be dry-cleaned.

▶ Vacuum shades regularly using the brush attachment. Lower the shades completely before vacuuming to clean the full length; don't forget the tops and valances.

▶ Remove finger marks with a sponge or a quick spray of an all-purpose spray cleaner.

▶ To thoroughly clean the shades, remove them from the window and spread them out on a flat surface. Test a corner of the shade with a detergent to see if the color bleeds.

SHUTTERS

Painted or stained shutters are the most common, but some people choose only to seal or varnish their wood shutters. For painted shutters, the best care is probably the least

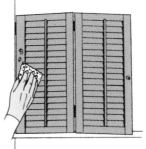

since some polishes and waxes can damage the color and/or decoration.

▶ Vacuum all shutters regularly with a brush attachment and wipe occasionally with a sponge to remove

smudges and finger marks.

▶ Use warm soapy water and a cloth to wash painted shutters; wash each louver separately on both sides. If you feel you must wax, use a hard paste wax only once a year.

▶ Shutters finished with varnish, lacquer, or wax can be cleaned with commercial aerosol polishing/waxing products. Choose a product that is appropriate for the high-gloss or satin finish of your shutters.

If you don't want to wash dishes, you can eat out. If you don't want to polish brass candlesticks, you can put them in storage. But if you don't keep up with the laundry, you won't have any clean items to wear. Although automatic washing machines/dryers and permanent press fabrics have removed much of the misery, someone still has to sort the laundry, load the clothes in the washer, select detergent and water temperature, move the clothes to the dryer, fold the dried clothes, and press some garments. In other words, it's still a chore. And the multitude of fabrics, trademarks, and special care instructions can complicate the job. With guidelines and tips on how to care for your favorite silk blouse and your child's cloth diapers, you can speed through piles of laundry and save some time for more enjoyable activities.

KNOWING YOUR MATERIALS

Although it may not seem obvious, the first step in doing your laundry quickly and efficiently is to know what an item is made of and the best way to care for it. Most garments and many other fabric items—including those made of suede and leather—manufactured and sold in the United States have permanently attached care labels. These labels can be of enormous help in determining exactly how you should remove stains and clean an item.

Certain information is not included on care labels. Neither the manufacturer nor the retailer is required to inform a consumer that a certain fabric will shrink. The label assumes that the purchaser knows that an item labeled "Hand-wash Only" should be washed in lukewarm water and that all nonwhite articles should not be treated with chlorine bleach. Check the accompanying chart—

"Understanding Fabric Care Labels" on page 108—if you don't understand the meaning of a care label or if you want to clarify how to care for a particular garment.

Another important piece of information contained on fabric care labels is the fiber content of the material. This is especially important with blends. These fabrics are

combinations of fibers, such as cotton and wool, cotton and polyester, or wool and acrylic. Blends should be cared for in the same way as the fiber with the highest percentage in the fabric. For example, a blend of 60 percent cotton and 40 percent polyester should be cleaned as though it were 100 percent cotton. However, when you remove spots and stains, you should follow procedures recommended for the most delicate fiber in the blend. For example, to remove stains from a blend of cotton and silk, use the procedure recommended for silk. If the stain is still apparent after such treatment, follow the procedure for cotton, the most durable fiber in this blend.

NATURAL FABRICS

Cotton

Cotton fabric is strong, long-wearing, and absorbent. It will shrink and wrinkle unless it is given special treatment. Cotton is often blended with other fibers or treated with a finish to make it wrinkle-resistant. It is available in a wide variety of weights and textures, from denim and corduroy to percale.

▶ Machine-wash and tumble-dry cotton fabrics, using a water temperature ranging from cold to hot, depending on the manufacturer's care instructions, and an all-purpose detergent.

▶ If needed, a chlorine bleach can be used on white or colorfast cotton unless a fabric finish has been applied. Do not use more than the recommended amount of bleach; this can damage the fibers.

▶ Use a fabric softener to improve softness and to reduce wrinkling, but be aware that fabric softener makes cotton less absorbent and should not be used on towels, washcloths, or diapers.

▶ Pretreat oil-based spots and stains with a prewash.

▶ Wash and shrink cotton fabrics before using them for home sewing.

▶ Iron cotton with a hot iron for best results. Use spray starch or spray sizing to restore a crisp appearance.

Linen

Pure linen fabric wrinkles easily, so many manufacturers make linen blends or add wrinkle-resistant finishes to overcome this problem. Linen is absorbent and comfortable to wear, but it can crack or show wear at the seams, along the creases, or on the finished edges of the garment.

▶ Machine-wash and tumble-dry linen. An all-purpose detergent is the best cleaning agent.

▶ Chlorine bleach can be used on white linen, following the manufacturer's recommended amount so as not to damage the fabric.

▶ Linen may also be dry-cleaned.

▶ To iron, press with a hot iron while the fabric is still slightly damp for the best results.

Silk

Silk is a delight to wear, but it requires special care. Most silk garments are marked "Dry-clean Only," but some can be washed by hand. If you intend to make a washable silk garment, be sure to wash a piece of the fabric by hand to make sure it is washable. Always test a corner of the fabric for colorfastness before washing a whole piece of silk. Some dyed silk will bleed.

▶ Use a hair shampoo containing protein and warm or cool water for hand-washing. The protein in the shampoo feeds the protein in the silk. Handle washable silk gently during washing; never twist or wring it. Hang silk out of direct sunlight to drip-dry.

▶ Press silk while it is still damp with a warm iron (below 275°) or use a steam iron.

▶ To remove stains from washable white or light-colored silk, use only oxygen bleach or mix 1 part hydrogen peroxide (3 percent) to 8 parts water.

Wool

Wool fabric is highly resilient, absorbent, and sheds wrinkles well, but it will shrink and mat if exposed to heat and rubbing. It is popular in both knit and woven fabrics. Wool fabric textures range from fine wool crepe and jersey to felt and mohair.

▶ Treat spots and stains on wool fabrics with solvent-based spot removers.

▶ Wool should always be dry-cleaned unless it is specifically marked "Washable."

▶ Use light-duty detergent in cold water to wash wool. Allow the article to soak for a few minutes before starting the washing process. Machine-washing is appropriate only if the care label indicates that it is, and then use only cold water and a gentle cycle.

▶ Handle woolens carefully when they are wet to avoid stretching. Remove excess moisture by rolling a wool article in a towel, then block it into shape and dry it on a flat surface.

▶ Clean felt by wiping it with a dry sponge; for a more thorough treatment, hold the material over the steam from a teakettle, brushing lightly with a dry sponge or lint-free cloth to smoothe the surface.

▶ Machine-dry woolens only if the manufacturer's instructions recommend it.

▶ Press wool with a hot iron, using lots of steam. Cover the article with a damp cloth or chemically treated press cloth.

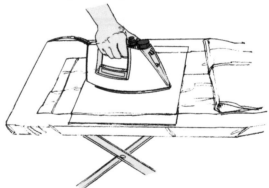

▶ Allow any wool garment to dry thoroughly before storing it.

SYNTHETIC FABRICS

Acetate

Acetate is made from cellulose and has a silklike appearance. It is closely related to rayon and has good body and drapes well. Taffeta, satin, crepe, brocade, and double knits often contain acetate. It is not very absorbent or colorfast and easily loses its strength when it is wet.

▶ If the care label specifies that the article is washable, hand-wash it carefully in warm water, using a light-duty detergent. Otherwise have it dry-cleaned.

▶ Do not soak colored items or wash them with white articles.

▶ Add fabric softener to the rinse water to reduce wrinkles.

▶ Line-dry acetate away from heat or direct sunlight.

▶ Press acetate at the coolest setting, on the wrong side, while the article is damp. Use a press cloth when pressing the right side of the fabric.

▶ Nail-polish remover and perfumes will permanently damage acetate.

Acrylic

Many acrylic weaves resemble wool's softness, bulk, and fluffiness. Acrylics are wrinkle-resistant and are usually machine-washable. Often acrylic fibers are blended with wool or polyester fibers. Acrylic's biggest drawback is its tendency to pill. Blends will do this less than pure acrylic.

▶ Dry-clean acrylic garments or wash them by hand or in the machine.

▶ Pretreat oil-based stains and turn garments inside out before laundering to reduce pilling.

▶ Wash delicate items by hand in warm water, gently squeezing out the excess. Machine-wash sturdy articles with an all-purpose detergent and tumble-dry at low temperatures.

▶ If the fabric is labeled "Colorfast," it can be bleached with either a chlorine or oxygen bleach.

▶ Adding fabric softener to the rinse water every third or fourth time an article is washed reduces static electricity.

Fiberglass

Fiberglass fabrics are wrinkle- and soil-resistant, but they have poor resistance to abrasion. They are not absorbent, but stand up well to sun and weather, which makes fiberglass fabrics ideal for curtains and draperies. Fiberglass is never made into wearing apparel because it sheds small glass fibers.

▶ Dust fiberglass periodically with the upholstery attachment of your vacuum cleaner.

▶ For best results, hand-wash fiberglass using an all-purpose detergent. Wear rubber gloves to protect your hands from glass fibers.

▶ If you wash machine-washable fiberglass in the washing machine, rinse out the tub to remove the glass fibers. Never wash fiberglass articles with items made of anything else.

▶ Drip-dry fiberglass articles; do not iron them.

Modacrylic

Modacrylic is a fiber often used in fake furs, fleece robes, blankets, stuffed toys, and wigs. It is resilient, soft, and warm, and it resists moths, mildew, sunlight damage, and wrinkling.

▶ Hand-wash delicate modacrylic items, such as wigs, and machine-wash sturdy items in warm water with a gentle cycle and a light-duty detergent. Use fabric softener to reduce static electricity.

▶ Use a low-heat setting in the dryer, removing modacrylic articles as soon as the tumbling stops.

▶ If pressing is needed, use a cool iron.

▶ Deep-pile modacrylic coats should be dry-cleaned for best results.

Nylon

Nylon fabrics are extremely strong, lightweight, smooth, and lustrous. They are also nonabsorbent and have excellent abrasion and wrinkle resistance. Often combined with spandex, nylon knits are very stretchy, but hold and recover their original shape. Available in many textures, nylon is used to make all kinds of items, including lingerie, carpets, rainwear, and tents. Always follow the manufacturer's cleaning instructions.

▶ Pretreat oil-based stains on nylon.

▶ Machine-wash sturdy articles in warm water with an all-purpose detergent.

▶ Hand-wash lingerie and hosiery, using warm water and a light-duty detergent, or machine-wash in a mesh bag to prevent stretching or tearing.

▶ Do not launder white nylon with colored fabrics of any kind.

▶ Use a chlorine bleach only if a nylon article is colorfast.

▶ Use fabric softener to significantly reduce static electricity.

▶ Tumble-dry nylon at a low temperature setting. Press at a cool temperature setting.

Olefin

Olefin fabrics are nonabsorbent and hold in body heat, but they are also very heat-sensitive and melt immediately upon contact with heat. Olefin is used as a filling for outerwear and upholstery. The fabric is bulky, but lightweight.

▶ Machine-wash olefin in warm water, using an all-purpose detergent. Add fabric softener to the final rinse.

▶ Ironing olefin is not recommended, since even the slightest amount of heat will melt the fabric.

▶ Tumble-dry olefin at the lowest possible heat setting.

Polyester

Polyester fabrics are strong, resilient, wrinkle-resistant, colorfast, crisp, and hold pleats and creases well. But they are also nonabsorbent, attract and hold oil-based stains, may pill when rubbed, and may yellow with age. Polyester is used for clothing and filling; some bed linens and towels are also made from polyester blends. It can be safely dry-cleaned or machine-washed.

▶ Pretreat oil-based stains with a prewash.

▶ Turn polyester-knit garments inside out before washing to prevent snags.

▶ Machine-wash polyester in warm water, using an all-purpose detergent. Use a chlorine bleach, if necessary. Fabric softener will reduce static electricity.

▶ Tumble-dry at a low temperature setting. Do not overly dry polyester; this will cause gradual shrinkage.

▶ Press polyester fabrics at a moderate temperature setting or use steam.

Rayon

Rayon is a strong, absorbent fabric, but it tends to lose its strength when it is wet. It is used for drapery and upholstery fabrics as well as for clothing.

▶ Dry-clean rayon or wash it by hand unless it is labeled "Machine-washable."

▶ For hand wash, use lukewarm water with a light-duty detergent. Squeeze moisture out gently when washing rayon fabrics by hand.

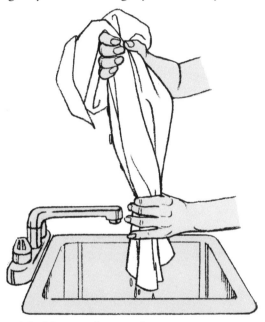

▶ Machine-wash rayon in warm water on a gentle cycle with a light-duty detergent.

▶ Chlorine bleach can be used on rayon unless it has been treated with a resin finish.

▶ Drip-dry and press rayon on the wrong side with an iron at a medium temperature setting while the fabric is damp.

Spandex

Spandex is a lightweight fiber that resembles rubber in durability. It has good stretch and recovery, and it is resistant to damage from sunlight, abrasion, and oils. Always blended with other fibers, spandex provides the stretch in waistbands, foundation garments, swimwear, and dancewear.

▶ Pretreat oil-based stains.

▶ Hand- or machine-wash spandex-blend garments in warm water using an all-purpose

detergent. Do not wash white spandex with colored fabrics of any kind.

▶ Use only oxygen or sodium-perborate bleach. Rinse thoroughly.

▶ Line-dry or tumble-dry garments made with spandex at a low temperature setting.

Triacetate

Triacetate resembles acetate, but it is less sensitive to heat; this allows it to be creased and crisply pleated. Triacetate is often used in jersey, textured knits, and taffeta.

▶ Pleated garments can be hand- or machine-washed in cold water. Set the gentle cycle to agitate for three minutes. Drip-dry permanently pleated garments or air-dry them in a dryer.

▶ Most triacetate articles can be machine-washed with an all-purpose detergent in hot or warm water.

▶ Tumble- or line-dry triacetate. Press, if necessary, using a hot temperature setting.

THE BASICS OF LAUNDRY

One way to do your laundry is to jam as many dirty clothes as possible into the

continued on page 110

UNDERSTANDING FABRIC CARE LABELS

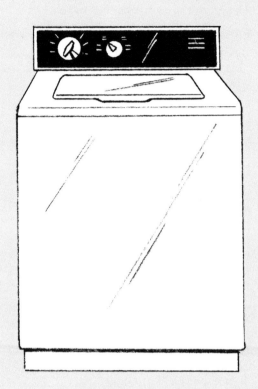

When label reads	It means
Cold Wash/ Cold Rinse	Use cold water or cold washing machine setting.
Warm Wash/ Warm Rinse	Use warm water or warm washing machine setting.
Hot Wash	Use hot water or hot washing machine setting.
No Spin	Remove wash load before final machine spin cycle.
Delicate Cycle/ Gentle Cycle	Use appropriate machine setting; otherwise, wash by hand.
Durable Press/ Permanent Press Cycle	Use appropriate machine setting; otherwise, use warm wash, cold rinse, and short spin cycle.
Wash Separately	Wash alone or with like colors.

Nonmachine Washing

Hand-wash	Launder only by hand in lukewarm (hand-comfortable) water; may be bleached; may be dry-cleaned.
Hand-wash Only	Same as above, but do not dry-clean.

Machine Washable

When label reads	It means
Machine-wash	Wash, bleach, dry, and press by any customary method, including commercial laundering and dry-cleaning.
Home Launder Only	Same as above, but do not use commercial laundering.
No Chlorine Bleach	Do not use chlorine bleach. Oxygen bleach may be used.
No Bleach	Do not use any type of bleach.

When label reads	It means
Hand-wash Separately	Hand-wash alone or with like colors.
No Bleach	Do not use bleach.
Damp-wipe	Surface-clean with damp cloth or sponge.

Home Drying

When label reads	It means
Tumble-dry	Dry in tumble dryer at specified setting—high, medium, low, or no heat.
Tumble-dry/ Remove Promptly	Same as above, but in absence of cool-down cycle, remove at once when tumbling stops.
Drip-dry	Hang wet and allow to dry with hand-shaping only.
Line-dry	Hang damp and allow to dry.
No Wring	Hang-dry, drip-dry, or dry flat only.
No Twist	Handle to prevent wrinkles.
Dry Flat	Lay garment on flat surface.

Ironing and Pressing

When label reads	It means
Cool Iron	Set iron at lowest setting.
Warm Iron	Set iron at medium setting.

When label reads	It means
Hot Iron	Set iron at hot setting.
Do Not Iron	Do not iron or press with heat.
Steam-iron	Iron or press with steam.
Iron Damp	Dampen garment before ironing.

Miscellaneous

When label reads	It means
Dry-clean Only	Garment should be dry-cleaned only, including self-service.
Professionally Dry-clean Only	Do not use self-service dry-cleaning.
No Dry-clean	Use recommended care instructions. No dry-cleaning materials.

continued from page 107

washing machine, run it through whatever wash cycle happens to be programmed, and hope for the best. This method may leave your sweater doll-sized or turn your white silk shirt pink, but it's quick—if you don't count the time you'll spend replacing your ruined clothes. It's also expensive. Doing the laundry properly will take more time, but it will extend the life of your clothes and they'll look better. Once you know the basics—how to sort clothes, pretreat stains, select laundry products, and use the washer and dryer— getting the laundry done is quite simple.

SORTING THE WASH

Sorting the laundry is the first step to a clean wash and helps to keep clothes, linens, and other household items looking their best through repeated washings. First sort the laundry by color. Put all the white or predominantly white articles in one pile, the light colors and pastels in another pile, and the bright and dark-colored items into a third. Then separate the dark pile into two piles: one for colorfast items and one for noncolorfast items. Further separate each pile into three smaller piles based on how dirty they are: lightly soiled, moderately soiled, and heavily soiled. Now you may have up to 12 various-sized piles of laundry. You'll want to make sure to sort them until you come up with a reasonable number of compatible, washer-sized loads. The following hints will help you with the final sorting:

▶ Combine white and light-colored items that have similar degrees of soil into the same pile.

▶ Combine noncolorfast items with similarly colored colorfast items with the same degree of soil.

▶ Create a separate pile for delicate items that must be hand-washed.

▶ Separate white synthetic articles, and wash them only with other white fabrics.

▶ Separate synthetics, blends, and permanent-press fabrics from natural-fiber fabrics without special finishes.

▶ Separate items made from fabrics that produce lint from fabrics that attract lint.

PREPARING THE WASH

Follow these hints to minimize damage to the articles you are washing and to help clean them thoroughly:

▶ Pretreat spots, stains, and heavily soiled items with either a prewash spot-and-stain remover, a liquid detergent, a paste made from granular soap or detergent, a bar of soap, or a presoak.

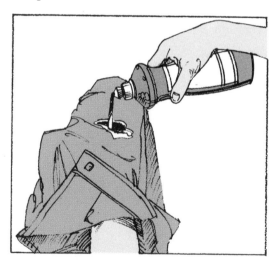

▶ Know the fiber content and finishes of fabrics so you can select the proper water temperature and cleaning products.

▶ Save care information so you can follow the recommended cleaning procedures.

▶ Close all zippers, hook all hooks, and button all buttons.

► Turn pockets inside out to get rid of debris.

► Remove any nonwashable trim, decorations, pins, or buckles that might make holes or snag other articles in the wash.

► Tie and buckle all belts and sashes to prevent tangling.

► Mend seams, tears, holes, or loose hems to prevent further damage during the wash cycle.

► Turn sweaters and corduroy garments inside out to prevent pilling and to combat their tendency to collect lint.

PREWASH SPOT-AND-STAIN REMOVERS

While soaps and detergents can be worked directly into spots and heavily soiled areas before you put the laundry into the washer, a special product designed just for removing spots and stains is more convenient to use. These are called prewash spot-and-stain removers and typically come in aerosols or pump sprays. They are excellent for spot-treating stubborn soil and stains, especially grease marks on synthetic fabrics.

► Treat the stain while it is still fresh. Saturate the soiled area completely, then lightly rub the fabric together to work the prewash product into the fibers.

► Some prewash products can damage the exterior finish of the washer and dryer, so be careful where you spray them.

► Granular presoak products containing enzymes can break down stubborn stains such as milk, blood, baby formula, chocolate, gravy, some fruits and vegetables, and grass. They are not effective on rust, ink, oil, or grease.

► Following the manufacturer's directions, mix a solution in a large sink or in the washer. Before adding the soiled laundry, make sure that the presoak has dissolved thoroughly. Soak for the recommended length of time; an overnight soak is suitable for articles that look dull and dingy.

► Do not soak dark- and light-colored fabrics together for long periods of time; this can cause colors to run.

► Wash the laundry as usual after using a presoak.

► You can also use a presoak for diaper-pail solutions and as a detergent booster.

SELECTING LAUNDRY PRODUCTS

Most commercial laundry preparations are designed to be used in washing machines, but some can be used for both hand- and machine-washing. Read the label carefully before purchasing any product to make sure it is the right one for the job you want it to do. When you use a laundry product, follow the directions precisely and measure accurately.

Detergents and Soaps

Soap, a mixture of alkalies and fats, is a good cleaner in soft water, breaks down well in city sewer systems, and does not harm the environment. Soap is less effective in hard water, however, because it reacts with the high mineral content to form a curd that leaves a gray scum on clothing.

Detergents are synthetic washing products derived from petroleum and other nonfatty materials. They are less affected by hard water than soap and have excellent cleaning power. Detergents contain a wetting agent that lifts off dirt and agents that help to make hard water minerals inactive, which is why they do not create scum. Many detergents contain phosphates, which are harmful to the environment because they promote an overgrowth of algae in water, but some detergents are phosphate-free. The cleaning ability of phosphate-free detergents is not as effective in hard water and in cold-water washes, and these detergents cause excessive wear to many fabrics.

Use liquid detergents in cold-water washes for best results, or dissolve powder or granular detergents in 1 quart hot water, then add the solution to the cold wash water.

Bleach

Bleach works with detergent or soap to remove stains and soil, whiten white items, and brighten the colors of some fabrics. It also acts as a mild disinfectant. The two basic types of laundry bleach are chlorine and oxygen. Common liquid chlorine bleach is the most effective and least expensive, but it cannot be used on all fabrics. Oxygen bleach is safer for all washable fabrics, resin-finished fibers, and most washable colors, but it is much less strong than chlorine bleach.

▶ Always give colored fabrics a colorfastness test before using any bleach by mixing 1 tablespoon chlorine bleach with ¼ cup water or 1 tablespoon oxygen bleach with 2 quarts hot water. Apply this solution to an inconspicuous place; wait a few minutes and check for a color change. If the color does not bleed, use the bleach according to the manufacturer's directions.

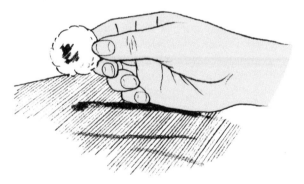

▶ Add diluted chlorine bleach to the wash water about 5 minutes after the wash cycle has begun or use an automatic bleach dispenser.

▶ When you use laundry bleach it should be poured into the wash water or otherwise diluted. Bleach should never be poured directly onto fabrics.

▶ Always bleach the whole item and not just a single stain.

▶ Use the hottest water possible when using a bleach; this improves its performance.

▶ Bleach clothes only in the wash cycle so the bleach can be completely removed during the rinse cycle.

▶ When washing synthetics that contain spandex (foundation garments or swimwear, for example), use only an oxygen or sodium perborate bleach.

▶ Whiten diapers with less bleach by adding ⅓ cup baking soda to the beginning of the wash cycle.

▶ Avoid using chlorine bleach on resin-finished rayon; it may cause the fabric to discolor.

▶ If you find an unexpected rip or tear in a garment and want to know if it has been caused by bleach, inspect the edges around the area. If the fabric has been damaged by bleach, the edges will be weak and will tear easily. Yellowish discoloration is also an indication of bleach damage.

Fabric Softeners

Fabric softeners add softness and fluffiness, reduce static electricity on synthetics so they will not cling, help decrease lint, and make pressing easier. They are available in liquid, sheet, or solid form. Liquid fabric softeners are added to the wash or rinse cycle; sheet and solid products are used in the dryer.

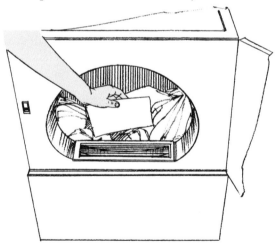

▶ Read the instructions for using a fabric softener to determine at what time in the laundering cycle to add it.

▶ Dilute liquid fabric softeners with water before adding them to the automatic fabric-softener dispenser or to the rinse.

▶ Fabric softener can stain fabric if it is poured or sprayed directly onto clothes or if it is used with a water conditioner.

▶ Sheet fabric softeners will stain polyester articles if they are used in the dryer when these fabrics are drying. If you stain an item with fabric softener, rub the stained area with liquid detergent or a prewash spot-and-stain remover and rewash the article.

▶ Fabric softener should not be used in combination with another laundry product, such as a water conditioner, in the rinse cycle. Stains may result.

▶ When laundering baby clothes, it's best to use fabric softener sparingly because some babies are sensitive to softener buildup.

▶ If a laundered garment feels greasy or slick, you may have used too much fabric softener. Leave the softener out of the next few washes to see if the condition improves.

▶ If you use a sheet-type fabric softener, you can use it in the washing machine's rinse cycle for loads that you plan to air-dry rather than machine-dry.

USING AN AUTOMATIC CLOTHES WASHER

When you consider the alternative of a washtub in the backyard, the automatic clothes washer is a great timesaver. For the best results from your washing machine, you must know how to combine multiple load capacities, water levels, temperature settings, and cycles properly.

Loading the Machine

Read the washer manufacturer's instruction booklet thoroughly, put it away in a safe place for reference, and follow the recommended laundry procedures.

▶ Do not overload the machine; garments should not pile up past the top of the agitator.

▶ Loading the washer to full capacity each time you wash will save time and energy;

USING WATER CONDITIONERS

The amount and type of chemicals and minerals dissolved in water determine whether it is hard or soft. The condition of the water affects the cleaning potential of laundry products: The softer the water, the more effective it is for cleaning. Determine the hardness of your water so you will know if you need to condition it for effective cleaning.

Hard water leaves a residue on laundered articles; this is known as washing film. To soften water, the minerals must be removed or locked up. Water that measures under four grains hardness per gallon will probably clean effectively, especially if a detergent rather than soap is used. You can soften hard water with a mechanical water softener that attaches to your home's water tank or by adding a water-conditioning product to the wash and rinse water.

▶ Follow the directions on product labels precisely.

▶ Use a nonprecipitating water conditioner to remove previously formed washing film or soap/detergent buildup. You can also remove light hard-water washing film from diapers, towels, or fabrics by soaking them in a solution of 1 cup white vinegar and 1 gallon water in a plastic container.

▶ Use a nonprecipitating conditioner if you use soap in hard water or if you use a phosphate-free detergent.

don't be tempted to throw dark bath towels in a bleach load or sweaters in a permanent press load just to fill it.

▶ Mix small and large items in each load for the best circulation, and distribute the load evenly around the wash basket.

Selecting Water Temperature

The correct water temperature(s) for a load of wash varies according to the kinds of fabric being washed and the amount of soil. Use the chart on page 108 to help you select the proper wash and rinse settings. Be aware of the actual temperature of the water in the washing machine; it can vary during the year. If the water temperature is below 80°F, it is too cold to do a good job even if you use a cold-water detergent. Adjust the amounts of cold and hot water flowing into the machine to get the right temperature for each temperature setting.

Selecting Water Level

Use enough water to provide good circulation, but do not use so much that you waste water and energy. Most machines have a water-level control, and you should adjust this control to match each load you wash. Refer to the manufacturer's instructions for this information. To minimize wrinkling and shrinkage when washing delicate and permanent-press items, always use at least a medium water level setting for both the wash and rinse cycles, no matter how small the load.

Selecting Machine Cycle

Select the type of cycle and the length of washing time according to the kind of load and the degree of soil. Follow these guidelines, using a longer cycle for heavily soiled laundry:

▶ Sturdy white and colorfast items: Use normal cycle, with a 10-to-12-minute wash time.

▶ Sturdy noncolorfast items: Use normal cycle, with a 6-to-8-minute wash time.

▶ Sturdy permanent press and wash and wear: Use permanent press cycle, with a 6-to-8-minute wash time.

▶ Delicate fabrics and knits: Use gentle or delicate cycle, with a 4-to-6-minute wash time.

DRYING CLOTHES

Most clothes dried in an automatic dryer come out soft and almost wrinkle-free. If you have time and a backyard, you may prefer to dry the laundry on the clothesline on sunny days, reserving the dryer for inclement weather and for your permanent-press fabrics.

Machine Drying

▶ Read the manufacturer's instruction book to familiarize yourself with the dryer's operating procedures and recommended cycles.

▶ Shake out each article before placing it in the dryer to speed the drying time and cut down on wrinkles.

▶ Do not overload the dryer; this will cause uneven drying and excessive wrinkling.

▶ Remove items from the dryer as soon as it stops, and hang or fold them to keep them from getting wrinkled.

▶ Dry clothes until they are "almost dry" rather than "bone dry" if you are going to iron them.

▶ Clean the lint filter after each use of the dryer.

▶ Polyester knits should be removed promptly from the clothes dryer to prevent wrinkling and shrinking.

Line Drying

▶ Attach items to the clothesline by their most sturdy edges. Smooth the clothes as you hang them, running your fingers down seams and along the front, collar, and cuff edges. Dry white and light-colored items in the sun and bright-colored items in the shade.

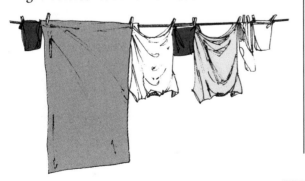

▶ If you are going to the trouble of hanging clothes outside to dry, make sure that clothespins and clotheslines are clean.

▶ Use plastic rope or plastic-coated wire for your clothesline, and wipe it with a damp cloth before using it.

IRONING TIMESAVERS

Ironing is a tedious task, but thanks to permanent press and other innovations, Tuesdays are no longer devoted to an all-day stint of ironing. Still, some garments must be ironed to look their best. The following should help you make short work of the ironing you still have to do in your home:

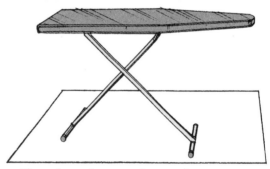

▶ If you have the space in your home, set up an ironing center. You will save time by not having to set up the board and collecting the iron and ironing supplies.

▶ If you have to set up your board every time, do your ironing in the bedroom. You'll be able to use the bed to sort your laundry, and you'll have hangers close at hand in the closet.

▶ A piece of lightweight muslin or batiste makes a perfect, inexpensive pressing cloth.

▶ When ironing, keep thread, needle, and extra buttons handy for making necessary repairs before an item is pressed and stored in the closet.

▶ Progress from articles or garments needing the lowest temperature to those requiring the highest temperature.

▶ Start with small areas on a garment, such as cuffs, before progressing to larger areas.

▶ To make your ironing board cover fit perfectly, place it on the board while it's still damp from the washer, and let it dry in place.

▶ To prevent wrinkles, keep moving freshly ironed surfaces away from you.

▶ Starch pillowcases lightly to make the fabric more resistant to stains from face and hair creams and oils.

▶ To prevent collars, cuffs, and hems from puckering, iron them on the wrong side first.

▶ Iron collars and cuffs from the ends toward the center for best results.

▶ Iron double-thickness fabric on the inside first, then on the outside.

▶ To prevent large items from dragging on the floor while you're ironing, slide a card table under the narrow end of your ironing board.

▶ Unwanted creases in a permanent-press fabric can sometimes be banished by pressing with a cloth moistened with a solution of 2 parts water and 1 part white vinegar.

▶ Acrylic knits can stretch out of shape if moved when wet and warm. Press each section dry and let it cool completely before moving it on the ironing board.

▶ When pressing badly wrinkled corduroy, hold the iron just above the garment and steam the fabric thoroughly. Then, while the corduroy is still damp and hot, quickly smooth

HAND-WASHING

Most washable fabrics can be put into the machine, but some items are marked "Hand-wash Only." Never disregard this label—even when you're in a hurry. Although the washing machine is usually the fastest and best way to do your wash, hand-washing is quicker and cheaper than using the machine when you have only a few items to clean.

Sort hand wash in the same way you sort machine wash. Separate the clothes into piles by color, putting white and light colors together, dark and noncolorfast items into separate piles. Pretreat stains and heavily soiled areas with a prewash spot-and-stain remover or by rubbing liquid detergent into the area.

Use a light-duty soap or detergent and dissolve it in the warm or cool wash water before adding the clothes. Submerge the articles in the water and let them soak for 3 to 5 minutes. Gently squeeze the suds through the fabric,

being careful not to rub, twist, or wring excessively. Rinse articles thoroughly in cool water until the water runs clear. Add a few drops of fabric softener to the last rinse, if desired.

Hang blouses, dresses, scarfs, and lingerie to drip-dry. The shower is a good place for this. Use towels to blot up excess moisture from sweaters, stockings, panties, and bras. Hang these items to dry only if the weight of the water will not stretch them out of shape; otherwise, dry them on a towel on a flat surface.

it along the ribs with your palm. This technique will eliminate even bad creases.

▶ Revive the nap of velvet or corduroy by pressing it right-side down on a piece of the same fabric.

▶ If you don't have a sleeve board, insert a rolled-up towel in sleeves so they can be pressed without leaving creases. You can make your own sleeve board from a heavy cardboard tube covered with a soft fabric.

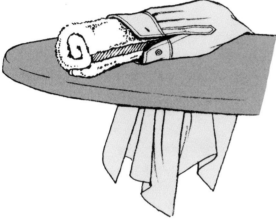

▶ Quick spray starch can be made at home by slowly adding ½ teaspoon of cornstarch and 1½ teaspoons of wheat starch to 1 cup of cold water. Stir until the starch is dissolved and pour the blend into a clean pump-spray bottle. You can use it to spray fabrics lightly when ironing.

▶ Ironing reduces the fluffiness and absorbency of cloth diapers.

▶ Restore a shiny look to chintz by ironing the fabric right-side down on waxed paper. This also adds body to the fabric.

▶ To keep from giving your wash-and-wear garments a sheen when you do touch-up ironing, turn the clothing inside out and iron the wrong side.

▶ To remove wrinkles from a tie, insert a piece of cardboard cut to fit its inside. Cover the tie with cheesecloth, and press lightly with a steam iron.

▶ To avoid flattening embroidery or eyelets when ironing, iron them facedown on a thick towel. A towel is also a good cushion for napped fabrics.

▶ Hold pleats in place with paper clips when ironing. Be careful that the clips don't snag the fabric—particularly if the fabric has a loose weave.

▶ To avoid clogging the inside of a steam iron with mineral deposits from tap water, use distilled water.

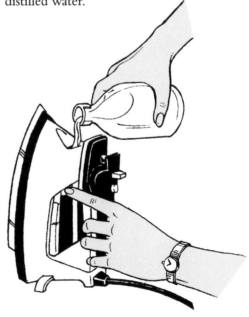

▶ If your iron is sticky from pressing starched clothes, clean it by running it across a piece of aluminum foil, fine sandpaper, or paper

SOLVING LAUNDRY PROBLEMS

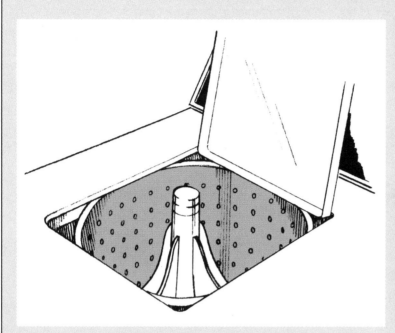

Here are some of the most common laundry problems and simple, quick ways to solve them.

Brown Stains
Cause: Soap, detergent, or bleach reacting with iron or manganese in the water.
Solution: Install an iron filter on your water system. Do not use chlorine bleach in the wash. Use a nonprecipitating water conditioner in both the wash and rinse water.

Excessive Wear
Cause: Improper use of bleach.
Solution: Always dilute chlorine bleach before adding it to the washer.

Cause: Tears, holes, snags, split seams, and loose hems.
Solution: Make all repairs before washing an item and hook all hooks, close zippers, and remove pins or other sharp objects before putting articles in the washer.

Gray and Dingy Fabric
Cause: Incorrect sorting, insufficient detergent, or water temperature too low.
Solution: Follow the suggestions for sorting and proper washing techniques.

Greasy Spots
Cause: Undiluted liquid fabric softener coming into contact with fabric.
Solution: Dilute liquid fabric softeners.

Cause: Fabric softener sheets in the dryer with lightweight fabrics.
Solution: Use liquid softener in the washing machine when washing delicate fabrics. Greasy spots can be removed by rubbing in liquid detergent and then washing again. Also use a lower temperature setting on the dryer.
Cause: Hard water.
Solution: Use a water conditioner appropriate for your detergent or install a water softener.
Cause: Overloaded washer.
Solution: Reduce the load size so the clothes can circulate more freely.

Harsh-Feeling Fabrics
Cause: Spin speed not adequate.
Solution: Increase the spin speed or check to make sure the load is balanced so the spin can reach its maximum speed.
Cause: Hard water.
Solution: Increase the amount of detergent, install a mechanical water softener, or use a water conditioning product.
Cause: Using soap in hard water.
Solution: Switch to a detergent, install a mechanical

water softener, or use a water conditioner.

Linting

Cause: Incorrect sorting.
Solution: Read and follow suggestions for sorting.
Cause: Not enough detergent.
Solution: Increase the amount of detergent to help hold lint in suspension so it can be flushed down the drain.
Cause: Overloaded washer.
Solution: Reduce load size or increase the water level so the wash can circulate freely.
Cause: Improper use of fabric softener.
Solution: Do not add softener directly to wash water unless directed to do so.

Cause: Debris in cuffs or pockets.
Solution: Remove any tissues, paper, or loose dirt before washing.

Scorching During Ironing

Cause: Iron temperature setting too high.
Solution: Reduce the heat setting on the iron.
Cause: Heat of iron reacting with a buildup of laundry products.
Solution: Run clothes through one or two complete washing cycles with 1 cup nonprecipitating water conditioner and no other laundry product, then wash as usual.

Static Electricity

Cause: Synthetic fabrics tend to produce static electricity.
Solution: Use a fabric softener in the washer or dryer.

Yellowing

Cause: Incomplete removal of soil, especially body oils.
Solution: Pretreat heavily soiled areas, increase the amount of detergent, use hotter water and bleach.
Cause: Iron in the water.
Solution: Install an iron filter, use extra detergent, and use a nonprecipitating water conditioner.
Cause: Aging of some fabrics.
Solution: No solution, except routine washing.

---

sprinkled with salt. If your iron is plastic-coated, though, avoid salt or other abrasives.

▶ Remove cleaning-product residues from the soleplate vent areas of an electric iron with a cotton swab or a pipe cleaner.

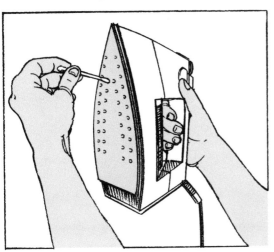

DEFEATING SPOTS AND STAINS

If all we had to worry about was ring-around-the-collar, laundering would be a much easier job. Unfortunately, stains are easy to come by in the normal course of living. Grass stains on jeans, mustard on T-shirts, and chocolate on just about anything are part of life. With the right treatment, however, most stains can be eliminated.

BASIC RULES FOR STAIN REMOVAL

Successful stain removal relies on the correct technique and the appropriate removal

TIPS FOR SPECIAL CARE ITEMS

▶ Place panty hose, knee-highs, and other small items in a mesh bag before washing them in a machine; they will be less likely to get tangled or damaged.

▶ To machine-wash fragile garments, put them in a pillowcase and close it with a plastic-bag tie. Wash the bundle on a gentle cycle.

▶ Unless the label states otherwise, you can wash suede-look-alike skirts and shirts. Add a couple of towels to the washing machine at the same time and you'll find mock suede items come out of the machine with a softer, smoother surface.

▶ Turn a turtleneck sweater wrong-side out before you put it in the laundry hamper. When it's washed, any makeup or skin oils that have come off on the neck area will be exposed to the suds and will come clean faster.

▶ To prevent fraying, wash a foam rubber pillow in its case. Then air-dry the pillow. Do not put it in the dryer.

▶ Glycerin will keep plastic items such as shower curtains and baby pants soft and pliable; add to the rinse water.

▶ Plastic or rubber rainwear should be air-dried, not put in a clothes dryer.

▶ Some down-filled garments can be machine-washed using cold water and a mild detergent. Rinse well until the water shows no more suds, then machine-dry at very low heat. Add a large bath towel or sneaker to the dryer to help rotate the garment.

▶ A little liquid detergent may be all you need to remove grass stains from washable fabric shoes; you can also try a prewash spot-and-stain remover.

▶ Hand-wash quilts filled with cotton batting; machine-washing is too harsh and will cause the batting to bunch.

▶ Launder a patchwork quilt using the method recommended for the most delicate fabric in the quilt.

▶ Lift a fresh grease spot from nonwashable fabric by sprinkling the spot with cornstarch; allow the cornstarch to soak up the grease for a few minutes and then brush it away.

▶ Hand-wash leather gloves in saddle soap while they're on your hands, but don't rub them. Rinse them well and remove them. If they're hard to remove after washing, run a stream of water into them.

▶ Before drying leather gloves you've just hand-washed, blow into them to help reshape the fingers. When the gloves are almost dry, put them on once more, flexing the fingers to soften the leather. Then take off the gloves, and dry them flat.

▶ Once leather gloves have been dry-cleaned, they should not be washed.

▶ If you spray new tennis shoes with starch before wearing them, dirt can't become embedded in the canvas and the shoes will always be easy to clean.

▶ When washing white tennis shoes, bleach them ultra-white by adding lemon juice to the final rinse.

▶ Tennis shoes can be cleaned in the washing machine, or cleaned by hand with a soap-filled plastic scouring pad.

▶ You won't lose shoelaces in the wash if you string them through the buttonholes in a shirt and tie the ends together.

agent for the particular stain and the material that is stained. If you ignore the basic rules for stain removal, you may be stymied in your attempt to get rid of a spot. The following basic rules should be kept in mind:

▶ The quicker the better. The best time to treat a stain is the moment after it occurs. The longer it sets, the more likely it is that a stain will become permanent.

▶ Know what you're cleaning. Identify both the staining agent and the stained surface. Both will affect the way in which you treat the stain.

▶ Clean it off before you clean it. Remove as much of the staining agent as you possibly can before you begin the stain-removal process.

▶ Be gentle. Rubbing, folding, wringing, and squeezing cause stains to penetrate more deeply and may damage delicate fibers.

▶ Keep it cool. Avoid using hot water, high-heat clothes dryers, and irons on stains; heat makes some stains impossible to remove.

▶ Pretest stain removers. Even water can damage some fabrics, so test every cleaner you plan to use in an inconspicuous spot.

▶ Follow directions. Read manufacturers' care labels and directions on product containers before you start to clean a stain.

▶ Work from the edges into the center. You won't spread the stain or leave a ring.

DIFFERENTIATING STAINS

There are many different types of stains. In general, they break down into three major categories: greasy stains, nongreasy stains, and combination stains.

Greasy Stains

Greasy stains come in all flavors—from butter, and even margarine, to the oil from your car. You can sometimes remove grease spots from washable fabrics by laundering. Pretreating by rubbing a little detergent directly into the spot often helps, as does using a dry-cleaning solution on the stain. If you are treating an old stain or one that has been ironed, a yellow stain may remain after treatment with a solvent. Bleach is often effective at eliminating this yellow residue.

To remove grease spots from nonwashable fabrics, sponge the stain from the edges to the center with a dry-cleaning solution. Total elimination of the stain may require several applications, and you must allow the spot to dry completely between each sponging. Greasy stains may also be removed from nonwashable fabrics by using an absorbent substance, such as cornstarch, cornmeal, French chalk, or fuller's earth (a natural mineral clay). Dust it on the greasy spots. When the absorbent material begins to look caked, shake or brush it off. Repeat this procedure until the stain is gone.

Absorbents are easy to use and will not harm fabrics; however, other stain-removal agents, such as detergents, dry-cleaning solvents, and bleach, can damage fibers. Before using any of these products, you should carefully read the care label on the stained item and the label on the product container. If you do not have either one of these labels, test the cleaning product on the fabric in an inconspicuous area.

Nongreasy Stains

Fruit juice, black coffee, tea, food coloring, ink—nongreasy stains are easy to acquire, but not impossible to remove. If you are treating a nongreasy stain on a washable fabric, sponge the stain with cool water as soon as possible. If this doesn't remove the stain, try soaking the fabric in cool water. The stain may soak out within half an hour, or you may need to leave the item in water overnight. If some of the stain still remains after this treatment, try gently rubbing liquid detergent into it, then rinse with cool water. The very last resort is to use bleach, but always read the fabric-care label before you bleach. If the stain is old or has already been ironed, it may be impossible to remove it completely.

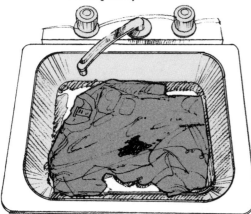

A nongreasy stain on fabric that cannot be washed can be sponged with cool water. Place an absorbent pad under the stained area and slowly drip water through the fabric with an eye dropper or plastic pump/trigger spray bottle. This method of flushing the stain lets you control the amount of water and the rate at which it flows through the fabric so that you don't inadvertently spread the stain. If you treat a nongreasy stain with water while it is still fresh, you can often remove it entirely. If water fails to remove the stain, work liquid detergent into the stain and rinse it by sponging or flushing with cool water. Sponge the spot with rubbing alcohol after you've rinsed it to remove any detergent residue and

to speed drying. (Caution: If you're treating acetate, acrylic, modacrylic, rayon, triacetate, or vinyl, be sure to dilute the alcohol with water, 1 part alcohol to 2 parts water.)

Combination Stains

Some stains are double trouble. Coffee with cream, salad dressing, and lipstick leave a trail of combination stains behind them; they're both greasy and nongreasy. Getting rid of combination stains is a two-part operation. First you need to eliminate the nongreasy stain and then attack the greasy residue. On most fabrics, you'll need to sponge the stain with cool water, then work liquid detergent into the stain and rinse thoroughly. After the fabric has dried, apply a dry-cleaning solution to the greasy part of the stain. Allow the fabric to dry. Repeat the application of cleaning fluid until the stain is gone.

YOUR STAIN-REMOVAL KIT

To beat stains, you have to be prepared. A well-stocked stain-removal kit, like a first-aid kit, should be ready to help you handle cleaning emergencies whenever they occur. Here are the tools you'll need to have:

► Clean white cotton cloths

► Disposable diapers for absorbing flushed cleaning solutions

► White blotting paper

► White paper towels

► A spoon, blunt knife, or spatula for scraping

► An eyedropper or pump/trigger spray bottle

► A small brush

► Several colorfast weights

Your kit will also need to include a variety of stain-removal agents. What you need depends on what you are likely to have to clean. You will be able to purchase most of them at your local hardware store, grocery store, or pharmacy.

Absorbents

▶ **Absorbents** "soak up" grease stains. Cornmeal is the best absorbent for light colors, and fuller's earth the best for dark colors. Spread the absorbent material on the stained areas and allow it to work. As the grease is soaked up, the absorbent material will cake or become gummy. It should then be shaken or brushed off. Repeat the process until the stain has been removed. This process may take up to eight hours or more.

Bleaches

▶ **Chlorine** is commonly used to bleach white cotton, linen, and synthetic fabrics. It is a powerful stain remover, which can weaken fibers if it is allowed to stay on fabric for too long a time. Never use chlorine bleach on silk, wool, or fabrics that are exposed to sunlight, such as curtains. Always pretest chlorine bleach. Caution: Chlorine bleach is poisonous. If it comes in contact with the skin or eyes, it will cause burns and irritation.

▶ **Color remover** contains hydrosulfite chemicals, which lighten the color of fabrics before they are redyed a lighter color. They also remove some stains from colorfast fibers. Always pretest color remover. If the product causes a distinct color change instead of fading the fabric, you may be able to restore the original color by rinsing immediately with cool water. If the color fades when color remover is applied, the original color cannot be restored. Color remover should not be used in a metal container. Caution: Color removers are poisonous. Avoid prolonged contact with skin. Observe all precautions on the label.

▶ **Hydrogen peroxide** is sold in a 3-percent solution and is a mild antiseptic. It is a safe bleach for most fibers. A stronger solution used for lightening hair is too strong to use on fabric and other household surfaces. Buy peroxide in small quantities and store it in a cool, dark place; it loses strength quickly after it is opened and if it is exposed to light.

▶ **Sodium perborate** can be purchased in crystal form at pharmacies under trade names or generically. It is safe for all fabrics and surfaces. This oxygen-type bleach is slower-acting than hydrogen peroxide. When you use this bleach, be sure to rinse the treated articles.

Chemicals

▶ **Acetic acid** can be bought in a 10-percent solution at pharmacies. White vinegar is a 5-percent acetic acid and can be used as a substitute for the stronger solution. Acetic acid is a clear fluid that can be used to remove stains on silk and wool. It must be diluted with 2 parts water for use on cotton and linen (test for colorfastness). Never use this chemical on acetate. If acetic acid causes a color change, try sponging the affected areas with ammonia; this may restore the color.

▶ **Acetone** is the base for nail-polish remover and household cement thinner, but they should not be substituted for pure acetone because they contain other ingredients that can worsen stains. You can purchase acetone at pharmacies and paint stores. The colorless liquid smells like peppermint, and it can be used on stains caused by substances such as nail polish or household cement. Although acetone will damage neither natural fibers nor most synthetics, it should be tested to make sure that dyed fabrics will not be harmed. Acetone should not be used on fabrics containing acetate; it will dissolve them.

▶ **Isopropyl alcohol** in a 70-percent solution is sufficient for most stain-removal jobs that call for alcohol. Stronger, denatured alcohol (90-percent solution) can also be used. Be sure you do not buy alcohol with added color or fragrance. Since alcohol will fade some dyes, test it on the fabric you will be cleaning. Alcohol will damage acetate, triacetate, modacrylic, and acrylic fibers. If you must use it on fibers in the acetate family, dilute the alcohol with two parts water.

▶ **Ammonia,** the plain household variety without added color or fragrance, can be used for stain removal. Because ammonia affects some dyes, test it on the stained article. To restore color changed by ammonia, rinse the affected area in water and apply a few drops of white vinegar, then rinse with clear water. Ammonia damages silk and wool; if you must use it on these fibers, dilute it with an equal amount of water and use sparingly.

▶ **Amyl acetate,** as chemically pure amyl acetate, or banana oil, is available in drugstores; it's safe for use on fibers that could be damaged by acetone, but it should not be allowed to come in contact with plastics or furniture finishes.

▶ **Coconut oil** can be bought in drug and health-food stores. It is used in the preparation of dry spotters that are used to remove many kinds of stains. If you cannot obtain coconut oil, you may substitute mineral oil, which is almost as effective. To make a dry spotter, combine 1 part coconut oil and 8 parts liquid dry-cleaning solvent. Store this solution in a tightly capped container to prevent evaporation.

▶ **Glycerin** is used in the preparation of wet spotters that are used to remove many kinds of stains. To make a wet spotter, mix 1 part glycerin, 1 part white dishwashing detergent, and 8 parts water. Store the solution in a plastic squeeze bottle, and shake well before each use.

▶ **Oxalic acid,** sold in many pharmacies, is effective in treating ink and rust stains. The crystals must be dissolved in water (1 tablespoon crystals to 1 cup warm water). Test the solution on a hidden corner of the spotted item before using it on the stain. Moisten the stained area with the solution. Allow it to dry, then reapply. Be sure all traces of the solution are rinsed out.

▶ **Sodium thiosulfate,** also known as photographic "hypo" or "fixer," is available in crystal form at drugstores and photo-supply houses. Although considered safe for all fibers and harmless to dyes, this chemical should be tested on an inconspicuous area before use.

▶ **Turpentine** is most often used as a thinner for oil-base paints, but it is effective on paint and grease stains.

▶ **Vinegar** for stain removal refers to white (clear) vinegar. It is a 5-percent acetic acid solution and should be diluted if you use it on cotton or linen. Vinegar is safe for all other colorfast fibers, but it can change the color of some dyes, so always test it on an inconspicuous area first. If an article changes color, rinse the affected area with water to which you've added a few drops of ammonia. Rinse thoroughly with clear water. This may restore the color.

Dry-cleaning Solvents

▶ **Perchloroethylene, trichlorethane, and trichloroethylene** are three of the most common and effective ingredients in dry-cleaning solvents. Not all dry-cleaning solvents can be used on all surfaces and not all of these products remove all stains, so be sure to read the label before using a solution.

Washing Agents

▶ **Detergents** for stain removal, when instructions call for a mild detergent, should be limited to a white dishwashing liquid detergent; the dyes in nonwhite detergents may worsen the stain. When instructions call for a pretreating paste made of detergent and water, use a powdered detergent that does not contain bleach. When the stain-removal directions specify that you should apply a liquid laundry detergent directly to the spot or stain, be sure to read the directions on the product's label carefully. Some products cannot safely be used in this manner.

▶ **Enzyme presoaks** are most effective on protein stains, such as meat juices, eggs, and blood; they may harm silk and wool. Make sure you have exhausted every alternative before you use enzyme presoaks on these two fabrics. Use a presoak as soon as possible; enzyme-presoak solutions become inactive in storage.

▶ **Pretreaters** can be used on spots and stains when you think that a stain might not respond to normal laundering procedures. They start the cleaning process before the stained item is put in the washer. Pretreaters must be used in conjunction with the rest of the laundering process; do not try to use a pretreater alone, as though it were a spot remover. After applying a pretreater, you should not allow the fabric to dry before washing.

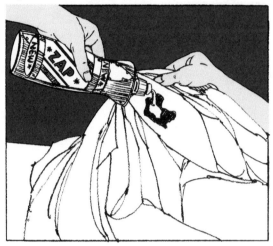

▶ **Soaps,** such as bath soaps with added moisturizers, fragrance, dyes, or deodorant, should not be used to treat spots. Purchase either laundry soap or pure white soap.

EIGHT WAYS TO BEAT STAINS

It would be nice to be able to squirt a little dab of the right solution on a stain, stand back, and watch the spot fade away forever. Unfortunately, stain removal is not that simple. You need the right cleaning agents and to know how these tools and products are used to remove stains quickly and effectively.

There are eight basic techniques for stain removal: brushing, flushing, freezing, presoaking, pretreating, scraping, sponging, and tamping. The right technique for a particular spot or stain depends on what was spilled and where it fell.

Brushing

Use brushing to remove dried stains. Some kinds of spots, such as dried mud, can be

removed completely by brushing. For other kinds of stains, brushing is only a step in the cleaning process. A small, stiff-bristled brush, such as a toothbrush, is best for this technique. When you're working on fabric, stretch the piece on a firm, clean surface. Hold a sheet of paper next to the stain, and brush the staining material onto the paper. A gentle motion with the brush pulls the stain up off the surface and onto the paper.

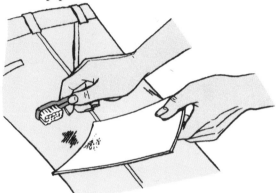

Flushing

Use flushing to remove loosened staining materials and the residue from stain-removal agents. If cleaning products are left in the material, they may cause additional staining or even damage the treated article. When you are flushing a stain, especially one on nonwashable fabric, you need to control the flow of water carefully so that you don't spread the stain or get the fabric wetter than you need to. An eyedropper or a plastic pump/trigger spray bottle that can be adjusted to a fine stream lets you precisely control the amount of water flushed through the fabric. Before you begin this treatment, place a clean absorbent pad, such as a disposable diaper, under the spot. Work slowly, replacing the absorbent pad frequently to prevent the deposited staining material from restaining the fabric. If you're treating a stain on a washable fabric, just rinse the article in warm water after you have flushed the stain.

Freezing

Candle wax, chewing gum, and other gooey messes are easier to remove when they

SAFETY PRECAUTIONS

To treat stains and spots as soon as they occur, you have to be prepared. But many of the products you stock in your stain-removal kit are flammable or toxic, and certain safety tips should be kept in mind when storing and using these products.

▶ Store stain-removing products carefully and out of the reach of children. The storage area should be cool, dry, and apart from a food storage area. Keep bottles tightly capped, and boxes closed.

▶ Do not transfer cleaning products to new containers.

▶ Follow the directions on the product label and heed all warnings.

▶ Glass and unchipped porcelain containers are preferable to metal or plastic when working with stain-removal agents. Never use plastic with solvents. Never use any container that is rusty. Clean all containers thoroughly after use.

▶ Protect your hands with rubber gloves. Don't touch your eyes or skin while handling stain-removal chemicals. If you do accidentally touch your eyes or spill chemicals on your skin, flush immediately with clear water.

▶ Remember that the fumes of solvents are toxic; work in a well-ventilated area.

▶ Do not use chemicals near an open flame or electrical outlet. Do not smoke while using chemicals.

▶ Do not use a solvent as a laundry additive.

▶ When using a solvent on a washable fabric, be sure to rinse all traces of the solvent out of the fabric.

▶ Do not experiment with mixtures of stain-removal agents. Never combine products unless specifically directed to do so in the home recipes for cleaning solutions. Many combinations can be dangerous.

▶ If the cleaning process requires the use of more than one stain-removal agent, rinse out each product thoroughly before applying the next.

are cold and hard. Hold an ice cube against the stain to freeze it. If the stained item is not washable, place the ice in a plastic bag. You can put a small stained item in a plastic bag and place the whole thing in the freezer. After the stain has solidified, it can usually be gently lifted or scraped from the surface.

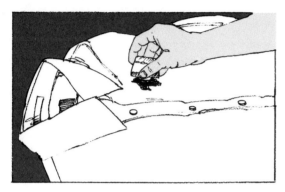

Presoaking

When your wash is grayed, yellowed, or heavily soiled, washing alone will not get it clean and bright—you will have to presoak. Sort the soiled items before presoaking; items that are not colorfast should be presoaked separately from colorfast items because their colors may bleed. You may add bleach, laundry detergent, or an enzyme presoak to the soaking water. But don't use chlorine bleach and an enzyme product at the same time. You can leave colorfast, stained articles in a presoak for as long as it takes to get them clean, but for most stains, 30 minutes is long enough. Items that aren't colorfast should be soaked only briefly. Before you wash a load of presoaked laundry, make sure that it has been thoroughly rinsed and that no residue of the presoak is left on the items.

Pretreating

Pretreat oily, greasy stains with liquid laundry detergent, a soil-and-spot-removing spray, bar soap, or a pretreating paste made from powdered detergent and water. After you apply a pretreater, rub it into the stain gently, and wash the item as you would normally.

Scraping

Scrape away excess solid staining material with a dull knife, spoon, or spatula before you apply stain remover. Don't press too hard; move the edge of your scraping tool back and forth across the stain in short strokes.

Sponging

Put an absorbent pad, such as a disposable diaper, under the stain before you sponge it. On a carpet you will have to work without an absorbent pad, so be especially careful not to use an excessive amount of the cleaning solution or water. Use another pad or a sponge to apply the stain-removing agent. Sponge the stain gently using light strokes. Change either pad as soon as any of the stain is deposited on it. Some fabrics, such as acetate, triacetate, and rayon, are likely to develop rings when they are sponged. When you work on stains on these fabrics, barely wet the pad with stain remover and touch the fabric lightly so that the stain remover is absorbed as slowly as possible. Blot the treated area between absorbent pads. Allow it to air-dry. Ironing or drying with heat may cause the stain remover itself to stain the fabric.

Tamping

The best way to get some stains out of durable, tightly woven fabrics is to tamp them with a soft-bristled brush, such as a toothbrush. Place the stained article on a hard work surface, not on a pad, and lightly rap the stain with the tips of the bristles. Repeat until the stain is removed. Use this technique sparingly since tamping will harm most fabrics.

MENDING AND REPAIR

Even if the only time you'll want to take up needle and thread is to replace a button or snap, resew a ripped seam, or hem a skirt or slacks, every stitch you sew saves you the expense of a tailor's bill and extends the life of your clothes. There's no reason to dread making repairs—replacing buttons and minor alterations can be learned in minutes. With a few supplies and a little patience, basic mending at home will have your family's wardrobe up to par in short order. Although most mending jobs can be done by hand without a sewing machine, make sure you have the essentials of the basic sewing kit so that you can follow the step-by-step instructions of basic mending techniques.

THE BASIC SEWING KIT

- ▶ A selection of buttons
- ▶ A selection of needles
- ▶ A selection of threads
- ▶ Sewing scissors
- ▶ Pins and pin cushion
- ▶ Thimble

- ▶ Measure
- ▶ Fasteners, such as snaps and hooks and eyes
- ▶ Self-fastening tape
- ▶ Patches

If you don't have these items already, keep the following tips in mind when shopping for them:

▶ Light trimming scissors or small bent-handled shears in a 6- or 7-inch length are best. Use these scissors only for sewing. Special bent-handled shears are available for left-handed sewers.

▶ Pins with large glass or plastic heads are the easiest to use. Buy the longest ones you can find—up to 1½ inches. Be sure to get a pin cushion or a container to store them.

▶ A package of assorted sharps—medium-length needles with round eyes—are suitable for all fabric weights.

▶ A few small spools of 100 percent polyester or cotton-wrapped polyester general-purpose thread in size 50 will handle most mending needs. Buy basic colors—white, black, brown, navy. Cotton thread is also acceptable, but it is not strong enough for stretchy seams.

▶ Thimbles come in various sizes, so you'll want to try them on until you find one that fits the middle finger of your sewing hand.

▶ Hooks and eyes in assorted sizes (1, 2, and 3) and snaps in sizes 3/0, 2/0, and 0 solve most replacement problems.

▶ Velcro-type self-fastening tape, purchased by the yard or in squares and circles, can substitute for zippers, buttons, and other fasteners in many cases.

▶ A 6-inch metal sewing gauge is more useful for sewing than a tape measure, particularly in hemming where it can be used for keeping a desired measurement.

▶ Luxuries, those items that make sewing a lot easier, include a seam ripper—the sharp, curved edge is used to cut seams open, the fine point is used to pick out threads; a needle threader, which saves lots of time and frustration; and pinking shears, which have zigzag edges, allowing you to trim fabric without fraying.

THE BASIC TECHNIQUES

The ground rules for simple mending are just that—simple:

► Fix it when you find it. The old adage that the longer you take to fix something, the worse it gets holds true in mending.

► Make it like the original. Study the garment before you repair it. You'll quickly see how to match the buttons, thread, and stitch patterns. Be sure to buy a replacement zipper of the same length and type.

► Press as you go. This holds especially true for repairs of hems, seams, or patches, which should be pressed often during the mending period. Pressing prepares fabric for smooth stitching, helps keep folds flat and in place, and makes it easy to achieve professional results. When you press, lift the iron up and down with a light touch, rather than sliding it back and forth. This method prevents distortion of the mended area.

► Follow the manufacturer's directions. This is especially true for patches, gripper-type snaps, and zippers.

Threading the Needle

Hold the needle upright with one hand and rotate it in your fingers until you can see the eye. Hold the cut thread about ³/₄ inch from the end with the fingers of the other hand and push the thread through the eye of the needle until about ¹/₂ inch extends beyond the eye. Pull about one-third of the thread length through for a single thread; match the ends if a double thread is needed for the mending job. If you have trouble threading the needle, the following tricks may help:

► Position the needle in front of a white surface so the eye is more visible.

► Stiffen the thread end by moistening it or running it through some beeswax.

► Spray your fingertips with hair spray and then stiffen the tip of the thread by rolling it back and forth in your fingers.

► Try a needle with a larger eye, or use a needle threader.

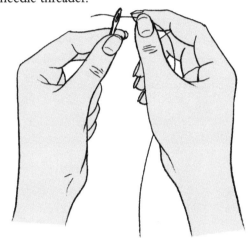

Knotting the Thread

Place the end of the thread along the ball of the index finger of your left hand (right hand if you're left-handed). Hold the thread with your left thumb and position the point of the needle over the thread about ¹/₂ inch from the end of the thread. Hold the end of the thread and the needle in place with the left thumb. With your right hand, wrap the thread snugly around the tip of the needle, twice for a small knot or four times for a large knot.

Pinch the wrapped thread between the thumb and index finger of the left hand. Push the needle up between those fingers as far as you can with the second finger of the right hand. Then grasp the point of the needle with the thumb and index finger of the right hand and slide the wrapped thread slowly and smoothly down the needle, over the eye, and down the length of the thread into a snug knot. Trim away the excess thread below the knot.

Use a small knot for a single thread or on lightweight fabrics. Use a large knot with double thread or with loosely woven or knit fabrics. Make sure no knot is so large that it

  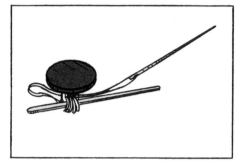

(Left) Replacing some sew-through buttons requires shank-builders. (Middle) When removing a shank-builder, wind the thread under the button bottom. (Right) A shank button has a small loop on its underside.

shows through or creates a lump on the garment.

Replacing a Button

Most buttons can be sewn with general purpose sewing thread. Use heavy-duty thread for coats and heavy jackets. Buttons should be sewn on loosely enough to allow for the overlapping garment layer containing the buttonholes. Buttons sewn too tightly will make the button too difficult to close. Sew-through buttons usually have two or four holes through which the button is sewn to the garment. Shank buttons have a small loop on the back side through which they are sewn to the garment.

To replace a sew-through button, you will need a shank builder—either a toothpick or a thick matchstick. Insert the needle into the fabric on the side of the garment where the button will be and bring the point up 1/8 inch away. Pull through to the knot. Make two small stitches to mark the spot for the button and to give your work a firm base—the button will cover the knot and stitches. Now insert the needle through one of the holes of the button from the wrong side. Let the button fall down the needle and the thread to the garment. Place your shank-builder across the top of the button. Hold it in place with your finger and stitch over the shank-builder as you sew on the button. In most cases, you will want to match your stitches to the stitch design of the other buttons, choosing from one of four stitch patterns. Take three to six

stitches through each pair of the button's holes, depending on how much stress the button will receive. Then bring the needle up through the fabric but not through the button. Remove the shank-builder, hold the button tightly away from the garment, and wind the thread snugly two or three times around the threads under the button. Insert the needle through to the wrong side of the garment, and push the needle under the button stitches. Pull the thread partially through, forming a loop. Insert the needle through the loop, and pull the thread snugly to form a knot. Cut the threads close to the knot.

To replace a shank button, begin by inserting the needle on the side of the garment where the button will be located. Bring the needle up 1/8 inch away, and pull the thread through to the knot. Make two small stitches to mark the spot for the button and to give a firm base for your work. The button will cover the knot and stitches. Position the button at the marking with the shank parallel to the buttonhole. Insert the needle through the shank and then down through the fabric. Stitch through the shank four to eight times. Be careful to keep the stitches on the underside of the garment small and neat. Finally, make a knot. Insert the needle under the button stitches under the wrong side of the garment. Pull the thread partially through, forming a loop. Insert the needle through the loop, and pull the thread snugly to form a knot. Trim the threads close to the knot.

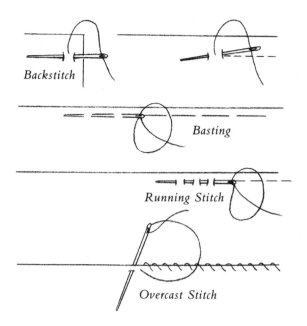

Backstitch

Basting

Running Stitch

Overcast Stitch

Basic Stitches

Four basic stitches can get you through almost any type of hand-sewing repair. If you haven't sewn before, you may want to practice a bit to develop the ability to stitch evenly in a straight line.

▶ **BACKSTITCH**—This is the easiest alternative to a machine straight stitch. Viewed from the top, backstitching appears as a continuous line of even stitches; viewed underneath, the stitches are twice as long as those on top and they overlap at the ends. Use a single knotted thread and work from right to left. Insert the needle from the underside of the fabric layers $1/8$ inch to the left of where your stitching will begin. Pull the thread through to the knot. Insert the needle $1/8$ inch behind where the thread emerges (that is, where your stitching will begin). Bring the needle up $1/4$ inch beyond this insertion, and pull the thread snugly. Bring the needle up $1/4$ inch beyond the insertion, and pull the thread through. Continue in this manner, forming evenly spaced stitches about $1/8$ inch long.

▶ **BASTING**—Basting is used to hold two or more layers of fabric together temporarily during fitting or construction. You may want to baste a hem or cuff to make sure you like the length before completing the hem with a

more permanent stitch. Use an unknotted, single thread, so it will be easy to pull out, and work from right to left. Insert the needle from the right side and weave the point of the needle in and out two or three times. Basting stitches may be as long as 1 inch. Pull the thread partially through, securing the unknotted end between your thumb and forefinger so that you don't pull it through entirely. Reinsert the needle and repeat the process. Do not backstitch at the end of your work, but leave the thread loose so that it can be easily removed.

▶ **RUNNING STITCH**—The running stitch, used for delicate repairs, topstitching, and gathering, is worked in much the same way as basting, but the stitches are shorter and even. Because they're permanent, you'll want to secure the thread at both ends with a knot. Use a single knotted thread and work from right to left. Insert the needle from the wrong side, then weave the point evenly in and out of the fabric two or three times. Pull the thread through firmly, but avoid puckering the fabric.

▶ **OVERCAST STITCH**—This stitch is used to keep a fabric edge from fraying. Use a single, knotted thread, and work from right to left. Insert the needle from the underside of your work. Pull the thread through to the knot, and insert the needle from the wrong side again, $1/8$ to $1/4$ inch to the left of the knot. Pull the thread through again, but not too tightly or the fabric will curl. The more your fabric frays, the closer together the stitches should be. Keep the depth of the stitches uniform, and make them as shallow as possible without pulling the fabric apart.

BEYOND THE BASICS

With a sewing machine and expertise, you can accomplish most repair jobs much more quickly than you can by hand, as well as do alterations and make garments. No matter what your level of sewing expertise is, some or all of the following tips should help you hone your skills.

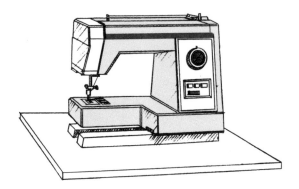

Organizing Your Supplies

▶ Attach your tape measure to the sewing table so that you won't have to rummage through all your equipment to find it.

▶ Keep a small magnet in your sewing basket. When needles and pins drop on the carpet while you're sewing, retrieve them quickly with the magnet.

▶ Sewing needles can get rusty and dull. Rub off any rust with an abrasive soap pad or steel wool.

▶ To help you thread needles, keep a magnifying glass in your sewing basket.

▶ Make a habit of leaving a length of thread in a needle before storing it in a pincushion (or whatever you use as a pincushion). You'll be able to see it more easily, and the needle will be less likely to slip all the way into the pincushion.

▶ A bar of soap makes a perfect pincushion. As well as storing pins and needles, it lubricates the tips so that they slide easily through stiff fabrics.

▶ To keep scissors from damaging other items in your sewing basket, cover the points with the rubber protectors sold for knitting needles.

▶ Use a chair that is adjustable and designed to support the back when sewing.

▶ File your clothes patterns by storing them upright in a shoe box.

▶ Egg cartons make convenient storage containers for spools of thread.

▶ Store tiny buttons in empty pill bottles.

▶ When throwing out clothing you no longer wear, first stock up on notions by saving any usable zippers, buttons, or decorative trim. These can come in handy when you're trying to replace a fastener.

▶ Thread looks darker on the spool than it will on fabric. Choose a thread a shade darker than the material you'll be using it on.

Hemming Techniques

▶ Before hemming a skirt, a dress, or pants, let the garment hang for a day on a hanger. The fabric will settle, and you'll get a more accurate hem.

▶ You can make your own hem gauge from any lightweight cardboard such as a postcard or index card. Notch the card at the depth required and pin up the hem.

▶ You can often steam out small puckers at the top edge of a hem. Don't redo a slightly puckered hem until you've tried to press out the pucker.

▶ Clip-type clothespins can be more convenient than pins for holding a hem in place while you sew it.

▶ Hem markers make the marking process much simpler.

▶ If neither washing nor dry-cleaning will remove an old hemline, disguise it with trim.

Dressmaking Techniques

▶ Before sewing in a zipper, shrink it: Set the zipper in very hot water for a couple of minutes, then let it dry. Repeat the whole process once more before sewing in the zipper.

▶ Smooth wrinkled pattern pieces by pressing them with a warm, dry iron. Don't use steam; it will distort the pattern size.

▶ If you're sewing a woman's blouse, sweater, or dress that will button down the front, make the buttonholes horizontal instead of vertical. The buttons will always stay firmly shut.

► In order to sew for yourself, you must know your body measurements accurately. Ask a friend to help you, and take measurements over your usual undergarments using a nonstretch tape measure.

► Cutting heavy fabrics, such as quilts or coatings, will be more accurate if you pin through only one layer of fabric. If you pin all the way through, the fabric will pucker.

► You can use a glue stick instead of pins and/or basting when making lapped seams. Apply the glue to the underside of the overlapping section. Press in place, allow to dry a minute or two, and topstitch.

► You can temporarily hold nonfusible interfacing in place with adhesive from a glue stick. This eliminates the need to baste interfacing to the garment piece.

► Stitch darts from the widest portion toward the narrowest.

► You can make a facing lie flat by stitching it to the seam allowance—not the fabric that will show—just inside the seam. Or, simply tack it at the seams. If you tack it all around the edge, the stitching will show on the right side of the fabric.

► To prevent heavy materials from dragging on the floor while you're sewing, support them on an ironing board placed next to the sewing machine table.

► Tissue paper can be useful when machine-sewing delicate or hard-to-handle fabrics. Lay the tissue under nylon fabric to keep it from slipping. When sewing lace, place tissue between the fabric and the machine to keep the lace from snagging.

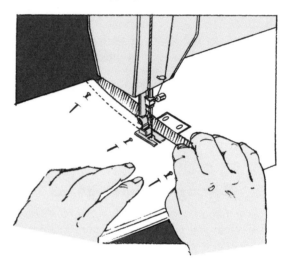

► Some fabrics tend to pucker slightly when sewn. This can usually be prevented if the fabric layers are held taut as they go under the presser foot. Hold the fabric in front of and behind the presser foot, keeping it taut without stretching it or pulling it.

► When a design calls for gathering the fabric, test-gather a scrap of your fabric to see if you're getting the desired look. This step will save time in the long run.

► When sewing cuffs, you'll have more room for seam allowance when they're turned inside the cuff if you take one or more diagonal stitches across the points of square corners. The heavier the fabric, the longer the diagonal needs to be.

► Shortening the stitch length when stitching around collar curves reinforces the seam and makes the curves smoother. On collar corners, shorten the stitch length and sew one or more diagonal stitches to reinforce the corners and make room for the seam allowances when the collar is turned.

▶ When making an elastic waistband, fasten the ends of the elastic with a safety pin for the first few wearings and washings to make sure that the fit of the waistband is comfortable. Elastic sometimes shrinks or relaxes after the first washings. When you are confident that the fit is right, remove the safety pin and stitch together the ends of the elastic to finish the waistband.

▶ When sewing snaps in place, stitch in the top half and rub a little chalk over its tip. Press it against the other side of the garment to mark the exact spot where you should sew in the bottom half of the fastener.

▶ If very small snaps slip out of your fingers, tape them in place on the fabric and sew through the tape. Lift off the tape when you're done.

Sewing Machine Smarts

▶ Take care of your machine. Keeping it clean, well oiled, and protected will extend its life. Follow the manufacturer's instructions for oiling.

▶ Always keep a supply of replacement needles on hand.

▶ Use a small paintbrush to clean dust and loose threads from your sewing machine.

▶ After you've oiled your sewing machine, stitch through a blotter to soak up any excess lubricant that might remain in the machine and leak onto your fabric.

▶ Rejuvenate a blunted machine needle, at least temporarily, by carefully rubbing it at an angle across the fine side of an emery board.

▶ If the foot control of your portable sewing machine creeps on the floor when you sew, glue a piece of foam rubber to its bottom surface.

▶ When you embark on a large-scale dressmaking project, fill a number of bobbins before you start. Then you won't find that just when you've gotten into the swing of it you have to stop to rewind the bobbin.

CARING FOR YOUR CLOTHES

Along with good laundering and mending techniques, your clothes will benefit from proper care and both short-term and long-term storage. Clothes that need to be stored for a season or longer need to be free of moths, moisture, and sunlight.

GENERAL CLOTHING CARE

▶ When you buy a new garment, dab the center of each button with clear nail polish to seal the threads. The buttons will stay on longer.

▶ Wrap adhesive or cellophane tape around your finger with the sticky side out to remove lint from a small area quickly.

▶ For a do-it-yourself lint remover, roll up a magazine and wrap wide adhesive tape around it, sticky side out. Pass it over lint, threads, and hairs.

▶ When brushing clothes to remove dust and lint, you'll get better results if you brush with the nap rather than against it.

▶ Rub zipper teeth occasionally with wax to keep the zipper working smoothly. The stub of a candle works well for this procedure.

▶ To remove tobacco odors from wool clothing, run hot water into the bathtub and add vinegar. Then hang the garment on the shower rod and close the bathroom door. The vinegar in the rising steam will remove the smell of the smoke.

▶ When the weather turns rainy or snowy, spray the hem of your coat with a stain repellant to protect it from mud and splashes.

▶ Before trying a chemical stain or spot remover, test the remover on a hem, seam, or other hidden part of the garment. If the liquid discolors or stains the cloth, you won't have ruined the entire garment, and you'll know that you should take the garment to a professional dry cleaner.

▶ You can de-wrinkle clothing in a hurry by running hot water into the bathtub and hanging the garment on the shower rod. The steam will remove the wrinkles.

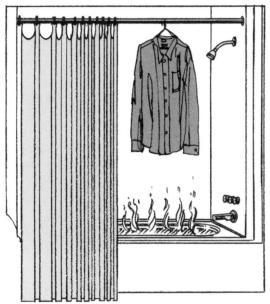

▶ Club soda, either straight from the bottle or flat, is a great emergency cleaner. Apply it with a damp cloth.

▶ When taking soiled garments to the dry cleaner, be sure no spots or stains are overlooked. Pin a note to each spot, explaining what the substance is, to call it to the dry cleaner's attention. Always have belts and accessories cleaned with the main garment to be sure the whole outfit remains the same color.

▶ Leather-look fabrics such as vinyl or polyurethane are easily cleaned with soap and water applied with a damp cloth.

EVERYDAY CLOTHES STORAGE

The next time you search for a specific item in the closet, you won't be disappointed to

HINTS FOR QUILTERS

▶ If you prefer not to mark up your quilt face with a pencil, "draw" in the straight lines with strips of masking tape.

▶ Cardboard templates become worn quickly. Edge templates with tape so that repeated use won't change the size.

▶ Keep track of patchwork squares by storing them in large-size coffee cans. Note the number of pieces on the lid.

▶ Make a sturdy master pattern for patchwork pieces from an iron-on mending patch. It won't slip or fray, and it will hold its shape for a long time.

▶ Iron some fusible bond onto the backs of lightweight quilting appliqués. They'll stay flat and keep their shape. You can get the same effect by treating them with spray starch and then ironing.

▶ After sorting patchwork pieces, slip a doubled thread through a pile of patches, leaving the knotted end of the thread at the bottom of the stack. With the top end left unknotted, you can peel off each square as it's needed.

find a wrinkled, misshapen garment if you take the time to store it properly. The same goes for folding clothes.

Hanging Clothes

▶ Hang your clothes on wooden or plastic hangers, making sure that zippers and buttons are closed. Shoulders, sleeves, and creases should be straight and collars should lie flat in place.

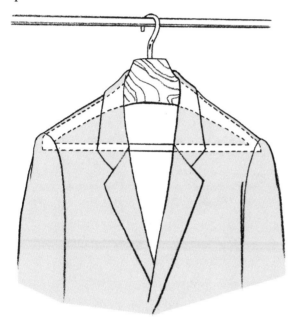

▶ Use hangers that fit the garment.

▶ Hang up a suit or dress immediately after wearing. The wrinkles fall out more easily while the fabric still retains heat from your body.

▶ Get into the habit of buttoning at least the top button of your coat or jacket when you hang it up. It will keep its shape better.

▶ For longer wear and a better fit, cashmere and wool clothing should be shaken briskly after each wearing, and then hung to air before being put away in the closet.

▶ To prevent a horizontal crease midway up the trouser leg, put newspaper or tissue over a hanger rod, then fold the trousers over that. (Don't use newspaper for pale-colored pants—it may mark the fabric.)

▶ Slip rubber bands on the ends of wire hangers to keep clothes from falling off.

▶ Double the strength of wire hangers by taping two together with adhesive or cellophane.

▶ When storing a hanging garment in a plastic bag from the cleaners, use a twist tie to seal any openings against dust.

▶ Recycle cardboard stiffeners that the laundry uses in your shirts to support the collars of shirts and turtleneck sweaters while they're hanging in the closet.

▶ Keep scarves wrinkle-free by pinning them with plastic clothespins to a coat hanger in your closet.

▶ To prevent sleeveless garments from slipping off wire hangers, bend up both ends of the hanger.

Folding Clothes

▶ To store sweaters, fold them in a bureau drawer. Hangers can distort the shoulder shape of a sweater and stretch the garment unnecessarily.

▶ To reduce wrinkles, lay a panel of tissue paper over the back of a garment before folding it.

▶ Hanging embroidered or sequined garments will distort their shape; store them flat.

▶ Line your bureau drawers with tissue paper to prevent clothing from catching and snagging on rough edges.

▶ When storing heirloom linens or baby clothing, don't starch or iron them. Wash and rinse them; then rinse again in a vinegar-and-water solution. If possible, allow them to dry in the sun. Finally, wrap each item separately in pale blue tissue paper, with extra paper between the folds.

SEASONAL STORAGE

If your wool sweaters need to be protected from moths or your heirloom items require

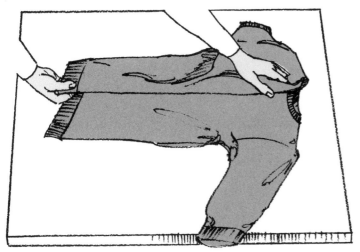
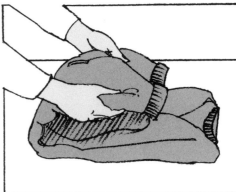

To fold a sweater, lay it facedown. Fold one side and arm to the middle. Then fold the arm back down on itself. Repeat on the other side. Finish by folding the sweater in two.

special care, you'll find that the time spent on storing your clothes properly will reward you the next time you get them out of storage. There will be no moth holes, no mildew, and no need for replacements.

Repelling Moths

▶ If your area has moths, and most do, you will want to store all wool garments, as well as wool afghans and blankets, to prevent moths from laying eggs.

▶ New garbage cans, either of metal or plastic, make good storage containers for clothing. If they are airtight and you are storing freshly cleaned or dry-cleaned clothes, you won't need to add mothballs.

▶ If your cedar closet is old and no longer smells of cedar—which deters moths—lightly sand its surfaces. The sanding will open the wood's pores and release a new cedar odor.

▶ The cedar odor only repels moths; it doesn't kill them. Clean all clothes before storage to remove any moth eggs.

▶ Mothproofing products should be placed as high as possible in the closet because the fumes filter downward. Otherwise, your garments get only partial protection.

▶ Convert a closet or chest to a cedar closet or chest by installing thin cedar slats over the inside surfaces.

Deterring Moisture

▶ To prevent mildew from forming in a leather-lined purse during storage, fill the purse with crumpled newspaper and leave it unfastened.

▶ In humid climates, corrugated boxes can be used for clothes storage if you first coat the box with thinned shellac to keep out moisture.

Caring for Furs

All furs need breathing space, so give them plenty of room between other garments in your closet. Good air circulation keeps the hairs from drying and breaking.

▶ After wearing a fur, just shake it gently, rather than combing or brushing the garment.

▶ Never store your fur coat in a plastic, cloth, or paper bag, because the lack of air will age it quickly.

▶ Avoid sitting for long periods of time or carrying a shoulder bag when you wear a fur. The friction will wear down the hair.

KNITTING AND CROCHET TIPS

► When buying yarn, check the label on each ball or skein to be sure it's all from the same dye lot; otherwise you could end up with yarn of slightly different shades. Keep a note of the dye lot in case you unexpectedly run short.

► Recycle still usable yarn from knitted items you no longer wear. After unraveling the yarn, wind it loosely around a cake rack, dip the rack into water, and then let the whole thing dry out. All the kinks will be "ironed out" of the yarn, and you can rewind it.

► Attach a paper clip to the page of your knitting book, and move the clip up or down the page to keep your place when following detailed instructions.

► When teaching a beginner how to knit, use a red needle to mark the purl row and a white needle to work the plain row.

► It's easy to pick up the wrong directions for size when working with a knitting pattern. Before you begin, use a black felt-tip marker to circle the directions that apply to your size. If you decide to make the same pattern in a different size later on, use a different colored marker to circle the new directions.

► Before buying yarn, consider the advantages and disadvantages of both wool and synthetics. Although wool will keep you warm even when wet, it needs special handling when laundering. Most synthetic yarns can be machine-washed, but some synthetics may gradually stretch out of shape. Wool may be irritating or allergenic to some people; synthetics are less likely to cause an allergic reaction.

► Make markers for your knitting from the little plastic price tags used to fasten bread wrappers. Or, if you're working with fine yarns, tie a piece of yarn of a contrasting color into a circle for use as a marker.

► If you carry your knitting around, you can make a carrier from a well-washed

plastic bleach bottle. Cut off about two inches from the top of the handle and spout, and drop in the ball of yarn. Draw up the end of the skein through the spout as you work.

► Test your knitting pattern for gauge size by doing a test run. Using the needles and yarn required by the pattern, knit a sample piece about four inches square. When you measure this, you'll have a good idea of any adjustments that may be required.

► To wind a hank of yarn into a manageable ball, have a friend hold the hank taut between two hands while you wind the ball. If no help is available, a ladder-backed chair works just as well. Always wind the ball loosely to keep from stretching the yarn out of shape.

► The plastic hairpins that come with brush hair rollers are better than straight pins for pinning seams on a knitted garment. The plastic pins are longer and stay firmly in place.

► To make sure knitted sleeves are identical, knit them on the needle at the same time.

► For a smoother look, try splicing instead of knotting the ends of your knitting. Unravel about an inch of each yarn end, then loosely weave the strands together.

► It's easier to camouflage the place where you've knotted two lengths of yarn if you do it at the edge rather than in the middle of an item. At the edge, you can cover the knot with a seam or edging.

► A knitting needle can do double duty as a ruler. Starting from the top down, mark off every inch with nail polish or with a waterproof marking pen.

► To keep yarn clean while you knit or crochet, put the ball of yarn into a plastic bag, and thread the end of the skein through a hole in the bottom of the bag. Draw out the yarn a little at a time as you work.

► Knitted cuffs have a tendency to lose shape. To help them keep their shape, interweave elastic thread through the cuffs or knit sewing silk of the same color into the first couple of rows.

► Knitted cuffs and other ribbed edges will keep their shape better if you use needles a size or two smaller than those used for the rest of the garment.

► Ribbed edges should never be ironed with steam. This causes the ribbing to flatten out and lose its flexibility.

► Prevent the strap of a knitted or crocheted shoulder bag from curling up or stretching out of shape by using two separate knitted or crocheted pieces. Bind them together with fusible webbing.

► To make a sweater for an expected baby, make buttonholes down both sides of the front opening of the garment. It'll be easy enough to sew buttons on the correct side, thus closing the extra openings, when you find out if the baby is a boy or a girl.

► Use a length of leftover yarn instead of ribbon when you gift-wrap a knitted or crocheted gift. The recipient can use this remnant for future mending. Slip the washing instructions from the yarn label into the package as well.

► Treat crochet hooks to a paraffin rub from time to time to keep them in good working condition.

► Use plastic toothbrush tubes to store crochet hooks.

STAIN REMOVAL CHART

ADHESIVE TAPE

ACETATE
CARPET/SYNTHETIC
CARPET/WOOL
FIBERGLASS
RAYON
SILK
TRIACETATE

Scrape gummy matter from the material very gently. Use a dry-cleaning solvent. If stain persists, apply a dry spotter to the stain and cover with an absorbent pad dampened with the spotter. Change the pad as it picks up the stain. Let it stand as long as any stain is being removed, keeping both the stain and pad moist. Sponge the area with dry-cleaning solvent. Allow surface to dry completely.

ACRYLIC FABRIC
BURLAP
NYLON
OLEFIN
POLYESTER
SPANDEX

Gently scrape off excess. Very carefully, apply cleaning fluid to the stain. If any remains, apply a wet spotter, with a few drops of ammonia added, to the stain. Tamp and blot occasionally with an absorbent pad. Flush with water and dry thoroughly.

COTTON
LINEN

Scrape to remove excess. Place facedown on an absorbent pad and sponge area with spot remover or cleaning fluid. Allow fluid to dry thoroughly; launder soon to remove all traces of fluid.

ALCOHOLIC BEVERAGES

ACETATE
BURLAP
FELT
FIBERGLASS
RAYON
ROPE
SILK
TRIACETATE
WOOL

Blot up any excess liquid. Spray on fabric spot cleaner, or flush area with cool water. Apply a wet spotter and a few drops of white vinegar. Cover with an absorbent pad dampened with the wet spotter and let stand as long as any stain is being removed. Keep the stain and pad moist, changing the pad as it picks up the stain. Flush with cool water, blotting excess liquid with a clean absorbent pad. Dry thoroughly.

ACRYLIC FABRIC
COTTON
LINEN
NYLON
OLEFIN
POLYESTER
SPANDEX

Apply fabric spot cleaner, or sponge stain promptly with cool water. If possible, presoak the stain in cool water for at least 30 minutes or overnight. Work undiluted dishwashing or liquid laundry detergent into stain. Rinse well. Launder as soon as possible. Old or ironed-in stains may be impossible to remove.

BABY FOOD/FORMULA

ACETATE
BURLAP
CARPET/SYNTHETIC
CARPET/WOOL
FIBERGLASS
RAYON
ROPE
SILK
TRIACETATE
WOOL

Blot up excess liquid or scrape excess solids from fabric. Sponge with a dry-cleaning solvent, or apply a dry spotter to the stain and cover with an absorbent pad dampened with the dry spotter. Let it stand as long as any stain is being removed. Keep pad and stain moist, changing the pad as it picks up the stain. Flush with one of the recommended liquid solvents. Allow to dry completely.

ACRYLIC FABRIC
COTTON
LINEN
NYLON
OLEFIN
POLYESTER
SPANDEX

Blot up or scrape excess material and rinse stain in cool water. Presoak for 30 minutes in an enzyme presoak. Launder immediately, if possible. If not, flush with cool water and allow to dry thoroughly. If stain has dried, repeated laundering may be necessary.

BERRIES (BLUEBERRY, CRANBERRY, RASPBERRY, STRAWBERRY)

ACETATE
CARPET/SYNTHETIC
CARPET/WOOL
FIBERGLASS
RAYON
ROPE
TRIACETATE

Spray on fabric spot cleaner. If stain remains, sponge with cool water. Then sponge the area with lemon juice. Flush with water. Blot as much excess liquid as possible and allow to dry. If stain still persists, apply a wet spotter. Cover with an absorbent pad moistened with wet spotter. Let stand as long as any stain is being removed. Change the pad as it picks up the stain. Keep the pad and stained area moist with wet spotter. Flush with water. If any trace of stain still appears, moisten the area with a solution of 1 cup warm water and 1 teaspoon enzyme presoak product—do not use on silk or wool. Cover with a clean absorbent pad that has been dipped in the solution and wrung almost dry. Let it stand for 30 minutes. Flush with water and allow to air-dry.

ACETATE
BURLAP
FIBERGLASS
RAYON
ROPE
SILK
TRIACETATE
WOOL

Spray on fabric spot cleaner. If stain remains, sponge with cool water immediately. Then sponge with lemon juice or rub a lemon slice over the stain. Flush with water. Blot as much excess liquid as possible and allow to dry. If any trace of stain still exists, presoak in a solution of 1 quart warm water, $1/2$ teaspoon liquid dishwashing or laundry detergent, and 1 tablespoon white vinegar for 15 minutes. Rinse with water and launder, if possible. If not, presoak in a solution of 1 quart warm water and 1 tablespoon enzyme presoak product for 30 minutes. Rinse well with water and launder as soon as possible.

BLOOD

ACETATE
BURLAP
FIBERGLASS
RAYON
ROPE
SILK
TRIACETATE
WOOL

Treat the stain as soon as possible. Sponge the stain with cold water. If any stain remains, apply a wet spotter and a few drops of ammonia (do not use ammonia on silk and wool). Cover with an absorbent pad dampened with the wet spotter and ammonia. Let it stand as long as any stain is being removed, changing the pad as it picks up the stain. Keep the stain and pad moist with the wet spotter and ammonia. Flush thoroughly with cool water. If stain persists, moisten it with a solution of $^1/_2$ teaspoon enzyme presoak—except on silk or wool—and $^1/_2$ cup warm water. Cover the stain with an absorbent pad dampened slightly with the enzyme solution. Let it stand for 30 minutes.

ACRYLIC FABRIC
COTTON
LINEN
NYLON
OLEFIN
POLYESTER
SPANDEX

Fresh blood stains can usually be removed by a thorough laundering in cold water. If any stain remains, soak it in a solution of 1 quart warm water, $^1/_2$ teaspoon dishwashing or liquid laundry detergent, and 1 tablespoon ammonia for 15 minutes. Tamp or scrape, blotting occasionally with an absorbent pad. Continue as long as any stain is being removed. Rinse well with water, making sure to remove all traces of the ammonia. If stain persists, presoak in a solution of 1 quart warm water and 1 tablespoon enzyme presoak product. After 30 minutes, rinse well, then dry or launder.

BUTTER/MARGARINE

ACETATE
BURLAP
CARPET/SYNTHETIC
CARPET/WOOL
FIBERGLASS
RAYON
ROPE
SILK
TRIACETATE

Scrape as much of the solid butter as you can without driving any of it further into the fibers. Apply an absorbent (cornmeal for light colors, fuller's earth for darks), but do not press it in. Give the absorbent plenty of time to work. Remove the absorbent and, if needed, repeat the application. If any residue remains, sponge the spot with cleaning fluid or spot remover.

ACRYLIC FABRIC
COTTON
LINEN
MODACRYLIC
NYLON
OLEFIN
POLYESTER
SPANDEX

Scrape any excess. Pretreat with stain remover, blot the stained area, and launder as usual. If the stain remains, or if immediate laundering is impossible, place the fabric stain-side down on an absorbent pad. Flush with cleaning fluid through the back of the stain and blot with a clean absorbent pad. Pretreat again and rinse well or launder.

CHEWING GUM

ACETATE
ACRYLIC FABRIC
BURLAP
CARPET/SYNTHETIC
CARPET/WOOL
COTTON
FIBERGLASS
LINEN
MODACRYLIC
NYLON
OLEFIN
POLYESTER
RAYON
SILK
SPANDEX
TRIACETATE
WOOL

Freeze until gum gets hard. Carefully scrape or rub the matter from the fabric. Sponge with a dry-cleaning solvent. Apply a dry spotter to the stain and cover with an absorbent pad dampened with the dry spotter. Let it stand as long as any stain is being removed. Change the pad as it picks up the stain. Keep the stain and pad moist with the dry spotter. Flush with dry-cleaning solvent. If stain remains, reapply the dry spotter and cover. Check the stain every 5 minutes and press hard against the stain when you are checking. Continue the alternate soaking and pressing until all the stain has been removed. Flush with dry-cleaning solvent. Dry.

CHOCOLATE/COCOA

ACETATE
BURLAP
FIBERGLASS
RAYON
ROPE
SILK
TRIACETATE
WOOL

Blot up any excess, or scrape any matter from the surface. Flush the stain with club soda to prevent setting. Sponge the stain with a dry-cleaning solvent. Then apply a dry spotter to the stain and cover with an absorbent pad dampened with the dry spotter. Keep the stain and pad moist with the dry spotter. Let it stand as long as any stain is being removed. Change the pad as it picks up the stain. Flush with dry-cleaning solvent. If a stain remains, moisten it with a solution of 1 cup warm water and 1 teaspoon enzyme presoak product—but do not use on silk or wool. Cover with a clean pad that has been dipped in the solution and wrung almost dry. Let it stand at least 30 minutes. Add more solution if needed to keep the stain warm and moist, but do not allow the wet area to spread. When the stain is lifted, flush thoroughly with water and allow to dry.

ACRYLIC FABRIC
COTTON
LINEN
NYLON
MODACRYLIC
OLEFIN
POLYESTER
SPANDEX

Wipe up as much excess as possible without driving the stain further into the fibers. Flush the stain with club soda. Sponge the area with a dry-cleaning solvent. Apply a dry spotter to the stain and cover with an absorbent pad dampened with the dry spotter. Keep the stain moist with dry spotter. Let it stand as long as any stain is being lifted. Change the pad as it picks up the stain. Flush with dry-cleaning solvent. If any stain remains, apply a few drops of dishwashing detergent and a few drops of ammonia to the stain, then tamp or scrape. Keep the stain moist with the detergent and ammonia and blot occasionally with an absorbent pad. Flush well with water to remove all traces of ammonia.

COFFEE

ACETATE FIBERGLASS RAYON TRIACETATE	Blot up with a clean cloth. Sponge the stain with water. Apply fabric spot cleaner or a wet spotter and a few drops of white vinegar. Cover with an absorbent pad dampened with the wet spotter. Keep the stain and pad moist with the wet spotter and vinegar. Let it stand as long as any stain is being removed. Change the pad as it picks up the stain. Flush with water. Repeat until no more stain is removed. If a stain remains, moisten it with a solution of 1 teaspoon enzyme presoak product and 1 cup warm water. Cover with a clean pad that has been dipped in the solution and wrung almost dry. Let it stand for at least 30 minutes. Add more solution, if needed, to keep the area warm and moist, but do not allow the wet area to spread. When the stain is removed, or no more is being lifted, flush thoroughly with water and allow to dry.
ACRYLIC FABRIC MODACRYLIC NYLON OLEFIN POLYESTER SPANDEX	Blot up any excess with a clean cloth. Presoak the stain in a solution of 1 quart warm water, 1/2 teaspoon dishwashing detergent, and 1 tablespoon white vinegar for 15 minutes. Rinse with water. Sponge the remaining stain with rubbing alcohol and launder, if possible. If not, presoak it in a solution of 1 quart warm water and 1 tablespoon enzyme presoak product for 30 minutes. Rinse well with water. Allow to dry, but launder as soon as possible.

CRAYON

ACETATE BURLAP FIBERGLASS RAYON ROPE SILK TRIACETATE WOOL/NONWASHABLE	Gently scrape to remove excess matter. Place an absorbent pad under the stain and flush with a dry-cleaning solvent. Allow to dry. Repeat, if necessary.
ACRYLIC FABRIC COTTON LINEN MODACRYLIC NYLON OLEFIN POLYESTER SPANDEX WOOL/WASHABLE	Scrape to remove the excess. Place the stain between two pieces of white blotting paper and press with a warm iron. Change the papers as the stain is absorbed. This stain can easily spread, so use care while pressing. On colorfast white cotton or linen, try pouring boiling water through the stain. After using either method, allow fabric to dry. If any trace remains, flush it with a dry-cleaning solvent. If any dye remains, sponge it with 1 part rubbing alcohol (do not use on acrylic or modacrylic) in 2 parts water. Rinse well with clear water and allow to dry.

CREAM

ACETATE BURLAP CARPET/SYNTHETIC CARPET/WOOL FIBERGLASS RAYON ROPE SILK TRIACETATE WOOL/NONWASHABLE	Remove any excess immediately. Sponge with dry-cleaning solvent. Then apply dry spotter to the stain and cover with an absorbent pad dampened with dry spotter. Let it stand as long as any stain is being removed. Change the pad as it picks up the stain. Keep the pad and stain moist with dry spotter. Flush with a dry-cleaning solvent. If any stain remains, moisten the area with a solution of 1 cup warm water and 1 teaspoon enzyme presoak—do not use on silk or wool. Cover with a clean pad that has been dipped in the solution and wrung almost dry. Let it stand for 30 minutes. Add more solution, if needed, to keep the area warm and damp, but do not allow the wet area to spread. When no more stain is being lifted, flush the area thoroughly with water and allow to dry.
ACRYLIC FABRIC COTTON LINEN MODACRYLIC NYLON OLEFIN POLYESTER SPANDEX WOOL/WASHABLE	Immediately remove any excess matter. Sponge the stain with a dry-cleaning solvent. Apply a dry spotter and cover with an absorbent pad dampened with dry spotter. Let it stand as long as any stain is being removed. Change pad as it picks up the stain. Keep stain and pad moist with dry spotter. Flush with one of the liquid dry-cleaning solvents. If any stain remains, apply a few drops of dishwashing detergent and a few drops of ammonia to the area, then tamp or scrape. Keep the stain moist with detergent and ammonia and blot occasionally with an absorbent pad. Flush well with water to remove all ammonia and allow to dry completely.

DEODORANT

ACETATE BURLAP CARPET/SYNTHETIC CARPET/WOOL COTTON FIBERGLASS LINEN RAYON SILK TRIACETATE WOOL	Spray on fabric spot cleaner. Another method is to apply rubbing alcohol to the stain and cover with an absorbent pad dampened with alcohol (dilute alcohol with 2 parts water for acetate, rayon, and triacetate; test silk for colorfastness before using alcohol). Keep both moist. Allow to stand as long as any stain is being removed. If the stain remains (and as a last resort), flush with a solution of warm sudsy water with a little ammonia added (use special care on silk and wool). Rinse with clear water. Apply a solution of warm water with a little white vinegar added, taking special care with this solution on cotton and linen. Rinse again with clear water. Dry thoroughly. (If the color of the fabric has been changed, it may possibly be restored by sponging lightly with a solution of 2 parts water and 1 part ammonia.) Caution: Never iron material with a deodorant stain. The combination of chemical and heat interaction will ruin most fabrics.

ACRYLIC FABRIC
MODACRYLIC
NYLON
OLEFIN
POLYESTER
SPANDEX

Most deodorant stains can be removed by pretreating with a liquid detergent or prespotter and laundering as usual. If the stain doesn't seem to be loosening with the pretreatment, rinse out the detergent and flush with white vinegar. Rinse in clear water. If the stain remains, flush the area with denatured alcohol. Rinse with clear water and dry or launder as usual.

FINGERNAIL POLISH

ACETATE
FIBERGLASS
RAYON
SILK
TRIACETATE
WOOL

Immediately scrape any excess with a dull knife or spatula. Apply a dry spotter to the stain and cover with an absorbent pad dampened with dry spotter. Let it stand as long as any stain is being removed. Keep the pad and stain moist. Flush with a dry-cleaning solvent. Allow to dry.

ACRYLIC FABRIC
BURLAP
COTTON
LINEN
MODACRYLIC
NYLON
OLEFIN
POLYESTER
ROPE
SPANDEX

Scrape the excess. Test acetone on an inconspicuous place. If fiber color doesn't change, flush acetone through the stain to an absorbent pad. When no more stain is being removed, change pads and flush well with a dry-cleaning solvent. Allow to dry thoroughly.

GLUE

ACETATE
FIBERGLASS
RAYON
SILK
TRIACETATE
WOOL

Immediately sponge the area with water. Spray on fabric spot remover. Then apply a wet spotter and a few drops of white vinegar. Cover with an absorbent pad dampened with wet spotter. Let it stand as long as any stain is being picked up. Change the pad as it removes the stain. Keep both the stain and pad moist with wet spotter and vinegar. Flush with water and repeat until no more stain is removed. For a lingering stain, moisten the area with a solution of 1 cup warm water and 1 teaspoon enzyme presoak product—do not use on silk or wool. Cover with a clean pad that has been dipped in the solution and wrung dry. Let it stand 30 minutes. Keep the area and pad moist and warm, but do not let the wet area spread. When no more stain is removed, flush thoroughly with water and allow to dry.

ACRYLIC FABRIC COTTON LINEN MODACRYLIC OLEFIN POLYESTER RAYON SPANDEX	Soak in a solution of 1 quart warm water, $1/2$ teaspoon liquid dishwashing or laundry detergent, and 1 tablespoon white vinegar. (Omit vinegar when treating cotton and linen.) Let soak for 15 minutes and rinse well with water. Sponge cotton or linen only with rubbing alcohol. Launder, if possible. If not, presoak in a solution of 1 quart warm water and 1 tablespoon enzyme presoak product for 30 minutes. Rinse well and launder as soon as possible.

GRASS

ACETATE CARPET/SYNTHETIC CARPET/WOOL RAYON SILK TRIACETATE WOOL	Sponge the area with a dry-cleaning solvent. Apply a dry spotter to the stain and cover with an absorbent pad dampened with the dry spotter. Let it stand as long as any stain is being removed. Change the pad as it picks up the stain. Keep both the stain and pad moist with dry spotter. Flush with one of the dry-cleaning solvents and allow to dry thoroughly. When working on carpets, be sure to blot up the excess liquid during the procedure and before drying.

ACRYLIC FABRIC COTTON LINEN MODACRYLIC NYLON OLEFIN POLYESTER SPANDEX	Work liquid dishwashing or laundry detergent into the stain and rinse well with water. If any stain remains, presoak in enzyme presoak product. Rinse thoroughly and launder as soon as possible. If any stain still remains, test for colorfastness in an inconspicuous place, then use a mild sodium perborate bleach or 3 percent hydrogen peroxide. Thoroughly rinse with clear water, then launder as usual.

GRAVY

ACETATE FIBERGLASS RAYON SILK TRIACETATE WOOL	Gently scrape any excess spill. Sponge the area with a dry-cleaning solvent. Apply a dry spotter to the stain and cover with an absorbent pad dampened with dry spotter. Let it stand as long as any stain is being removed. Change the pad as it begins to pick up the stain. Keep both the stain and pad moist with dry spotter. Flush with liquid dry-cleaning solvent. If any stain persists, moisten the stain with a solution of 1 cup warm water and 1 teaspoon enzyme presoak product—do not use on silk or wool. Cover with a clean pad that has been dipped in the solution and wrung dry. Let it remain for 30 minutes. Add enough solution to keep the area warm and moist, but do not let the stained area spread. When no more stain is being lifted, flush thoroughly with water and let dry.

ACRYLIC FABRIC
COTTON
LINEN
MODACRYLIC
NYLON
OLEFIN
POLYESTER
SPANDEX

Gently scrape any excess spill. Sponge the area with a dry-cleaning solvent. Then apply a dry spotter to the stain and cover it with an absorbent pad dampened with dry spotter. Let it stand as long as any stain is being removed. Change the pad as it picks up the stain. Flush the area with liquid dry-cleaning solvent and allow to dry. If any stain persists, apply a few drops of dishwashing detergent and a few drops of ammonia to the stain, then gently tamp or scrape to loosen the material. Keep the stain moist with detergent and ammonia and blot occasionally with an absorbent pad. Flush with water to remove all traces of ammonia. Allow to dry. If the stain still remains, moisten the stain with a solution of 1 cup warm water and 1 teaspoon enzyme presoak product. Cover with a clean pad that has been dipped in the solution and wrung almost dry. Let it stand for 30 minutes. Add enough solution to keep the stained area warm and moist. When no more stain is being lifted, flush thoroughly with water and allow to dry.

GREASE/AUTOMOTIVE, COOKING

ACETATE
CARPET/SYNTHETIC
CARPET/WOOL
RAYON
SILK
TRIACETATE
WOOL

Blot up as much excess as possible and apply an absorbent, such as cornmeal. After letting the absorbent work, brush it out of the fabric. If a stain remains, sponge with a dry-cleaning solvent. Then apply a dry spotter to the area. Cover the stain with an absorbent pad dampened with dry spotter. Let it remain in place as long as any stain is being lifted. Change the pad as it picks up the stain. Keep both the stain and pad moist with dry spotter. Flush with dry-cleaning solvent. If a stain still persists, sponge stain with water and apply a wet spotter with a few drops of white vinegar. Cover the area with an absorbent pad moistened with wet spotter. Let it stand as long as any stain is being removed. Change the pad as it picks up the stain. Keep both the stain and pad moist with wet spotter and vinegar. Flush the area with water and repeat above procedure until no more stain is removed. Allow to dry.

ACRYLIC FABRIC
COTTON
LINEN
MODACRYLIC
OLEFIN
POLYESTER
SPANDEX

Blot up the excess grease as soon as possible. Apply an absorbent and let it soak up the spill. After brushing out the powder, sponge the area with a dry-cleaning solvent. Then apply a dry spotter to any remaining stain. Cover the stain with an absorbent pad dampened with dry spotter and let it remain in place until no more stain is lifted. Change the pad as it picks up the stain. To help loosen the stain, occasionally tamp the area, blotting up any loosened material. Flush with liquid dry-cleaning solvent. If any trace of stain remains, sponge stain with water and apply a wet spotter and a few drops of ammonia. Tamp the stain again, blotting with an absorbent pad to remove any loosened material. Flush the area with water and repeat until no more stain is removed. Allow to dry.

MUD/DIRT

ACETATE
BURLAP
FIBERGLASS
RAYON
ROPE
SILK
TRIACETATE
WOOL

Let mud dry, then brush off the excess. This should remove the stain, but if any remains, sponge the area with water and apply a few drops of wet spotter and a few drops of white vinegar. Cover with an absorbent pad dampened with wet spotter. Let stand as long as any stain is being removed. Change the pad as it picks up the stain. Keep stain and pad moist with wet spotter and vinegar. Flush with water and repeat wet spotter/flushing until no more stain is removed. If stain remains, apply rubbing alcohol to the area and cover with an absorbent pad dampened with alcohol. (Do not use alcohol on acetate, rayon, or triacetate.) Let the pad stand as long as any stain is being removed. Change the pad as it picks up the stain. Keep the stain and pad moist with alcohol. If stain persists, moisten the area with a solution of 1 cup warm water and 1 teaspoon enzyme presoak, but do not use on silk or wool. Cover with a clean pad that has been dipped in the solution and wrung almost dry. Let it stand for 30 minutes. Add enough solution to keep the area warm and just moist. When no more stain is being lifted, flush thoroughly with water and allow to dry.

ACRYLIC FABRIC
COTTON
LINEN
MODACRYLIC
NYLON
OLEFIN
POLYESTER
SPANDEX

Let mud dry, then brush off excess. Laundering should remove any remaining stain. If more treatment is needed, sponge the stain with rubbing alcohol. (Do not use alcohol on acrylic or modacrylic.) Flush with water. If stain persists, sponge it with a dry-cleaning solvent. Allow to dry, then launder.

MUSTARD

ACETATE
BURLAP
CARPET/SYNTHETIC
CARPET/WOOL
FIBERGLASS
RAYON
SILK
TRIACETATE
WOOL

Mustard contains turmeric, a yellow dye. If not treated immediately, it can be impossible to remove. Lift off any excess spill with a dull knife or spatula. Flush the area with a dry-cleaning solvent. If fabric is strong enough, tamp or scrape to loosen the stain. Flush with the dry-cleaning solvent. While tamping stain, blot excess material with an absorbent pad. If stain remains, sponge with water and apply a wet spotter and a few drops of white vinegar. Tamp again to loosen stain. Flush with water. If stain persists, moisten area with 3-percent hydrogen peroxide and add a drop of ammonia (except on silk and wool). Do not let it bleach any longer than 15 minutes, then flush with water and allow to dry. When treating carpets, blot all excess liquid, then weight down an absorbent pad with a heavy object. When all liquid has been absorbed, allow to dry.

ACRYLIC FABRIC
COTTON
LINEN
MODACRYLIC
NYLON
OLEFIN
POLYESTER
SPANDEX

Mustard contains turmeric, a yellow dye. If not treated immediately, it can be impossible to remove. If stain has just occurred, spray on fabric spot cleaner. Or, if stain is older, scrape as much of the spill as possible. Flush with water, apply liquid detergent to the stain, and flush again. If the stain remains, presoak for several hours or overnight in a warm-to-hot solution of detergent. Rinse and launder as soon as possible.

OIL/AUTOMOTIVE, HAIR, LUBRICATING, MINERAL, VEGETABLE

ACETATE
CARPET/SYNTHETIC
CARPET/WOOL
RAYON
SILK
TRIACETATE
WOOL

Blot up as much excess as possible and apply an absorbent such as cornmeal. After letting the absorbent work, brush the powder off the fabric. If a stain remains, sponge with a dry-cleaning solvent. Apply a dry spotter. Cover with an absorbent pad that has been dampened with dry spotter. Let it remain in place as long as any stain is being removed. Change the pad as it picks up the stain. Keep both the stain and pad moist with dry spotter. Flush the area with the dry-cleaning solvent. If a stain persists, sponge the area with water and apply a wet spotter with a few drops of white vinegar. Cover the stain with an absorbent pad moistened with wet spotter. Let the pad stay in place as long as any stain is being removed. Change the pad as it picks up the stain. Keep both the stain and pad moist with wet spotter and vinegar. Flush with water and repeat the procedure until no more stain is removed. Allow to dry.

ACRYLIC FABRIC
COTTON
LINEN
MODACRYLIC
NYLON
OLEFIN
POLYESTER
SPANDEX

Blot excess spill as soon as possible. Apply an absorbent and allow it to soak up remaining spill. After brushing out the powder, sponge the area with a dry-cleaning solvent. Apply a dry spotter and cover with an absorbent pad moistened with dry spotter. Let it remain in place until no more stain is removed. Change the pad as it picks up the stain. To help loosen the stain, occasionally tamp the area, blotting any loosened material. Flush with one of the liquid dry-cleaning solvents. If any trace of the stain remains, sponge the stain with water and apply a wet spotter and a few drops of ammonia. Tamp the stain again, blotting with an absorbent pad. Flush the area with water and repeat until no more stain is removed. Allow to dry.

SOFT DRINKS/COLA

ACETATE FIBERGLASS RAYON SILK TRIACETATE WOOL	Blot up what you can with a clean cloth. Sponge the remaining stain with water. It is imperative that all the sugar be removed. Usually water will completely remove the stain, but if any remains, spray on fabric spot cleaner or apply a wet spotter and a few drops of white vinegar. Cover with an absorbent pad and let it stand as long as any stain is being lifted. Change the pad as it picks up the stain. Keep the stain and pad moist with the wet spotter and vinegar. Flush well with water. Repeat until the stain is lifted. If any sugar remains and turns yellow, it cannot be removed.
ACRYLIC FABRIC COTTON LINEN MODACRYLIC NYLON OLEFIN POLYESTER SPANDEX	Blot up any excess with a clean cloth and flush the area thoroughly with water. This is usually enough to remove the stain, but to be certain the sugar is removed, launder immediately. If that is not possible, soak the stain in a solution of 1 quart warm water, 1/2 teaspoon liquid detergent, and 1 tablespoon white vinegar for 15 minutes. Rinse with water. If it is an old stain, and the sugar has not been caramelized by heat, presoak the stain in a solution of 1 quart warm water and 1 tablespoon enzyme presoak for 30 minutes. Rinse well with water to remove enzyme and sugar residues. Allow to dry, but launder as soon as possible.

SOFT DRINKS/NONCOLA

ACETATE CARPET/SYNTHETIC CARPET/WOOL FIBERGLASS RAYON SILK TRIACETATE WOOL	Blot up as much excess as possible and sponge the area with cool water. Spray on fabric spot cleaner or apply a wet spotter and a few drops of white vinegar. Cover with an absorbent pad dampened with the wet spotter. Let it stand as long as any stain is being removed. Keep both the stain and the pad wet with the wet spotter. Flush with water. Repeat, if necessary. If the stain persists, moisten the area with a solution of 1 teaspoon enzyme presoak and 1 cup warm water—do not use on silk or wool. Cover with a damp cloth that has been dipped in the solution and wrung almost dry. Let it stand 30 minutes. Add more solution as needed to keep the stain warm and moist, but be careful not to let the wet area spread. When the stain is gone, flush thoroughly with water to remove all sugar residue.
ACRYLIC FABRIC COTTON LINEN MODACRYLIC NYLON OLEFIN POLYESTER SPANDEX	Blot up as much of the liquid as you can. Launder as soon as possible—washing usually removes all traces of the soft drink. If laundering isn't possible, presoak the stain in a solution of 1 quart warm water, 1/2 teaspoon liquid detergent, and 1 tablespoon white vinegar for 15 minutes. Rinse with water, allow to dry, then launder.

UNKNOWN STAINING AGENT

ACETATE
CARPET/SYNTHETIC
CARPET/WOOL
FIBERGLASS
RAYON
SILK
TRIACETATE
WOOL

Sponge the area with a dry-cleaning solvent. Tamp or scrape to help loosen the stain. Flush with the dry-cleaning solvent. If stain persists, apply amyl acetate and tamp again. Flush with the solvent and allow to dry. If stain still remains, sponge stain with water and apply a few drops of white vinegar. Tamp again. Apply a wet spotter and a few drops of ammonia (do not use ammonia on silk or wool). Tamp again. Allow to dry. Sponge with rubbing alcohol and pat with an absorbent pad dampened with alcohol (do not use full-strength alcohol on acetate, rayon, or triacetate).

ACRYLIC FABRIC
COTTON
LINEN
MODACRYLIC
NYLON
OLEFIN
POLYESTER
SPANDEX

Cover the stain with a rubbing alcohol compress. Let it remain on the stain for a few minutes, then wipe with a cloth moistened with ammonia. If stain persists, sponge the area with a dry-cleaning solvent. Apply a dry spotter. Tamp or scrape to help loosen the stain. Flush with one of the liquid dry-cleaning solvents. If stain remains, apply amyl acetate and tamp again. Flush with the dry-cleaning solvent. If stain still persists, sponge with water, then apply a wet spotter and a few drops of white vinegar. (Do not use vinegar on cotton or linen.) Tamp again and apply a wet spotter and a few drops of ammonia. Flush with the dry-cleaning solvent and allow to dry.

URINE

ACETATE
CARPET/SYNTHETIC
CARPET/WOOL
FIBERGLASS
RAYON
SILK
TRIACETATE
WOOL

Sponge the area with water or club soda immediately to dilute the stain. Apply a wet spotter and a few drops of ammonia. (Do not use ammonia on silk or wool.) Cover with an absorbent pad moistened with wet spotter. Let it stand as long as any stain is being removed. Change the pad as it picks up the stain. Keep both the pad and stain moist with wet spotter and ammonia. Flush with water, then apply wet spotter with a few drops of white vinegar. Flush well with water and repeat, if necessary. Allow to dry. Apply rug shampoo.

ACRYLIC FABRIC
COTTON
LINEN
MODACRYLIC
NYLON
OLEFIN
POLYESTER
SPANDEX

Flush immediately with water or club soda. Soak the stain in a solution of 1 quart warm water, 1/2 teaspoon liquid detergent, and 1 tablespoon ammonia for 30 minutes. Rinse well with water. If stain persists, soak in a solution of 1 quart warm water and 1 tablespoon white vinegar for 1 hour. (Use white vinegar with care on cotton and linen.) Rinse well and allow to dry. If stain is set, try applying rubbing alcohol to the area and tamping (do not apply full-strength rubbing alcohol to acrylic or modacrylic—dilute with 2 parts water). As stain loosens, blot the liquid and stain with an absorbent pad. Keep both the stain and pad moist with alcohol and change the pad as it picks up the stain. Allow to dry.

VOMIT

ACETATE
BURLAP
FIBERGLASS
RAYON
ROPE
SILK
TRIACETATE
WOOL

Gently scrape up solids. Sponge the area with water and apply a wet spotter and a few drops of ammonia. (Do not use ammonia on silk and wool.) Cover with an absorbent pad moistened with wet spotter and ammonia. Let it stand as long as any stain is being picked up. Change the pad as it picks up the stain. Keep the stain and pad moist with wet spotter and ammonia. Flush thoroughly with cool water, making sure to remove all traces of ammonia. If a stain persists, moisten it with a solution of $1/2$ teaspoon enzyme presoak and $1/2$ cup warm water—do not use on silk or wool. Cover stain with an absorbent pad dampened with the solution and let it stand for 30 minutes. Add enough solution to keep the area warm and barely moist. Flush with water and dry thoroughly.

ACRYLIC FABRIC
COTTON
LINEN
MODACRYLIC
NYLON
OLEFIN
POLYESTER
SPANDEX

Quickly scrape to remove solids. Soak the stain in a solution of 1 quart warm water, $1/2$ teaspoon liquid detergent, and 1 tablespoon ammonia. Tamp or scrape to help loosen the stain. Blot occasionally with an absorbent pad. Rinse well with water, making sure to remove all ammonia traces. If stain persists, presoak in a solution of 1 quart warm water and 1 tablespoon enzyme presoak for 30 minutes. Rinse well and launder as soon as possible.

Buying, preparing, and storing food are activities that take quite a bit of planning and effort. As a result, most cooks are quite receptive to tips that help make these chores quicker and easier. The following pages have information for all kinds of kitchen questions. Whether you are a cooking novice who wants to learn food basics in order to prepare simple meals or an old pro who needs to catch up on the latest information on dietary requirements, you'll find details to help you fine-tune your individual cooking style and diet.

STOCKING THE KITCHEN

CUPBOARD OF EQUIPMENT

*FOR THE TOP OF
THE STOVE*
1 double boiler
2 skillets with lids (8- and 9-inch)
1 Dutch oven with lid (5-quart)
2 saucepans with lids (2- and 3-quart)
Teakettle

FOR THE OVEN
1 roasting pan
2 racks (roasting and wire cooling)
1 broiler pan or equivalent
2 round cake pans (9-inch)
1 cake pan (13-×9-inch)
2 pie pans (9-inch)
2 large baking sheets
3 ovenproof casserole dishes (1-quart, 1½-quart, and 2-quart)
1 muffin tin

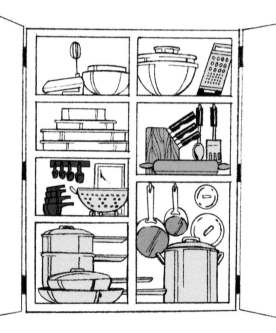

FOR FOOD PREPARATION
1 set of mixing bowls
1 set of measuring spoons
1 set of dry measuring cups
1 liquid measuring cup
Flour sifter
Rolling pin
Cutting boards (wood and plastic)
Grater

Colander
2 to 3 wooden spoons
Slotted spoon
Plastic spatula
Long-handled fork
Ladle
Tongs
2 small sharp knives
1 to 2 large sharp knives
Serrated bread knife
Sharpening stone
Sieve
Garlic press
Vegetable peeler
Vegetable brush
Pastry brush
Potato masher
Wire whisk (preferably
    stainless steel)
Meat thermometer
3 to 4 storage containers
    with lids
ELECTRIC APPLIANCES
Blender or food processor
Coffee maker
Hand mixer
Stand mixer
Toaster
        ACCESSORIES
Bottle opener
Can opener
Corkscrew
Pepper grinder
1 trivet (for hot plates)
3 to 4 pot holders
3 to 4 dish towels
2 to 3 dishcloths
Aluminum foil
Plastic wrap
Resealable plastic bags in
    all sizes
Waxed paper
        EXTRAS
Bread loaf pans
Bread maker
Coffee grinder
Cookie cutters
Deep fryer
Dessert molds
Griddle

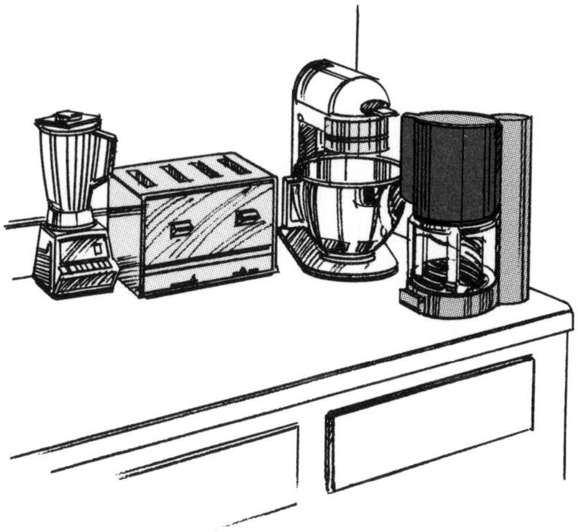

Kitchen shears
Kitchen timer
Ice-cream maker
Mallet
Microwave oven
Pastry bag with decorating
    tips
Pizza pan
Pizza cutting wheel
Popcorn popper
Pressure cooker
Salad spinner
Soufflé dish
Springform pan (9-inch)
Steamer
Tube pan (6-cup)
Waffle iron
Wok

FOOD ESSENTIALS FOR THE PANTRY

Baking powder
Baking soda
Beans (dried and canned)
Bread crumbs
Bouillon cubes (chicken
    and beef)
Broths (canned beef and
    chicken)
Chocolate (unsweetened
    and semisweet)
Cocoa (unsweetened)
Cornmeal
Cornstarch

Flour (unbleached, all-purpose;
    whole wheat)
Gelatin (unflavored)
Honey
Instant coffee
Ketchup
Mustard
Nuts (pecans and walnuts)
Oils (olive and corn, soybean,
    or canola)
Pasta (dried macaroni, spaghetti)
Peanut butter
Rice (white)
Salt
Syrup (corn and maple)
Sugar (brown, confectioners',
    and granulated)
Tomato (canned paste, sauce,
    and whole)
Vanilla extract
Vinegar (white and red wine)
Worcestershire sauce
Yeast (dry)

EXTRAS
Almond extract
Capers
Coconut
Flour (cake and rye)
Horseradish
Nuts (almonds, hazelnuts, pine
    nuts)
Oatmeal
Oils (peanut, virgin olive)
Olives (green and ripe)
Pasta (dried angel hair,
    linguine, orzo, rigatoni)

Raisins
Rice (brown, wild)
Sauces (barbecue, soy, hot
    pepper, tamari, teriyaki)
Vinegar (balsamic, rice, and
    fruit-flavored)

HERBS, SPICES, AND SEASONINGS

BASICS
Basil
Bay leaves
Chili powder
Cinnamon
Nutmeg
Oregano
Pepper (black and red)
Paprika
Parsley flakes
Tarragon
Thyme

EXTRAS
Allspice
Aniseed
Caraway seed
Cardamon
Celery seed
Chervil
Chives
Cloves (whole and ground)
Coriander
Cumin

Curry powder
Dillweed
Fennel
Ginger
Mace
Marjoram
Mint
Mustard (dry)
Red pepper flakes
Peppercorns
Rosemary
Saffron
Sage
Savory
Turmeric
SEASONING BLENDS
Italian seasoning
Garlic powder
Onion powder
Seasoned salt

STORAGE TIPS

▶ Purchase food-storage containers that do several jobs—freezer-to-oven casserole dishes are very useful.

▶ Since pots, pans, and casseroles can be heavy, store them at lower levels to avoid having to reach up for them.

▶ Toss a few extra plastic clothespins into your kitchen drawer to seal packages of partially used foods.

▶ Save screw-top glass containers for storing dry goods in the pantry.

▶ A small plastic or glass salt shaker with no metal parts makes an excellent sprinkler for lemon juice.

▶ The shaker bottles and containers that some spices come in can be filled with flour for no-mess flouring of cutlets and other foods. If you add seasonings to the flour, you've got an instant seasoned coating mix.

▶ If you store your sharp knives in drawers, keep them in a holder to prevent the blades from getting dull.

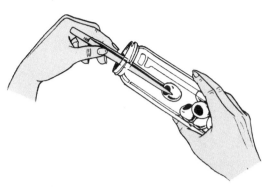

▶ A large pair of tweezers or needle-nose pliers can help you get olives and pickles out of narrow jars; they are also useful for placing garnishes on food without touching the food with your hands, or for removing bones from fish fillets.

▶ Most plastic food containers can be recycled for storing or refrigerating food.

▶ Mesh bags and wire baskets make good storage containers for potatoes and onions because they allow necessary air circulation.

HEALTHY COOKING, HEALTHY EATING

For the two out of three Americans who neither smoke nor drink, eating patterns may shape their long-term health prospects more than any other personal choice, according to a report from the U.S. Surgeon General in 1988. While food alone cannot make you healthy, good nutritional habits are an important component of a healthy lifestyle that includes regular exercise.

DIETARY GUIDELINES FOR AMERICANS AGE 2 AND OVER

▶ Eat a variety of foods.

▶ Maintain healthy weight.

BUYING SAFE COOKWARE

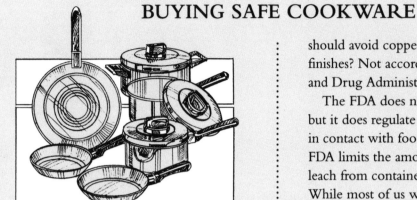

Cookware is made of a variety of materials, including aluminum, cast iron, clay, copper, and stainless steel. When you buy cookware, the two primary questions you should ask yourself are how practical and safe it is.

Most people know what they like. When a recipe demands that temperature be exact, good cooks who do not mind the expensive price choose a copper pan, because copper conducts heat evenly. On the other hand, for those who do a lot of low-fat cooking, nonstick finishes are often preferred, since they minimize the amount of fat needed to fry or sauté a dish.

Few cooks are experts on safety. Copper, for example, is toxic, and is easily dissolved by some foods, which is why the FDA cautions against using unlined copper for general cooking. (Most copper cookware, however, is lined with tin or nickel, and does not constitute a problem.) Many nonstick finishes are made of plastics that can break down when exposed to high heat over time. Does this mean that cooks

should avoid copper pans and nonstick finishes? Not according to the U.S. Food and Drug Administration.

The FDA does not regulate cookware, but it does regulate chemicals that come in contact with food. For example, the FDA limits the amount of lead that may leach from containers used to hold food. While most of us would prefer using lead-free cookware, it would be almost impossible to cook foods at even very low heat without using cookware that contained some metal. Concerns about aluminum cookware in the 1970s prompted many Americans to toss out their uncoated aluminum pots and pans. They were worried that aluminum particles would leach into their food cooked in these pans. Today, aluminum cookware, which represents a substantial portion of the market, is coated with nonstick finishes or is made of anodized aluminum (aluminum that is subjected to a process that makes it extremely hard and smooth). Unlike uncoated aluminum, anodized aluminum doesn't react to acid foods so it can be used to cook foods made with tomatoes, lemons, and wine.

Stainless steel is one of the most popular choices for cookware because of its durability and easy cleanup. Steel, of course, is an alloy of iron and other metals. To be considered stainless, it must be comprised of at least 11 percent chromium. Additionally, most stainless steel pots and pans have copper or aluminum bottoms, which conduct heat much better than stainless steel. Manufacturers advise consumers to avoid putting acid or salty foods in stainless steel containers for long periods to prevent undissolved salt from pitting the surface.

Like copper, cast iron is preferred because it conducts heat so evenly. There are no known hazards in cooking with cast iron, and some nutritionists suggest that there may be benefits when food is cooked with additional iron in unglazed cast iron. Be particularly careful, however, to keep the pan free of rust by coating it frequently with unsalted cooking oil.

Enamel-coated cookware could pose a hazard if it contains lead. It is possible that enamel-coated housewares manufactured and sold before 1971 could be problematic. Avoid using old enamel-coated containers to hold or cook food. Today, lead is not used in the manufacture of enamel-coated cookware, although it is present in some glazes for crockpots.

When it comes to nonstick coatings, which are made out of plastics, today's pots and pans are often coated with the same materials that are used to make surgical implants such as artificial arteries. Although they are extremely durable, manufacturers recommend that wooden or plastic utensils be used to avoid scratches. Consumers should also avoid cleaning them with scouring pads or abrasive powders.

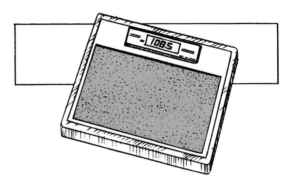

► Choose a diet low in fat, saturated fat, and cholesterol.

► Choose a diet with plenty of vegetables, fruits, and grain products.

► Use sugar only in moderation.

► Use salt and sodium only in moderation.

► If you drink alcoholic beverages, do so in moderation.

VARYING YOUR FAMILY'S DIET

Remember the five food groups from your school days? Well, the five groups remain the same, but the allocation of servings has changed. A varied diet does not mean equal portions from the five groups. Instead more emphasis is placed on leaner foods, such as breads, cereals, fruit, and vegetables. This emphasis is designed to help Americans maximize the intake of nutrients and reduce the fat in their diets. A reduction of fats to under 30 percent (and saturated fat to less than ten percent) of total daily calories is suggested.

The belief that too much fat in one's diet is a cause of obesity, heart disease, and diabetes is only one reason to reduce fats. More than 40 nutrients are required for good nutrition, including vitamins, minerals, amino acids from protein, certain fatty acids from fat, and sources of calories—protein, carbohydrates, and fat. No single food can supply all these nutrients. Vegetables are important sources of vitamins A and B, folic acid, minerals, and fiber. Milk provides protein, B vitamins, vitamins A and D, calcium, and phosphorus.

Meat, fish, and poultry provide protein, B vitamins, iron, and zinc. No one food provides all the nutrients for a healthy diet, which is why a nutritious diet must be a varied diet. By eating servings in the proportion suggested by the dietary guidelines, Americans can assure themselves of a nutritional diet. People who cannot eat foods from all five groups, due to allergies or even tastes, should consult a nutritionist or dietician to learn how to meet nutritional requirements.

MAINTAINING A HEALTHY WEIGHT

Being too fat or too thin can cause health problems. Obesity is linked to high blood pressure, heart disease, stroke, and other illnesses. While being too thin is a less common problem, thinness is associated with osteoporosis (a bone disease) in women and early death in both men and women. While there is no definition for "healthy weight," most people can take a look in the mirror to see if they're in the ballpark. Additionally, it isn't that difficult to check whether you're eating more than the recommended number of calories per day, which is the most common cause of overweight.

Recommendations of the food and nutrition board of the National Academy of Sciences suggest that men should consume between 1,840 and 3,600 calories per day, with 61 to 120 grams of fat; women need 1,520 to 2,640 calories with 51 to 88 grams of fat. The calorie ranges should reflect age and amount of activity; the older and less active you are, the closer you should be to the low end of the range. Additionally, no more than $\frac{1}{3}$ of the fat should be from saturated fat.

To decrease calorie intake:

▶ Reduce your intake of fat and fatty foods.

▶ Eat more fruits and vegetables, along with breads and cereals without added fats and sugars.

▶ Reduce sugar and sweets in your diet.

▶ Eat smaller portions and limit second helpings.

▶ Reduce consumption of alcoholic beverages.

LIMITING FAT AND CHOLESTEROL

Dietary fat is the single most important factor related to chronic illness, according to the 1988 Surgeon General's Report.

WEIGHTS AND MEASURES

Dash = less than $\frac{1}{8}$ teaspoon
$\frac{1}{2}$ tablespoon = $1\frac{1}{2}$ teaspoons
1 tablespoon = 3 teaspoons
2 tablespoons = $\frac{1}{8}$ cup
$\frac{1}{4}$ cup = 4 tablespoons
$\frac{1}{3}$ cup = 5 tablespoons plus 1 teaspoon
$\frac{1}{2}$ cup = 8 tablespoons
$\frac{3}{4}$ cup = 12 tablespoons
1 cup = 16 tablespoons
$\frac{1}{2}$ pint = 1 cup or 8 fluid ounces
1 pint = 2 cups or 16 fluid ounces
1 quart = 4 cups or 2 pints or 32 fluid ounces
1 gallon = 16 cups or 4 quarts
1 pound = 16 ounces

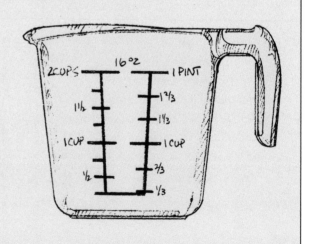

LIST OF EQUIVALENTS

Almonds, blanched, slivered	4 oz. = 1 cup
Apples	1 medium = 1 cup sliced
Bananas	1 medium, mashed = 1/3 cup
Butter or margarine	2 cups = 1 lb. or 4 sticks; 1 cup = 1/2 lb. or 2 sticks
	1/2 cup = 1 stick or 8 tablespoons
	1/4 cup = 1/2 stick or 4 tablespoons
Chocolate	1 (6-ounce) package chocolate chips = 1 cup chips or 6 (1-ounce) squares semisweet chocolate
Cocoa, unsweetened	1 (8-ounce) can = about 2 cups
Coconut, flaked	3 1/2 oz. = 1 1/3 cup
Cream cheese	3-oz. package = 6 tablespoons; 8-oz. package = 1 cup
Flour	
White or all-purpose	1 lb. = 3 1/2 to 4 cups
Whole-wheat	1 lb. = 3 3/4 to 4 cups
Honey, liquid	16 oz. = 1 1/3 cups
Lemons	1 medium = 1 to 3 tablespoons juice and 2 to 3 teaspoons grated peel
Milk	
Evaporated	5-oz. can = 2/3 cup; 12-oz. can = 1 2/3 cups
Sweetened, condensed	14-oz. can = 1 1/4 cups
Pecans, shelled	1 lb. = 4 cups halved; 3 1/2 to 4 cups chopped
Raisins, seedless, whole	1 lb. = 2 3/4 to 3 cups
Shortening	1 lb. = 2 1/2 cups
Sugar	
Granulated	1 lb. = 2 1/2 cups
Brown, packed	1 lb. = 2 1/4 cups
Confectioners'	1 lb. = 3 3/4 to 4 cups unsifted
Walnuts, chopped	4 1/2 oz. = 1 cup

Additionally, a diet low in saturated fat and cholesterol can help maintain a desirable level of blood cholesterol. For adults, this level is below 200 mg/dl. Greater risk of heart disease is believed associated with higher cholesterol levels.

A total daily intake of no more than 30 percent of calories from fat is recommended. Less than 10 percent of the 30 percent should be from saturated fats. The major sources of saturated fat are from animal products, with lesser amounts from tropical oils, such as coconut, palm kernel, and palm oils, and hydrogenated oils, which are processed oils typically used in preserved food.

By following the serving portions on the Food Group Chart, you can reduce your fat intake as well as balance your diet nutritionally. In addition, the following tips should help you reduce fats in your diet:

▶ Use fats and oils sparingly in cooking.

▶ Limit amounts of salad dressings and spreads, such as butter and margarine. One tablespoon of most spreads provides 10 to 11 grams of fat.

▶ Check food labels to see how much fat and saturated fats are in a serving.

▶ Trim fat from meat and remove skin from poultry.

▶ Moderate the use of egg yolks.

▶ Avoid organ meats, which contain high levels of fat and cholesterol.

▶ Keep your total daily servings of meat, poultry, fish, dry beans, and eggs to between 2 and 3 servings.

▶ Choose skim or nonfat milk, fat-free or low-fat yogurt, and low-fat cheeses. One cup of skim milk has only a trace of fat; 1 cup of 2-percent milk has 5 grams of fat; and 1 cup of whole milk has 8 grams of fat. Yogurt and cheese, which are made from milk, can also contain a lot of fat.

▶ Limit avocados and nuts, which are high in fats, in your diet.

▶ Shellfish, other than scallops, typically have more cholesterol than other fish and should be eaten sparingly by those on a low-cholesterol diet.

EMPHASIZING VEGETABLES, FRUITS, AND GRAINS

Along with being naturally low in fat, vegetables, fruits, and grain products provide

complex carbohydrates, dietary fiber, and a host of nutrients. Complex carbohydrates are important, because they are digested slowly and help to curb the appetite and sustain body energy. Complex carbohydrates, such as starches, are in breads, cereals, pasta, rice, dry beans, and a variety of vegetables. Dietary fiber is essential for proper bowel function.

MODERATING SUGAR

Sugar isn't just found in a box. *Sugar* takes the form of table sugar, brown sugar, raw sugar, glucose, fructose, maltose, lactose, honey, syrup, corn sweetener, molasses, and fruit juice concentrate. Sugars and starches, which break down into sugars, are in many healthy foods, including milk, fruits, some vegetables, breads, and cereals. We probably get plenty of sugar in a well-balanced diet without adding it. So what's wrong with sugar? Along with promoting tooth decay, sugars add calories without providing nutrients. The guidelines suggest that sugar should be used in moderation by healthy people and sparingly by people with low calorie needs.

MINIMIZING SALT AND SODIUM

Sodium and chloride, found in table salt, are essential to the diet, but high salt intake is associated with high blood pressure, and most people eat far more salt than is needed. Much of the sodium in our diets is added during processing and manufacturing. Daily sodium intake should not exceed 2,400 milligrams, according to the food and nutrition board of the National Academy of Sciences. While that sounds like a lot, some frozen dinners have 1,900 milligrams; a cup of lowfat milk has 158 milligrams; and one pretzel has 101 milligrams.

FOOD GROUP CHART

Food Group	Number of Servings	Serving Size
Breads, cereal, rice, and pasta	6–11	1 slice of bread; bun, bagel, or English muffin; ½ cup of cooked cereal, rice, or pasta
Vegetables	3–5	1 cup of raw leafy greens; ½ cup of other vegetables
Fruit	2–4	1 piece medium-size fruit
Milk, yogurt, and cheese	2–3	1 cup of milk or yogurt; 1½ ounces of cheese
Meat, poultry, fish, dry beans, eggs, and nuts	2–3	Daily total of 6 ounces
Fats, oils, and sweets		Use sparingly

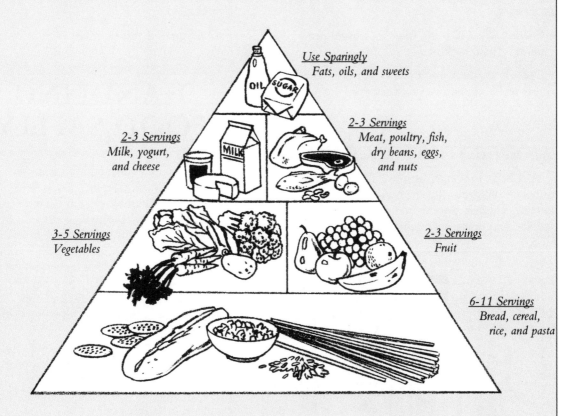

Use Sparingly
Fats, oils, and sweets

2-3 Servings
Milk, yogurt, and cheese

2-3 Servings
Meat, poultry, fish, dry beans, eggs, and nuts

3-5 Servings
Vegetables

2-3 Servings
Fruit

6-11 Servings
Bread, cereal, rice, and pasta

To reduce sodium intake, try the following:

▶ Do not use salt or use it sparingly in cooking and at the table.

▶ Check labels of frozen dinners, packaged mixes, canned soups, and salad dressings, which can contain high amounts of sodium.

▶ Limit salted snacks, such as pretzels, chips, crackers, and salted nuts.

▶ Choose fresh or frozen vegetables, which have less sodium than canned varieties.

▶ Ready-to-eat cereals have much higher amounts of sodium than most cereals that need to be cooked.

▶ Lunch meat, hot dogs, processed hams, sausages, and other cured meats are generally high in sodium that is added during processing.

▶ Foods packed in brine (pickles, olives, and sauerkraut) are high in salt.

▶ Use salt substitutes and plenty of herbs and spices to flavor food usually enhanced with salt.

MODERATING ALCOHOL

Alcoholic beverages supply calories but few nutrients. Additionally, drinking alcoholic beverages is linked to many health problems. Adults who drink may reduce their health risk

by drinking in moderation. For men, this is no more than two drinks a day; for women, this is no more than one drink a day. A drink is considered to be 12 ounces of regular beer; 5 ounces of wine, or 1½ ounces of 80-proof distilled spirits.

The U.S. Departments of Agriculture and Health and Human Services suggest that the following groups should avoid alcohol completely:

▶ Women who are pregnant or trying to conceive.

▶ Individuals who plan to drive or engage in other activities that require attention or skill.

▶ Individuals using medicines, including over-the-counter varieties.

▶ Individuals who cannot moderate their drinking.

▶ Children and adolescents.

HANDLING FOOD SAFELY

Handling and cooking food is just as important as healthy eating. Food-borne illnesses are caused by various bacteria that contaminate food, prompting ailments from diarrhea to botulism. While most food-borne illnesses are not life threatening for healthy people, they can be severe and even fatal for young children, the elderly, and people who are already sick. Careful handling and complete cooking of food can prevent most food-borne illness.

While you'll want to check other sections in this book for additional information about individual foods, make sure you know how to properly buy, store, and cook perishables to ensure your family's safety.

BUYING FOOD

▶ If you live a long way from the grocery store, be especially careful of how you handle perishable food between purchase and home storage, particularly in hot weather. Pick up perishables last at the supermarket and, if you live more than 30 miles from the store, keep an ice chest in your car and transfer perishables to it for the journey home.

▶ When you unload your groceries into the freezer, be sure to place the new items behind previously purchased items of the same type. Then you'll automatically reach for the older items at the front of the freezer first.

▶ Never buy food that is for sale after its "Sell By" date.

▶ Be conservative about following the "Sell By" and "Use By" dates on purchased products; they do not tell you how much the food has been handled or how well it has been refrigerated before you buy it.

▶ Don't buy canned foods that have dents, which could indicate a problem with the contents.

▶ Don't buy cans that are sticky, which could indicate a leak. If you inadvertently buy such a can, return it to the store.

▶ Buy eggs graded A or better that are refrigerated in the store.

▶ Make sure your market is clean and that perishables are stored properly.

▶ Buy shellfish from markets supplied by state-approved sources.

SAFE FOOD STORAGE

Storing food properly not only ensures that you will be cooking with fresh food, it will prevent contamination. You need to know what can be stored as well as how long products can be stored in the refrigerator, freezer, and at room temperature. The following are general rules for food storage.

Storing Food at Room Temperature

▶ Always check the label on boxed and canned goods to see how they should be stored. If you have not refrigerated items that should be refrigerated, don't use them; throw them out.

▶ Few foods benefit from light and warmth. If you have storage cabinets above your kitchen range, use them only for nonfood items.

▶ To avoid spoilage and explosions, home canned foods should be stored out of direct light and away from direct heat sources.

▶ Not all boxed or canned foods can be kept at room temperature. Check the labels for instructions.

▶ Store new cans and dried foods behind those on the shelf to be sure you use the older ones first.

▶ Canned foods do not keep forever. High-acid canned foods, such as tomatoes, keep for between 12 and 18 months, while low-acid foods can keep up to five years. To be on the safe side, try to use canned food within a year.

▶ Don't store foods in cupboards under the sink where they could be damaged by sweating pipes or in cupboards that also contain cleaning supplies.

▶ Potatoes and onions, which should not be refrigerated, need to be kept cooler than most foods stored in cupboards. If you don't have a cellar, make sure you store them in the coolest place possible.

Refrigerating and Freezing Food

Few perishables don't need to be refrigerated or frozen. The exceptions include apples, which keep relatively well for months, and some other fruits and vegetables that keep at room temperature for a few days to a week. In all other cases, and particularly with meats, poultry, seafood, and dairy products, food should be refrigerated or frozen as soon as you bring it home to ensure maximum freshness and to prevent the growth of bacteria. Make sure you know how long foods can be refrigerated or frozen, and don't use food that has been stored past the time it should be stored.

▶ Refrigerator temperatures should be 40 to 45°F, and the freezer should be 0°. Check temperatures frequently with a thermometer.

▶ Don't crowd the refrigerator or freezer. Air needs to circulate to keep temperatures even.

▶ Plastic-coated milk cartons or cottage cheese or ice-cream containers are not airtight enough to be reused as freezer containers. Use them only for short-term refrigerator storage.

▶ When you freeze food, label each package to avoid future guesswork and to make sure you don't freeze it too long. Mark the contents and the date on each package.

▶ Use home-frozen fruits and vegetables within a year.

▶ To prevent the spoilage of frozen foods and retain their best flavors and textures, thaw them in the refrigerator before reheating. Never thaw frozen poultry and seafood at room temperature; use the refrigerator or microwave.

▶ Containers for freezing should be odorless, moistureproof, and airtight. The best wraps and containers include rigid plastic or glass containers with tight-sealing lids, zip-top plastic freezer bags, and heavy-duty plastic film or aluminum foil. Glass containers should be labeled freezer-safe. Plastic storage bags, sandwich bags, produce bags, bread bags, and plastic dairy tubs are not good choices for freezer containers because they don't seal well and could promote freezer-burn in foods left frozen for a long period of time.

▶ Never refreeze fish that has been previously frozen and thawed.

DETECTING FOOD-BORNE ILLNESS

If you suspect any kind of food poisoning or illness associated with contaminated food or water, call your doctor immediately. With most food-borne illness, symptoms can develop early—within half an hour of eating—to within a few days. Common symptoms of food-borne illness include diarrhea, abdominal cramping, fever, and sometimes blood or pus in the stools. Severe exhaustion, nausea, and vomiting can also be signs of these illnesses.

The most critical disease—botulism, which can be fatal—is caused by the botulinum toxin in canned foods, lunch meats, and some seafood. Symptoms are double vision, inability to swallow, speech difficulty, and progressive paralysis of the respiratory system. If you suspect botulism, get medical help immediately.

FOOD STORAGE CHART

Product	Storage Period	
	Refrigerate	Freeze
Fresh meat:		
Beef, ground	1-2 days	3-4 months
Beef, steaks and chops	3-5 days	6-12 months
Pork, chops	3-5 days	3-4 months
Pork, ground	1-2 days	1-2 months
Pork, roasts	3-5 days	4-8 months
Cured meat:		
Lunch meat	3-5 days	1-2 months
Sausage	1-2 days	1-2 months
Gravy	1-2 days	3 months
Fish:		
Lean, such as cod	1-2 days	6 months
Fatty, such as salmon	1-2 days	2-3 months
Chicken:		
Whole	1-2 days	12 months
Parts	1-2 days	9 months
Giblets	1-2 days	3-4 months
Dairy products:		
Swiss, brick, and processed cheese	3-4 weeks	Do not freeze
Milk	5 days	1 month
Eggs, fresh in shell	3-5 weeks	Do not freeze
Eggs, hard cooked	1 week	Do not freeze

SAFE FOOD PREPARATION

Careless food preparation and incomplete cooking are responsible for many food-borne illnesses. Cross-contamination of foods occurs when a bacteria from one food is transferred to another. For example, if you use a cutting board to cut up a raw chicken and neglect to wash it before using it to slice vegetables for a salad, any salmonella bacteria on a raw chicken could be transferred to the raw vegetables. While you won't be exposed to the bacteria if the contaminated chicken is thoroughly cooked, you could pick it up from the salad. The best way to protect yourself from food-borne illnesses is to make sure you know how to properly prepare and cook food.

▶ Thoroughly wash all fresh fruits and vegetables before eating or cooking.

▶ Wash hands before preparing meals. If you have a cut or sore on your hands, wear gloves or don't cook.

▶ Once prepared, keep hot foods hot and cold foods cold. Disease-causing bacteria grow quickly in temperatures between 40 to 140°F.

▶ Do not put cooked food on an unwashed plate or platter that has held raw meat.

▶ Wash the lid of canned goods before opening.

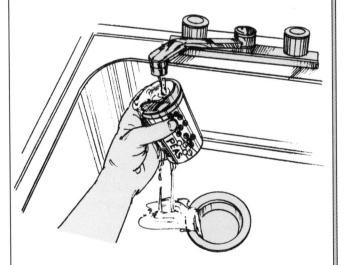

▶ Clean the blade of the can opener after each time you use it.

▶ Wash kitchen linens frequently. Bacteria can lodge in tea towels and washcloths that are reused a lot without laundering. Throw out dish sponges when they get dirty.

▶ Don't handle meat or poultry more than necessary, because frequent handling can introduce bacteria into these products.

COOKING FOOD SAFELY

▶ Use a thermometer to assure that meats, particularly poultry, are thoroughly cooked. Beef and lamb should be cooked to at least 140°F; pork to 150°; and poultry to 180°.

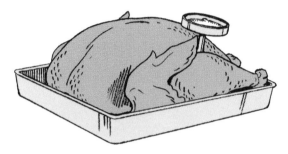

▶ Egg dishes are particularly susceptible to bacteria growth and should be handled carefully. Serve egg-rich hot dishes immediately after cooking and refrigerate leftovers quickly. If the dish is to be served cold, put it in the refrigerator immediately after preparation and keep it there until you're ready to serve it.

▶ Although the acid in a marinade will help slow the growth of dangerous bacteria, it won't prevent it altogether; do not allow food to marinate on the countertop. If the marinating process takes longer than an hour, refrigerate the container.

▶ Foods should not be marinated in any container (metal, for example) that can be affected by the acid in the marinade. Use only glass or plastic containers for marinating.

▶ When using a marinade as a basting sauce, marinades should only be applied up to the last five minutes of grilling or broiling. This precaution is necessary because the marinade could have become contaminated with harmful bacteria from the raw food during the marinading process. The marinade must be cooked over the heat for a minimum of five

minutes to ensure that the harmful bacteria are destroyed if you intend to use it on cooked food.

▶ Although cooking destroys most of the bacteria that can lead to food poisoning, it does not destroy the staph (staphylococcus aureus) organism. For this reason, two hours is the longest that prepared foods—especially starchy foods, cheese, and meat dishes such as cooked meats and meat salads—should be allowed to sit at room temperature.

▶ Partial cooking may speed up food preparation, but it's not advisable because partial cooking may encourage bacteria growth before cooking is complete. Don't interrupt cooking of meat and poultry; cook it completely at one time.

▶ Refrigerate leftovers as soon as possible in shallow containers to hasten cooling. Use them within three days.

▶ Reheated foods should be brought to a temperature of at least 165°F.

▶ Cook frozen foods 1½ times as long as thawed foods.

FREEZING FOODS AT HOME

▶ To save freezer space, freeze a single layer of well-sealed foods at -10°F for about 24 hours

THE LOWDOWN ON POULTRY AND SEAFOOD

Although most people know that pork should be cooked thoroughly to avoid any danger of trichinosis, many people are unaware of the potential danger in underdone chicken and raw fish.

Sixty percent or more of raw poultry sold probably carries some disease-causing bacteria. To avoid any danger of bacteria or parasites to which poultry is susceptible, make sure it is thoroughly cooked, regardless of the cooking methods used. Do not partially cook it and then store it to finish cooking later.

There are several ways to test chicken to see if it is completely cooked. The most accurate method for whole chickens is to use a meat thermometer. Before roasting, insert the thermometer into the thickest part of the inner thigh away from any bones. The chicken is done when the temperature registers 180°F. Temperature can also be measured with a handy, instant-reading thermometer that is inserted and then removed. Insert this thermometer into the thigh as described above. To test chicken pieces, insert a fork into the thickest part of the piece. If the fork goes in easily, the juices are clear, not pink, and the chicken is tender throughout, then it is fully cooked.

Additionally, take special care to be sure to wash cutting surfaces, utensils, and your hands with hot soapy water when handling raw poultry and seafood to avoid cross-contaminating other foods.

The U.S. Food and Drug Administration estimates that 85 percent of all illnesses caused by eating seafood comes from eating raw mollusks—oysters, clams, and mussels. These shellfish feed by filtering water through their systems. Along with nutrients, they pull bacteria and viruses into their bodies, which can cause serious illnesses in humans who eat them. Persons with liver, stomach, blood, and immune disorders are particularly vulnerable.

Some fish are also known to accumulate mercury and PCBs in their bodies, which are not destroyed by cooking. Swordfish, for example, are known for accumulating methylmercury, according to the U.S. Food and Drug Administration. Consumption on a regular basis may not be advisable for women who are pregnant or who intend to become pregnant.

Although preparation methods depend on the type of seafood, make sure it is thoroughly cooked but not overdone. Just about any fish is done when it flakes. It's a little trickier with shellfish. Fish dries out quickly, and shellfish gets rubbery if cooked too long.

While consuming seafood can cause some illnesses, the risk is small. An FDA study showed about one illness per million servings of seafood when raw shellfish were excluded. That compares to about one illness for every 25,000 servings of chicken.

or until frozen solid, then reset the thermostat to 0°F and stack the containers on top of each other. Repeat for new batches as necessary.

▶ For quick-freezing, freeze only two to three pounds of food per cubic foot of freezer space at any one time.

▶ Use your hands to press as much air as possible out of a filled freezer bag before sealing it.

▶ It's sometimes hard to get the air out of an odd-shaped bag of produce to be frozen. Make it easier by lowering the filled bag into a sink full of water and letting the water press the air out. Then twist the top of the bag, fold the twisted section over, and fasten it with a rubber band, pipe cleaner, or twist tie.

▶ For fastest freezing, foods newly prepared for freezing should be placed in a single layer in the coldest part of your freezer. Leave the freezer closed for 24 hours, then move the packages—which should be frozen solid—to another area of the freezer to free up the coldest area for the next batch.

▶ Remember that your freezer can only freeze a limited amount of food at a time. A good estimate is two to three pounds of food for each cubic foot of freezer space.

▶ Foods that are packed in liquid expand as they freeze, and room—or head space—must be allowed for this expansion to keep lids from popping off or freezer bags from bursting. Allow 1/4-inch of head space for pints, 1/2-inch for quarts.

▶ If you pack foods in containers with narrow mouths, the food expands upward in the container even more and you must allow more head space: 3/4 inch for pint containers; 1 1/2 inches for quarts.

▶ Avoid ice crystals forming in the foods you freeze by freezing them fast at zero temperatures. If foods freeze too slowly, moisture from the cells in the food fibers forms ice crystals between the fibers, and the product loses liquid and may darken. Quick-freezing at very low temperatures locks the cells in the food fiber in their proper places.

▶ Liquid foods are safest frozen in plastic bags that are then placed in cardboard boxes.

▶ Foods that don't take well to the freezer include cooked egg whites (because they get tough), salad greens (which lose their crisp texture), mayonnaise (because it separates when frozen), and foods cooked with onion, cloves, pepper, and garlic (because these flavors can get stronger and bitter when frozen).

▶ To cool prepared foods for freezing, place food in its cooking container, uncovered, in shallow, ice-cold water in the kitchen sink. This is quicker and more energy efficient than cooling warm foods in the refrigerator.

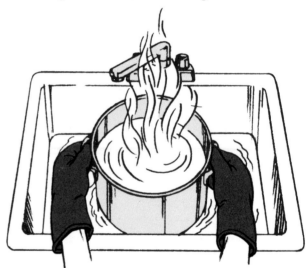

▶ Foods with a high salt or fat content—Canadian bacon, ham, and bacon, for example—do not freeze well because they can become rancid after only one month.

▶ Don't worry about the separation of the fat from the meat and the oil from the marinade that occurs when you freeze marinated meat. The components will combine satisfactorily when reheated. If you're health conscious, you may even want to skim off some of the fat and oil while the dish is still frozen.

▶ To freeze fish, do so immediately after it's been caught or purchased. Rinse it under cold water and pat very dry with paper towels. Wrap in plastic and then in aluminum foil

DEALING WITH SPOILED FOOD

▶ Mold is a sure sign of spoilage. Throw out any moldy food, with the exception of cheese. Mold can be trimmed from cheese, but make sure you trim a large section around the mold, because mold lies beneath the surface as well as on top.

▶ What do you do with a product you suspect to be a potential source of food poisoning? Seal it in a strong plastic bag, mark the bag to indicate that the contents are dangerous, and place it on a high shelf in the refrigerator (where children can't reach it). Place a paper plate under the package to avoid leakage. Then report it to health officials.

▶ When you open a jar of canned food that has been stored for some time, watch for spurting liquid. If any liquid does spurt out, the contents have spoiled.

▶ If canned food smells strange or looks cloudy after opening, discard it immediately without tasting it.

▶ If the lid on a canning jar is bulging, the contents may be spoiled.

▶ Spoiled home-canned products may be contaminated with botulism toxins that are not necessarily destroyed by sewage treatment plants. This is why spoiled food cannot safely be flushed down the toilet. Instead, bury it deeply enough that it cannot be dug up by animals and none of it can seep up to the surface.

▶ Another way of making spoiled food safe for disposal is to boil it for ten minutes. This will produce a horrible smell, but it will destroy the toxins. After boiling, you can safely dispose of the food.

▶ Spoiled food can also be chemically inactivated. Put the food in a glass container and mix in ½ to 1 cup of chlorine bleach or several tablespoons of strong lye. Let it stand overnight somewhere where you are quite certain it is out of reach of children and animals. After treatment, the spoiled food can be flushed down the toilet or wrapped in newspaper and put in the garbage.

▶ Protect yourself. Always wear rubber or plastic gloves when handling spoiled food, and dispose of the gloves afterward.

▶ You don't have to throw out jars that have held spoiled food. If you boil the jars and screw bands for 15 minutes in a strong detergent solution, they can be safely reused. Do not reuse the lids; dispose of them along with the spoiled food.

before placing it in the freezer. Plan to use it as soon as possible for best quality.

▸ Don't try to freeze salads made with mayonnaise.

▸ Freeze slightly underripe vegetables rather than those that are past their prime. Underripe vegetables retain flavor and shape when frozen.

▸ To prevent foods such as berries from sticking together when frozen, flash-freeze them first. Separate them on a cookie sheet, freeze, remove, and—while still frozen—pack them together in airtight containers before replacing them in the freezer.

▸ Fruits with pits, like plums and cherries, must be pitted before freezing. The stone can change the flavor of the fruit during long-term freezer storage.

▸ To freeze whole lemons or limes, wash and dry the fruit; twist a freezer bag tightly around it; seal and freeze.

GLOSSARY OF FOODS

DAIRY PRODUCTS

All dairy products are made from milk, whether it be from cows, goats, or sheep.

With the exception of nonfat dried milk, store dairy products in the refrigerator or freezer.

Butter and Margarine

Butter is made from cream and must have a milk fat content of 80 percent. It is sold both unsalted (sweet) and salted. Margarine is made from milk, milk emulsions, and vegetable oil. Fat content can be 80 percent or lower, with some spreads now offering almost fat-free margarine.

▸ Always store butter and other spreads in the butter keeper or on the bottom shelf of the refrigerator; otherwise it will absorb flavors from other foods.

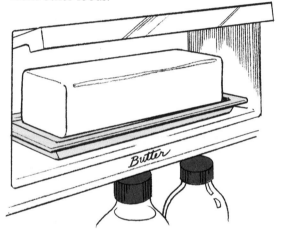

▸ If you're going to store unsalted butter in your freezer for a long time, wrap it carefully and seal it airtight. Salted butter that you're freezing for a short time can be stored in its original container.

▸ Use unsalted (often labeled sweet) butter, rather than salted butter, for cooking. It's generally fresher than salted butter, because salt is a preservative that can mask flavors.

▸ If you're short on butter, stretch it by adding evaporated milk. Two cups of evaporated milk added to 1 pound of butter makes almost 2 pounds of butter. Add the milk a little at a time to butter that has been brought to room temperature and beaten until creamy. Chill. (Don't use this mixture in cakes such as pound cake.)

Creams

Creams, made from the fatty part of milk, differ according to the percentage of fat. Half-and-half, the lightest, has about 12 percent fat. Light cream and sour cream have about 20 percent fat, although nonfat sour creams are now available. Whipping cream is about 40 percent fat.

▶ Half-and-half or undiluted evaporated milk can be substituted in a recipe that calls for light cream. In a pinch, just use whole milk.

▶ For best results when beating heavy or whipping cream, chill the cream, bowl, and beaters first—the cold keeps the fat in the cream solid, thus increasing the volume.

▶ For optimum volume, beat whipped cream in a deep, narrow bowl. Generally 1 cup of

WHAT TO DO IF THE FREEZER FAILS

▶ If your freezer goes out but you expect the stoppage to be temporary, avoid opening the freezer to check on the contents.

▶ If you expect your freezer to be out of action for more than a day or two, call around to find a school, church, or store with a freezer in which you can store your frozen goods temporarily.

▶ It may be possible to rent space in a commercial freezer or cold-storage plant if you expect it to take a while to get your freezer repaired.

▶ Dry ice will keep your food frozen in a freezer that's temporarily out of commission, but it must be handled carefully. Caution: Never touch dry ice with your bare hands—it freezes everything, including skin. Also, work in a well-ventilated area.

▶ If you use dry ice to preserve the contents of a nonfunctioning freezer, avoid letting it touch the packages. Place the ice on empty shelves, or cover the frozen goods with a layer of cardboard and place the dry ice on top.

▶ To determine how much dry ice you need to keep your frozen foods in good condition, use the following calculation: If you have a 10-cubic-foot freezer that is full, figure on 25 pounds of dry ice to keep the contents below freezing for three to four days. If the freezer is only half full, the same amount of ice will only keep the produce frozen for two to three days.

▶ After a thaw, check if meat or poultry still contains ice crystals. If it does, you can refreeze it safely. Otherwise it should be cooked. Of course, you can refreeze the food after cooking.

cream will yield 2 cups of whipped cream, so be sure to choose a bowl that will accommodate the increased volume.

▶ Do not overbeat or whipped cream will clump together and form butter.

▶ Add flavorings, such as powdered sugar and vanilla extract, to the cream after it has begun to thicken. Sweetened whipped cream will have a softer texture than unsweetened.

▶ Sour cream will curdle if it becomes too hot, and there are no culinary tricks to restore it. Always add sour cream at the end of the cooking time and heat it only until it is warm, not hot, and never to a boil.

▶ Homemade crème fraîche has a more natural taste and texture than the store-bought kind and can be prepared much more economically. Mix one teaspoon of buttermilk and one pint of heavy cream in a glass jar. Put the covered jar in a warm spot (75-85°F) for about 24 hours, until the cream is the consistency of pudding. This cream can be refrigerated for several weeks.

Cheeses

Cheeses, all made from animal milk, range from fresh, unripened cheeses to aged, hard cheeses. Fat content varies as well.

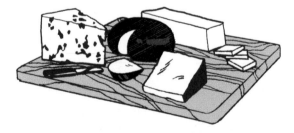

Types of Cheeses

▶ Unripened cheeses include cottage cheese, farmer's cheese, cream cheese, and ricotta.

▶ Soft cheeses, which have been ripened for a short time, include feta, Brie, Camembert, and chèvre.

▶ Hard cheeses, ripened for various lengths of time, range from semi-hard to hard and can be cut or grated. They include cheddar, Edam, Emmenthaler, fontina, Gouda, Gruyère, Havarti, Muenster, Parmesan, provolone, and Romano.

▶ Blue cheeses, which are ripened by green molds, include Gorgonzola, Roquefort, and Stilton.

Tips on Cheese

▶ Refrigerate all cheeses with the exception of Parmesan. While some grated Parmesan cheese products can be kept out of the refrigerator after opening, others cannot. Check the label.

▶ Cheese should not be exposed to air, which will dry it out.

▶ Serve all cheeses at room temperature.

▶ Always check the labels on cheese, particularly if you are looking for low-fat, low-cholesterol varieties. Fat content should be listed in grams of fat per ounce. Given that cheese can be very fatty, a "low-fat cheese" isn't necessarily low fat.

▶ Frozen cream cheese that appears grainy after defrosting can be whipped smooth again.

▶ To soften cream cheese quickly, remove from wrapper and place it in a medium-size microwave-safe bowl. Microwave on MEDIUM (50 percent) 1½ to 2 minutes or until slightly softened, turning the bowl after 1 minute.

▶ When using ricotta cheese in recipes, first dry it thoroughly. Place the cheese in a clean cotton or linen towel and, holding it over a large bowl or sink, squeeze it into a tight ball and wring. Keep moving the ricotta to dry parts of the towel and wring it until all excess moisture is gone. To remove all ricotta from the towel, use a spatula or pastry scraper.

▶ Cheese will have added freshness and flavor if it's wrapped in a cloth soaked in wine and vinegar and then stored in the refrigerator.

▶ Store cottage cheese upside down in the refrigerator to keep it fresh longer.

▶ Mold won't form on cheese if you store it with a few sugar cubes in a tightly covered container. If cheese does get moldy, cut or scrape the mold off and then dab the exposed surfaces with vinegar to retard mold growth.

▶ If you don't have a cheese slicer, you can cut cheese easily with extra-strength thread held taut.

▶ When cheese gets too hard, you can soften it by soaking it in buttermilk. To prevent cheese from drying out and hardening, apply butter to the cut end, or wrap tightly in aluminum foil.

▶ It's easier to grate cheddar or any soft cheese if you chill it in the freezer for a few minutes before grating.

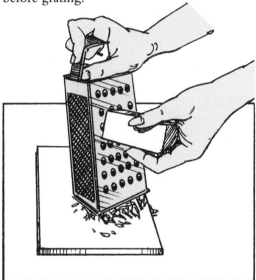

▶ You can make thinner, neater slices of processed cheese if you dip your knife in hot water before cutting.

▶ If you like to use cheese strips in salads and as garnish, try cutting strips with a potato peeler.

▶ A good way of cleaning the grater after grating cheese is to rub a slice of bread over it. As a bonus, you've made cheese-flavored bread crumbs for topping a casserole.

Eggs

Rich in protein, calcium, iron, and vitamins, chicken eggs are a nearly perfect food—unless you're watching your cholesterol intake. Although eggs are relatively low in calories, they're very high in fat and cholesterol. Eggs are classified as to size, jumbo being the largest. For most recipes, medium or large eggs suffice. The color of the shell—brown or white—has nothing to do with the nutrient value.

▶ Always use clean, uncracked, grade A eggs and cook them until the yolks are thickened and set.

▶ Always use fresh eggs. To check if an egg is fresh, place it in a bowl of cold water. A fresh egg will sink; a stale egg will float.

▶ Store fresh eggs in the refrigerator for 3 to 5 weeks; hard-cooked eggs can be refrigerated for up to 1 week. Egg whites will keep in the freezer for up to 1 year; after you defrost them remember that 2 tablespoons of egg white that's been frozen equal 1 tablespoon of fresh egg white. Egg yolks do not freeze well.

▶ Store eggs with the large end up to maintain quality.

▶ Eggs absorb odors through their shells and should be kept away from foods with strong aromas.

▶ To check if an egg has been hard cooked, spin it like a top. If it spins on its end, it is cooked; if it turns on its side, it is raw.

▶ When slicing hard-boiled eggs, the yolk will not crumble if you first dip your knife or egg slicer in cold water.

Milk

Whether it's homogenized, whole, nonfat dried, evaporated, or condensed, milk is a basic product, because it provides so many nutrients. Milk also contains various amounts of fat. The percentages on milk labels refer to the amount of fat in the milk. No fat is removed from whole milk; fat is removed from 2 percent, 1 percent milk, and skim milk. Nonfat milk contains no fat.

Buttermilk used to be the part of the milk that was left behind after butter was churned. Today, buttermilk is made from pasteurized skim milk to which a bacterial culture is added to produce the tart flavor. Fresh milk

BOILING AN EGG

▶ To hard-boil eggs, put the eggs in a single layer in a saucepan. Add enough water to come at least 1 inch above the eggs. Cover and quickly bring the water to a boil. Turn off heat. If necessary, remove the pan from the burner to prevent further boiling. Let eggs stand, covered, in the hot water for 15 to 17 minutes. Immediately run cold water over the eggs or put them in ice water until completely cooled.

▶ If an egg cracks when you boil it, add a little vinegar to the water. The vinegar will prevent the white from streaming out of the shell.

▶ If you want to keep yolks perfectly centered in hard-boiled eggs (perhaps for deviled eggs), stir the water constantly while cooking.

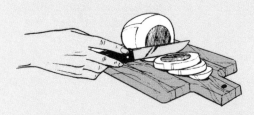

▶ Hard-boiled eggs will be easier to shell if you submerge them in cold water for a minute or so after cooking. When you crack the egg's shell, gently roll the egg between the palms of your hands. The shell should slip right off, or you can easily peel it under cold running water.

can be soured and used as a substitute for buttermilk. If a recipe calls for 1 cup of buttermilk, place 1 tablespoon lemon juice or distilled white vinegar in a measuring cup and add enough milk to measure 1 cup. Stir and let the mixture stand at room temperature for 5 minutes.

▶ It's safe to store milk in the freezer, but be sure to defrost it in the refrigerator, not at room temperature.

▶ Keep nonfat dried milk in the cupboard and reliquefy it for use in place of whole or skim milk.

▶ Soy milk can be used in most recipes that call for cow's milk. The tastes are similar enough in cooked dishes.

Yogurt

Once scorned, yogurt has become a popular dairy product for snacks, desserts, and in cooking. Yogurt is made from milk and a culture. Most of the fat is removed in low-fat yogurt, and nonfat yogurt contains no fat. There's even a nondairy soy yogurt for people who do not eat dairy products.

▶ Store yogurt in the refrigerator and watch the labels. Throw out any yogurt with mold.

▶ Plain (nonflavored) yogurt can be substituted in many recipes for sour cream and mayonnaise. Take care when adding yogurt to hot foods. Too much heat or over-vigorous stirring can cause yogurt to become stringy or to separate. Always add it at the last minute and stir gently.

▶ You can save money by making your own fruit yogurts by simply adding fresh fruit to plain yogurt.

Frozen Dairy Products

Frozen ice milk, frozen yogurt, and even milkless frozen dairy products should all be stored in the freezer, where they will keep for varying lengths of time. These products will take on a cardboard taste if frozen too long. Ice cream that's been opened and put back in the freezer may develop a waxlike film on its exposed surface. A film won't form if you press a piece of waxed paper against the exposed surface before resealing the carton. Melted ice cream shouldn't be refrozen, but you can refrigerate it and use it on cereal.

FRUIT

Nearly every variety of fruit is a nutritionally perfect food. Along with providing fiber and vitamins to the diet, they have a very low fat content and are low in sodium. Since most fruits can be eaten raw, the only real trick to serving delicious fruit is to make sure they're ripe, when their taste and texture are at their peak. Fruits also need to be carefully watched for perishability. Along with the following tips, be sure to check the explanations under individual categories for more information.

▶ Although their appearance might not be perfect, standard grades of fruits are as high in nutrition as the more expensive grades.

▶ Whenever possible, avoid buying prepackaged fruits; the packaging may disguise rotten spots.

▶ Use stainless steel knives to cut fruit, because carbon steel knives react with fruit and cause discoloration.

▶ To easily peel thick-skinned fruit, put the fruit in a bowl, pour boiling water over it, and wait 60 seconds. Remove the fruit and peel the skin with a paring knife.

▶ To prevent freshly cut fruit from browning, keep the fruit submerged in water to which you've added juice from half a lemon.

▶ To keep dried fruit fresh for a longer period, keep it in the freezer.

Types of Fruit

Apples

For adaptability, availability, nutritional content, and taste, you simply can't beat apples. Refrigerate apples to slow down the ripening process. If you don't have room in the refrigerator, keep your apples stored in a cool place, with a wet towel placed over the top of the container to keep the apples moist but not wet. Don't let apples freeze—they will spoil. When you keep apples in the refrigerator, store them in a separate compartment away from other fruits or vegetables. Apples absorb odors from strong-flavored vegetables. Apples also give off gases that can cause other fruits and vegetables to ripen too quickly (which can be helpful if you are trying to ripen other fruit).

▶ To tell if an unpicked apple is ripe, twist it clockwise on the stem. A ripe apple should come away from the tree easily.

▶ If you have an apple tree in your garden, you can test apples for ripeness by cutting one open and looking at the seeds. A mature apple will have dark brown seeds. In an immature apple the seeds are pale tan or white in color.

▶ Store apples in clear plastic rather than in a paper bag. You'll be able to spot any that are spoiling and remove them before they contaminate other fruit.

▶ To maintain the crispness of apple slices and to prevent them from browning, immerse them in salted water for ten minutes before you use them.

▶ When dicing several apples to make a large apple salad, mix them with dressing or mayonnaise as you chop. If you wait until you've cut all the apples, the first ones cut may discolor; coating them with mayonnaise will prevent this.

▶ To prevent apples from shrinking when you bake them, remove a horizontal belt of peel from around the middle of each one. To prevent wrinkling during baking, cut random slits in each one before placing them in the oven.

SORTING OUT APPLES

If you've ever made an apple pie that wasn't a winner, it's probably because you used the wrong apples. Some apples are great for eating; some are great for cooking; and a few varieties are great whether they're eaten raw, cooked, or baked in a pie.

All-Purpose:
Baldwin, Granny Smith, Jonathan, Winesap

Eating:
Golden Delicious, McIntosh, Red Delicious

Cooking:
Rhode Island, Greening, Rome Beauty, York Imperial

Berries

While the many varieties of berries differ in taste, they're very similar when it comes to choosing and handling. Nearly all berries are fragile and perishable. Select berries that are firm, but not hard. If they're covered with plastic, look at the container bottoms. If they are wet or stained, much of the fruit is probably moldy or mushy. Select only those containers that have dry bottoms. If you discover one or two bruised and spoiled berries when you get home, discard them; molds quickly spread from berry to berry. To keep berries in prime condition, don't wash them until you're ready to eat them. They can be stored for a few days in the refrigerator in a colander, which helps the air circulate around them to keep them fresh.

▶ **Blackberries** grow on thorny shrubs. Like raspberries, blackberries are extremely fragile. Their peak months are June, July, and August. In addition to making a wonderful pie, blackberries combine beautifully with other berries for a fruit salad. Puréed, strained, and combined with a little sugar, they make a splendid sauce for ice cream.

▶ **Blueberries** are either commercial or wild. Wild blueberries, which are much smaller than commercial berries and have much more flavor, are available only in certain parts of the country, because they are very perishable and hard to find. Look for plump, fresh berries of good blue color with a waxy bloom; they should not have stems attached. If you're lucky enough to pick wild blueberries, use them immediately or pack clean, dry fresh blueberries in freezer containers and freeze for later use in baking. Keep fresh blueberries cold and covered and use within two to three days for peak freshness. Rinse gently before using and remove any stems.

▶ **Cranberries**—small, sour, red berries—are native to North America. They are usually cooked with sweetener to make them edible. Cooking cranberries requires less sugar if you add a 1/4-teaspoon of baking soda to the pot. When cooking cranberries, add a teaspoon of butter to each pound of berries to prevent overboiling and "foaming." Cranberries are done cooking when they look as though they're ready to burst. If you cook them until they actually pop, they'll taste bitter.

▶ **Raspberries** are extremely perishable and expensive. Look for berries that are plump and fresh looking and use them as soon as possible after purchase. Wash gently just before using. For recipes that require the juice to be separated from the frozen raspberries, thaw the raspberries in a strainer that is set over a bowl.

▶ **Strawberries** come in a wide assortment. Although some are huge, bright red, and well shaped, the flavor of these berries does not always measure up to their appearance. Often, the smaller berries have a sweeter, more distinct strawberry flavor. Choose fruit that is fresh, clean, and bright red, with green caps attached. Strawberries should be stored in the refrigerator, caps attached, until ready to use. Rinse gently just before preparing, and use fresh strawberries as soon as possible for maximum freshness. Always be sure to hull strawberries after they are washed, never before, or they will absorb some of the water causing the fruit to soften. For coarsely crushed strawberries, use a potato masher.

Citrus Fruits

▶ **Grapefruit** are low in calories, natural diuretics, and perfect palate cleansers. Although grapefruit look the same on the outside, they can be either white or pink inside. The pink or "red" grapefruit are sweeter. To select the juiciest grapefruits, look for firm, heavy fruit with the thinnest skins. The "yellowness" of grapefruit skin doesn't indicate anything. Grapefruit do not ripen once picked, so they can be refrigerated immediately, where they will keep for up to six weeks.

▶ **Oranges** come in a variety of shapes, sizes, colors, and degrees of sweetness, which is why it is important to use the right orange for the right purpose. Eating oranges, such as navels, temples, and Jaffas, have a sweet-tart flavor and thick peels that are easy to remove. They can also be separated into segments with ease. Valencias and Parson Browns are two varieties of juicing oranges. They are sweet, have a thin, difficult-to-remove peel, and lots of seeds. When selecting oranges, don't be misled by the intensity of their color—most oranges are dyed to make them look more appetizing. Instead, look for brown spots— surprisingly enough, they indicate top quality. Oranges store well and can be purchased in large quantities according to need. To maximize the amount of juice from an orange, roll it on the counter with the palm of your hand before squeezing it. One medium

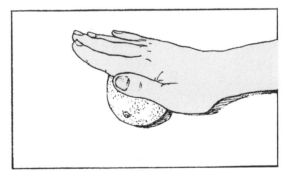

orange yields ⅓ to ½ cup of juice. The rind of 1 medium orange yields 2 to 3 tablespoons of grated peel. Grated orange peel may be frozen if it is tightly wrapped.

▶ **Tangerines** are best when they're juicy. When selecting tangerines, choose heavy fruit, which indicates good juice content. They may feel slightly puffy, which is normal, since the skin zips off easily. Fresh tangerines are very perishable—handle them with care.

Keep them cold and humid and use as soon as possible.

Grapes and Raisins

▶ **Grapes** are grown all over the world in warm climates, but nearly all the grapes sold in the U.S. are grown in California. The same grapes that are eaten fresh are used for making wine and raisins. Although seedless grapes—especially the white Thompson variety—are by far the most popular, growers are convinced that the ones with seeds have a better flavor. Select grapes with deep color and firm fruit, and refrigerate immediately. Rinse them with water only before eating, or they will get soft. A quick way to remove seeds from grapes is to slice the grapes slightly off-center. This exposes the seeds and makes them easy to flick away. Frozen grapes make cooling warm-weather snacks.

▶ **Raisins** are most often made from Thompson seedless grapes. Some have been dried naturally by the sun, although the

GETTING THE MOST FROM LEMONS AND LIMES

Lemons and limes are rarely eaten on their own, but they are probably used more than any other fruit—in everything from flavoring beverages and pies to adding zest to vegetables, fish, and poultry. Lemons can even prevent some fruits (such as apples and bananas) from turning brown when sliced. Fresh lemons and limes are found in supermarkets year-round, and bottled juice is also widely available. The most familiar green limes—known as Persian limes—are grown in California, Florida, and Mexico. Florida also produces the key lime—a small, round yellow lime with more flavor than Persian limes that is used to make Florida's famous key lime pie, a creamy and sweet dessert.

▶ A medium-size lemon will yield about 3 to 4 tablespoons of juice and 1 to 2 teaspoons of grated rind.

▶ To get the juiciest, most flavorful lemons and limes, pick those with smooth skins and small points at each end. As soon as you bring them home from the store, put them in the refrigerator in a tightly sealed container of water. Doing so encourages them to yield more juice. (You can get the same result by immersing a lemon in hot water for about 15 minutes before squeezing it.)

▶ To get the most juice from your lemons and limes, warm the fruit to room temperature and press down as you roll them on the countertop with the palm of your hand before squeezing.

▶ If only a small amount of juice is needed, make a hole in the lemon or lime with a toothpick. Squeeze out the amount you need, then seal the hole by inserting the toothpick in it; store it in the refrigerator.

▶ To remove peel in strips, use a very sharp knife or vegetable peeler (or special gadget called a lemon zester). Remove only the colored part of the peel. If necessary, scrape any white left on a peel before adding it to the recipe.

▶ When using both the juice and peel of a lime or lemon, grate the peel first, then squeeze the juice.

▶ Limes should be kept out of the sunlight to prevent them from turning yellow.

majority are usually dried by artificial heat. They are loaded with sugar and crammed with vitamins and iron. When incorporating raisins into a batter or dough, dust them lightly with flour first. This will prevent them from sticking together and from sinking to the bottom of the pan. Store leftover raisins in a tightly covered glass jar or place the opened package in an airtight plastic bag.

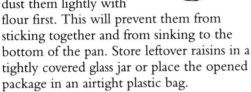

Melons

From cantaloupes to watermelons, melons are great to eat on their own and a perfect basis for a fruit salad. Select melons that are heavy. A melon will smell like a melon if it is ripe. If you hold it to your ear, shake it, and hear the juice and seeds sloshing around, it's overripe. Ripen melons for a few days before refrigerating. For maximum enjoyment, let melons develop in flavor and juiciness at room temperature, then serve or keep cool and use soon. Enhance the good fresh taste of cantaloupes or honeydew melons by sprinkling them with a few drops of lemon juice.

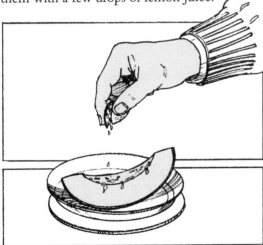

▸ **Cantaloupes** should be well shaped with a smoothly rounded, depressed area at the stem end. A fragrant aroma is also a sign of good quality. Allow cantaloupes to mellow at room temperature for a few days after purchase.

▸ **Crenshaw melons** have a golden rind tinged with green when ripe. It can be smooth or slightly ribbed. The flesh is salmon-pink in color. Look for those that are round at the base and taper to a point at the stem end.

▸ **Honeydew melons** have a smooth, velvety surface and a creamy white or yellow rind. Avoid honeydews with a stark-white rind tinged with green, as these are likely to be unripe. For maximum flavor and juiciness, keep honeydews at room temperature for a few days before serving or using in recipes. When ripe, use immediately or refrigerate.

▸ **Persian melons** resemble cantaloupe, but the rind is dark green and covered with a pale yellowish netting. The rind turns lighter green as the melon ripens. The flesh of the Persian melon is thick and orange-pink in color. Keep this melon at room temperature for a few days before enjoying its delicate flavor.

▸ If you want to take a watermelon on a picnic, wrap it in dry newspaper or burlap as soon as you remove it from the refrigerator. It will stay refreshingly cool till you're ready to eat it.

Stone Fruits

▸ **Apricots** are usually dried, because they are very fragile when they are ripe for picking and they do not ripen once picked. Nearly all domestic apricots are grown in California, and most of them are sold to be canned or dried. If you're lucky enough to find fresh apricots in a grocery store, look for ones that are both soft and juicy.

▶ **Cherries** should be plump, firm, and fresh. Depending on the variety, cherries should be brightly colored, ranging from yellow, red, deep red, reddish brown, mahogany to black. Avoid buying immature fruit, which is hard, smaller, and light in color, or overly soft and shriveled. Fresh cherries are usually available only in the summer, but they can be frozen for enjoyment later in the year. Simply wash the fruit, remove stems and pits, drain well, and place in a plastic bag. Seal tightly and store in the freezer. They'll keep up to one year. When ready to use, remove fruit from the freezer and use before completely thawed.

▶ **Dates** are usually sold dried, but fresh dates have an excellent flavor. If you have never tasted them, try to track them down at a specialty food store. They are a good source of vitamins but are very sweet, because they are half sugar.

▶ **Nectarines** are the result of a cross between a plum and a peach. Choose fruit that is smooth, plump, highly colored, and free from blemishes. Yellow skin should be brightly blushed with red. Avoid hard, dull-looking nectarines. Nectarines do not gain sugar after harvest, but should mellow and soften at room temperature for maximum enjoyment. They can be easily substituted for peaches in recipes.

▶ **Olives**, the fruit of the olive tree, must be cured in brine to be fit to eat. The size of an olive is no indication of its flavor. Some tiny varieties are bitter, while others are quite mild, and the same is true for large olives. Green olives are harvested before they are fully ripe; black olives have ripened on the tree. Most imported olives come from France, Greece, or Italy. In the United States, California produces both Greek- and Italian-style olives. Try to use the kind of olive called for or a very similar one in recipes.

▶ **Peaches** are widely available canned, but fresh peaches are usually only available from June to September. Freestone peaches, named

because the pit separates easily from the fruit, are the most common. The pit is harder to get out of clingstone peaches, which are less juicy. Select plump, well-shaped peaches with a creamy or golden undercolor. The red blush differs with varieties and is not a sign of ripeness. Avoid peaches tinged with green because they will not ripen properly. Most peaches are sold before they are ripe. To ripen them, store at room temperature in a loosely closed paper bag or fruit-ripening bowl until they yield to gentle palm pressure. Once ripe, use immediately or refrigerate for a few days. To easily peel peaches for pies or other desserts, put them in boiling water for 10 to 20 seconds, then run them under very cold or ice water. The peels will be easily removed.

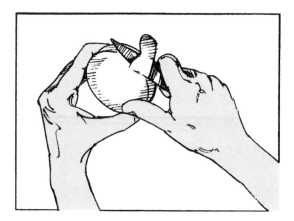

▶ **Plums** come in a rainbow of colors—purple, blue, scarlet, green, and yellow—and shapes. Tastes range from tart to sweet. When selecting plums, choose those with good color. They should be fairly firm to slightly soft and should yield to slight pressure under your thumb. At home, allow plums to soften at room temperature for a few days to bring out their full flavor; then refrigerate and use as soon as possible. Prunes are made from dried plums.

Tropical Fruits
▶ **Bananas** contain nearly 5 teaspoons of sugar—almost twice as much as many popular candy bars—but an average-size banana only has 80 to 90 calories because they're low in

fat. Choose bananas that are plump and not bruised or split. Select bananas that have not yet become fully yellow so that they will be firm and free of bruises when you get them home (where they will ripen easily at room temperature). To hasten the ripening of green bananas, place them so that they touch overripe ones, or wrap them in a damp cloth and put them in a bag. Fully ripe bananas will keep a few days longer in the refrigerator. Although the skin will darken, the inside will taste great.

▶ **Coconut,** easily available in packages, is best when it's fresh. When choosing a coconut from the display, check that the three soft "eyes" on the shell are intact, dry, and free of mold. Shake it to make sure that it is full of "milk." To release the milk, pierce the three "eyes" on the shell and drain the liquid. Coconut milk can be refrigerated for 24 hours or frozen for future use. To remove the shell from a coconut, heat the coconut in the oven for 15 minutes at 350°F. Tap it all over with a hammer, remove the cracked shell, and peel away the brown skin. The full flavor of shredded coconut is released when it is toasted. Spread the coconut in an even layer on a baking sheet and place it in a preheated 350°F oven for 8 to 10 minutes. Peek at it after 7 minutes to make sure it is not in any danger of burning. If the coconut is fresh and moist, it will take a little longer to toast to a nice golden color than drier coconut. Store leftover shredded coconut in an airtight container for up to one week in the refrigerator or up to six months in the freezer. Cream of coconut is made by pressing the white meat of tree-ripened coconuts into a thick liquid. The liquid is then processed into a creamy consistency. It is available in supermarkets in the beverage, baking, or specialty foods sections.

▶ **Kiwifruit** has fuzzy, brown skin covering emerald flesh that is often described as a combination of melon, pineapple, and strawberry. Dotted with edible black seeds, slices of kiwi are a festive addition to any recipe. For best eating, firm kiwifruit needs to be ripened for full tangy sweet flavor. Most kiwifruit sold in stores has probably been harvested when mature but still hard. To ripen the fruit at home, place it in a plastic bag with an apple, and leave it at room temperature until it yields to gentle palm pressure. Use immediately or refrigerate. For slower ripening, just refrigerate it for several weeks. When storing ripe kiwifruit in the refrigerator, place it in the fruit bin away from other fruits so that the flavors don't get mixed. Kiwis contain an enzyme that prevents gelatin from setting, so don't include them in a gelatin salad mold. Ice cream and dairy products are good with kiwifruit, but another enzyme in the fruit causes composition changes when combined with milk. If you use the two together, serve the dish immediately after combining the kiwifruit and the dairy product.

▶ **Mangoes** vary in size, shape, and color, but the yellowish orange flesh of the mango has a rich flavor and a spicy aroma. They must be fully ripe before eating or using in recipes.

The skin of most mangoes becomes tinged with more red or yellow as the fruit ripens. Mangoes are ready to eat when they yield to gentle pressure. Allow them to ripen at room temperature until soft, then use or refrigerate for a few days. For a change from raw mangoes, cook the peeled, chopped fruit with water, sugar, and orange juice to make a hot or cold sauce for ice cream or fruit salad.

▶ **Papayas** are a tropical fruit native to the Americas and available year-round; they range in both size and shape. When ripe, the skin is usually deep yellow and the flesh is light orange to salmon in color and has a soft texture. Fresh papayas will be soft when gently squeezed. Allow fruit to ripen at room temperature until the skin has turned at least half yellow. Once ripe, it can be refrigerated. It can be served either raw or cooked. The center of the papaya contains lots of edible black seeds that have a peppery taste and can be used as a garnish or added to salad dressings. The flesh contains an enzyme called papain, which is an ingredient in commercial meat tenderizers. If you make a gelatin mold with papaya, cook the fruit first or the papain will prevent it from gelling.

▶ **Pineapples** do not ripen after they are picked. If they have been harvested too early, the fruit will not be very sweet. Select fruit that is firm, plump, and heavy for its size. Serve it as soon as possible or cut it up in rings or wedges and refrigerate, where it will keep for one week. If a fresh pineapple isn't quite ripe, you can make it taste ripe this way: Prepare it as usual and then put the pieces in a pot, cover them with water, add sugar, and

boil for a few minutes. Then drain off the water, let the fruit cool, and chill it in the refrigerator. The center ring of a doughnut cutter is ideal for removing the core from slices of fresh pineapple. Just press the ring on each pineapple slice. If a recipe calls for gelatin and pineapple, use either canned fruit or fresh pineapple that has been boiled for five minutes. There is an enzyme in fresh pineapple that will prevent gelatin from setting.

▶ **Starfruit,** or carambola, is a tropical fruit that ranges in taste from tart to sweet. The flavor of a sweet carambola is likened to a combination of orange and pineapple; tart varieties are similar to lemon. Carambolas are golden yellow when ripe. Ripe carambolas may also be tinged with brown along the ribs.

Other Fruits

▶ **Currants** are actually the names for two very different fruits. One, made from the tiny, dark, Zante grape, is most often dried and used in baking. Raisins and currants may be used interchangeably in recipes. The second variety is a tiny berry related to the gooseberry. It comes in black, red, and white varieties and is used in preserves and jellies, liqueurs, and pie fillings.

▶ **Pears** are available throughout the year. America's most popular variety is the Bartlett pear. Other favorites include the Anjou, Bosc, Comice, and Seckel. Pears do not ripen on the tree, which is why they are hard when harvested. Choose firm fruit of good color for the variety of pear. Surface blemishes and russeting are natural for some varieties and do not affect fruit quality. Ripen pears at room temperature until they yield to gentle pressure at the stem end. Don't wait until pears feel soft. Pears ripen from the inside out and should not be kept until they feel soft on the outside. When ripe, refrigerate pears immediately. For cooking or baking, use firm, slightly underripe pears.

▶ **Rhubarb** is also known as "pieplant," because it is frequently teamed with strawberries and used as a filling for pies. The long pink or red stalks of the rhubarb are very tart and must be sweetened with a generous dose of honey or sugar. When cooking rhubarb into a sauce, take care not to overcook it and add only a small amount of water to the pan. Too much cooking or water will turn it into mush. Always discard the rhubarb leaves; they contain oxalic acid and are toxic.

GRAINS

Grains are the seeds of grasses that are either used whole or ground into flour. The type of grass—barley, corn, oats, rice, wheat—determines the nutrient value and taste of the grain. When combined with legumes, grains provide the building blocks of protein, such as in the traditional Southern dish of beans and rice.

Grains are purchased dried and keep well for about six months if stored in an airtight container in a cool, dark place. Some grains, such as cornmeal and oats, are more susceptible to insect larvae and should be used faster than barley and rice. Cooking times vary, and package directions should be followed closely. Overcooking grains robs them of nutrients.

▶ **Barley** needs to be rinsed well before cooking if the whole grain is used. The outer husk is removed to produce pearl barley, often used in soups and casseroles.

▶ **Buckwheat** is ground from the seeds of a plant in the rhubarb family. It is a Japanese staple and used to make flour and soba noodles. Because it is gluten free, it is a good choice for people sensitive to wheat.

▶ **Corn** is ground into both coarse cornmeal (polenta) and fine cornmeal, hominy, or grits.

▶ **Couscous** is a quick-cooking, tiny grain made from semolina, or the hard part of durum wheat. A staple in Middle Eastern cooking, couscous combines well with vegetables and spices.

▶ **Oats** are a gluten-free grain typically used for oatmeal by removing the hulls from whole oats. The resulting oat groats are then steamed and rolled to flatten them into flakes. Thus, they are often called rolled oats.

▶ **Rye,** when ground, is added to white and whole-wheat flours to make dark breads.

▶ **Quinoa** is a South American grain loaded with nutrients. It can be substituted for rice in many dishes.

▶ **Wheat** is typically ground into flour and is available as cracked wheat, wheat flakes, and wheat germ (the heart of the grain and thus especially nutritious). Whole-wheat flour is more nutritious than white flour, but it does not store as well. Freeze whole-wheat flour in airtight containers for longer storage.

MEAT

Meat is typically considered one of four types of red meat—beef (from cattle); pork (from pigs); lamb (from young sheep); and veal (from calves or young cattle). All meat in the United States is inspected for wholesomeness, and most meat is graded. In most supermarkets beef, pork, and veal cuts are graded choice, while pork sold in supermarkets is usually graded U.S. No. 2—the equivalent of choice. Only a prime grade (for beef, veal, and lamb) and U.S. No. 1 (for pork) are superior. These are usually only available at specialty markets. Avoid buying beef, veal, or lamb that is graded good or standard, along with pork grades of U.S. Nos. 3 and 4.

Most shoppers and cooks differentiate meat by the cut, such as a chop, roast, or steak. The cut is determined by where the piece of meat comes from on the animal's body. While the names of cuts may vary across the country, the important thing to remember about cuts of meat is that not all cuts can be cooked in the same way.

Usually cuts that require more cooking time will be less expensive, but they are often more flavorful. The most tender cuts, which come from little-used muscle, can be cooked most quickly. Pork chops, for example, come from the mid, upper side of the pig, and can be easily broiled or grilled very quickly at high heat. A flank steak, which comes from the well-used lower, rear side of a steer, needs to be marinated or pounded before broiling or grilling. At the other extreme are round steaks and round roasts, from the lower, rear part of the steer. Because these cuts are from heavily used muscle, they require slow cooking at low heat to release their flavor and make them tender.

Always make sure you're buying the type of cut of meat called for in a recipe. If you're unsure, ask your butcher. The most well-known and common cuts of meat are described in the following sections, along with buying tips. Some tips that apply to meats in general follow on page 188:

WILD ABOUT RICE

Rice comes in dozens of varieties and flavors. Generally, there are two types of rice—long grain, which produces a fluffy texture when cooked, and short grain, which sticks together. Rice is sold in packages and generally will keep well in a cool, dark place in an airtight container. Some rices need to be rinsed before cooking, but most rices can be cooked quickly in boiling water. Follow directions on the packaging, but check the pot to make sure the liquid isn't absorbed too fast and the rice begins to burn. To keep rice from sticking together, add a tablespoon of oil to the water. Don't stir rice while it's cooking—it can mash the grains.

White rice is the food staple of many countries. Converted white rice contains more nutrients than ordinary white rice, which is parboiled before milling. Some of the varieties of white rice are arborio, an Italian rice used to make the classic dish, risotto; basmati, an Indian long-grain, flavorful rice; and pearl rice, a tiny rice.

Brown rice, available in both short and long-grain versions, is more nutritious than white rice, because it contains the bran and germ of the rice kernel. These are removed during milling to produce white rice, which is the staple food for about one-third of the world's population. Brown rice typically needs about twice the cooking time of white rice.

Wild rice is a cereal grain, but not a true rice. Native to the upper Great Lakes region, it was originally grown and gathered by the Chippewa Indians. Wild rice has a nutty flavor and is higher in protein than ordinary rice.

PERFECT PASTA

It's no surprise that pasta is becoming an essential part of the American diet. Pasta, the Italian word for "dough," is rich in energizing complex carbohydrates, essential B vitamins, and iron; easy to prepare; and adaptable to various types of meals. And when pasta is served with legumes, all the essential amino acids are present, making it a good choice for a "meatless" meal that still provides plenty of protein.

Pasta is used to describe all the various products made with wheat flour and water, such as linguine, spaghetti, and ravioli. These specific names describe the shape, not the content, of the particular dough. Pasta can be made from whole or white wheat; when eggs are added, it's usually called a noodle. Today, however, egg-free noodles, as well as rice noodles, are readily available in pasta forms. Ingredients added to give pasta color include beets and tomatoes to make it reddish, carrots for an orange hue, and spinach for a green color.

Fresh pasta should be stored in the refrigerator and used within 24 hours. Dried pasta should be stored in a cool, dry place. It will keep almost indefinitely. Cooking pasta is quick, but tricky. For both store-bought fresh and dried pasta, follow package directions. Pasta should be cooked at a fast boil. This method circulates the pasta during cooking so that the cooking results will be more consistent. A faster cooking time makes fresh pasta more convenient than dried; fresh pasta usually cooks in 3

minutes or less, depending on desired doneness, while dried pasta requires 7 to 12 minutes cooking time. When substituting dried pasta for fresh, make sure to allow extra cooking time. Pasta that is al dente is tender, but firm. Leftover pasta can be frozen and reheated or microwaved. Refrigerated pasta can be freshened by rinsing with hot or cold water, depending on how you plan to use it. Of the dozens of pastas available, the following are the most commonly available:

▶ Fettuccini, lasagna, and tagliatelle are basically flat-type pastas used with heavy sauces and other thick ingredients.

▶ Linguine, spaghetti, spaghettini, and vermicelli are all very thin pastas, typically used with thin sauces, either meatless or with meatballs or ground meat.

▶ Elbow macaroni, spiral macaroni, fusilli, penne, rigatoni, and shells are particularly good at absorbing sauces.

▶ Cannelloni and ravioli are filled with cheese or other fillings. Cannelloni has open ends, while ravioli is sealed.

▶ Orzo, which actually means barley, is a tiny pasta that looks more like rice.

▶ To save money, trim beef and veal roasts yourself. Store the bones in a heavy bag in the freezer, and use them to make beef stock.

▶ A more expensive cut that has no bones or fat may be more economical in the long run than a cheap cut with a lot of bone and fat.

▶ Thaw meat in the refrigerator or microwave, not at room temperature. Allow about 5 hours for each pound of meat to thaw in the refrigerator. Follow your microwave's instructions for thawing meat. Never refreeze meat that has been thawed and not cooked.

▶ Marinating less tender cuts of meat in a bath of oil, vinegar, and herbs provides a twofold benefit—it infuses the meat with a wonderful flavor and also penetrates the meat fibers to help tenderize them.

▶ To french a bone means to scrape it clean of fat and meat so that a 2-inch length of clean bone is exposed. This is usually done to beef and pork rib bones. In lamb, the most common cut that is frenched is the rack. In addition to enhancing the appearance of the meat (frenched bones are often decorated with paper frills), exposing the bones makes it easier to carve between them.

Beef

For years, beef was considered the mainstay of American families. Today per capita beef consumption has declined, both because of interest in other meats and increasing emphasis on beans, grains, and vegetables. But Americans continue to consume beef in much higher proportions than other countries, due to its availability, cost, and ease of preparation.

▶ To meet USDA standards, all ground beef must be at least 70 percent lean. Ground sirloin and ground round are the leanest; ground chuck contains more fat. Usually, the higher the fat content, the lower the cost per pound. Ground beef is typically used for burgers, which can be broiled, fried, or grilled; meatballs; and meatloaf. Use or freeze ground beef within 24 hours after purchase.

▶ **Roasts**—with the exception of a standing rib roast, which is more like uncut rib steaks—need time and added moisture to release their flavors. Rump roasts, rolled roasts, and chuck roasts can be browned and then roasted until well done or cooked on top of the stove in a pot with added vegetables and stock. The larger the roast, the longer it can keep in the refrigerator, but freeze any roast if you do not plan to cook it within three to four days, depending on size.

▶ **Steaks** come in various types. Steaks from the short loin portion include club, T-bone, and porterhouse. They're more tender—and expensive—than sirloins. Tournedos are small beef steaks cut from the tenderloin. Rib steaks come from the rib portion. All of these can be broiled or grilled. Flank and round steaks, from the lower part of the animal, need to be marinated before grilling or cooked slowly at lower heat. Steaks can last only a little longer in the refrigerator than ground beef. Freeze it if you do not plan to use it within two to three days.

Lamb

From six weeks to a year old, a lamb produces lightly flavored, relatively lean meat. Mutton, the meat from sheep older than a year, is common in England and Australia. Ground lamb, often used in Middle Eastern recipes, can be substituted for ground beef, but it has a distinctive flavor and more fat. Lamb riblets or spareribs come from the breast portion of the lamb, not the rib portion. The lamb breast is cut between the ribs to form riblets. They are best braised, or marinated

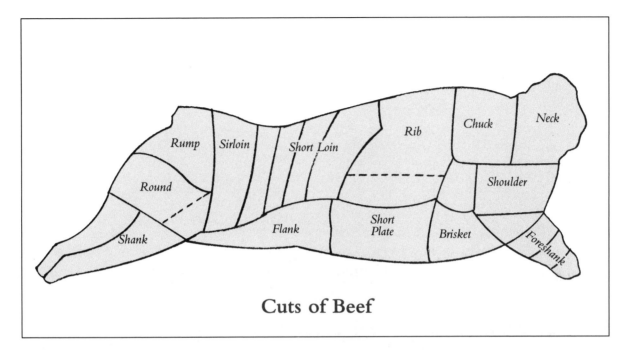

Cuts of Beef

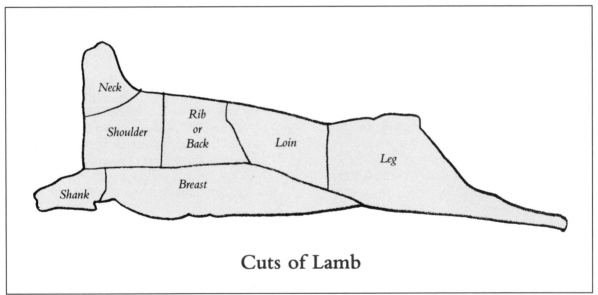

Cuts of Lamb

and grilled. Like beef, refrigerator storage depends on size. Cook ground lamb within 24 hours; roasts within three to four days.

Pork

Pork is available cured or uncured in a wide variety of cuts. Curing refers to a variety of processes by which the meat is prepared before sale, but it does not mean that the meat is precooked. Bacon, for example, is cured, but requires further cooking. A fully cooked ham does not need to be cooked. Pork chops, the equivalent of beef steaks cut from the loin, are not cured. All pork must be thoroughly cooked because of the possible presence of the trichina parasite.

▶ Bacon is highly perishable and should be used soon after purchasing. It will keep in the

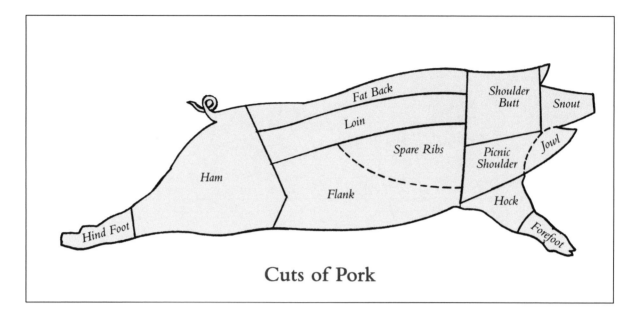

Cuts of Pork

refrigerator about ten days or can be frozen for up to three months. Canadian bacon is a lean smoked meat and a popular breakfast food. Because it is purchased fully cooked, it heats quickly in a skillet over medium–high heat.

▶ **Pork chops and roasts** refer to center-cut, loin, and rib chops and sirloin roasts cut from the loin. They can be broiled, grilled, roasted, and even baked. The tenderloin, the most tender meat cut from the loin, is a strip of meat that lies along each side of the backbone. When it is cut crosswise into slices, it forms circles that are called medallions. To be on the safe side, freeze pork chops and roasts if you don't plan to cook them within two to three days.

▶ **Ham** comes from the hind leg of a pig. It is usually thought of as a cured meat, although it can be purchased uncured and is then referred to as fresh ham or pork leg. The distinctive flavors of hams are produced by the pigs' diets—peanuts, acorns, apples, corn, or peaches—and the type of wood over which they are smoked—apple, hickory, or oak. Fully cooked hams and even canned hams should be refrigerated. Check the label for storage information. Packaged ham slices or whole hams should be stored in the coldest part of the refrigerator. Use ham slices within three or four days; whole hams within a week. Ham does not freeze well; it loses flavor and texture when frozen. If you must freeze ham, try to use it within a month or so.

▶ When a recipe calls for ribs, you must choose between spareribs, baby ribs, country-style ribs, and back ribs. Basically, they all come from the midsection of the pig, and most of the weight is in the bones. Spareribs have the least amount of meat; baby or baby-back ribs, which are cut from the loin, have more meat; and country-style ribs have much more meat per pound. All of them can be grilled, broiled, or baked. Because they are mostly bone, you'll want to buy more per serving than you would for most meats. Cook ribs within one to two days of purchase.

Veal

Veal refers to the meat from young calves fed a special diet to produce lean, light-colored meat. It is typically the most expensive meat per pound. Because of its delicacy, nearly all cuts of veal benefit from sautéing, braising, or low-temperature roasting. The most well-known cuts are chops, which are cut from the shoulder and can be braised or fried; roasts, cut from the

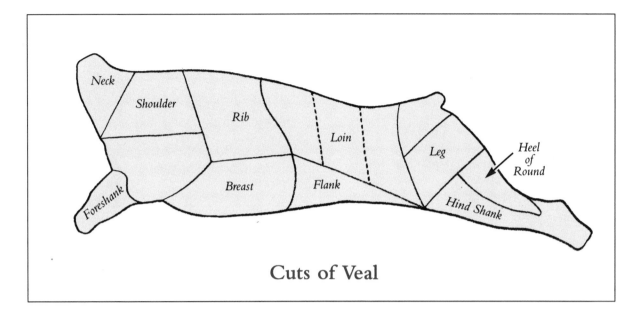

Cuts of Veal

shoulder or loin; and breast, which can be cooked slowly. Veal should be cooked within one to two days of purchase.

NUTS

Whether they're whole, chopped, or ground, nuts add nutrition and flavor to meals and dishes. Their high oil content, however, negates some of the benefits of their high protein content. Varieties include almond, brazil, cashew, chestnut, coconut, hazelnut (or filbert), macadamia, peanut, pecan, pine (or pignoli), pistachio, and walnut, both black and English. Most varieties can be bought whole, chopped, or ground; salted or unsalted; roasted or spiced. Generally, whole, unshelled nuts are the least expensive.

When purchasing whole nuts, estimate 2 pounds unshelled for 1 pound shelled to make sure you have enough. Most unshelled nuts will keep at room temperature for up to six months, but shelled nuts should be stored in airtight containers in the refrigerator or freezer to keep them from becoming rancid. Throw out any that have mold.

▸ To remove thin skins, place the nuts on a baking sheet and bake them in a preheated 350°F oven until the skins begin to flake off.

This will vary with the variety. They can easily burn, so watch them closely. Remove them from the oven, wrap them in a heavy towel, and rub them against the towel to remove as much of the skins as possible.

▸ To grind nuts, use a nut grater or grinder and grind only a few nuts at a time to prevent them from becoming oily.

▸ To toast nuts, place them in a single layer on a baking sheet and toast in a preheated 350°F oven until very lightly browned. Again, watch them closely. Depending on the variety, this should take from 3 to 10 minutes. Use them immediately or store them in a covered container in the refrigerator.

POULTRY

Poultry refers to domesticated birds, including chicken, Rock Cornish hens, duck, goose, and turkey. Game birds include wild ducks/geese and pheasants.

Families no longer have to fight for their favorite parts of the chicken. Chickens are no longer packaged either whole or cut up. You can buy packages of breasts, thighs, legs, and wings. At the same time, turkey is no longer restricted to the Thanksgiving table. Its relatively low fat content makes it a good substitute for beef and pork in hot dogs, lunch meat, and even sausages.

Ground turkey and fresh turkey parts, now available year-round in supermarket meat cases, are finding their way to the dinner table with increasing frequency. Ground turkey's low fat content and excellent flavor make it a popular replacement for ground beef in a wide variety of recipes.

Poultry Packaging

Most poultry sold today is packaged according to size:

▶ **Broilers or fryers** are young chickens weighing between 2½ to 4 pounds. They are available whole, cut up, or in packaged parts.

▶ **Roasters,** weighing between 4 and 8 pounds, are sold whole. The smaller-size roasters can be cut up for baking or frying.

▶ **Stewing hens,** weighing between 3 and 7 pounds, are older birds with tougher meat. They are best for making stocks and stews.

▶ **Capons,** young cocks that were castrated, are tender and fat and command a premium price.

▶ **Rock Cornish hens,** the result of two breeds of chicken, are small, young birds weighing between 1 and 2 pounds.

▶ **Turkeys,** sold by weight, include small (4 to 10 pounds); medium (10 to 20 pounds); and large (over 20 pounds).

▶ **Ducks** usually weigh between 5 and 6 pounds, while a goose usually weighs between 8 and 15 pounds.

Buying and Storing Poultry

▶ Although it's difficult to see through the packaging, avoid poultry that has bruised or dry-looking skin.

▶ Fresh, uncooked chicken can be refrigerated for up to two days. If the chicken is packaged in plastic bags or on plastic-sealed trays, it may be refrigerated in the original packaging.

▶ If the chicken comes wrapped in butcher paper, unwrap and repackage it in airtight plastic bags or plastic wrap. When you are ready to cook the chicken, rinse it under cold water, pat dry with paper towels, and trim away any excess fat.

▶ While whole birds are less perishable than cut-up birds, poultry should never be refrigerated more than 48 hours.

▶ To properly freeze fresh chicken or turkey, remove it from its original packaging. Rinse it under cold water, pat dry with paper towels, and trim away excess fat. For a whole chicken, remove the giblets from the body cavity. Wrap the chicken in moistureproof freezer paper, label it with the date, and freeze. Wrap, label, and freeze the giblets separately. Use this same procedure to freeze chicken pieces, but be sure to separate the pieces into several packages so they freeze quickly.

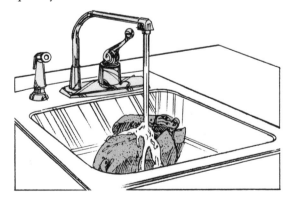

▶ Freeze whole chickens for up to eight months, chicken pieces for up to six months, and giblets for up to three months.

▶ Store-purchased frozen turkeys should be put in the freezer in their original wrappings as soon as possible after purchase.

▶ To defrost uncooked frozen chicken, thaw it in its wrapping in the refrigerator. Allow enough time for it to thaw completely, about three to four hours per pound. Caution: Never defrost chicken on the countertop at room temperature.

▶ Defrost a frozen turkey in its original wrapper inside the refrigerator. Be sure to allow enough time for complete thawing—about two days for a 12-pound turkey, three to four days for larger birds.

▶ Remember that ground chicken and turkey are more perishable than ground beef. Use them within 24 hours of purchase or freeze.

SEASONINGS

Onions, garlic, salt, and pepper are basic seasonings; it's hard to cook without these staples. But herbs and spices are becoming more important in American cooking, because we can use them to replace sodium and fats in our diets. These healthier seasonings can make the difference between a bland, lean dish and a dinner without leftovers. The trick is in learning to use herbs and spices correctly.

Essentially, herbs are the leaves of various herbal plants. They are often available fresh, and many more are available dried or ground. Spices are the seeds, buds, fruits, flowers, bark, and roots of plants. Spices are much more pungent than herbs. In some cases, a plant produces both a spice and an herb. Fresh or dried cilantro is made from the leaves of the herb. Coriander is the name of the seeds, either ground or whole, from the same herb. Other seasonings are made from a mix of spices, such as chili powder, or a mix of herbs, such as bouquet garni.

Specific seasonings work best with specific foods. For example, some seasonings work

BONING A CHICKEN BREAST

1. For easier handling, freeze the chicken until it is firm, but not hard. Remove the skin.

2. For each breast half, use a sharp knife to make three or four arched cuts between the meat and the bone, lifting the meat away with your free hand. (Or, slip your fingers between the meat and the bone and work the meat free without the aid of a knife.)

3. When the meat and bone are separated, remove the heavy white tendon that runs along the length of the breast. This will prevent the meat from shrinking as it cooks.

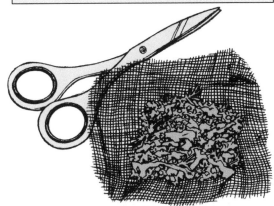

well with meat and poultry but overpower seafood. And because some herbs and spices work wonderfully together, while others fight each other, it's wise to follow a recipe unless you know that a specific herb or spice can be substituted in a dish.

In cooking, herbs are more delicate than spices. If added too soon, they can lose their flavor. Conversely, spices need longer cooking time, both to burn off bitter oils and to bring out their flavor. Generally, you'll want to add spices at the beginning of cooking and herbs near the end.

Until recently, the only fresh herb available at supermarkets was parsley, but now hot-house variety herbs of all kinds are available year-round. The flavor in fresh herbs comes from aromatic essential oils that are released by chopping or heating. When herbs are dried these oils become concentrated. When substituting dried herbs for fresh, use about one-third as much. Make sure fresh herbs are really fresh and not limp when you buy them. They will keep refrigerated for varying lengths of time, but most herbs should be used quickly.

Herbs and spices should be stored away from the heat of the range to preserve their full strength and pungency. It's best to store them in airtight containers in a cool cupboard. Most ground spices store well for about a year, twice as long as ground or dried herbs, which only have a shelf life of about six months.

Of the various herbs and spices available, the following are the most used in cooking:

Herbs

Basil: Available fresh and dried, the sweet taste of basil is an essential herb in Italian dishes and the basis for the most popular Italian pesto sauce.

Bay leaf: The dried whole leaves of this herb add tang to stews and meat dishes, but make certain that you remove the bay leaf before serving.

Chives: As a member of the onion family, chives have a delicate flavor and are generally used as a fresh garnish. Mince fresh chives with a knife or snip with kitchen scissors just before using.

Dill: A member of the parsley family, dill weed is the dried soft feathery leaves of the dill plant. Its distinctive flavor can easily dominate a dish, so use it sparingly at first.

Marjoram: With a taste close to oregano, marjoram is typically used in fish, meat, and poultry dishes and in tomato sauces.

Mint: Available both fresh and dried in dozens of varieties, mint is used in vegetable and fruit-based dishes, as well as teas.

Oregano: A strongly flavored herb, oregano can easily overpower delicate dishes, but is perfect in tomato sauces, soups, and most Italian dishes.

Parsley: When purchasing fresh parsley, look for bright green bunches with a fresh aroma. To store, wash parsley well, shaking off excess water. Wrap parsley in paper towels before placing it in a plastic bag. Refrigerate until ready to use.

Rosemary: Although it does not combine well with other herbs, the distinctive pine flavor of rosemary makes it a good choice for meats and poultry, particularly tucked inside a chicken or lamb roast, and on grilled food.

Sage: Fresh sage is much stronger than dried sage, but either combines well with game, poultry, and stuffings, to impart the characteristic sage flavor.

Salt substitutes: Various varieties of salt substitutes comprised of a mix of dried herbs and/or spices are available. They can be used in equal amounts for salt.

Tarragon: Tarragon is widely used on chicken, fish, and vegetables, as well as in many sauces. Dried tarragon loses much of the pungency of the fresh leaf.

Thyme: Thyme is widely used to add flavor to vegetables, meat, poultry, fish dishes, soups, and cream sauces. English thyme is probably the most popular of the many varieties of thyme.

Spices

Allspice: Made from dried spice berries, this spice gets its name because it resembles the combined flavors of cinnamon, nutmeg, and cloves.

Capers: These are the small, pea-size buds of a flower from the caper bush. Found mostly in Central America and the Mediterranean, capers add pungency to sauces, dips, and relishes. Usually these green buds are pickled and can be found in the condiment section of the supermarket.

Cayenne: This hot red pepper needs to be used sparingly to avoid overpowering a dish, but it is essential in many Latin American and Southwestern dishes.

Cinnamon: While the ground bark is used mainly in desserts, whole bark sticks can be used to flavor cider and other hot drinks.

Clove: This sweet spice is available in whole cloves and ground and used in both baked meat dishes and many desserts.

Cumin: Ground from cumin seeds, cumin is used in many Latin American and Southwestern dishes for its smokey and hot flavor. Use it sparingly.

Curry powder: Curry powder is formed by blending together a number of spices, including turmeric, cardamom, cumin, pepper, cloves, cinnamon, nutmeg, and sometimes ginger. Chilies give it heat, and ground dried garlic provides a depth of taste. Curry blends vary depending on their use. Milder powders are used for fish and eggs; stronger ones season meats and poultry.

Chili powder: Like curry powder, chili powder is a blend of fairly hot spices and ground chilies.

Ginger: A gnarled, tan-colored root, fresh ginger adds its own distinctive pungency and aroma to foods and is used extensively in the dishes of the Far East.

Nutmeg: This spice has a distinctive, pungent fragrance and a warm, slightly sweet taste that is used to flavor baked goods, candy, puddings, meats, sauces, vegetables, and eggnog.

Paprika: Ground paprika adds zip without the heat to dishes such as potato salad, as well as a good flavor to seafood.

Saffron: Given that it's the most expensive spice in the world, it's fortunate that it doesn't take much saffron to flavor a dish. This fragrant spice is used most often in soups and rice dishes, reflecting its Far East heritage.

Tumeric: Related to ginger, tumeric is an essential component of curry powder and was once know as Indian saffron. Use it sparingly—a little turmeric goes a long way.

SEAFOOD

Low in cholesterol, fat, and sodium, seafood makes for a nutritious entrée. It's also quick and easy to prepare, which is probably another reason why Americans are eating more fish every year. Freshwater fish live in lakes and rivers, while saltwater fish come from the ocean or ocean bays. Shellfish refer to fish that live in hard shells.

FRESHWATER FISH
Brook Trout
Buffalo Fish
Carp
Catfish
Crappie
Lake Trout
Mullet
Pickerel
Salmon (some varieties)
Whitefish
Yellow Perch
Yellow Pike

OCEAN FISH
Atlantic Herring
Bluefish
Flounder
Grouper
Haddock
Halibut
Pollack
Pompano
Red Snapper
Salmon (some varieties)
Sea Bass
Scrod

Sole
Swordfish
Tuna
Turbot
Whiting

SHELLFISH
Abalone
Clams
Crab
Crawfish
Lobster
Oysters
Mussels
Prawns
Shrimp
Snails
Squid

Buying Seafood

The best way to tell if a fish is fresh is to look it in the eye, examine its gills, and smell it. If the eyes are clear and bulge a little, if the gills are pink, and the smell is fresh, it is fresh. There are only a few exceptions to this rule. If fish are already cut into fillets or steaks, the test is more difficult. You then have to rely on firm and shiny flesh. There should be no darkening around the edges of the fish or discolorations. One of the best ways to make sure you are consistently buying fresh seafood is to shop at a reputable fish store.

▶ Fresh fish should not be accompanied by a fishy or ammonia smell.

▶ Avoid prepackaged fresh fish, because there is no way to tell if is really old.

▶ When buying shellfish—such as clams and mussels—in the shells, be sure shells are tightly closed. If the shell is slightly open, tap it lightly. It should immediately snap shut. If it doesn't, the fish is dead and should be discarded.

▶ Make sure live lobsters are really alive. Their legs should move, and the tails should not be limp.

▶ Most shrimp are previously frozen and thawed for sale. They shouldn't smell or be

mushy. If they are, discard them immediately and find a different fish store.

▶ Don't buy crabs with slimy or greasy shells.

Storing Seafood

▶ If you store fish in the refrigerator too long, you'll defeat the whole point of buying fresh fish. It won't be fresh, and it won't taste fresh.

▶ Before refrigerating, take off any wrappings, rinse the fish under cold water, and pat dry with a paper towel. Then refrigerate fish immediately at between 32 and 37°F. Use within 24 hours of purchase.

▶ To freeze fish, do so immediately after it's been caught or purchased. Remove wrappings, rinse it under cold water, and pat very dry with paper towels. Wrap in plastic and then in aluminum foil before placing it in the freezer. Plan to use it as soon as possible for best quality, at least within one month.

▶ Never refreeze fish that has been previously frozen and thawed.

▶ Always thaw frozen fish in the refrigerator, not at room temperature.

▶ Store live shellfish—such as clams, mussels, and oysters—in the refrigerator for no more than 24 hours. Keep them moist with a damp cloth or paper towel, but make sure they can breathe. Live lobsters and crabs can be stored in brown paper bags, but again, make sure the wrapping is not airtight.

▶ Most fish do not freeze well. The exceptions are shrimp, lobster tails, and some thick fish, such as salmon.

VEGETABLES

Vegetables are a bulb, leaf, root, shoot, or even seed of various plants. While they vary in nutritional content, storage, and ways to be cooked, there are a few tips to keep in mind about all vegetables:

▶ Fresh vegetables in season can be considerably cheaper than the same foods frozen or canned.

▶ Vegetables stored in the crisper of your refrigerator will keep better if the crisper is at least ⅔ full. If it is empty or almost empty, the vegetables will dry out. When storing only a few vegetables in the refrigerator, put them into airtight plastic bags or plastic containers, then into the crisper.

▶ To freshen blemished or wilted produce, snip off all brown edges, sprinkle the vegetables with cold water, wrap them in towels, and place them in your refrigerator for an hour or more.

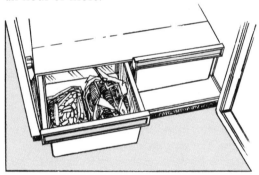

▶ When slicing raw vegetables, it sometimes helps to cut a small slice off one side to form a steady base.

▶ If you're simmering vegetables and you need to add more water, use hot water, not cold. Adding cold water may toughen the vegetable fibers.

▶ Economize on time and fuel by steaming two vegetables simultaneously in the same pot. If you want to serve them separately, keep each vegetable wrapped in aluminum foil during cooking.

▶ To make frozen vegetables taste as much as possible like fresh ones, pour boiling water on them before cooking. This flushes away all traces of frozen water.

▶ If you've purchased fresh vegetables and find live insects in them, drive them out by soaking the food for 30 minutes in cold water to which you've added a few tablespoons of salt or vinegar.

BRASSICAS

Bok choy
Broccoli
Brussels sprouts
Cabbage
Cauliflower
Kale

The most familiar brassicas—broccoli, brussels sprouts, cabbage, and cauliflower—are available year-round. As with leafy vegetables, choose brassicas that have bright leaves and no signs of wilting. Store them unwashed in the refrigerator, and use as soon as possible. To prepare, remove hard stems and hard outer leaves, and rinse them well. Broccoli, cabbage, and cauliflower can be eaten raw or cooked. Be sure not to overcook these vegetables. Not only do they become mushy, they lose their

nutrients quickly if overcooked.

▶ To ensure even cooking of broccoli stems over 1 inch in diameter, cut lengthwise gashes in stem ends before cooking.

▶ Peel the thick skin off broccoli stalks (the part you're often tempted to throw out), then slice the stalks very thinly and add the slices to a tossed salad. They're crisp and delicious.

▶ For brussels sprouts with the best flavor, look for tightly closed buds with fresh green leaves.

▶ Speed the cooking time for brussels sprouts by marking an "X" with a knife on the bottom of each before putting it in the pot.

▶ To soften and peel whole cabbage leaves for stuffed cabbage, core the cabbage head and freeze it for several days. Put the head into a large bowl of hot water, and the leaves will peel right off.

▶ Cabbage that has been frozen before cooking will not have the characteristic overpowering odor. After defrosting, there will be no odor when the vegetable is boiled.

▶ Prevent red cabbage from turning purple during cooking by adding a tablespoon of vinegar to the cooking water.

▶ To retain the fresh white appearance of cauliflower while cooking, add the juice of half a lemon or lime or 1 tablespoon of milk to the cooking water.

BULB VEGETABLES

    Garlic
    Leeks
    Onions
    Scallions
    Shallots

This group of vegetables is typically used to flavor other foods, although baked garlic and onions are increasingly showing up on their own as a sidedish. Scallions or green onions are baby onions used raw or lightly cooked. Leeks, a versatile and mild-tasting member of the onion family, add a subtle, yet distinctive flavor to recipes. Shallots, sort of a cross between garlic and onions, have a very mild flavor. The name "onion" actually refers to a wide variety of onions—pearl, white, red, yellow, Spanish, and even Vidalia, a sweet onion grown in Georgia. Leeks and scallions are sold fresh and should be refrigerated where they'll keep for about one week. The rest of the onion family and garlic are cured after harvesting. Look for firm garlic and onions with no signs of sprouting. Store them in a cool dark place where they'll keep for about one month.

▶ The easiest and fastest way to peel garlic cloves is to trim off the ends and crush the cloves with the bottom of a heavy saucepan or the flat side of a large knife. The peels can then be easily removed. If the cloves are to be left whole, trim them and drop them into boiling water for 5 to 10 seconds, then place them in cold water and drain. The peels should slip right off.

▶ Avoid burning garlic, which makes its flavor very bitter.

▶ Look for leeks with fresh tops that are small to medium in size. They should be no more than 1½ inches in diameter; larger leeks are not as tender or flavorful.

▶ Leeks grow in sand, and they have to be thoroughly washed before using. To clean them thoroughly, cut two perpendicular slits, starting about three inches from the root end and running all the way through the stem end. Wash the vegetables thoroughly under cold running water to remove all dirt.

▶ When exposed to the air through peeling or chopping, an enzyme in onions can irritate the tear ducts causing your eyes to water. Sometimes chilling the onion before cutting can reduce this effect. It also helps to breathe only through your nose.

▶ Peel fresh white onions quickly if you first immerse them in boiling water for a minute or two.

▶ If you make an "X" at the root end of an onion with a sharp knife, the onion won't pop apart during cooking.

▶ Soak onion rings in cold water for an hour to make them milder and more suitable for use in salads.

CUCUMBERS AND SQUASHES

Acorn squash
Butternut squash
Cucumber
Pumpkin
Summer squash
Zucchini

Characterized by their thick skins and many seeds, this group of vegetables is not as nutritious as most. Cucumbers, for example, are 96 percent water. Those sold in the supermarket produce section are often waxed to preserve the moisture content. Squashes vary in size and shape. Acorn squash, named for its resemblance to an acorn, has dark green, fluted skin and yellow-to-orange pulp. With their thinner, edible skins and seeds, summer squash vary from dark-skinned zucchini to yellow summer squash. The mild, delicate flavor found in all varieties of summer squash make them largely interchangeable in recipes.

▶ Wash cucumbers thoroughly in cold water to remove the waxy protective covering if you're using the cucumbers unpeeled. Refrigerate whole cucumbers in a plastic bag for up to one week. To seed cucumbers, cut cucumbers in half lengthwise and scrape out the seeds with a small spoon.

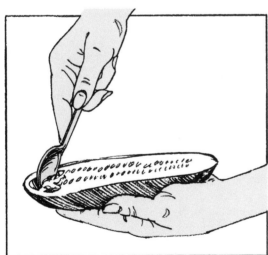

▶ Expert gardeners usually recommend summer squash when it is no more than 5

inches in length. It can be steamed, fried, stuffed, or eaten raw.

▶ Pumpkins can be used in ravioli, cheesecakes, relishes, and, of course, baked in a pie.

LEAFY VEGETABLES

Arugula
Chicory
Escarole
Boston and iceberg lettuce
Radicchio
Romaine
Sorrel
Spinach
Swiss chard
Watercress

Once reserved almost exclusively for salads, leafy vegetables are making their way into other dishes, and spinach, the one leafy vegetable that used to be cooked, is fast becoming a salad staple. Leafy vegetables range in flavor from the very mild, nearly bland taste of iceberg lettuce, to the hot tang of watercress. Radicchio, the only vegetable in this group that is not green, resembles a small head of red lettuce.

Select leafy vegetables that are crisp with no signs of withering. With the exception of iceberg lettuce, all leafy vegetables have a relatively short shelf life and should be eaten as soon as possible, within two to three days. Wash them in plenty of cold water and spin-dry in a salad spinner; you can also drain them thoroughly and dry them with paper towels. If they are not to be eaten immediately, refrigerate them with two or three wet paper towels in a closed plastic bag to keep the leaves crisp.

▶ Lettuce will rust more slowly if there is no excess moisture in its container. To keep your lettuce bag or refrigerator vegetable compartment relatively dry, put in a few dry paper towels or dry sponges to absorb excess water.

▶ To core a head of iceberg lettuce, strip off any coarse outside leaves. Holding the head core-end down, whack it onto the kitchen counter, and lift or twist out the core with your fingers. You can also core a head using a knife, but the cut edges will discolor.

▶ Wash spinach by plunging it into a bowl of water two or three times to get rid of any grit.

▶ To lock color and flavor into cooked spinach, begin by washing the spinach well in cold water and removing the stems and spines. Lift the spinach leaves from the water and place them in a heavy nonaluminum pan. The spinach should fit in tightly. Cover and steam over medium heat, tossing occasionally until the spinach is just wilted.

▶ When you want to use cooked spinach in stuffings or molded vegetable dishes, cook it, then drain well. Place the spinach in a cotton or linen towel. Holding it over a bowl or the sink, squeeze the spinach until all excess moisture has been removed.

▶ Feel free to use both the stems and tangy leaves of watercress.

MUSHROOMS

All mushrooms are fungi, but we use the term "mushroom" to distinguish edible fungi from poisonous toadstools. Recently there has been an explosion of mushrooms in the marketplace. In fancy produce stores you can now find many varieties of both fresh and dried mushrooms—cèpes (otherwise known as porcini), chanterelles, enokitake, morels, and shiitake, to name just a few. The domestic white button mushroom, however, continues to be the most popular and widely available. Choose button mushrooms that have caps tightly closed around the stems. Do not peel mushrooms, and do not wash mushrooms until you are ready to use them. Wipe mushrooms clean with a damp paper towel— do not soak them in water. Cut off a small slice from the bottom of each mushroom, and they are ready to use.

▶ Canned mushrooms cost more than fresh ones, so you'll save if you buy fresh ones— especially if they're on sale—and freeze them for future use.

▶ Don't refrigerate mushrooms in a sealed plastic bag where they can become slimy very quickly. Use a brown paper bag, which confines the humidity that keeps mushrooms fresh and permits them to breathe.

▶ To cut fresh mushrooms into uniform sections, try using an egg slicer.

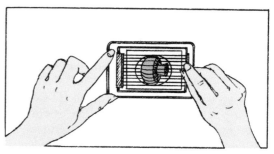

▶ To maintain the whiteness and firmness of mushrooms while sautéing them, add a teaspoon of lemon juice to ¼-pound of melted butter.

PODS AND SEEDS

Corn
Fava beans
Green beans
Okra
Peas
Runner beans
Snow peas
String beans

Highly nutritious pods and seeds are staples in our diet. Because they retain their nutritional content when frozen right after picking, they are easily available year-round. Some of the varieties in this group are also dried and then cooked as a grain or legume. If purchased fresh, these vegetables lose their nutrient value—and flavor—very quickly. Use them as soon as possible or refrigerate for one to two days. They should be cooked very lightly to preserve their nutrients.

▶ Sweet corn varieties can be golden yellow, white, or a mixture of both.

▶ In selecting fresh sweet corn, choose ears with fresh-looking husks that are cool to the touch. If displayed without husks, look for fully developed kernels with good color. Use corn promptly for the freshest and sweetest flavor.

▶ To maintain maximum quality of fresh sweet corn if you can't serve it immediately, shuck the corn, wrap in plastic, and refrigerate.

▶ When cooking corn in boiling water, do not add salt while corn is cooking. Salted water will toughen kernels.

▶ To grate fresh corn, place a four-sided grater in a large bowl, and grate it over the largest grate.

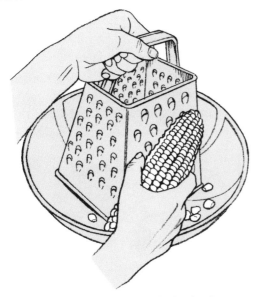

▶ If you like to grill corn with the husks on, try it this way: First soak the cobs—husks and all—in water for 60 minutes. Then, fasten the ends with wire twist ties so that the husks won't slip off and place the corn on the grill. Turn it every ten minutes for 40 minutes, remove it from the grill, peel off the husks, and serve.

▶ For extra succulent corn on the cob, strip green leaves from the cobs and use the most tender ones to line the bottom of the pot before adding water and cooking.

▶ A damp paper towel rubbed over corn on the cob easily removes the corn silk.

▶ Snow peas (also known as sugar peas and Chinese pea pods) are translucent green pods. Choose fresh, crisp, thin pods in which the outline of the peas is barely visible. Keep peas refrigerated in plastic bags and use promptly.

▶ The delicate flavor of okra is best if you choose 2 to 3-inch pods that are deep green in color, firm, and free of blemishes. You should be able to easily snap the pods and puncture them with slight pressure.

▶ To easily shell peas, drop the pods in boiling water. The pods will split open and release the peas, and the pods will float to the surface.

ROOT VEGETABLES

Beet
Carrot
Jicama
Parsnip
Radish
Rutabaga
Turnip

Root vegetables, so named because they are the root of a plant, are a great source of vitamin A, as well as other vitamins and iron. Carrots are probably the most popular root vegetable in the U.S., because they are readily available year-round, store well, can be eaten raw or cooked, and are very versatile, used in salads, stews, and even cakes. Turnips have never achieved the popularity of the potato, even though they can be mashed, baked, boiled, steamed, and served in many of the same ways as potatoes. Purchase root vegetables when they are as fresh as possible and avoid ones that have any sign of wrinkling. They will keep longer if refrigerated. Small young root vegetables only need to be scrubbed to prepare them for eating or cooking. Larger root vegetables should be pared or scraped.

▶ To prevent beets from fading during cooking, leave an inch or two of stem attached and add a few tablespoons of vinegar to the water.

▶ Most carrots are sold in film bags with the tops removed. When you buy carrots, look to see that the bag contains fresh-looking, smooth, and well-shaped carrots of good orange color. If you buy fresh carrots that are not packaged, look for those with fresh green tops and well-shaped, brightly colored roots.

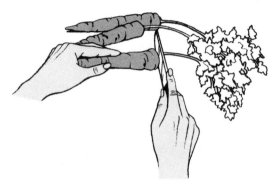

▶ Because carrot tops can rob the vegetable of moisture during storage, slice off the tops before refrigerating.

▶ Carrots can be skinned in seconds if they're first dropped into boiling hot water for five minutes and then plunged into cold water. The skins will slip right off.

▶ Jicama, often referred to as the "Mexican potato," has a sweet, nutty flavor. It can be purchased in Mexican markets or in the produce section of most large supermarkets. Cut leftover jicama into julienned strips and use as dippers with your favorite dip.

▶ Select small, young turnips for a mild, sweet flavor and crisp texture; older turnips can be woody and bitter.

Shoot Vegetables

Artichokes
Asparagus
Bamboo shoots
Celery
Endive
Fennel

With the exception of celery, this group of vegetables might be called the exotics. Asparagus lovers pay a premium price for this fresh vegetable in the spring, although like the other vegetables in this group, asparagus are not highly nutritious. To maximize their

LEGUMES

The term "legume" is used to describe the dried seeds of pod-bearing plants. In countries where meat is scarce, legumes are dietary staples because they are extremely nutritious and very low in fat. When combined with grains, they provide essential amino acids to form protein and thus are an important food for vegetarians and those restricting their meat intake. Legumes are much less expensive than meat.

Store legumes in an airtight container or in their packaging for up to a year. Most legumes need to be rinsed and soaked, preferably overnight, before they can be cooked. Put the dried legumes in a bowl of water and then strain through a colander, removing any pebbles or withered beans. Legumes are frequently

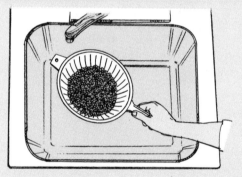

soaked to shorten their cooking time. To soak them, place them in a bowl of water for at least 8 hours. You may also use the quick-soak method: Add dry beans to a large pot. Cover them with water. Bring to a boil and continue boiling for 2 minutes, uncovered. Take them off the heat, cover, and let them sit for 1 hour. Beans will be ready to use.

Legumes may be easier to digest if you change the water frequently, but they will also lose some of their nutrients.

Cooking times vary, and package directions should be carefully followed. The best way to cook legumes is to simmer them slowly and skim off any foam that collects on the surface. They are done when they can be easily mashed. Be careful not to overcook legumes, because this makes them mushy and can affect their flavor. Unfortunately, beans do not cook well in a microwave oven, so it is difficult to shorten the cooking time. Cooked beans freeze well, however, so you can cook a whole package of beans and seal them in freezer bags for storage in the freezer.

► **Aduki beans** are small, red Japanese beans that are gaining popularity, because they can be cooked much faster than most beans and are considered to be easier to digest. They can be substituted for kidney beans in most recipes.

► **Black beans,** also called turtle beans, are very flavorful. They are often used in Latin American cooking and are great in tacos, burritos, soups, and stews.

► **Cannellini beans** are cultivated white beans, similar to kidney beans, which are used extensively in Italian cooking. In the U.S., they are most often canned. Great Northern beans may be substituted.

► **Chick-peas,** also called garbanzo beans, are available canned as well as dried and are the basis for many Middle Eastern dishes, such as hummus.

► **Dried peas** are great in soups and can be used in place of lentils in many recipes.

► **Fava beans** are Mediterranean beans with a nutty flavor. They make a rich addition to soups and stews. Unlike most beans, the skins of fava beans need to be removed after soaking to avoid a bitter taste. Canned fava beans are easily substituted for dried beans.

► **Kidney beans** are available in white or red varieties. They can be used interchangeably with pintos and are available dried and canned. They are the usual basis for chili.

► **Lentils,** whether brown, green, or red, are popular because they don't have to be soaked and cook very quickly. Most often used in soups and stews, lentils can be substituted for ground meat in various recipes.

► **Lima beans,** also known as butter beans and calico beans, are usually sold frozen or canned, although dried forms are available.

► **Pinto beans,** like kidney beans, are often used in Southwestern dishes and are usually the basis for refried beans, which are served at almost every meal in Mexico.

► **Split peas** are most often used in soups. Like lentils, these do not require soaking before cooking.

► **Soybeans** are rich in protein, but they are seldom served cooked because they are difficult to digest. They are more often used to make various protein-rich sauces, soy milk, tofu, soy sauce, and even flour.

nutrients, asparagus and artichokes should be only lightly steamed and never boiled. The rest can be eaten raw. Any sign of limpness in this group indicates an old vegetable. Refrigerate after purchase and use quickly.

▶ During spring months artichokes should be bright green. They may appear bronzed in winter.

▶ Cooking artichokes in iron or aluminum pots will turn the pots gray; use stainless steel or glass pots instead.

▶ To keep artichokes from discoloring as you clean them, squeeze a lemon half into a bowl of cold water. As you clean each artichoke, rub it with the other half of the lemon, and then drop it into the acidy water.

▶ The size of the asparagus stalk has no relationship to tenderness. Whether thick or thin, select asparagus with firm, straight stalks and closed, compact tips. Open tips are a sign of over-maturity. Always choose asparagus stalks that show the most green color.

▶ To maintain the moisture content that keeps asparagus fresh, cut a small slice off the bottom of each stalk, then stand all stalks upright in a container with an inch of water at the bottom and store in the refrigerator.

▶ If you've purchased asparagus with thick, tough stalks, peel the lower parts of the stalks with a potato peeler until you reach the soft interior. Cook as usual and the stalks will taste as tender as the flowers.

▶ To firm uncooked limp asparagus stalks, position them upright in a deep pot. Add ice

water, and cover the pot with a plastic bag. Put the pot in the refrigerator for an hour, and when you're ready to cook the asparagus, the stalks will be firm.

▶ Avoid damaging the delicate tips of canned asparagus by opening the can from the bottom rather than the top.

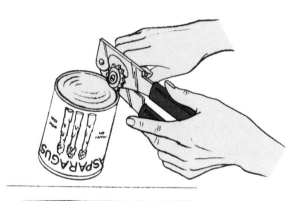

▶ Noted for its pleasant, flavorful sharpness, Belgian endive adds elegance to meals, either fresh in a salad or gently braised. Look for tightly furled stalks of creamy white color. The leaves should be pale yellow, not green, at the tips.

TUBERS

Potatoes
Sweet potatoes
Yams

The most famous tuber—the potato—ranks first among the most important agricultural products in Western Europe and the Americas. It is highly nutritious, easily grown, and extremely versatile. Sweet potatoes come in many varieties, but despite their resemblance to yams, the two are unrelated. Rich in vitamin A, vitamin C, and minerals, they pack more nutrition than white potatoes. Their sweetness is due to a remarkably high sugar content that is increased even further during cooking. Yams are also very sweet and can be cooked similar to sweet potatoes.

Choose firm, relatively smooth, clean tubers. They should be reasonably well shaped and free from cuts or bruises. Avoid green-colored tubers and those with sprouts. Store tubers in a cool, dark, dry, well-ventilated place; do not refrigerate. Protect them from light, which can cause them to turn green and lose their vitamin C content.

▶ Exposure to air turns peeled potatoes dark, so if you want to peel potatoes ahead of time, cover them with water and refrigerate.

▶ To quickly peel sweet potatoes, boil them until just tender and drop them into cold water. The skins will slip right off.

▶ When cooking potatoes, leave skins on when possible—they add extra nutrition and good taste.

▶ To firm raw potatoes that have gone soft, immerse them in ice water for 30 minutes.

▶ To cook a baked potato in half the usual time, boil it for 5 minutes before putting it in a hot oven to get the "baked" flavor.

▶ If you need to bake potatoes quickly, use baking nails. Insert a nail lengthwise in each potato; it will heat rapidly and then radiate heat to the inside of the potato, decreasing baking time by as much as 15 minutes.

▶ Bake potatoes quickly by slicing them in half lengthwise and cooking them on a lightly greased baking sheet, cut side down.

▶ To make delicious, fat-free "French fries," cut the potatoes into 1/2-inch thick pieces and soak them in a large bowl of cold water for at least two hours. Place the "fries" on a baking sheet with at least 1 inch of space between the pieces. Preheat your oven to 400°F and bake the "fries" about 35 or 40 minutes, until they're nicely puffed and browned.

▶ Sprinkle a little flour on potatoes before frying them and they'll be extra crisp and crunchy.

▶ Use unpeeled potatoes when making hash browns. Just run them through the grater, skin and all, and you won't lose the nutrients that are just under the potato skin.

▶ To prevent potato pancakes from discoloring, add sour cream to the grated potatoes; you can also grate the potatoes into a bowl of ice water, draining before use.

COOKING METHODS

KNOW YOUR OVEN

While modern ovens have become more precise, oven cooking times can vary according to the oven. Although most people use a conventional oven, convection ovens, which are popular in Europe, are now being sold by American manufacturers.

In a conventional oven, the air does not circulate, and it's important to preheat the oven to the desired temperature and not to overcrowd the inside of the oven. With a convection oven, a fan circulates the hot air, which eliminates the need to preheat and allows more food to be baked or roasted at one time. Be sure to allow less time for most cooking in a convection oven.

▶ For even cooking in a conventional oven, allow 2 inches between pans and 2 inches between pans and the oven wall. This allows adequate room for circulation of the hot air.

continued on page 209

FRUITS MASKING AS VEGETABLES

Fruit vegetables are technically fruits, but we treat them as vegetables. They include avocados, a wide variety of chilies, eggplant, peppers, and tomatoes. Although dissimilar, they share one important characteristic—they're more perishable than most vegetables.

Avocados

Although they're loaded with vitamins, especially vitamin C, avocados pose a major problem for anyone on a low-fat diet—they're loaded with fat. In fact, 1 tablespoon of avocado contains 2.4 grams of fat. Most avocados are sold when they're green and hard and must be ripened so that the skin is brown and the pulp is soft but not mushy. To test if an avocado is ripe, stick a toothpick in the stem end. If it slides in and out with ease, the avocado is ready to eat. To

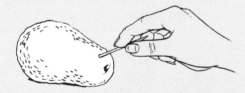

speed up the ripening of avocados, place them in a brown paper bag and store the bag in a warm place. Once ripe, you can retard spoilage by keeping them in the refrigerator. Avocados can be sliced into salads, mashed for guacamole, and even baked.

▶ Only peel the avocado and remove the pit immediately before serving. The flesh darkens very quickly.

▶ For a perfect avocado half, cut the fruit in half lengthwise, pull the halves apart, and plunge a very sharp chef's knife into the pit. The pit will pull away cleanly with the knife. Remove the avocado halves from the shell with a spoon, or very gently with your fingers.

▶ To keep an unused avocado half from turning dark, press the pit back into place before refrigerating the uneaten half.

Chilies

The difference in flavor and hotness found among chili peppers depends on the variety. Among the most familiar chilies, the Anaheim (or California when dried) pepper is the mildest. Chili peppers contain volatile oils that may burn your skin and make your eyes smart. When handling them, it is best to wear rubber gloves and avoid touching your face or eyes. Thoroughly wash any skin that comes in contact with chili oil.

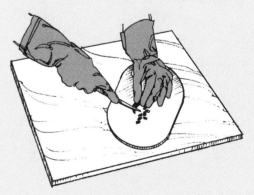

▶ Canned chilies should be rinsed in cold water before using. Much of the "fire" is in the seeds and canning liquid. The canners who pack chilies rate their hotness on a scale of 1 to 200—with 1

being the mildest. A jalapeno chili, hot enough to burn your mouth, bring tears to your eyes, and make your hair curl, rates 15 on this scale!

▶ Dried chilies can be found in markets that specialize in Mexican, Puerto Rican, and Spanish foods. The following are the most common:

Ancho chilies are large, full-flavored, and range from mild to medium-hot. They are frequently used in Mexican cooking.

Mulato chilies are usually larger than anchos and have a more pungent flavor—usually medium-hot.

Pasilla chilies are long, slender, medium-size, and dark brown in color. Flavor ranges from mild to quite hot, and they are sold in dried and powdered forms.

Chipotle chilies are brownish red with wrinkled skin; dried, smoked, and often canned, this chili is very hot and has a distinctive, smoky flavor.

Eggplant

Eggplant comes in a variety of shapes, colors, and sizes—the small white eggplant is round and white and actually resembles an egg. The most common form of eggplant is dark purple. When purchasing eggplant, look for a firm eggplant that is heavy for its size, with a tight, glossy, deeply colored skin. The stem should be bright green. Dull skin and rust-colored spots are a sign of old age. Refrigerate unwashed eggplant in a plastic bag for up to five days. To remove the bitter juices from eggplant before cooking, cut it into slices or cubes as directed in the recipe. Sprinkle the eggplant liberally with coarse or kosher salt, and set the pieces on several layers of paper towels for 30 minutes. Rinse the slices or cubes quickly under cold running water and pat them dry before continuing with the recipe. A potato peeler works well to peel the skin of eggplant.

Peppers

Bell peppers have come a long way since they existed only in a single color—green. Now it's easy to find yellow, red, orange, purple, and brown bell peppers. Apart from their visual appeal, they each have their own distinctively pleasant taste. Sweet green peppers should be fresh looking, firm, thick-fleshed, and of bright green color. Avoid peppers that are soft and dull looking. At home, keep peppers cool and humid and use within a few days for maximum freshness. Red sweet peppers are simply green peppers that have matured and changed color. Fresh red peppers are high in vitamin C and are also a fair source of vitamin A and potassium.

▶ Peppers will stay bright green during baking if you coat them with salad oil or olive oil before stuffing and cooking them.

▶ To save time, roast a lot of red peppers at one time by using the just-lit coals of a barbecue. Char the peppers on all sides, then place them in a heavy plastic bag and seal for 10 minutes. Use a small, sharp knife or your fingers to lift off the skin, stem, and seeds of each pepper. Slice and store the peppers in a jar in the refrigerator. They'll keep for several weeks and can be used in hot vegetable dishes, in salads, or as an antipasto.

▶ To roast peppers in the oven, put them on a rack in a broiler pan 3 to 5 inches from heat. Turn often until blistered and charred on all sides. Transfer to a plastic bag; seal the bag and let it stand 15 to 20 minutes to loosen the skins. Remove loosened skins with a paring knife. Cut peppers in half and remove the seeds and stems.

Tomatoes

From bite-size cherry tomatoes to hefty beefsteaks, fresh tomatoes should be chosen for their color and aroma. Firm, underripe tomatoes can be placed, stem side down, in a warm, sunny spot for a few days. They will soften and improve in flavor. Store ripe tomatoes at cool temperatures to slow down loss of vitamin C. Wash tomatoes just before using and remove any caps that are present.

Sun-dried tomatoes are a new addition to many supermarket produce departments. The oil-packed variety

tends to be more expensive but benefits from being soaked in liquid, making them ready to use. The dry variety needs to be poached in liquid before being used (see package directions). Both varieties can be used either whole or chopped.

▶ Allow unripe tomatoes to ripen at room temperature away from direct sunlight.

▶ To hasten ripening, place an apple in a paper bag along with a tomato.

▶ To peel tomatoes, place them, one at a time, in a saucepan of simmering water for about 10 seconds. (Add about 30 seconds if they are not fully ripened.) Then immediately plunge them into a bowl of cold water for another 10 seconds. The skins will peel off easily with a knife. Do not add more than one tomato at a time to the water or the temperature will drop rapidly and the tomatoes will stew before their skins can be removed.

▶ For firm tomato slices, try cutting parallel to the stem axis.

▶ To heighten the flavor when cooking tomatoes, add a pinch of sugar to the cooking water.

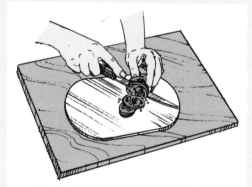

continued from page 205

▶ If your oven doesn't have an indicator light, allow 10 minutes for preheating before putting in breads or cookies. Preheat at the setting required in the recipes.

▶ If you want to use aluminum foil in the oven to catch spills, place it on the rack below the one used for baking. If it is directly under the utensil it will reduce air circulation. Use foil only on the part of the lower rack that is directly under the utensil; do not cover the entire rack.

BAKING AND ROASTING

Both baking and roasting involve cooking food with dry, hot air. Although similar to baking, roasting usually begins with a higher heat (400°F and above) to brown meats or vegetables. Then the heat is lowered to finish the cooking. Typically, one temperature is maintained during baking, and very often the meat is cooked in some form of liquid.

Roasting is best for whole chickens and turkeys; beef, pork, and veal roasts; and leg of lamb. Baking is best for chicken parts, chops, meat loafs, and fish. Vegetables like bell peppers and potatoes respond well to roasting. If you're roasting them with a meat roast or whole chicken, delay adding them to the oven because vegetables take less time to cook.

▶ Meat will shrink less during roasting if it's cooked longer at a lower temperature.

▶ A shallow pan is better than a deep one for cooking a roast because it allows heat to circulate around the meat.

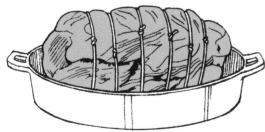

▶ Slice a roast more easily by letting it stand for about 15 minutes after taking it from the oven.

▶ Dropping a few tomatoes in the pan will help tenderize a pot roast. Acid from the tomatoes helps break down the roast's stringy fibers.

▶ A chicken will baste itself if you cover the bird with strips of bacon during roasting. Remove the bacon before the end of cooking to brown the bird further.

▶ It's best to baste a chicken only during the final 30 minutes of cooking. Sauce won't penetrate during the early cooking stages and may cause the chicken to brown too quickly.

▶ When a recipe calls for fish to be baked "en papillote" (in a parchment paper casing), aluminum foil can be substituted for the parchment paper.

▶ Fish won't stick to the pan during baking if you lay it on a bed of parsley, celery, and onions. This vegetable bed also adds flavor.

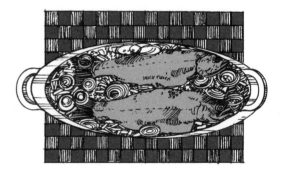

BOILING, SIMMERING, AND POACHING

The important difference between boiling, simmering, and poaching is the temperature of the cooking liquid. Boiled foods are cooked in boiling liquid at 212°F. Simmered foods are cooked in gently bubbling liquid at 185 to 205°F. Poached foods are cooked in liquid that is hot but not actually bubbling (160 to 180°F).

Vegetables cook very quickly when boiled. It's best to get a small amount of water boiling, add the vegetables, turn down the heat to a simmer, and let them cook gently. With large whole vegetables, such as

SAVORY STUFFING

Whether you call it dressing or stuffing, what goes inside the bird can be delicious, but it takes a few tips to get it just right:

▶ Stuff a chicken or turkey just before roasting. If you need to make the stuffing ahead of time, store it in an airtight container in the refrigerator separately from the bird. Make sure the stuffing is cool before you stuff the bird.

▶ Always stuff a chicken or turkey loosely—don't cram dressing into the cavity. If the bird is stuffed loosely, the oven heat will penetrate more easily to cook the stuffing all the way through.

▶ When stuffing a chicken, allow about ¾ cup of stuffing for each pound of chicken.

▶ For the most accurate thermometer reading of a roasting turkey, immerse the thermometer in warm water before sliding it into the turkey. When you insert it, keep it away from fat and bones, both of which render inaccurate readings.

▶ To hold in stuffing, truss a turkey with unwaxed dental floss—it's extra strong and doesn't burn. You can also use two heels of dampened bread to block the cavity and keep the dressing in place. Position the crusts so that they face out and then overlap each other. One or two raw potatoes could also be used to seal the cavity.

▶ When preparing a stuffed chicken or turkey, check the stuffing as well as the

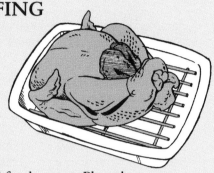

bird for doneness. Place the thermometer in the stuffing and leave it for 5 minutes before taking a reading. For complete cooking, the stuffing should register 165°F and the bird 185°F.

▶ You'll be able to remove the dressing from a turkey easily if it is held in a cheesecloth bag that you've pushed into the cavity. When you're ready to serve, pull out the bag and turn the dressing into a bowl.

▶ To prepare fresh chestnuts for a stuffing, use a small, sharp knife to slit the flat side of each chestnut. Put the nuts in a saucepan, cover them with cold water, and bring to a boil. Cook for several minutes, then remove the pan from the heat. Working quickly with only a few nuts at a time, peel the outer and inner shells. Cook the peeled nuts covered with water or stock in a saucepan. Simmer until tender (about 30 minutes).

▶ When storing leftovers, always remove the stuffing from the cavity and store separately.

▶ Stuffed poultry that has been commercially frozen should not be defrosted before cooking.

artichokes, you'll want to make sure the vegetables are covered with water.

Parboiled vegetables are boiled in water until they are almost halfway cooked. They are then drained and rinsed in cold water to stop further cooking. This process tenderizes long-cooking vegetables so their final cooking time will be less and they can then be combined with quicker-cooking ingredients. Stir-fries and kabobs are two examples of dishes that can benefit from parboiling.

▶ Prevent boil-overs by inserting a toothpick horizontally between pot and lid so that steam can escape harmlessly.

▶ Prevent steam from scalding your wrists and hands when you drain boiling water from a pot of vegetables by first turning on the cold water tap.

▶ Using the wrong size cooking utensils on your range top is inefficient and wastes energy. If a pan is larger than the electric element, it may overheat. It it's too small, fuel is wasted.

▶ When poaching a whole fish, wrap it in a length of cheesecloth for easy removal from the poaching liquid.

BROILING

Cooking food on very high heat under a broiler is the essence of broiling. Usually, meat is broiled on a wire rack over a pan. The high heat seals in the juices of the food and browns the outside, while the fat drips into the pan under the food. Because the grease from meat falls into the broiler pan away from the meat, broiling is an important alternative to low-fat cooking.

▶ Dripping fat can smoke and catch fire while you're broiling meat. Guard against this by placing dry bread in the broiler pan to soak up the fat.

▶ If grease on your broiler catches fire, sprinkle salt or baking soda on the flames. Don't try to use flour as a fire extinguisher— it's explosive.

▶ Broiling with gas is different from broiling with electricity. When you broil with gas, you should keep the oven door closed because gas flames absorb moisture and consume smoke. When you broil with electricity, keep the door slightly open so the oven can expel moisture.

▶ If you use a rack, you can line the broiler pan with foil for easy cleanup. If you're not using a rack, foil prevents fat from draining away.

▶ To prevent chicken from drying out when broiling, brush it with lemon juice to keep it moist and add a touch of extra flavor.

▶ Save time and effort when broiling sausages by putting the links on a skewer so you can turn them all with one movement. They'll all be evenly browned, too.

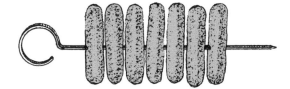

FRYING

To fry food, you cook at high heat in a skillet on top of the range. Almost all foods to be fried require some liquid or fat to prevent them from sticking to the pan, which is why it is difficult to fry "fat-free." Sautéing generally involves much shorter cooking times and is reserved for foods that cook very quickly.

▶ When frying meats, be careful not to overcrowd the pan. If there are too many pieces in the pan, the meat will steam instead of brown.

▶ Make sure meats are completely dry before frying or sautéing.

▶ To sauté food in butter, add the food just after the foam on the butter subsides.

▶ Sprinkle a little salt in the frying pan before you start cooking to prevent hot fat from splattering.

▶ Don't use the same vegetable oil for frying more than a few times. Old oil soaks into fried foods.

▶ Instead of clarifying butter for sautéing foods, add a small amount of vegetable oil to unsalted butter. The vegetable oil will allow the butter to reach a higher temperature without burning.

▶ You can give your skillet a nonstick finish by sprinkling the pan with salt and then warming it for 5 minutes. Remove, wipe out the salt, and use as usual.

▶ When frying, broiling, or grilling chicken, always use tongs to turn the pieces. If you use a fork you're likely to pierce the skin, and natural juices will escape.

▶ Chicken livers won't splatter during frying if you first perforate them with a fork. Puncture several holes in each.

▶ When sautéing boneless chicken breasts or other chicken pieces, use a shallow skillet if you want the chicken to stay crisp. A deep pan creates steam, causing a buildup of moisture and a loss of crispness.

▶ If you chill a chicken for an hour after flouring it for frying, the coating will adhere better during cooking.

▶ If you can't get a fishy odor out of a pan used for frying fish, sprinkle the pan with salt, pour hot water in it, let it stand for a while, and then wash as usual.

COOKING FROZEN FOODS

▶ Most frozen vegetables should be cooked without thawing, but one major exception is corn on the cob. It should be thawed completely before cooking; otherwise you'll have to cook it too long and it will get tough.

▶ If you have leftover tomatoes, freeze them for later use in stews and soups. Freezing makes them soft, but this won't affect their taste.

▶ Thaw frozen foods by placing the container under cold running water for a few minutes. Then place the container in a pan of lukewarm water until the food slips out easily.

STIR-FRYING

Follow these simple steps for successful stir-frying:

1. Prepare all the ingredients in advance, including cleaning, cutting, measuring, and combining.

2. Cut the meat and vegetables into uniform sizes and shapes to ensure even cooking.

3. Make sure the oil is hot before adding any food to the wok or pan. (The best oils to use for stir-frying are peanut, corn, or soybean.)

4. Add the thickest foods that take the longest time to cook first. Add food that requires little cooking time, such as mushrooms, at the end.

5. While you don't have to stir constantly, the reason it's called stir-fry is that you stir the food often enough so that it cooks evenly on all sides.

TIPS FOR COOKING PASTA AND RICE

Pasta

▶ A large strainer or a French fry basket can make it easy to drain pasta. Set either device inside the cooking pot before you add the pasta; after cooking you can simply lift the pasta from the pot.

▶ When buying pasta, make sure it's made from semolina rather than ordinary flour. Pasta made from semolina holds its shape better and doesn't become mushy.

▶ When boiling water for spaghetti or macaroni, add a teaspoon or so of cooking oil to prevent the pasta from sticking together (or to the pot).

▶ For perfect al dente pasta every time, use the old Italian method of testing for doneness. Remove a strand of pasta from the boiling water and throw it against the wall or refrigerator. If it sticks, the pasta is cooked al dente and should be drained and served immediately.

▶ There are several ways to prevent the pot boiling over when cooking pasta. You can lay a large metal spatula across the top of the pot; rub shortening around the rim before cooking; or add several teaspoons of cooking oil or a dab of butter to the cooking water.

▶ To preserve the freshness of the unused portion of pasta in a box you've opened, store the remaining pasta in a tightly covered glass container.

▶ For superior pasta, let salted water come to a boil, stir the pasta into the water, cover the

HOW TO COOK BACON

To cook bacon in a skillet, place it in a single layer over medium-high heat, turning it two to three times for even cooking. To bake it, place bacon in a single layer on a rack in a baking pan and bake at 350°F 15 to 20 minutes or until crisp. The least messy way to cook bacon is in the microwave, although it can be tricky. Put two layers of paper towel on a microwave-safe rack or dish and arrange the bacon rashers in a single layer. Cover with another paper towel. Microwave at HIGH (100 percent) about 1 minute per slice. (This is highly dependent on the power of your microwave, the thickness of the bacon, and the number of slices you are cooking at one time. Because bacon cooks so quickly, it will burn very fast. Whatever the method, always be extremely careful—bacon grease gets very hot and can catch on fire very quickly.)

STEAMING

Using only a small amount of water in a pan on top of the range, this cooking method relies on the steam, rather than the heat of the water, to cook food. This low-fat method is great for vegetables, because they also retain more nutrients when steamed than when boiled.

pot, and turn off the heat. After the pasta sits for 15 minutes, it will be ready to eat.

▶ To prevent cooked spaghetti strands from becoming sticky, run fresh, hot water into the spaghetti pot before draining.

▶ If you've made a pot of spaghetti but can't serve it at once, leave it in water, but make it cool enough to stop the cooking process. To reheat the spaghetti, put it in a strainer and shake it thoroughly as you run it under hot tap water.

▶ If you're going to use pasta in a dish that requires further cooking, reduce the pasta cooking time by one-third.

Rice

▶ If you've cooked too much rice, freeze it. When ready to use, put it in a sieve and run hot water through it.

▶ For rice that's snowy white, add some lemon juice to the cooking water.

▶ If the rice you're cooking has burned slightly, remove the burned flavor by adding a heel from a loaf of fresh white bread and covering the pot for a few minutes.

▶ When cooking rice, add a pinch of rosemary to the water instead of salt for a special flavor.

COOKING IN THE MICROWAVE OVEN

Microwave ovens are great timesavers, but cooking in a microwave is much different than cooking in an oven or on top of the range. Along with following the manufacturer's directions, keep the following in mind:

▶ Be sure to use nonmetal utensils in the microwave. To ensure that a nonmetal utensil will be safe in the microwave, place the utensil in the oven and put a cup of cool water on it or next to it. Microwave on HIGH for 1 minute. If the utensil is hot after 1 minute, it is not safe for microwave oven use. If it's

warm, use it only for short-term heating. If it's cold, but the water is hot, you can use the utensil safely in the microwave oven.

▶ Paper plates, cups, and napkins can be used in the microwave oven. But don't use foil-lined paper products, paper towels that include nylon or synthetic fibers, or newspaper.

▶ When using plastic roasting or cooking bags in the microwave oven, discard the wire twist tie and use a plastic fastener or a piece of string instead.

▶ For microwave cooking, cut meats and vegetables in uniform sizes to make sure that they cook evenly.

▶ Baked foods rise higher in a microwave oven. To avoid spillage, fill cake and bread pans only half-full with batter.

▶ To ensure that food cooks fully and evenly in the microwave oven, stir food pieces and turn dishes periodically while they're cooking.

▶ Remove large bones from meat before microwaving it, because the dense bone may keep the area around it from cooking. The deboned meat will cook more evenly if you use a middle temperature range.

▶ When microwaving a food that needs thorough cooking to destroy possibly harmful organisms, be particularly careful to observe the recommended standing time. Let the food stand outside the oven for the full recommended time to complete cooking; cover with foil to keep hot.

▶ To get more juice from a lemon, pop it in the microwave on HIGH power for 30 seconds. The same process works for other citrus fruits.

▶ Paper towels around sandwiches, rolls, or other baked goods will absorb moisture that would otherwise make the food soggy.

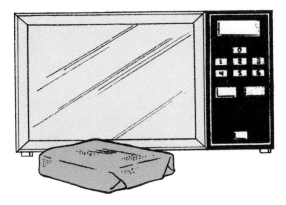

▶ Potato chips that have lost their crunch can be placed on paper towels in the microwave oven and heated briefly. The towels will absorb moisture and restore the chips to crispness.

▶ Thick-skinned foods, such as potatoes, squash, and tomatoes, trap steam during microwave cooking. Pierce the skins before cooking to allow steam to escape. The same applies to eggs in the shell.

▶ Use your microwave to make short work of shelling nuts. Put 2 cups of nuts into a 1-quart casserole with a cup of water, and microwave it for 4 to 5 minutes on HIGH. When you crack the nuts, the meats will come out in one piece.

▶ If your brown sugar has turned into an intractable lump, just place a piece of dampened paper towel in the box, close the box tightly, and put the whole thing in the microwave for 20 to 30 seconds on HIGH to soften up the sugar.

▶ Ease the chore of peeling such foods as tomatoes or peaches. Heat for 30 seconds on HIGH, then allow to stand for 2 minutes. The peel will slip off easily.

▶ Ice cream that has hardened too much in the freezer can be returned to usable consistency

if you microwave it on WARM for 10 to 15 seconds.

▶ Several food items (such as potatoes) will cook more evenly in a microwave oven if they are arranged in a circle around the center with 2 inches between them to allow the microwave energy to circulate adequately. Similarly, chicken pieces will cook more evenly if arranged in the dish with the thicker or bigger portions toward the outside edges of the dish.

▶ With foods that require browning, such as breads, cookies, and some meats, a conventional oven produces better results than a microwave oven unless the microwave oven has a broiling element.

THE BEST BARBECUE

The smoky taste of food grilled over an open fire isn't the only reason Americans love to barbecue, but it's one of the best. If you have a gas grill, you'll want to skip right to the techniques section, but if you're grilling with coals, try the following tips to get your barbecue burning just right:

Arranging Coals

For **direct cooking,** arrange the coals in a single layer directly under the food. Use this method for quick-cooking foods, such as hamburgers, steaks, and fish.

For **indirect cooking,** arrange coals to one side of the grill. Place a drip pan under the food at the other side. For more heat, divide the coals on either side of the drip pan. Use this method for slow-cooking foods, such as roasts and whole chicken.

Checking Charcoal Temperature

To check the temperature of the coals, cautiously hold the palm of your hand at grid level—over the coals for direct heat and over the drip pan for indirect heat—and count the number of seconds you can hold your hand in that position before the heat forces you to pull it away.

Seconds	Coal Temperature
2	Hot (about 375°F or more)
3	Medium-hot (about 350°F to 375°F)
4	Medium (about 300°F to 350°F)
5	Low (about 200°F to 300°F)

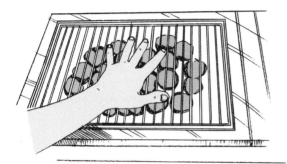

GRILLING TECHNIQUES

▶ Watch foods carefully during grilling. Total cooking time will vary with the type of food, position on the grill, weather, temperature of the coals, and degree of doneness you desire.

▶ If you plan on grilling for more than 45 minutes, add 10 to 12 new coals around the edges of the coals just before you begin to cook. When the new coals are ready, move them to the center of the fire.

▶ Spray your barbecue grill with nonstick cooking spray so you'll be able to turn

chicken pieces without tearing. Hamburger patties will stay whole, too. The spray also means that cleanup will be much easier.

▶ Use long-handled tongs or a spatula to turn meat. A fork or knife punctures meat and lets the juices escape.

▶ Use a meat thermometer to accurately determine the doneness of large cuts of meat or poultry cooked on the rotisserie or covered grill.

▶ Spice up the flavor of food on the barbecue by sprinkling the coals with fresh herbs that have been soaked in water.

▶ To tenderize pork chops or chicken pieces before barbecuing, boil them in a saucepan for 15 minutes, drain them, and then marinate them in barbecue sauce for 30 minutes. Then position them on the grill and barbecue as usual.

▶ To cook a whole turkey on the barbecue grill, allow 15 to 18 minutes a pound for an unstuffed turkey, 18 to 24 minutes for a stuffed one.

▶ If you're cooking a variety of vegetables on skewers on the grill, make sure they all finish cooking at the same time by blanching or parboiling long-cooking vegetables (such as potatoes or carrot chunks) ahead of time.

▶ Chunks of fresh vegetables, threaded on a skewer and grilled, make a tasty accompaniment to barbecued meats, or a satisfying alternative to meat for vegetarians. The same applies to fruit. Skewer chunks of peach, pineapple, banana, and other fruits and barbecue over medium heat. Baste with a mixture of melted butter, sugar, and cinnamon, and turn the skewers often.

▶ Add zip to skewered vegetables by brushing them with salad dressing instead of butter.

▶ Cook potatoes, carrots, or winter squash directly on the coals by first wrapping the vegetables thoroughly in foil. They'll take 30 to 45 minutes to cook.

▶ Use spare space on your barbecue grill to heat bread or rolls. Either brush the bread or rolls with butter and heat face-down on the grill for a minute or two, or wrap in foil and heat for 10 to 20 minutes.

▶ For the best kabobs, parboil solid or starchy vegetables, such as carrots or potatoes, before using.

▶ For additional flavor and for a very different taste, toss water-soaked wood chips, such as hickory or mesquite, on hot coals before adding food. Adding wood chips to the coals will create smoke, so make sure the grill is in a well-ventilated area away from any open windows.

GRILLING SEAFOOD

▶ Seafood generally cooks much faster than meats. Watch it carefully.

▶ If you use a marinade, remove excess before placing seafood on the grill.

▶ Use bacon strips to hold shrimp and scallops on skewers. Simply thread one end of the bacon on the skewer, add a shrimp or scallop, bring the bacon through the skewer again, add another shrimp or scallop, and continue until you reach the end of the bacon rasher. The bacon gives a great flavor to the seafood and anchors the pieces on the skewer. Use turkey bacon if you're watching fat content.

▶ Many cookware and hardware stores offer special grills for holding fish that can be used on top of your grill. They also make cleanup easier.

CLEANUP

▶ A grill will steam-clean itself if wrapped in wet newspapers or sprayed with window cleaner while it's still hot.

▶ Wipe the grill with crumpled aluminum foil while it's still warm.

▶ To coat the grill protectively before cooking, use vegetable oil and wipe it off as soon as the grill is cool enough to touch.

▶ A beer-can opener makes a great scraper for cleaning barbecue grills; file a notch in the end of the opener opposite the sharp point.

SAFETY TIPS

▶ Position the grill on a heatproof surface, away from trees and bushes that could catch a spark and out of the path of traffic.

▶ Make sure the grill's vents are not clogged with ashes before starting a fire.

▶ To avoid flare-ups and charred food when grilling, remove visible fat from meat.

▶ When you barbecue juicy meat, fat dripping on the hot coals can cause flames to flare up. Put out the flames by dropping lettuce leaves on the coals, or by squirting water on the coals with a spray bottle or turkey baster.

► If you partially cook foods in the microwave or on the range, immediately finish cooking the food on the grill. Do not refrigerate partially cooked foods or let them sit at room temperature before you complete cooking on the grill.

► Always serve cooked food from the grill on a clean plate, not one that held the raw food.

► In hot weather, food should never sit out for over 1 hour. Remember, keep hot foods hot and cold foods cold.

SALADS AND SALAD DRESSINGS

► Crisp up soggy lettuce by submerging it in a bowl of cold water and lemon juice and putting it in the refrigerator. After an hour, remove the lettuce from the refrigerator and dip it briefly in hot water, then in ice water to which you've added a dash of apple cider vinegar. Pat the lettuce dry.

► Another way to make lettuce (or celery) crisp is to place it in a pan of cold water to which you've added slices of raw potato.

► If you put washed salad greens in the freezer about 10 minutes before preparing the salad they will be even crunchier.

► A salad can be prepared up to 6 hours ahead of time if you place the vinaigrette dressing in the bottom of the bowl and carefully place well-dried salad greens on top. Cover and refrigerate, but don't toss until just before serving.

► To make scalloped edges on cucumber rounds you use in salads, simply run fork tines over a peeled cucumber, then slice as usual.

► For a more elegant presentation, remove the seeds from cucumbers before serving them in a salad or as a vegetable side dish. Cut the peeled or unpeeled cucumber in half lengthwise; remove the seeds with a melon baller or a small spoon.

► For extra-crisp cucumber slices, soak them in salted ice water for 30 minutes. Just before serving, drain and rinse well under cold running water. Pat dry and toss with dressing.

► Be sure that lettuce leaves are well dried before tossing, or the salad dressing won't cling.

► When dressing a salad with vinegar and oil, remember to pour the vinegar first. If you pour the oil first, the vinegar won't stick to the greens.

► Don't pour vinaigrette dressing over salad greens until the moment before serving. Only shredded cabbage or tomatoes can stand a vinaigrette bath for up to an hour before serving without losing firmness.

► Don't toss sliced tomatoes into your salad. Their water content will dilute the salad dressing. Add them on top at the last minute, or use whole cherry tomatoes.

► A soggy salad never garners compliments for the chef. You can keep your salads crisp if you invert a saucer in the bottom of the bowl to allow any liquid to drain and collect under the saucer, away from the greens.

► For instantly cold, well-blended oil and vinegar salad dressing, pour the dressing into a screw-top jar, add an ice cube, and shake. Remove the ice cube before pouring the dressing.

► If you want crumbled Roquefort or blue cheese for your salads, freeze it; it will crumble easily when scraped with a paring knife. (This does not work well with other cheeses.)

► For extra-creamy salad dressings, place dressing ingredients in a slow-running blender and slowly add the oil.

► If salt is used as a salad seasoning, it's best to add it at the last minute. If you add the salt ahead of time, the lettuce will wilt.

► A crushed garlic clove rubbed on the inside of a salad bowl will heighten the taste of the salad ingredients.

► For easy unmolding of gelatin salads or aspics, lightly grease the mold with vegetable oil (or sweet almond oil for desserts) before pouring in the gelatin mixture. Chill until solid.

▶ When you make a gelatin salad with cream cheese, mix the cheese with dry gelatin before adding liquid to avoid lumps.

▶ To save money and enjoy fresher flavor, make gourmet mustards and vinegars at home. For mustards: Add freshly ground or cracked spices or chopped fresh herb leaves to Dijon mustard. Flavor to taste. Store in the refrigerator. For herb vinegars: Heat 1 quart of white wine vinegar with 1 cup of minced fresh herbs (or ¼ cup dried herbs) in a nonaluminum saucepan. Steep at room temperature overnight, then strain through a fine sieve lined with cheesecloth. Add a few sprigs of the appropriate herb into the bottle used to store the vinegar, so that you know the flavor. Store in airtight glass bottles.

SOUPS AND SAUCES

A soup is any combination of vegetables, meat, or fish cooked in a liquid. The stock—the strained liquid that is the result of cooking vegetables, meat, or fish—determines its flavor.

TYPES OF SOUPS

Bisque—A bisque is a thick soup made from puréed shellfish, fowl, or vegetables, and cream.

Broth—Broth is the liquid resulting from cooking vegetables, meat, or fish in water. Bouillon is another term for broth.

Chowder—Chowder is a thick, chunky seafood soup. It can contain any of several varieties of seafood and vegetables. The term is also used to describe any thick, rich soup containing chunks of food (corn chowder, for example).

Consommé—Consommé is a rich clear broth made by straining all "sediment" out of the soup or seasoned stock.

Fruit Soup—Fruit soup is made of cooked, puréed fruit combined with water, wine, milk or cream, spices, and other flavorings. Sugar is sometimes added. Fruit soups are served either hot or cold.

STOCK-MAKING BASICS

▶ Begin with a good soup pot, one that is heavy and conducts and distributes heat evenly.

▶ For meat-based stocks, place the meat and bones in a soup pot and cover them with cold water. Heat the water slowly to a boil without stirring. Use a ladle to remove the scum as it collects on the surface of the water. When boiling, add the vegetables and seasonings of your choice; add salt sparingly. Reduce the heat and simmer gently, partially covered, for at least 2 hours. Strain the stock through dampened cheesecloth.

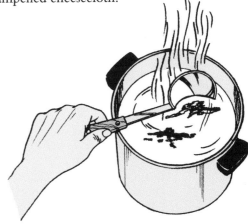

▶ To remove the fat from stock, cover and refrigerate. The fat will solidify on the surface for easy removal.

▶ When making stock, never allow the liquid to boil. Boiling will make the stock cloudy.

▶ Puréed leftover vegetables lend additional flavoring to soup stocks.

▶ If you want rich, brown beef stock, add beef bones that have been browned in the broiler (about 6 inches from the heating unit).

▶ To make a concentrated stock that will add a chef's touch to your soups, reduce brown beef or chicken stock to a heavy, syruplike consistency, being careful not to burn the stock. Store it in the refrigerator or freezer and just break or cut off small pieces as needed to flavor soups or sauces.

▶ Freeze water from boiling or steaming vegetables and use it in soup stock. You'll have the added benefit of nutrients from the vegetables.

▶ When saving meat juices for stock, leave the fat in place on the surface. When it solidifies, it will seal the stock and its flavor.

▶ When cutting chickens into pieces, save the carcasses, necks, and gizzards. The same applies if you skin and debone your chickens. Freeze them, along with roast turkey and chicken carcasses. When you have enough, use the carcasses to make chicken stock.

▶ To avoid scorching and boil-overs when cooking soup in a large stock pot, position two or three bricks around the burner so that the pot is elevated above the heating coils or the gas flames. Then simmer the contents as long as necessary over low heat.

▶ For tastier clam chowder, add the minced clams at the last moment and cook just long enough to heat. As a bonus, the clams won't become mushy.

▶ To keep milk from curdling when you prepare tomato soup, add the soup stock to the milk, instead of the milk to the stock.

▶ Except for fresh fruit soups, most soups can be refrigerated for one to two days. In fact, some people think the flavor of the soup is enhanced.

SAUCES

▶ Brown sauce won't thicken if you add acids, such as citrus juice or vinegar, before the sauce has been reduced.

▶ If brown sauce is too thick, thin it with more meat stock or one to two tablespoons of light cream.

▶ Don't cover meat sauces while keeping them warm. Moisture will build up and will dilute your sauce.

▶ Substitute beef, veal, or pork fat for butter when making a brown sauce for gravies.

▶ To give your sauce an extra-shiny appearance, whip in 2 tablespoons of cold butter just before serving.

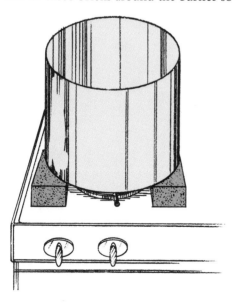

▶ If a sauce begins to separate, add a little cold water. If the sauce begins to cool too quickly, alternate cold and hot water.

▶ If you make béarnaise sauce several hours ahead of time, keep it in a tightly closed, preheated vacuum bottle.

▶ If an egg-based sauce curdles, it's probably because it's been boiled. Keep the temperature moderate when making egg sauces.

Gravies

▶ If gravy's too salty, add several pinches of brown sugar. It will remove the salty taste without sweetening.

▶ If your gravy tastes burned, stir in a teaspoon of peanut butter.

▶ There are two quick ways to darken gravy. The first is to mix 1 tablespoon of water with 1 tablespoon of sugar, heating the blend in a pan until the sugar browns and the water evaporates. Pour the gravy into this pan. The second method is to add coffee to the gravy; it will add color without affecting the flavor.

▶ One way to make rich brown gravy for a roast is to put flour in a pie pan and let it brown in the oven along with the roast. When the meat is done, mix the toasty brown flour with a little cold water and heat it with the meat juice.

▶ If you want greaseless gravy, let the pan drippings sit for a few minutes. The grease will rise to the top where it can be skimmed off, leaving stock for grease-free gravy.

ALL ABOUT BAKING

MEASURING INGREDIENTS

Dry Ingredients

▶ Always use standardized measuring spoons and cups.

▶ Fill the correct measuring spoon or cup to overflowing and level it off with a metal spatula or knife.

▶ When measuring flour, lightly spoon it into a measuring cup and then level it off. Do not

FREEZING SOUPS AND STOCKS

▶ Before freezing, refrigerate the soup until the fat rises to the surface. Skim the fat and discard bones, bay leaves, or any other ingredients that will not be eaten.

▶ Divide the soup into portions to serve two, four, or more, depending on the number of people you are most likely to be feeding at one time.

▶ To save freezer space, store the soup in self-sealing plastic bags, stacking them in the freezer like pages in a book.

▶ To avoid having all your plastic containers filled with frozen stock, line each container with a heavy-duty freezer

bag and fill it with stock. Cover and freeze. Slide the bag with the frozen stock from the plastic container. Seal the bag with tape or a twist tie, and return it to the freezer.

▶ There's no need to thaw frozen stock before using. Just pop a frozen block of stock into a covered saucepan and heat it gently until boiling.

▶ If freezer space is tight and you want to store homemade stocks, simply cook down the stock until it's reduced by half, then freeze it. Restore the stock to its original volume by adding water.

tap or bang the measuring cup—this will pack the flour.

▶ If a recipe calls for sifted flour, sift the flour before it is measured. If a recipe calls for "flour, sifted," measure the flour first and then sift it.

Liquid Ingredients

▶ Use a standardized glass or plastic measuring cup with a pouring spout. Place the cup on a flat surface, fill to the desired mark, and check the measurement at eye level.

▶ When measuring sticky liquids such as honey and molasses, grease the measuring cup or spray it with vegetable cooking spray before adding the liquid to make removal easier.

BREADS

In most breads, yeast is to used to make dough rise. Quick breads rely on other agents—such as baking powder—to make them rise.

Dissolving Yeast

Dissolving yeast properly is the most important step in successful yeast breads and coffeecakes.

▶ Dissolve the yeast with a small amount of sugar in warm (105–115°F) water or milk, depending on the recipe. The warmth and sugar cause the yeast to grow and multiply. It is best to use a thermometer to check the temperature of the liquid.

▶ After about 5 minutes the yeast will start to foam and bubble. If it doesn't, throw out the yeast mixture and start over.

▶ Be sure to use yeast before its expiration date. It quickly loses its effectiveness as it ages.

▶ Yeast doughs need to rise before baking to ensure proper volume and texture. Be sure to cover the dough and set it in a warm (70–75°F), draft-free place.

Kneading

Although bread dough starts out soft and sticky, it becomes smooth and elastic when kneaded. The purpose of kneading is to develop the gluten, a protein present in wheat flour that gives the bread structure. The gluten forms long elastic strands in the dough that trap carbon dioxide gas produced by the yeast. It is the trapped gas that causes the bread to rise.

▶ Knead bread dough on a lightly floured surface.

▶ Always use the heel of your hand—not your fingers—to knead.

▶ Push the dough away from you with the heel of your hand, then bring the far end down to fold the dough in half. Give the dough a quarter turn and repeat the process, adding more flour as needed to prevent sticking. You should develop a rhythm to your kneading, making the motion fluid and continuous.

▶ Knead the dough until it is smooth, satiny, and springy when pressed with a finger (8 to

10 minutes). Air bubbles or blisters should appear just below the surface.

▶ You can also use an electric mixer with a dough-hook attachment

Rising

▶ Shape the kneaded dough into a ball and place in a lightly oiled bowl; turn the ball to coat the entire surface with oil. This prevents the bread from forming a crust that could hinder rising.

▶ Cover the bowl with a cloth towel and set it in a warm (70–75°F), draft-free place. A gas oven with the pilot light on, or an electric oven that has been heated for 1 minute and then turned off, are good places.

▶ Let the dough rise until it has doubled in size, usually about 1 hour. One way to test if the dough has doubled is to press two fingertips about ½ inch into the dough; the indentations should remain when you remove your fingers.

Shaping and Second Rising

▶ After the dough has doubled, punch it down with your fist. This removes large air bubbles, giving the bread a fine, even texture.

▶ Pull the edges of the dough to the center to form a ball.

▶ Shape the dough according to the recipe directions and place it on a greased baking sheet or in a greased loaf pan.

▶ Cover the shaped loaves and let them rise again in a warm place until they have doubled

MARVELOUS MARINADES

Marinades add unique flavors to foods and help tenderize less tender cuts of meat, but they require special care. After food is removed from a marinade, the marinade may be used as a basting or dipping sauce. When used as a basting sauce, marinades should only be applied up to the last 5 minutes of grilling or broiling. This precaution is necessary because the marinade could have become contaminated with harmful bacteria from the raw food during the marinading process. The marinade must be cooked over the heat for a minimum of 5 minutes to ensure that the harmful bacteria are destroyed. If you wish to use marinade as a dipping sauce, place it in a small saucepan and bring it to a full boil.

▶ Turn marinating foods occasionally to let the flavor infuse evenly. Heavy-duty plastic bags are great to hold foods as they marinate.

▶ The safest way to apply basting sauce is to brush it on the food before turning it over.

▶ Basting sauces containing sugar, honey, or tomato products should be applied only during the last 15 to 30 minutes of grilling. This will prevent the food from charring. Basting sauces made from seasoned oils and butters may be brushed on throughout grilling.

in size, about 1 hour. (Do *not* use your fingertips to test if the loaf has doubled; judge this by appearance.)

Baking

▶ Place the bread on the center rack of an oven preheated to the temperature called for in the recipe.

▶ The bread is done when it is golden brown, well rounded, and sounds hollow when lightly tapped.

▶ For a crisp crust, place a pan of water in the bottom of the oven during baking, or brush the top of the loaf with water.

▶ For a softer crust, brush the loaves with softened butter immediately after baking.

Cooling and Storing

▶ Immediately remove the bread from the pan or baking sheet and place it on a wire rack to cool.

▶ Once the bread has completely cooled, wrap it in plastic wrap or place in an airtight plastic bag or container.

▶ Store the bread at room temperature; placing it in the refrigerator actually causes it to become stale faster.

▶ If wrapped well, bread can be frozen for up to six months.

▶ Freeze coffeecakes before adding glazes or icings; frost them after thawing. Thaw unwrapped yeast breads at room temperature for 2 to 3 hours; you can also heat them partially unwrapped in a 375°F oven for 20 minutes.

▶ Allow a freshly baked loaf to cool for at least 3 hours on a wire rack before freezing. Place the loaf in the freezer on a flat surface for 2 hours or until it is solidly frozen. Wrap the frozen loaf in plastic wrap and then in heavy-duty aluminum foil. Label it with the date and the type of bread and return it to the freezer. Bread can be frozen for up to 6 months. Thaw frozen bread in its wrapping at room temperature for 2 to 3 hours. Freshen the loaf by heating it in a 300°F oven for 20 minutes.

QUICK BREADS

These breads are quick to make because they rely on quick-acting leavening agents such as baking soda, baking powder, and eggs—rather than yeast—to make them rise. Quick breads include biscuits, scones, muffins, popovers, and puff pancakes.

Biscuits and Scones

▶ When preparing biscuits, cut the shortening or butter into the dry ingredients with a pastry blender or two knives until the mixture forms coarse crumbs. Blending the fat in any further produces mealy biscuits.

MAKING PASTRY IN THE FOOD PROCESSOR

The food processor can make a delightful pastry dough in a very short time. Be sure the shortening is fully chilled (put it in the freezer for 15 to 20 minutes, if desired). Combine the flour and salt and add half of the shortening. Process with quick pulses until the mixture resembles coarse crumbs. Add the remaining shortening and repeat the process. Quickly add the ice water through the feed tube while pulsing; stop as soon as the dough looks like it will gather into a ball. Gather it into a ball and refrigerate before rolling it out.

▶ Mix the dough gently and quickly to achieve light and tender results. Overworking the dough makes the biscuits tough.

▶ On a lightly floured surface, roll or pat out the dough to the desired thickness.

▶ Press a floured cutter straight down through the dough; twisting produces lopsided biscuits.

▶ For crusty biscuits, place them at least one inch apart on the baking sheet. For soft, fluffy biscuits, place them close together.

▶ Scones are similar to biscuits, but the dough is richer due to the addition of cream and eggs. While the dough can be cut into any shape, scones are usually cut into wedges or triangles.

Muffins

▶ For most muffin recipes, mix the dry ingredients together first to evenly distribute the baking powder and/or baking soda.

▶ Combine the liquid ingredients and add them all at once to the dry ingredients. Stir just until the dry ingredients are moistened. The batter should be lumpy; the lumps will disappear during baking.

▶ Overbeating the batter will result in tunnels, peaked tops, and a tough texture.

BEATING EGG WHITES

▶ Separate eggs while they are cold because the yolk is firm and less likely to break. Remember that egg whites won't beat properly if any trace of yolk remains. Flecks of yolk can be removed with the moistened tip of a cotton swab.

▶ Let the whites sit out at room temperature for 30 minutes before beating to achieve their highest volume.

▶ Make sure that the bowl and beaters you are using are clean and dry; any grease or yolk that is present will decrease the volume of the egg whites.

▶ For best results, use a copper, stainless steel, or glass bowl (plastic bowls have an oily film, even after repeated washings).

▶ Add a pinch of cream of tartar and salt to the egg whites after they have been beaten slightly and are foamy; this will prevent them from collapsing.

▶ When a recipe calls for sugar, add it slowly to the egg whites, beating well after each addition. If the mixture feels grainy to the touch, continue beating before adding more.

▶ If the egg whites are to be folded into other ingredients, this should be done immediately after they are beaten.

▶ Standard-size muffin pans have cups that are 2½ or 2¾ inches in diameter.

▶ Grease the cups or use paper baking liners and fill them ⅔ to ¾ full with batter. Pour water into any empty cups to prevent the pan from warping in the oven.

▶ Muffins are done when the center springs back when lightly touched and a wooden toothpick inserted into the center comes out clean and dry.

▶ Remove muffins from their cups immediately after baking and cool them on a wire rack.

▶ Stored in an airtight plastic bag, muffins will stay fresh for several days.

▶ For longer storage, wrap and freeze. To reheat, wrap frozen muffins in foil and heat in a 350°F oven for 15 to 20 minutes. For best flavor, use frozen muffins within one month.

Popovers and Puff Pancakes

▶ Popovers and puff pancakes are leavened by steam. A shell is formed by the flour and liquid in the batter. This shell stretches as the steam inside expands during cooking. The steam comes from the unusually high liquid content of the batter.

▶ When baking popovers and puff pancakes, be sure the oven is fully preheated and do not peek during baking. Opening the oven door lets in cold air that may cause them to collapse.

CAKES

Cakes are divided into two basic categories according to what makes them rise. Butter cakes rely primarily on baking powder or baking soda for height, while sponge cakes depend on the air trapped in the eggs during beating. Tortes are simply several layers of cake separated by a filling.

Butter Cakes

Butter cakes include pound cakes and yellow, white, spice, and chocolate layer cakes. These cakes use butter, shortening, or oil for moistness and richness and are leavened with baking powder and/or baking soda.

▶ Before mixing the batter, soften the butter so that it mixes easily with the sugar.

▶ Grease and flour the pans before mixing the cake batter so that the cake can be baked immediately. To grease and flour cake pans, use a paper towel, waxed paper, or your fingers to apply a thin, even layer of shortening. Sprinkle flour into the greased pan; shake or tilt the pan to coat evenly with flour; then tap lightly to remove any excess.

▶ A butter cake is done when it begins to pull away from the sides of the pan, the top springs back when lightly touched, and a cake tester or wooden toothpick inserted into the center comes out clean and dry.

▶ After removing butter cakes from the oven, let them stand in their pans on wire racks for 10 minutes, or as the recipe directs. Run a knife around the edge of the cake to loosen it from the sides of the pan and invert it on a wire rack. Turn the cake top-side up onto a second rack to finish cooling.

Sponge Cakes

These cakes achieve their high volume from beaten eggs. Sponge cakes do not contain butter, oil, or shortening. Angel food cakes are the most popular and can be literally fat-free since they use only egg whites, not yolks. Yellow sponge cakes are prepared with whole eggs. Chiffon cakes are also lightened with beaten eggs, but they are not true sponge cakes because they contain vegetable oil.

▶ When preparing sponge cakes, be sure to beat the eggs to the proper stage. Handle the beaten eggs gently when folding the other ingredients into them to prevent them from losing air and volume.

▶ Sponge cakes are usually baked in tube pans. The center tube helps the heat circulate during baking and also supports the delicate structure of the cake. Do not grease the pans for sponge cake batters. The ungreased pan lets the batter cling to the sides as it rises.

▶ A sponge cake is done when it is delicately browned and the top springs back when lightly touched.

▶ Invert a sponge cake baked in a tube pan onto a funnel or bottle immediately after removing it from the oven. If it is cooled top-side up, it will fall. Do not remove a sponge cake from the pan until it is completely cool.

Tips for a Flawless Cake

▶ Some cake recipes specifically call for cake flour, which contains less protein than all-purpose flour and produces a more tender cake. Use cake flour if the recipe calls for it.

▶ Be sure to use the pan sizes specified in cake recipes.

▶ Place the cake pan(s) in the center of a preheated oven. Oven racks may need to be set lower for cakes baked in tube pans.

▶ If two racks are used, arrange them so they divide the oven into thirds and then stagger the pans so they are not directly over each other. Avoid opening the oven door during the first half of the baking time. The oven temperature must remain constant to allow the cake to rise properly.

▶ When a cake is baked all the way through, it will begin to shrink away from the side of the pan. Insert a wooden toothpick into the center; if it comes out clean without a trace of moisture, the cake is done. Lighter cakes will also spring back if gently pressed in the center.

▶ Let the cake cool in the pan on a wire rack for about 10 minutes, then loosen it from the side of the pan with a knife or metal spatula. Invert it on the rack and let it cool completely before frosting or cutting.

▶ Make sure the cake is completely cool before frosting it. Brush off any loose crumbs from the cake's surface. To keep the cake plate clean, place small pieces of waxed paper under the edges of the cake; remove them after the cake has been frosted.

▶ Use a flat metal spatula for applying frosting to achieve a more professional look. First apply a thin layer of frosting on the cake as a base coat to help seal in any remaining crumbs.

▶ To evenly halve a cake horizontally, remove the cake from the pan and place on a flat surface. Measure the cake with a ruler and mark a cutting line with toothpicks. Cut through the cake with a long serrated knife, just above the toothpicks.

▶ To cut an angel food cake, use a long serrated knife and cut with a sawing motion.

▶ To easily fill muffin cups, place batter in a 4-cup glass measure. Fill each cup ¾ full. Use a plastic spatula to control the flow of the batter.

Storing Cakes

▶ Store one-layer cakes in their baking pan, tightly covered.

▶ Store 2- or 3-layer cakes in a cake-saver or under a large inverted bowl.

▶ If the cake has a fluffy or cooked frosting, insert a teaspoon handle under the edge of the cover to prevent an airtight seal and moisture buildup.

▶ Cakes with whipped cream frostings or cream fillings should be stored in the refrigerator.

▶ Unfrosted cakes can be frozen for up to four months if well wrapped in plastic. Thaw them in their wrapping at room temperature.

▶ Frosted cakes should be frozen unwrapped until the frosting hardens, and then wrapped and sealed; freeze for up to two months. To thaw, remove the wrapping and thaw at room temperature or in the refrigerator.

▶ Cakes with fruit or custard fillings do not freeze well, because they become soggy when thawed.

▶ Store cakes in the refrigerator covered with plastic wrap to help prevent them from picking up flavors of other foods.

THE ABCs OF BAKING

Whether you're taking on bread, cakes, cookies, pies, or other baked desserts, take the guesswork out of baking by practicing the following techniques:

▶ Read the entire recipe before beginning to make sure you have all the necessary ingredients and baking utensils.

▶ Remove butter, margarine, and cream cheese from the refrigerator to soften, if necessary.

▶ Toast and chop nuts, pare and slice fruit, and melt chocolate before preparing the cookie dough.

▶ Measure all the ingredients accurately and assemble them in the order they are called for in the recipe.

▶ Use the pan size specified in each recipe and prepare it as stated. The wrong-size pan may cause a burned bottom or edges or a sunken middle.

▶ Warped or bent pans cause uneven baking results and unevenly shaped baked goods. Find another use for warped pans (put them under your houseplants, for example), and buy new ones for baking.

▶ Shiny aluminum pans reflect heat and give a golden color to breads and cookies. For pies, use dark pans to absorb heat and keep the crust from getting soggy.

▶ Oven temperatures can vary significantly depending on the oven model and manufacturer, so watch your baked dish carefully and check for doneness using the test given in the recipe.

▶ Adjust oven racks and preheat the oven. Check oven temperature for accuracy with an oven thermometer.

▶ Follow recipe directions and baking times exactly.

COOKIES

Despite the multitude of flavors, shapes and sizes, cookies can actually be divided into five basic types: bar, drop, refrigerator, rolled, and shaped. These types are determined by the consistency of the dough and how it is formed into cookies.

Bar Cookies

Bar cookies and brownies are very easy to make—simply mix the batter, spread in the pan, and bake. These cookies are also quick to prepare since they bake all at once, rather than in batches on a cookie sheet.

▶ Always use the pan size called for in the recipe. Substituting a different pan will affect the cookies' texture. A smaller pan will give the bars a more cakelike texture, and a larger pan will produce a flatter bar with a drier texture.

▶ Most bar cookies should cool in the pan on a wire rack until barely warm before cutting into bars or squares.

▶ To make serving easy, remove a corner piece first; then remove the rest.

Drop Cookies

These cookies are named for the way they are formed on the cookie sheet. The soft dough mounds when dropped from a spoon and then flattens slightly during baking.

▶ Space the mounds of dough about 2 inches apart on cookie sheets to allow for spreading, unless the recipe directs otherwise.

▶ Cookies that are uniform in size and shape will finish baking at the same time. To easily shape drop cookies into a uniform size, use an ice-cream scoop (Nos. 80 or 90 are best) with a release bar.

Refrigerator Cookies

Refrigerator doughs are perfect for preparing in advance. Tightly wrapped rolls of dough can be stored in the refrigerator for up to one week or frozen for up to 6 weeks. These rich doughs are ready to be sliced and baked at a moment's notice.

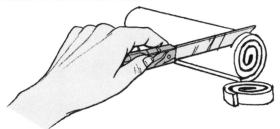

▶ Always shape the dough into rolls before chilling.

▶ Shaping is easier if you first place the dough on a piece of waxed paper or plastic wrap.

▶ If desired, you can gently press chopped nuts, flaked coconut, or colored sugar into the roll.

▶ Before chilling, wrap the rolls securely in plastic wrap to prevent air from penetrating the dough and causing it to dry out.

▶ Use gentle pressure and a back-and-forth sawing motion when slicing the rolls so the cookies will keep their nice round shape. Rotating the roll while slicing also prevents one side from flattening.

Rolled Cookies

Rolled or cutout cookies are made from stiff doughs that are rolled out and cut into fancy shapes with floured cookie cutters, a knife, or a pastry wheel.

▶ Chill the cookie dough thoroughly before rolling for easier handling. Remove only

ALL ABOUT CHOCOLATE

When a recipe calls for chocolate, you'll want to make sure you have the right chocolate on hand. For cooking or baking, you'll need to use semisweet, unsweetened, milk, white chocolate, or cocoa. It's not a good idea to substitute one chocolate for another.

▶ Store chocolate in a cool, dry place. If chocolate gets too warm, the cocoa butter rises to the surface and causes a grayish white appearance, which is called a bloom. The bloom will not affect the chocolate's taste or baking quality.

▶ Chill chocolate to make it easier to grate.

▶ Warm a wrapped chocolate square in your hands to make it easier to shave it for curls. Unwrap the chocolate and use a vegetable peeler or a sharp knife to "shave" the chocolate.

Types of Chocolate

▶ **Unsweetened chocolate** contains no sugar. It is usually sold in 1-ounce squares.

▶ **Semisweet chocolate** is usually about 40 percent sugar. It is sold in squares or chips. Bittersweet chocolate contains even less sugar.

▶ **Milk chocolate** contains milk solids and is rarely used in baking.

▶ **White chocolate** is not really chocolate at all, but is cocoa butter with added sugar, milk, and flavorings. It is more delicate than other chocolates.

▶ **Unsweetened cocoa** is formed by extracting most of the cocoa butter from

pure chocolate and grinding the remaining chocolate solids into a powder.

Melting Chocolate

Make sure the utensils you use for melting chocolate are completely dry. Be careful not to scorch chocolate when you melt it.

▶ **Double Boiler**—The safest method of scorch-free melting is to use a double boiler. Place the chocolate in the top of a double boiler or in a bowl over hot, not boiling, water; stir until smooth.

▶ **Direct Heat**—Place the chocolate in a heavy saucepan and melt it over very low heat, stirring constantly. Remove the chocolate from the heat as soon as it is melted. Be sure to watch the chocolate carefully since it is easily scorched with this method.

▶ **Microwave Oven**—Place an unwrapped 1-ounce square or 1 cup of chips in a small microwavable bowl. Microwave on HIGH (100 percent) 1 to 1½ minutes. Stir the chocolate at 30-second intervals until smooth, since it will retains its original shape.

enough to work with at one time from the refrigerator.

▶ Save trimmings and reroll them all at once to keep the dough from becoming tough.

▶ To make your own custom-designed cookie cutters, cut a simple shape out of clean, heavy cardboard or poster board. Place the cardboard pattern on the rolled-out dough and cut around it using a sharp knife.

Shaped Cookies

These cookies can be simply hand-shaped into balls or crescents, forced through a cookie press into more complex shapes, or baked in cookie molds.

▶ Be sure to use the specific cookie press or mold called for in the recipe. The consistency of the dough may not lend itself to using a different tool.

▶ By using different plates in a cookie press, spritz cookies can be formed into many shapes. If your first efforts are not successful, just transfer the dough back to the cookie press and try again.

WHEN YOU RUN OUT, SUBSTITUTE

If you don't have:	Use:
1 teaspoon baking powder	¼ teaspoon baking soda plus ½ teaspoon cream of tartar
½ cup firmly packed brown sugar	½ cup sugar mixed with 2 tablespoons molasses
1 cup buttermilk	1 tablespoon lemon juice or vinegar plus milk to equal 1 cup (Stir; let mixture stand 5 minutes.)
1 ounce (1 square) unsweetened baking chocolate	3 tablespoons unsweetened cocoa plus 1 tablespoon shortening
3 ounces (3 squares) semi-sweet baking chocolate	3 ounces (½ cup) semi-sweet chocolate morsels
½ cup corn syrup	½ cup granulated sugar plus 2 tablespoons liquid
1 tablespoon cornstarch	2 tablespoons all-purpose flour or 4 teaspoons quick-cooking tapioca
1 cup sweetened whipped cream	4½ oz. frozen whipped topping, thawed
1 cup heavy cream (for baking, not whipping)	¾ cup whole milk plus ¼ cup butter
1 whole egg	2 egg yolks plus 1 tablespoon water
1 cup cake flour	1 cup minus 2 tablespoons all-purpose flour
1 cup honey	1¼ cups granulated sugar plus ¼ cup water
1 teaspoon freshly grated orange or lemon peel	½ teaspoon dried peel
1 teaspoon apple or pumpkin pie spice	Combine: ½ teaspoon cinnamon, ¼ teaspoon nutmeg, ⅛ teaspoon *each* allspice and cardamom
1 package active dry yeast	1 packed tablespoon compressed yeast

▶ Flavor or tint the dough with food coloring; pressed shapes can be decorated before baking with colored sugar or candied fruit.

▶ To flatten cookies, use the bottom of a greased and sugared glass. Place balls of cookie dough on the cookie sheet, then flatten with the glass.

Tips for Flawless Cookies

▶ Use shiny cookie sheets with little or no sides for best baking results.

▶ When a recipe calls for greasing the cookie sheets, use shortening or a vegetable cooking spray for best results.

▶ Lining the cookie sheets with parchment paper is an alternative to greasing. It eliminates cleanup, bakes the cookies more evenly, and allows them to cool.

▶ Promote even baking and browning by placing only one cookie sheet at a time in the center of a conventional oven. If you use more than one sheet at a time, rotate the cookie sheets from top to bottom halfway through the baking time. If the cookies brown unevenly just with one cookie sheet in the oven, rotate the cookie sheet from front to back halfway through the baking time.

▶ Most cookies bake quickly and should be watched carefully to avoid overbaking. Check them at the minimum baking time, then

watch carefully to make sure they don't burn. It is generally better to slightly underbake, rather than to overbake, cookies.

▶ Allow cookie sheets to cool between batches; the dough will spread if placed on a hot cookie sheet.

▶ Most cookies should be removed from cookie sheets immediately after baking and placed in a single layer on wire racks to cool. Fragile cookies may need to cool slightly on the cookie sheet before being moved. Always cool cookies completely before stacking and storing. Bar cookies and brownies may be cooled and stored in the baking pan.

▶ Before drizzling cookies with chocolate or icing or dusting with powdered sugar, place waxed paper under the wire rack to make cleanup easier.

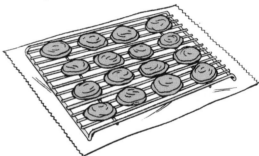

Storing Cookies

▶ Store soft and crisp cookies separately at room temperature to prevent changes in texture and flavor.

▶ Keep soft cookies in airtight containers. If they begin to dry out, add a piece of apple or bread to the container to help them retain moisture.

▶ Store crisp cookies in containers with loose-fitting lids to prevent moisture buildup. If they become soggy, heat undecorated cookies in a 300°F oven for 3 to 5 minutes.

▶ Store cookies with sticky glazes, fragile decorations, and icings in single layers between sheets of waxed paper.

▶ Bar cookies and brownies may be stored in their own baking pan, covered with aluminum foil or plastic wrap. Make sure the cookies or brownies are cool.

▶ As a rule, crisp cookies freeze better than soft, moist cookies. Rich, buttery bar cookies and brownies are an exception to this rule since they freeze extremely well.

▶ Freeze baked cookies in airtight containers or freezer bags for up to six months. Thaw cookies and brownies unwrapped at room temperature. Meringue-based cookies do not freeze well, and chocolate-dipped cookies will discolor if frozen.

PASTRIES

The only real secrets to tender, flaky pie crusts are to keep the ingredients cold and handle the dough as little as possible. Tough crusts are the result of overdeveloped gluten, a protein present in flour.

Preparing Pastry Dough

▶ If you use butter in your pastry dough, it must be chilled. Vegetable shortening and lard, although soft at room temperature, do not need to be chilled. Also make sure that the liquid you add is cold. The cold liquid, such as ice water, keeps the fat solid.

▶ Blend the flour and salt together, then cut the fat in quickly with a pastry blender, two knives, or your fingertips until the shortening lumps are the size of peas.

▶ Add cold water (or any liquid) gradually, a tablespoon at a time, stirring lightly with a fork. The amount of liquid needed will vary depending on the type of flour and the humidity; the dough should be just moist enough to hold together with slight pressure and be gathered into a ball.

▶ To create a tender pie crust, add a small amount of acid, such as lemon juice, vinegar, sour cream, or even crème fraîche, to the pastry dough along with the liquid.

▶ Handle the pastry dough quickly; overworking it will make it tough. If the dough is difficult to handle, refrigerate it until firm.

▶ Wrap the ball of dough in plastic wrap and refrigerate it for at least 1 hour. Chilling the

dough makes it easier to handle and helps prevent shrinkage during baking.

▶ Flour the rolling pin and surface just enough to prevent sticking. Place the chilled dough on a lightly floured surface and flatten it into a ½-inch thick circle. Roll the dough with a floured rolling pin, pressing out from the center to the edge using quick, short strokes. Continue rolling until the dough is ⅛-inch thick and 2 inches larger than the inverted pie pan. For less mess, roll the dough between two pieces of wax paper and peel off the paper when the dough is the size you need.

▶ Loosely fold the dough into quarters and place the point of the folded dough into the center of the pie pan. Gently unfold the dough and ease it into the pan; do not stretch the dough or it will shrink during baking.

▶ For a single-crust pie, trim the dough and flute the edge.

Baking Pastry

▶ **Single-crust pies**—Some single-crust pies, like custard pies, are baked in an unbaked pastry shell. Others require the shell to be prebaked so that it does not become soggy. If the pastry shell is to be baked without the filling, prick the dough all over with a fork. Line the pastry with aluminum foil, waxed paper, or parchment paper and spread dried beans (or peas) or pie weights over the bottom. Weighing down the pastry prevents it from puffing and losing its shape during baking. The pastry can be fully or partially baked in this manner. Cool it completely before adding the filling.

▶ **Double-crust pies**—These pies are made by placing the filling (usually fruit) between two unbaked layers of pastry. Spoon the filling into the pastry shell and brush the rim of the shell with water. Roll out the top crust and place it over the filling. Press the pastry edges together to seal, then trim and flute. Cut a few slits or vents in the top crust to allow steam to escape. Before baking a double-crust pie, try glazing the top crust with milk or cream to promote browning. Brushing it with beaten egg will add color and shine; sprinkling it with granulated sugar will add a little sparkle.

▶ If the top crust or edges of the pie shell are browning too quickly, cover the pie loosely with aluminum foil and continue baking.

Storing Pastry

▶ Meringue-topped pies are best when served the day they are made; refrigerate any leftovers.

▶ Refrigerate custard or cream pies immediately after cooling.

▶ Fruit pies can be covered and stored at room temperature overnight; refrigerate them for longer storage.

▶ To freeze unbaked pies, do not cut steam vents in the top crust. Cover the top with an inverted paper plate for extra protection, packaging it in freezer bags or freezer wrap. To bake, do not thaw. Cut slits in the top crust and allow an additional 15 to 20 minutes of baking time.

▶ Baked pies can also be cooled and frozen. To serve, let the pie thaw at room temperature for two hours, then heat until warm.

▶ Freezing is not recommended for pies with cream or custard fillings or meringue toppings.

▶ Unbaked pie dough can be frozen in bulk for later use. Simply flatten the dough into circles and stack them in a freezer bag with waxed paper separating each layer. Freeze prepared pastry shells in pie pans with waxed paper between the shells. Bulk pie dough must be thawed before using.

BAKING THE PERFECT CHEESECAKE

With cheesecakes, a picture-perfect appearance isn't just cosmetic. A smooth top is a good indication of a well-baked, moist interior. While some cheesecakes develop small cracks around the rim during baking or cooling, there should never be center cracks, which is a sure sign that the inside of the cake will be too dry. If you're having trouble smoothing out those cracks, check the causes and cures below. Cheesecakes can be stored in the refrigerator for up to one week, but for the best flavor, bring them to room temperature before serving. Freezing is not recommended for cheesecakes.

COMMON CAUSES OF CRACKS IN CHEESECAKES	CURES
Overbaking or baking in a too-hot oven	Test for doneness by gently shaking the cheesecake. A 1-inch area in the center of the cheesecake should jiggle slightly. This area will firm during cooling.
Overbeating the batter, which incorporates too much air into the batter	Soften cream cheese before beginning the recipe. It will then combine easily with other ingredients and prevent lumps from forming in the batter. Beat the batter gently—only as long as the recipe specifies.
Jarring the cake during baking or cooling	Don't coddle the cheesecake. Keep the oven door closed until it's time to check for doneness.
Refrigerating the cake before it's completely cooled	After baking, run a knife around the inside of the pan to loosen the edges of the crust. Let cool and then remove the rim of the pan. Make sure the cheesecake is no longer warm before refrigerating.
Wrong pan size	Don't substitute. A springform pan is your best bet for a perfect cake.

SOLUTIONS TO COMMON BAKING PROBLEMS

PROBLEM	SOLUTION(S)
QUICK BREADS	
BITTER TASTE	Distribute baking soda/baking powder evenly with other dry ingredients.
FAILURE TO RISE	Use fresh baking soda and baking powder.
TOUGH TEXTURE, TUNNELS, PEAKED TOPS	Avoid overstirring; batter should be lumpy.
RAISINS OR OTHER DRIED FRUIT SINK TO BOTTOM OF LOAF	Toss fruit lightly with flour before adding to batter.
LOPSIDED BISCUITS	Press floured cutter straight down into dough without twisting.
YEAST BREADS	
BREAD IS HEAVY AND COMPACT	Liquid used to dissolve yeast may have been too hot or too cold; check temperature with a thermometer. Too much flour was added during kneading; do not exceed maximum amount called for in recipe.
BREAD IS CRUMBLY	Dough has risen too much. Let rise just until double for first rising and until nearly double for second rising.
CRUST IS TOO THICK	Oven temperature may be too low; use oven thermometer to check for accuracy.
BREAD HAS LARGE HOLES	Press or punch air bubbles out of dough thoroughly before shaping into loaf.

COOKIES

UNEVEN BROWNING	Bake on only one rack at a time; use cookie sheets with little or no sides.
COOKIES SPREAD TOO MUCH	Allow cookie sheets to cool between batches before reusing.
CUT-OUT COOKIES ARE TOUGH	Save dough scraps to reroll all at once; handle dough as little as possible. Use just enough flour on board to prevent sticking.

CAKES

CAKES FALL IN MIDDLE	Avoid overbeating—too much air is incorporated into batter. Avoid opening oven door before cake sets.
CAKE PEAKS IN CENTER	Oven temperature may be too high and cake will rise too quickly; use oven thermometer to check for accuracy.
CAKE IS DRY	Avoid overbeating egg whites. Avoid overbaking. Check cake for doneness at lower end of baking time range.

PIE CRUSTS

PASTRY IS CRUMBLY	Add additional water, one teaspoon at a time.
PASTRY IS TOUGH	Add water gradually, stirring lightly after each addition. Avoid overworking dough; toss flour mixture and water together just until evenly moistened. Handle dough as little as possible.
CRUST SHRINKS EXCESSIVELY	Roll pastry from the center outward; roll to an even thickness. Avoid stretching pastry when transferring from rolling surface to pie plate.

I t probably goes without saying that a nicely maintained home, lawn, and garden take a lot of work. It's also true that many potential problems can be avoided with a scheduled maintenance program. However, it is a fact of life that things break down and require repair. The more a homeowner is prepared to fix problems on his or her own, the less expensive and time-consuming they are. The following pages contain a lot of information on how to take good care of your home and property and how to do common repairs.

BASIC TOOLS AND SUPPLIES

Y ou don't need expensive power tools or even a full workshop of hand tools for many home repair and maintenance chores. To tackle most minor home repairs, you'll need an electric drill and between 12 and 15 hand tools, including:

- Two or three chisels
- Claw hammer
- Assortment of nails and screws
- Measuring tape
- Level
- Pliers
- Saws (crosscut and hacksaw)
- Screwdrivers (slotted and Phillips-head)
- Adjustable wrench

The most important rule about selecting tools is to go for quality. Metal parts should be smooth and shiny, and the tool well balanced. Poor-quality tools can be unsafe and may be difficult to use. Inexpensive tools are often painted to hide defects or roughness of the metal parts, and the machining of the tool is crude. While you'll pay more for quality

equipment, you'll have tools that are safer and more durable.

Choose your tools from the following list depending on the projects you want to tackle yourself.

Chisels

- Wood chisel, preferably a pocket chisel
- Cold chisel, preferably a flat chisel

Wood chisels are used to remove wood and cut mortises; cold chisels are used to cut metal, such as bolts, and other hard materials, like brick or concrete.

Measuring and Marking Tools

▶ **Flexible measuring tape**—The most helpful are at least 1 inch wide and 25 feet long. An automatic power return is handy.

▶ **Folding rule**.

▶ **Level**—Used for finding correct horizontal and vertical readings when installing cabinets, appliances, hanging wallpaper, etc. A 30-inch level is adequate for most home repairs.

▶ **Chalk line**—Used for marking a straight line over long distances, such as for wallpaper and in carpentry.

For more advanced woodworking projects, you may also want a carpenter's square, used for figuring board-foot requirements, rafter height, angles, etc.; and a try square, used for testing the squareness of edges, marking saw cuts, and establishing a 45-degree miter. A stud finder comes in handy if you need to find the studs behind walls (density sensors work best).

Handsaws

▶ **Crosscut saw**—Used to saw cuts across the grain of the wood, particularly in plywood and hardboard panels.

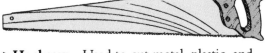

▶ **Hacksaw**—Used to cut metal, plastic, and pipe.

For woodworking projects, you may also want a ripsaw, used to cut along the grain of the wood; a backsaw, to make miter cuts and for trimming molding; a drywall saw, used to cut openings for pipes and electrical boxes; and a coping saw, which has thin and replaceable blades to be used for multiple projects.

Hammers

▶ **Claw hammer**—Preferably a 16-ounce curved claw hammer with a cushioned grip.

A rubber mallet comes in handy when you're trying to unstick painted windows or have to do light hammering on surfaces that can be damaged. Other specialty hammers include a ball-peen hammer for metal working and a mason's hammer for brick and concrete projects.

Screwdrivers

▶ **Slotted (blade)** for flathead screws.

▶ **Phillips head (blade)** for Phillips-type screws.

One of each type of screwdriver is essential, but since slots in screws come in various lengths and depths, neither may fit into a screw you are using for a particular project. Screwdrivers are relatively inexpensive, and a good set will include standard blade sizes.

Wrenches

▶ **Adjustable wrench** (6 to 10 inches long).

This type of wrench adjusts to various widths to accommodate various bolt head and nut sizes. For plumbing repairs, you may need a pipe wrench. To work with appliances, cars, and machinery, you'll need various sizes of open-end and box-end (or combination) wrenches, which must precisely fit on the nut or bolt. An Allen or hex-key wrench is necessary when tightening set screws and other screws with Allen-type heads. Frequently the appropriate Allen wrench is included in kits in which it is needed.

Power Tools

▶ **Electric drill**—A ³⁄₈-inch drill is good for most projects. For flexibility, a cordless, reversible, variable speed drill is helpful.

▶ **Electric sander**—An orbital sander is the handiest for most small projects.

Electric drills can be fitted with various accessories to perform all kinds of chores. Other handy drills, although not power drills, are a hand drill, which is used to make holes in wood and soft materials, and a push drill, used to make pilot holes and set hinges.

For woodworking projects, you'll want a circular saw and a saber saw, sometimes called a jigsaw. A circular, the power version of a crosscut saw and a ripsaw, can be mounted and used as a small table saw. A saber saw, the power version of a keyhole and coping saw, can hold many different blades and cut many materials, such as wood, plastic, and metal.

Other Tools

▶ **Clamps**—These come in various sizes to hold materials together; start with several sizes of C-clamps and a set of bar clamps.

▶ **Planes**—A jack plane is used to remove excess wood and bring the surface of the wood to trueness and smoothness; a smoothing plane is used to bring wood to a final finish. A block plane can do both, plus it is used to smooth and cut the end grain of wood.

SANDPAPER				
Grit	**Number**	**Grade**	**Available Coating**[1]	**Common Uses**
Very Coarse	30 36	2½ 2	F,G,S F,G,S	Rust removal on rough finished metals
Coarse	40 50 60	1½ 1 ½	F,G,S F,G,S F,G,A,S	Rough sanding of wood; paint removal
Medium	80 100 120	0(1/0) 00(2/0) 3/0	F,G,A,S F,G,A,S F,G,A,S	General wood sanding; plaster smoothing; preliminary smoothing of previously painted surfaces
Fine	150 180	4/0 5/0	F,G,A,S F,G,A,S	Final sanding of bare wood or previously painted surfaces
Very Fine	220 240 280	6/0 7/0 8/0	F,G,A,S F,A,S F,A,S	Light sanding between final coats; dry sanding
Extra Fine	320 360 400	9/0 —[2] 10/0	F,A,S S S	High-satinized finish on lacquer, varnish, or shellac; wet sanding
Super Fine	500 600	—[2] —[2]	S S	High-satinized finishes; wet sanding

F=flint; G=garnet; A=aluminum oxide; S=silicon carbide. Silicon carbide is used dry or wet, with water or oil.
[2]No grade designation.

► **Router**—This is the power equivalent of chisels, files, planes, and saws, and can cut dados, mortise joints, and step moldings. You can also use a router to trim plastic and laminate.

STORING AND MAINTAINING TOOLS

► To protect tools, store them so they aren't subjected to moisture. Keep a thin coating of oil on metal parts, wrap them in plastic wrap, or keep carpenter's chalk, which absorbs moisture, in the toolbox.

► A piece of garden hose—slit open—is a handy protective cover for the teeth of a handsaw between projects.

► To guard the teeth of circular saw blades when not in use, store the blades in record album covers. You can even store them in an ordinary record rack in your workshop.

► Store tools in a box containing oil-soaked sand if moisture is a problem.

► If you hang tools on pegboard walls, outline each tool with an artist's brush so you'll know at a glance where each tool goes. You'll also know when a tool hasn't been replaced.

► If you want to remind yourself to unplug an electric drill when changing accessories, fasten the chuck key near the plug end of the cord.

► Keep screwdrivers handy—slide the blades through the mesh in plastic berry baskets nailed to the shop wall.

► An empty soft-drink carton makes a convenient kit for holding and carrying lubricants.

► To retard moisture and rust, keep mothballs with your tools. If rust spots appear, rub them away with a typewriter eraser.

SELECTING NAILS

The easiest way to fasten two pieces of wood together is with nails, which are manufactured in a wide variety of shapes, sizes, and metals. Most nails are made of steel, but aluminum, brass, nickel, bronze, copper, and stainless-steel nails are available. To prevent rusting and to add holding power, nails are also manufactured with coatings—either galvanized, blued, or cemented.

Nail size is designated by penny size, originally the price per hundred nails. Size ranges from 2 penny (or 2d), 1 inch long, to 60 penny (or 60d), 6 inches long. Nails shorter than 1 inch are called brads; nails longer than 6 inches are called spikes.

The length of the nail is crucial in repair jobs. At least two-thirds of the nail should be driven into the underlying material.

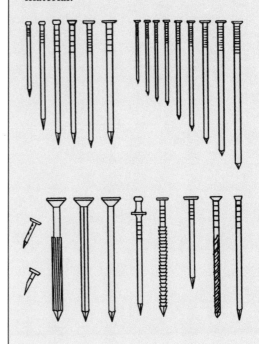

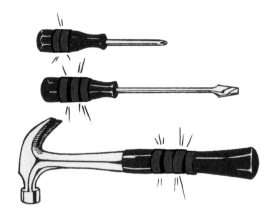

▶ Use a pocketed shoebag in your workshop. The bag holds more and takes up less space than a shelf.

▶ Paint all tool handles with an unusual, bright color, or wrap reflective tape around them so they'll be easy to identify.

▶ To increase workbench storage space, slide an old dresser under the bench and use the drawers for storage.

▶ Tack rags will last longer if they're stored in an airtight container to keep them from

STEEL WOOL

Grade	Number	Common Uses
Coarse	3	Paint and varnish removal; removing paint spots from resilient floors
Medium Coarse	2	Removing scratches from brass; removing paint spots from ceramic tile; rubbing floors between finish coats
Medium	1	Rust removal; cleaning glazed tiles; removing marks from wood floors, removing finishes with paint and varnish removers
Medium Fine	0	Brass finishing, cleaning tile; removing stubborn finishes with paint and varnish remover
Fine	00	Satinizing high-gloss finishes with linseed oil
Extra Fine	000	Removing paint spots or stains from wood; cleaning polished metals; rubbing between finishing coats
Super Fine	0000	Final rubbing of finish; stain removal

ABRASIVE CLOTHS

Type	Grades	Common Uses
Emery	Very coarse through fine	General light metal polishing; removing rust corrosion from metal; wet or dry sanding
Crocus	Very fine	High gloss finishing for metals
Aluminum Oxide	Very coarse through fine	Power sanding belts

ABRASIVE POWDERS

Type	Grades	Common Uses
Pumice	F through FF	Rubbing between finish coats; final buffing; stain removal
Rottenstone	None	Buffing between finish coats; final buffing; stain removal
Rouge	None	Metal polishing

drying out. Airtight storage also prevents spontaneous combustion, which can be very dangerous. (This safety tip applies equally well to other rags, coveralls, work gloves, and any other clothes that might absorb flammable oils and solvents.)

▶ To sharpen scissors, use them to slice up several pieces of sandpaper.

▶ Clean tools without expensive cleaners. Pour a small amount of kerosene on the metal part of a tool and rub vigorously with a soap-filled steel-wool pad. Then wad a piece of

continued on page 246

SELECTING SCREWS

Screws provide more strength and holding power than nails. Additionally, if something needs to be disassembled, screws can easily be removed. For most woodworking projects, screws replace nails. Screws are available in four different categories: wood, sheet-metal, machine, and lag.

Wood screws are usually made of steel, although brass, nickel, bronze, and copper screws are used if corrosion is possible. Like nails, screws are available with different coatings to deter rust. Screws are manufactured with four basic heads and with different kinds of slots. Flathead screws are almost always countersunk into the material being fastened so that the head of the screw is flush (or lower) with the surface. Oval-head screws are partially countersunk, with about half the screw head above the surface. Round-head screws are not countersunk; the entire screw head lies above the surface. Filister-head screws are raised above the surface on a flat base to keep the screwdriver from damaging the surface as the screw is tightened.

Most screws have slot heads and are driven with slotted screwdrivers. Phillips-head screws have crossed slots and are driven with Phillips screwdrivers.

Screws are measured in both length and diameter at the shank, which is designated by gauge number from 0 to 24. Length is measured in inches. The length of a screw is important, because at least half the length of the screw should extend into the base material. To prevent screws from splitting the material, pilot holes must be made with a drill before the screws are driven.

For most home-repair purposes, wood screws will suffice. Sheet-metal screws, machine screws, and lag screws also come in various types. If you're trying to replace one of these screws, take an old screw with you to the hardware store.

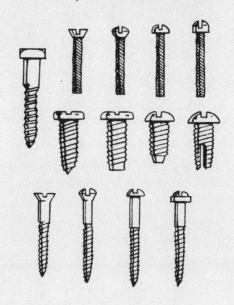

ADHESIVES

If you fail to use the correct adhesive in the appropriate way, you'll end up with a poor joining job. Follow the manufacturer's instructions for projects, or use the following chart to determine what kind of adhesive you need for a particular job.

Multipurpose Adhesives

▶ **White glue**—This white liquid is usually sold in plastic squeeze bottles for use on porous materials, such as wood, paper, cloth, and pottery. It is not water-resistant. Clamping for the entire curing time is usually required.

▶ **Epoxy**—The two parts, resin and hardener, must be mixed for use on metal, ceramics, some plastics, and rubber. Clamping is required for about 2 hours.

▶ **Contact cement**—This rubber-based liquid is used for bonding laminates, veneers, and other large areas. Clamping is not required.

▶ **Instant glue**—This one-part glue, similar to epoxy, is used for metal, ceramics, glass, some plastics, and rubber. Clamping is not required.

▶ **Polyurethane glue**—This high-strength glue is used for wood, metal, ceramics, glass, most plastics, and fiberglass. Clamping is usually required.

▶ **Silicone rubber adhesive or sealant**—This rubber glue and sealant, similar to silicone rubber caulk, is used for gutters and on building materials. It is highly durable and waterproof. Clamping is not required.

▶ **Household cement**—This fast-setting, low-strength glue is used for wood, ceramics, glass, paper, and some plastics. Clamping is usually not required.

▶ **Hot-melt adhesive**—Hot-melt glue is sold in stick form and used with hot-glue guns for temporary bonds of wood, metal, paper, some plastics, and composition materials. Clamping isn't required.

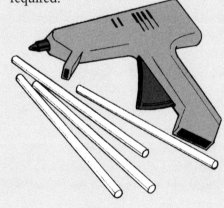

Wood Glues

▶ **Yellow glue**—Also called aliphatic resin and carpenter's glue, this yellow liquid is used for general woodworking and is more water-resistant than white glue. Clamping is usually required for the entire curing time. Yellow glue does not accept wood stains.

▶ **Plastic resin glue**—Urea formaldehyde is sold in powder form and mixed with water. It is used for laminating layers of wood and for gluing structural joints. Plastic resin glue is water-resistant but not waterproof. Clamping is required for up to 8 hours.

▶ **Resorcinol glue**—This waterproof two-part glue consisting of liquid and powder is used in repairing outdoor furniture, kitchen counters, structural bonding, boats, and sporting gear. It is also used on cork, fabrics, leather, and some plastics. Clamping is required.

▶ **Hide glue**—The traditional woodworker's glue is available in liquid or flake form. It is not moisture-resistant, and it does not accept wood stains. Clamping is required.

▶ **Casein glue**—Sold in powder form and mixed with water, this glue is used for resinous or oil woods. It is moisture-resistant but not recommended for outdoor use. Clamping is required for about 4 hours.

Adhesives for Ceramics and Glass

▶ **China and glass cement**—Acrylic latex-based cements have good resistance to water and heat. Clamping is required.

▶ **Silicone rubber adhesive**—It is specifically recommended for glass and china because of its excellent resistance to water and temperature extremes. Clamping is required.

Metal Adhesives and Fillers

▶ **Steel epoxy**—This compound is heat- and water-resistant. It is used for patching gutters and gas tanks, sealing pipes, and filling rust holes.

▶ **Steel putty**—It is used for patching and sealing pipes that aren't under pressure, ceramics, and masonry.

▶ **Plastic metal cement**—This one-part adhesive and filler is moisture-resistant but cannot withstand temperature extremes. It is used for metal, glass, concrete, and wood.

Plastic Adhesives

▶ **Model cement**—This adhesive is used for most plastics. Clamping is required until set.

▶ **Vinyl adhesive**—This adhesive does not usually require clamping.

▶ **Acrylic solvent**—These products melt the acrylic bonding surfaces. They are used for acrylics and polycarbonates. Clamping is required.

continued from page 243

aluminum foil into a ball and rub it on the surface. Wipe away the residue with newspaper, and coat the tool lightly with olive oil before storing. Caution: Kerosene is flammable; do not pour it or use it near an open flame.

▶ Snow won't stick to your shovel if you coat it with floor wax.

▶ Don't take a chance of hitting a thumb or finger when hammering a small brad, tack, or nail. Slip the fastener between the teeth of a pocket comb; the comb holds the nail while you hold the comb. A bobby pin or a paper clip can be used the same way as a comb.

▶ For easy workshop measuring, fasten a yardstick to the edge of your workbench. Cut keyhole slots in the yardstick so you can remove it when you need it elsewhere.

DO-IT-YOURSELF COATING FOR TOOLS

To make a rust-preventive coating for tools, outdoor furniture, and other metal objects: Combine ¼ cup of lanolin and 1 cup of petroleum jelly in a double boiler over low heat. Stir until the mixture melts and blends completely, and then remove from heat and pour it into a clean jar, letting the mixture partially cool. Use the mixture while it's still warm, and don't wipe it off—just let it dry on the object. If there's any extra, cover it tightly, and rewarm it before you use it again.

TIMESAVERS

▶ Wipe a thin coat of shaving cream on your hands before starting a messy task.

▶ You won't waste time when picking up spilled nails, screws, or tacks if you collect them with a magnet covered with a paper towel. When the spilled items are attracted toward the magnet, gather the towel corners over the pieces and then pull the "bag" away from the magnet.

▶ As an aid in measuring lumber or pipe, paint lines a foot apart on a concrete floor.

▶ If you know the exact width of your hand with thumb and fingers spread, you can make rough measurements without using a ruler or tape measure.

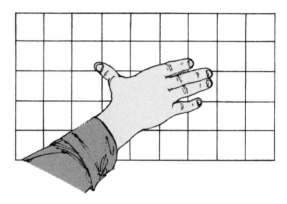

▶ Prevent a knot in nylon rope from working loose by holding it briefly over a small flame. The heat will melt and bond the fibers.

▶ Loosen a stubborn screw, bolt, or nut from a metal surface with a shot of penetrating oil. (Don't use this with a wood surface—it could absorb the oil.) If you don't have oil, use hydrogen peroxide, white vinegar, kerosene, or household ammonia. Should these prove ineffective, heat the metal with an iron, rap it sharply with a hammer while it's still hot, and try again to loosen it. Caution: Kerosene is flammable; do not pour it or use it near an open flame.

▶ Many rusted bolts can easily be worked loose by pouring a carbonated beverage directly on them.

▶ If a bolt repeatedly loosens due to vibrations, coat the threads with fingernail polish and reinsert it; it won't loosen again. If you need to remove it, you can easily break the seal with very little effort and strength involved.

▶ If you don't have a carpenter's level, substitute a tall, straight-sided jar with a lid. Fill the jar three-quarters full of water. Lay it on its side on the surface you're testing—when the water is level, the surface is, too.

▶ If you're out of penetrating oil, substitute hydrogen peroxide or lemon juice.

▶ An old nylon stocking makes an effective strainer as a substitute for cheesecloth.

▶ Use a coping saw blade to remove a broken-off key from a lock. Slide the blade in beside the key, turn it toward the key so its teeth sink into the key's soft brass, and then pull the blade out along with the key fragment.

▶ Dipping the ends of a rope in shellac will keep them from unraveling.

EXTERIOR MAINTENANCE

DOWNSPOUTS, FLASHING, AND GUTTERS

▶ Inspect your gutters frequently, depending on the amount of leaves and tree seeds in your area. They should be cleaned at least in the autumn after all leaves have fallen and again in the spring. If you have heavy rains and lots of trees in your area, you'll want to clean them more frequently to avoid buildup of debris.

▶ When inspecting flashings for leaks, use roof cement to patch any thin spots or gaps along a flashing joint, at a chimney, or along a valley. This will prevent major repairs.

▶ Use a ladder tall enough to reach the gutters, but take care if you prop your ladder on the gutter—it could bend the gutter out of shape, causing low spots where pools of water will collect when it rains.

▶ Clean gutters by hand using a whisk broom to remove leaves. Remember to wear gloves. Then hose them down after you've removed the debris. This flushes out the debris remnants and gives you an opportunity to observe the flow of water and check for low spots or improper pitch.

▶ When cleaning gutters, inspect each hanger for bent straps and popped nails as you work your way along the gutter. If the house has a fascia or board trim, check the gutter's alignment with it. The gutter should rest firmly against the fascia for maximum support.

▶ Check the nails or screws in the straps holding the downspout to your house. These can work themselves loose with use or age, or when a downspout has been used as a ladder support.

▶ To keep downspouts clear, flush them frequently with a garden hose. If necessary, remove stubborn clogs by forcing the running hose down the downspout.

▶ For best wear and protection, paint the outsides of gutters with oil-based exterior house paint, and coat the insides with asphalt roofing paint, which will make them resistant to rust. When painting galvanized gutters, you'll first need to neutralize the zinc coating. If you don't, the paint will quickly peel. While commercial washes are available, an inexpensive and effective home remedy is to

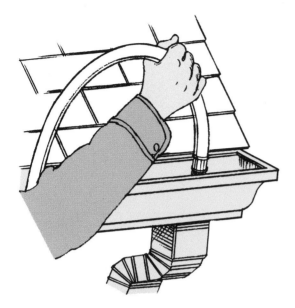

mix a 50/50 solution of warm water and white vinegar. Apply at least three coats of this solution to the gutters, allowing for drying time between coats, and rinse thoroughly before painting.

▶ If you are replacing only a section or two of gutter, take a cross-sectional piece with you when buying a new one. You'll need an exact match of shape and material.

▶ Using a spray-on auto undercoating is a quick and easy way to repair your rain gutters. If you notice any gaps in the gutter, simply spray. If you have to patch a small hole, put a piece of screen wire over the hole and then spray on the undercoating.

▶ When installing a new gutter, get someone to help with lifting the gutter sections. Positioning long sections cannot be done by one person.

GATES AND FENCES

▶ Use pressure-treated lumber for posts that will be sunk in the ground. While more costly, they will last many years.

▶ Don't procrastinate on fence repairs; one weak post can bring down the entire fence.

▶ Shore up a broken fence rail with a two-by-four scrap, securing it with galvanized nails.

▶ Steady a wobbly post by driving a pair of stakes into the ground on either side of the post and bolting them down. Another solution would be to soak the ground with water and then tamp the soil around the post hole.

▶ Use galvanized steel T-braces, available at most hardware stores, to repair a rail. Level the rail, drill pilot holes into the post and rail, and secure with galvanized screws. Caulk the joint, then paint the braces to match the fences.

▶ If a gate sags or won't close properly, replace its hinges with heavier ones. Make sure to use galvanized screws.

▶ A slight sag in a gate can sometimes be repaired by shimming under the bottom hinge. Prop up the gate in the open position, remove screws from the post side of the hinge, and cut a thin piece of cedar shake to fit into the hinge mortise. Reattach the hinge by driving longer screws through the shim.

▶ To square up a gate, drive a screw eye into the upper corner of the gate on the hinge side and another into the lower corner on the gate side. Run wire and a heavy-duty turnbuckle from one screw eye to the other and tighten the turnbuckle until the gate frame is square.

▶ Before installing a new fence, make sure you know where your property line is and be aware of any zoning setback requirements about the placement of your fence.

OUTDOOR ROOMS
Decks

▶ Inspect your deck frequently for popped nails and loose railings or boards. Remove and replace any nails that have popped with coated screws, and immediately repair or replace loose railings to avoid hazards.

▶ To clean everyday dirt from a wood deck, use a mild household detergent in water to wash it. Rinse thoroughly.

continued on page 252

WORKING SAFELY WITH LADDERS

▶ Always make sure your ladder is in good condition. Replace any missing or broken rungs or discard the ladder. An unsafe ladder is very dangerous.

▶ To keep your hands free while you're making repairs, make a holster for the nails and screws you'll need. Take a paper cup and make two vertical slits in it about 1 inch apart; the slits should be wide enough to let you slip your belt through them.

▶ When working on a steeply sloped roof, keep your tools on a sheet of plastic foam to prevent them from sliding off.

▶ Attach a shower curtain ring to your belt and slip your hammer through it to keep it handy when you're on the roof.

▶ To avoid marring a paint job when leaning a ladder against clapboard siding, cover the top ends of the ladder with heavy woolen socks. The paint will remain unmarked.

▶ When using an aluminum ladder, watch out for power lines: Aluminum conducts electricity.

▶ If you're planning to work on a ladder extended to its full height, increase stability by lashing the bottom rung to two stakes driven into the ground under and to the sides of the ladder.

▶ Before climbing up a ladder, test the bottom rung to make sure the ladder is solidly footed.

▶ When positioning a ladder against a house or tree, it is safest to position it so that the distance from the base of the ladder to the house or tree is one-quarter of the ladder's extended length. Otherwise the ladder may fall forward or tip backward.

▶ The best way for a lone worker to raise a ladder is to pin its feet against the base of the house and push the ladder up from the other end, hand over hand, until it is upright.

▶ Keep your hips within the ladder's rails. Extend the top two rungs higher than the place where you're working. The ladder should always extend up above the roof.

▶ Make sure your ladder has firm support at the top. If you place it against a window sash or close to an edge, a slight shift could cause you to fall.

MONTH-TO-MONTH
ROUTINE MAINTENANCE SCHEDULE

Some homeowners like to schedule routine maintenance on a seasonal basis, which works well for those who don't procrastinate. Others prefer work on a monthly basis, which makes for tighter deadlines and prevents procrastinators from delaying their spring work until the end of June.

The following monthly schedule is a guide that should be adjusted for your climate, your home, and your lifestyle. If your fall schedule will be packed with football games, children's soccer games, music lessons, and other weekend activities, you may want to start activities earlier. Likewise, if you're planning major gardening, you may want to hurry up the spring chores so that you have lots of time to garden. Notice that periodic chores that can be done

any time are relegated to the least active months. The important thing about a routine maintenance schedule is to get your chores completed so that minor maintenance doesn't become a major problem.

January
▶ Change disposable filters on forced-air furnaces; wash permanent filters.

▶ Give major appliances a thorough dusting. Clean dust from behind refrigerator compressor panel and move refrigerator away from wall to clean behind back panel; clean range thoroughly according to manufacturer's instructions; clean sediment from washing machine hose lines and filters.

▶ Check wood ladders for loose rungs; repair or replace any defective ladders.

February
▶ Change disposable filters on forced-air furnaces; wash permanent filters.

▶ Pour water into the sump pump to make sure it's in good working order and that the float can rise and fall freely. Clean any sediment accumulated on the strainer screen.

▶ Check cords on appliances and extension cords for wear and/or fraying. Repair or replace any defective cords.

March
▶ Change disposable filters on forced-air furnaces; wash permanent filters.

▶ Turn on outside faucets after the threat of a hard freeze has passed.

▶ Check window and storm door screens for holes. Patch them now or have them rescreened.

▶ Inspect roof shingles or shakes for damage from winter storms; replace any missing shingles.

▶ Inspect siding for popped nails and weathering; check brick for crumbling mortar.

April
▶ Change disposable filters on forced-air furnaces; wash permanent filters.

▶ If needed, paint or stain the exterior of your home when it gets warm enough, but avoid postponing the job until the summer when paint and stain dry too quickly.

▶ Wash windows and put up screens.

▶ Change batteries in smoke alarms on the weekend that daylight savings time begins.

▶ Check the exterior of your home for insect infestations; plug any small holes where wasps and hornets could try to make a nest. Inspect for termite tunnels.

▶ Inspect caulked areas; recaulk, if necessary.

May

▶ Inspect outdoor furniture and barbecue for wear; make necessary repairs.

▶ Check deck, patio, walkway, and driveway for split wood, cracks, etc.

June

▶ Call a professional service person to inspect and adjust the central air conditioning. Install window air conditioners; clean the filter with a solution of mild household detergent and water; and clean the evaporator and condenser coils with a vacuum cleaner.

July

▶ Flush the hot water tank to remove sediment that accumulates and that can eventually cause deterioration of the inside of the tank. (Be sure to shut off the power source to the water heater.)

Follow the manufacturer's instructions for draining.

August

▶ Check the exterior for signs of weathering and to see if you need to make time to touch up peeling paint when cooler weather arrives.

▶ Patch any cracks in concrete sidewalks or driveways to prevent major cracks. Fill any cracks in asphalt drives.

▶ Improve drainage around your home to accommodate the expansion of wet soil when it freezes. This will help eliminate buckled basement walls.

September

▶ Have your furnace and chimney cleaned.

▶ Inspect the roof for any problems. If you have skylights, make sure to check that the flashing is intact.

▶ Store outside furniture.

October

▶ Change disposable filters on forced-air furnaces; wash permanent filters.

▶ Change batteries in smoke alarms on the weekend that daylight savings time ends.

▶ Remove or cover window air conditioners.

▶ Check thermostat. Remove faceplate and blow away any lint that's collected.

▶ Remove and clean screens before storing them for the winter.

November

▶ Change disposable filters on forced-air furnaces; wash permanent filters.

▶ Clean gutters and downspouts, preferably after the last leaves have fallen.

▶ Put up storm windows.

▶ Put weatherstripping on windows and doors that require additional help in keeping out cold air.

▶ Get your humidifier ready. Clean filters and use a humidifier cleaning solution to clean the reservoir.

▶ Empty gas-powered lawn mowers and remove any accumulated debris. Follow manufacturer's instructions for cleaning lawn mowers and sharpening blades.

December

▶ Change disposable filters on forced-air furnaces; wash permanent filters.

▶ Make sure your electrical system is operating well before using holiday lights.

continued from page 248

▶ To remove stains caused by tree sap, use mineral spirits and rinse thoroughly.

▶ To remove mildew, wash the deck with a bleach and water solution (1 cup of bleach to 1 gallon of warm water). Flush the area with clear water and allow it to dry. Commercial brighteners are also available; follow the manufacturer's instructions.

▶ If mildew is a continual problem, you probably have too much shade on your deck. Check to see if you can trim some tree branches or bushes to expose more of the deck to the sun's drying effects.

▶ Deck stains make routine cleanup much easier and preserve the life of the wood. Apply stains specially formulated for decks immediately over new wood, except for pressure-treated lumber, which should age for six months before being stained. The deck will benefit from a new coat of stain every one to two years (be sure the stain contains commercial sealant). Follow the manufacturer's instructions for applying the stain. If your deck has been painted, you will have to remove the paint before a stain can be applied.

▶ Avoid applying clear finishes, such as varnish or shellac, to wood decks. They don't withstand sun and moisture, and they must be removed if they start to peel.

Furnishings

▶ When storing folding patio chairs, use old pillowcases as protective covers. Slip a case over each folded chair and pin it closed. The fabric guards against scratches and dirt.

▶ Waxing the ends and bottoms of wooden patio furniture legs helps protect against

PATCHING HOLES IN GUTTERS

1. Remove all rust and any other loose metal by cleaning the area with a wire brush. Cover the bad spot with paint thinner.

2. Cut a patch from wire window screen material. The patch must be large enough to cover the hole and extend about ½ inch beyond it. If a screen patch seems too daunting, consider one of the factory patch kits now on the market. The primary component of these kits is rubberized-foil sheet material that has an adhesive backing. As always, you'll need to clean the rusted area and arrest its further progress with paint thinner or a commercial rust inhibitor. Then just peel the backing from the foil and press the foil over the degraded area. The foil patch will match a galvanized gutter fairly closely. It can also be painted.

3. Coat the area around the hole with asphalt roofing cement.

4. Put the patch down over the cement and press it in place.

5. Brush the cement over the screen.

6. When the first coat sets, cover it again with cement.

7. Tiny holes can be patched without the screen; the cement will fill in by itself, but you will have to apply several coats.

moisture that might be absorbed from standing rainwater.

▶ The metal edges of tubular patio chairs won't be able to cut through the rubber cups on the leg bottoms if metal washers are first inserted in the protective cups.

▶ Drilling holes in solid metal patio furniture will allow rainwater to drain. If water is allowed to collect, the furniture will rust prematurely and take a much longer time to dry.

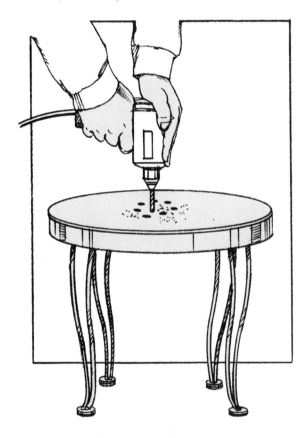

▶ Lowering rolled-up awnings after a storm will allow them to dry.

▶ Cleaning awnings in the direction of the seam, not against it, will prevent seam weakening.

▶ Rejuvenating faded canvas awnings with a special paint available from awning dealers or paint stores extends their life.

ROOFS

The best way to preserve your roof is to inspect it annually for wear and make repairs as soon as possible. Once you have a leak, however, you have to know where it's coming from. The water leaking may often travel before dripping into a room below.

If there's an unfinished attic below a leaky roof, finding a leak isn't too difficult. Climb into this space and look around with a flashlight—it's easier to see a leak in the semidark, so don't turn on a light. When you find the leak, outline the wet area with chalk. If possible, push a piece of wire up through the leaky spot, so that it protrudes from the roof. This makes it easier to find the leak when you're working outside. A good place to start your search is at flashing and valleys.

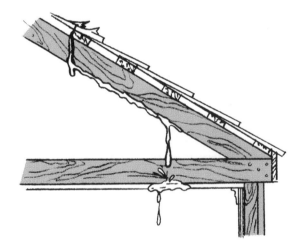

Pitched Roofs

▶ It's not necessary to replace a cracked shingle if all the pieces are still in place. Slide a piece of roofing felt or roll roofing under the shingle until it is behind the cracks. Drill holes for the new nails needed, then drive in the nails gently. Cover the nail heads with roof cement.

▶ When repairing shingles, use the new synthetic cement or a fiber-impregnated cement.

▶ New asphalt shingles can be put down over old asphalt, wood, and roll roofing if it's only one or two layers. If it's in three layers, the old roofing must be stripped off. Cedar shakes, slate shingles, or tiles must be taken off.

▸ For emergency repair of a shingle, cut a patch to fit from a piece of sheet metal and slip it well under the shingle above the one you're repairing. Apply a coat of roof cement to the bottom of the patch, and tack it in place. Cover the tack heads with cement. When you return to make a more permanent repair, pry up the patch.

Flat Roofs

▸ A leak in a flat roof may be seen under the damaged spot, making the damage to the roof easy to see. But built-up roof layers often cause water to migrate laterally, not straight down.

▸ Any water pooled in the leak area should be mopped up so that the surface can dry before attempting repairs.

WALLS AND SURFACES

Brick and Concrete

▸ To remove white powdery surfaces on brick or concrete, go over them with a stiff brush.

SAFE ROOF REPAIRS

▸ Roof repairs should be done on a sunny day when the roof is completely dry. A wet roof is slippery and very dangerous.

▸ Adequate safety measures must be taken for any roof repairs. Always use safety ropes.

▸ On steep roofs, use a ladder framework to provide secure anchoring.

▸ Rubber-soled shoes provide the best traction when working on a roof.

▸ The location of power lines should be kept in mind when working on a roof.

Wet the surface with a weak 5-percent solution of muriatic acid and water, leaving it on for five minutes. Brush the wall and rinse it immediately with clear water. Work a 4-foot-square section at a time.

▸ When you're pouring concrete steps, be sure to use solid objects as fillers; hollow objects buried in concrete—pieces of pipe, for example—have a tendency to float to the surface.

▸ A smooth concrete surface is a hazard on outdoor steps. After the concrete has set, but while it is still workable, run a stiff broom across the steps to roughen the surface.

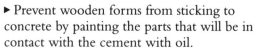

▸ Drilling in masonry can be made easier by making a pilot hole with a masonry nail at the exact spot where you want to drill.

▸ Prevent wooden forms from sticking to concrete by painting the parts that will be in contact with the cement with oil.

▶ When laying a brick patio, start from a corner of the patio near the house and work outward toward the edges.

▶ Laying a dry brick patio is quite simple. Dig out the area needed, edge the excavation with weather-resistant boards staked into place, and spread out a sand base 2¼ inches deep. Spray the base gently with water, tamp it down until it's at a 2-inch level, and let it dry. Position the bricks, fitting them tightly and making sure they're level. Pour sand on the bricks, sweep it into the crevices, sprinkle with water, and repeat as necessary to fill any gaps.

▶ When you're building a stone retaining wall, make sure you dig below the frost line for your footing. Otherwise, the wall could fall apart.

▶ If you put sand on top of asphalt sealer it will prevent the sealer from sticking to your shoes.

▶ Small cracks in blacktop can be patched with sand and liquid blacktop sealer. Pour sand along the crack to fill it partway. Then pour the blacktop sealer into the crack over the sand, which will absorb the sealer quickly. If necessary, repeat until the surface is smooth.

CAULKING

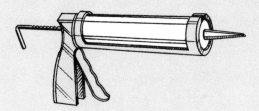

Caulking is a great way to repair minor holes in walls, joints between different materials, and other small jobs. Gaps that measure more than ½ inch wide and ½ inch deep, however, are not good candidates for caulk. Fiberglass insulation, expandable foam, or sponge rubber strips are better insulators.

▶ To open a caulking tube, cut off the tip at an angle to the width of the narrowest point to be filled. Punch out the foil seal with a nail.

▶ To use a caulking gun, pull out the plunger arm to disengage the notches and insert a tube of caulk, base first, so that the nozzle sticks out through the slot at the end of the gun. Turn the plunger arm and push it in to engage it. Hold the nozzle at a 45-degree angle to the joint you want to fill. Squeeze the handle firmly.

▶ Use a steady movement to caulk. Don't try to smooth by smearing.

▶ Dry all surfaces before you apply caulking compound for best results.

▶ Remove all old caulking before applying new caulking to any repair job. If it doesn't peel out, use a putty knife to cut out the old caulk. Use a dry paintbrush to remove dust and other debris.

▶ Never caulk when the temperature falls below 50°F. For an emergency job in cold weather, use polybutane cord.

▶ Caulk when painting the house. Apply primer to the seams first, then caulk. (Primer helps the caulking stick.) Allow the caulking to cure as directed by the manufacturer, then apply a finish coat. Be sure to use a compound that will take paint.

▶ Plug a tube of leftover caulk with a large nail in order to keep the caulk from drying out.

Siding

▶ Cracked, warped, or loose siding should be repaired as soon as you notice it. Water works its way through such defects into the interior wall where rotting can take place undetected.

▶ If you don't have time for a thorough repair, seal splits with oil-based caulking compound and clamp them together by driving nails and clinching them over the boards.

▶ To remove mildew from house siding, scrub the surface with a bleach and water solution (1 cup of bleach to 1 gallon of warm water). Flush the area with clear water and allow it to dry thoroughly before painting.

▶ To replace an unstained shake or shingle, take replacement shakes or shingles from an inconspicuous area of the house, reserving the new shingles for that spot. This eliminates an unweathered patch in the repair area.

INTERIOR MAINTENANCE

ELECTRICITY

Working Safely With Electricity

An electric shock is always distressing, always hazardous, and often fatal. The concept behind electrical safety is that you must avoid physical contact with any live or

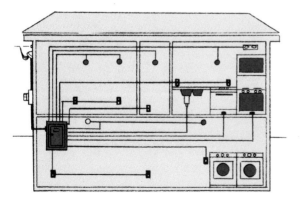

"hot" part of the circuit. All electrical devices are designed to provide the greatest measure of safety, but you can defeat any built-in safeguards through carelessness and ignorance. Understanding the hazards and the precautions required by those hazards are mandatory for safe electrical work.

▶ Everyone in the family should know how to throw the master switch that cuts off all electrical current.

▶ If there's a chance of contact between water and electricity, do not wade in water until the master switch has been shut off.

▶ It is the insulation around a conductor that protects you from danger. Never do anything that would compromise the integrity of the conductor insulation, such as stapling an extension cord to a baseboard or to a wall. The staple can cut through the insulation and create a short circuit, which, in turn, can start a fire.

▶ A regular examination of all wiring and discarding any cord that has brittle insulation should be routine home maintenance.

▶ You should always avoid contact with any part of a live circuit.

▶ You must unplug any portable electrical device or any appliance if you plan to work on it.

▶ You should wait to work on a switched outlet or lighting fixture—even though you've flicked off the switch—until you have also deactivated the circuit. In many switching systems, parts of the circuit are still energized when the switch is off.

▶ You must always remove a plug fuse entirely and put it in your pocket or toolbox when you deenergize a circuit. To avoid the chance of accidentally reenergizing the circuit, securely tape a circuit breaker handle in the "Off" position.

▶ A sign letting people know that you are making electrical repairs is always a good idea.

▶ You should always assume that an electrical outlet or apparatus is energized until you prove otherwise with a circuit tester or by pulling a fuse or tripping the disconnect plug.

▶ Insulating your pliers by slipping a length of small-diameter rubber hose on each handle is a necessity when you work with electricity. Wrap other metal parts with electrician's tape. Insulate the shank of a screwdriver by slipping a section of rubber or plastic tubing over it. Be sure to cut the tubing so that it extends from the handle down to the blade.

▶ A fuse should always be replaced with a fuse of the amperage indicated on the panel. You risk causing an electrical fire if you use a fuse rated to carry more amps.

▶ Stand on a dry board or wooden platform when working with a fuse box or a circuit breaker box. Also use a wooden rather than an aluminum stepladder to minimize the risk of shock when working with electrical wiring.

▶ When maneuvering a section of electrical cable through a wall, you should play it safe and use roughly 20 percent more than a straight-line measurement indicates that you need. Often there are unexpected obstructions and the cable must be moved around.

▶ A blown fuse or a tripped circuit breaker is a sign of trouble. Locate and eliminate the problem before you replace a blown fuse or reset a tripped circuit breaker.

▶ You can save time ahead of time by determining which circuits activate which outlets in your home; diagram or print the information on a card attached to your circuit breaker or fuse box. When your electricity fails, you'll be able to solve the problem.

Fuses and Circuit Breakers

Fuses and circuit breakers are safety devices built into your electrical system. Because the typical homeowner does not know about wire current-carrying capacity, the fuses or circuit breakers on the electric panel are there to prevent overloading of a particular circuit. Without fuses or circuit breakers, if too many

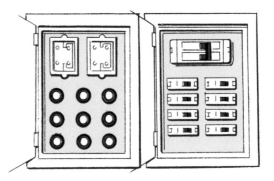

appliances are operating on a single circuit, the cable would get extremely hot, melt, and possibly start a fire.

To prevent prolonged electrical overloads, fuses are designed to blow and circuit breakers are designed to trip. Either device stops the flow of current to the overloaded cable. For example, a 15-ampere fuse should blow when the current passing through it exceeds 15 amperes. A fuse that blows or a circuit that trips is not necessarily faulty; it is doing its job properly, indicating that there is trouble somewhere in the circuit. Either there are too many devices plugged in or some malfunctioning device, such as an appliance with an internal short, is connected to the circuit.

A blown fuse or a tripped circuit breaker is the signal to look for trouble. A blown fuse must be replaced with a new one, while a tripped circuit breaker must be pushed to "On" to restore power. Some circuit breakers flip to a neutral position and must be turned off before being turned on. It makes no sense to replace a blown fuse or to reset a tripped circuit breaker until you have located and eliminated the cause of the trouble.

Caution: Never try to defeat this built-in safety system by replacing a fuse with one of a larger current-carrying capacity. Likewise, placing a copper penny behind a blown fuse is sure to lead to disaster.

HEATING AND COOLING

The basic components of heating and cooling systems are troublefree and easy to

continued on page 260

REPLACING A WALL SWITCH

Whether the switch doesn't work properly or you want to add a dimmer, you don't need an electrician to change a wall switch. There are four primary symptoms of switch failure:

▶ When the switch loses its snap, when the handle hangs loosely in any position, or when there is no clear distinction between the "Off" and "On" position.

▶ When the switch no longer turns the light on or off.

▶ When flipping the switch only makes the light flicker.

▶ When the switch may work occasionally but you have to jiggle the handle back and forth several times to keep the light on.

If any of these switch problems is noticed, you should replace the wall switch as soon as possible.

To begin, first deenergize the electrical circuit that powers the switch. (See "Fuses and Circuit Breakers.") Tools needed are screwdrivers, an electrician's multitool, and an auxiliary light source. You will also need a replacement wall switch. But first you will need to look at the switch you are

replacing before you can determine what kind of switch to buy.

Remove the switch cover plate. If the cover plate doesn't come off easily, it is probably being held in place by several layers of paint. Use a razor blade or a craft or utility knife to cut the paint closely around the edge of the plate to free it.

Inspect the old switch to find out what replacement model you will need to purchase. (You must use the same kind of switch, but you can install a better grade of switch.)

The traditional single-pole toggle switch is still the most popular. When the toggle switch is mounted properly, the words "On" and "Off" are upright on the toggle lever, and the light goes on when

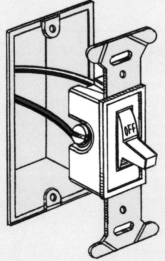

you flip up the switch. You can replace this with a silent toggle switch, which is slightly more expensive. One version contains a capsule of mercury that the toggle handle tilts to make electrical contact. It is particularly important that you mount such a switch properly; otherwise, the mercury will not make the correct contact.

A variation of the traditional toggle switch is called the lever-action switch, which is designed to lie almost flush against the wall. It turns the fixture on when the top of the switch is pushed in. Another type, the push-button switch, has a single button that turns the light on when pressed and off when pressed again. Push-button switches often feature a built-in neon lamp that glows when the switch is off. The translucent plastic push button allows you to see the glowing lamp, making it easy to locate the switch in the dark. You can install the push-button switch with the built-in glowing lamp as a replacement for the single-pole switches you have in your home.

Some kinds of wall switches have no terminal screws for conductor attachments. Instead, the switch has small holes that are only slightly larger than the bare copper conductors. Once you remove about ½ inch of insulation from the end of the wires, push the bare ends into the holes. Locking tabs make the electrical connection and grip the wires so that they cannot pull out. To release the wires from the switch, all you have to do is insert a narrow-bladed screwdriver in the slot that is right next to the wire-grip holes.

After you decide and purchase the type of replacement switch you want to install—and turn off the electric current to the old switch—you are ready to go to work.

With the switch cover plate removed, you will see two screws holding the switch in the switch box. Remove the screws and carefully pull the switch out of the box as far as the attached wires allow. If there are two screws with wires attached, the switch is a simple on-off (single-pole) type. Do not disconnect any wires until you compare the old switch with the replacement switch to make sure you know which wire goes to which terminal screw. If your light can be switched on from just one location, it is a single-pole switch; if it can be switched on

from two locations, it is a three-way switch; it if can be switched on from three locations, it is a four-way switch.

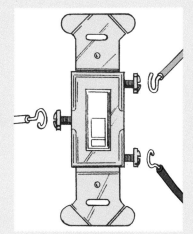

Loosen one of the old terminal screws, remove the wire, and attach the wire to the corresponding terminal screw on the new switch (the wire should wrap around the screw in a clockwise direction). Then do the same with the remaining wires. Take care to connect the wires so that all the bare wire is safely under the binding screws, and clip off any excess uninsulated wire. The procedure is the same with all switches. Verify your wiring by comparing it with the diagram on the package your new switch came in.

If you're installing the modern, stab-in type of wall switch, strip ½ inch of

insulation. Push the bare end of the wire into each stab-in hole, and check that the wires have caught properly by tugging gently on them. Caution: If the wire insulation or the conductors coming into the switch box are brittle or frayed, that part of the circuit or switch loop should be rewired.

The only tasks remaining are to replace the switch in the switch box and install the cover plate. Push the switch into the box carefully, and make sure the wires fold neatly into the box behind the switch. There are small tabs extending from the switch's mounting bracket; these tabs are supposed to lie flat against the wall outside the electrical box. They hold the switch flush with the wall no matter how the electrical box is angled inside.

Put the switch back into place, using the two mounting screws provided with the new switch. Oval holes in the mounting bracket allow you to fasten the switch so that it's straight up and down, even when the screw holes in the electrical box are tilted. Finally, attach the cover plate with the screws you removed earlier, and replace the circuit fuse or reset the circuit breaker.

continued from page 257

maintain. Efficient operation depends on regular maintenance. To keep your heating and cooling systems in top shape, have them professionally serviced once a year. The best time to have this done is at the end of the heating season when service is prompt.

When a heating or cooling system malfunctions, any one of its three basic components (heat-cold source, distribution system, or thermostat) may be causing the problem. Heating systems can be powered by electricity, gas, heating oil, and even wood, in the case of a wood-burning stove used to heat an entire house. First of all, know what kind of system you have.

Heating Systems

▶ Forced-air systems distribute heat produced by the furnace with an electrically powered fan, called a blower. Air is forced into the structure through a system of metal ducts.

▶ Gravity systems are based on the principle that hot air rises and cold air settles; they cannot be used to distribute cool air from an air conditioner. Warmed air rises and flows through ducts to registers in the floors throughout the house.

▶ Radiant heating systems function by warming either the walls, floors, or ceilings, or, more commonly, by warming radiators or convectors in rooms. These objects then warm the air in the room.

Basic Maintenance Procedures

▶ Check to make sure the unit is receiving power; look for blown fuses or tripped circuit breakers at the main service panel. Some furnaces have a separate fused disconnect, usually at a different panel near the main service panel. Other furnaces have fuses mounted in or on the unit.

▶ If the unit has a reset button, wait 30 minutes to let the motor cool, and then press the button. If the unit still doesn't start, wait 30 minutes and press the reset button again. (Gas furnaces don't have a reset button.)

▶ If the unit has a separate power switch, make sure the switch is turned on.

▶ Check to make sure the thermostat is properly set. If necessary, raise (or for an air conditioner, lower) the setting 5 degrees.

▶ If the unit uses gas, check to make sure the gas supply is turned on; if necessary, turn it on. If the unit uses oil, check to make sure there is an adequate supply of oil. If necessary, have the tank refilled.

TROUBLESHOOTING DOORBELLS AND CHIMES

If a doorbell or chime does not ring, follow these steps to determine which parts, if any, should be replaced:

1. Test the button. Remove the button and touch the two wires together. If the bell rings, the button is defective.

2. Test the bell. Detach the wires at the bell or chime and connect them to a spare bell. If the substitute bell rings when the doorbell button is depressed, the present bell is defective.

3. Connect the test bell to the transformer and press the door button. If the bell does not ring, the transformer is defective.

4. If the transformer is not receiving power, check to see that the circuit is turned on. Check for a loose connection at the transformer primary. Then trace and check all wiring to detect a break in the circuit. Replace the faulty wiring segment if the circuit is broken.

▶ Clean or replace furnace filters at the beginning of the heating season and when necessary throughout the season (monthly or every other month). Take out the filter and hold it up to the light; if it looks clogged or dust has accumulated on the surface, replace it, despite the length of time it's been in use.

▶ Use a new filter of exactly the same kind, material, and size as the old filter; don't try to substitute.

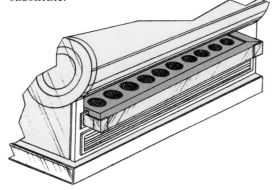

▶ Clean permanent filters according to the manufacturer's instructions.

▶ With steam systems, follow the manufacturer's maintenance procedures. If you don't have instructions, hire a furnace professional to do this for you and take notes on how it's done so you can do it yourself the next time.

Cooling Systems

Other than routine cleaning of a cooling system, a professional service person should be called for any maintenance. There are some cleaning procedures, however, that will help your system function properly:

▶ The condenser is located outside the house, where it accumulates dirt and dust, which need to be removed periodically. Clean the condenser with a commercial coil cleaner, available at refrigerator supply stores; follow the instructions supplied.

▶ Clean the fins on the condenser with a soft brush to remove accumulated dirt; you will have to remove a protective grille and cabinet to vacuum the fins. Do not clean the fins with water, which could turn the dirt into mud and compact it between the fins. Be careful

when cleaning the fins; they're made of light-gauge aluminum and are easily damaged.

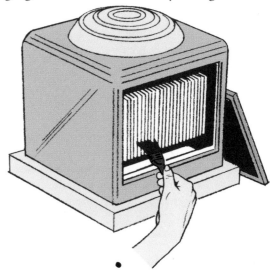

▶ If the fins are bent, straighten them with a fin comb, sold at most appliance parts stores.

▶ Check the concrete pad under the condenser to make sure it's level; set a carpenter's level front to back and side to side on top of the unit. If the pad has settled, lift the pad with a pry bar or a piece of two-by-four and force gravel or rocks under the concrete to level it. This will maintain efficiency and ensure longer life.

▶ Protect outside condensers during the fall and winter with a commercial condenser cover made to fit the shape of the unit or with heavy plastic sheeting, secured with sturdy cord.

▶ Keep away cut grass, weeds, vines, or dryer lint that could grow around the condenser and obstruct the flow of air.

Safety Procedures with Heating Systems

▶ Before doing any work on any heating or cooling system, make sure all power to the system is turned off. At the service panel, remove the fuse or trip the circuit breaker that controls the power to the unit. If you're not sure which circuit that is, remove the main fuse or trip the main circuit breaker to cut off all power to the house.

▶ Some furnaces have a separate disconnect switch. If so, remove the fuse or trip the circuit breaker.

▶ If the fuse blows or the circuit trips repeatedly when the furnace or air conditioner turns on, there is a problem in the electrical system. Do not try to fix the furnace; call a professional.

▶ If the unit uses gas and there is a smell of gas in your home, do not try to shut off the gas or turn any lights on or off. Get out of the house, leaving the door open, and go to a telephone; call the gas company or the fire department immediately to report a leak. Do not reenter your home.

PLUMBING

Plumbing actually refers to two complementary but entirely separate systems in your home—one system brings fresh water in, and the other subsystem takes wastewater out. Any cross-connection of these systems could jeopardize your water supply.

In most urban and suburban areas, water is pumped to your home by a community water department, and wastewater is carried off to a collective sewage-treatment facility via a main sewer line. In rural areas, you may depend on a private well for your water supply and a septic system for waste disposal.

All water that enters your home is cold; it is piped through the cold-water trunk lines

EMERGENCY BLACKOUT KIT

▶ Candles or oil lamps and matches for area lighting.

▶ Flashlight, battery lantern, or other auxiliary light source for troubleshooting.

▶ Correct and up-to-date circuit directory posted on main entrance panel door.

▶ Tool kit with appropriate tools for making electrical repairs.

▶ Circuit tester, preferably the voltage-readout type.

Spare Parts for Fuse Boxes
▶ Two replacement plug fuses of each amperage rating in use, preferably Type S.

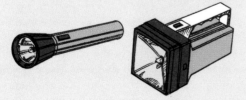

▶ Four replacement cartridge fuses, including main fuses, of each amperage rating in use.

Spare Parts for Circuit Breaker Boxes
▶ One replacement pull circuit breaker of a rating equal to the smallest size in use or one of each size in use.

▶ One replacement double-pull circuit breaker of each amperage rating in use. These are 240 breakers, and are not likely to be part of power failure.

General Parts
▶ Selection of light bulbs.

▶ One replacement duplex receptacle to match existing units.

▶ One replacement single-pole switch to match existing units.

▶ One replacement three-way or other special switches to match existing units.

▶ Miscellaneous supplies—wirenuts and electrician's tape.

directly to all fixtures and appliances that use unheated water; offshoots to individual fixtures are called branches. Pipes that run vertically, extending upward, are called risers. One pipe carries water to your water heater, while a hot water line from the water heater carries water to all the fixtures and appliances that require hot water.

Plumbing Essentials

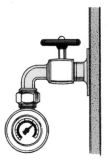

▶ Some fixtures have—or should have—individual supply shutoff valves so that you need not close the main shutoff to repair them. But it's a good idea to make sure everyone in the family knows the location of the main shutoff valve in your house, as well as how to use it. This could prevent flooding if a pipe bursts and will minimize damage. Tag the main shutoff valve so that anyone can easily find it and know how to turn it off.

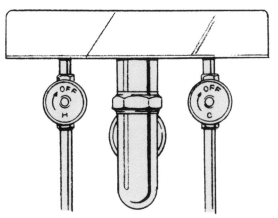

▶ You should always remember to turn off the water supply before attempting any repair. (Minor repairs to the toilet can be done without turning off the water supply.)

▶ Check with your local plumbing code official before you add or change any pipe in your house. You will learn what is allowed and what is prohibited, and whether or not a homeowner is allowed to do his or her own work.

Drains

▶ Keep drains free of clogging and odors by pouring boiled water into them.

▶ For better suction when plunging a clogged drain, cover the rubber cap of the plunger with water and plug the fixture's other openings with wet rags.

▶ Unclog a moderately clogged drain by pouring down ½ cup of baking soda followed by ½ cup of vinegar. Caution: The two ingredients interact with foaming and fumes, so replace the drain cover loosely. Flush after about 3 hours.

▶ Fix greasy drains with this treatment: Pour in ½ cup of salt and ½ cup of baking soda, followed by a teakettle of boiling water. Allow to sit overnight, if possible.

▶ For a homemade, noncorrosive drain cleaner, mix 1 cup of baking soda, 1 cup of table salt, and ¼ cup of cream of tartar in a small bowl. Stir thoroughly and pour into a clean, covered jar. To use, pour ¼ cup of the mixture into the drain and immediately add 1 cup of boiling water. Wait 10 seconds, then flush with cold water. Do this weekly to keep drains clogfree and odorless. (One blending of this mixture equals 2¼ cups of cleaner.) Flushing drains with plenty of boiled water on a weekly basis also works well.

Faucets

▶ If a dripping faucet is getting on your nerves before the plumber arrives or before you have time to fix it yourself, tie a 2-foot-long string

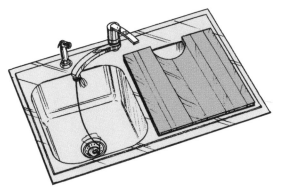

around the nozzle, and drop the string's end into the drain. As the faucet drips, the drops will run silently down the string.

▶ You can avoid having the teeth of the wrench scar a chrome-plated plumbing fixture during installation by first wrapping the fixture with a double coating of plastic electrical tape.

Pipes

▶ If a water pipe is banging against a wall and causing noise, you can silence it by wedging the pipe off the wall with a wood block and clamping the pipe to the wedge with a pipe strap.

▶ If you have a stretch of water pipe that often freezes, consider wrapping it with insulation.

▶ The easiest way to thaw a pipe is to wrap and secure a heavy towel or a burlap bag around it to concentrate and hold heat against it. Pour the hottest water you can obtain over the towel. Be careful, because most of the water will run off the towel on you or the floor. A properly positioned pan or bucket can save you a scalding mess.

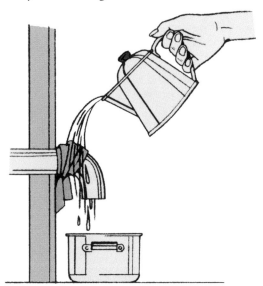

▶ A good way to clean copper pipe before sweat-soldering is to wrap a strip of emery cloth around the end of the pipe and move it back and forth as if you were buffing a shoe.

▶ Most amateur plumbers are so proud of their first sweat-soldered joints that they immediately turn on the water. Allow the joint to cool a bit, because the sudden cooling effect of rushing water could weaken the joint and cause it to crack.

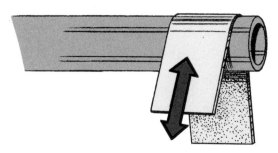

▶ If a pipe springs a leak, you should consider replacing an entire section rather than just patching the leak. A pipe that is compromised to the point of leaking in one place will often start leaking in other places.

▶ Whenever you secure a plastic pipe, be careful to anchor it so that it can expand and contract with temperature changes. If you place a bracket on a pipe, include a buffer fashioned from garden hose, radiator hose, foam rubber, rubber cut from old inner tubes, or kitchen sponges.

▶ When you are adding or replacing drainpipes, they must be pitched so that the downward flow will carry out the waste. The maximum degree of pitch is $1/4$ inch per foot—$1/16$ to $1/8$ inch is better.

Valves

▶ To keep the water shutoff valve in good working order, you should make a habit of turning it off and then on again once every six months.

▶ When shutting down your water system, you should remember to open all the faucets and outdoor hose spigots to drain. Flush the toilet and sponge out remaining water from the tank. Drain or blow water out of fixture traps, including the toilet. After removing all the tap water from the sink and lavatory traps, fill the traps with RV antifreeze.

DOORS

▶ If hinge screws on a door are loose because the screw holes have become enlarged, try using longer screws. Another option would be to fill the holes with pieces of wood toothpick dipped in glue. When the glue dries, reinsert the screws. You can also wrap hinge screws with steel wool and reinsert.

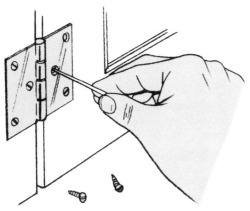

▶ If a door binds on the knob side when the door is closed, its hinges may be misaligned. If the top of the knob side binds, try putting a cardboard shim behind the bottom hinge. If the bottom corner binds, slip a cardboard shim behind the top hinge. To shim a door hinge, loosen the screws on the door frame side. Cut a shim from thin cardboard with slots to fit around the screws, slide it behind the hinge, and tighten the screws.

▶ If you're trying to remove a door's hinge pin and the pin won't budge, press a nail against the hinge bottom and tap upward against the nail with a hammer.

▶ If a doorknob bangs against a wall, protect the wall by installing a door stop.

▶ For better control when lifting a door off its hinges, remove the bottom pin first. When replacing a door on its hinges, insert the top pin first.

▶ To prevent people from mistaking a closed sliding glass door for an open one, apply eye-level decals—at both adult and child levels, if necessary—to alert people before they walk into the pane and possibly injure themselves. You can use the same trick to mark lightweight screens.

▶ You needn't worry about oil dripping on the floor if you quiet a squeaky hinge by lubricating its pin with petroleum jelly rather than oil.

▶ Cardboard shields will protect the finish on a door when you clean and polish door hardware. Fit the shields around the metal parts, holding them in place with masking tape.

continued on page 268

TROUBLESHOOTING THE TOILET

PROBLEM	CAUSES	REPAIRS
Water in tank runs constantly	1. Float ball or rod misaligned	1. Bend float rod down carefully to move ball so that it will not rub against side of tank.
	2. Float ball contains water	2. Replace float ball.
	3. Float ball not rising high enough	3. Carefully bend float rod up, but only slightly.
	4. Tank ball not seating properly	4. Remove any corrosion from lip at bottom of tank of valve seat. Replace tank ball, if worn.
	5. Ballcock valve does not shut	5. Replace washers in ballcock off water assembly or, if necessary, replace entire assembly.
Toilet does not flush or flushes inadequately	1. Drain is clogged	1. Remove blockage in drain with closet auger.
	2. Not enough water in tank	2. Raise water level in tank by bending up float rod slightly.
	3. Tank ball falls before enough water leaves tank	3. Move guide up so that back tank ball can rise higher. You may also replace tank ball.
	4. Leak where tank joins toilet bowl	4. Tighten nuts on tank; replace spud washer, only if necessary.
	5. Ports around underside of bowl rim clogged	5. Ream out residue from ports.
Tank whines filling	1. Ballcock valve not operating properly	1. Replace diaphragm washers or install new ballcock assembly.
	2. Water supply is restricted	2. Check shutoff to see if it is completely open. Check for scale or corrosion at entry into tank or on valve.
Moisture around fixture	1. Condensation	1. Install foam liner, tank cover, drip catcher, or temperator valve.

PROBLEM	CAUSES	REPAIRS
Moisture around fixture (cont.)	2. Leak at flange wax seal	2. Tighten closet bolts first, but not too tight—you could crack the fixture. If leak persists, replace wax seal.
	3. Leak at bowl tank connection	3. Tighten tank bolts; replace worn spud washer, if necessary.
	4. Leak at water inlet connection	4. Tighten compression and coupling nut; replace washers and gasket, if necessary.
	5. Crack in bowl	5. Replace entire fixture.

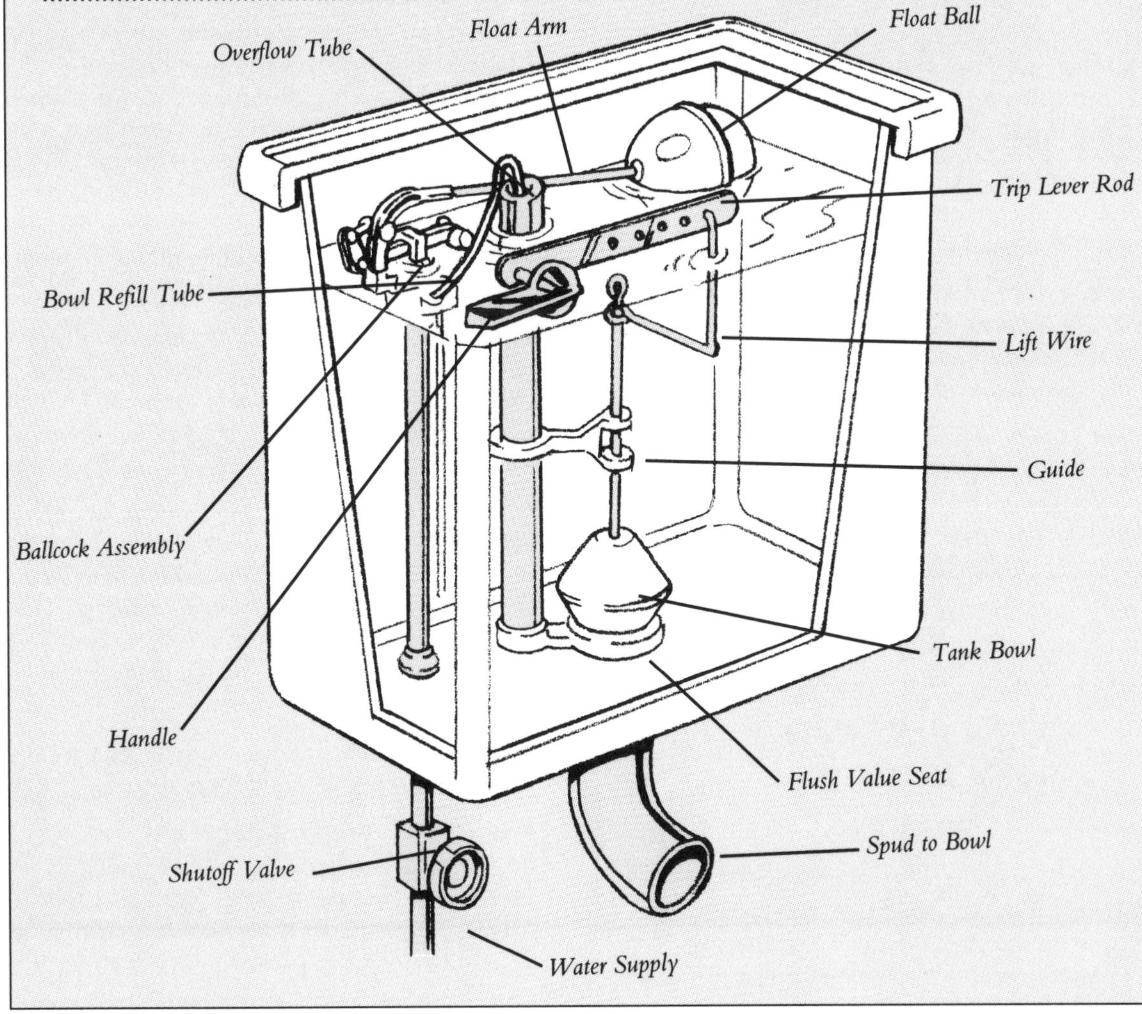

Overflow Tube

Float Arm

Float Ball

Trip Lever Rod

Bowl Refill Tube

Lift Wire

Guide

Ballcock Assembly

Tank Bowl

Handle

Flush Value Seat

Shutoff Valve

Spud to Bowl

Water Supply

continued from page 265

▶ If you need to plane the bottom of a door because it scrapes the threshold or the floor, you can do so without removing the door. Place sandpaper on the threshold or floor, then move the door back and forth over this abrasive surface. Slide a newspaper or magazine under the sandpaper if it needs to be raised in order to make contact.

▶ To remove ¼ inch or more from a door, score with a utility knife to prevent chipping and finish with a circular saw.

▶ When you've fashioned a door to the exact size for hanging, bevel the latch edge backward to let it clear the jamb as it swings open and shut.

▶ Before you replace a door that you have planed, seal the planed edges. If you don't, the door will swell and stick again.

▶ Graphite from a soft pencil can be used to lubricate a resistant door lock. Rub the key across the pencil point, and then slide it in and out of the lock several times.

▶ If you want to replace an existing lock but you can't find a new one that will fit the existing holes, cover the old holes with a large decorative escutcheon plate.

▶ To reduce noise in your home and cut energy costs at the same time, weather-strip all doors and windows.

FLOORS AND WOODWORK

Floors

▶ If you have a squeaky wood floor under tile or carpet, you may be able to eliminate the squeak without removing the floor covering. Try to reset loose boards by pounding a

hammer on a block of scrap wood in the area over the squeaky boards. The pressure may force loose nails back into place.

▶ To silence squeaky hardwood floors, try using talcum powder as a dry lubricant. Sprinkle powder over the offending areas, and sweep it back and forth until it filters down between the cracks.

▶ Try filling dents in a hardwood floor with clear nail polish or shellac. Because the floor's color will show through, the dents will not be apparent.

▶ To prevent scratching the floor when moving heavy furniture across uncarpeted areas, slip scraps of old carpeting, facedown, under all furniture legs.

Floor Coverings

▶ Sometimes bulges or curled seams in a linoleum or vinyl resilient floor can be flattened by placing aluminum foil over them and "ironing" them with your steam iron. (The heat will soften and reactivate the adhesive.) Position weights, such as stacks of books, over treated areas to keep them flat until the adhesive cools and hardens.

▶ To remove a resilient floor tile for replacement, lay a piece of aluminum foil on it, pressing down with an ordinary iron set at medium. The iron's heat will soften the mastic, and you can easily pry up the tile with a putty knife.

▶ Remove a resilient tile by covering it with dry ice. (Caution: Wear work gloves to protect your hands.) Let it stand for ten minutes and then remove any remaining ice. The cold will make the tile brittle, so it will shatter easily. Chisel out the tile from the edges to the center.

▶ After laying floor tiles, help them lie flat by going over them with a rolling pin.

▶ To replace a damaged area of resilient flooring, make a perfect patch from scrap flooring by placing the scrap piece over the damaged area so that it overlaps sufficiently. Tape it to hold it in place. Cut through both layers at the same time to make a patch that is an exact duplicate. Replace the damaged area with the tightly fitting patch.

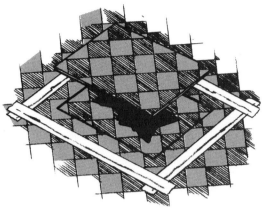

▶ To patch a gouge (not a dent) in a resilient floor, take a scrap of the flooring and grate it with a food grater. Mix the resulting dust with clear nail polish and plug the hole.

▶ Another way to camouflage a gouge or hole in a resilient floor is with crayon wax. Choose a crayon that matches the floor color, melt it, fill the gouge or hole, and then wax the floor.

▶ Laying resilient floor tile is easier if the room temperature is at least 70°F before you start, because tile is more pliable at higher temperatures. Put all boxes of tile in the room for at least 24 hours prior to positioning them on the floor. Try to keep the room temperature at the same level for about a week after laying the tiles, and then wait at least a week before washing the floor.

▶ Burns in carpet can sometimes be repaired. If only the tips of the carpet are burned, carefully cut off the charred fiber with small sharp scissors. Sponge the area lightly with a mild detergent solution and again with clean water. The low spot won't be noticeable when the carpet dries.

FURNITURE

Repairing Furniture

▶ You can treat scratches on natural wood or antique finishes by polishing them with a mixture of equal amounts of turpentine and

REPAIRING A BURN HOLE IN CARPET

If a burn goes all the way to the backing but the backing isn't burned, the carpet can be repaired by removing the charred fibers and inserting new ones.

▶ Carefully cut out the burned fibers, and then pull the stubs out of the backing with tweezers. Clean out the entire burn area, so that the woven backing is exposed in the hole.

▶ To fill the hole, ravel fibers from the edge of a scrap piece of carpet; you'll need enough individual tufts of yarn to place one tuft in each opening in the backing. If you don't have a scrap piece, use tufts from an inconspicuous area of the carpet, such as the back of a closet.

▶ Apply a little latex adhesive to the exposed backing.

▶ Use a carpet tuft-setting tool to insert the new fibers. Fold each fiber in half to form a V, and place the folded tuft into the tuft-setter. Set the tip of the tuft-setter into the opening on the backing and strike the handle lightly with a hammer. When you lift the tuft-setter, the fiber will stay in the carpet backing.

▶ Set fibers across the entire burn area, one at a time. The repair area should match the rest of the carpet in density and depth; if a tuft doesn't match in height, you can adjust it by pulling it up a little with tweezers. You can also tap it down again with the tuft-setter.

▶ When the hole is completely filled, cut off any protruding fibers flush with the rest of the pile.

boiled linseed oil. Apply with a clean, soft, damp cloth.

▶ Any scratch made by a match can be removed by rubbing with a lemon wedge.

▶ There are several ways to remove white spots, such as those left by wet drinking glasses. Rub them with toothpaste on a damp cloth, or rub them with paste furniture polish, any mild abrasive, or oil. Appropriate abrasives are ashes, salt, soda, or pumice: suitable oils are olive oil, petroleum jelly, cooking oil, or lemon-oil furniture polish.

▶ Paper stuck to a polished table can be lifted after saturating the paper with cooking oil.

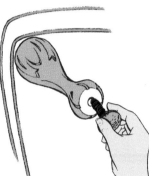

▶ You can tighten a loose furniture leg caster by wrapping a rubber band around its stem and reinserting it.

▶ When wood fibers in a piece of furniture are merely bent, but not cut, you can straighten out any dents with an iron—set on medium—and a damp cloth. Place the damp cloth on a dent, hold the iron on it until the cloth begins to dry, redampen the cloth, and repeat the process as needed.

▶ A cabinet or dresser knob can be tightened by dipping its screw or screws in fingernail polish or shellac and reinserting the knob. When the polish or shellac hardens, the screws will be set and the knobs will be tight.

▶ Wooden drawers can be unstuck by rubbing contact surfaces with a bar of soap or a candle.

▶ Decals will easily lift off painted furniture if you sponge them with vinegar.

▶ To tighten wobbly wicker furniture, wash it outdoors with hot soapy water, rinse it with a hose, and let it air-dry. The wood and cane will shrink and tighten.

▶ Saggy wicker or cane seats can be similarly tightened by sponging them with hot water.

▶ Cigarette burns can usually be rubbed out of wooden furniture with very fine sandpaper or steel wool. If necessary, color the area with stain pens or shoe polish to match the rest of the surface.

▶ If you need to pound apart sections of a chair that needs regluing, a soft mallet will provide enough power but will be much kinder to the wood than a hammer.

▶ Thread can serve as packing around a chair rung before it is reglued.

▶ When disassembling a piece of furniture for repair, label or number the parts with pieces of masking tape so you'll know how to put them back together. Make a list describing which part of the piece of furniture each number represents.

▶ If loose cane on a rattan chair is snagging your clothing or stockings, tame it with clear tape, or blunt it by dabbing on clear nail polish.

▶ Instead of straining your back when rearranging a heavy piece of furniture, simply position a child's roller skate or skateboard under each end, and then wheel the piece to its new location.

▶ Use a tourniquet to hold a freshly glued chair rung firmly in place. Clamp the glued rung with a heavy cord wrapped around the chair legs. Use a dowel to twist the cord until the proper tension is reached, propping the dowel to maintain pressure.

▶ If a chair wobbles because one leg is shorter than the others, steady the chair by forming an appropriately shaped piece of wood putty to "extend" the short leg. When the putty dries, sand and stain it to match the leg and glue it in place.

▶ Always remember to tape the drawers shut before moving a piece of furniture—and remember to remove the tape quickly; otherwise it will leave marks.

Refinishing Furniture

▶ If your home has central heating, turn it off before starting to varnish a piece of furniture.

This will help to keep dust from circulating and settling on the wet varnish. Don't let the temperature drop below 70°F, however, because varnishes (or glues) don't work well in a cool environment. Remember that your work space should be well ventilated.

▶ When using paint stripper on a piece of furniture that has legs, put a tin can under each leg to catch drips.

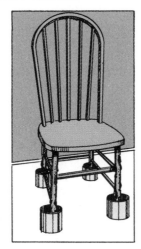

▶ When gluing dowels, a dowel that's exactly the size of the hole it fits into can push much of the glue to the bottom of the hole and not hold as well as it should. To avoid this, cut a few grooves in the dowel so the glue is distributed along its surface for a more secure bond.

▶ When you're working with varnish, hold the container as still as possible so that bubbles don't form and spoil the smooth finish.

▶ If you'd like to know how your unfinished furniture would look if it were stained, try the "wet test." Dampen a cloth with turpentine and wipe it over the surface; the moisture will bring out the grain, showing any contrasts and giving the wood the appearance it would have if stained.

▶ To sand a furniture spindle or rung without flattening it, hold a sandpaper strip behind the part, one end in each hand, and saw the ends back and forth, rotating the spindle as you work, to buff-sand the wood.

▶ When refinishing, a flat rubber kitchen scraper can be useful for removing paint from curved or rounded surfaces, especially since it can be used even on delicate carvings. For greater versatility, buy both wide and narrow sizes.

▶ Sanding concave curves will be easier if you hold the sandpaper around a piece of dowel the same diameter or smaller as the curve. You can also slit a length of rubber garden hose and wrap the paper around it with the ends held in the slit.

▶ Many small items are useful for cleaning furniture crevices and cracks when you're refinishing. Enlist the aid of a nut pick, a plastic playing card, a plastic credit card, the broken end of an ice cream stick, the tine of an old fork, an orange stick, wooden toothpicks, or an old spoon.

▶ It's a practical idea to use newspaper to protect your floor or workbench when you're refinishing a piece of furniture, but the legs may stick to the paper. To avoid this, drive a nail partway into the bottom of each leg.

▶ If you need an unusually shaped smoothing tool for use on wet spackling compound and other wood fillers, try whittling an ice cream stick to the required contour.

▶ To smooth wood evenly and thoroughly in the refinishing process, work with successively finer steel wool or sandpaper grades. Between sandings, brush off or vacuum the sanding debris; then wipe the wood clean with a tack cloth.

▶ Remember that treatment with any bleach raises the wood grain, even when the furniture piece has been thoroughly sanded.

To prevent the raised grain from affecting the finish, resand to the level of the wood surface after the wood dries.

▶ A heavy string is useful when stripping the narrow turnings of a spindle furniture leg. Gently "saw" the string back and forth to remove the finish.

▶ To avoid gouging wood when using a putty knife to strip furniture, round the putty knife's sharp corners with a fine-toothed file. If you're working on large flat surfaces, dull a paint scraper the same way.

▶ If wood still shows ink stains, white water marks, splotches, or traces of any previous stain or filler after stripping, try wiping them away with liquid laundry bleach. To remove black water marks or to lighten chemically darkened wood, use oxalic acid (available in paint stores and drugstores).

▶ To obtain a smooth, evenly finished surface on open-grained woods, treat them with a filler after staining. First apply filler in the direction of the grain; then work across the grain to completely fill all pores.

▶ If large knots in unfinished furniture are loose, remove them, apply carpenter's glue around their edges, and replace them flush with the surface. If small knots (pin knots) are loose, remove and discard them and plug the resulting holes with plastic wood.

▶ For the most professional patching job, use shellac sticks to fill cracks and gouges since they leave the least conspicuous patch.

▶ It will be easier to apply paint or varnish remover to a piece of furniture if all hardware has been removed. If you label the hardware along with a sketch of the furniture, it will also be easier to reassemble it correctly.

▶ To help slow evaporation after applying a coat of paint remover—and give it more time to work—cover the surface with aluminum foil. Keep in mind, though, that paint remover stops working after about 40 minutes.

▶ To make a template to patch damaged veneer, lay a sheet of bond paper over the damaged area and rub a soft lead pencil gently over it. The edges of the damaged area will be precisely indicated on the paper so you can cut a pattern.

▶ If hardware is spotted with paint or finish, drop it into a pan filled with paint remover. Let it soak while you work on the wood, then wipe it clean.

▶ Small blisters on a veneered surface can sometimes be flattened with heat. Lay a sheet of smooth cardboard over the blistered area and press firmly with a medium-hot iron, moving the iron slowly and evenly until the blisters soften and flatten. Leave the cardboard in place and weight the smoothed-out area for 24 hours.

▶ For more durability, top an antiqued finish with a coat of semigloss or high-gloss varnish.

▶ Cane chairs will last longer and be easier to clean if you apply a protective shellac coating.

▶ Wash-away paint and varnish removers should not be used on veneered or inlaid furniture pieces, since water is the natural enemy of wood and certain glues. Water used to remove the chemicals must be removed from any wood furniture as soon as possible to avoid raising the wood grain or dissolving the glue.

Upholstering Furniture

▶ When you reupholster furniture, put fabric scraps in an envelope and staple the envelope to the underside of the newly covered piece. That way you'll have scraps for patching.

▶ When using ornamental tacks for upholstery, push extras into the frame in an inconspicuous spot so you have replacements if needed.

▶ Before covering kitchen chair seats with plastic, warm the plastic with a heating pad so it will be more pliable and easier to handle.

▶ To hammer decorative furniture tacks without damaging their heads, place a wooden spool over each tack and pound on the spool.

▶ When you're refinishing a piece of upholstered furniture and want to keep the upholstery, it's best to remove the fabric before you work on the finish—but only if you are sure you can put it back on again. If the piece is large, have a professional upholsterer remove and replace the fabric.

▶ When examining a sample of upholstery fabric, fold the sample and rub the backs together to make sure that the backing is firmly bonded to the fabric.

▶ Test whether a fabric is likely to "pill" by rubbing it with a pencil eraser to see if bits of fabric appear.

▶ For speed and convenience, cut foam rubber upholstery padding with an electric carving knife.

STAIRS

▶ Stairs are put together with three basic components—the tread, the riser, and the stringers (the side supports). In most cases, squeaks are caused by the tread flexing against the riser or the stringer. Have someone walk up and down the stairs to locate the squeak.

▶ To stop squeaks at the front of a stair tread, drive pairs of screw-shank flooring nails, each pair angled in a V, across the tread and into the top of the riser below it.

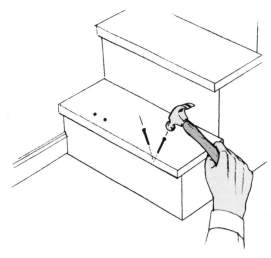

▶ Try eliminating squeaks in stairs by using packaged graphite powder or talcum powder in a squeeze bottle. Apply the lubricant along the joints in the problem area.

▶ If an application of graphite powder or talcum powder fails to eliminate a stair squeak, go under the stairs and drive wedges into the gaps between the moving components. If the gaps between stair components aren't wide enough to accept wedges, brace the joints with one-by-two blocks to stop the movement of the stairs.

DRYWALL

▶ To save your arm muscles when installing ceiling drywall, construct two "deadman" supports. Use floor-to-ceiling two-by-fours, including T-bars at the tops. They will support the panels while you do the final positioning and securing.

▶ Instead of carrying large drywall sheets into the house and possibly damaging them while navigating awkward corners, measure and cut them to fit before bringing them inside.

▶ Drive nails in pairs, spaced 2 inches apart, when installing drywall to discourage nails from popping out.

▶ Small cracks or holes in drywall can be repaired with spackling compound. Follow the manufacturer's instructions and lightly sand before priming or painting.

▶ To ensure that a nail stays in a stud, drive another drywall nail through the wall into the stud; set the new nail about 2 inches above or below the old one. Don't use a nail set on the new nail. Just pound it flush with the wall and then give it one more light hammer whack to "dimple" the drywall surface around the nail head. Cover the nail head and hole with drywall compound and then lightly sand when dry.

WINDOWS AND SCREENS

Windows

▶ Applying a reflective vinyl coating on the inside of your windows will both protect your furniture upholstery or drapery fabric from the fading effects of strong sunlight and help keep your home cooler in the summertime.

▶ To free a window that's been painted shut, use a scraper, knife, or spatula to cut the paint

PATCHING PLASTER

▶ To fill a large crack in a plaster wall, remove loose plaster with a putty knife. Make sure to widen the opening slightly in a V-shape.

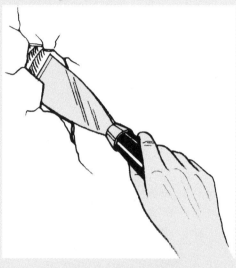

▶ Clean the loose plaster and dust from the crack with a vacuum cleaner.

▶ Mix a thick paste of plaster of paris, and then wet the crack thoroughly with a wet paint brush.

▶ Pack plaster of paris into the hole to its full depth, and smooth the surface with a scraper or trowel.

▶ Let the filled crack dry until the plaster turns bright white—at least 24 hours.

▶ Sand the patch lightly when the plaster is drying, using medium- or fine-grade sandpaper wrapped around a wood block.

▶ Prime before painting the wall.

▶ Large cracks will have to be replastered at least twice (once with perlitic plaster, then with plaster of paris) to make the surface smooth.

seal between the sash and the window frame. Then, working from the outside, insert the blade of a pry bar under the sash and pry gently in from the corners. Lever the bar over a block of scrap wood.

▶ When replacing a broken sash cord, consider using nylon rope or a sash chain, both of which last much longer.

▶ To prevent a windowpane crack from spreading, score a small arc with a glass cutter just beyond the crack, curving around it. Most of the time the crack will travel only as far as the arc.

▶ To remove cracked glass from a window without excessive splintering, crisscross the pane on both sides with several strips of masking tape, then rap it with a hammer. Most of the pane will be held together.

▶ When installing a new windowpane, speed up the process by rolling the glazing compound between the palms of your hands to form a long string the diameter of a pencil. Lay the "string" along the frame, over the glass, and smooth it in place with a putty knife.

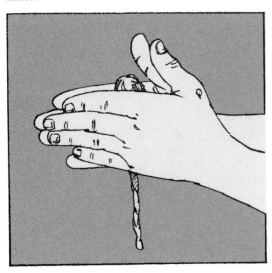

▶ To make dried-out putty workable again, sprinkle it with a few drops of raw linseed oil and knead it until it is soft and pliable. You can also ask someone at your hardware store to put the can on a paint shaker.

▶ Before attempting to chisel dried and hardened putty from a wooden window frame, brush raw linseed oil over the putty's surface. Let it soak in to soften the putty.

▶ If you try to open a window and it refuses to budge, tap a hammer on a block of wood at various places on the sash.

▶ Fill a pellet gun hole in a windowpane with clear nail polish or shellac. Dab at the hole; when the application dries, dab again and reapply until the hole is filled. The pane will appear clear.

REPAIRING WALLPAPER

▶ Make sure to save extra wallpaper for patching. Tape a piece or two on a closet wall so that it will correspond in color density and pattern to the paper on the wall.

▶ To repair a damaged wallpaper section, tear, don't cut, a patch from a piece that's been weathered. Because less-defined torn edges blend imperceptibly with paper already on the wall, the patch will be virtually invisible. Don't remove the damaged wallpaper; simply paste the patch directly over the damaged surface. Caution: This will not work on vinyl or foil wallpaper.

► To cover a clear bathroom window without putting up curtains, make the glass opaque by brushing on a mixture of 4 tablespoons of Epsom salts and ½ pint of stale beer.

► When painting glazing compound, lap the paint slightly over the edge of the compound and onto the glass.

Screens

► To keep aluminum screens from pitting, clean them outdoors (never indoors) with kerosene. Dip a rag in the kerosene and rub both sides of the mesh and the frames, then wipe off the excess. This is a particularly good rust inhibitor for older screens. (Caution: Kerosene is highly flammable and should always be stored in small amounts in a cool place. Never pour or use kerosene near an open flame.)

► To repair a small tear in a wire window screen, fold the wire strands back into place. If the hole doesn't close completely, brush clear nail polish or shellac sparingly across the remaining opening. Let the sealer dry, and

REPAIRING A LARGE DRYWALL HOLE

► Cut a scrap piece of drywall into a square or rectangle a little bigger than the hole or damaged area.

► Set the patch against the damaged area and trace around it lightly with a pencil.

► Cut out the outlined area with a keyhole saw. Keep your saw cut on the inside of the traced line so that the hole will be the same size as the patch.

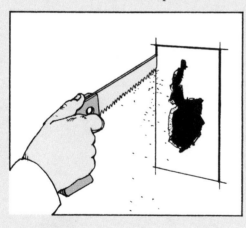

► Make a backing board about 6 inches longer than the long dimension of the hole.

► Insert the backing board coated with panel adhesive into the hole and hold it firmly against the inside of the wallboard. Fasten the ends of the board to the drywall with drywall screws driven through the walls at the sides of the hole.

► Countersink the screws below the surface of the drywall.

► To hold the patch in place, spread panel adhesive on the back of the drywall patch and around its edges.

► Set the patch into the hole and adjust it so that it's exactly even with the surrounding wall. Hold it in place until the compound starts to set.

► Let the patch dry at least overnight.

► Fill the patch outline with seam tape and at least three coats of joint compound. Cover the exposed screw heads with drywall compound. Let dry overnight.

► Sand lightly and then prime.

reapply until the pinhole is transparently sealed. (Be careful not to let any sealer run down the screen; immediately blot any excess.)

▶ If there's a clean cut or tear in a window screen, stitch it together. Use a long needle and monofilament fishing line, a strong nylon thread, or a fine wire. Zigzag-stitch across the cut, being careful not to pull the thread or wire so tight that the patch puckers. After stretching, apply clear nail polish to keep the thread or wire from pulling loose.

▶ To close a large hole in a window screen, cut a patch from a scrap piece of screening that is the same type as the damaged screen. Zigzag-stitch the patch into place, and then apply clear nail polish to the stitching.

WOODWORKING

▶ Plywood frequently splits when you begin sawing it. Prevent this by applying a strip of masking tape at the point where you plan to start.

▶ To prevent splintering or splitting when sawing, prescore the top layer on both sides—at the cutoff point—with a utility knife with a sharp razor blade.

▶ If you're buying plywood to use where only one side will be visible, you can save money by buying a piece that is less expensive because it's perfect on only one side.

▶ Use expensive exterior grade (CCA-treated) plywood only for outside use. Use less expensive water-resistant bond plywood when panels will be exposed to weather infrequently. And use relatively inexpensive dry bond CDX plywood when panels will be used indoors.

▶ To hide a screw head, drill a counterbored hole, seat the screw, glue a piece of doweling into the counterbore, and sand it flush.

▶ Saws cut more easily across the grain than with it. In ripping cuts there's a tendency for the blade to follow the grain, rather than a marked or scribed line. Use a ripsaw or be

very careful when making rip cuts to be sure the cut does not turn out wavy.

▶ To prevent dimpling a wood surface when removing a nail with a hammer, protect the surface with a small block of wood or a shim; this will also increase your leverage and keep the nail from coming out crooked and making the nail hole oblong.

▶ To extract a nail without widening its hole or denting surrounding stock, use long-nose pliers and roll the pliers in your hand or over the edge of a small block of wood.

▶ To prevent a saw from binding when ripping a long board, hold the initial cut open with a nail or wedge. Move the nail or wedge down the cut as you continue to saw.

▶ Check that wood is perfectly smooth after sanding by covering your hand with a nylon stocking and rubbing it over the surface. You'll be able to detect any remaining rough spots.

▶ To make any sawing task smoother and easier, lubricate a saw's blade frequently by running a bar of soap or a candle stub over its sides.

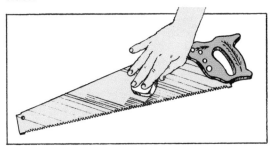

▶ You can clean clogged sandpaper and give it new life by vacuuming it or rubbing a fine-bristled brush back and forth across its grit.

▶ When you drill through any kind of wood, a certain amount of splintering will occur at the breakout point. (This is true regardless of the type of bit used, because the composition of wood causes it to fracture rather than break.) Prevent this breakout splintering by backing the stock with a piece of scrap.

▶ Whenever there's danger of splitting a narrow section of wood with a screw, predrill a hole. Then the wood won't crack when you insert the screw. With hardwoods, you should also wax the screw threads.

▸ A plastic playing card or credit card can serve as a scraper for removing excess wood filler from a surface being repaired.

▸ A salt shaker makes a good applicator for distributing pumice evenly on a wood surface.

▸ When gluing two pieces of wood together, position the grain in the same direction. If the pieces are cross-grained and later swell due to moisture absorption, the joint will pull apart because the two surfaces will slide past each other.

LAWN AND GARDEN

Basic Gardening Tools

If you're a beginning gardener, avoid investing in a lot of tools until you're sure you enjoy gardening. A great many tools are available on the market, and many of them are entirely unnecessary. The following are the most useful for gardening:

▸ **Bow saw** for trimming trees.

▸ **Flexible hose,** with length depending on the size of your property.

▸ **Gloves**—While thin, cotton "garden" gloves are good for working with plants, you'll want sturdy thick gloves for pruning, cleaning gutters, etc.

▸ **Hoe.**

▸ **Rakes,** both leaf and soil types.

▸ **Shovel;** a snow shovel in winter climates comes in handy, too.

▸ **Spading fork or pitchfork** for moving perennials, turning compost.

▸ **Small spade.**

▸ **Sprayer.**

▸ **Trowel.**

▸ **Wheelbarrow.**

Tips on Garden Tools

▸ Invest in good-quality tools; cheap tools increase your work and break under stress.

▸ Make sure the sizes and weights of your tools suit you.

▸ Select tools with wood handles made of hickory or ash with the grain running straight along the full length of the hand.

▸ Avoid tools where a single rivet holds the metal portion to the wood portion.

▸ Make sure blade shanks are reinforced.

▸ Use a rake with short, sturdy metal prongs for leveling and grading soil. Use rakes with long, flexible fingers for raking leaves and collecting trash from between plants.

▸ Buy a watering can that's short enough to fit under both the kitchen tap and the outside faucet so that you can fill it easily without a lot of twisting and maneuvering.

▶ Keep tools in good condition by storing them carefully and protecting them from the weather.

▶ Periodically sharpen the blades on shovels and hoes.

▶ Paint the handles of your small garden tools a bright color—anything but green—so that you can easily find them.

LAWNS, SHRUBS, AND TREES

Outside jobs are more than just keeping up appearances. Regular maintenance of your lawn and landscaping will actually minimize work. A neglected lawn soon goes to seed and begins to erode, and getting the lawn back into shape by resodding or reseeding takes a lot of work. Neglected trees and shrubs die easily, and their replacements cost money and require more care than established specimens. Fortunately, keeping up a lawn and landscaping elements is neither time consuming nor expensive. Keep the following tips in mind to reduce maintenance time:

▶ Don't separate the lawn into sections, which requires more mowing and raking time.

▶ Don't try to grow grass where it won't grow, especially in deep shade. Substitute with hardy groundcovers.

▶ Plant shrubs and trees native to your area, because they will require less time and effort.

▶ Plant for the future. Some trees and shrubs grow fast and spread. Don't plant them too

closely, causing yourself transplant work down the road.

▶ Mulch flower beds to retain moisture and deter weeds.

Lawns

▶ The kind of grass that grows best in your area is determined by the climate, moisture, and soil. If you're planning to sow or sod a new lawn, talk to the experts in your area about what kind of grass seed or sod is the most successful.

▶ Choose sprinklers appropriate for your lawn.

▶ Water only when the lawn needs it. Overwatering or everyday shallow watering isn't as good as deep-watering, because it causes shallow root systems that require frequent watering.

▶ All fertilizer is numbered, with groups of numbers such as 5-10-5. The numbers stand for plant nutrient contents of the product. The first number is the amount of nitrogen, the second is the amount of phosphoric acid, and the third is the amount of potassium.

▶ Be sure not to allow leaves to remain on your lawn all winter, because they will mat down and smother the grass.

▶ When laying sod, set succeeding rows of strips with staggered joints, as if you were laying brick.

▶ As the hot weather approaches, set your lawn mower blade higher; longer grass will provide shade protection for the roots.

Shrubs and Trees

▶ Avoid buying shrubs with cankers, leaf rot, spots, insects, or other problems. Shrubs that are already weak won't have much chance of surviving a transplant to your yard.

▶ Transplant balled-root shrubs into a hole that is 8 inches wider and 6 inches deeper than the balled roots of the plant.

▶ Remove any plastic or metal twine or wrap from a shrub or tree that you intend to plant. While burlap will rot, plastic and metal won't and will more than likely strangle the roots later.

▶ When you plant or transplant a bare-root shrub or tree, be sure to spread out the plant's root system in the hole and cover the roots with top soil or a rich soil mixture.

▶ Deeply water newly planted trees and shrubs.

OUTDOOR GARDENS

To a large extent, climate and soil dictate the composition of gardens. While you can't change the climate, you can modify the soil. And with a few tricks, you can even grow plants and vegetables that may be only marginally hardy in your area.

The United States is divided into zones according to climate conditions for gardening purposes. Trees, shrubs, and plants—the ones that do best in a given location because of the light, water, temperature, and soil conditions—are then assigned to these various zones. If you're attempting to grow a plant in a nonnative area, you'll have to consider how to adjust your soil and protect plants from temperature extremes that would otherwise kill them.

Soil Testing and Preparation

Soil types vary from the extremes of constantly dry, nutrient-poor sand to 90 percent rocks held together with 10 percent soil. Most soil conditions fall somewhere between these extremes. To find out what kind of soil you have in your yard, try this do-it-yourself texture test:

Take a small handful of moist garden soil and hold some of it between your thumb and the first knuckle of your forefinger. Gradually squeeze the soil out with your thumb to form a ribbon.

▶ If you can form a ribbon that stays together for more than 1 inch, you have a heavy clay soil.

▶ If a ribbon forms but holds together for between ¾ to 1 inch, you have a silty clay loam.

▶ If the ribbon breaks into shorter pieces, the soil is silty.

▶ If a ribbon doesn't form at all, the soil is sandy.

This test will tell you the general type of soil that is adequate for many gardens. To determine soil content for vegetable or flower gardens, you'll want to have your soil professionally tested. Many county Cooperative Extension offices perform this service, and private testing labs do this, too. To obtain a soil sample to use for this test, take several slices of soil from the area where you plan a garden bed. Dig 4 to 6 inches down before taking the samples, and mix

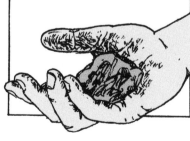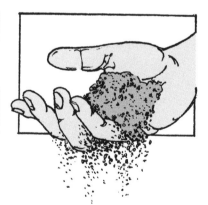

Soil may vary from light sand to heavy clay. A rough test can be made by squeezing a wettened sample in your hand. If it falls apart easily, it's primarily sand (left); if it forms a solid, sticky glob, it's primarily clay (center). The ideal growing medium is somewhere between the two (right).

them all together. Collect samples for each type of garden—i.e., lawns, vegetables, flowers—separately.

One test will be a pH test that reads for acidity or alkalinity. A pH test result between 6.0 and 7.0 is ideal for most horticultural plants and requires no adjustment. A result below 6.0 indicates the soil is acid—good for rhododendrons and azaleas—but not for most plants. Ground limestone can be applied to reduce soil acidity. A pH test result of over 7.2 means the soil is too alkaline for most plants. To solve this problem, add powdered sulfur or iron sulfate.

A complete test will also provide information about the nutrients and percentage of organic matter in your soil. Both of these results will help you in determining whether and how to fertilize your soil.

After testing your soil, keep these other tips in mind:

► Smooth the soil surface with an iron rake.

► Adjusting the nutrient and pH levels in soil will not improve its consistency. To correct soil texture requires the addition of one of several soil conditioners, such as leaf mold, compost, well-rotted cow manure, and peat moss.

► For flower and vegetable gardens, thoroughly turn and loosen the soil to about a 6-inch depth, removing any rocks.

► When cultivating the soil in your garden, remember that good soil is slightly lumpy. If you work it until it's too fine, it will pack hard when it rains or blow away in a strong wind.

► Work the soil well before planting root crops. If they have to negotiate lumps, stones, or other obstructions, vegetables such as carrots and parsnips will grow forked or distorted instead of straight.

► If your soil is extremely poor, but you still want to grow vegetables, consider container gardening in pots, hanging baskets, and raised beds. Many small vegetable varieties, such as cherry tomatoes, can be successfully grown in hanging baskets.

Planning the Garden

► Avoid setting your plants in the shade of buildings and large trees. In addition to blocking sun from your garden bed, trees will also compete for the available soil nutrients and moisture—remember that a tree's root system can reach beyond the span of its branches.

► If you garden in containers or raised beds, remember that your plants will dry out faster than those in a regular garden bed and will need more frequent watering.

► Try to position your tall-growing plants on the north and northeast side of your garden so that they won't overshadow other plants.

▶ Each year, keep a notebook in which you record your garden's progress. Note dates of plantings and fertilizings, which plants did well or not so well, harvest dates, and problems with weeds, bugs, or lack of rain. You'll have a useful gardening guide to refer to next season.

▶ Remember that vegetables grown for their fruits—tomatoes, peppers, eggplants, for example—need a minimum of 6 to 8 hours of direct light a day. If they don't get enough light they may produce a leafy green plant but little or no fruit. Crops that are grown for their leaves and roots will produce satisfactory crops in light shade.

▶ Save garden space by interplanting, such as planting fast-growing lettuce between your tomato seedlings. By the time the tomatoes need the space, the lettuce will have been harvested.

▶ A garden can be organized to give you both flowers and vegetables. Try planting beans with sweet peas, tomatoes behind the marigolds, and peppers among the petunias.

▶ To make sure you plant seeds in straight rows, make a simple planting guide from two stakes with a string stretched between them. Or use the handle of your rake to make a trench in which to plant the seeds.

Watering

▶ The best time to water gardens and lawns is early in the morning. Early morning watering lets the sun dry the leaves quickly, preventing the spread of fungal diseases that thrive in moist conditions.

▶ Avoid watering from above, if possible, because many diseases are encouraged by wet leaves. Gently water at the soil level to avoid washing the soil away and exposing the roots.

▶ Water gently, because a sharp jet of water can wash away the soil and expose the roots. Use a nozzle that breaks the force of the water at the end of the hose.

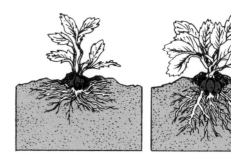

▶ Select a watering can made of lightweight material. Remember that you'll have to lift and carry it when it's filled with water.

▶ Always soak the soil thoroughly when watering. A light sprinkling can do more harm than no water at all because it promotes shallow root growth.

Fertilizing

▶ Remember that phosphoric acid encourages root growth and fruit production; nitrogen is necessary for leafy growth; and potassium promotes root growth and disease resistance. A complete, well-balanced fertilizer contains these ingredients in fairly equal proportions.

▶ Apply fertilizer at the rate suggested on the product label.

▶ A way to supply fertilizer quickly is by spraying a solution directly on the plant foliage with a sprayer, watering can, or hose-feeding attachment. Buy foliar fertilizers that are specially formulated for this purpose and follow the manufacturer's instructions carefully to avoid burning the foliage.

Seeds and Seedlings

▶ Keep seed packets in the refrigerator or some other cool place till you're ready to plant the seeds. The refrigerator is also the best place to store leftover seeds. Put them in a glass jar with a bit of silica gel and screw the cap on the jar tightly.

▶ Never transplant seedlings directly from indoors into the garden. They must be hardened off by being exposed gradually to outdoor conditions: Put the containers outside during the day and bring them in again at night for a couple of weeks before setting the seedlings out.

▶ Plastic jugs—such as milk jugs—with the bottoms removed make good insulators to

PRUNING SHRUBS AND TREES

Most shrubs and trees benefit from a pruning that allows more air and light into dense growth and rids the shrub or tree of weak branches.

▶ Keep your pruning shears sharp; dull blades cause bruising and ragged cuts that invite pests and disease.

▶ Use the appropriate tool for the branch or limb to be pruned. Too large or too small a tool can make ragged cuts.

▶ Make all cuts as close as possible to the base of the branch being removed without damaging the ridged collar where it attaches to the larger limb.

▶ Prune most shrubs and trees—with the exception of trees that exude sap and early spring flowering species—in the winter when trees are dormant. Spring-flowering trees, such as lilacs, should be pruned immediately after bloom.

▶ Prune lightly in the spring for shaping purposes, if needed.

▶ Remove damaged or dead limbs anytime during the year.

▶ If a tree or shrub needs heavy pruning (when as much as a third of the plant's live tissue will be removed), do the pruning in stages over a two-to-three-year period.

▶ Make sure that any limbs will not fall on power lines when cut.

▶ Remove crossovers, suckers from root system, and other unwanted branches.

▶ While shearing is great for hedges, it makes for unusual new growth on trees and shrubs.

protect young transplants from cold night temperatures. Two-pound coffee cans with both ends removed also work well.

▶ Seeds won't germinate if they're planted too deeply. Follow this guide: Small seeds should be planted ¼ to ½ inch deep; medium seeds ½ to 1 inch deep; and large seeds 1 to 1½ inches deep. Very tiny seeds can just be pressed into the soil.

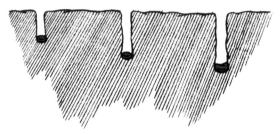

▶ Many beginning gardeners hate to thin plants because of the "waste." But unless

EQUIPMENT AND SUPPLIES FOR STARTING PLANTS INDOORS

▶ A fluorescent light fixture with full-spectrum growlamp bulbs.

▶ An automatic timer to turn the light fixture on and off each day. Never leave the lights on all the time; plants need time to rest in the dark.

▶ White or silver-colored reflectors placed around three, or all four, sides to bounce light onto plants from all angles. Make a reflector card by covering cardboard with aluminum foil.

▶ A thermostatically controlled soil heating cable if the setup is in a cool room.

▶ A drip tray, which allows watering of seedlings from the bottom.

plants are thinned you'll get a poor crop, because individual seedlings will be fighting each other for space, moisture, and soil nutrients. Always thin as directed on the seed packet.

▶ If the weather becomes very hot before your transplanted seedlings have had time to become accustomed to garden conditions, provide shelter by propping a board so that it will shade the young plants.

Pest Control

▶ Use insecticidal soap on plants to control pests. You may also make a homemade insecticide by mixing 2½ tablespoons of biodegradable detergent to 1 gallon of water and using it to spray both sides of the plant leaves. After an hour, spray or hose them down with clear water.

▶ During the early stages of infestation by larger insects, you can often hand-pick the bugs and their eggs from the leaves or brush them into a jar coated with detergent.

▶ Always follow the manufacturer's instructions precisely when using any commercial pesticide.

Herb Gardening

▶ Low-growing herbs, such as thyme, marjoram, and chives, should be planted where they won't be overshadowed by other plants. They make a delightful edging for a flower bed or a path.

▶ Coriander, tarragon, and dill grow to a height of 2 feet or more, so plant them against a wall or toward the back of a flower bed that backs onto a fence or wall.

▶ Certain herbs spread so fast outdoors that they'll take over the garden unless you control them. For example, wild marjoram, tarragon, and mint are perennials that flare out in all directions from season to season. Restrict them with a sunken section of stovepipe that confines their roots; a large coffee can with both ends removed works well, too.

▶ Herbs can be frozen, dried, or stored in oil or vinegar. Cut them just before they flower, when their oils are most abundant. The best time to cut herbs for storage is at midmorning on a sunny day.

▶ Grow rosemary and bay in clay pots buried just beneath the surface of the soil in your garden. This makes it easier to move them indoors when the weather gets cold; they're temperature-sensitive and may not survive winter conditions outdoors.

Vegetable Gardens

▶ To protect your corn crop from birds, tie paper bags over the ears.

▶ If you're short on garden space, try growing corn in an old washtub.

▶ Peas don't like hot weather; harvest them before the summer heat gets too intense.

▶ Harvest radishes when they're 1 inch in diameter; larger radishes are tough.

▶ When buying tomato plants for the garden, look for plants that are short, stocky, and bright green in color. Be sure not to plant your tomatoes until the soil is warm and the danger of frost has passed.

▶ If your tomato seedlings are too "leggy," plant them deeper and on a slant, so that the plants don't get top heavy.

▶ If you want your garden vegetables to ripen faster outdoors, place aluminum foil beneath them to reflect the sunlight.

GARDENING WITH INDOOR PLANTS

All plants need light, water, and nutrients in varying degrees to grow properly. While it's easy to kill succulents, like cacti, with too much water, other plants will die quickly if

COMPOSTING

▶ A bin, a wire cage, or even a pile can be the start of a compost. Locate your compost on a well-drained, level area, preferably in the shade.

▶ A 3- to 4-foot-tall compost pile is the most efficient size.

▶ To start a compost pile in the fall, use leaves that have been shredded. Don't use large whole leaves, such as oak leaves, which take years to deteriorate.

▶ Keep vegetable and fruit peelings, tea and coffee grounds, garden plants, weeds, grass clippings, etc., in a plastic bag and empty them onto the pile when the bag is full. Apply more leaves over the scraps.

▶ Water the pile when it's dry and turn it periodically to accelerate decomposition.

▶ Compost is ready for garden beds when it is dark and crumbles easily. It should smell woody, not rotten.

▶ Never start a compost pile when there is the danger of attracting rats, and never put scraps or bones from animal matter, including meat, poultry, and fish, in the compost pile.

▶ Never use grass clippings from a lawn that has been recently treated with a herbicide as mulch or compost on your garden.

LAWN AND GARDEN MAINTENANCE SCHEDULE

Winter
- Order seed catalogues and begin planning your garden.
- Prune deciduous trees and shrubs.
- Start perennial seeds in seed trays indoors under lights.

Early Spring
- Rake up any leaves and debris that have accumulated during the winter.
- Remove top layer of winter mulch.
- Loosen turf with a leaf rake to remove brown, matted material without disturbing grass.
- Reseed bare lawn patches.
- Plant bare-root and container-grown perennials.
- Work the soil in the vegetable garden.
- Apply superior dormant oil sprays to control insects when tree buds just begin to show new growth.
- Check trees and shrubs for winter damage. Prune where needed before buds begin new growth.
- Prune roses as new growth begins.
- Transplant shrubs and small trees while plants are still dormant.
- Plant hardy vegetable plants.

Late Spring
- Apply fertilizer to lawns and beds of spring bulbs in May to avoid early spring diseases.
- Fertilize shrubs and plants.
- Fertilize vegetable garden.
- If the spring is dry, be sure to water shrubs and plants.
- Mulch flower beds and shrubs.
- Stake plants if needed.
- Transplant perennial seedlings.
- Thin new growth in flower and vegetable gardens.
- Plant warm-season annual flowers and vegetable transplants after last danger of frost has passed.

Summer
- Keep weeds under control in vegetable and flower gardens.
- Keep shrubs and plants watered if the summer is dry.
- Check trees, shrubs, and plants for insect infestations and disease, and eliminate them, if necessary.
- Prune late-flowering shrubs and trees.
- Pinch off dead flowers.

Early Fall
- Divide and replant perennial flowers.

- Plant new trees and shrubs, except in areas with extreme winter temperatures.
- Reseed or sod new lawns.
- Fertilize lawns, shrubs, and trees.
- Remove dead branches from deciduous trees and shrubs.
- Cut back stems of flowering plants—except hardy plants—after the first frost.

Late Fall
- Clean out all old vines, stalks, stems, and rotten fruit.
- Harvest vegetable garden.
- Rake remaining leaves and shred for winter mulch.
- Plant bulbs; dig up dahlia and canna roots, gladiolus, and other bulbs that do not survive the winter.
- Use hand pruners to cut back dead stems on perennials that die down. Leave only 2 to 3 inches of stem.
- Continue deep-watering perennials until the ground has frozen solidly.
- Apply winter mulch to perennial beds when the ground is frozen hard.
- Protect perennials that are marginally hardy in your zone.
- Drain and store hoses.
- Clean and store tools.

they dry out. Flowering plants need lots of light and fertilizer to bloom, while many plants prefer diffuse light. Consequently, the first rule of indoor gardening is to know the individual needs of your plant.

▶ Choose plants that will fit your household, both in terms of light and humidity, as well as tolerance of pets, children, and how much time you want to spend tending to them.

▶ Plants that are highly tolerant of indoor growing and even careless owners include:

Bamboo palm *(Chamaedorea erumpens)*
Burro tail *(Sedum Morganianum)*
Cast-iron plant *(Aspidistra elatior)*
Chinese evergreen *(Aglaonema commutatum)*
Corn plant *(Dracaena fragrans 'Massangeana')*
Crown of thorns *(Euphorbia 'Milii')*
Fiddle-leaf *(Ficus lyrata)*
Milk bush *(Euphorbia Tirucalli)*
Monkey-puzzle tree *(Araucaria araucana)*
Mother-in-law's tongue *(Sansevieria trifasciata)*
Norfolk Island pine *(Araucaria heterophylla)*
Philodendron *(Philodendron Selloum)*
Ponytail *(Beaucarnea recurvata)*
Pothos *(Epipremnum aureum)*
Rubber plant *(Ficus elastica)*
Sago palm *(Cycas revoluta)*
Spider plant *(Chlorophytum comosum)*
Swedish ivy *(Plectranthus australis)*
Swiss cheese plant *(Monstera deliciosa)*
Tahitian bridal veil *(Tripogandra multiflora)*
Wax plant *(Hoya carnosa)*

▶ Avoid eating plants that are poisonous. Among the more common ones are:

Elephant ear *(Caladium* species)
Dumb cane *(Dieffenbachia* species)
Spurges *(Euphorbia* species)
Ivy *(Hedera* helix)
Holly *(Ilex* species)
Daffodils *(Narcissus* species)
Elephant ears *(Philodendron* species)
Azaleas *(Rhododendron* species)
Castor oil bean plant *(Ricinus communis)*
Yew *(Taxus* species)

Lighting

▶ To test how much light your plants will get in a given location, place a sheet of paper where you want to put a plant, and hold your hand a foot above the paper. If your hand casts a sharp, well-defined shadow, you have bright light. If the shadow is fuzzy but recognizable, you have filtered light. If all you get is a blur on the paper, your light is shady and you will have to choose your plants carefully or consider supplementing the available light.

▶ Plants grow toward light (this process is called phototropism). Keep a plant standing straight by periodically turning the pot a quarter-turn.

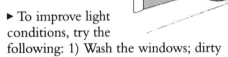

▶ To improve light conditions, try the following: 1) Wash the windows; dirty

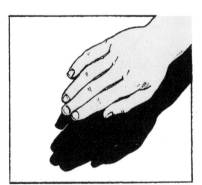
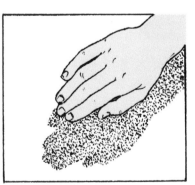

windows can cut down on light transmittal by as much as 40 percent. 2) Move the plants around. 3) Add artificial light. 4) Increase light reflection by using aluminum foil or sharp white rocks on top of the soil in the pots.

▶ Give newly potted plants a little less light for the first few days.

Watering

▶ If you're not sure whether a houseplant needs watering or not, poke your index finger 1 inch into the topsoil. If the soil is moist, don't water. If it's dry, do. You can also use a knitting needle. If the needle inserted into the soil comes out dry, water the plant.

▶ Water houseplants slowly and thoroughly until the water runs out of the bottom of the pot. If the plant is in a saucer, empty the saucer after the plant finishes draining.

▶ Plants originating in deserts and dry areas like to be drenched and permitted to dry out.

▶ Water bulb houseplants, like cyclamen, from the bottom. Fill a pie pan with water and let the plants sit in it for a while.

▶ To "water" a terrarium, simply pat the inside of the glass with a wet paper towel or use an ordinary basting syringe.

▶ During cold-weather months, a room filled with houseplants will benefit from the moisture provided by a portable vaporizer.

▶ Water that has been sitting for some time is best for watering plants. It will have reached room temperature (some plants dislike cold water).

▶ Plants don't like softened water. If you have an ion exchange water softener, get your plant water from the tap before it goes into the softener.

▶ Humidity for plants can be increased in several ways. Group the plants closer together. Put a layer of pebbles or perlite in a metal or plastic pan, place the pots on the pebbles, and keep the water in the pan just below the bottoms of the pots.

▶ A dried-out houseplant can be revived by sinking the pot in tepid water until air bubbles come out. Next time, remember to water before the soil shrinks away from the edge of the pot, which indicates that the root ball has dried out.

▶ There's nothing you can do to save an overwatered plant that has rotted; however, you can clip still-healthy leaves or stems and root them to start new plants.

▶ Slip shower caps over the bottoms of hanging planters to catch the overflow when watering. The caps can be removed after an hour or so.

Drainage

▶ Any container used as a plant pot must have drainage holes. If you're recycling a container such as a yogurt cup or margarine tub, make holes in the bottom and stand the pot on a saucer.

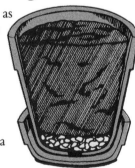

▶ Use pieces of plastic foam for a lightweight drainage layer in the bottom of a hanging planter.

▶ Sand or perlite added to your plant mix will improve drainage; you can also enlarge the hole in the bottom of the pot or use more crocking (broken clay pots).

▶ Old sponges cut into squares are great for covering drainage holes in flowerpots.

Feeding

▶ Phosphorus encourages root growth and fruit production; nitrogen is necessary for leafy growth; and potassium promotes root growth and disease resistance. A complete, well-balanced fertilizer contains these ingredients in fairly equal proportions.

▶ Usual signs of nitrogen deficiency are stunted growth, pale yellow lower leaves, and rusty brown edges.

▶ Usual signs of phosphorus deficiency are slow growth and spindly stems, although these could also indicate a lack of adequate light.

▶ Potassium deficiency is usually indicated by scorched edges on leaves, weak stems, and shriveled seeds or fruit.

MAKE YOUR OWN POTTING SOIL

To make a suitable potting soil for most houseplants, mix together 4 cups of black soil or potting soil; 4 cups of leaf mold, peat moss, or spaghnum moss; 4 cups of coarse sand; 2 to 4 cups of activated charcoal; and 1 tablespoon of steamed bone meal. This mix should be "cooked" in the oven so that it reaches 180°F for 30 minutes before use. Allow soil mix to cool before planting.

For plants with very fine roots, adjust the recipe by decreasing the black soil and sand to 3 cups each and increasing the peat or spaghnum moss to 6 cups.

To make potting soil for cacti, decrease the black soil and leaf mold or moss to 2 cups each, and increase the sand to 6 cups.

▶ It's best to fertilize plants periodically, once a month, but give your plants a breather from fertilizer from January to March, the usual dormancy period of plants.

▶ Don't fertilize a plant that is sick or droopy or plants that have been recently purchased or repotted.

▶ Unflavored gelatin dissolved in water is a good, nitrogen-rich plant food. Use one envelope of gelatin to a quart of liquid, and water the plants with this mixture (freshly made) once a month.

Repotting

▶ Repot plants only when needed.

▶ If you have plants that need to be brought in and potted for the winter, line the pots with plastic. Leave some excess plastic over the edge of the pot, and punch a couple of holes in the bottom for drainage. In spring, when it's time for transplanting, lift the soil and the plant out of the pot by the plastic.

▶ When reusing old pots, free them of pests or disease by washing them in hot water and soaking them overnight in a solution of 1 part chlorine bleach to 8 parts water. Rinse well.

▶ If children or pets keep knocking your plants over, try double-potting. Put the plant and its original pot inside another larger pot with rocks or gravel between the two. This will add both size and weight and should stabilize the plant.

Deterring Pests

▶ You can unwittingly bring bugs into a house by taking houseplants outside for extra sun and then returning them to their places indoors. If you take plants outdoors, keep them isolated from other houseplants for 3 to 4 weeks after you bring them back into the house. If you detect bugs on the plants, wipe the stems and leaves with a mild soap-and-water solution.

▶ To keep your pets away from your plants, remember that cats are territorial animals.

Don't position a plant in the cat's favorite place in the sun. Also, if your dog likes to people-watch through the window, leave that spot free.

Working with Seedlings

▶ Use a cardboard egg carton for a seedling nursery. Fill with loam and your plant seeds. When the seedlings are ready to be transplanted, plant the shell and the plant. The carton will decompose and enrich the soil. Egg cartons only work, however, for small-rooted seedlings; fast-growing young plants—like tomatoes—need more space.

▶ To speed up seed germination, place seed trays on top of your refrigerator, where the 72° to 75°F emitted heat will promote steady growth.

▶ Use a mister to water delicate seedlings.

TENDING PLANTS WHILE YOU TRAVEL

▶ Houseplants that like to be evenly moist will survive your absence for a couple of weeks if you water them well and put them on a tray of wet gravel inside a large, clear-plastic dry cleaning bag (a terrarium tent).

▶ Before going away, put water in the bathtub and set your large plants on top of bricks; the bricks should be placed on end with the tops just out of the water. Cover the plants and tub with a sheet of

clear plastic, and set your bathroom light on a timer to give them 12 hours of light a day.

▶ As an alternative when you go on vacation, set all your houseplants on old towels folded in a few inches of water in the bathtub. The plants will absorb the water as they need it.

▶ Succulents (such as cacti) will survive your absence if you water them well and move them out of direct light before you leave.

▶ Self-watering pots and plant waterers that work by means of wicks, gravity, or capillary action should be used only with plants that prefer to be evenly moist or wet. Some of these devices do a beautiful job on water-loving plants, but they are not satisfactory for plants that like to dry out between waterings.

► To avoid dislodging newly planted seeds, place the containers in a shallow dish of water so that moisture can be absorbed from underneath.

Timesavers

► If you love indoor plants but don't want to invest a lot of time and effort in taking care of them, select large, mature, well-established plants. They usually need less attention than young plants that are just getting started.

► To cut down on the time you spend on your indoor garden, choose plants that have more or less the same water, light, and temperature requirements. Pot them in the same mix in containers of the same type and size. Then all you will have to do is give them all the same amount of light and water.

► For an easy-to-care-for indoor garden, choose plants that are tolerant of varying light intensity, water requirements, and humidity.

► Clean the leaves of a houseplant quickly with a feather duster.

► Pinch new shoots at the growing points to encourage branching, which produces more growth for flowering. Palms are an exception to this rule; it's fatal to pinch back palms.

► Simplify the task of rotating a big, heavy planter so that the plant gets sun all around by setting the pot on a lazy Susan.

PEST CONTROL

Bats

► Bat-proofing your property is a good idea if you've been infested once and want to eliminate future colonies. The strong odor a colony leaves behind attracts other bats even after the first group has been evicted.

► If you see a bat in your house, try to chase it out through an open window or door. Remember to always wear gloves when dealing with bats.

Insects

► Keep ants away from your home with a concoction of borax and sugar. Mix 1 cup of sugar and 1 cup of borax in a quart jar. Punch holes in the jar's lid and sprinkle its contents outdoors around the foundation of your home and around the baseboards inside your house. The ants are attracted by the sugar and poisoned by the borax.

► If you have cockroaches, sprinkle borax powder in the kitchen and bathroom cabinets. Avoid sprinkling where children and pets could be affected.

► Some people are allergic to bee or wasp stings. If you know or suspect that you are one of them, never try to exterminate a nest yourself. Hire an exterminator.

► If there's a hornet, wasp, bee, or other flying insect in your house and you have no insect spray, kill it with hair spray.

► If your home becomes infested with fleas, vacuum rugs thoroughly before spraying and throw out the dust bag at once.

► Change the water in a birdbath every 3 days to help reduce the mosquito population, because mosquito larvae thrive in water.

► The presence of carpenter ants indicates another problem. Because they're fond of damp wood, you should check your pipes, roof, and windowsills for water leaks.

▶ In the spring, moving leftover firewood away from the house will help discourage insect infestations.

▶ Centipedes prey on other bugs, so the presence of centipedes in your house may indicate the presence of other insects as well.

▶ You can distinguish termite damage from other insect damage by examining any holes you find in wood. Termites usually eat only the soft part of wood, leaving the annual rings intact.

▶ Remember that supermarkets and grocery stores almost always have roaches, so check bags and boxes when unpacking food at home.

▶ If you live in a multiunit building, any pest control measures you take individually will be ineffective in the long run simply because insects can travel from one apartment to another. To eliminate bugs completely, the entire building should be treated at one time.

Raccoons and Rodents

▶ Carefully wrap all food in containers so that mice cannot get to it.

▶ Raw bacon or peanut butter makes good bait for a mousetrap; so does a cotton ball saturated with bacon grease. Make sure a mouse will have to tug the trap to remove the

bait. If you're using peanut butter, dab some on the triggering device and let it harden before setting the trap. If bacon is your bait, tie it around the triggering device.

▶ If a raccoon sets up housekeeping in your attic or chimney, chemical repellents—such as oil of mustard—are temporarily effective. The smell may bother you as much as it does the raccoon. Your best bet is to let the animal leave, and then cover its entrance hole with wire mesh so that it cannot return.

▶ To keep rodents out of your house, seal every opening they could squeeze through. Some need less than $\frac{1}{4}$ inch of space. Put poison in deep cracks or holes, and stuff these with steel wool or scouring pads pushed in with a screwdriver. Close the spaces with spackling compound mixed with steel wool fragments.

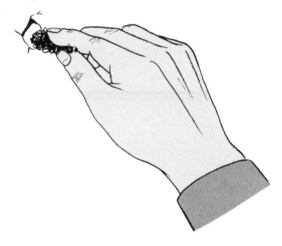

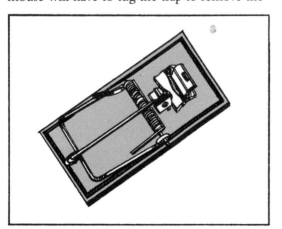

WHAT'S WRONG WITH MY PLANT?

Most difficulties with plants are not due to disease or insects, but to cultural practices that can be easily corrected. Even if pests are involved, there is an increasingly wide range of biological pesticides, such as insecticidal soap, that can be used around the home without harming its other inhabitants.

SYMPTOM	CAUSE	TREATMENT
CULTURAL PROBLEMS		
Pale growth with new leaves smaller than normal. The plant stretches toward the light.	Insufficient light	Move plants to a brighter spot or closer to the light source. Supply artificial light.
Foliage wilts, potting mix is dry.	Lack of water	Water thoroughly.
Foliage wilts, potting mix is moist. Soil smells of decaying vegetation.	Overwatering	Water less frequently. Increase light so the plant can better absorb the water it is given.
Growth is slow and leaves are pale in color.	Lack of fertilizer.	Apply an appropriate fertilizer regularly throughout the growing season.
Growth is stunted and leaves are yellowed. A crustlike accumulation appears at the base of the plant's stem and on the pot rim.	Buildup of mineral salts in the soil	In light cases, leach the soil thoroughly with clear water. In more severe cases, repot into fresh soil.
Plant does not bloom.	Various causes (too little light, too much water, etc.)	Improve growing conditions.
INSECTS AND OTHER PESTS		
Leaves take on a mottled appearance and appear dusty underneath. If the leaves are shaken over a sheet of white paper, tiny moving "spiders" can be seen. In severe cases, a spidery webbing stretches between leaves.	Spider mites	Clean plant thoroughly with soapy water. Spray with insecticidal soap. Keep the air humid to prevent a recurrence.
Little balls of "cotton" (actually slow-moving insects or their egg cases) are seen on stems, at leaf axils, or on the plant's root system. Leaves yellow and may become covered with secretions.	Mealybugs	Touch individual insects and egg cases with a cotton swab dipped in rubbing alcohol. Spray the entire plant with a solution composed of 7 parts water and 1 part rubbing alcohol.

SYMPTOM	CAUSE	TREATMENT
Shell- or scalelike bumps are seen on leaves and stems. Plants may yellow or become covered with secretions.	Scale insects	Scrape off the shells with an old toothbrush dipped in soapy water. Treat with insecticidal soap.
Green to black, round-bodied, translucent insects cluster together on new growth. Plants may yellow or become covered with secretions.	Aphids	Wash the plant thoroughly with a damp cloth dipped in soapy water. Treat with insecticidal soap.
Tiny, white, dandrufflike insects rise up when the plant is touched. Small translucent bumps are seen underneath the leaves.	Whiteflies	Use a vacuum to suck up flying adults, then wash the plant thoroughly with a damp cloth dipped in soapy water. Treat with insecticidal soap.
Leaves and foliage are streaked and mottled. Hyphen-sized insects scatter about when the plant is breathed upon. Tiny black excrements are found on infected plant parts.	Thrips	Remove severely infested flowers and foliage. Treat with insecticidal soap.
New growth is distorted and turns brown and dry, eventually ceasing altogether. This problem is very host-specific, affecting mostly African violets, begonias, and cyclamens.	Cyclamen mites	This problem is very difficult to treat. It is often best to get rid of infected plant. An appropriate miticide or repeated insecticidal soap treatments can be used if the plant has great value.
Tiny insects are seen jumping on the soil surface during watering.	Springtails	Springtails are basically harmless. Letting the soil dry out between waterings will discourage them.
Tiny black midges are seen hovering around plants and elsewhere in the house. Grublike larvae are seen in the soil.	Fungus gnats and sand flies	These insects are annoying but relatively harmless to indoor plants. Letting the soil dry out between waterings will discourage them.

DISEASES

White mold appears on leaves and flowers. Plant parts yellow and die.	Mildew	Improve air circulation. Treat with an appropriate fungicide.
Gray, fluffy mold appears on leaves and flowers. Plants yellow and die.	Gray mold (botrytis)	Improve air circulation. Treat with an appropriate fungicide.
Black patches appear at base of stem underground on the roots. The plant wilts and doesn't recover even when watered.	Root or stem rot	Can be caused by various disease or organisms, but is usually linked to overwatering. Start the plant over from cuttings.

Do you spend too much time chasing lost papers, going on futile shopping trips, and rummaging through overstuffed closets for missing items? Chances are that your household needs to be better organized. Structure comes easily to some people, but others seem to have no idea how to organize their day, let alone a week. If you fall into the latter category, the good news is that there are plenty of tricks to help you get organized. It's not that difficult, nor does it take a lot of time. And although we can't promise that an organized household won't face a crisis now and then, we can promise that you'll be much better prepared to cope with the inevitable emergencies that crop up.

MANAGING TIME

Missed appointments and slapdash meals aren't the result of hectic schedules—they're the consequences of disorganization. To efficiently manage time, papers need to be where you can find them, agendas must be set and followed, and items needed for daily life should be on hand. In other words, papers, schedules, and shopping must be organized. The following gives you some helpful ideas of how to do just that—without wasting too much time in the process.

ORGANIZING HOUSEHOLD PAPERS

Chasing papers wastes time and energy. And when bills aren't paid or permission slips aren't turned in, the price for disorganization is paid in interest payments and lost field trips. If your idea of organizing your papers is to stack them on the dining room table, try some of the following hints:

▶ Designate one area of your home, even if it's only one drawer somewhere, for filing business papers, bills, letters, and clippings.

▶ Set up a filing system for your important papers and receipts. This can be as simple as an accordion file that can be stored in a closet or a file cabinet that can do double duty as an end table. Use the categories in "Setting Up a Filing System" to organize your file folders.

▶ Use a "Miscellaneous" file for items that don't easily fit into a category, but be sure to go through this file when it fills up. You'll find that new categories will stand out, and unneeded items will be easily recognizable.

▶ Keep your mail in one location in the house and open up and file everything at least once a week. If you can't file papers on a regular basis, use a folder labeled "To File" to temporarily store items and set aside time to file these papers when it fills up.

▶ Hang a basket near the front door and keep your keys in it, so you'll always know where they are. Also use this basket for bills and letters that need to be mailed. When you grab your keys, you'll remember the mail.

▶ For households with children, keep a special clipboard in a prominent place for all those permission slips and other school documents that are easily mislaid. It's hard enough to get a child to deliver these papers to you, but at least once you've got your hands on them you'll know where they are and when they have to be processed.

▶ Instead of using an address book, try using index cards stored in a file box. Along with names, addresses, and phone numbers, you'll have room to keep track of birthdays, anniversaries, clothing sizes, and even presents you've given in recent years. If someone moves, substitute an updated card.

▶ Keep instruction booklets that come with appliances in a notebook. Paste the back cover of each booklet against one of the notebook's three-hole-punched sheets, and you'll know just where to find the information when you need it.

▶ Review your filing system periodically and toss out items no longer needed, such as last year's utility bills or warranties on discarded items.

Using Lists and Planners

▶ Make lists, both daily and weekly, to make sure you remember what needs to get done.

Checking off the items will give you a sense of accomplishment, as well as remind you of what you still need to do.

▶ Create a weekly "Family Chore List" where family members can sign up for chores. This gives everyone some say in what they're going to do and also shares the responsibility of getting things done.

▶ Use a yearly planner to set long-term goals, such as saving money or planning vacations.

▶ Use a large wall calendar to keep track of appointments, meetings, visits, birthdays, and other events. Keeping this near the phone makes it easier to mark in dates and remind you of upcoming events.

Setting Priorities

▶ Decide on the time of day when your energy level is highest to do your least favorite chore. You'll find you can get through it much more easily. Wind down the day with one of your favorite activities.

▶ If you have trouble getting started in the morning, get organized the night before. Lay out your clothes, measure the coffee, and set the breakfast table before you go to bed.

▶ Set realistic goals. Don't try to cram too much into one day or even one year. If you

SETTING UP A FILING SYSTEM

What to File:

Banking—check registers, extra checks, passbooks, canceled checks

Car—title, insurance policies, maintenance records, payments

Credit cards—list of all credit cards with numbers; statements

Guarantees and warranties, including instruction pamphlets

House records—insurance policy and mortgage papers; list of home improvements and receipts; lease and renter's insurance policy, if renting

Investment records—mutual fund and broker statements

Life insurance policies

Medical records—immunizations, insurance forms, insurance payments, prescriptions

Tax records—copies of tax records for previous years and receipts for deductible expenses you plan to claim in next year's return

Copy of will (keep other copy at your attorney's office)

What to Store in the Bank Deposit Box:

Personal papers, including birth certificates, marriage license, passports, military service records, divorce decrees

House deed and title

Financial holdings, including savings bonds, bank certificates of deposit, stock certificates

List of valuables (include room-by-room videotape of home, if possible)

---

find yourself constantly behind schedule, keep a notepad with you and write down everything you do for a few days. Then look at the list objectively to determine whether you've attempted to do too much.

► Separate a major project into manageable parts. For example, spend an extra hour each month to thoroughly clean a room, instead of trying to do "spring" or "fall" cleaning.

► Get the family involved in day-to-day chores. Even young children can set the table or put newspapers in the recycling bin. If school activities and homework prevent older children from carrying out weekday chores, get them involved for an hour or two on the weekends.

SHOPPING EFFICIENTLY

All too often shopping trips end up with few or meaningless purchases. Unless shopping is your passion, you can avoid futile shopping trips and make necessary trips more efficient.

Groceries

► Create menus for the week before you go shopping and make sure you have everything needed to make the meals selected.

► Pin menus for the week on a bulletin board—with the recipe titles and cookbook page references. The first one home can start the meal.

► Post a list in the kitchen—on the refrigerator, if possible—and establish a rule that every time something is used up, it goes on the list. This method goes a long way in avoiding last-minute shopping trips for missing items.

► Make out your shopping list in the same order as the food is stocked in the store aisles.

▶ Go grocery shopping when it's least crowded. Depending on your area and the store, this might be very early in the morning or late in the evening.

▶ Keep coupons in an envelope or folder that can be taken along to the grocery store.

▶ Keep a good supply of staples on hand, and make sure that you can make at least one or two meals from canned and packaged items, such as rice and beans or pasta with sauce.

▶ Make good use of your freezer by cooking double quantities and freezing a meal.

Clothing

▶ If you're looking for a particular item, wear the kind of clothes and accessories that would work with this item. If you're looking for a jacket, for example, wear a shirt and tie. This takes the guesswork out of how the item will look once you get it home and reduces the possibility of returns.

▶ Keep an updated index card in your purse or wallet with the sizes and measurements of all your family members. You'll be prepared to

take advantage of an unexpected bargain and avoid returns of items that don't fit.

▶ If you're trying to match a color perfectly, be sure to take the item with you. Your eye may not be as color-aware as you think.

▶ To save yourself the time and trouble of going from store to store, phone ahead to see which store has what you're looking for.

▶ Staple fabric scraps snipped from skirt and pants hems or seams to a card, and carry it with you for help in coordinating shirts, sweaters, and accessories.

Hardware

▶ Make a list of basic tools you need to function efficiently in the home. For some, this may be as simple as a group of basic hand tools, some nails and screws, and a few necessities. The trick is to anticipate the kinds of jobs you need to do in the months ahead, and be sure that you keep a supply of what's necessary. Avoid time-consuming trips to the hardware store for basic necessities.

▶ If you have a tool bench or tool area, keep a notepad around to jot down lists for the next hardware run. Otherwise, you'll end up spending hours browsing around the store trying to remember what you need.

TIMESAVERS

▶ Put a check from your checkbook in your wallet so that you'll always have an extra when you find yourself down to your last check—or if you've forgotten your checkbook. Be sure to record the amount of this extra check in your checkbook when you use it.

▶ Use printed address labels to fill in your name on coupons; label items that you lend; label the bowl or casserole dish you take to a potluck or dinner; or identify an item left for repair.

▶ Keep a seam ripper (with the safety cap on) near your favorite reading chair. It's perfect for clipping recipes and coupons from newspapers and magazines.

▶ Use a portable phone in the kitchen to allow you to do some cleaning up when you're involved in a long phone call.

▶ Help your children learn to make their beds by marking the centers of sheets, blankets, and spreads with an appliquéd design or colored thread. Even a young child will see that when the little line of teddy bears is in the middle of the bed, the sheet is on straight.

▶ Keep extra clothespins in the coat closet and have your family use them to clip together gloves, boots, and sneakers so that you waste less time rummaging through piles of partnerless items. If your child takes a clothespin to school in his or her tote bag, it can be used to clip boots or gym shoes

together for easy retrieval at the end of the day.

▶ Put compartmented hanging closet organizers for shoes to work all around the house. They're ideal for storing sweaters, underwear, socks, needlework supplies, and many other space-hungry household items. And you can see at a glance just what's in there.

▶ Assign a color to each family member and color-code items throughout the house. Schoolbags, umbrellas, ponchos, coat hooks, storage boxes, and lunch boxes can all be color-coded this way.

▶ Label film as soon as it's developed with place, date, and any other information needed for identification.

MANAGING A HOME OFFICE

A home office can be as small as a folding file or as large as a room. If you're running a business out of your home, you'll obviously need much more space and equipment than a family looking for a corner to file papers and tend to correspondence. The important thing to remember about creating a home office is to make it suit your family's needs. For example, if your children need to use a computer, you'll want to set up space that can be shared—not a corner in your bedroom. Likewise, equipment and supplies should be selected for versatility.

CREATING OFFICE SPACE

▶ Use a wall or part of a wall to set up an office. If you're extremely short on space, mount shelves on the top portion of a wall to store files and use a table that can be folded down.

▶ Use a screen to separate a corner of a room and create office space. While not ideal, it may be the best space you can find in small apartments.

▶ Find a niche—under the stairs, on a landing, or in an odd-sized room or hallway. Use a roll-down window blind to enclose the niche when not in use.

▶ Convert a closet into an office with a folding door. If there is no power inside the closet, you'll want to have it wired to provide good lighting at a minimum. This works particularly well in a guest-room closet. Keep a portable wardrobe hanger on hand for guests when they arrive.

▶ Replace a double bed with a sofa bed in a guest room or extra bedroom to allow space for your office.

Outfitting a Home Office

Equipment is almost secondary to some of the intangibles that a home office must have to work properly. Along with good lighting, make your office a place that you like. This doesn't require a lot of space. In fact, sometimes it's easier to plan a small space than a large area. If your office ends up looking like a sterile cubicle in a high-rise, you're not going to want to spend time there.

The Basics	**The Extras**
Folding file folder	File cabinet
Phone jack	Phone with
	answering
	machine

Electric typewriter	Computer with word-processing and financial software and printer
Hand-held calculator	Desktop calculator
Writing area	Desk
Comfortable chair	Adjustable chair on casters
Task lighting	Natural light, overhead light, and task lighting
Shelf	Bookshelves
Storage space	Storage cabinets Photocopier and fax machine

▶ If you intend to outfit a room, draw up a floor plan before purchasing equipment. Use a 1-inch scale and draw in windows and doors. Then plan various design plans for such items as your desk and computer.

▶ Try to include some shelving or storage that can be reached while sitting at your desk or work counter.

▶ Plan your work space so you have room to keep items such as the phone within reach while still retaining space to jot notes.

▶ Make sure you allow room for file cabinets to open. They're deeper than a desk.

▶ Use bulletin boards to hold reminders, calendars, and a "To Do" list. Put up the board where you can see it easily.

▶ If you're working on a small counter space, it's a good idea to get computers out of the way and save space on the desk for the monitor and keyboard. You'll need to purchase longer computer cables, however, to make this work.

MANAGING SPACE

Some people manage to work quite well in disarray, but most of us find that crammed closets and cluttered countertops and tables hide more than they store. When it comes to closets and shelving, you have two options: You can either do it yourself or call in a professional organizer. Most professional organizing companies are limited to dealing with closets or garages, leaving the rest of the house to your own devices. Other companies may help with custom cabinetry for dens, kitchens, or bathrooms, and their professional designers can help with pricing and selection of materials. No one, however, can help with the principles of organizing. The good news is that you don't need carpentry skills to maximize the efficiency and organization of storage areas. With a little ingenuity, you can easily make basic organizing principles work for you.

GETTING STARTED

Start with the principle of first things first. If you're running out of room in your home,

TAX CONSIDERATIONS

Unless a home office is used exclusively and regularly as a principal place of business, there are no tax deductions allowed for a home office. If you think your home office meets these qualifications, consult with an accountant. Some available tax deductions are: expense for a second phone line, depreciation of the portion of the home that constitutes the office; a percentage of expenses, such as utility bills; and purchase of equipment as business expenses. Be aware, however, that deductions can be made only against income generated by a home business, not against income generated in other employment, and that a home office cannot generate a tax loss.

first determine whether you're storing too many items.

▶ Employ the one-year rule about possessions in your home. If you haven't worn or used something over the last year, store it in the basement or attic. If it continues to gather dust, give it away or discard it.

▶ Be ruthless about old clothes and paperback books that you don't intend to read again. They'll serve a much better use if given to a charity or library book sale than they will cluttering up your closets and shelves.

▶ Store out-of-season clothes in basement closets or boxes. The time spent in doing this twice a year is much less than the time spent in trying to find clothes in a cluttered closet every morning. Moving clothes that you haven't worn also provides incentive to get rid of them.

▶ Make sure your coat closets and bedroom closets are used only for clothes worn regularly, not for storing infrequently used sports items.

▶ Go through your kitchen cupboards and drawers and get rid of items that you don't use. Throw out junk, donate anything that

CARING FOR COMPUTERS

▶ Try not to position your computer in a carpeted room. Static from the carpet may damage the computer circuits or even wipe out data on your disks. If you must keep the computer in a carpeted room, buy an antistatic mat or use an antistatic spray to reduce buildup on the carpet.

▶ Occasionally wipe your computer keyboard with a clean, lint-free wiper. You can use an antistatic cleaning fluid if necessary, but spray it on the cloth, not on the keyboard.

▶ Air must circulate freely around the computer and peripherals to avoid building up heat. Never block the slots that allow cooling air to circulate.

▶ Cigarette smoke, humidity, and dust can harm your computer. Try to keep the appliance clear of such conditions. Cover the keyboard, printer, and peripherals when not in use.

▶ Be sure to use correctly wired three-wire electrical outlets for your computer system. The three-wire plug grounds the equipment, avoids electrical "noise" from the motor of your refrigerator, and minimizes interference with TVs and radios.

▶ When you buy a computer, check your homeowner's insurance policy to find out if you're covered if your computer is stolen or damaged.

might be useful to someone else, and store things that you rarely use elsewhere, such as in the cellar or basement.

▶ Go through the "junk" drawer. Chances are that you'll find something that you are ready to throw out.

▶ Evaluate each of the areas you plan to organize and determine which is the most troublesome. Make it a goal to start there first.

▶ Manufacturers display a constant stream of new products and gadgets for organizing. Don't be swayed or confused by advertising or the many products on the market. Decide what you need for the space you're organizing and then search for the product or materials that will do the job.

▶ If you have an estimate from a professional organizing company, compare it with the cost of doing it yourself. Nearly every product and accessory is available to the everyday consumer. Doing it yourself will reduce labor costs, but be sure to include the cost of any tools or special equipment required. Also, remember that when existing structures are removed, holes, scratches, and other unsightly conditions will be left behind. It demands less time and less energy if the closet or storage area is patched, prepped, and repainted before the new system is installed. Don't forget to add this extra expenditure to the total budget for the project.

MAXIMIZING CLOSET STORAGE

The key to success in organizing or reorganizing is to have a clear, well-conceived plan, whether the plan is your own or a scheme designed by you and the organizer/designer. If you're adding a new closet or putting in a closet system, if you don't plan the space well, you'll simply end up with space that will become as cluttered as your old closet. In their haste to get going, many people tend to disregard the planning stage. If you don't have a plan, you'll probably end up taking everything out of the closet and you'll be facing a mound of stuff with no idea how to organize it better than the way it was.

Planning a Closet Remodeling

▶ Draw an exact replica of your closet, including positive and negative features, and include all dimensions.

▶ Assess your wardrobe and other storage items to see what needs to be stored. Keep in mind that you want to store like items together, such as all blouses in one section and all slacks in another.

▶ To avoid crowding, allow 1 inch of horizontal space per garment; allow 2 to 3 inches of horizontal space for each suit, sportcoat, and blazer or jacket, depending on the bulk of the shoulder padding. Based on these allocations, when categories of clothes are hung together, you can easily figure out how much space you need. For example, 12 skirts would occupy 12 inches of horizontal space, and 3 suits would occupy 6 to 9 inches of horizontal space.

► To prevent clutter from sneaking its way back into your closet, a portion of your clothes rod should be the "work space" section. This work space is nothing more than an area designated and left empty for "clothes-in-process." Dry cleaning, both incoming and outgoing, will occupy this rod space.

► Take advantage of all your closet space. Check whether your closet can accommodate a main clothes-hanging rod high enough to allow another rod to be installed beneath it. Hang the shorter rod at least 36 inches from the floor for slacks and shirts.

► Be sure to plan on hanging clothes rods at least 1 foot from the back of the closet to avoid crushing garments. Allow at least a 3-inch minimum clearance for rods hung under shelves so you can remove hangers freely.

► Plan for hooks, shelves, or hanging bins to transform the inside surfaces of closet doors into useful storage areas.

► Assign your clothes and accessories to specific locations inside your closet. Since different clothes and accessories possess completely different characteristics, you cannot treat them as one entity. Also, individuals have personal preferences for storing clothes, and people come in different proportions, sizes, and shapes. Determine what needs to be hung on hangers, hung from hooks, or stored on shelves or in baskets. Everything should be allotted rod space, shelf space, floor space, or space on a specialty rack.

► When it comes to closets, men and women aren't equal. Men's shoes take up more room, and jackets tend to be bulkier. Don't assume a particular storage piece works equally well and that each and every shoe rack on the market will serve both sizes. Be sure to examine any potential purchase of closet materials to make certain it can accommodate your size.

► Allow for any irregularities. A closet with a sloped or lower-than-normal ceiling, masonry/plaster/brick walls rather than wall-board, windows inside the closet, vents, or other unusual structural components will restrict the materials that you may be able to

use. The shape and size of your closet may also limit the location and installation of any organizing materials you buy.

► Plan for grids on the sides of closets to store belts, bags, and scarves that take up little space but lots of shelf room.

► If you have obstacles inside your closet—air ducts or even space taken by water heaters—utilize the space by storing objects that fit the space. For example, if you have a narrow space between the closet wall and an air duct, fit it with shelves, hung on the wall, and store items such as bags and shoes.

► The position of the door can be either a hindrance or a help because it determines whether the adjoining wall space (on the inside of your closet) is accessible or large enough to be used in some way. The wall space on either side of the door and above the door can often supply usable space. For example, extra wall space can be used to install boots on hooks.

► Take advantage of cubbyholes, which work well for keeping stacks of sweaters conveniently contained and categorized or for keeping handbags and purses in an upright and standing position for easy access. This method allows you to clearly see each item without digging through various layers. This also opens up shelf space inside the closet.

► Don't forget about the back of the door. The inside of the closet door works well for belt racks, scarves, necklaces, and other articles meant to hang. Laundry bags are not appropriate here. Any type of storage rack that is bulky or protrudes is going to get in the way, or it could brush against the clothes inside the closet when the door is closed.

Sample Closet Configurations

STANDARD WALL CLOSET

A standard wall closet only 42 inches wide is just about the smallest clothes closet anyone is likely to have. Saving space here is very important.

► Shoes are placed on a shoe rack on the left side wall because of the door's position. This

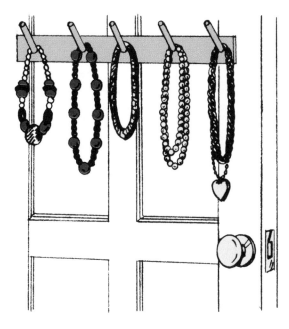

shoe-storage method requires only 5 inches of space to operate efficiently.

▶ Racks for ties, belts, and scarves are placed on the opposite side wall. Since the racks are at the same heights as the ventilated shelving, there is sufficient space for the lengths of the belts.

▶ Boots are hung from the ceiling, but not directly in front of the shelf. You may hang as many pairs as you like as long as they don't block access to the shelves. Placing the boots on the ceiling stores them without using any storage space.

▶ Purse and sweater cubbyholes on the shelf could be substituted for other kinds of shelf dividers. The main idea is to divide the height and length of the ventilated shelf into smaller compartments.

▶ Using attachable or add-on hangers increases the number of garments the closet can hold (from about 58 to about 99). A stool is also a permanent fixture in this closet, so that the boots and top shelf are not out of reach.

LARGE CLOSET (100-INCH CLOSET)

A much larger closet, as much as 100 inches wide, provides some alternatives to the smaller 42-inch closet. The primary objective of this design is to provide maximum hanging capabilities. But the closet manages to incorporate an extra 6 feet of shelf space, in addition to the full-length top shelf, by adding cubbyholes in a vertical alignment. Only 12 inches of hanging space was exchanged for this extra shelf space. The ventilated system allows the lower shelf and rod to stand free. With a modular system, a supporting wall would be needed.

LARGE CLOSET (106-INCH CLOSET)

Although this closet seems to be the same as the 100-inch wide closet, there is a major difference—there is wall space on the wall that also holds the closet door. This provides 24 inches of additional space on each side of the closet for shoe racks or belt/tie racks without any reduction in visibility or accessibility.

WALK-IN CLOSET

Many people seem more intimidated by the prospect of designing a walk-in closet than a standard wall closet. But the same factors are applicable in both—nothing changes except that you draw more than one wall for a complete design. Only one thing can cause failure: not understanding how each piece comes together in the corners of the closet. When the rods and shelves of two walls butt into each other in the corner, that corner space can be functional in only one direction.

▶ The main advantage of a walk-in closet over a standard wall closet is the walk-in closet's capability to keep each closet function separate from the others. One entire wall can be used for hanging, and another entire wall can be used for shelving. The standard wall closet must combine hanging and shelving on the same wall.

▶ Walk-in closets offer so much increased wall space that it is seldom necessary to conserve space to the same degree as in a standard wall closet.

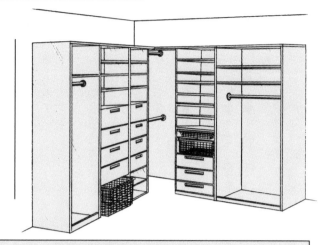

MEASURING YOUR GARMENTS

Measure the lengths of your garments from the top of the closet rod to the bottom edge of the garment itself. This tells you how much vertical space is required for slacks, dresses, or suits, so they can hang without obstruction. Also consider the type of hanger your clothes hang from; this can alter your closet design. Chrome hangers positon a garment 3 to 4 inches closer to the rod than a conventional hanger, giving your closet more vertical space.

Following is a list of average lengths for various garments. This should provide a basis for comparison as you measure your own clothes. Fashions with extremely short or long tails are the exception to these averages. They should not take precedence over the lengths of the majority of your clothes.

Man's suit/sportcoat	40 to 42 inches
Man's shirt	39 inches
Man's or woman's slacks (folded over a hanger)	26 inches
Man's or woman's slacks (hanging from cuffs)	46 inches

Woman's blouse	30 to 34 inches
Woman's suit skirt (street length)	34 inches
Woman's dress skirt	38 inches
Woman's blazer/ suit jacket	32 to 34 inches
Dress	45 to 50 inches

▶ The shorter "inset" walls or the inside surface of the doors supply the perfect spot for belt/tie racks or wall shoe racks.

▶ A closet with a door that opens inward and is flush with the side wall prevents use of part of the wall for any major closet component. Instead, mirrors can be installed on both the wall and the inside of the door.

MAXIMIZING EXISTING STORAGE

▶ Ready-made shelves, available in wood finish, laminate, and glass, can be installed just about anywhere to create storage for books and decorative items, toys, glassware, china, and just about anything that will fit on a 6- or 12-inch ledge. If you intend to store heavy items, make sure the brackets are securely anchored.

▶ A hallway that's wide enough can double as a storage area if you line the walls with shelvers or shallow cabinets.

▶ Create a "closet" by storing bulky items such as golf clubs, skis, and camping equipment behind a decorative folding screen in a little-used corner.

▶ Most new homes, and many old homes, have enclosed staircases, which hide valuable space. These often can be opened up to create closets, niches, or even shelf space.

▶ Put the space under a stairway to work. Construct a wheeled, wedge-shaped container

continued on page 311

QUICK TRICKS FOR YOUR CLOSET

▶ For simple remodeling, consider adding a second shelf above the existing one. This can be a good place for little-used, bulky items that take up space.

▶ Consider an over-door shoe rack, which holds 18 to 21 pairs of shoes, for the inside of a closet door. Shoes in their boxes on the shelf occupy more space.

▶ Install two rows of coat hooks on your closet doors—one down low for a child to use, another higher up for you to use.

▶ Pegboard is most often used on walls, but it can also be used to make the inside of a closet or cabinet door more functional. Remember that you'll need to provide space behind the panels for the hooks.

▶ If you're a total klutz with a hammer, there are all kinds of ways to cheat. For example, use sturdy boxes stacked on their sides to make compartmented shelf space—you can see at a glance what's stored in the boxes, and you can use the tops for little-used items.

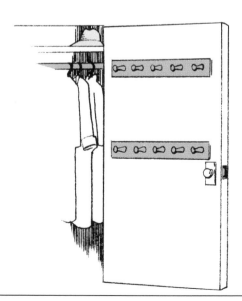

EVALUATING CLOSET SYSTEMS

While cost is usually a factor, most closet systems fall into one of the following categories. The final decision to install one system rather than another shouldn't be based strictly on cost but on how much the system can be adapted to your needs.

Separate Shelf/ Separate Rod System

This traditional style of closet is typically seen in most older homes where the closet hasn't already been renovated. Both the shelf (or shelves) and the closet rod are usually either metal or wood. The shelf is supported on each side wall and along the back wall by strips of wood that are nailed to wall studs. The shelf itself isn't permanently attached; it can be lifted off the wood strips and removed from the closet. The rod is either separate from or fused with the hardware, which is attached to strips of wood installed on the side walls. When these wood strips are removed, holes are left in the wall.

Advantages: Since no extra amenities, such as racks for shoes, ties, or belts, are included or programmed into the structure, you have the freedom to place them where you want them.

Disadvantages: At least a small degree of carpentry skill is required. The system must be installed between two supporting walls.

Costs: The cost of this system depends almost entirely on the quality of the wood you use. This system is usually comparably priced to a ventilated system and costs approximately a third to a quarter less than even the cheapest prepackaged modular system. Designing, purchasing, and installing the components yourself will cut the cost by almost half.

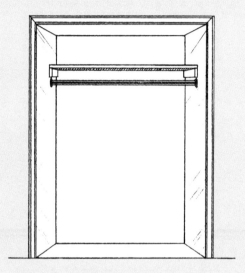

Modular Systems

Modular systems consist of presized cubicles and shelves with structural dividers, giving more definition to the closet space. They are still a separate shelf/separate rod system but with an upscale appearance. The structural dividers enable you to create compartments to confine your belongings to a specific area in your closet with either a wood or metal rod. Sometimes, a plastic-coated metal rod is offered in a range of decorative colors.

Advantages: When modular systems can be modified or custom-designed to your own specifications to match the size of your closet and its possessions, they are definitely worth looking into. Some of these systems provide a wide variety of features that makes them very flexible.

Disadvantages: The structural dividers eat into your closet's space, reducing the actual space you have available for storing your belongings. This isn't a problem when you have a closet of reasonable size and dimensions, but it can be critical in a smaller closet where every inch counts. The preconstructed modular systems offer only a limited number of sizes and shapes, forcing you to accept someone else's concept of where things should be placed or hung in your closet. These systems seldom match up exactly with your individual needs. Accommodating a modular system to closets that are especially small or oddly shaped will be particularly difficult.

Costs: The quality of the materials used in construction, as well as the number of "specialty" features you choose, will cause great fluctuations in price, ranging from affordable to extravagant. Cost is also affected by the amount of personal participation you are willing or able to give to the project. Certainly, the more you do on the project, the more you save.

Ventilated Closet Systems

Although these systems have been around for quite some time, they are still the newest type of closet material. The systems are constructed from metal rods covered with a vinyl or epoxy chip-resistant coating. The diameter of the rod inside the coating is the most important factor to consider: The smaller it is, the less sturdy and

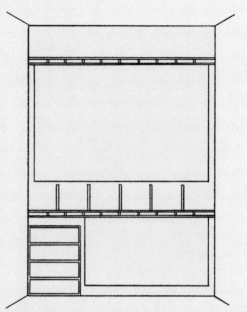

dependable the system will be. Take your time investigating the hardware used for installing these systems; some of it isn't reliable. Purchase only those systems with the attached wall "anchor" and not the ones that only supply an unsheathed screw. Precise measurements are a must, and a bit of know-how in handling a drill is helpful.

Advantages: Ventilated systems save space, because the overhanging front edge actually becomes the closet rod, extending a mere 2 inches below the shelf itself. All other closet systems require at least 4 to 6 inches for the same service. Ventilated systems allow the corner area of your closet to hold hanging garments, something no other system can do. These systems can resolve the problems presented by unusual wall configurations that otherwise would just be wasted space. There is also a "track system" variation offered in the ventilated line that allows the heights of

continued on page 310

continued from page 309

the shelves to be adjusted easily.

Disadvantages: Ventilated systems have vertical struts built into the front edge every 12 inches for added stability. These struts prohibit sliding your hangers the full length of the clothes rod. However, if your closet is properly organized, there should be no reason to shove the hangers aside. Ventilated systems need support braces every 12 to 24 inches, and these also prohibit sliding your hangers the length of the rod. Newer versions have corrected this problem by redesigning the brace so it is secured at the top of the shelf, leaving the rod area clear.

Costs: The cost of a ventilated system is comparable with that of the "Separate Shelf/Separate Rod System."

Prepackaged Kits

These kits actually come in a box containing the necessary pieces to

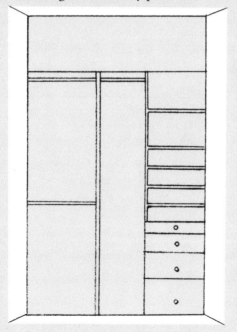

assemble a ventilated system yourself.

Advantages: If you find a kit that fits your specific needs, it's certainly less trouble to carry home just one box. Kits include instructions to guide you through the installation process.

Disadvantages: For any given closet, there are a limited number of possible configurations, restricting the number of possible designs. You might see an unassembled kit designed precisely as you would like your own finished closet to be, but that kit may not be suitable for your closet's size and shape. Choosing a kit becomes a hit-or-miss proposition; you're lucky when all the pieces fit and disappointed when they don't.

Costs: Unless they're on sale, prepackaged kits seldom cost any less than buying the components separately. In fact, kits can cost a bit more because you're paying for precut lengths.

Instant Closets

For all intents and purposes, instant closets are the same as the prepackaged kits. The only difference is that prepackaged kits are permanently attached to the walls of your closet while instant closets are simply assembled and slid into the closet.

Advantages: There's nothing quicker or easier than an instant closet.

Disadvantages: Instant closets have a tendency to offer a less clearly defined layout. There is also less usable space.

Costs: Unless you can peek inside the box before you buy, you can't tell the quality of the product. And no matter how low the price, if the quality is low, the purchase is costly.

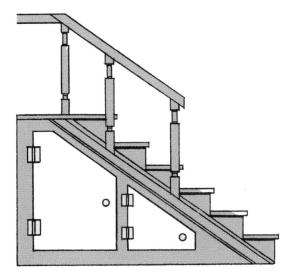

continued from page 307

that fits into the farthest area beneath the steps.

▶ Replace ordinary nailed-in-place steps with hinged steps. Use the space under the hinged steps to hold boots or sports equipment.

▶ Create a storage area by enclosing the underside of the staircase that leads to your basement. This can be a good space for a pantry, holiday decorations, or even children's toys.

ROOM-BY-ROOM ORGANIZATION

BATHROOM

▶ Hang a wicker basket on the bathroom wall for storing towels, tissues, soap, bath toys, and other incidentals.

▶ Keep toothbrushes handy but neatly out of the way on cup hooks attached to a wall or under a cabinet.

ALL ABOUT CLOTHES HANGERS

▶ Don't use wire hangers. They tangle because their necks are too small and narrow, they can damage your clothing, and they are always falling off the rod.

▶ Plastic tubular hangers, usually the first alternative, are available and inexpensive. Many of these hangers include "notches," but when the thin shoulder straps or the hanging loops inside the waistband of a skirt are put in the notch, they slip and slide out.

▶ Use "attachable" hangers to efficiently use space. Typically, all your clothes are hung from a closet rod that runs the length of the closet, creating an empty area just made for these hangers. These are also known as add-ons because these hangers have an extra hook in the center

that allows other hangers to be attached to the hanger above. Clothes can then be aligned vertically in the closet rather than horizontally across the closet rod. If additional hanging space isn't essential, using attachable hangers opens up space for shelves, cubby holes, drawer units, or other storage devices.

▶ Use open-end slacks hangers, which allow slacks to slide on and off the unencumbered opening of the hanger. The neck is bigger and rounder than most any other types of hanger, so it won't snarl or snag with the other hangers on the rod. These hangers are also shorter in length and width than most hangers, opening up areas of the closet where a standard-size hanger cannot go.

ACCESSORY STORAGE SELECTING

▶ Divide larger spaces into smaller, more manageable segments that more closely resemble the size and shape of the items they hold. This eliminates the stacks and piles of garments and accessories that are so common in closets.

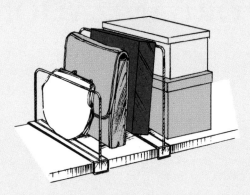

▶ Drawer organizers work well for positioning and arranging articles in a drawer so that each article is plainly visible.

▶ Acrylic shelf dividers provide an adaptable and easy way to segregate a whole shelf into specifically assigned storage compartments. These dividers are perfect for handbags, sweaters, hats, or any other conceivable item.

▶ Don't use rod space for shoe storage, even if you own a perfectly good shoe bag designed for the rod.

▶ If drawers are your only recourse for sweater storage, roll the sweaters rather than folding them. Place the rolled edge up and align the sweaters in the drawer single file from front to back or side to side so that each sweater is visible and handy.

▶ Avoid using a belt ring—your belts get jumbled. Any style of belt rack that provides an ample number of hooks for the placement of individual belts and that can be installed on the side or back walls of your closet is the best type of rack for belts.

▶ A style of tie rack that has hooks for each individual tie and that can be installed on a closet wall is the best type of tie rack to use. You can see the full complement of ties by extending their arms outward for easy selection and access. Afterward, the arms fold back into the unit, and the unit slides back into its original position.

▶ Store jewelry in containers that are scaled to their size— jewelry boxes, bags, pouches, chests, and cases. Hang necklaces from padded hooks.

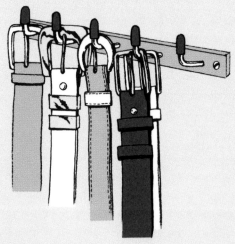

▶ Color-code cups and toothbrushes. Have each family member choose a different color, and there will be no confusion over belongings.

▶ Make your shower rod do double duty. Attach extra hooks to hold a back brush and a net bag for bath toys and washcloths.

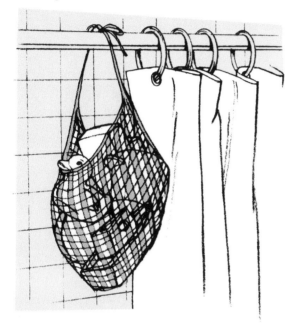

▶ Erect shelves in the "dead" wall space beside the vanity, over the toilet, or behind the door. Such shelves offer convenient storage without intruding on floor space.

▶ Consider installing "over-the-door" towel racks, or install hooks on the inside of the bathroom door for towels and robes.

▶ To avoid misplacing frequently used items, glue small magnets on the walls of the medicine cabinet to hold nail files, cuticle scissors, clippers, and other small metal objects.

BEDROOM

▶ Add more storage space in your bedroom by building a headboard storage unit. You can place books, lamps, or a radio on the lid of the unit and store extra linens and blankets on the inside.

▶ Use flat, roll-out bins for under-the-bed storage. They can hold bed linens, sewing supplies, and infrequently used items.

▶ Use hooks or an accordion rack on the wall to hang attractive hats, jewelry, and scarves.

▶ For a double-duty ottoman, build a plywood box with a hinged cover. Paint the outside or cover it with fabric, and then cover the top with scrap carpeting. Add a cushion for comfortable sitting, and store your magazines in style. (This also works well for the family room.)

KITCHEN

▶ An efficient kitchen saves both time and steps. Make sure your kitchen offers an efficient and effective work triangle. This means that the total distance from sink to range to refrigerator should not be less than 12 feet nor more than 22 feet. The work areas should be no closer than 4 feet nor farther than 9 feet from one another. Shorter distances mean you are too cramped; longer ones mean you must take tiring extra steps. If you're not remodeling, consider moving the refrigerator or the range if your kitchen is extremely inefficient.

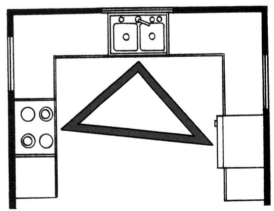

▶ Store dinnerware and cutlery near the dishwasher so that it can be emptied quickly and easily.

▶ Keep place mats flat and out of the way by hanging them on a clipboard hung from a hook inside a cabinet or pantry door.

▶ Free up counter space by putting your microwave on a shelf above the counter.

▶ To increase the capacity and efficiency of a drawer, outfit it with a lift-out tray. Fill the tray with items you frequently use, and use the space beneath the tray for articles you seldom need.

▶ If you're short on storage, add open shelving with a depth of between 6 to 10 inches.

▶ If your kitchen is too small to accommodate a table and chairs permanently, install a pull-out extension table or work space that slides back into a "drawer." Or, make a flip-up counter and eating area that folds back down when not in use.

▶ To make the most of available space when storing tapered glassware, position every other glass upside down.

BUILDING BETWEEN-STUDS SHELVING

If your home is built with studs and drywall, you can add cabinets or shallow shelves between the studs anywhere you need them. Because they are recessed and don't project into the wall, they won't take up any space. Although these cabinets or shelves will be narrow in depth, they can be used for any of the following: a canned-goods pantry in the kitchen, paperback shelves in bedrooms and family rooms, a second medicine cabinet or towel storage in the bathroom, shelves for stuffed animals in a child's room, or storage for hanging long tools, such as shovels and rakes, in the basement or garage. To build either a shelf space or cabinet, use the following tips:

▶ Locate the studs with a stud finder. Make sure that no plumbing pipes or electrical wires are behind the space.

▶ Lay out the dimensions of your planned storage on the wall. To avoid cutting through studs, plan your storage between the studs.

▶ Turn off the power to the room you're working in.

▶ Using a keyhole saw or saber saw, cut the wall opening along the layout lines. Go slowly and watch for electrical and plumbing lines. Then remove the drywall or plaster.

▶ If you're creating storage wider than the space between two studs, you'll have to cut out the stud in the middle.

▶ Cut two two-by-fours to fit the top and bottom of the opening and toenail them into the studs.

▶ To finish an open storage unit, line the enclosure with wallboard or wood, and paint or wallpaper the opening. Ready-made laminated shelves are easy to install and easy to clean, but you can also make your own shelving. Trim the front edge with molding to hide the joints.

▶ To make an enclosed recessed cabinet, you will need to buy a door the size of your opening and install a magnetic hinge inside a side panel.

▶ A wall-hung canvas "apron" with lots of pockets makes a decorative and space-saving holder for all sorts of kitchen gadgets and utensils.

▶ Hang your sharp knives inside or on the side of a high cabinet to save drawer space and keep these utensils out of the reach of children.

▶ To economize on drawer space, arrange wooden spoons and other utensils bouquet-style in a handsome pitcher, canister, or wooden bucket near the range or on the counter.

▶ If you lack drawer space for kitchen linens and towels, store them in attractive baskets on the counter.

▶ If you don't have cabinet space for your pots and pans, put a small wooden ladder—painted to match your kitchen—in a corner and place the pots and pans on the steps.

▶ Hang pots and pans from a ceiling rack. Use hooks meant for hanging swag lamps and screw them directly into the joists.

▶ Hang mugs on cup hooks underneath your cabinets.

▶ Use lazy susans in deep cupboards, or install cabinet organizers with pull-out shelving to create more efficient storage.

▶ Extension cords won't get tangled when stored in a drawer if you wind them and secure them with rubber bands.

▶ If possible, install a peninsula or island in your kitchen. An island only 18 inches wide can hold 12- or 18-inch cabinets underneath. To install a sink or range in the island, it should be at least 3 feet wide.

LAUNDRY ROOM

▶ Add shelves above your washer and dryer to hold colored plastic baskets—one color for each family member. When you take clean clothes out of the dryer, sort each person's clothes into the appropriate basket. Family members can then pick up their baskets and fold and put away their own clothes.

▶ Keep two large paper bags near your washing machine or dryer. As you notice items that need mending or items that should be discarded, you can simply store them in your "mending" bag or "give-away" bag until you're ready to deal with them.

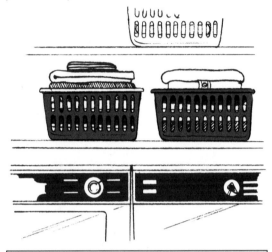

OFF-THE-FLOOR GARAGE STORAGE

▶ Hang as many items as possible on the walls to maximize floor space.

▶ Install shelves or cabinets on the top half of the garage's front wall. Make sure you install them high enough so that the hood of your car can tuck under the shelves.

▶ Install a platform across the garage ceiling joints to create a large storage place for infrequently used items.

▶ Store nails and screws in glass baby food jars.

▶ Put a wine rack next to the door and use it to store your sandy beach shoes and muddy running or gardening shoes.

▶ Use a metal garbage can to store long-handled yard tools. Hooks can also be attached to the outside of the can for hanging up smaller tools. You can lift up the whole can and move it to whichever part of the yard you're working in.

Keeping up a home is a never-ending chore. It seems as though you just finish one job when another one pops up, not to mention time-consuming, preplanned chores such as painting and decorating. These will always entail a lot of work, but they can be made more manageable if you understand certain basic rules and techniques. Just a few routine procedures can save you time and help you do a more efficient job in the process.

EXTERIOR PAINTING AND STAINING

No one realizes how big their house is until they start to paint it. Exterior painting is no more difficult than interior painting, and the tools and techniques are similar. It is a major job, however, requiring time, energy, patience, and no small sum of money. Doing the work yourself is a lot cheaper. Depending on how old the previous coat of exterior paint is, you may have a major job of scraping, sanding, and washing.

Required Tools and Materials

▶ Exterior paint or stain, stir sticks, and a large container for mixing paint

▶ Primer suitable for paint or stain

▶ 3- or 4-inch-wide brush and 1½- to 2-inch-wide brush; buy brushes suitable for paint or stain

▶ Extension ladder or scaffolding

▶ Putty knife, wire brush, and scraper

▶ Sandpaper block or orbital electric sander and medium-grit sandpaper

▶ Caulking gun and high-grade exterior caulk

▶ Nail set and hammer

▶ Garden hose, scrub brush, pail, and household detergent or high-pressure sprayer

▶ Drop cloths and rags

▶ Measure your home to determine how much paint or stain you will need. Multiply the average height of the house (distance between foundation and eaves and soffit area) by the distance around the foundation to get the surface area. If you have lots of full-length windows or doors, you can subtract this from the surface area. A gallon of exterior paint usually covers about 500 square feet; stain coverage varies. Usually a gallon of paint for trim is sufficient for large homes. Be sure to check the manufacturer's estimate for coverage and to consider how many coats of paint or stain you are applying. Ask your paint dealer for help in verifying your calculations.

▶ Make sure you buy enough paint to cover all surfaces.

▶ Select paint or stain appropriate for your home's surfaces. Don't try to put alkyd-based paint on a surface previously painted with latex paint. Likewise, stain cannot be used over paint, although you can restain a house in a different color by using a stain primer and a solid stain.

▶ Select colors appropriate for the style of your home.

▶ Make sure the color is compatible with your roof, brick, and stone work.

▶ Never use more than three colors on a home, although some Victorian-style homes blend shades of color for a "gingerbread" effect. Choose one color for the siding, one contrasting color for the trim, and perhaps a separate color for the door.

▶ For a monochromatic scheme, use three shades of the same color.

▶ Check out your neighborhood for exterior colors that you like and are compatible with the style of your house.

▶ If you're considering painting masonry—brick walls and chimneys—be aware that once you paint them, they will require painting forever, and paint is not as durable on masonry as it is on wood.

▶ Paint the downspouts and gutters to match the siding. (If you don't paint these, your choice of siding color may be affected.) Galvanized gutters must be specially treated before they can be painted; commercial products are available.

Preparing Surfaces

Thorough preparation is the key to a good paint job. It could take you two or three times as long to prepare the surfaces as it will to paint. If you attempt to get by this stage of the house-painting chore, you'll be repainting very quickly.

▶ Make an inventory of all required prep work by inspecting your house thoroughly.

▶ Scrape all loose paint with a wire brush or wide-blade paint scraper and sand surfaces. Washing before you scrape will loosen paint chips and make scraping easier. An orbital electric sander can save time on this job if you have a lot of sanding work to do.

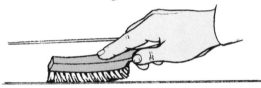

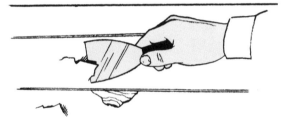

▶ Correct any problems or defects in the previous paint job. (See "Identifying Paint Problems" for guidance.)

▶ For particularly heavy deposits of paint, you may need to use a heat gun. Hold the heat gun above the surface and scrape off paint with a putty knife right behind it. Be sure to follow the manufacturer's instructions for proper use of the heat gun. If the wood is old and dry, extreme caution must be used with the heat gun.

▶ Use a hammer to reset popped nails.

▶ Tightly nail any loose boards.

▶ If your house isn't too dirty, wash it with a garden hose to remove dust; for caked-on dirt, use a scrub brush or sponge and a pail of warm water with a strong household detergent. For a major job, rent a high-pressure spray cleaner to remove grime and peeling paint. Scrape peeling paint; sand to feather the edges.

▶ Caulk around windows, doors, chimneys, etc., with a high-quality exterior caulk that accepts paint or stain; use caulk to fill large cracks.

▶ Replace any loose glaze in windows.

▶ Tie back and cover shrubs and trees that would impede your movements; cover light posts and sidewalks. This step is particularly important with stains, which are thin and tend to spatter much more than paint.

▶ Loosen downspouts, light fixtures, and other accessories for easier painting.

Applying Paint or Stain

▶ The best time to paint is in late spring or early fall on a dry day that is not too sunny. Temperatures below 40° F and direct hot sun can ruin paint jobs.

▶ Make sure all surfaces are dry. Do not paint within 24 hours of a heavy rain and do not paint when rain is forecast.

▶ If you are not applying a full coat of primer, apply it to bare spots and allow them to dry thoroughly according to the manufacturer's instructions.

▶ If possible, mix all the paint or stain you will be using into a large container and stir carefully. This will avoid a color change in the middle of a wall. Then pour what you need into a smaller can for easier work.

▶ Plan your painting carefully. Paint from top to bottom to avoid dripping paint on freshly painted areas. Do the walls first, followed by the trim.

▶ Try to follow the sun, working in the shade after the sun has dried the early-morning dew.

▶ Use a solid extension ladder set firmly against the house. The top of the ladder should stick up above the roof. Make sure the ladder is on firm footing, with about one-quarter of its length out from the foundation of the house. Make sure both extension hooks are firmly locked on the supporting rungs. When moving the ladder, watch for power lines.

▶ Use a 3-inch brush to paint clapboard siding. Dip the bristles in the paint and coat the underside edges of four or five clapboards to a length of 3 feet. With a fully loaded brush, paint the face of each board, using short strokes to cover the surface. To finish, level the paint with smooth, horizontal strokes.

▶ For shingles and shakes, use the same technique but apply the paint vertically.

▶ Use a brush specially made for stain and avoid getting too much stain on the brush. Use broad, horizontal strokes and try to come

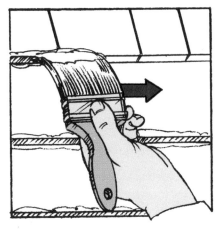  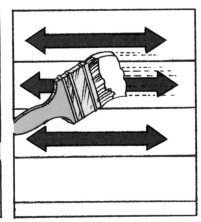

to a natural ending point—like a corner—to prevent lap marks.

▶ Stir the paint or stain frequently to avoid pigment settling to the bottom.

▶ To paint high places, work in horizontal sections across the top of a wall. Never lean away from an extension ladder or reach more than an arm's length to either side of it. Paint one high section, move the ladder, and paint another, creating a painted band as you go. Repeat all the way across the wall. Then lower the ladder to work on a lower section.

▶ Be sure to paint a tight seal between metal and wood around doors and windows.

▶ On downspouts, paint in the direction of the flutes, usually up and down.

INTERIOR PAINTING

Required Tools and Materials

▶ Interior paint plus large container for mixing paint

▶ Primer suitable for paint

▶ A 9-inch-wide roller and paint tray; extension handle if painting high walls or ceilings

▶ A 1- or 1½-inch sash brush for window frames; a 2-inch brush for baseboards and moldings

▶ Stir sticks

▶ Tall stepladder or scaffolding

▶ Putty knife, wire brush, and scraper

▶ Sandpaper block or orbital electric sander and medium-grit sandpaper

▶ Spackling compound

▶ Nail set and hammer

▶ Bucket, sponge, and household detergent

▶ Drop cloths and rags

Selecting Paints

Interior paints are available in both latex and alkyd bases. The main advantages of latex are that it dries quickly, has little odor, and requires only soap and water for cleanup.

Alkyd-based paints are often used on wood trim and doors for increased durability. A wide variety of finishes is available in both types of paints—flat, semigloss, satin, and high-gloss. While high-gloss is the most durable and washable, it must be sanded or

IDENTIFYING PAINT PROBLEMS

▶ **Peeling**—When paint curls away from the surface, it is usually caused by moisture in the wood. The source of the moisture should be located and eliminated. Siding vents may help dispel moisture vapor. Latex paint may also help with moisture problems. A second cause of peeling is that paint was applied over a glossy surface. Scrape off all loose paint flakes with a wire brush and sand the surface to feather sharp edges. Prime any bare spots before painting.

▶ **Alligatoring**—When paint shrinks into individual islands exposing the previous surfaces, the result is a surface that resembles an alligator skin. Noncompatible paints, old surfaces of paints containing lead, and second coats applied when the surface wasn't dry can all be responsible for this condition. The surface should be scraped, sanded, and primed before repainting. If you suspect lead paint as a cause, you may want to consider hiring a professional to deal with this problem.

▶ **Blistering**—Moisture or improper painting is usually the culprit when paint rises from the surface and forms blisters. To make sure, scrape off a blister; if dry wood is behind the blister, the problem is moisture. If you find paint, it's probably a solvent blister caused by using

oil- or alkyd-based coating in hot weather. The heat forms a skin on the paint and traps the solvent in a bubble.

▶ **Wrinkling**—New paint can run and sag into a series of droops when the paint is too thick and forms a surface film over the still-liquid paint below or if the surface was painted in cold weather. Sand the wrinkled area smooth or remove the old paint. To recoat, make sure the new paint is the proper consistency and be sure to brush it out as you apply.

▶ **Chalking**—When paint has a dusty surface, it is considered to be chalking. Some alkyd-based paints are designed to chalk so that when it rains a powdery layer is released, automatically cleaning the surface. If the chalking stains foundations and sidewalks, too much chalking is occurring. Thoroughly wash down the chalking surfaces, then paint over them with a nonchalking paint.

▶ **Mildew**—This moldy growth appears where there is dampness and shade. If you paint over it, it's likely to come right through the new paint. Use a fungicide, such as a chlorine bleach or commercial solution, to kill patches of mildew before repainting. Follow the manufacturer's instructions carefully when using such solutions.

"deglossed" when it's time to repaint. Flat paints are the least durable; reserve them for walls and ceilings that won't need to be scrubbed.

▶ A gallon of interior paint will cover about 450 square feet. For estimating purposes, figure 400 square feet of coverage per gallon of paint. To determine the amount of paint required to cover a room, figure the area of the walls (length × height × 2 for each wall), then divide by 400. With this method, a gallon of paint will cover a 10×15-foot room with one coat. Two coats will take two gallons.

▶ A rough-textured wall requires more paint than a smooth-textured wall. To be on the safe side, estimate about 350 square feet per gallon.

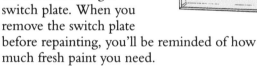

▶ Record how much paint you used for each room on the back of the light-switch plate. When you remove the switch plate before repainting, you'll be reminded of how much fresh paint you need.

Choosing Colors

Even those who decide on white walls and ceilings can be overwhelmed by the many options among "white" paints. Color is mood setting. A creamy white will be softer than a blue white. Red, yellow, and orange shades are bright, warm, and cheering. Blues, silvers, and whites are soothing and cooling. To select color, you need to think about the mood and atmosphere you want to create, along with the colors in furniture and carpets and the light in your rooms.

▶ Fluorescent light changes color. If you are in doubt at the paint store, take the paint chip outside to examine the color.

▶ Color is much more intense on four walls than on a small 1-inch paint chip. Choose a lighter shade of a color you like or have the paint mixed to one-half of the color.

▶ Bring home paint chip samples and look at them in various kinds of light.

▶ If you're in doubt about a color, buy a quart of paint and paint one wall. Wait until it dries and look at it in various lights to make sure it's what you want.

▶ Color can saturate your eyes. When mixing paint, look away at a white surface for several minutes to allow your eyes to adjust so that you can judge the color accurately.

▶ A darker color on the ceiling will make a room with a high ceiling seem more in proportion.

▶ In a long, narrow room, paint the end walls contrasting colors for a striking effect.

▶ A favorite painting can be the inspiration for the color scheme of a room. Select one dominant color and several toning shades to create a pleasing combination.

▶ Warm a cold, north-facing room with cream colors and warm pastels, such as peach and rose.

▶ Tone down a south-facing room with cool colors, such as blue and violet.

Preparing Surfaces

▶ Patch any holes or cracks in plaster walls; prime them before painting.

▶ Use a hammer to reset any popped nails in drywall. Fill the "dimple" created by the hammer with spackling compound, let it dry, and sand lightly.

▶ Sand woodwork and any surfaces having high-gloss paint.

▶ Cut the gloss on walls with a solution of trisodium phosphate. Rinse well and then sponge dry.

▶ Dust thoroughly, including ceilings.

▶ Use masking tape to separate areas where different paints will be used, such as on window frames and trim. Use the bowl of a spoon to press the masking tape tightly to the

HOW TO USE A PAINTBRUSH

▶ The wide brushes used for exterior painting require a heavy grip, much as a tennis racket. Hold smaller trim brushes as you would a pencil.

▶ Before getting paint or stain on the brush, condition it. For latex paints, dampen the brush with water; remove the excess moisture by gently striking the metal band around the handle's base over the edge of your palm and into a sink or pail. For alkyd paints, soak the brush for a day in a can of linseed oil. The brush will last longer and be easier to clean.

▶ Never dip a brush more than about one-third of the length of the bristles into the paint.

▶ To remove excess paint, gently tap the brush against the inside of the paint can or lightly drag it across the lip of the can.

Cleanup and Storage

▶ Clean latex paint and stain off brushes with a mixture of household detergent and water. Be sure to rinse thoroughly.

▶ Clean alkyd paint and stain off brushes with mineral spirits or paint thinner. Use a specially designed "comb" to get the thinner completely through the brush.

▶ An empty coffee can with a plastic lid makes a perfect container for soaking brushes. Just make two slits in the center of the plastic lid to form an "X," push the brush handle up through the "X," and replace the lid. The lid seals the can so the solvent can't evaporate, and the brush is suspended without the bristles resting on the bottom.

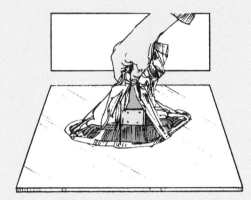

▶ To clean a paintbrush without making a mess of your hands, pour solvent into a strong, clear plastic bag, and insert the brush. Your hands will stay clean as you work the solvent into the bristles through the plastic.

▶ To reuse paint thinner, pour it into an empty coffee can. After you've cleaned your brushes, cover the can tightly and let it stand for several days. When paint from the brushes settles to the bottom as sediment, drain off the "clean" thinner into another can and store it for reuse.

▶ A paste-type paint remover will remove paint spots from brick.

▶ Before capping leftover paint for storage, mark the label at the level of the remaining paint so you'll know without opening the can how much is left inside. Label the cans by rooms so there's no question which paint to reorder or use for touch-ups.

▶ Store a partially used can of paint upside down to prevent "skin" from forming on the surface of the paint. (Be sure the lid is tight.)

surface to keep paint from seeping under it. Be sure to remove the tape before the paint is dry. With latex paints, wait only 30 minutes to remove tape. With alkyd paints, you can wait two or three hours.

▶ If you want to paint a window frame and have no masking tape, use strips of newspaper dampened so that they will stick to the glass. Peel off the paper as you finish each frame.

▶ Before painting a ceiling, turn off the light fixture, loosen it, and let it hang down. Then wrap it in a plastic bag for protection against paint splatters. Bring in a secondary light source. In general, if you want to improve your painting, improve your light.

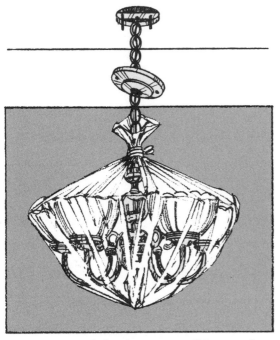

▶ Move as much furniture as possible out of the room or to the center of the room. Cover it and the floor with drop cloths.

▶ Glue paper plates to the bottom of paint cans to serve as drip catchers. The plates move along with the cans and are more convenient than newspapers.

▶ If you don't want to—or can't—remove hardware when painting adjacent areas, coat the hardware with petroleum jelly before painting. Any paint that gets on the metal by accident can be easily wiped off.

▶ If your wall-switch cover plate was painted over and you need to remove it, avoid flaking or chipping any paint by cutting carefully around the plate's edge with a single-edge razor blade. Remove the screws and lift off the plate.

Painting Ceilings

▶ Paint the ceiling before painting the walls. You'll not only eliminate the risk of spattering paint on the walls, it gets the worst job over first.

▶ Maintain a wet edge at all times to avoid creating lines or ridges.

▶ If you're using fast-drying paint, you may have to work more quickly and avoid taking a break.

▶ When painting a ceiling with a roller, it's not necessary to try to keep the roller strokes all the same length; the lines won't show when the paint dries.

▶ Use the zigzag pattern, starting about 3 feet out from one corner; work across the narrow dimension of the room in 3-foot-square areas.

Painting Walls

▶ Paint an entire wall before taking a break so that the painted portions won't lose their wet edge.

▶ Always stand back when done and check for any missed spots or smears. Using a movable light source, walk along the wall to detect any missed or thin areas.

▶ Paint in sections from top to bottom or from side to side. If you're using an extension handle, it's more convenient to start in one higher corner and go all the way across the room, so you won't have to change the handle on your roller until you no longer need it for that wall.

▶ Where you don't have enough room to do the zigzag pattern—over and under windows and above doors—roll the paint on horizontally.

USING A PAINT ROLLER

▶ Choose a roller cover to obtain the texture you want on the walls and a roller appropriate to the paint you are using.

▶ Moisten the roller with water or thinner, depending on whether you're using latex or alkyd paint. Roll out the excess on a piece of scrap lumber, craft paper, or a paper grocery bag. Don't use newspapers, because the roller could pick up the ink.

▶ Fill the well of the roller pan about half-full and set the roller into the middle of the well.

▶ Lift the roller and roll it down the slope of the pan, stopping just short of the well. Do this two or three times to allow the paint to work into the roller. Then dip the roller into the well once more and roll it on the slope until the pile is saturated.

▶ If the roller is overloaded, it will drip on the way to the wall and have a tendency to slide and smear—instead of roll—across the surface.

▶ Work on a 2- or 3-foot-square area at a time. Roll on the paint in a zigzag pattern without lifting the roller from the wall or ceiling, as if you're painting a capital "M" or "W." Without lifting the roller, fill in the blanks of the letters with more vertical zigzag strokes.

▶ Finish the area with light strokes that start in the unpainted area and roll into the paint. At the end of the stroke, raise

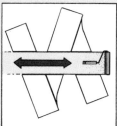

the roller slowly so that it leaves no mark.

▶ Go on to the next area and repeat the zigzag technique, ending it just below or next to the first painted patch.

▶ Always start with a roller stroke away from you. On walls, the first stroke should be up. If you roll down on the first stroke, the paint may puddle under the roller and run down the wall.

▶ Be careful not to run the roller so rapidly across the wall that centrifugal force causes it to spray droplets of paint.

▶ Avoid bumping the roller into the walls as you paint the ceiling or into the ceiling as you paint the walls, even if you're using the same paint. The roller may leave a visible ridge of paint each time it touches the ceiling or the wall.

▶ Wear a scarf or painter's hat when working with a roller, because even the neatest painter will get spatters. If you wear glasses, stop to wash them frequently to remove paint.

▶ Use an extension handle rather than a ladder to speed your work. It's also safer. When you're finished, be sure to stretch out your muscles to avoid aches.

▶ Use a 4-inch roller or a paintbrush between windows and around doors.

Painting Trim

▶ Trim can be painted before or after walls; if you paint trim before walls, any spatters only need to be feathered out, not removed, because the wall will be painted anyway. If you paint trim after walls, you'll have to take care to avoid touching the walls, which most good painters do anyway. The best argument for painting trim first is that you get the most tedious job out of the way.

▶ If you paint trim first, you'll want to mask it before painting walls.

▶ Use spackling compound to repair any holes in trim.

CUTTING-IN CORNERS

Rollers make quick work of vast expanses of flat surfaces, but they are not effective for painting in wall-to-wall or wall-to-ceiling corners or even around woodwork. At these junctions, you'll need a trim brush to paint a 3-inch-wide border around the ceilings, walls, windows, doors, and baseboards. This border-painting technique is called "cutting-in," and it should be done before you use a roller, whether or not the surfaces will be painted with the same color. When the surfaces are painted different colors, the cutting-in technique is called "beading."

When Same-Color Surfaces Meet

Use a dry trim brush with beveled edges to paint five or six strokes perpendicular to the edge of the ceiling or the wall.

Smooth over these strokes with a single, long stroke. Where two walls meet, first paint out from the corner, then paint vertically. Where the wall and ceiling come together, use downward strokes on the wall first, followed by smoothing horizontal strokes. On the ceiling itself, your first cutting-in strokes will be toward the center of the room, away from the wall. Then paint a smoothing horizontal stroke on the ceiling that follows the direction of the wall.

When Different-Color Surfaces Meet

Use a dry beveled trim brush with long bristles. Hold the brush so that your thumb is on one side of the metal ferrule and your fingers are on the other. Press the brush lightly against the surface; as you move the brush, add just enough pressure to make the bristles bend away from the direction of your brush stroke. Keep the brush about $1/16$ inch away from the other colored surface. The bent bristles and the pressure will release a fine bead of paint that will spread into the gap. Go slowly and only cut in 4 or 5 inches at a time. Although tedious at first, speed and accuracy improve with practice.

▶ Sand glossy wood trim to allow the next coat to adhere.

▶ Run a bead of high-quality interior caulk between floor moldings and wall and ceiling moldings and walls. Wet your finger and smooth the caulk into the gap, avoiding the creation of ridges. Allow to dry thoroughly before painting.

▶ Try to keep your brush strokes even to avoid brush marks.

▶ If you use a shield, try to get it just under the bottom molding. Don't push too hard or you may wedge the molding away from the wall.

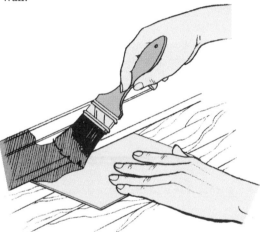

Painting Windows

▶ Some painters prefer to use masking tape on windows; others believe that the time it takes to get the masking tape on just right (on the glass and butted up to the seal) isn't worth the time. Whether you use masking tape or not, you still need to paint smoothly and avoid getting too much paint on the tape.

▶ To paint double-hung windows, raise the bottom sash more than half-way up and lower the top sash until its bottom rail is several inches below the bottom sash. Paint the bottom rail of the top sash and on up the stiles (or sides) as far as you can go. Paint all the surfaces of the bottom sash except the top edge.

▶ Next, reverse the position of the sashes—top sash up to within 1 inch of the window frame, bottom sash down to within 1 inch of the sill. Paint the formerly obstructed surfaces of the top sash and the top edges of both sashes.

▶ Next, paint the window frame, working from top to bottom, including the sill.

▶ When the paint is dry to the touch on the sashes, move them both down as far as they will go and paint the exposed jambs. (Don't paint metal jambs.) Let the paint dry and raise both sashes all the way and paint the lower jambs. To keep the sashes from sticking in the jambs, put on only as much paint as necessary to cover the old coat.

▶ When the window is completely dry, lubricate the channels with paraffin or a silicone spray.

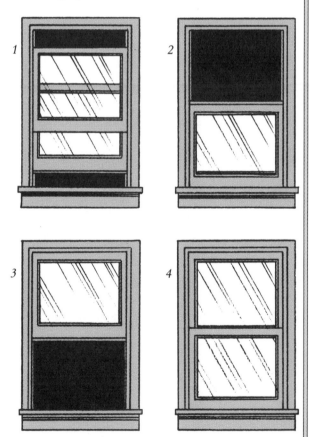

When painting double-hung windows, paint horizontal frames first, then verticals; sash channels first, then frames.

Painting Doors

▶ Flush doors—those with smooth, flat surfaces—can be painted with either a brush or roller.

▶ No matter what type of door you are painting, finish the entire door without stopping. Otherwise, the marks may show.

▶ If possible, remove doorknobs, the plates behind them, and the latch plate at the top of the door.

▶ If you can't remove doorknobs, protect them by wrapping the knobs with aluminum foil or by slipping plastic sandwich bags over them.

▶ For doors that are not flush, begin by painting the inset panels at the top of the door. Paint all the panels and the molding around them, before working your way down from the top to the bottom.

▶ Paint the top rail, middle rail, and bottom rail (the horizontal rails) with back-and-forth strokes. Paint the stiles (the verticals) with up-and-down strokes.

▶ Paint the top edge of a door last, but only give it a light coat. Over time, paint can build up on the top edge, causing the door to stick.

▶ Paint the door's hinge edge and latch edge last. Paint the bottom edge of the door or it may warp from moisture infiltration.

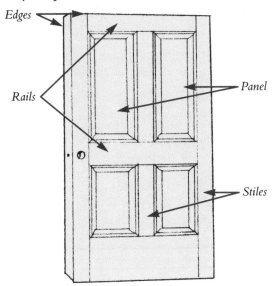

Edges

Rails

Panel

Stiles

Painting Stairways

▶ When painting stairs, paint alternate steps so that you'll have a way out. When those dry, paint the others. You can also paint one side of each step at a time. Use the other side for foot traffic until the painted side dries, then reverse the process.

▶ Where appearance isn't important, steps will be safer if you sprinkle in a little silica sand over the wet paint (so that they'll be less slippery) and edge them with luminous paint (so that they'll be more visible).

Painting Cabinets and Cupboards

▶ Remove all obstructions, including handles, hinges, pulls, knobs, latches, and drawers.

▶ If the hinges have pins that can be removed easily, take off the doors until the cabinet and cupboard interior surfaces have been painted and dried.

► Paint interiors before exteriors in the following order: 1) inside back wall; 2) inside top; 3) side walls; 4) bottom; 5) top and edges of shelves.

► Work from the top down to paint the exteriors.

► If the doors are still in place, swing them open and paint the inside surface of the doors; close them part-way and paint the outside.

► Stand drawers up on newspapers and paint only their fronts. Do not paint the exterior sides or exterior bottoms of the drawers.

► If necessary, paint the inside bottom of drawers last.

► Be sure to let everything dry thoroughly before putting them back together. Doors and drawers have an annoying tendency to stick to still-tacky surfaces.

Cleanup and Storage

► Clean up immediately. Fresh paint comes out easily from brushes and pans, but once dry, it's almost impossible to restore them.

► To avoid having to clean a paint roller pan, use a disposable plastic pan liner. When you're finished, simply dispose of it.

PAINTING SHUTTERS

► If possible, spray shutters, using either a canned spray paint or a power sprayer. This makes quick work of a tedious job.

► To get the correct "feel" for spray painting and to determine the correct spray distance from the object to be painted, first experiment with a sheet of cardboard as the target area. To avoid paint running at the edges, release the spray trigger at the edge.

► To paint with a brush, take down the shutters and make sure they are smooth; sand any rough edges.

► Lay the shutters flat so that paint doesn't run at corners of slats.

► Avoid loading your brush with paint; a too-wet brush will result in runs and sags, and, if the shutters are adjustable, sticking problems.

► Paint the window side of the shutter first.

► On adjustable shutters, place a wooden matchstick or a little wood wedge between the adjusting rod and one or two of its staples to keep the rod away from the louvers, making both easier to paint.

► Paint the louvers first with a ½-inch or 1-inch trim brush. Then paint the frame with a 2-inch brush.

► Leave the shutter edges until last, so you can periodically check for runs. If you find any, smooth them out with an almost-dry brush before they set.

► Wait until the front is dry to paint the back.

SELECTING PAINTS AND STAINS

PAINTS	ADVANTAGES	DISADVANTAGES
Latex	Dries quickly; allows wood to breathe; durable; soap and water cleanup; available in flat, satin, semi-gloss, or gloss finish	May leave lap marks if you aren't careful
Alkyd	More durable; available in flat or gloss finish; good for high-traffic areas	Thinner required for cleanup; dries slowly
STAINS	**ADVANTAGES**	**DISADVANTAGES**
Latex	Minimizes moisture problems; durable; soap and water cleanup	Dries extremely fast; hard to avoid lap marks
Alkyd	Durable	Dries slowly; thinner required for cleanup
Semi-transparent	Less prone to peeling; easy application; only one coat needed when restaining	Can only be used on new wood or same color stain
Solid stain	Can be used over different color stain (with stain primer); easy application; only one coat needed when restaining	Cannot be applied over paint

▶ Inexpensive roller covers may leave fiber on the painted surface. If you can afford it, buy a top-of-the-line product and wash it thoroughly before using.

▶ To clean a paint roller after its first use, roll it as dry as possible, first on the newly painted surface and then on several sheets of newspaper. Then slide the roller from its support and clean it with water or a solvent, depending on the type of paint used.

▶ As with leftover exterior paints, mark the cans with the level of paint inside of them, the color, and where they were used.

▶ Leftover paint that is lumpy or contains shreds of paint "skin" can be strained through window screening.

▶ Remove paint splatter from your hair by rubbing the spots with baby oil.

▶ If you use masking tape around windows while painting the woodwork, remove the masking tape immediately after painting. Otherwise it may pull off some of the paint.

▶ To get paint drips off hardwood, ceramic tile, or resilient flooring, wrap a cloth around a putty knife and gently scrape up the paint. Then wash the areas with warm, soapy water. Don't use solvent if you can avoid it.

▶ Wipe off major paint splotches from reusable drop cloths. Don't use solvents on drop cloths; they may dissolve plastic ones and ruin the rubber backing on canvas ones. Allow drop cloths to dry thoroughly.

WALL COVERINGS

While painting is easier, covering your walls with paper, fabric, or even paneling lends an almost instantaneous decorative touch. And in the case of rooms lacking decorative details and rooms with poor walls, a wall covering can turn a liability into an asset. Papering walls is the least expensive and easiest way to achieve a new effect in a room, although it is not recommended that novices begin with silk-screened paper that has not been precut. Fabric is more expensive than wallpaper, but it's no more difficult to hang. Paneling is the most expensive, time consuming, and permanent option.

WALLPAPERS

Required Tools and Materials

▶ Appropriate adhesive for nonprepasted coverings

TAKING A BREAK

Although not difficult, painting can be tiring. It's worth taking a break to rest your muscles, especially those in the shoulders, neck, arms, and back. To keep your break easy, try the following tips:

▶ Try not to stop in the middle of a wall or the ceiling. You'll lose the wet edge and risk visible lap marks when the paint dries.

▶ Try to use up all the paint in your paint tray, particularly if it's latex; otherwise it will dry out very quickly.

▶ If you want to take a short break or if you're interrupted in the middle of a painting job, wrap a plastic bag or aluminum foil around your brushes and rollers just tight enough to keep the air out. The wrapping should be loose enough to avoid crushing the bristles on brushes or the pile on rollers. Put it in the refrigerator if your break will last longer than one hour.

▶ Leave brushes on a flat surface or hang them up. Do not leave your brush standing up in the can. The bristles may bend or paint may be drawn up into the top of the brush.

▶ Leftover paint in trays should be poured back into the can and the cans should be sealed. Wipe out the rim of the can first with the tip of the brush, then with a paper towel or cotton swab. Drape a cloth over the lid and lightly hammer it down.

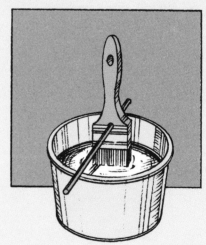

▶ Paste brush and bucket for wall covering that must be pasted

▶ Water tray for prepasted coverings

▶ Sponge

▶ Plumb line

▶ Metal tape measure

▶ Scissors and utility knife

▶ Putty knife or scraper

▶ Seam roller

▶ Vinyl or nonvinyl smoothing brush, depending on whether you're using a vinyl covering

TAKING PRECAUTIONS WHEN PAINTING

▶ Both water-thinned and solvent-thinned paint ingredients are poisonous and should be kept away from children and pets.

▶ Always work in well-ventilated areas, even if you're using odorless paints. Wear a painter's mask, particularly if you are using alkyd paints indoors.

▶ Do not smoke while painting. Extinguish all pilot lights on gas appliances.

▶ Wear long-sleeved shirts and pants, and wash up as soon as you can after painting to avoid toxic paint chemicals being absorbed through your skin.

▶ If you are working on a ladder in front of a closed door, lock the door so that no one can inadvertently swing the door open and send you sprawling.

▶ When painting overhead, wear goggles to keep paint out of your eyes.

▶ Screwdriver to remove screws from outlet and switch covers

▶ A pasting table—while this isn't mandatory, it makes the job a lot easier

Estimating Number of Rolls

Wallpapers (used generically to refer to paper, vinyl-coated, vinyl, burlap, and grass cloth) are sold in rolls that are between 15 and 54 inches wide. Regardless of the width, a single roll contains about 36 square feet. With trimming and waste, you can safely estimate obtaining about 30 square feet of coverage from a roll of wallpaper. (European rolls are slightly different; ask your wallpaper dealer for advice.)

To calculate how many rolls you need for a room, find the perimeter of the room by measuring the length of each wall and adding

the measurements together. Then measure the height. Multiply the first figure by the second, and then divide by 30. The result will be the number of rolls you need. For example, in a 9- by 12-foot room, the perimeter equals 42 feet (9 + 9 + 12 + 12). With 8-foot ceilings, you would multiply 42 by 8 to get the total square footage, 336 square feet. Dividing this number by 30 equals 11, which means that it would take 11 rolls to wallpaper the room.

If there is only one door and one window in the room, ignore these openings in your calculations. If you have multiple windows and doors, calculate their square foot totals by multiplying the height by the width of each and adding them together to get a square foot total you can subtract from your overall total. If you want to be on the safe side and have plenty of spare paper for mistakes and to set aside, add 10 percent.

If you are covering a ceiling, multiply its width by its length to determine the surface area in square feet and again divide the number by 30.

To make sure your estimates are accurate, ask your wallpaper dealer to check your figures, and don't scrimp. If you are uing a patterned wallpaper, you'll need extra paper to accommodate the inches of paper that are lost in order to match the pattern. You'll want some extra paper in case you make a mistake or need to make repairs later.

Choosing a Wallpaper

Color, pattern, and texture aren't the only things to consider. First and foremost your choice should be influenced by the room and your family's lifestyle. In some rooms, like a child's bedroom, kitchen, or family room, durability is critical. A nonwashable wallpaper might be appropriate for a dining room that is reserved for special meals, but walls that will be exposed to regular doses of fingerprints and spills should be covered with durable, scrubbable vinyl.

Fabric-backed, solid vinyls tolerate the most abuse. They're more washable than painted surfaces and resistant to scuffs and scratches. Vinyl-covered paper is slightly less durable; it is usually considered washable but not

scrubbable. Printed papers, flocked papers, foils, grass cloths, and hand-painted papers should be reserved for rooms that won't be subject to much abuse.

You'll also want to consider whether a wallpaper needs a liner, whether it can be used on rough walls, and whether it is prepasted or must be pasted. Prepasted papers have a dry, factory-applied adhesive on the back that becomes sticky when moistened with warm water. Other wallpapers require an appropriate premixed or mix-it-yourself solution that must be applied to the back of the paper.

Typically, paper-backed burlaps, flocks, hand prints, foils, murals, and vinyls should be hung with vinyl adhesive. Regular papers and unbacked burlaps require wheat paste or stainless adhesive. For strippable wallpapers, you'll need to use strippable adhesive or wheat paste. In areas or rooms subject to high humidity, mildew-resistant adhesives should be used. Ask your wallpaper dealer to help you make the correct selection of adhesive for nonprepasted coverings.

Once you narrow your choice to the type of wallpaper you'll need, you'll want to consider colors, patterns, and textures. Keep the following tips in mind:

▶ If you're planning your first attempt at hanging wallpaper, choose a covering that's easy to work with—pretrimmed, vinyl-coated paper with a simple pattern.

▶ Machine-printed wallpapers are less expensive than silkscreens, which are printed by hand.

▶ Small and random patterns are much easier to match than stripes and large patterns.

▶ Vertical patterns tend to make the ceiling seem higher; horizontal patterns do the reverse.

▶ A large room will seem smaller or cozier if covered with a large, bold pattern; small patterns with lots of light background open up a room.

▶ Consider the dominant colors and patterns already present in the room you intend to paper. One or more of those colors should be present in the wallpaper to tie the color scheme together. And, unless you're a professional or an amateur with a very keen eye, avoid mixing too many patterns.

▶ To raise the height of the room or to draw attention to the ceiling (particularly if it has decorative moldings), choose a simple pattern and use a more strongly patterned or colored border at the top of the walls.

▶ Pay attention to texture. Shiny surfaces, such as foils, attract light and tend to "cool" a room; heavier textures, such as burlap and grass cloth, absorb the light and "warm" the room.

▶ The reflective surface of foil wallpapers tends to emphasize the smallest bumps or imperfections in the wall surface. To minimize irregularities, use a lining paper under these wallpapers.

▶ If you've found an unusual wallpaper pattern but aren't sure whether you can actually live with it, order a sample and tape it to the wall of the room where you're thinking of using it and leave it there for a while.

▶ Color is uniform on machine-printed rolls cut from one continuous run, but it may differ from previous or subsequent runs. Because of this, wallpaper manufacturers assign lot or run numbers to each roll. When you buy

machine-printed paper, make sure to get rolls that have the same lot number on them.

Preparing Surfaces

▶ Turn off the power and remove electrical cover plates and, if possible, all fixtures on the walls. If possible, keep the power off while you're hanging paper.

▶ Strip or scrape old paper from walls. While you can successfully paper over some wallpapers, it's not a good idea, because the moisture in adhesives can cause both the old and new coverings to peel away from the wall.

▶ Sand any bumps and fill any holes with spackling compound, dry, and then sand smooth.

▶ Wash walls to remove any dirt or grime.

▶ Size new plaster or drywall. Sizing, sold in most hardware stores, is mixed with water and then sponged on walls. It is helpful for formerly pasted walls and painted walls, because it helps the wallpaper adhesive stick better.

▶ Plan your first strip. Choose an inconspicuous corner, preferably behind a door. It's almost inevitable that the pattern won't match perfectly as you return to the start.

Hanging Wallpaper

▶ Use a 4-foot level or chalk line to mark where your first strip of paper should hang. Remember that few walls are perfectly plumb. If you begin by hanging your first strip in the corner without establishing a level line, the last strip may be seriously out of plumb.

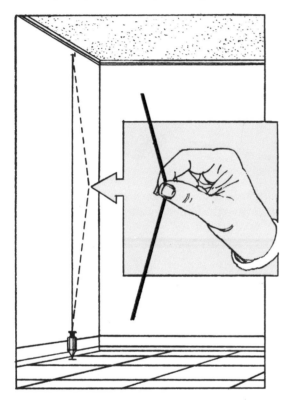

▶ Cut the first strip of wallpaper 4 to 6 inches longer than the height of the room. Make sure it's the correct length and then place it pattern-side up on the pasting table.

▶ Patternless coverings do not have to match. If you have a pattern that matches, you'll want to match your second strip before you paste or wet down the first strip.

▶ To hang the first strip of prepasted paper, position the water tray under the place you plan to begin and fill the water tray about two-thirds full. Roll the cut strip so the pattern is on the inside and soak in the tray as

directed by the wallpaper manufacturer. Unroll the paper from the tray. Remove the paper from the water and gradually unroll it. It should unroll fairly easily.

▶ To hang the first strip of nonprepasted covering, mix adhesive according to directions. It shouldn't be lumpy. Use a brush to apply the paste to the center of the strip and work outward to the corners, spreading the paste evenly. Follow the instructions of the wallpaper manufacturer on how much paste should be applied. When finished, fold the paper toward the middle from each short edge.

▶ To hang prepasted paper, position the top of the paper at ceiling level. After trimming the paper to length (leaving several inches at the top and bottom for minor adjustments), roll the paper loosely with the pasted side out. Then place the roll in a tray of warm water. Allow it to soak for one minute and slowly unroll it from the tray. In this way any areas that did not get wet in the soak will get a coating of water as you pull it from the tray.

▶ Before laying each length of paper, be sure to "book" it. When booking, lay the paper out on a clean floor, pasted side up. Then fold it in half, top-to-bottom, so that the pasted sides of the paper are in full contact. Be careful not to crease the fold area. Allow each roll to book approximately five minutes. This paste-to-paste resting period will better activate the adhesive and will greatly simplify the hanging.

▶ Using your plumb line (to see when it is vertically level), mark to align one side. Leave about 2 inches at the top to be trimmed. Use the wallpaper brush to smooth the paper on the wall, gradually working your way to the sides and down. Make sure the bottom is aligned before trimming the top with a utility knife.

▶ For nonprepasted papers, unfold the top half of the strip and position in place as suggested above. Then pull the other half of the paper out from under it before fully smoothing it on the walls.

▶ Repeat the basic procedure for each strip. To place each strip correctly, match the pattern near the top edge, set the paper against the wall next to the previous strip, and slide it to butt exactly against the already pasted paper.

▶ Correct small mistakes in placement with the smoothing brush. Poorly set strips can be peeled off and repositioned.

▶ Foil wallpapers are easily damaged, so instead of using a regular smoothing brush on them, smooth them in place with a sponge or folded towel. Bond the seams in the same way.

▶ Seams may be overlapped, but butted seams are preferred. To overlap seams, simply overlap the strips and use a sharp knife to cut through both layers. Then lift out the bottom layer and smooth the top layer. To butt seams, which

REMOVING OLD PAPER

▶ Strippable paper has a smooth, plasticlike texture that allows the paper to be stripped from the walls. You'll simply have to sponge off any remaining adhesive.

▶ "Peelable" papers are just that—you can peel them off, but a papery surface will be left on the walls. This is easily removed with commercial wallpaper remover, which is mixed with water and sponged on the walls.

▶ If thick, old paper or layers of paper don't come off the walls easily, you'll need a putty knife or scraper to slash or

score the old paper and allow the wallpaper remover to get under to the adhesive. This is necessary to thoroughly saturate the old glue behind the backing. Be careful not to slash into the actual wall to avoid making repairs. Make slits 8 to 10 inches apart and sponge remover into the holes. Let set and use a wide drywall knife or putty knife to scrape off the paper when it starts to look soft.

▶ When preparing to remove old wallpaper, first soak it with very hot water applied with a paint roller; add a touch of detergent to the water to hasten the process. If the paper is foil or vinyl coated, score its surface so water can penetrate.

▶ For major removal jobs, you may want to rent a wallpaper steamer. This softens the adhesive while you use a scraper to remove the paper. When removing old wallpaper with a steamer, save the ceiling for last. As you work on the walls, steam rising from the applicator will loosen the ceiling paper. Much of it will start sagging from its own weight, and peeling it off will be easy.

▶ To remove any remaining adhesive, use fine steel wool.

must be done with patterns that match, the edges should fit tightly with no overlap. Make sure the seams are very tight, because the seams will pull away slightly as the adhesive dries. Use a seam roller to make sure the covering is adhering tightly to the wall.

▶ Paper over all outlet openings and simply trim the paper at these holes when you're finished. The switch and outlet covers will hide any ragged trims. If you've left the power on, be particularly careful when working around electrical openings.

▶ To work around a door, window, or other opening, set the precut short strip into place above the opening, handling it just as you would a full-length strip.

▶ To paper around corners, try to make sure the strip doesn't fit exactly into a corner but goes beyond it by at least an inch. If your strip does end up in a corner, it's unlikely that your pattern will match exactly, because corners are rarely plumb.

▶ Blisters result from excess adhesive. Use a smoothing brush to try to work them out to the sides of the strip. While small blisters may disappear as the adhesive dries, large blisters are unlikely to disappear. After about 2 hours, use a pin to puncture the blister. Gently squeeze out the trapped adhesive with your thumbs.

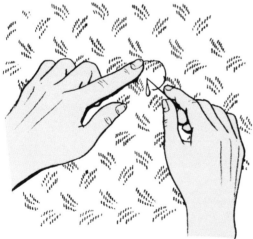

▶ To repair loose seams, lift the seam and use an artist's brush to apply adhesive under the seam.

HANGING BORDERS

Borders provide an easy, inexpensive way to dress up a room. You can hang them over wallpaper or painted walls. Border paper is available in various widths—usually between 2 and 8 inches—in a wide variety of designs. It can be hung under the ceiling molding to attract attention upward; slightly below the ceiling to make a tall room seem lower and cozier; at chair-rail height in a breakfast room or children's room; or around a door or window as a decorative "frame."

Wallpaper borders are sold by the yard. To find out how much you need, add up the distance all around the room in feet, then divide by three to give you the yardage. You will want to make sure that it's perfectly level, because any "wave" in the border will show up immediately.

If you're hanging the border around a window or door, be sure to miter the corners for a neat edge. Overlap the border strips at the corner with each strip extending past the other about 1 inch. Use a sharp utility knife to make a 45-degree cut through both papers. Remove the waste from the top border, then lift the other side and remove the waste from below.

Installing Paneling

If you're looking for a way to cover deteriorated walls, finish off a basement room, or give any area a new look, consider manufactured wall paneling designed for do-it-yourselfers. Large but lightweight sheets of paneling go up fast, and once they're up, the job is usually over, because most paneling requires no finishing.

Paneling can be purchased finished or ready to finish. Hardboard panels that simulate everything from barn siding to marble are also available. Some paneling has a composition core, which breaks easily, and should be used only over drywall or plaster walls. Modern adhesives reduce nailing, and the preparation

and basic installation steps are the same for both plywood panels and hardboard. Many building codes require a drywall backing, particularly in basements.

With existing walls, remove the molding and trim and check for high or low spots by moving a long, straight board against the wall and watching for any gaps as you draw it along. Build up any low spots with drywall

TIMESAVERS

▶ Save time when applying wallpaper paste by using a short-napped paint roller.

▶ To make wallpaper hanging easier, a right-handed person should work from left to right and a left-handed person from right to left.

▶ Change the blade in a utility knife as soon as it is dull.

▶ If there are stubborn grease spots on walls that you're going to paper, seal them with clear nail polish or shellac so that the grease won't soak through the new wallpaper.

▶ Wallpaper a ceiling with the strips positioned crosswise—they're shorter and more manageable. Accordion-fold each strip, pasted area against pasted area,

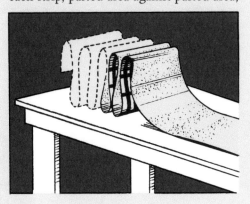

and unfold it as you go along, supporting the paper with one hand and smoothing it onto the ceiling with the other.

▶ When folding wallpaper accordion-style before hanging, the pasted side should not touch the patterned side at any point, and the paper should never be allowed to crease.

▶ When papering over wall anchors or places where you plan to reposition shelves or pictures, insert toothpicks in holes left by screws or picture hooks. As you cover these sections, force the toothpick points through the paper to mark reinstallation points for screws or hooks.

▶ Use a razor or small, pointed scissors to make tiny cuts to allow paper to lie flat next to openings and tight corners.

▶ If you don't have a seam roller to tame a loose wallpaper seam, rub the seam with the back of a spoon.

▶ If you're stapling fabric to a wall and you want to mask the staples at the top and bottom, glue a band of fabric—or even a wide, contrasting ribbon—over these seams. The staples can also be covered with molding strips.

joint compound and sand down any high spots. If the walls are badly cracked or extremely uneven, you should install furring strips on which to attach the paneling. Masonry walls must always be furred and possibly waterproofed. (Furring strips are two-by-twos or two-by-fours that are nailed or glued to the wall, with pieces of cedar shingle under them to even up low spots. Use two-by-fours because they provide a better bearing surface.)

Exactly how much furring you need depends on how uneven your walls are. If they're smooth, with a variation of only ½ inch or so between high and low spots, you only need to put up two-by-four vertical strips with soleplates and top plates at the floor and ceiling.

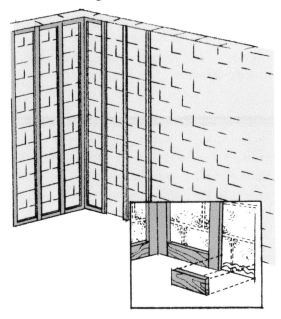

You'll need to compensate for the increased thickness of the wall at electrical wall switches and outlets. Electrical codes will prohibit leaving a gap between an existing box and its coverplate, as this would expose the cable connections to combustible materials. Don't bother trying to move the box forward, as this is always a difficult chore and you're likely to damage at least some of the boxes. Instead pull the receptacles from the existing boxes (without removing the wires) and install insert-type box extensions. These extensions

look like standard boxes, but don't have backs in them. As they are slightly smaller than standard boxes, they can be inserted into existing boxes. Front flanges keep them from going in too far. With the extensions in place, mount the receptacles and coverplates normally.

Stack the panels in the room to be paneled, placing strips of boards between each one. Leave them there for at least 48 hours before installing them to allow the panels to adjust to the moisture content of the room.

After the panels have stabilized to the humidity and temperature in the room, lean them against the walls where you want them. When you have the panels arranged the way you want them, number them.

Measure the distance from floor to ceiling at several different points. If the panels have to be cut for height, you can cut all of them the same, provided the height varies by no more than ¼ inch. If the variance is more than ¼ inch, you should measure the height for each panel and cut it to fit. If you are using ceiling moldings, leave a ¼-inch gap at the ceiling line. There should also be a ¼-inch gap at the floor, which will be concealed by the baseboard. If you are not going to use a ceiling molding, each panel must be cut to conform to the ceiling line.

Because few corners are plumb (vertically level), place the first panel in a corner next to the wall and check for plumb with a level. Get the panel plumb and close enough to the corner so that you can span the space with a scribing compass. Then run the compass down the corner, with the point in the corner and the pencil marking a line on the panel. Cut the panel along the marked line using a saber saw equipped with a fine-toothed blade. Install the first panel so that it is plumb. If it isn't, the error will compound itself with each additional panel you install.

If you plan to nail the panels, use nails of a matching color. You can use 3d finishing nails to attach the panels to furring strips. If you must go through wall material to reach the studs, be sure to use nails that are long enough to penetrate about 1 inch into the studs. Drive nails about every 6 inches along the edges of

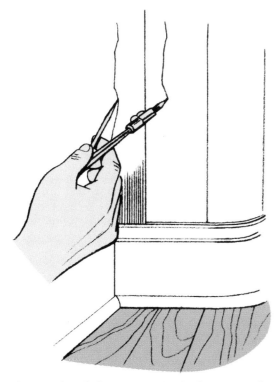

the panel and about every 16 inches across the center. Check frequently to make sure you are nailing into the furring strips.

If you are using panel adhesive, it is applied with a caulking gun. Run a ribbon of adhesive down all the furring strips, or if there are no strips, along the perimeter and in the pattern of an "X". Nail the panel in place at the top and bottom with a pair of nails.

When you come to a door or window, use one of the large sheets of paper that came between the sheets of paneling to make a pattern. Tape the paper in place, press it against the door or window frame, mark it with a pencil, and cut it to fit with scissors. Use this pattern to transfer the marks to the panel; then cut with a fine-toothed crosscut handsaw or with a saber saw equipped with a fine-toothed blade. If you use a handsaw, cut the panel with the face-side up. If you use a hand-held power saw, cut with the face-side down.

To make cutouts for electrical outlets or switches, measure carefully, trace the outline of the switch or outlet box on the panel and drill pilot holes at opposite corners. Then use a keyhole or saber saw to connect the corners with a saw cut.

Most panel manufacturers offer prefinished moldings to match. These include floor and ceiling moldings, as well as inside and outside corner moldings. Use a miter box and a fine-toothed backsaw to cut moldings. Nail the moldings into place with nails of a matching color.

DESIGN AND DECORATION

GETTING STARTED

Before doing any redecorating or buying furniture, ask yourself questions about the room and its current furnishings:

▶ Does a room seem too dreary or the ceiling too low?

▶ Does the family room need storage for children's toys?

▶ Do you want a dining room table that can double as a bridge table?

These types of questions will help you determine what the room or house requires. Next, you'll want to use the basic elements of design to help you determine what style of furnishings you prefer. If you have absolutely no idea of what you want, buy some decorating magazines or get some back issues from the library and leaf through them. When you find a photograph you like, ask yourself why. Is it the color, the carpeting, the furniture style, or even the lighting? Make a list of what you like and then reconsider the room or furnishings you intend to decorate.

If you're still at a loss and you can't afford professional help with your home decoration, consider swapping talents with an artistic friend or neighbor who would love to redesign or redecorate your room in return for your services in some other area.

Creating a Plan

Before shopping for furniture, make a floor plan of your room. Use grid paper and a scale of 1 square on the grid to 1 square foot of floor space. Mark in doors, windows, heating outlets, electrical outlets, and other features that will influence where you can and cannot position a piece of furniture. You don't want to buy a bookcase that blocks your most conveniently placed electrical outlets. Also consider the traffic patterns. A handsome coffee table that looks wonderful on the showroom floor will be a lot less attractive if it's going to block everyone's route to the kitchen or the stairs.

Take your floor plan and tape measure when you shop—a chair that looks quite small on the showroom floor may look a lot bigger when you get it into your living room or den.

Design Basics

▶ A room will appear larger if you match the wall color with an oversized piece of furniture, particularly if both the walls and furniture are a light color.

▶ Tie the decor of a room together by using the same fabric on two different chairs.

▶ In a low-ceilinged room, use vertical lines— high-backed chairs, straight draperies—to carry the eye upward and give an illusion of height. Horizontal lines—a long sofa or low bookcases—give a feeling of space and make high ceilings appear lower.

▶ Small rooms will seem even smaller if filled with elaborate patterns or designs. Keep the furniture for a small room simple and the colors fairly restrained.

▶ Low-placed, eye-catching objects such as a low coffee table, low-slung chairs, and floor plants, will make a room with a low ceiling appear more in proportion.

▶ Room dividers or furniture positioned in the middle of the room will give the effect of two rooms in one.

▶ The texture of furnishings can brighten or darken a room. Glossy surfaces—such as satin, glass, and tile—reflect light and add brightness to a room; surfaces such as brick, carpet, and burlap absorb light and create a soft atmosphere.

▶ Installing mirrors on one wall that reflect the rest of the room will make a small room appear larger.

▶ Give any room a quick facelift by updating hardware, such as doorknobs, drawer pulls, and curtain rods.

SELECTING FURNITURE
Beds and Bedding

▶ When shopping for a mattress, be sure that the clerk offering you advice is employed by the store and not by any particular bed manufacturer. A manufacturer's representative will have a vested interest in selling you his or her company's brand, which might be less suited to your needs than a product by another manufacturer.

▶ When buying an innerspring mattress, make sure it has thick, strong wire along its borders and a machine-stitched tape covering its outside edges.

▶ Before purchasing a double, queen, or king mattress, lie down on it with your partner to be sure it gives both of you the desired support side by side and at your heads, shoulders, and hips. If one person rolls over, the mattress definitely shouldn't sway. If it does, try another mattress.

▶ Make sure any mattress you buy is warranted against defects in workmanship and details for 10 to 15 years. Some guarantees aren't valid if the mattress isn't positioned on a frame that conforms to the manufacturer's specifications.

▶ Bed manufacturers don't share a common system for rating mattress firmness. You'll have to judge each mattress by testing it, not by relying on a "soft," "medium," or "firm" tag.

▶ When you purchase a new bedspread, consider buying a larger size than you need

and then cutting the excess to make a matching headboard.

Floor Coverings

▶ Consider your family's lifestyle when purchasing carpet. You'll want carpeting that is easy to clean and stain resistant in just about every room, but in some rooms these criteria are more important than others.

▶ Light colors tend to show dirt more easily, while dark colors tend to show lint.

▶ Traffic patterns appear more prominent on high-pile than on low-pile carpeting.

▶ The more densely tufted the carpet, the better for wearability, no matter what the fabric.

▶ Use densely packed, low-pile carpet in medium-tone colors for high traffic areas, such as halls and stairs.

▶ Good padding is essential; you should always invest in dense padding to preserve the life of your carpet. You'll also get less noise and a more cushioned flooring as well.

▶ Use area rugs to break up large amounts of space, but avoid using many small rugs in a large room.

▶ If you're using carpeting in the kitchen or bathroom, make sure you pick a style that is resistant to moisture, mildew, and stains.

► Use the same carpet throughout to unify a small house or apartment.

► Take a carpet sample home and look at it in various lights against your other furnishings.

► Use carpet tape or rubber skid grips to attach area rugs to floors to avoid slips.

► Almost all tiles can be used on walls, but be sure to use floor tiles on floors. Thinner wall tiles will crack quickly under pressure, no matter how well they're installed.

► If you use unglazed tiles, remember that they will have to be sealed to prevent stains from seeping into the porous tiles and grout.

► Use nonskid ceramic tiles in kitchens and bathrooms to avoid slips.

► Extra high-gloss vinyl flooring, often used on submarines and ships' decks, makes fine flooring for lofts, darkrooms, and photo studios. This is often sold by army surplus stores.

Furniture

► Furniture items advertised for sale "as is" can make wonderful bargains, but be sure to identify the damage before the purchase. A minor scratch may be something you can live with (or fix yourself), but avoid structural damage unless you're willing to pay for repairs.

► Good bargains are often available at "closeout" sales, but it is unlikely that you will be able to match the piece later. A closeout is a style the manufacturer is discontinuing and you will not be able to find replacements or additions once the consignment is gone.

► Push hard on the arms and back of an upholstered chair. You shouldn't be able to feel hard frame edges through the fabric. If you can, the chair is poorly padded and will wear out quickly.

► Whether the spring construction consists of coil springs or wire, make sure it is solid.

► If you move frequently, be wary of buying furniture with a specific location in mind.

Look instead for items that are adaptable in style and color.

► Look for a quality frame when buying major pieces of furniture—sofas, dining tables, easy chairs. Check the frame that supports upholstered furniture. Lift one end of the piece; it shouldn't wobble or creak. If it does, the construction may be inferior. The best framing material is 100-percent kiln-dried hardwood.

► After quality, comfort should be at the top of your list of criteria. You'll grow tired of even the most elegant chair if it's not comfortable.

► Visit department stores that display furniture in room-style groupings. It's sometimes much easier to imagine how furniture will look in your own home if you see it in a homelike setting.

Fabrics

► The fabric used to upholster a piece of furniture can boost the price to a surprising degree. If you suspect that a piece you like owes its price to a lush fabric, ask if the piece is available with a less expensive fabric.

► Make sure cushions are made of high-density material for comfort and durability.

► A fabric that has its design woven in is likely to be more serviceable than one that is printed only on one side.

► Lightweight fabrics wear better when they are quilted; the quilting allows the fabric to "stretch" under stress.

► If your household is particularly hard on furniture—or if you have cats—keep in mind

that nubby fabrics are more likely to snag and pill than smooth ones.

▶ The fabric on the arms of upholstered chairs and sofas will wear twice as long if the piece comes with matching arm caps.

▶ Vinyl-covered furniture may be a good choice for a family room or high-traffic area, but it's not invulnerable. Body oils and perspiration can harden vinyls, and tears are difficult to repair.

▶ Fold a printed fabric and rub the printed sides together. If any of the print comes off, don't buy the fabric. It's an inferior product.

▶ Tightly woven fabrics wear better than loosely woven ones. To check the weave, hold the fabric up to the light. Spots of light will show through a loose weave.

▶ Furniture upholstered in sturdy fabrics with a high content of durable fibers like nylon and olefin are good choices for households with adventurous children or playful pets—or adults who forget to take off their shoes before putting their feet up on the sofa.

▶ Upholstered furniture should not be placed in constant direct sunlight or near heating outlets; these can cause fading or discoloration.

▶ If anyone in your family has allergies, check the materials used to fill upholstered furniture to avoid those that would affect an allergy. Most states require furniture manufacturers to attach a label stating the materials—such as down, feathers, kapok, horsehair, or polyurethane—used to pad the frame and fill the cushions.

Lighting

▶ To eliminate shadows that reduce visibility in your kitchen or workshop, replace incandescent fixtures with fluorescent lamps that provide even, shadow-free illumination. Or, you can spend a bit more money and get color-balanced lamps.

▶ If you're planning to replace a lamp socket, consider installing a three-way socket for greater lighting versatility. Wiring a three-way socket is as simple as wiring a standard on/off fixture.

▶ Any change in a fluorescent lamp's normal performance, such as flickering or noticeable dimming, is a warning that the bulb should be replaced.

▶ Good lighting is important in any area where you apply makeup or fix your hair. A light-colored counter helps reflect light up on to your face. Luminous fixtures spaced about 3 feet apart on either side of a mirror and about 60 inches above floor level provide an ideal setting for personal grooming.

▶ If you have a dark hall where it's necessary to use a light all day, choose a fluorescent fixture for maximum energy efficiency. You'll also need to change the bulb less often.

▶ For maximum comfort and illumination, position lighting fixtures so that the bottom of the shade is at your eye level when you're sitting down.

▶ Floor-level lights directed upward toward houseplants or paintings add drama and make interesting shadow patterns on walls and ceilings.

▶ Chandeliers are dramatic and dress up a dining area. A chandelier between 24 and 30

inches in diameter works well in a typical dining room. If your dining area is less than 10 feet wide, choose a smaller fixture. As a general rule, a chandelier should not be larger than the width of your dining table less 12 inches.

▶ To give a room a soft glow, light objects in a room instead of the whole room. For example, spotlight a piece of art or a bookcase.

Window Treatments

▶ Don't invest in drapes if your budget is tight. Instead, brighten up your room with inexpensive shades that complement the wall color or wallpaper. You can also glue fabric over them.

▶ Hang shiny, metallic blinds vertically or horizontally to help reflect summer sun. This works especially well in south and west windows where you can't construct awnings.

▶ Make a curtain panel from a bedsheet by knotting the top corners around a bamboo pole.

▶ Old removable-slat wooden blinds can be renovated. Spread the slats outdoors on newspaper and refinish them with high-gloss spray paint or brush-on enamel.

▶ Substitute a screen of hanging plants for curtains.

▶ For an unusual window covering, attach wooden rings to a patchwork quilt and hang it from a wide, wooden rod. Don't do this, however, if the quilt is an antique that could fade or otherwise be damaged by exposure to sunlight.

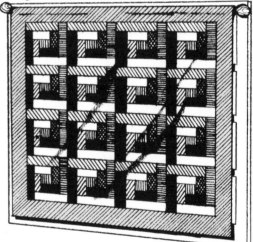

▶ Hang an Indian print bedspread full-width across a window. Open it diagonally across half the window and secure it with a tieback.

▶ Old, carved doorknobs, attached to each end of a dowel, make an attractive curtain rod. Paint or stain the knobs to match your furniture.

▶ In a beach house, use roll-down window blinds to make a door for a doorless room.

DECORATIVE TOUCHES

Style is personal. Whether you prefer traditional, country, contemporary, or even postmodern styles in furnishings, you'll want to add personal touches that will make your house or apartment a home.

Arranging Flowers

▶ Stems of different lengths make bouquets more interesting.

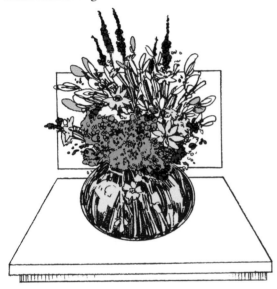

▶ Flowers in different stages of bloom provide more variety of form than when they're all at the same stage.

▶ Matching vase size to bouquet size keeps a good balance between flowers and containers.

▶ Use a sharp knife and cut stems on the slant. Scissors and shears can pinch some water channels closed.

▶ When you're cutting flowers from your garden, carry a bucket of water in which to place the blooms as soon as they're cut.

▶ Cut flowers early in the morning when they're full of moisture from the previous night.

▶ Remove all leaves from any portion of the stems that will be under water to extend flower life.

▶ To give short-stemmed flowers more length, slide them into soft-drink straws before putting them in a vase.

▶ Refrigerate a vase of flowers each night so the flowers will last longer.

▶ To speed the opening of flower buds, put the stems in a container of warm water.

▶ When you receive a box of cut flowers from a florist, recut the stems to encourage maximum water intake.

▶ Cut flowers from the florist are expensive. Fill out a small bouquet with interesting foliage. Foliage is generally more long lasting than flowers, and with luck and good care some foliage can be kept attractive for months. Fresh cut flowers can be added to the foliage arrangement as the old ones die off.

▶ Cut flowers last longer if you cut their stems at an angle. To avoid mashing, use a very sharp knife. Cut the stems under water to prevent air bubbles from forming.

▶ Long-stemmed flowers will stand erect in a wide-mouthed vase if you make a lattice across the top of the vase with transparent tape.

▶ Flowers loosely arranged in a vase will last longer than tightly packed ones.

▶ Fix a small hole in a flower vase by dripping melted candle wax over it from the inside of the container and allowing the wax to harden. As an alternative, drip epoxy glue on a hole or crack and let it harden.

▶ To keep drying flowers dust-free, cover them with plastic bags punched with air holes. When the flowers have dried, spray them with hair spray. This will serve several purposes: The hair spray will give the flowers a clear matte finish, keep them from shedding, keep insects away, and protect them from moisture.

▶ Some flowers and foliage can be placed in a vase without water and dried upright. Try pussy willows, wild grasses, and grains and flowers with large composite heads and sturdy stalks, such as Queen Anne's lace and cockscomb.

▶ A branch cut from any blossoming tree or bush makes an unusual centerpiece on a dining or coffee table.

▶ Glue corn pads or pieces of felt to the rough bottoms of vases and art objects to keep them from scratching tables.

Hanging Pictures and Mirrors

▶ If a picture that was positioned correctly won't hang straight, wrap masking tape around the wire on both sides of the hook so that the wire can't slip. You can also install parallel nails and hooks a short distance apart; two hooks are better than one for keeping pictures in their places.

▶ Squares of double-faced tape affixed to the two lower back corners of the frame will keep a picture from moving. If you don't have double-faced tape, make two loops with masking tape, sticky side out. Apply to each of the lower back corners and press the picture against the wall.

▶ Take the guesswork out of arranging several pictures on the wall. Spread a large sheet of wrapping paper or several taped-together newspapers on the floor and experiment with frame positions. When you decide on a pleasing grouping, outline the frames on the paper, tape the paper to the wall, and drive hooks through the paper into the wall. Then remove the paper and hang the pictures.

▶ Picture-hanging can be frustrating if you simply try to "eyeball" the right spot to put the hook. Instead, place a picture exactly where you want it the first time with the following method:

Cut a sheet of paper to the exact size of the frame. Position the pattern on the back of the picture, pull up the wire from which the picture will hang taut, and mark the inverted "V" point on the pattern. Adjust the pattern on the wall, and then poke through it to mark the "V" point on the wall. If you nail the hook there, the picture will hang precisely where you wanted it.

▶ If the picture isn't too heavy, another timesaving method is to hold the picture by its wire and decide where you want it positioned. Wet a fingertip and press it on the wall to mark the wire's inverted "V" point.

▶ Don't lose a perfect picture grouping when you repaint a room—insert toothpicks in the hook holes and paint right over them; when the paint dries, remove the toothpicks and rehang your pictures.

▶ To prevent a plaster wall from crumbling when driving in a nail and hook, first form an "X" over the nail spot with two strips of masking or transparent tape.

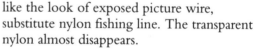
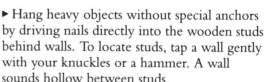

▶ If you're hanging a picture from molding but don't like the look of exposed picture wire, substitute nylon fishing line. The transparent nylon almost disappears.

▶ Hang heavy objects without special anchors by driving nails directly into the wooden studs behind walls. To locate studs, tap a wall gently with your knuckles or a hammer. A wall sounds hollow between studs.

▶ Hang mirrors to reflect you but not the sun.

▶ Sometimes a picture that has been hanging for a while will leave darkish outlines on the wall, because dust and dirt have collected against the frame. To prevent such buildup, allow better air circulation by holding pictures slightly away from the wall with thumb tacks pressed firmly into the backs of their frames.

A house equipped with an expensive burglar alarm won't alert you to a fire, and smoke detectors won't prevent a family member from slipping and falling on the stairs. To create a safe home for your family, you need to take steps to prevent accidents, fires, and theft. You and your family need to know what to do in an emergency. While these measures won't guarantee your family's safety, they will limit your vulnerability. Smoke detectors save lives. If you have children—or grandchildren—in your home, be sure to refer to the safety precautions in the "Child Care" section. If you have pets, refer to the safety precautions in the "Pet Care" section.

ACCIDENT PREVENTION

H ome accidents are one of the leading causes of death among children and injuries among adults. In many cases, these accidents could have been avoided by taking simple precautions. Check your house—and your habits—to ensure that your home isn't a danger zone.

▶ Wipe up spilled water, grease, and other liquids from your kitchen, bathroom, and garage floors as soon as possible to avoid slips.

▶ Secure throw rugs with nonskid pads or slip-resistant backing. You also can use double-faced adhesive carpet tape on the backs of rugs or rubber matting under rugs to keep them in place.

▶ Staple burlap to the bottom step of a ladder to use as a scraper for your shoes. This limits the risk of a fall caused by slippery substances left on your shoes. Remember, serious injuries can and have resulted from falls off ladders.

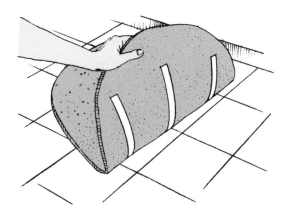

▶ Don't put hot tea, coffee, or other hot liquids on a tablecloth that hangs way over the side of the table. Someone could trip on the cloth and spill the scalding liquid.

▶ Never keep a loaded gun in the house; store ammunition and weaponry separately.

▶ If an older person, or someone who is unsteady on his or her feet, lives in your home, install one (or preferably two) grab bars in bathtubs or showers. A stool with nonskid tips can be used as a seat while showering or bathing.

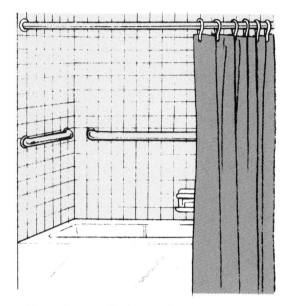

▶ One of your telephones should be accessible in the event of an accident that leaves a family member unable to stand to reach a wall telephone. This is especially important if there is an older person in your home.

▶ Keep a telephone close to your bed so you don't have to get out of bed or go to another room to call for help in an emergency.

▶ When buying a step stool that you can use to reach high shelves or cupboards, choose one with a handrail to hold on to when standing on the top step. Always make sure the step stool is fully open and steady before climbing on it.

▶ Elderly people and children are often at risk of burns from scalding water. By setting the hot-water heater below 115°F, you can avoid this risk. If your hot-water heater does not have a thermostat, use a thermometer to check the water at the faucet.

▶ Never place an electric appliance where it can fall in water.

▶ Never touch an electric appliance while you are standing in water.

▶ Don't place electric heaters near combustible materials.

▶ When working in a darkroom, avoid using a fan when you're mixing chemicals. The fan may blow dry chemicals into the air, causing a serious health risk.

▶ Use disposable utensils such as plastic spoons and paper cups when mixing dry chemicals.

▶ Do you use your basement or garage as a general storage area? If so, there are probably many things you can trip over, including tools and sharp or pointed objects. Look at these areas with an eye to accident prevention and remove or move any objects that are potential hazards.

▶ If there's no light switch at the entrance to the storage area, keep a flashlight handy or consider having switches installed.

▶ Never remove the guards from your power tools. Tools used with the guards removed pose a serious risk of injury.

▶ Guard your pet from drinking from pools of poisonous antifreeze that gather under cars.

Safe Use and Storage of Pesticides

Many pests and insects can be eliminated without the aid of an exterminator, but it's extremely important to know how to safely use and store these poisonous substances. Read the instructions on any pesticide before using it and keep the following in mind:

▶ Never spray insecticides near a flame, furnace, lighted stove, or pilot light.

▶ Keep insecticide sprays away from children, pets, dishes, foods, and cooking utensils.

▶ When fumigating, use only the amount of pesticide required for the job.

▶ Avoid contact with any pesticide.

▶ Never flush insecticides down the toilet, sewer, or drains.

▶ Never smoke while using pesticide, and thoroughly wash your hands immediately after using the materials.

▶ As soon as you have used a space spray (bomb), leave the room. Close the room up tightly for at least ½ hour before ventilating, then air out the room carefully.

▶ Follow the manufacturer's instructions for storage. Most pesticides should be tightly sealed and stored in a cool, dark place. If possible, store them in a locked cabinet or at least on high shelves away from children.

▶ Do not reuse insecticide containers. Wrap them in brown-paper bags or newspaper and dispose of them properly.

STAIR SAFETY

Stairs can be particularly dangerous, but you can do a lot to minimize risks:

▶ Handrails that don't run the full length of a staircase can be dangerous— someone may assume that the stairs end where the handrail ends and miss the last step. If necessary, consider extending or replacing the handrail.

▶ If stair carpeting becomes loose, fix it immediately. It's very easy to slip on loose carpeting.

▶ If you're in the habit of placing items on the stairs to remind you to put them away next time you go upstairs or downstairs, try to work out a different reminder system for yourself. Someone may trip over items left on the stairs— especially in an emergency.

▶ Be sure not to use throw rugs at the top or bottom of a flight of stairs.

▶ If you intend to paint basement stairs, either add a little sand to the paint for a better grip or install rubber or abrasive treads.

▶ If the outside of your house is not very well lit, either paint the edges of outside steps white so that they are easier to see in the dark or install outdoor lighting.

▶ Never hang a chemically treated pest strip in a room where people will be present for any length of time, especially the sick, the elderly, or children.

▶ Wear rubber gloves when spraying with anything poisonous.

FIRE PREVENTION

Fires can strike just about anywhere at any time. The first step in protecting your family from a fire is to make sure your home and family are equipped to deal with a fire. Along with installing smoke detectors in your home, you should have a fire extinguisher in key areas such as the kitchen, bedrooms, workshop, and garage. Additionally, everyone should know what to do in case of a fire. Walk your family through a fire drill so everyone knows what to do and where to go in case of fire. Every room in the house should have at least two escape exits. If one of these is a window from a second story, install ladders that can be dropped from the windows. Make sure children know just where the family will reunite if they have to leave the house in case of fire. School-age children should also know where to go and what to do in case of a fire at school. Make sure that the school carries out regular fire drills and that your children are familiar with proper procedures. The following simple precautions will go a long way in minimizing the risk of a fire in your home:

▶ Assign a special closet to combustible materials and dangerous tools that you don't want your children to touch. Put a good lock on the door and a heat detector inside to alert you to any fire danger.

▶ Don't overload electrical circuits with too many appliances. If your fuses are blowing or your circuit breakers are popping, hire an electrician to look at your system.

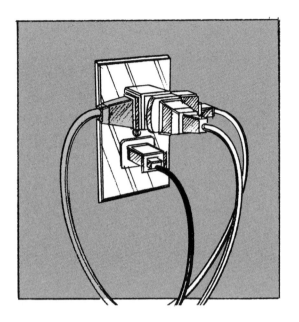

▶ Don't run extension cords under the rugs. The cords wear easily and may short out, causing a fire.

▶ Nails or staples used to attach electrical cords to the walls or baseboards can damage the cords and cause fire or shock hazards. Tape cords to walls or floors instead of using nails or staples.

▶ Replace frayed electrical cords before they burn or cause a fire.

▶ Keep combustibles away from the furnace, which can emit flames or sparks.

▶ Some fire departments supply stickers that can be placed in a window to alert firefighters to the presence of a child or an elderly or handicapped person. Inquire if such stickers are available in your locality.

▶ An electrical outlet or switch that is unusually warm or hot to the touch may indicate a potentially dangerous wiring condition. In such a situation unplug cords, avoid using switches, and call an electrician to check the wiring.

▶ Ceiling fixtures and recessed lights trap heat. Since overheating can lead to fire, don't use a bulb of too high wattage in such a fixture. If you don't know the correct wattage, use a bulb of 60 or fewer watts.

▶ If you have a wood-burning stove in your home, be sure it's installed according to local codes. Some insurance companies will not cover fire losses if the stove is not correctly installed.

▶ Always extinguish the fire in a wood stove before leaving the house or before going to bed at night.

▶ Unplug your hair dryer or any other small appliance used in the bathroom when you're not in the room. If a plugged-in appliance falls in the sink or tub, it could cause a serious shock.

▶ An electric blanket should not be tucked in at the sides. It may overheat and start a fire.

▶ Be sure to turn a heating pad off before you go to sleep. It can cause burns even at a relatively low setting.

▶ To make a dry fire extinguisher, pour six pounds of fine sand into a large container and add two pounds of baking soda. Stir the mixture thoroughly. Keep the container in your shop, garage, or kitchen. This mixture can be sprinkled directly on small oil, grease, and petroleum product fires.

▶ If you live or work in a high-rise building, locate the fire exits on your floor. If an alarm sounds, remember that you should always use the fire stairs, not the elevator.

▶ Learn to distinguish the sound of a fire alarm in your building from the sound of an elevator alarm bell. If you think someone's trapped in the elevator when, in fact, the building is starting to go up in flames, you could be in serious trouble.

STORM SAFETY

▶ Always keep a battery-powered radio in a handy spot in your home so that you can tune to radio stations if you lose electricity. Check or change the batteries frequently.

▶ Keep a flashlight in an easily accessible spot on every floor of your home. Check the

SAFETY IN THE KITCHEN

The kitchen is one of the more dangerous rooms in the house. Open flames, sharp knives, hot pots, and scalding liquids can cause serious injuries. Look at your kitchen from the perspective of an accident waiting to happen. Are papers stacked too close to the range or cooktop? Are knives easily accessible to children? Do low kitchen cupboards conceal poisonous cleaning substances? Additionally, you'll want to keep the following in mind:

▶ Keep the gas cooktop away from open windows where curtains could blow into the flames or where wind could extinguish the cooking flames.

▶ Keep the handles of pots and frying pans turned inward on the kitchen range so that they cannot be knocked or tipped over by accident. This is especially important if there are young children in the household.

▶ When handing a knife to someone else, always hold the point turned away from the other person.

▶ To prevent grease fires, keep the stove clear of anything flammable, including pot holders, paper napkins, and towels when frying food.

▶ Keep baking soda on hand for extinguishing a kitchen fire in an emergency.

batteries every now and then and replace them as soon as needed.

▶ Keep a supply of candles on hand for power failures.

▶ As a safety precaution before leaving the house on vacation, unplug all electrical appliances except for those lights connected to automatic timers.

▶ If you live in a storm-prone area, nail down roof shingles or use adequate adhesive to keep them from blowing off in a violent wind. For roofs with shingles that are not the seal-down type, apply a little dab of roofing cement under each tab.

SMOKING OUT A FIRE

Smoke detectors won't prevent a fire, but they can and do save lives by alerting you to smoke. If you don't have smoke detectors, install them now. In most jurisdictions, landlords are required to have smoke detectors in rental units. If your landlord won't provide them, buy them yourself. For basic protection at minimum expense, locate one smoke detector in the hallway near each separate sleeping area. Ask your city or town's fire department for advice on locating detectors. And be sure to check the batteries in your smoke detectors at least twice a year. Many people find that they remember to do this if they take care of it when daylight savings time begins in April and ends in October. Don't mount a smoke detector in areas where the alarm can be triggered inappropriately—such as by smoke from cooking, steam from the shower, or in the garage where combustion products from the car's engine can set it off.

▶ Alert your local police department if you discover downed power lines. Set up barricades to keep others away from the area until help arrives.

▶ A lightning-protection system should offer an easy, direct path for the bolt to follow into the ground and thus prevent injury or damage while the bolt is traveling that path.

▶ Grounding rods (at least two for a small house) should be placed at opposite corners of the house.

▶ In a hurricane, don't go out unless you have to; however, if flooding threatens, seek high ground and follow the instructions of civil defense personnel.

▶ When a major storm is imminent, close shutters, board windows, or tape the inside of larger panes with an "X" along the full length of their diagonals. Even a light material like masking tape may give the glass the extra margin of strength it needs to resist cracking.

▶ When a tornado threatens, leave windows slightly ajar.

▶ Store a lantern, pick, shovel, crowbar, hammer, screwdriver, and pliers in your storm shelter. If the exit becomes blocked, you may have to dig your way out.

▶ The basement is not a good shelter during a tornado because it's too close to gas pipes, sewer pipes, drains, and cesspools. A better shelter would be underground, far from the house (in case the roof falls) and away from the gas and sewer systems. Let all family members know where the shelter is.

▶ Keep an eye on large trees—even healthy ones—that could damage your house if felled in a storm. Cut them back, if necessary.

▶ A spare tire in the trunk of your car can be used as a life preserver in a flooding or drowning emergency. Make sure the tire is in good condition, and keep it inflated to the correct pressure.

SECURING YOUR PROPERTY

While it's difficult to protect your home from professional thieves, most home burglaries are done by amateurs. These thieves are much more easily thwarted if you employ some fairly simple security precautions:

▶ Plan to burglarize yourself. You'll discover any weaknesses in your home-protection system that may have previously escaped your notice.

▶ Lock up your home, even if you go out only for a short time. Many burglars just walk in through an unlocked door or window.

▶ Change all the locks and tumblers when you move into a new house.

▶ For the most effective alarm system, conceal all wiring. A professional burglar looks for places where he or she can disconnect the security system.

▶ Your house should appear occupied at all times. Use timers to switch lights and radios on and off when you're not at home.

▶ If you have a faulty alarm that frequently goes off, get it fixed immediately and tell your neighbors that it's been repaired. Many people ignore an alarm that goes off periodically.

▶ A spring-latch lock is easy prey for burglars who are "loiding" experts. Loiding is the method of slipping a plastic credit card against the latch tongue to depress it and unlock the door. A deadbolt defies any such attack. It is only vulnerable when there is enough space between the door and its frame to allow an intruder to use power tools or a hacksaw. But using tools takes time, which is not advantageous to the burglar.

▶ If you lose your keys, change the cylinder immediately.

▶ Before turning your house key over to a professional house cleaner for several hours, make sure the person is honest and reputable as well as hard-working. Check all references thoroughly by telephone. If the house cleaner is from a firm, call your local Better Business Bureau to check on the firm's reputation. Make sure the firm insures its employees against accidents and theft.

▶ Instead of keeping a spare key in a mailbox, under the doormat, or on a nail behind the garage, wrap the key in foil—or put it in a 35mm film can or a pipe-tobacco can—and bury it where you can easily find it if you need it.

▶ Don't leave notes for workmen or family members on the door. These act as a welcome mat to a burglar.

▶ If the entrances to your home are dark, consider installing lighting with an infrared detector. Most thieves don't want to be observed trying to get in a door.

▶ Talk to your neighbors about any suspicious-looking person or strange cars you notice lurking about.

▶ To prevent burglars from stealing ladders stored outdoors, padlock them to something that cannot be moved.

HOW TO HANDLE A FIRE

▶ If you smell smoke or your smoke detectors sound, get your family out of the house immediately. Call the fire department from a neighbor's house.

▶ Never reenter a burning house for any reason. Leave fire fighting to the professionals as soon as they're on the scene.

▶ Never use water on electric, oil, or grease fires. Water will only spatter the flames. Turn off the heat immediately and use a lid or some large piece of metal baking ware to smother the flames.

▶ If you can't shut off the gas before fighting a gas fire, get out of the house immediately.

▶ If you can't remove the fuel from a wood, paper, or fabric fire, cut off its air by smothering the fire with a coat or heavy woolen blanket. You might also cool the fire with water, a fire extinguisher, sand, or earth.

▶ Even if a fire is confined to a frying pan or wastebasket, never spend more than 30 seconds fighting the fire. Small fires can grow with frightening speed.

▶ Don't use liquids to put out a fire around an electrical appliance. Throw heavy blankets on the appliance.

▶ If someone's clothes are on fire, douse the flames with water or use a heavy blanket to smother the fire.

▶ To keep your tools from being stolen, paint the handles. Thieves avoid items that are easy to identify.

▶ Trees, located near windows or shrubbery that might shield a burglar from view, can be major flaws in your home-protection plan.

▶ Ask for credentials from any salesperson who requests entry to your home—even security-system salesmen. Ask for the ID to be pushed under the door. Many professional burglars use this cover to check out homes, and if you're doubtful, check with the person's office before letting him or her in. If you want to buy an electronic alarm system, make your own contacts with reputable firms.

▸ There's no need to let people know that you live alone—especially if you are a woman. Do not list your full name on your mailbox or your entry in the telephone book. Use only your initial and your last name.

▸ If someone comes to your door asking to use the phone to call a mechanic or the police, keep the door locked and make the call yourself.

▸ Dogs are good deterrents to burglars; even a small, noisy dog can be effective—burglars do not like to have attention drawn to their presence. Be aware, however, that trained guard dogs do not make good pets. Obedience training and attack training are entirely different, and only the former is appropriate for a house pet.

Securing Doors

▸ To help burglar-proof your home, install 1-inch throw deadbolt locks on all exterior doors.

▸ A door with too much space between the door and the frame is an invitation for the burglar to use a jimmy. Reinforce such a door by attaching a panel of ¾-inch plywood or a piece of sheet metal to it.

▸ If there are door hinges on the outside of your house, take down the door and reset the hinges inside. Otherwise all a thief has to do to gain entry to your home is knock out the hinge pin.

▸ You can burglar-proof your glass patio doors by setting a pipe or metal bar in the inside bottom track of the door slide. The pipe should be the same length as the track.

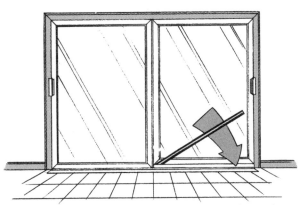

▸ It's easy for a burglar to pry his way through rot. Replace rotted door frames with new, solid wood.

▸ It's simple for a thief to break glass panels and then reach in and open a doorknob from the inside. A door with glass panels should be either fortified, replaced, or secured with deadbolts that can only be opened with a key.

Securing Windows

▸ Protect your windows with one or more good locks, an alarm system, burglar-resistant glass, or many small panes instead of one large area of glass.

▸ When installing window locks, have all the locks keyed alike and give each family member a key. Keep a key near the window where children can get it (but a burglar can't reach) in case of fire.

▸ After installing a window lock, drip some solder on the screw heads. It will stop a burglar from unscrewing the lock after cutting a small hole in the windowpane.

▶ It can be a problem to lock an aluminum sliding window in a ventilating position. A locking sliding window bolt allows high security as it foils entry even if the glass is broken.

When You're Away

▶ If your plans to be away from home have been publicized through a funeral, wedding, or similar newspaper notice, hire a house sitter. Burglars often read the newspapers to see who's planning to be away from home all day or for several days.

▶ Ask your neighbors to use your garbage cans when you're on vacation so your absence won't be so evident.

▶ If you're going to be away from home for several days—or even for just one day—adjust your telephone ring to its lowest volume. To a prowler, an unanswered phone is a quick tip that your home is empty.

PROTECTING YOUR VALUABLES

The most obvious way to protect your valuables is to store them in a safety-deposit box at a financial institution or in a secure home safe that is too heavy to be moved. When buying a wall safe, be sure it's fireproof as well as burglarproof. If you don't want to invest in a safe, other less expensive alternatives can limit theft potential:

▶ A chiseled-out space in the top of a door makes a great "safe" for small valuables.

▶ Devise a hiding place in an acoustical ceiling. Remove a tile and restore it afterward with magnetic fasteners or a similar device. However, be careful not to leave finger marks.

▶ Fireplace logs can be hollowed out to make hiding places, too. Other ideas include the underside of desktops, linings of drapes, underneath insulation in the attic, and inside a lamp.

▶ Hollow out the leg of a table or chair for hiding small objects. Drill from the bottom, then cap all the legs with rubber tips.

▶ Avoid obvious places such as mattresses, drawers, inside figurines, behind pictures, and under carpets.

▶ Many police departments offer a free "operation identification" program that includes home inspection, advice on protective measures, and use of an engraving tool to mark a code number that will identify your valuables in case of theft. Call your police department to find out if they offer such a service.

GARAGE SECURITY

▶ If you frost or cover your garage windows, burglars won't be able to tell if your car is gone.

▶ Keep your garage door closed and locked even when your car is not in the garage.

▶ Are you worried about someone entering your house through your attached garage? If the garage door lifts on a track, a C-clamp can provide extra security since the door cannot be opened if you tighten the C-clamp on the track next to the roller.

▶ Install a peephole in the door separating the house from the garage. If you hear suspicious sounds, you can check without opening the door.

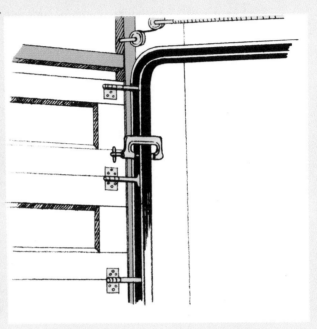

Parenthood is filled with joys, challenges, rewards, frustrations, surprises—and above all, questions. Unfortunately, infants don't come with instruction manuals; and babies, toddlers, children, adolescents, and even parents are individuals. Along with the following information about child care, there's a wealth of knowledge about parenting available at bookstores and libraries that will answer your questions. Remember, however, your children will grow and develop at their own pace, and everyone in the family will do a lot of learning along the way.

CHILDREN'S SAFETY ISSUES

SAFE-PROOFING YOUR HOME

Accidents remain the leading cause of injury and death in children up to 5 years of age. Most of these accidents occur in and around the home, and many are preventable.

Around the House

▶ Don't hold a child on your lap while you drink or pass a hot beverage, or while you smoke.

▶ Store all your poisonous materials on high shelves, out of the reach of children. Never keep poisonous products in containers or bottles used for beverages or food. Toxic products should have safety caps and should be properly closed.

▶ The following houseplants are poisonous if swallowed or chewed and should be kept out of the reach of children: poinsettia, mistletoe,

dieffenbachia, philodendron, rhubarb, laurel, rhododendron, azalea, and cherry boughs.

▶ Make sure that your child cannot accidentally get locked in a closet or other confined space. Check all knobs and locks in the house and remove any that suggest possible hazards.

▶ Set the water heater no higher than 120°F to protect a child from being scalded.

▶ Make sure all electrical outlets are sealed off with safety caps. Also, check all electrical cords to make sure that the insulation has not become frayed and that the wires are not exposed.

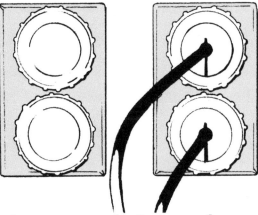

▶ Remove any unstable furniture or floor lamps.

▶ All dangling cords should be taped down, unplugged, or moved up out of your baby's reach. Place cribs away from windows where cords are potential strangulation hazards.

▶ Make sure that all windows your child might be able to get to are either locked or barred, or adapted with window stops, screens, or grilles so that they may open no more than 6 inches.

▶ Keep home workshop tools disconnected, and lock switches and power supplies so a child cannot turn them on.

▶ Check all toys to be sure any eyes, noses, buttons, knobs, or other parts will not come off when pulled or chewed.

▶ Keep small unsupervised children away from toys or games containing disc batteries. The batteries are small enough to be swallowed and are potentially lethal. Household appliances, watches, and hearing aids containing these batteries should also be kept out of reach.

▶ Avoid using caustic drain cleaners. The "metal snake" or standard rubber plunger are more effective in cleaning drains and offer no toxic hazard. Dispose of bottles containing caustics out of the reach of children. Even if rinsed or empty, they may contain crystals which, if mouthed by a child, could cause injury.

▶ When an infant is with a closely spaced older sibling, it's wise to supervise the situation closely. Also, be sure to set aside some special time each day when you can give undivided attention to your older child.

The Kitchen

▶ Install childproof latches on all drawers, closets, and cabinets containing poisonous materials and dangerous items.

▶ Unplug all small electrical appliances when they are not in use; when they are in use, be sure that the cords are not dangling down where your infant or child can reach them.

▶ When using the stove, remember to keep all pot and pan handles turned toward the back of the stove; be extra careful in handling hot liquids that could spill or splatter; and repeatedly remind your child to stay far away when someone is cooking.

▶ When serving or consuming hot foods or liquids, be sure to set them down on the middle of the table, not near the edge where a child could pull them off. Use broad-based cups and bowls with hot foods, and do not use tablecloths that hang over the table and can easily be yanked off.

▶ Fold and put away all step stools.

▶ Keep knives, forks, graters, and other such utensils out of reach of infants and toddlers.

Bedrooms

▶ Do not leave jewelry around where children could find it and possibly choke if they put it into their mouths.

▶ Perfumes, deodorants, makeup, and other such substances can lead to accidental poisonings.

▶ Belts, ties, shoelaces, and especially plastic bags can cause strangulation and suffocation. Keep them out of the reach of infants and children.

▶ Never place pillows in an infant's crib, and keep the crib away from the cords of window shades, mini-blinds, or drapes.

▶ Never place a plastic bag or thin plastic covering within reach of an infant or small child, or near the child's bed.

Bathrooms

▶ Even if you could manage to secure all the medicines, soaps, shampoos, nail clippers, hair dryers, scissors, and tweezers, the basic materials and equipment that constitute the bathroom would still represent an unacceptable level of danger to infants and toddlers. There simply are too many slippery surfaces, hard tiles, hot water faucets, water receptacles, etc. Supervise children in the bathroom.

▶ To prevent children from accidentally locking themselves in the bathroom, make sure the door has no fastening—like an inside bolt—that cannot be opened from the outside. You may also remove the lock and instruct everyone in the family to knock when the door is closed.

▶ Face your child toward the hot water faucet in the bathtub to prevent accidentally bumping into the hot metal.

▶ If your small child can't distinguish or remember to stay away from the hot water tap, make it easier by marking it with red tape.

▶ Keep electrical appliances, such a shavers, hair dryers, and toothbrushes, away from small children. Teach older children the danger of using such appliances near water or with wet hands. The hair dryer is the appliance that causes most bathtub-related electrocutions of children.

Living Areas

▶ Sofas, coffee tables, desks, and end tables usually have hard edges with sharp corners, which can do damage to a newly crawling and climbing baby. Consider placing soft bumpers and round edge protectors on these trouble spots.

▶ Remove all unstable furniture (furniture that can be easily pulled or pushed over) to an area that is inaccessible to your child. Also, watch out for rocking chairs and recliners, where a child's fingers or toes can get crushed or caught.

▶ Placing a secure safety gate at the top of every staircase is highly recommended. Placing the lower gate at the third step up from the bottom will give your baby two or three steps on which to practice climbing stairs without risk of serious injury.

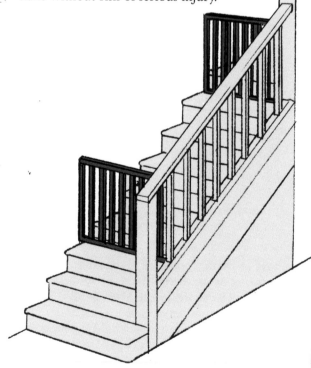

▶ If you have a piano in your home, guard against a toddler accidentally dropping the lid on fingers by fastening an upright cork at each end of the keyboard.

▶ Make it easy for small children to go up and down your stairs. Add a temporary handrail at child-height on the wall opposite the permanent handrail. Also, stairways are a lot safer when they are well lit and clear of toys, clothes, and debris.

▶ Whenever a fire is going, secure a screen or lock it in place to keep sparks from flying out;

PRECAUTIONS WHEN YOU'RE NOT AT HOME

▶ If you have young children and use baby-sitters, paste a name and address label near (or on) the telephone. Then the baby-sitter who knows you as "the lady across the road" but doesn't remember the street number of your house will have the full address right there if it's necessary to make an emergency call.

▶ Give a new baby-sitter a tour around the house, including the location of your first-aid kit.

▶ Write down instructions for baby-sitters; don't expect them to remember verbal instructions.

▶ If you will be inaccessible while away, arrange to call and make sure the sitter has the phone number of a nearby friend or relative who can be contacted in case of an emergency.

▶ School-age children should never reveal to callers that they are home alone. Teach them to tell phone callers that you can't come to the phone right now, but if they'll give a number you will call them back. Work out a strategy with your children—and remember that it need not require the child to tell a deliberate lie. Even if you are an adult, there is no need to let strange callers know if you are alone in your house or apartment.

▶ If your children won't be attended by a baby-sitter after school, make sure they understand that if they come home and find a door or window open or any signs that the home has been disturbed or entered, they should never enter. Be sure they know to go straight to the nearest phone and call the police, then you.

▶ Children old enough to answer the door should be able to see who's there, just as you do. Install a second peephole low enough for youngsters to use.

use only well-seasoned wood. A mesh screen is preferable to a glass screen because it won't get as hot nor is it as likely to be touched accidentally by your child.

▶ Never use gasoline or charcoal starter to light an indoor fire. Never burn Christmas trees indoors.

▶ If you have a wood-burning stove, it should not be used or it should be fenced in when your child is around.

▶ Store pokers, other instruments that are heavy and have sharp points, matches, lighters, and starter fluid out of the reach of infants and young children.

▶ Install smoke detectors on every floor of your home.

BUYING BABY EQUIPMENT

Security and stability are the key factors in buying equipment for your infant. First, look for the seal of approval from the Consumer Product Safety Commission, and examine items carefully to make sure they are stable and without safety hazards. Additional guidelines have been established by the Juvenile Products Manufacturers Association, and you may want to see if the product conforms to these voluntary standards.

▶ Run your fingers over the equipment, and touch every spot to which the infant is likely to come in contact. Avoid rough surfaces or surfaces that could become dangerously hot if exposed to the sun.

▶ Inspect all hinges, springs, or moving parts to make sure there are no places where your baby's hands, feet, fingers, or toes could get caught or pinched.

▶ Examine all small parts, straps, and coverings to make sure they are fastened securely.

▶ If equipment needs to be assembled, read and follow all manufacturer's directions.

▶ Extras can add to the cost of a product without necessarily increasing its quality. Ask

yourself whether you need a stroller that comes with a blanket or other extras.

Car Seats

▶ Car seats for infants and young children are mandatory in all 50 states and must conform to Federal Motor Vehicle Safety Standards. Infants weighing under 20 pounds must be belted into the seat, facing the rear of the car, and in a reclining position. Older children may sit upright facing forward. Except for infant seats, most car seats convert from a reclining position to upright and can be used by children weighing up to 40 pounds.

▶ The "child model" car seat has a protector that is lowered in front of the child and is padded to protect the child in case of a crash. Since it is locked in place with only the standard seat belt, this model is very convenient, although it limits a curious child's visibility.

▶ The harness model holds the child in place with shoulder, lap, and crotch straps. In recent years, the manufacturers of these devices have developed many excellent models that can be used in several different ways.

▶ Whichever seat you choose, make sure that it has a label indicating that it meets all federal requirements, that it is comfortable for your baby, and that it fits your car.

▶ Make sure the seat is not difficult to use or confusing to operate, particularly if you will need to use the seat in more than one car. Incorrect use of car seats can be dangerous as well as illegal.

Cribs

▶ The slats of a crib should be less than $2\frac{3}{8}$ inches apart so your baby's head cannot get caught between them. Cornerposts should be less than $\frac{5}{8}$-inch high so that they don't catch necklaces. Headboards should not have cutouts or decorations that could trap the head or neck.

▶ All hinges and screws should be well set and out of reach, and there should be secure safety latches on the drop side that cannot be

KEEPING CHILDREN SAFE AWAY FROM HOME

▶ A child's fingerprints are a sure means of identification, and many organizations recommend that parents have children fingerprinted. Some police stations offer this service—they make one set of prints that parents keep. Ask if this service is available in your locality. Do-it-yourself fingerprinting kits are also available.

▶ Make sure your children know your family's rules about talking to or accepting gifts or rides from strangers.

▶ Children love T-shirts, tote bags, buttons, and other items on which their name is displayed. Unfortunately, such identification makes it easier for a stranger to greet a child by name, thus appearing to be a friend. Teach young children that someone who knows their names can still be a stranger to whom "stranger danger" rules apply. To be on the safe side, avoid having your child wear identity-revealing items.

▶ Although it's not wise to have children wear clothing that reveals their name to strangers, they can carry an ID in an inconspicuous place when they go to a zoo, circus, or some other place where they might get lost. Attach a stick-on label listing the child's name and phone number inside a purse, tote bag, or a pocket. Then if a child gets lost, you will be notified over the loudspeaker system.

▶ When you take older children to a large, crowded place, such as a zoo or a ballpark, decide on a prearranged place where you will meet if you are accidentally separated. Agree to go directly to that location at a prearranged time, or if you have failed to meet up after a certain length of time. Be very clear about the location.

▶ For your child's safety when bicycling, insist on a helmet and identification including name, address, and phone number.

▶ Make sure your child is protected by sunscreen, hats, and clothing in the summer, and avoid midday sun.

▶ A child with a medical condition, such as diabetes, should always carry identification that includes medical condition, doctor's phone number, and details of medication or emergency treatment.

tripped, either by your baby or by any curious older children who may have access to the nursery.

▶ Make sure the mattress fits snugly—if you can fit two fingers between the mattress and the side of the crib, your baby's head could become wedged there. A rolled blanket could be used to fill the space between the mattress and end boards. The mattress should be firm.

▶ All finishes should be smooth, and all paints used should be nontoxic and lead-free.

▶ Don't use soft pillows or blankets that can become easily bunched; until infants can lift their heads high for long periods of time by themselves, suffocation when lying facedown in too-soft materials is a possibility.

▶ Make sure you can lift a portable crib without too much effort, that it folds and stores easily, and that it is stable. Shake the crib to test for stability. Also make sure it has a support bar underneath.

High Chairs, Infant Seats, and Strollers

▶ Anything the infant will be sitting in should have a wide base that keeps the device steady and decreases the chance of tipping.

▶ Make sure a high chair, infant seat, or stroller has a good harness, and that you fasten it firmly to prevent your baby from falling or climbing out.

▶ Never use an infant seat as a car seat.

▶ Make sure that the mechanism that keeps a collapsible high chair or stroller open is securely locked when in use.

▶ Good support is important, particularly during the early months when your baby's back, shoulder, and neck muscles are relatively weak. It is critical that such devices provide sufficient propping. Any minor shortcomings in this regard should be compensated for by folding and fitting in blankets or towels accordingly.

▶ Make sure that all surfaces are smooth and nontoxic, and that all hinges, latches, and other such features are in good working order and inaccessible to your baby's hands and fingers.

▶ Fold a stroller a few times and lift it into the folded position to see whether or not it will fit easily into the trunk of your car.

▶ Make sure a stroller has solid wheels; rear wheels should come with shock absorbers.

CLOTHES FOR INFANTS AND CHILDREN

Comfort, convenience, ease of cleaning, and safety factors are important in selecting clothing for infants and children:

▶ Try to buy clothing made from flame-retardant fabric. Many manufacturers are now using such materials exclusively, but it is wise to read all labels carefully.

▶ Make sure that any small items, such as buttons, ribbons, or decorative features, attached to your baby's clothing are fastened securely. If a button or whatever is pulled off or falls off, it can immediately become a choking hazard. Also, check to see that anything like zippers or elastics are stitched strongly into place. If the thread around such features begins to unravel, the article should be fixed or removed before accidental ingestion becomes a possibility.

▶ Layettes (a term used to describe the clothing/wardrobe for a newborn) are generally a matter of choice. Along with a plentiful supply of diapers, your baby will also need a couple of changes of clothing daily, such as sleepers, stretch suits, nightgowns, pajamas, undershirts, etc.; a receiving blanket and blanket for the crib; clothes for warm-weather outings or a knitted cap for cold-weather outings; socks or booties; and sweaters, bunting, or similar clothing for outings in cooler weather.

▶ Use plastic pants sparingly.

▶ Wash your baby's clothing in mild soap or mild detergent and double-rinse them. Do not wash them with the rest of your laundry, and do not use fabric softeners, since many of them contain chemicals that may irritate your baby's skin. It's best to continue washing your baby's things separately for the first few months until skin becomes less sensitive.

▶ Cloth diapers should be washed separately in hot water and double-rinsed.

▶ Bibs are useful for keeping drool and food off clothes.

SELECTING TOYS

▶ Safety is the most important consideration when selecting toys. Make sure that any item—or any removable part of an item—is no less than 1¼ inches in any dimension so that it cannot be swallowed or produce gagging.

▶ Avoid anything with sharp corners, jagged edges, or pointy protrusions.

▶ Avoid toys made with straight pins, sharp wires, nails, and other dangerous materials.

▶ Check to make sure that all materials and paints used in the production of any item are safe (not glass or brittle plastic) and labeled nontoxic.

▶ Stuffed toys should be labeled "nonflammable," "flame resistant," or "flame retardant," as well as "washable" and "made of hygienic materials."

▶ Check for durability and sturdy construction. Don't be shy about removing a toy from its box and giving it a good going-over. If it can be broken into little pieces, if buttons or other decorations can be torn off without too much effort, if parts can pinch or trap fingers or catch hair, etc., the toy is potentially dangerous.

▶ Regulations go a long way toward protecting your child from unsafe playthings, but they are not an absolute guarantee. It is always possible that a slightly defective item will slip past the safety checks and end up in a store. Moreover, many toys from other countries that are not subject to such regulations, and many toys that were produced before the regulations went into effect, end up on the more informal markets, such as rummage sales, flea markets, etc. Before purchasing any plaything for your baby, give it a good going-over yourself to make sure that all safety factors are in order.

▶ Check toys periodically to make sure they are in good repair. An item that passes all safety checks at the time of purchase can immediately become a serious hazard as soon as it is broken, chipped, or otherwise damaged.

▶ Fireworks are so dangerous that they should never be given to a small child to play with. It goes without saying that you should never give a gun (loaded or not) to a child of any age to play with.

INFANTS AND TODDLERS

FEEDING AND NUTRITION

During the first year of life a child's weight triples, while during the second year weight increases only by a third. After that, the rate of weight gain slows even more, and so does the need for increased calories. Be sure to follow your child's growth in height and weight through regular medical checkups. If your child is growing and gaining weight normally, quantity of food is not that important. If your baby is not growing as expected, consult your pediatrician.

Basic Guidelines

▶ The decision to breast-feed or bottle-feed is highly personal—you need to feel comfortable with whichever method you choose. If you feel that you'll be more comfortable bottle-feeding, you are better off using formula. On the whole, babies do well whichever way you decide to feed them.

▶ A healthy feeding schedule should be neither entirely flexible or inflexible. Especially for young babies, feeding on demand, within reason, is preferred. If a baby appears to want hourly feedings, something is wrong. On the other hand, a baby can be on a rigid 4-hour feeding schedule and do well, but there will be days when a child will be hungry every 3 to 5 hours. Since your goal is to satisfy your baby's needs, feeding when hungry is appropriate.

▶ Although babies can be overfed, it's generally not necessary to worry about a plump 3-month-old. Between 30 and 35 ounces a day is the maximum amount of formula babies should receive. If your baby takes this amount or less, everything is fine.

▶ Babies who are not getting enough to eat are usually easy to spot. They let you know by demanding feedings too frequently and by not sleeping for any reasonable length of time; they're unhappy babies.

▶ Both formula and breast milk have a high water content. Many babies, therefore, do just fine without water until they are old enough to use a cup. If your baby takes the maximum amount of formula and wants more, try offering water. If you're nursing your baby, it's more difficult to know, so you might try offering water from time to time. In either case, several wet diapers a day are a good indication that your baby is getting enough water.

► Remember that nothing that you intend to feed your baby, including a bottle, should be warmed in a microwave. Microwave ovens may warm foods unevenly, leaving "hot spots" that can burn your baby's mouth or lips. It is really not possible to test for these local hot areas, so it's best to use the tried-and-true, warm-water methods for warming bottles and food.

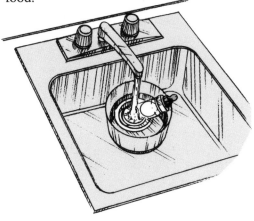

► If your baby is eating well and developing as expected, don't be concerned with an occasional spit-up. There are, however, some helpful hints to employ with babies who are "spitters," or who burp up milk after feeding. Keep plenty of cloth diapers handy to lay on your shoulder or lap when you burp your baby. Try burping the baby more frequently during feedings. Check the nipple flow from the bottle to make certain your baby isn't getting the formula too quickly. If you are worried about spitting up, or you can't seem to find a cause, discuss it with your pediatrician.

► A newborn's normal bowel movement is loose and largely fluid. It is normal for a newborn to pass as many as one stool per feeding. The definition of diarrhea, therefore, is more than one loose stool per feeding. If you notice this occurring or if your baby is acting ill, consult your pediatrician.

► Most babies are given supplemental vitamins beginning in the first month of life. These may be contained in the formula or given as drops to the breast-fed baby. Often, a pediatrician will prescribe a supplement of vitamins A, D, and C for the first year or so of life, just to be sure that the baby is getting enough of everything. Your pediatrician will let you know when it is no longer necessary to give these supplements, but it is generally agreed that no child over 18 to 24 months of age who is eating a varied, nutritious diet needs supplemental vitamins.

► In areas where there is no fluoride in the water, it is recommended that infants, children, and young adolescents receive fluoride daily. This is usually given as a vitamin/fluoride combination in children under 2, and later as a single daily chewable fluoride tablet. The fluoride promotes improved dental health by decreasing the rate of cavities in the baby teeth and, later, in the permanent teeth.

► Many babies outgrow their natural iron supply in the first months of life and may become anemic from iron deficiency. Breast-fed babies generally receive enough usable iron in the breast milk, but many formulas, especially those made from cow's milk, lack this important mineral. Therefore, most pediatricians recommend iron-fortified formulas for bottle-fed babies. Careful studies indicate that the amount of iron in these formulas does not cause constipation or stomach upset.

Burping an Infant

When nursing babies are sucking well and getting most of the areola plus the nipple in their mouths, they may not be swallowing much air and may not have to burp every time. The same is true for bottle-fed babies who are sucking well from nipples kept full of formula.

BOTTLE-FEEDING YOUR BABY

Preparing Formula and Sterilizing Bottles:

▶ To mix the formula, read the instructions on the formula container carefully. Most liquid concentrates are mixed by combining an equal amount of water and formula (such as 2 ounces of formula to 2 ounces of water). Most powdered formulas are mixed by adding 1 loose, level scoop (contained in can) of powder to every 2 ounces of water. To sterilize, you can use either of the following methods.

▶ The "terminal heating method" is safest because it sterilizes bottles, nipples, caps, formula, and water all at the same time. This method can be used for prepared concentrated formulas and for evaporated milk, since both of these must be diluted with sterilized water.
1. Clean bottles and nipples in warm, sudsy water; rinse well.
2. Prepare formula according to

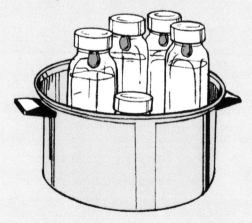

directions in a clean measuring cup or mixing bowl.

3. Pour prepared formula into bottles.
4. Place nipples (upside-down), collars, and caps loosely on bottles.
5. Using a bottle rack, place bottles into sterilizer or large pot containing 3 inches of water.
6. Boil water for 25 minutes.
7. Remove from heat, and cool for 1 to 2 hours to room temperature.
8. Tighten collars and caps, and refrigerate until needed; use within 48 hours.

▶ The "single bottle method" is useful when preparing single bottles with powdered formula.
1. Place desired amount of water in each clean bottle.
2. Loosely cover with nipple (upside-down), collar, and cap.
3. Place bottles on bottle rack in sterilizer or pot containing 3 inches of water.
4. Cover and boil for 25 minutes.
5. Remove from heat, and cool 1 to 2 hours to room temperature.
6. Tighten caps and store at room temperature or in refrigerator; use within 48 hours.
7. To use, remove cap and nipple from one bottle and add powdered formula as directed; tighten cap; and shake well to mix. (Note: Powdered formula mixes better in warm water, so slight reheating makes mixing easier.)

Giving the Bottle:

▶ Before giving your baby a bottle, you'll need to warm it and test the temperature.

1. To warm a bottle of prepared formula or milk, take the bottle out of the refrigerator, shake it, and run it under hot water.
2. Test the temperature by squeezing a few drops onto the inside of your wrist. It should feel warm, not hot.
3. Prop the baby in a semi-reclining position in the crook of your arm, and tilt the bottle slightly downward to keep the nipple full of formula.
4. Professionals agree that bottles should not be propped. You should hold your baby during feeding; then, put your baby to bed without it. If you put your baby to bed with the bottle, milk may pool in baby's mouth, promoting tooth decay. Also, because of the proximity of the eustachian tubes, babies who go to bed with their bottles have a greater tendency to develop ear infections.

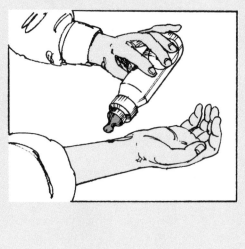

▶ If you're breast-feeding, stop to burp your baby when sucking slows down.

▶ If you're bottle-feeding, about midway through the feeding is a good time to stop and burp your baby.

▶ If your baby starts to fuss during the feeding, an air bubble possibly formed. You should stop feeding to burp the baby.

▶ If a baby starts to doze and you think that feeding is not done, stop to burp. Chances are feeding will start up again.

▶ When burping your baby, you may want to lay a cloth diaper or towel on your shoulder or lap to protect your clothing from spittle or burped-up milk.
1. With baby's bottom resting on your forearm and head resting on your shoulder, use your free hand to gently pat or rub the back.

2. Lay the baby on the stomach across your lap. Use one hand to cup the jaw and support the head; use the other to gently rub or pat the back. This is an especially useful position for larger babies.

BREAST-FEEDING

Many mothers choose to breast-feed their infants:

▶ Breast-feeding provides the baby with the best nutrition, because breast milk has a perfect balance of all the nutrients a baby requires (except, perhaps, for fluoride). Although today's formulas are close in composition to breast milk, they have not been able to duplicate it exactly.

▶ Some of the mother's immunities against disease and allergy are transferred to newborns during breast-feeding. Breast-fed newborns tend to have fewer and milder illnesses.

▶ Nursing causes the uterus to contract, which can help it return more quickly to its prepregnancy size.

▶ Breast milk is free, readily available, and at the perfect temperature for your baby. In addition, breast-feeding can be a wonderful and satisfying experience for both you and your baby.

Nursing Positions

When breast-feeding your baby, you need to be comfortable and relaxed. Before you leave the hospital, practice various nursing positions with the assistance of a maternity nurse or lactation specialist to help you become more confident.

▶ From a side-lying position, with pillows propped under your arm and behind your back, lay the baby side up in front of you and gently support the back with your hand. Roll forward slightly so that your nipple is level with your baby's mouth.

▶ From a sitting position, with a pillow on your lap to help support the baby, cradle baby's head and shoulders in your arm as you offer the breast. A rocking chair is both comfortable and relaxing for a nursing mother.

▶ From a sitting position, use the "football carry," with the baby's torso tucked under your arm. Your forearm should support baby's back and torso

while your hand supports the head.

Offering the Breast

▶ Before beginning, be sure that you and your baby are in a comfortable position. To avoid cracked or sore nipples, the baby needs to latch on to the entire nipple and as much of the areola (dark area) as possible.

▶ With your forefinger above the areola and your middle finger below, compress the breast; this will make it easier for baby to get all of the nipple and most of the areola into the mouth.

▶ Babies sometimes thrust their tongues on the underside of the nipple, which can cause breast soreness. If this occurs, or if your baby has not taken enough of the nipple in the mouth, gently remove your baby from the breast and try again.

▶ You may need to use one finger to press down slightly on a full breast so the baby can breathe through the nose.

▶ When sucking slows, or when it's time to switch to the other breast, gently break the sucking seal. Do this by sliding one finger between the inside of your baby's cheek and your breast. Do not allow your baby to tug on the nipple, since this can cause breast soreness and cracking.

Tips About Breast-Feeding

▶ You do not have to forego breast-feeding because you need to return to work soon after the birth. Breast-feed your baby whenever you are at home. At work, use a breast pump to express milk into bottles if you have a way to refrigerate them. Whoever takes care of the infant can use the bottled breast milk the next day. If expressing milk while at work is uncomfortable or impossible for you, leave formula for the baby during your work hours and then nurse when you are at home. If you don't express milk during the day, however, your milk supply will gradually decrease.

▶ Nursing moms do not need a special diet, just a nutritious, well-balanced one. You should be eating a variety of foods from the four major food groups (meat, dairy, grains, and fruits and vegetables) each day. You should drink at least two quarts a day, at least half of which should be milk. Some obstetricians like to keep new moms on a multiple vitamin plus iron as added insurance. Now is not the time to seriously limit calories or reduce weight, although you can be careful, especially with desserts and fats.

▶ Whenever you are ill, you should check with your doctor or your baby's pediatrician before taking any medication. Remember, anything you eat or drink is likely to be found in some increment in your breast milk. In addition, any kind of narcotic substance, in addition to being harmful to you, is damaging to your baby. If you are using any drug or are addicted to any drug or narcotic, give your baby a better deal and get some help. Meanwhile, don't breast-feed.

3. Sit the baby up crosswise on your lap. With one hand, grasp under the armpit and lean the baby forward slightly so that the torso is supported by your forearm. For a very young baby, you may need to cup the chin in your hand to support the head instead. Use your other hand to gently pat or rub the back.

Introducing Solid Foods

Most pediatricians believe that between 4 and 6 months is an optimum time to introduce solid foods. If your baby is very large and is still hungry after getting the maximum amount of formula, you might start as early as 4 months with your physician's approval. Parents who have allergies or allergic family histories will probably want to start later and be more cautious when introducing solids. Even if there are no allergies in the family, early exposure to some foods may produce a reaction that wouldn't occur if the food was introduced at a later age. If your infant shows signs of diarrhea or a skin rash shortly after the introduction of a new food, don't reintroduce the food for a few days. If the infant again reacts to the food, consult your pediatrician.

▶ Introduce no more than one new food a week. This allows time for you to see if the baby has an unfavorable reaction to a particular food. Many times, the same food can be introduced again later, when the child's digestive system is more mature.

▸ Begin introducing solids with a few tablespoons of infant cereal—usually rice cereal, since it is the mildest. Avoid sweetening cereal or mixing it with fruit. Never mix cereal in the bottle. Although the cereal will be fairly watery, it should be offered with a spoon. It's messy at first, but one of the important goals of introducing solids is to gradually teach the baby how to eat them.

▸ Gradually add fruits such as mashed bananas, applesauce, and strained fruits. Strained vegetables can be added once the infant has been taking solid foods for 2 to 4 weeks. Foods that are not naturally soft and watery should be puréed with a small amount of water before being served to the baby.

▸ Include strained meats once the infant has adjusted to strained vegetables for a few weeks. Consult your physician about how to balance an infant's diet if you intend to have your baby follow a vegetarian diet.

▸ You can make homemade baby food whenever your baby is ready for solids. It's preferable, however, to process your own foods only after you've introduced the baby to most baby foods. Using store-bought jars of baby food in the beginning can make it easier to introduce a variety of pure foods. When you do begin making your own baby food, you'll want to be discriminating about content and amount. Don't make more than enough for 1 or 2 meals unless you plan to freeze individual servings.

▸ Both store-bought baby food and homemade baby food require careful handling and refrigeration; opened jars of the store-bought variety as well as freshly processed homemade baby foods should be kept refrigerated, and neither should be kept for more than two days.

▸ Spoon only small amounts into your baby's dish and keep the rest in the refrigerator. If the baby requires more, retrieve the jar, put a small amount in the dish, and immediately refrigerate the remainder.

▸ Any cooked vegetable or cooked, soft meat, poultry, or fish (carefully deboned) can be processed and offered to your baby. If the food isn't liquid enough for the processor, add a small amount of water or broth. Cooked potatoes, squash, beets, carrots, and peas can all be mashed or puréed in small amounts for your baby. Applesauce, pear sauce, mashed bananas, and cooked, mashed peaches are good choices as well.

▸ Do not add salt, sugar, seasonings, or any other ingredients (other than water or broth) to your baby's food. If you intend to process food for the baby using a food that you'll be serving to the rest of the family, separate the baby's portion before adding seasonings for the rest of the family's meal.

HYGIENE

Bathing Infants

▸ In the first two to three weeks of life, before the umbilical cord heals, your baby shouldn't have a tub bath. A sponge bath (in which a baby is not actually sitting in water) given three to four times a week is usually adequate at this stage.

▶ Wash the baby's diaper area, face, and neck whenever necessary.

▶ Choose a convenient time for your baby's bath. You'll need to devote all your attention to the process, so aim for a time when you won't be disturbed. It's usually best to give a bath between feedings or before a feeding (although not when a baby is screaming from hunger). Avoid giving baths after a feeding—that's when the baby often sleeps. If the phone rings or someone comes to the door, have someone else answer it, or just ignore it. You

will not be able to leave, and taking the baby with you could cause your child to get chilled.

▶ Be sure to clean the stump of the umbilical cord until it falls off during the second or third week after birth. Until the stump has separated and the area has healed, you'll probably be advised to clean the area with isopropyl (rubbing) alcohol. This should be done three to four times a day (or with every diaper change if that's easier to remember).

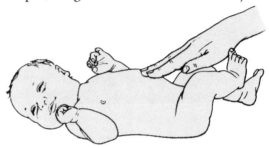

▶ Use a baby bathtub, a changing table with a built-in baby tub, or a dishpan in the sink to give your baby a tub bath. It is too difficult to do in the bathtub. Be sure that you cover all faucets and that you turn the cold water off last, so that the faucets are not scalding hot should your baby get near them.

▶ Support the baby's head and back with one hand as you wash with the other.

▶ Make sure the room is warm and that all slippery surfaces are lined with rubber mats or towels.

FOODS TO AVOID

▶ Do not feed your baby foods that have pieces that can break off and cause choking.

▶ Honey to babies under 1 year old is dangerous because of the risk of botulism (food poisoning).

▶ Eggs have a high likelihood of allergic reaction. Egg yolks should not be offered to babies under 6 months old; avoid giving egg whites until the baby is at least 1 year old.

▶ Chocolate and nuts are both highly allergenic; nuts are also dangerous because of the risk of choking, and therefore should not be given to children under 4 or 5.

▶ Sugary fruit drinks should be avoided; stick with watered fresh juices.

▶ It also goes without saying that you never give an infant beverages with caffeine or alcoholic drinks.

A PRUDENT DAILY DIET FOR TODDLERS AND PRESCHOOLERS

To provide toddlers and preschoolers with the nutrition they need for healthy growth and development, offer foods from the following food groups daily:

Meat or Meat Substitute (2 to 3 servings daily)

Single serving suggestions:

1 ounce cooked meat, fish, or poultry

1 whole egg (no more than 3 per week) or 2 egg whites

½ cup cooked beans or peas

2 tablespoons peanut butter spread on bread or crackers

2 ounces tofu

1 ounce high-protein pasta

Dairy Products (3 to 4 servings daily)

Single serving suggestions:

1 cup 2-percent milk

1 cup yogurt

1½ ounces cheese

½ cup cottage cheese

1 to 1½ cups ice cream (occasionally)

Grains (3 to 4 servings daily)

Single serving suggestions:

1 slice bread

½ hamburger bun or roll

½ bagel or English muffin

3 to 4 crackers (whole grain preferred)

½ cup cooked cereal

1 ounce cold cereal (not sugary type)

½ cup pasta or rice

Fruits and vegetables (3 to 4 servings daily)

Single serving suggestions:

½ cup raw or cooked vegetables (appropriate for age)

1 cup leafy cooked vegetables

1 whole fruit—soft and/or cooked (apricot, banana, pear, apple, plum, peach, fig, etc.)

½ grapefruit or other citrus fruit (including tomato)

½ cup soft cubed melon

▶ Offer small servings, and give your child choices whenever possible. Since toddlers dislike having to sit still for any length of time, try offering small meals 5 to 6 times a day rather than less frequent larger meals.

▶ Don't make meal time a battle of wills, and try not to put too much emphasis on eating.

▶ Start your child off with healthy choices. Serve whole grain breads and crackers rather than white commercial bread. Offer fruits as snacks.

▶ A toddler needs 30 percent of his daily calories from fat. Make sure your child is getting enough fat.

Remember that a serious problem in terms of health for infants and toddlers is the danger of choking incidents. Use the following tips to avoid choking accidents:

▶ Teach your child to chew slowly and enjoy mealtime.

▶ Always have your child eat in a high chair; chewing and swallowing need undivided attention at this point.

▶ Avoid salty and sugary foods and any foods that toddlers can choke on or inhale into their windpipes.

▶ Gather everything you will need, including a couple of soft towels, a washcloth, a mild baby soap, a clean diaper, and clean clothes.

▶ Fill the baby tub with a few inches of water. The water should feel pleasantly warm, not hot, to your elbow. Turn the cold water off last and push the faucets out of the way or cover them.

▶ Undress and wrap your baby in a towel. Dip the washcloth in plain warm water, and gently clean the baby's face and ears.

▶ Using the "football carry," hold the baby over the tub. Tilt the infant downward slightly so that soap does not run into the eyes. Gently wash the head using your fingertips or the washcloth and a small amount of soap. Rinse with plain water and pat the head dry.

▶ Gently lower baby, bottom first, into the tub, keeping one hand under the bottom and the other under head and neck. Grasp under the armpit so that the head and back are resting on your arm.

GIVING A NEWBORN A SPONGE BATH

Before you begin, gather your supplies, and then partially fill a container or sink with water that feels gently warm, not hot, to your elbow. Turn the cold water off last and be sure the faucets are pushed out of the way or covered.

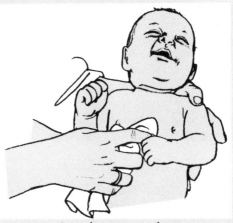

1. Keep your baby wrapped or partially clothed as you wash the face and ears with the washcloth dipped in plain warm water.

2. Hold your baby under your arm using the "football carry" with your arm supporting the neck and back and your hand supporting the head. Gently wash baby's head using your fingertips and a small amount of baby soap (or baby shampoo). Keep your baby tilted downward slightly, so the soap does not run into the eyes. Rinse thoroughly with plain warm water and pat the head dry.

3. Hold your baby on your lap or on the bathing surface and remove the shirt. Gently wash the chest, arms, and legs using your fingers or the washcloth and a small amount of soap. Dip the washcloth in plain water, rinse the areas, and pat them dry.

4. Support the neck and head as you gently turn baby on the side. Wash the back, rinse with the washcloth dipped in plain water, and pat the back dry.

5. Remove the diaper. Using the washcloth and a small amount of soap, gently clean the diaper area, especially between the folds for girls and around the penis for boys. Dip the washcloth in plain water, rinse the area, and pat it dry.

6. Diaper and dress your baby quickly to avoid a chill.

▶ Using the other hand, wash the chest, abdomen, arms, and legs. Gently wash the genital area, especially between the folds for girls and around the penis for boys. Be sure to clean in skin creases. Rinse with bath water.

▶ Gently sit baby up, use your free hand to grasp under the armpit from the front, leaning the infant forward so that the head and torso are supported by your arm. Once you have a secure hold on your baby, use the other hand to wash and rinse the back.

▶ Slip your hands under the armpits and carefully lift the baby out of the tub. Wrap the baby in a towel and pat dry.

▶ Clean your baby's outer ears at bath time using a soft, wet cloth. Gently wipe the outer ear and ear folds. Be sure to wipe behind the ears, since this is a good hiding place for cradle cap. The baby's inner ears, or ear canals, are self cleaning. Never use cotton swabs in the baby's ear canals. Not only is it unnecessary, it can be harmful. Never put anything smaller than your elbow into the ear.

Bathing Toddlers

▶ Toddlers and preschoolers should be bathed two to three times a week. More frequent bathing can cause dry skin.

▶ Sponge-bathe hands, arms, face, and bottom whenever necessary.

▶ Avoid using bubble bath in the water, since it can be both drying and irritating to the skin.

▶ If your preschooler prefers to take a shower, make sure the child knows how to operate everything.

▶ Lightly spread a little lotion over the skin before you towel your child off to help

---

CARE OF THE GENITALS

Careful skin care in the genital area can help prevent diaper rash and infections.

▶ Use a soft washcloth.

▶ Use warm water or warm water with a small amount of gentle soap, and be sure to rinse thoroughly with clear water.

▶ For newborn girls, wash gently in the folds of the genital area; be sure to gently wipe (not rub) from front to back.

▶ For newborn boys who have been circumcised, be sure to follow your pediatrician's recommendations for caring for the penis. If you notice bleeding or any sign of infection (pus, redness, or swelling), notify your pediatrician.

▶ For newborn boys who have not been circumcised, external washing and rinsing is recommended. Since the natural separation of the foreskin from the glans may not be complete for several years, do not attempt to forcibly retract the foreskin. If you can partially retract the foreskin without using pressure or causing pain, you can clean the part of the glans that is exposed. Otherwise, leave it alone until the foreskin has separated from the glans.

▶ If you have any questions about the care of your newborn's genitals, contact your pediatrician.

prevent dryness. Avoid lotions with perfumes, however, since they can cause irritation.

▶ Dry scalp and dry or damaged hair can result from too much shampooing. Unless your child rolls in dirt every day, daily shampooing is not necessary and not recommended; once or twice a week—or whenever it looks and smells grimy—should do it.

▶ If necessary, rinse a child's hair without washing it.

▶ Use a mild shampoo, and only shampoo once. Be sure to rinse hair and scalp thoroughly. Use clean water for rinsing, since using bath water won't get hair clean enough.

▶ If hair is very tangled after shampooing, use a creme rinse to make combing easier.

Trimming Nails

▶ Use baby nail scissors with blunt ends to prevent injury if the baby pulls away unexpectedly.

▶ You can use a soft emery board to file nails down. It may take two of you to get the job done at first. One can hold the baby while the other grasps one of the baby's fingers at a time and carefully files.

▶ Better yet, babies' nails can be cut when they sleep. Try clippers—they make the job easy and quick.

▶ Trim the fingernails as often as necessary to keep them short; this may mean once a week or once every other week.

▶ A baby's toenails grow more slowly than fingernails, but they require attention, too. Trim them as you do the fingernails, just not as often.

Dealing with Diapers

▶ Cloth diapers are generally the least expensive option if you have easy access to a washer and dryer and can wash them yourself. Cloth diapers are not as airtight as disposables, but may actually be better for baby's skin, because they allow moisture to evaporate and may decrease diaper rash. When using diaper pins, be careful not to prick the baby. Another option is to enclose cloth diapers in the soft plastic "tie at the hip" covers or diaper holders.

▶ Disposable diapers are the most expensive option, but they are convenient, especially when you're away from home. They eliminate the need for diaper pins, because they come with sticky tabs that hold them in place; they save time because there's no laundering; and they tend to be less likely to leak.

Unfortunately, some of the disposables with pleating and elastic around the tummy and thighs are too efficient; they keep urine in very well, but they don't allow air circulation. So while they protect clothing and bedding, they may also help promote diaper rash. Keeping the diaper fairly loose and checking it frequently for urine or feces can help.

▶ Never take your hands off your baby or leave during diapering. Even new babies can wriggle and fall off a raised surface. Diapering on the floor or using a changing table with a belt that fastens around your infant's tummy may help to prevent such accidents.

▶ Make sure that everything you need is within reach before you begin diapering. If you discover that you've forgotten something, take the baby with you to get it. Never leave your baby unattended for even a second unless in a crib or strapped into a carrier.

▶ Change your baby's diaper whenever it is wet or soiled, which will be many times throughout the day and night. This is true no matter which type of diaper you use, but is especially important if you use disposables or plastic pants over cloth, which can trap moisture against the skin and cause irritation.

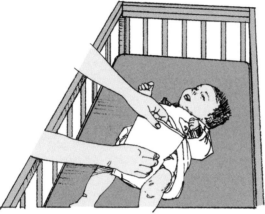

▶ Be sure to thoroughly clean the baby's diaper area using a washcloth and warm, slightly soapy water (use only mild soap made especially for babies). Once you've rinsed the diaper area thoroughly, pat it dry.

▶ If you use diaper pins or any type of ointment, lotion, or powder, be sure to keep them out of your baby's reach as you are diapering.

▶ If you use powder, pour a small amount into your hand, keeping it away from your baby's face; inhaling powder can irritate the respiratory tract.

▶ Store soiled or wet cloth diapers in a diaper pail containing ½ cup of vinegar and enough water to cover the soiled diapers. Diapers that are merely wet can be tossed directly into the pail. Rinse soiled diapers before placing them in the pail.

DAILY CARE BASICS

Dental Hygiene for Infants and Toddlers

▶ Clean your child's teeth at least twice a day, and especially after dinner.

MAKING HYGIENE FUN FOR TODDLERS

Helping your child develop good hygiene habits will help ensure their continuation later on.

▶ The time allotted for cleaning up should always be considered an important part of the everyday schedule.

▶ You should praise your child for having clean teeth, hair, hands, and nails.

▶ Your child should be allowed to choose new products for hygiene—such as a toothbrush, comb, nail brush, soap dispenser, and cup.

▶ Your child should have a mirror at the proper height to watch while face and teeth are cleaned and hair is combed.

▶ Give your child a nonskid stool or a set of little steps to reach the sink with ease.

▶ Parents and child should be hygiene pals—washing hands, brushing teeth, and combing hair together.

► For infants and young toddlers, use gauze wrapped around your finger to wipe teeth and the gum line. Once your child is willing, introduce a small, soft toothbrush (with or without a small amount of toothpaste). Gently brush a child's teeth using an up-and-down motion.

► After brushing, floss the teeth by gently sliding the dental floss along the side of each tooth, massaging slightly down and a little bit under the tooth.

► Let your child watch you as you brush your teeth. Make sure to encourage independent brushing, too.

► Most pediatric dentists suggest that children have their initial visit at age 2 or 3. It is best to make the first appointment once all 20 of the deciduous (baby) teeth have erupted.

► If you have a concern or see a problem before then, consult your pediatrician and/or pediatric dentist. Any problems with baby teeth should be attended to because of the risks of pain and infection.

Naps and Bedtime

► Most newborns sleep most of the time. Although some babies sleep only 10 hours a day, and some as many as 23, the average is about 17 hours, equally divided between day and night. Periods of wakefulness and alertness are very brief and irregular at first. They usually last no more than a few minutes at a time.

► By 3 months of age, babies typically sleep 15 hours—10 at night and 5 during the day. By 6 months of age, the average is about 14 hours—11 during the night and 3 during the day. Remember that there is great variability in sleep patterns among individual babies. Don't be alarmed if your baby is awake and alert more or less than these averages during the early months.

► There is no set age at which all babies routinely begin sleeping through the night. At first, sleeping is tied closely to feeding; babies will tend to fall asleep when they're full and wake up as soon as they're hungry. It is not until about 3 or 4 months of age that being tired generally takes priority over being hungry. This is also when babies can stay awake for relatively long stretches.

► Most 2-year-olds still need a nap (or even two) every day. Some toddlers skip them from time to time or prefer to go without, but not many. Sometimes when toddlers are tired, they will let you know or simply fall asleep. Sometimes parents need to decide.

► If your child regularly skips a nap and is unbearably cranky for the rest of the day, too tired to wait for the night, or you simply need some quiet time for yourself, encourage a nap. If your child is not sleepy, you could encourage some quiet playtime—with or without you—instead.

► Avoid any rough-and-tumble play for an hour or more before your toddler's usual bedtime. Instead, set up and follow a bedtime ritual. This ritual can include brushing teeth; bathing (2 to 3 times a week, not every night); changing diapers; and getting into pajamas.

► Make bedtime special. Read a book, tell a story, sing a lullaby, and/or say prayers together.

► If your child is climbing out of the crib, check to see if you are keeping anything in the crib (bumper guards, stuffed toys, etc.) that can be used as a stepping stool to make

climbing out easier. If your child is clearly climbing out alone, try adjusting the mattress to its lowest level.

▶ If it's clear that your toddler can get in and out of the crib without getting hurt, your child may still be able to sleep in it until it is outgrown. Be sure to leave the crib rail down, however, and put padding or carpeting on the floor at the side of the crib where your child gets out. If you think there's still a chance of falling while climbing out, you can move the crib mattress to the floor and let your child sleep there.

▶ Keep in mind that a toddler who is no longer confined in a crib is capable of getting up in the middle of the night and roaming about the house unsupervised. If your child no longer stays in the crib, confine the child to the bedroom and make sure the room is safe even if you are not around.

▶ Some parents move their toddler out of the crib and into a bed as soon as another baby comes along and needs the crib. Although this practice may be economical, it is not advisable—toddlers should not have to make this move before they're ready. Buy, rent, or borrow another crib for the new little one, instead.

AVOIDING DIAPER RASH

Careful skin care, frequent diaper changes, and proper diaper care all help to prevent diaper rash. Babies of the most conscientious parents can and do get diaper rash, but the number and severity can be cut down by doing the following:

▶ Change the baby frequently.

▶ Dress your child in loosely fitting diapers, allowing time to go bare-bottomed whenever practical.

▶ Avoid using plastic pants or diapers with gathers around the tummy and thighs.

▶ When cleaning the diaper area during changing, use water or water with a small amount of soap. If you use wipes, alternate their use with plain water.

▶ Wash gently in the folds of the genital area for girls and below the penis for boys. Also, make certain the anal area is thoroughly clean.

▶ After washing the diaper area, rinse thoroughly with a clean, wet cloth or plain water.

▶ Pat baby's bottom dry before putting on a clean diaper. If you use powder or lotion, remember that less is better and that neither is necessary.

▶ When laundering diapers, use a mild soap, and run the diapers through the rinse cycle twice. Avoid fabric softeners, which may leave a residue that can irritate your baby's skin.

Teething

Babies get their teeth at different ages and at different rates. On the average, babies begin to teethe at about 6 to 8 months of age and erupt about 1 tooth per month until they have 20 (at about 2½ years), which is the total number of deciduous or "baby" teeth. Babies have no symptoms from teething until a tooth starts to erupt (break through the surface) and the area of the gum around the tooth begins to swell or bulge. Although many babies erupt teeth without any symptoms, teething may cause fussiness, soreness of the gums, drooling, runny nose with clear mucus, slightly elevated temperature (rarely over 100.4°F), and slightly loose bowel movements.

▶ Keep your teething baby more comfortable by allowing cool, firm teething objects, like rubber teething rings. Avoid giving your baby toys made of thin, brittle plastic—pieces from these could be bitten off and choked on. Also keep baby from gnawing objects or furniture if it is possible that the paint used was made

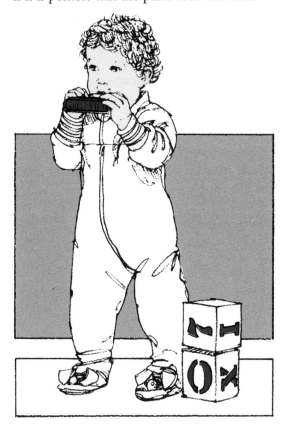

from lead. You may use an appropriate dose of acetaminophen drops (not aspirin) if baby is very uncomfortable. Check with your pediatrician, however, before giving your baby any medications.

WHEN CHILDREN AWAKE AT NIGHT

Sometimes toddlers experience separation anxiety and awake to make sure their parents are around. They can also have nightmares that cause them to be anxious and frightened when they wake up alone. If your child wakes up after falling asleep, try the following:

▶ Make certain that there's no physical reason for the reaction (such as a wet or dirty diaper, a cold room, or an empty stomach). Be sure there's a night-light in the room and that any transitional object (such as a favorite toy) is within reach.

▶ Shorten the amount of time you spend with your waking child. The next time it happens, offer comfort, but don't pick up the child. Leave the child in the crib, explaining in a reassuring voice that everything is all right.

▶ If your child continues to wake you up, offer comfort from the doorway of the room; let your child see you and explain in a reassuring voice that everything is fine, but that it's time for sleeping. If distress still continues, just call from your room and explain that everything is all right. Eventually your child will learn that it's time for sleeping.

▶ Don't give up, and by all means, don't bring your child back to your bed with you; once you do, such treatment will be demanded in the future.

▶ While teething can make toddlers uncomfortable and cranky, it will not make them ill. They may develop a low-grade fever of up to 100.4°F the day or two before a tooth erupts, but temperatures return to normal after the tooth erupts.

▶ To make your teething toddler more comfortable, offer cool liquids to drink and crackers or teething biscuits to gnaw on. Sucking on a pacifier, especially the one-piece variety that can be refrigerated or frozen, may also bring some relief.

▶ Some professionals recommend rubbing ice on the toddler's gums as a temporary pain reliever, but do this only if your toddler is willing.

Toilet Training

▶ Start using specific terms for the body parts and functions involved regularly, so your child will know exactly what you are talking about.

▶ Talk to your child about the advantages of being toilet trained in a positive, upbeat manner every now and then.

▶ Purchase a potty chair or adapter seat. A potty chair allows your child to be largely independent, since your help is not needed for getting off and on. The fact that it is easily portable can mean a lot in terms of convenience.

▶ Make sure that the potty chair is simple to use, stable, and has nonskid features to keep it from slipping on a tile floor.

▶ An adapter seat has the advantage of direct flushing, but it may create inconvenience for other family members who will have to remove and replace it. If you purchase one, make sure it fits your toilet securely.

▶ If your child is older and larger, you may want to train directly on the regular toilet.

▶ Make sure your child knows what is happening. Give your toddler several opportunities to practice the various steps involved—removing clothing, sitting on the potty chair, etc.

▶ Pick a time of day when your child usually eliminates to try the toilet. Explain in a pleasant and reassuring tone that from now on, waste products will begin going into the toilet instead of into diapers. Then place your child onto the potty chair, and encourage eliminating.

▶ Never strap your child in or in any way make the process seem like punishment. Be sure to be there at all times. While your child is trying, talk, read, or in other ways encourage entertainment and comfort.

▶ Praise every bit of progress lavishly—even if it's something as simple as sitting quietly on the potty chair for more than a few seconds.

▶ Be patient. Toilet training is rarely accomplished completely in one session; if things aren't going well, just forgetting about it for the moment and attempting it again later is often the best solution to whatever problems are arising. When children are pushed, the bathroom becomes a battleground, and the whole experience becomes extraordinarily unpleasant for everyone involved.

► If your preschooler does not approach this process with a positive attitude, the easiest thing to do is just wait a couple of weeks and try again.

► While most children will have accidents now and then, if you suspect it is a medical problem, consult your pediatrician.

ADOLESCENTS

Adolescence is a difficult time for your child. Along with getting used to the physical appearance of their changing bodies, they are dealing with hormonal change that can affect their moods as well as trying to adapt themselves to a teenage society. While your role as a parent should continue, you have to adapt as well. Few teenagers respond to parents who treat them like small children or those who ignore them. Make sure you and your child can talk to—not at—each other, so that you can serve as a guide, not an enforcer.

Talking with Your Teenager

► Take an active interest in your teenager's activities. You should know their where-abouts, their friends, and their activities. Avoid, however, being too snoopy about what they're doing. Don't read your child's mail or papers without permission.

► Set reasonable limits and make them stick. Set penalties, such as no television or grounding, ahead of time and make sure your adolescent knows the penalty for breaking the rules. Don't impose penalties you haven't discussed.

► Don't gossip about your teenagers with other parents. Teenagers especially resent when their friends report what you've said.

► If you have a problem, select a good time to discuss it, not when your adolescent is rushing out the door. Present your case calmly and let your teenager have a say.

► If you can't resolve a problem verbally or the discussion becomes heated, work out a compromise in writing.

WHEN TO KNOW A CHILD IS READY FOR TOILET TRAINING

Children are ready to begin toilet training at different times. Some begin to show signs of readiness as early as 20 months, while others are not ready until 3 or 4 years of age. Until certain specific signs of readiness are apparent, attempts to toilet train your child will be both frustrating and futile. If training is attempted too early, it often results in an inappropriate focus on the issue and actually may delay the time when the child uses the toilet independently. Begin, but don't try to rush the process, after your child demonstrates these signs:

► A dry diaper for increasingly long time periods, indicating bladder is able to store increasing amounts of urine.

► A bowel movement on a fairly regular schedule.

► A desire and ability to follow instructions.

► Anxiousness to be changed from a wet or dirty diaper.

► An attempt to copy bathroom activities of other family members.

► A demonstration in a recognizable way (by facial expression; by squatting or running to a particular place, such as the changing table; etc.) that urination or a bowel movement is about to occur.

► The motor skills to remove and at least partially replace the clothing that must be removed to use the toilet.

► The ability to get to the toilet or potty when the need to "go" is felt.

▶ Set aside time to spend with your teenager. If the evening meals are rushed because of activities, arrange weekend time for activities that your teenager enjoys.

▶ Assign chores, but don't expect teenagers to jump up whenever you want something done. Let them select the time that is convenient for everyone.

▶ Give teenagers a reasonable allowance but expect them to be responsible with the money. Let them pay for activities and school lunches. If they consistently run out of money and try to borrow, sit down and discuss whether the allowance isn't adequate or whether the teenager is spending money frivolously.

▶ If you and your teenager are having chronic disagreements or even hostility, get a counselor to help you resolve differences. Don't let arguments get out of hand or reach the shoving stage.

Coping with Acne

Acne is a skin disease that affects millions of Americans, particularly teenagers. Although heredity appears to be a factor in who gets acne, no one knows exactly what causes it. Typically acne occurs on the face, upper chest, and back, in adolescence when the body starts to mature.

If your teenager is suffering from acne, you can help. First, avoid belittling this disease. It is both unpleasant and embarrassing. Telling teenagers that they will "grow out of it" does not help, and may not be true. While some teenagers have few bouts with acne, others find the condition worsens. In noninflammatory acne, usually just a few whiteheads and blackheads appear now and then. With inflammatory acne, whiteheads become inflamed and pimples and pustules develop. A severe case can cause disfiguring cysts and scars. Prescription drugs and even surgery may be needed to treat this condition. If your adolescent is suffering from persistent and major outbreaks, consult a dermatologist.

Parents can help teenagers suffering from mild cases of acne by sharing information for acne sufferers. The following steps are recommended for mild cases of acne:

▶ Regular use of a nonprescription acne medicine containing sulfur, resorcinol, salicylic acid, and benzoyl peroxide.

▶ Washing the face once or twice daily with soap.

▶ Avoiding any food or drink that you suspect may trigger an outbreak.

▶ Not picking at or squeezing pimples, which can cause infections, injure the skin, and spread the acne.

▶ Consulting a dermatologist if none of these measures work or if the acne becomes severe.

Coping with Braces

Today, many preteens and adolescents—and even adults—have to cope with braces, which are designed to correct a "malocclusion," or a bad bite. Along with improving the smile, which is important for self-esteem, there are important reasons for having braces. Crooked and crowded teeth are hard to clean and can contribute to conditions that cause tooth decay and eventual gum disease. A bad bite can cause abnormal wear on tooth surfaces, excess stress on supporting bones and gum

COPING WITH TEMPER TANTRUMS

Temper tantrums are common among toddlers. They are the result of frustration, because the toddler has not yet learned more appropriate strategies for attaining goals and has not yet learned to accept that there are limits to what is allowed. During a tantrum, children may cry, scream, pound fists against the floor, and perhaps even hold their breath (although this is alarming, it is not dangerous; natural reflexes will force a breath before any damage is done).

During a tantrum, you cannot reason with your toddler. Generally the most effective way to deal with it is to simply ignore it until your child calms down. Make sure there is no danger of getting hurt, then just leave the room until the storm passes. When it does, offer a hug and reassurance that everything is all right, but do not give in to demands.

For example, if the tantrum was a result of your refusal to give a cookie, don't break down and give one. Doing so will only let your child know tantrums are an effective means of getting one's way. If the tantrum occurs in public, whisk your child off to a more private place to calm down or just go home.

While you may not be able to prevent all tantrums, you certainly can make them less likely to occur. The best way to help prevent them is to minimize the chance that your toddler will get frustrated in the first place. For example, instead of telling your toddler to put on a shirt—a demand that is likely to provoke a "no"—offer a choice between a green or blue shirt. This way leaves room for autonomy while you get your way.

Additionally, continued efforts on your part to make your toddler's environment safe, engrossing, and accessible can help prevent the frustration that comes from hearing "no, no, no" from you all the time. And finally, be sure to praise your toddler for appropriate strategies for dealing with frustration instead of only reacting to inappropriate behavior.

tissue, and misalignment of the jaw joints, which can result in chronic headaches or pain. Sharing the facts about braces can help your child or teenager cope with them better. And use the following tips to make life a little easier for someone who has braces:

▶ Keep a compact travel toothbrush, a small tube of toothpaste, and floss or interdental cleaners available to take when dining out.

▶ Don't belittle the aches and pains that come when the braces are first put on and then tightened. Plan meals around orthodontic appointments, so that you are not serving hard-to-chew food on the day of an appointment.

▶ If pain is a problem, ask your orthodontist about providing aspirin or an aspirin substitute or an orthodontic gel to soothe minor mouth irritations.

▶ Most food can be eaten if it is cut into small pieces so that it can be chewed, rather than bitten. Salads can be particularly difficult, however, so make sure your child or teenager is getting plenty of vegetables if he or she is avoiding salads.

▶ Peanut brittle, caramels, and bubble gum are off limits. Help your teenager by not having these around the house.

▶ Don't ask your child to smile or show off the braces to friends and relatives. It's better to let them get accustomed to the braces. They probably will smile normally once they're used to them.

▶ Don't be dismayed if it takes longer than originally proposed to correct a problem. Not everyone's face and mouth grow at the same speed.

DEALING WITH SUBSTANCE ABUSE

The prevalence of drugs among young people makes it imperative that parents take an active role in making sure their children are not using drugs. Along with teaching ethical and moral standards and demonstrating them through example, parents need to be informed about drugs and signs of drug use. It is up to parents to help their children resist peer pressure to use drugs and alcohol. There are many sources for information about alcohol and substance abuse among teenagers. Much of the information below is based on a publication of the U.S. Department of Education, "What Works: Schools Without Drugs." For a free copy of this handbook, call the Department of Education's toll-free number, 1-800-624-0100, or send your name and address to Schools Without Drugs, Pueblo, CO 81009.

Know the Facts

▶ There is no such thing as a safe drug or a safe or responsible use of drugs. However, marijuana, which is not physically addictive, is in a different category from the more dangerous drugs such as cocaine, heroin, and LSD.

▶ Drug use crosses all economic and racial boundaries; don't assume that it is confined to inner-city ghettos.

SIGNS OF SUBSTANCE ABUSE

Parents need to be aware of the signs of substance abuse, because detecting and facing the problem in its earliest stages may make it easier to overcome. Along with awareness of the following signs, make sure you know the extent of the drug problem at your child's school and in the community.

► Possession of drugs and equipment to use drugs, such as pipes, rolling papers, and eye drops. When there is clear evidence of substance abuse, take action immediately.

► Dramatic change in school performance, including increase in absenteeism or tardiness.

► Physical signs, including short attention span, poor physical appearance, slurred speech, bloodshot eyes, or dilated pupils.

► Behavioral changes, such as dishonesty, changes in friends, possession of money that is unaccounted for, hostility, reduced motivation and energy, and little or no interest in activities that once held their attention. Changes in behavior and appearance often accompany adolescence, so make sure you are looking for changes that reflect substance abuse, not a wish for independence.

► Identification with drug culture, including hostility about discussing drugs or alcohol.

► Elementary- and middle-school students, as well as high-school students, are exposed to drug use.

► Many teenagers are occasional users of alcohol and about 35 percent of adolescents are believed to be heavy drinkers, drinking 5 or more drinks on one occasion.

► Older students and young people are the source of most drugs to teenagers.

Take Action

If you suspect that your child is using drugs or alcohol, it is important that you take immediate action and not ignore the problem, hoping it will go away. Sometimes teenagers engage in this behavior purposely to get the attention of parents; your concern may be enough to stop the behavior. Substance abuse is a problem that only gets worse if it's ignored by parents who want to wish it away.

► Discuss your suspicions with your child in a calm manner. Don't confront a child under the influence of drugs or alcohol.

► Take disciplinary measures that help remove the child from circumstances where drug use or drinking might occur.

► Set up a plan of action; consult the child's counselor or a school social worker, if necessary.

► If the problem persists, seek professional help from drug-treatment or alcohol-abuse specialists as soon as possible. Don't delay, hoping that summer vacation or some other activity will change the behavior.

TOP 500 FIRST NAMES FOR BOYS
FREQUENCY RANK ORDER: U.S.A., 1990

NAME	RANK	NAME	RANK	NAME	RANK
Michael	1	Jeffrey	37	Edward	73
Christopher	2	Derek	38	Casey	74
Joshua	3	Richard	39	Alan	75
Matthew	4	Charles	40	Chad	76
James	5	Jeremy	41	Garrett	77
Justin	6	Travis	42	Jose	78
Andrew	7	Nathan	43	Donald	79
David	8	Patrick	44	Mitchell	80
John	9	Mark	45	Blake	81
Nicholas	10	Jason	46	Keith	82
Steven	11	Jesse	47	Ronald	83
Daniel	12	Jared	48	George	84
Ryan	13	Samuel	49	Vincent	85
Robert	14	Dustin	50	Peter	86
Joseph	15	Austin	51	Spencer	87
Jonathan	16	Kenneth	52	Douglas	88
William	17	Gregory	53	Seth	89
Zachary	18	Scott	54	Wesley	90
Brandon	19	Ethan	55	Antonio	91
Tyler	20	Bradley	56	Logan	92
Kyle	21	Paul	57	Colin	93
Anthony	22	Cameron	58	Raymond	94
Brian	23	Phillip	59	Lucas	95
Jacob	24	Taylor	60	Chase	96
Eric	25	Shane	61	Curtis	97
Sean	26	Devin	62	Gary	98
Cody	27	Dylan	63	Darryl	99
Jordan	28	Alex	64	Joel	100
Kevin	29	Christian	65	Colton	101
Thomas	30	Caleb	66	Craig	102
Timothy	31	Ian	67	Carl	103
Corey	32	Marcus	68	Luke	104
Alexander	33	Evan	69	Adrian	105
Benjamin	34	Trevor	70	Carlos	106
Aaron	35	Brett	71	Terrance	107
Adam	36	Nathaniel	72	Brent	108

NAME	RANK	NAME	RANK	NAME	RANK
Gabriel	109	Henry	148	Jorge	187
Juan	110	Colby	149	Neil	188
Darren	111	Dalton	150	Terrell	189
Frank	112	Gerald	151	Micah	190
Darius	113	Rodney	152	Demetrius	191
Luis	114	Martin	153	Danny	192
Victor	115	Grant	154	Albert	193
Troy	116	Jay	155	Ricardo	194
Dominic	117	Jack	156	Dwayne	195
Julian	118	Frederick	157	Glenn	196
Brendan	119	Lawrence	158	Arthur	197
Bryce	120	Damian	159	Bryant	198
Larry	121	Bobby	160	Trenton	199
Randy	122	Isaiah	161	Reginald	200
Johnny	123	Preston	162	Malcolm	201
Isaac	124	Dominique	163	Bruce	202
Jeremiah	125	Lance	164	Theodore	203
Dennis	126	Tanner	165	Alejandro	204
Clayton	127	Xavier	166	Rafael	205
Russell	128	Mason	167	Noah	206
Jerry	129	Mario	168	Hunter	207
Drew	130	Donte	169	Eddie	208
Todd	131	Max	170	DeAndre	209
Terry	132	Jamal	171	Ronnie	210
Levi	133	Billy	172	Brock	211
Andre	134	Lee	173	Wayne	212
Ricky	135	Roger	174	Jesus	213
Randall	136	Miguel	175	Elijah	214
Tony	137	Walter	176	Darrion	215
Louis	138	Antoine	177	Cole	216
Calvin	139	Quintin	178	Tyrone	217
Skyler	140	Maurice	179	Trent	218
Connor	141	Jamie	180	Jarrett	219
Jake	142	Emmanuel	181	Stuart	220
Stefan	143	Marquis	182	Riley	221
Dakota	144	Ross	183	Morgan	222
Jimmy	145	Maxwell	184	Alec	223
Willie	146	Miles	185	Tyson	224
Clinton	147	Elliott	186	Edwin	225

NAME	RANK	NAME	RANK	NAME	RANK
Kurt	226	Cedric	265	Angelo	304
Giovanni	227	Jackson	266	Eli	305
Marshall	228	Melvin	267	Forrest	306
Angel	229	Roberto	268	Hayden	307
Tommy	230	Roderick	269	Eduardo	308
Roy	231	Deontae	270	Sergio	309
Zachariah	232	Dean	271	Howard	310
Chance	233	Andres	272	Kelly	311
Francisco	234	Damon	273	Clarence	312
Francis	235	Gavin	274	Deon	313
Rashad	236	Brennan	275	Shannon	314
Courtney	237	Landon	276	Jaime	315
Kendall	238	Tristan	277	Earl	316
Dane	239	Keenan	278	Brad	317
Beau	240	Franklin	279	Nolan	318
Parker	241	Clifford	280	Dexter	319
Harrison	242	Trey	281	Zane	320
Ruben	243	Harold	282	Harry	321
Jaron	244	Wade	283	Andy	322
Donovan	245	Weston	284	Chaz	323
Braden	246	Sebastian	285	Jamar	324
Marvin	247	Lamar	286	Carlton	325
Ernest	248	Joe	287	Clint	326
Omar	249	Jerrell	288	Ashton	327
Dale	250	Hector	289	Darnell	328
Byron	251	Jarvis	290	Tyrel	329
Eugene	252	Kelvin	291	Leon	330
Jerome	253	Akeem	292	Julius	331
Jermaine	254	Blaine	293	DeAngelo	332
Manuel	255	Gage	294	Pedro	333
Barry	256	Ty	295	Alberto	334
Leonard	257	Kirk	296	Graham	335
Javier	258	Kendrick	297	Alvin	336
Desmond	259	Coty	298	Julio	337
Ivan	260	Dallas	299	Jace	338
Oscar	261	Warren	300	Lorenzo	339
Stanley	262	Josiah	301	Tevin	340
Brady	263	Nelson	302	DeMarcus	341
Quentin	264	Corbin	303	Ramon	342

NAME	RANK
Bernard	343
Keegan	344
Tory	345
Steve	346
Brenton	347
Marco	348
Mohammad	349
Wyatt	350
Chandler	351
Malik	352
Orlando	353
Ray	354
Reid	355
Marlon	356
Carson	357
Shea	358
Tucker	359
Sheldon	360
Cornelius	361
Clay	362
Alonzo	363
Leroy	364
Fernando	365
Kalin	366
Alfred	367
Jameson	368
Donnie	369
Mackenzie	370
Tracy	371
DeShawn	372
Abraham	373
Edgar	374
Joey	375
Simon	376
Raul	377
Alfonso	378
Armando	379
Kerry	380
Roman	381

NAME	RANK
Lane	382
Lonnie	383
Avery	384
Marquise	385
Gordon	386
Denzel	387
Dwight	388
Chris	389
Keaton	390
Norman	391
Tyree	392
Oliver	393
Jamel	394
Charlie	395
Perry	396
Enrique	397
Quinn	398
Owen	399
Chadwick	400
Heath	401
Bryson	402
Sam	403
Hakeem	404
Jamil	405
Tavaris	406
Sterling	407
Terron	408
Freddy	409
Alexis	410
Javon	411
Israel	412
Cesar	413
Ralph	414
Vernon	415
Marcos	416
Kareem	417
Thaddeus	418
Cortez	419
Fabian	420

NAME	RANK
DeJuan	421
Rory	422
Tremaine	423
Clifton	424
Kenny	425
Ezekiel	426
Shelby	427
Ben	428
Carter	429
Herbert	430
Keon	431
Khiry	432
Kadeem	433
Kyler	434
Khalil	435
Diego	436
Cary	437
Dallin	438
Everett	439
Felix	440
Scotty	441
Leo	442
Fred	443
Marcel	444
Toby	445
Cade	446
Dorian	447
Lloyd	448
Emilio	449
Amir	450
Stacy	451
Kent	452
Sidney	453
Kellen	454
Josue	455
Reese	456
Brant	457
Rico	458
Jackie	459

NAME	RANK	NAME	RANK	NAME	RANK
Jean	460	Kiefer	474	Rasheed	488
Kwame	461	Octavius	475	Tarik	489
Gilbert	462	Tobias	476	Rakeem	490
Noel	463	Rick	477	Ariel	491
Nico	464	Brody	478	Leonardo	492
Lamont	465	Alfredo	479	Pierre	493
Amos	466	DeRon	480	Grayson	494
Dontavius	467	Lester	481	Gerardo	495
Leslie	468	Hassan	482	Ahmad	496
Gerard	469	Wendell	483	Rudy	497
Raheem	470	Esteban	484	Pablo	498
Will	471	Ervin	485	Blair	499
Quincy	472	Addison	486	Rene	500
Sammy	473	Don	487		

TOP 500 FIRST NAMES FOR GIRLS
FREQUENCY RANK ORDER: U.S.A., 1990

NAME	RANK	NAME	RANK	NAME	RANK
Brittany	1	Hannah	37	Sierra	73
Ashley	2	Allison	38	Molly	74
Jessica	3	Kimberly	39	Holly	75
Amanda	4	Amy	40	Maria	76
Sarah	5	Jamie	41	Vanessa	77
Megan	6	Laura	42	Paige	78
Samantha	7	Mary	43	April	79
Stephanie	8	Erin	44	Stacy	80
Caitlin	9	Brianna	45	Alexandria	81
Katherine	10	Cassandra	46	Olivia	82
Kayla	11	Victoria	47	Lacey	83
Lauren	12	Alexandra	48	Shelby	84
Emily	13	Casey	49	Miranda	85
Jennifer	14	Katie	50	Abigail	86
Courtney	15	Anna	51	Natasha	87
Rachel	16	Taylor	52	Jenna	88
Nicole	17	Whitney	53	Carly	89
Elizabeth	18	Brandi	54	Breanna	90
Chelsea	19	Andrea	55	Julia	91
Amber	20	Jordan	56	Julie	92
Rebecca	21	Morgan	57	Monica	93
Christina	22	Haley	58	Marissa	94
Tiffany	23	Christine	59	Bethany	95
Kristen	24	Angela	60	Melanie	96
Heather	25	Alexis	61	Ariel	97
Danielle	26	Natalie	62	Felicia	98
Lindsey	27	Jacqueline	63	Krista	99
Michelle	28	Shannon	64	Kathleen	100
Melissa	29	Brooke	65	Desiree	101
Jasmine	30	Kaylee	66	Gabrielle	102
Erica	31	Kristy	67	Kylie	103
Kelsey	32	Candace	68	Margaret	104
Kelly	33	Tara	69	Kirsten	105
Alicia	34	Lisa	70	Patricia	106
Crystal	35	Kara	71	Kendra	107
Alyssa	36	Leah	72	Dana	108

NAME	RANK	NAME	RANK	NAME	RANK
Leslie	109	Alexa	148	Elise	187
Tabitha	110	Deanna	149	Jenny	188
Gina	111	Autumn	150	Alanna	189
Sydney	112	Mercedes	151	Karla	190
Anne	113	Carolyn	152	Lydia	191
Hillary	114	Jocelyn	153	Barbara	192
Bianca	115	Renee	154	Gabriela	193
Michaela	116	Kanisha	155	Meredith	194
Theresa	117	Claire	156	Nikki	195
Carrie	118	Audrey	157	Adrienne	196
Devon	119	Jessie	158	Tiara	197
Katrina	120	Madison	159	Yesenia	198
Bridget	121	Monique	160	Leticia	199
Caroline	122	Melinda	161	Linda	200
Jaclyn	123	Keri	162	Trisha	201
Karen	124	Ebony	163	Jade	202
Mallory	125	Angelica	164	Chanel	203
Jillian	126	Dominique	165	Iesha	204
Sabrina	127	Angel	166	Kierra	205
Madeline	128	Adriana	167	Sandra	206
Mackenzie	129	Bailey	168	Ciara	207
Diana	130	Tamara	169	Ellen	208
Cynthia	131	Katlyn	170	Misty	209
Savannah	132	Aubrey	171	Denise	210
Abby	133	Tasha	172	Christian	211
Kaylyn	134	Callie	173	Jaleesa	212
Robin	135	Colleen	174	Camille	213
Veronica	136	Keisha	175	Sherry	214
Carissa	137	Sasha	176	Virginia	215
Emma	138	Tanisha	177	Chloe	216
Shaina	139	Janelle	178	Nancy	217
Kiara	140	Susan	179	Marie	218
Shawna	141	Amelia	180	Mariah	219
Chantel	142	Deborah	181	Kiana	220
Cassie	143	Cori	182	Ariana	221
Destiny	144	Raven	183	Hope	222
Grace	145	Joanna	184	LaToya	223
Tracy	146	Arielle	185	Leanne	224
Valerie	147	Heidi	186	Toni	225

NAME	RANK	NAME	RANK	NAME	RANK
Porsha	226	Wendy	265	Donna	304
Justine	227	Cassidy	266	Maya	305
Lakeisha	228	Brianne	267	Lori	306
Rachelle	229	Shante	268	Carol	307
Summer	230	Kirstie	269	Selena	308
Shayla	231	Sharon	270	Linsey	309
Brenda	232	Faith	271	Jill	310
Cheyenne	233	Asia	272	Janet	311
Tierra	234	Tamika	273	Joy	312
Tia	235	Tonya	274	Annie	313
Tina	236	Melody	275	Macy	314
Maggie	237	Tessa	276	Antoinette	315
Karina	238	Corinne	277	Sadie	316
Nina	239	Kiersten	278	Bonnie	317
Sophia	240	Kate	279	Jana	318
Tiana	241	Jodi	280	Kendall	319
Janae	242	Randi	281	Ruth	320
Pamela	243	Dawn	282	Cherie	321
Raquel	244	Mia	283	Diane	322
Shaniqua	245	Rose	284	Clarissa	323
Simone	246	Maegan	285	Shanika	324
Priscilla	247	Mandy	286	Kali	325
Sonya	248	Anastasia	287	Shanna	326
Ashton	249	Shelly	288	Beth	327
LaTasha	250	Martha	289	Alice	328
Marisa	251	Alaina	290	Lillian	329
Ali	252	Tatiana	291	Rochelle	330
Tori	253	Suzanne	292	Bobbi	331
Jerrica	254	Skylar	293	Julianne	332
Breanne	255	Shanae	294	Loren	333
Regina	256	Chasity	295	Paula	334
Taryn	257	Charlene	296	Cecilia	335
Leanna	258	Naomi	297	Sylvia	336
Alisa	259	Terri	298	Mindy	337
Angelina	260	Shanice	299	Gloria	338
Carmen	261	Charlotte	300	Cindy	339
Tanya	262	Cheryl	301	Frances	340
Kari	263	Angelia	302	Lena	341
Kira	264	Leigh	303	Cherise	342

NAME	RANK	NAME	RANK	NAME	RANK
Sheena	343	Alyse	382	Shaylee	421
Shea	344	Chantal	383	Patrice	422
Sade	345	Marina	384	Rhonda	423
Sheila	346	Whitley	385	Alina	424
Evelyn	347	Yasmin	386	Rikki	425
Daniela	348	Lucy	387	Maureen	426
Jane	349	Johanna	388	Micah	427
Susanna	350	Shameka	389	Shirley	428
Carolina	351	Brenna	390	Reyna	429
Denisha	352	Roxanne	391	Maryann	430
Dorothy	353	Esther	392	Kyra	431
Kady	354	Elena	393	Shakira	432
Tammy	355	Cecily	394	Misha	433
Helen	356	Cherelle	395	Laurel	434
Codi	357	Natalia	396	Lara	435
Claudia	358	Kyla	397	Marilyn	436
Danica	359	Lily	398	Daisy	437
Jeanette	360	Eva	399	Alex	438
Ashlyn	361	Alexia	400	Quanisha	439
Nikita	362	Marcy	401	Janice	440
Serena	363	Jackie	402	Audriana	441
Marah	364	Latifah	403	Annelise	442
Alia	365	Janessa	404	Nadia	443
India	366	Nicolette	405	Diamond	444
Kami	367	Celeste	406	Cameron	445
Precious	368	Elaine	407	Rhiannon	446
Sally	369	Elisa	408	Adrian	447
Miriam	370	Yolanda	409	Stevie	448
Rosa	371	Jamila	410	Dakota	449
Larissa	372	Riley	411	Beverly	450
Eileen	373	Kathy	412	Candy	451
Blair	374	Isabel	413	Shaylyn	452
Juliana	375	Noelle	414	Charlee	453
Dena	376	Maura	415	Darci	454
Alysia	377	Joanne	416	Ayana	455
Elisha	378	Genevieve	417	Tawny	456
Keely	379	Josie	418	Skye	457
Charity	380	Lissette	419	Betty	458
Ruby	381	Tamesha	420	Deidra	459

NAME	RANK		NAME	RANK		NAME	RANK
Yvette	460		Elissa	474		Charmaine	488
Constance	461		Eliza	475		Ryan	489
Adrianne	462		Sandy	476		Rosemary	490
Lynn	463		Kenya	477		Nakia	491
Anita	464		Talisha	478		Bryn	492
Yvonne	465		Ansley	479		Marsha	493
Shawnee	466		Francesca	480		Nakisha	494
Amberly	467		Gretchen	481		Marisela	495
Beatriz	468		Tyler	482		Kamisha	496
Melisa	469		Paris	483		Janie	497
Sherika	470		Gianna	484		Zoe	498
Hallie	471		Jacy	485		Laken	499
Justina	472		Lashay	486		Lashonda	500
Kia	473		Michal	487			

ENTERTAINING & GIFTS

There are people who seem to be able to throw a party and think of creative gift ideas in a breeze. Most of us, however, need to put some thought and planning into hosting company or getting the "right" gift for Aunt Betty's birthday. Fortunately, there are some basic tricks that can make both jobs fairly easy and fun. In the following pages, you will find information galore—how much food to plan for each guest at a buffet, napkin-folding techniques to make your table look really unique, creative gift-wrapping ideas, and much more. You're sure to learn time-and-effort-saving tricks to make your life so much easier!

ENTERTAINING

The essence of entertaining is for everyone, including the host or hostess, to have a good time. If you're too wrapped up in how the party is going, you'll look like you're working, instead of having fun. And it's likely that your guests won't be relaxed. Successful party-givers all agree on one point—if you plan the party well, both you and your guests will enjoy your time together.

PARTY OPTIONS

Very few people have the dining space and kitchen help to accommodate a sit-down dinner for 20. Buffets offer the advantage of allowing you to dine with your guests, instead of running back and forth into the kitchen.

Sit-down dinners for small groups provide more intimacy and seem to inspire better conversation. Cocktail parties provide an easy way to entertain a large group of people, particularly if it is the prelude to another event.

When you're trying to decide what kind of party to have, forget about whether you have enough matching china for 12. Instead, consider the occasion, the number of guests you intend to invite, and your budget and space limitations.

Buffets

▶ If your guests will have to eat on their laps, avoid dishes that require the use of a knife. Serve pasta, stews, fish, or other foods instead.

▶ If you are using paper plates, make sure they're solidly constructed or consider putting the plates in holders. Flimsy paper plates around a buffet table are a disaster waiting to happen.

▶ Make sure you have enough hot trays to keep hot foods hot. If you don't, rent warming trays or opt for dishes that can be served at room temperature.

▶ Use tongs for serving salads and large serving spoons for other dishes.

▶ Have food arranged in portions, unless someone will preside at the buffet table to serve; don't expect your guests to slice meat or cheese or cut cake while they're balancing a plate at the buffet table.

▶ If elderly people or children will be attending the party, make sure that someone is assigned to help them get their food and find a seat.

▶ Just because you're having a buffet doesn't mean you can't seat your guests where you want them. Set up place cards ahead of time at your tables and ask your guests to check for their seats before they get their food.

Cocktail Parties

▶ If your party is a prelude to another event or not being held during a meal-time hour, limit the menu to appetizers. If the "cocktail party" is held during the dinner hour, plan on serving a light buffet of finger foods.

▶ Keep the food simple and small. Otherwise your floors and your guests' clothes will suffer.

▶ Use an electric serving tray to keep hot hors d'oeuvre warm. If you don't have a tray, enlist the help of an adolescent or a friend to help serve hot canapés to guests individually. If you simply set these on a table, they'll cool too quickly before everyone gets around to them.

▶ Have plenty of small napkins on hand to serve with drinks and canapés.

▶ If you're planning on a house full of guests, don't forget to rent or borrow an extra coat rack to avoid piling coats on a bed.

▶ For a cocktail party, you don't need to worry about seating. But make sure you have appetizers placed in all the rooms in which the party will be going on. Otherwise, you'll end up with everyone crowded in the room with the food.

Sit-Down Dinners

Matching china and silver aren't critical to a sit-down dinner, but comfortable chairs are crucial. To host a successful sit-down dinner, make sure you have the following criteria:

▶ Select a menu that will allow you to prepare most of the meal in advance.

▶ If you're serving separate courses, keep a tray handy between courses and at the end of the meal for clearing the table. It will save you a lot of trips between table and kitchen.

▶ If you don't feel confident about timing several courses, serve a casserole in an attractive dish.

▶ There's nothing wrong with serving a family-style sit-down dinner, but hot foods

ARRANGING A BUFFET TABLE

The best rule of thumb to use when setting up a buffet table is to arrange everything in a logical manner. At one end of the table set out the dinner plates. Follow these by the main course and the appropriate condiments and side dishes. Next arrange the vegetables, salads, breads, butter, etc. At the very end place the knives, forks, and napkins.

Desserts, dessert silverware, beverages (coffee and tea), and cups/saucers should be set out separately. Don't forget the cream, sugar, lemon, and spoons.

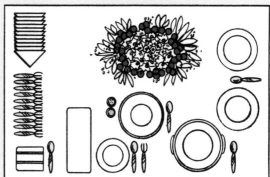

will cool too quickly if they have to be passed among more than eight people. Divide hot dishes into two servings to make sure everyone is able to serve themselves quickly. And check ahead of time to make sure you have enough room in the middle of the table for the serving dishes.

▶ If you've invited more guests than your dining table will accommodate, but still want to offer a sit-down dinner, extend the table by topping it with a large piece of plywood. Cover the table first with table pads or foam rubber to protect the surface and to keep the plywood from slipping. Then just cover everything with your favorite tablecloth.

Parties for Children

▶ For a birthday party, cover the party table with shelf paper and let each guest decorate his or her own place with nontoxic felt-tip markers. The kids can decorate white paper plates and cups the same way. It will keep the kids busy and save you money—plain paper utensils are much cheaper than the party kind.

▶ Create an autograph tablecloth at your child's next birthday party. Have the guests sign their names, then embroider over each signature or outline the names in permanent dye. Use the cloth at future birthday celebrations, adding new names each year.

SETTING A FORMAL TABLE

1. Napkin
2. Fish fork
3. Dinner fork
4. Salad fork
5. First-course soup and liner plate
6. Dinner or service plate
7. Dinner knife
8. Fish knife
9. Soup spoon
10. Bread and butter plate
11. Butter knife
12. Dessert spoon and fork
13. Place card

14. Water goblet
15. Red wine glass
16. White wine glass

▶ Allow at least 30 inches between place settings to avoid overcrowding your guests. If necessary, set up a separate table.

▶ Use a low centerpiece that won't interfere with your guests seeing one another.

▶ Serve from the left, remove plates from the right.

▶ To get children in the party spirit, send balloon invitations. Simply inflate the balloons with a balloon pump, write the invitation on the balloons with a felt-tip marker, and deflate the balloons. Put them in envelopes and mail to your guests.

▶ Have an undecorated frosted birthday cake ready, as well as a big dish of sugar cookies. Let the birthday child decorate the cake from jars of instant frosting while the rest of the kids decorate cookies with frosting, jelly beans, candy hearts, gumdrops, chocolate pieces, etc.

▶ Prevent birthday candles from dripping wax into the frosting by securing each candle with a marshmallow. This is much easier than trying to get the candles to stand straight in those tiny decorative holders.

▶ Cut circles of bread with a cookie cutter, and set out spreads—raisins, colored candies, pretzels, carrot and green pepper sticks, etc.—to make "face" decorations. Let the children design their own open-face sandwiches.

▶ Keep old wallpaper books or wrapping paper and have each child at a birthday party make his or her own hat. Provide blunt scissors, yarn for the ties, newspaper for making streamers, and a stapler.

▶ Instead of using one of your good tablecloths for a child's party, spread a large, colorful bath towel on the table. It looks festive, absorbs spills easily, and washes quickly. A bright sheet works well, too.

▶ For a child's summer birthday, plan an outdoor picnic or barbecue party—a great way to keep the birthday cake off your furniture. Plan the picnic for your own backyard or the playground, but make sure another adult or two is available to watch the children if you're minding the grill. Keep the insect repellent handy.

▶ If you're taking guest children to a restaurant, movie, or museum, take along a tote bag for mittens, scarves, hats, and all the other paraphernalia they need. You may have to carry the bag, but at least you won't spend half an hour trying to round up everyone's belongings. Make sure you have enough room and a seat belt for each child.

Theme Parties

▶ Potluck parties make for easy entertaining, but keep the following in mind if you are the host or hostess: Try to divide up dishes among the guests, so you don't end up with five plates of brownies and no salads; ask your guests not to bring food that has to be heated so you won't spend all your time in the kitchen; have extra serving plates and bowls on hand; and be sure to thank everyone for their offering, whether it's a box of store-bought cookies or a lavishly made dessert.

▶ For an easy summer party menu, set out different types of salad vegetables and a lot of toppings and let guests create their own salads. Make sure some of the ingredients are interesting or unusual enough to add a festive feel to the meal. Add some bread and wine to make the meal complete.

▶ Make sure not just one family is stuck with all the work and expense for major holiday meals. Invite family and friends over to help cook the holiday meal or make it a potluck with the exception of the main course.

▶ If you plan a costume party, give guests the option of dressing up.

PLANNING A PARTY

Planning is crucial to any successful party, whether it's a children's birthday party for ten or a cocktail party for 40. Along with selecting the guest list, the menu, and even entertainment, you will want to be sure all bases are covered before the invitations are sent out.

Selecting a Menu

▶ Adapt your menu to the party, your guest list, and the occasion. Few children appreciate beef Wellington, and few adults crave turkey hot dogs. Likewise, a heavy meal on a hot, humid day won't be appreciated.

HOSTING THE PERFECT PARTY

▶ Keep a record of the parties and get-togethers you've given, along with guest lists and menus and what aspects of the event were—or weren't—a success. It will make useful reading next time you plan to entertain, and you'll be less likely to serve your guests the same food you served at your last party.

▶ Make sure your guests understand your invitation. If you schedule the party during the dinner hour, guests will expect dinner. If you don't want children to attend, address the invitations to Mr. and Mrs.; if necessary, specify that children are not invited. If your invitations are clear, chances are your guests won't misinterpret them.

▶ Always greet your guests. At large parties, make sure you introduce an arriving guest or couple to someone else before leaving them.

▶ Don't get stuck in the kitchen. Spending time with your guests will help you evaluate how the party is going and allow you to pay attention to guests who may feel left out.

▶ Avoid inviting guests who dislike each other. Entertain them separately.

▶ Don't expect friends from work and social friends and relatives to become instant friends. Chances are that people will divide into separate groups at a large party. You may be able to initiate some new friendships by introducing people and launching a conversation about their mutual interests.

▶ If someone has reached his or her limit with alcohol, don't be afraid to offer that guest a glass of soda. And don't allow an inebriated guest to drive away from your home. Drive them yourself or call a taxi. If necessary, confiscate their keys.

▶ If you're having an adults-only party, hire a baby-sitter for your children, or see if they can sleep over with friends or relatives.

▶ Don't wear yourself to a frazzle cleaning the house. Spend at least a half-hour before your party relaxing. A tired, weary host or hostess makes for a very dull party.

▶ Don't be afraid to ask for help in throwing a large party. A friend may be only too happy to help in return for your help at his or her party.

▶ Keep your budget, space limitations, and even your cooking abilities in mind. Most guests will prefer a terrific bowl of chili to a poorly cooked or congealing roast.

▶ Avoid trying out a new recipe on guests. Prepare it first for family members or close friends. You'll be sure of the taste and the length of time it takes to prepare.

▶ Plan your menu to avoid cooking dishes that will need the oven or the top of the range at the same time. For example, if you need to use your oven for a roast, plan to cook side dishes on the top of the range.

▶ If you're planning on cooking most of the meal ahead of time, make sure you plan enough room in the refrigerator or freezer to accommodate the food until it is ready to warm or serve.

▶ Take advantage of seasonal fruits and vegetables. Not only will you save money, you'll be able to count on finding what you want at the market.

▶ To save shopping time, include alternatives in case your market doesn't have something your original menu would require.

▶ Avoid dishes that require last-minute preparation.

▶ Be sure to include a vegetarian entrée for those who don't eat meat.

Scheduling the Party

Plan your party on paper—and include a time schedule. By preparing this list well in advance, you'll also alert yourself to any problems, such as the creation of a menu that requires too much last-minute preparation. Be sure to include these elements in your list:

▶ Sending invitations—at least three weeks in advance for all but casual get-togethers.

▶ Guest list, with check-offs for responses.

▶ The complete menu, including quantities and estimated time to prepare each dish.

▶ A complete inventory of all food and beverage items needed for your menu. Check

spice racks ahead of time, and don't forget to check on supplies of coffee, tea, sugar, and other everyday items. Party day is not the time to run out.

▶ Schedule what can be precooked or prepared ahead of time. Vegetables, for example, can be prepared at least a day ahead. Cut them up, wrap them in damp paper towels, put them in plastic bags, and refrigerate.

▶ Inventory of your china, glassware, and flatware. Don't be afraid to mix and match, but be sure to have at least three to four settings beyond what you need. Borrow or rent extras ahead of time if you need them.

▶ Inventory of serving dishes and serving utensils. Make sure you have adequately sized bowls and platters for all items to be served. Don't forget about the hors d'oeuvre.

▶ Inventory of cookware. Check this at least a week before the party so that you can borrow or buy anything you will need to cook your food.

▶ Inventory of placemats, tablecloths, and napkins. Check to make sure they are clean and uncreased at least two to three days before the party.

▸ Centerpiece or flowers. Try to get these at least a day ahead. Unless they're dried, you don't want them to be wilted by the day of the party.

▸ On the morning of the party (or the night before), arrange flowers, set tables, and clear space in your closet for coats. Arrange a rubber mat near your front door for boots if you expect inclement weather.

▸ If possible, store your special supplies for entertaining in one place so that they're easy to find.

Estimating Quantities

There is nothing worse than running out of food at a party. To make sure that all of your guests go home full and happy, use the following guidelines to plan your next party. Just make sure to adjust the quantities upward if your guests include teenage boys or others who are known to be big eaters; adjust the figures downward for your full-of-dieters club lunch or friends who are small eaters.

Approximate quantities for multiple servings:

▸ 1 large head of lettuce for a salad for 6 people

▸ 1 large fruit pie for 8 people

▸ 1 loaf of bread for 16 people

▸ 1 two-layer cake for 10 to 12 people

▸ 1 large cheesecake for 10 to 12 people

Approximate quantities for single servings:

▸ ½ to 1 cup for a side dish or appetizer; 1 to 1½ cups for a main course dish

▸ 4 to 6 ounces of fish

▸ 6 to 8 ounces of meat (with bone)

▸ 4 to 6 ounces of meat (without bone)

▸ 2 ounces of rice (weight uncooked)

▸ 2 ounces of pasta (weight uncooked) for a main course dish; 1 ounce (weight uncooked) for a side dish

▸ ½ to ¾ cup of vegetables

▸ 2 rolls

▸ 1 to 2 tablespoons of sauce for main dishes or desserts; slightly less for appetizers or side dishes

▸ ½ cup of fruit salad

▸ ½ to ¾ cup of ice cream

▸ Two to three 6-ounce cups of coffee or tea per person

▸ Most recipes will double just fine, but avoid multiplying any recipe by more than four. Cook in batches instead.

▸ For a light cocktail party, plan on 6 to 10 canapés per guest. Plan on about one-third hot items.

▸ Make sure you have about ⅓ pound of ice per person, slightly more in the summer.

Setting Up a Bar

▸ Unless you want your guests in the kitchen, set up the bar in another room.

▸ An impromptu bar can be made by setting out an attractive tray of drinks, glasses, and accessories on a convenient table or counter.

▸ Make sure your bar has enough access for at least three people to serve themselves at one time or consider hiring a bartender.

▸ Provide nonalcoholic drinks—juices, soda, water—for guests who don't drink alcohol.

▸ When you buy ice for a party, keep it from melting by placing the bag of ice on dry ice.

▸ If you're making any kind of fruit juice punch, freeze some of the juice in a large bowl or container and use it instead of ice cubes to prevent the punch from becoming too watery.

▸ Wine that must be opened with a corkscrew should be stored on its side. This keeps moisture in the cork and makes opening the bottle easier.

▸ If you don't have the space in your refrigerator to keep soft drinks and beer cold during a party, fill your bathtub or washing machine with ice and store drinks there.

▸ Freeze an inch of water in the bottom of the ice bucket to help the ice last longer.

Party Beverages

When you serve drinks for company, remember that cocktails are before-meal drinks. The alcohol—be it gin, whiskey, rum, etc.—should be about 60 percent of the total drink and never below half. The home bartender should have bitters, carbonated sodas, lemons, oranges, limes, olives, and cherries on hand.

Standard before-dinner drink glasses are:
   Cocktail glass
   Old-fashioned glass
   Sour glass
   Daiquiri/champagne cocktail glass
   Straight whiskey glass

Standard wine glasses are:
   Tall tulip for champagne
   Rhine wine römer
   All-purpose tulip glass
   Bubble glass for sparkling Burgundy
   Pipe-stem sherry glass
   Brandy snifter
   Liqueur glass

Standard beer and ale glasses are:
   Heirloom stein
   Everyday stein

TENDING TO THE CHRISTMAS TREE

▸ To keep small children or pets from toppling the Christmas tree, place the tree in a playpen "fence."

▸ Fireproof the Christmas tree by spraying it with a ½-gallon of lukewarm water to which you've added 1 cup of alum, 4 ounces of boric acid, and 2 tablespoons of borax, thoroughly mixing all ingredients. If there's any solution left, pour it into the water in the tree stand.

▸ Make your fresh tree last longer by cutting the trunk by one inch on the diagonal and standing it in a water base; replenish the water daily.

▸ Never leave the lights on the tree or the lights plugged in when you're asleep or away from the house. A short in the wiring could start a fire.

▸ If you're going to plant a "living Christmas tree" on your property, do it long before the ground hardens. Dig a hole big enough to accommodate the burlap-covered roots of the tree, then cover the surface of surrounding ground with a thick layer of mulch. The tree should be well established by the first snowfall.

Pilsner glass (for light beer)
Ale glass
Ale mug
Standard mixed drink glasses are:
Collins glass
Lemonade glass
Highball glass
Silver cup with a handle (for mint juleps)
Tom and Jerry mug
Punch cup

▶ You can get about 16 1½-ounce drinks from a fifth of liquor.

▶ You can get about eight 3-ounce glasses from a standard 750-milliliter bottle of wine, if you expect to use 3 ounces of wine for each glass. If you are planning a big party, 1.5-liter bottles are a good economical idea.

▶ Beer should be served chilled, at about 45 to 50°F.

Wine Facts

Most of us probably already know that seafood, since it is light in flavor and texture, is best served with white wine. Beef, lamb, and pork need a more strongly flavored red wine. Poultry can go with either red or white, depending on how it's cooked.

If you are cooking a dish that has a wine-based sauce, serve the same wine that you used in the sauce. If the sauce is herby or creamy, choose a fruitier, sweeter wine—such as a Riesling or gewürztraminer. A brisk red wine—such as a Beaujolais or chianti—is great with tomato-based sauces or ones with high acidity.

Always remember that these are just guidelines. If you love Chardonnay, serve it. What you like is the most important thing to consider in the long run. Keep in mind that certain types of ethnic cuisines lend themselves very well to particular wines. Seafood-based Cantonese and Japanese cuisines work very well with crisp, white wines, while spicier cooking—Indian, Mexican, or Thai—seem to do best with robust reds.

Left to right: heirloom stein, everyday stein, pilsner stein, ale glass, and ale mug

Left to right: cocktail glass, other cocktail glass, old-fashioned glass, sour glass, daiquiri/champagne glass, and straight whiskey glass

Left to right: tall tulip glass, Römer, all-purpose tulip glass, bubble glass for sparkling burgundy, pipe-stem sherry glass, brandy snifter, and liqueur glass

Left to right: collins glass, lemonade glass, highball glass, silver cup, Tom and Jerry mug, and punch cup

HOSTING OVERNIGHT GUESTS

BEFORE THEY ARRIVE

▶ Try out your guest room or guest bed one night yourself. You may find that you need to replace a lumpy mattress or simply move a lamp to provide better lighting.

▶ Supply the guest room with books and magazines, an extra robe, and a tray to keep all personal things in one place.

▶ Keep a basket of toiletries—including soap, shampoo, toothpaste, shaving lotion—in your linen closet and put it in the guest room or bathroom before your guests arrive. They may

GARNISHES

Cucumber Twist

Slice unpeeled cucumbers into thin slices. Cut each slice from center to edge. Twist the cut edges in opposite directions. (You can do the same with lemon slices.)

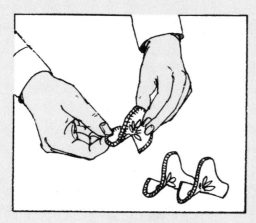

Maraschino Cherry Blossom

Cut canned maraschino cherries into 6 sections, cutting about ¾ of the way through. Spread open the petals and decorate them with leaves cut from a candied green cherry.

Radish Rose

Make 5 thin cuts almost to the stem end of a radish. Cut another 5 slices just above the first slices. Place the radish in iced water in a bowl and refrigerate until the "petals" open up.

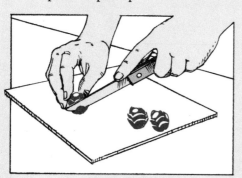

Carrot Flower

With a vegetable peeler, cut around the thick end of a carrot three times to make a spiral strip. Cut a cucumber slice and make a cut from the edge to the center. Lap one cut edge over the other to make a cone, securing with toothpick halves.

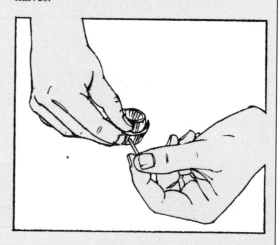

Twist to ruffle the carrot strip; place it in the cucumber to make a flower.

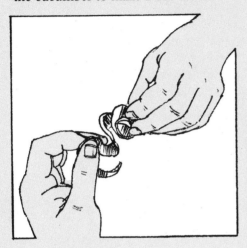

Carrot flowers liven up any dish that needs a touch of color. They are great decorations for salads, dips, rice dishes, cold meats, and roasts.

not need it, but they will appreciate your thoughtfulness.

► Don't expect guests to use the family towels. Supply them with their own.

► Keep a large empty drawer, storage box, or laundry basket handy for instant storage for an unexpected guest.

► Collect maps, transit information, tourist highlights, and pamphlets about your area and put them in basket in a convenient place in the guest room.

DURING THE VISIT

► Make sure you know the schedule of your guests and when they will be eating with you. If you're preparing meals, don't be afraid to ask them about any food allergies or dislikes.

► Most guests feel more comfortable if they don't feel you're doing all the work. If they ask to help, let them.

► Let your guests know where they can find breakfast supplies, in case they want to rise before you do. If you don't ask ahead and don't know what they prefer for breakfast, make sure you have coffee, decaffeinated coffee, tea, herbal tea, and juices on hand.

► Make sure your guests have enough blankets during the winter and a room fan during the summer.

► Don't feel you need to spend every minute with your guests. Let them know your schedule in advance and offer to help them with arranging transportation.

GUEST ETIQUETTE

► Don't expect your hosts to do all the work. Instead of asking if you can do something, pay attention and pitch in. Most hosts will appreciate your help.

► Don't expect your hosts to drop everything to entertain you, particularly if you're in for a long visit. Rent a car and plan your days.

► Keep your belongings in one place. Don't leave personal items in the bathroom.

continued on page 412

NAPKIN FOLDING

A great way to dress up your table is by mastering a few simple napkin folds. All they really involve is pleating, folding, and tucking. Experiment with different colors, textures, and sizes of napkins to make your table setting look really special.

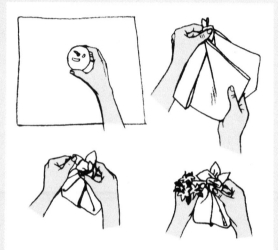

For Brunch

Place a round piece of fruit, such as an apple or orange, in the center of a large napkin. Lift up all four corners, folding down each loose end over to the right-hand side. Slip a napkin ring over the ends. Attach a decoration to the napkin ring.

For a variation, use small boxes of cereal or wrapped rolls instead of the fruit.

For a Festive Lunch

Fold the napkin into quarters so that the open ends are at the bottom. Fold up the top flap one-half of the way to the top. Fold up each remaining flap to

about one inch of the previous flap. Fold back both sides at a slight angle and lay the napkin flat. Tuck in the bottom three flaps to create horizontal lines. Loosely flip over the top flap and tuck a flower into the "vase" that is created.

Remember that this fold looks best with a two-sided print or solid color.

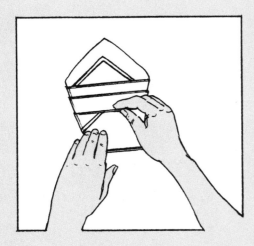

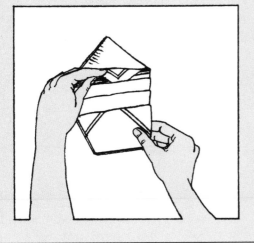

For Special Dinners

Accordion-pleat a napkin from top to bottom in one-inch folds. Being careful to keep the ends pleated, twist the center third of the napkin. Tie the twisted section into a low knot. The top of the napkin should look like a fan; the bottom should look like a fan handle. Slip a tassel through the knot and tie it carefully.

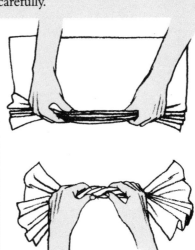

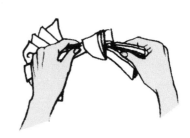

Napkin Folding (continued)

► Most folds require large, square napkins.

► Make sure that the napkins you plan to fold are clean and ironed. Work with clean hands on a clean work surface.

► Cut up an old stained tablecloth into napkin sizes and hem.

► Carefully launder delicate napkins in a mesh bag.

► If the space at your dining table is tight, use smooth, textured cotton napkins and place them directly on the dinner plates. Set the salad plates or bowls on top of the napkins.

► Bread sticks wrapped in a napkin are great kid-pleasers. They also keep extra-ravenous adults happy to wait for their dinner.

► At your next picnic or barbecue, try tucking moistened towelettes into the napkins.

► If you don't have enough matching napkins for all of your guests, just use what you have, but fold them all the same way.

► Roll flatware into napkins at your next buffet. It will make maneuvering a lot easier, and your friends will have less to carry.

► Use a flew blossoms from your centerpiece to decorate the napkins.

► You can use anything for napkin rings—plastic cookie cutters, party favors, pretzels, clip-on animals, oversize paper clips. Be creative!

continued from page 409
leave personal items in the bathroom.

► Keep your room or sleeping place tidy.

► Arrange to take your hosts out to lunch or dinner.

► If you need transportation to and from the airport or train station, ask your hosts when would be the most convenient time for them to pick you up or drop you off. If you're leaving at inconvenient times, take a taxi or a limo.

► Don't overstay your visit. The old rule about fish and visitors after three days still holds true.

► Be sure to thank your hosts for the time spent as their houseguests once you're home. A gift is not inappropriate, but a personal remembrance works just as well. Send photographs of your time together pasted into a scrapbook.

GIFT-GIVING

THE BASICS OF GIFT-GIVING

Gifts needn't be expensive or lavish to send the message that you care about the person you're remembering. The most important element in considering a gift is to think about the recipient, not yourself. Put aside your preferences and think what the recipient might appreciate. While you may look good in pale blue, don't buy a pale blue sweater for someone who never wears the color. Don't forget that the gracious acceptance and acknowledgement of a gift is also an important part of the custom, and get into the habit of sending thank-you notes.

► Keep a list of gifts you give so you don't give the same thing twice.

► If you don't know what someone wants, ask. Children—and even some adults—like making wish lists. You're bound to get at least some idea of their interests from the lists.

▶ To make sure you remember special events, take some time at the end of the year to mark up next year's calendar with birthdays, anniversaries, and other special days that you want to remember. A quick glance at the calendar will give you plenty of time to think about the gift you need to get.

▶ If money is tight, offer your time as a gift. Baby-sitting, cleaning the house, cooking a dinner, or planting a garden can be welcome. Make sure you write or type up your "gift" and schedule a time to follow through.

▶ Flowers, plants, and food are always welcome gifts, but make sure you don't give something that would affect allergies or pose a temptation for those on restricted diets.

▶ Don't give pets as a gift. This rule can be broken only with the absolute assurance of parents that a pet is appropriate for their child.

▶ Finding suitable gifts for adolescents can be difficult; tickets to a concert or a sporting event might be appreciated, but make sure their parents approve of the event and that transportation can be arranged.

▶ U.S. savings bonds are good gifts for older children and adolescents. Buy them in the child's name so their parents won't be taxed on the accumulated interest when they mature and are redeemed.

▶ You'll always have last-minute gifts on hand if you remember to buy doubles of things you need yourself. Such items as jams and preserves, correspondence notes, and toiletries make suitable gifts.

▶ Take advantage of sale items and specials that look like suitable standby gifts. Store these potential gift items in a particular spot. This is also a great way to stock up on holiday stocking stuffers.

▶ When you give stationery, include some stamps. This is an especially thoughtful touch if the recipient can't get around much.

▶ Gift certificates can be wonderful presents, but make sure it won't be difficult for the recipient to use the certificate. To make sure your gift certificate will be welcome, take advantage of hobbies and leisure activities, such as gift certificates to sporting goods stores for sports enthusiasts and yarn shops for needleworkers.

▶ For friends who enjoy the beach or have the luxury of their own swimming pool, a set of plush bath towels is a welcome gift.

▶ If you're in the habit of sending belated greeting cards, take some time one day to buy a number of cards for friends and relatives. Address them and stamp them immediately, and then keep them with your bills. You'll remember to send them when you pay your bills each month.

▶ To make sure you don't forget anyone on your Christmas list, make up next year's holiday card list from the return addresses on the envelopes of this year's cards.

GIFTS FOR SPECIAL OCCASIONS

Birthdays

Birthdays offer the best opportunity to give individualized presents, because your gift is going to only one person. You'll want to take special care to think of the recipient's interests and preferences, rather than your own. When you take the time to consider the recipient's hobbies, leisure interests, even profession, you can easily develop a list of gift ideas. Readers who enjoy mysteries will appreciate the latest new book by a favorite author, teenagers like a tape or compact disc by a favorite group (provided they don't have it already), and a good cook might like a new cookbook. Or you may choose to personalize someone's birthday by using the flower or gemstone traditionally associated with the month of their birth.

Baby Showers

▶ Think big when buying baby shower gifts. Babies are often ready for the six-month size within a couple of months of birth.

▶ Every new parent needs baby shampoo, soap, washcloths, crib sheets, soft towels, disposable diapers, and baby sleepwear.

▶ If you know a young couple needs a big-ticket item, such as a crib, go in with other people attending the shower to present a gift certificate. The present may not inspire oohs and aahs at the shower, but the couple will appreciate your thoughtfulness for years to come.

▶ Second and third children are likely to be using equipment handed down from their older siblings. Instead of baby clothes, think about the future with such ideas as U.S. savings bonds that can be used for college.

▶ Don't forget the new parents. Books on parenting or an offer to babysit can be wonderful presents.

Bridal Showers

▶ For a practical but pretty shower present, buy a laundry basket and attach kitchen gadgets and towels with colored ribbons.

Holidays

▶ To save time, schedule holiday shopping excursions at off hours, right after the stores open or in midafternoon. Avoid the crowds on weekends, lunch hours, and at quitting time if you can.

▶ If your family or circle of friends has expanded to the point where giving holiday gifts has become a burden rather than a pleasure, suggest that everyone draw names and buy a gift for just that person. Use a social occasion to draw names from a hat or designate one family member to draw the names for everyone else.

▶ If you're invited to a Christmas dinner, give a hurricane lamp filled with colored glass ornaments as a centerpiece to your hosts.

▶ Keep a few "general interest" items in stock to avoid embarrassment when you've forgotten to buy a gift. Holiday cookies, preserves, or other food gifts are acceptable to most people.

▶ Start children, teenagers, or young couples on a collection of tree ornaments.

▶ Use recycled lace and pretty fabrics to make individualized Christmas stockings.

Inexpensive Gifts

▶ Edible gifts, such as a loaf of freshly baked bread, a cookie jar or tin filled with home-made cookies, or a plate of fudge, are easy on the budget and almost always welcome.

GIVING FLOWERS

Fresh flowers or plants can become a special gift if you tie the flower to the person's birth month. Use the following list for ideas:

Month	Flower
January	Carnation
February	Violet
March	Daffodil
April	Daisy
May	Lily of the Valley
June	Rose
July	Larkspur
August	Poppy, gladiola
September	Aster, morning glory
October	Calendula
November	Chrysanthemum
December	Holly, narcissus

► Type up your favorite recipes on index cards for a recipe box.

► Dig up outdoor plants—such as begonias or cyclamen—in the fall. Repot the plants or plant the bulbs in decorative pots. After nurturing them for a few months, they'll make great holiday gifts for plant lovers.

► Flats of annuals, along with the offer to plant them, make a good gift for parents on Mother's Day in May and Father's Day in June.

► If you don't consider your time expensive, many homemade gifts—such as wood cutting boards crafted by a woodworker, dried flower arrangements, or handmade wreaths—can be inexpensive.

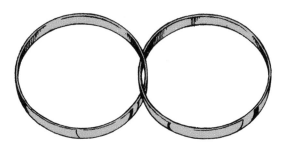

Weddings

► A gift of money in the form of a check is always appropriate; don't send or give cash, which could be lost in the mail or at the wedding.

► If the couple is registered with a gift registry, by all means use this listing. It's better to give the couple what they would like than another pair of candlesticks.

► If giving linens or towels, make sure you know the couple's preferences or be sure that the gift can be exchanged.

► If you intend to have gifts monogrammed or engraved, make sure you know the initials the bride will be using and make sure they want the gift.

► For relatives or special friends, a homemade gift—such as a quilt, afghan, or wooden

utensil or cabinet—is entirely appropriate and often more welcome than a store-bought one.

► Avoid cutesy gifts or gifts that are in bad taste. They speak volumes about the sender.

GIFT WRAPPING

First impressions are everything—how a package looks on the outside sets the tone for the gift inside. After all, even the most

BIRTHDAY GEMSTONES

Gemstones have long been associated with specific months and birthdays. In fact, opals are considered unlucky except for those born in October. Although jewelry is usually expensive, you can find simulated stones or even chips to commemorate someone's special birthday. And don't forget that with enough advance notice, local artisans can adapt their designs to include stones or chips in earrings, pendants, bracelets, rings, and cufflinks.

Month	Gemstone
January	Garnet
February	Amethyst
March	Bloodstone, jasper, or aquamarine
April	Diamond or sapphire
May	Emerald
June	Pearl, moonstone, or alexandrite
July	Ruby or turquoise
August	Carnelian or periodot
September	Sapphire or chrysolite
October	Opal, tourmaline, or beryl
November	Topaz
December	Lapis lazuli, turquoise, or zircon

wonderful gifts seem inadequate when presented in a shabby wrapping with little attention paid to small—but special—details. Today, choosing the perfect paper is not limited to traditional wrapping papers. Take a look at winning options such as versatile cellophane, brilliant mylar, interesting scraps of fabric, lacy doilies, handmade marbled and textured papers, newspaper pages, pearlized tissue papers, sturdy wallpaper, scented drawer liners—even bandannas, scarves, and ribbons. While the possibilities for a winning wrap are virtually endless, it's nice to know one failproof, quick and easy wrapping technique that works every time.

Be sure to organize your gift-wrapping chores by storing wrapping paper rolls in a narrow wastebasket, along with scissors, tags, transparent tape, and marking pens of assorted colors. If it's not too used-looking, smooth out wrapping paper from gifts you've received and use it again. Don't forget that you can iron paper that's not too flimsy.

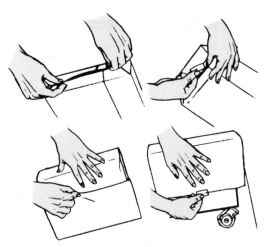

It's a Wrap

To get started, first decide how much paper you'll need using the following formulas:

Paper Width = Box Length + Box Height + 2 inches

Paper Length = (2×Box Width) + (2×Box Height) + 2 inches

For example, for a basic shirt box measuring 11½ (l) 8½ (w)×1½ (h) inches, you will need a 22×15-inch sheet of

WRAPPING CHILDREN'S GIFTS

▶ Let your children draw colorful designs on white craft paper. When they've finished, use the paper to wrap the gift and top with a few crayons.

▶ Roll or bundle bright-colored cellophane around an awkward-size gift. Tie it with yarn or a pair of neon sneaker shoelaces.

▶ Use a 21×21-inch bandanna and elastic cord to tie up a gift for a child or adolescent.

▶ Use a brightly colored mesh tote bag as a holder for small gifts or beach toys.

▶ Decorate a brown paper gift bag with stickers or acrylic paints.

▶ Use the Sunday comics for wrapping paper.

wrapping paper. For a square box measuring 7×7×7 inches, you will need a 30×16-inch sheet. If you're wrapping a box with slightly different measurements than those contained in this book, don't be discouraged. Simply adjust the sizes to fit your box.

Once you've determined how much paper to cut, rely on these quick and easy steps:

1. Place the sheet of wrapping paper on a work surface. Center the box, wrong-side up, on the wrapping paper so that the long side of the box runs parallel to the short side of the paper. Working with the long side of the box facing forward, bring the bottom edge of the paper

toward the center of the box. Secure with double-sided tape.

2. Fold down the top edge of the paper ½ inch. Place a length of tape along the fold. Bring the folded top portion toward the center of the box, pressing the taped fold firmly against the box to seal.

3. To wrap the ends, fold the sides of the paper in toward the center so that the paper forms triangular flaps at the top and bottom of the box. Press along the folds firmly to crease. Fold the top triangle down toward the center of the box, pressing firmly. Secure with double-sided tape.

GIFTS FOR ANNIVERSARIES

If you like to recognize anniversaries but don't know what to get a couple, use the following lists of traditional and contemporary wedding symbols to generate some gift ideas.

Year	Traditional Gifts	Contemporary Gifts	Other Gift Ideas
1	Paper	Clocks	Stationery, travel clock
2	Cotton, calico	China	Towels, serving bowl
3	Leather	Crystal, glass	Wallets, wine glasses
4	Books	Electrical appliances	Cookbook, juicer, coffee grinder
5	Wood	Silverware	Tree or shrub, wooden untensil, silver ladle
6	Iron, candy	Wood	Chocolates, cutting board, tray
7	Wool, copper	Desk sets	Afghan, copper bowl, picture frames
8	Bronze	Linens, laces	Figurine, bed linens, edged pillow
9	Pottery	Leather	Bowl, key chains
10	Tin, aluminum	Diamond jewelry	Cookware, cufflinks, pendant
11	Steel	Fashion jewelry	Cookware, earrings, tie tack
12	Silk, linen	Pearls	Bedding, necklace
13	Lace	Textiles	Shawl, pillows
14	Ivory	Gold jewelry	Synthetic ivory figurine, gold chains
15	Crystal, glass	Watches	Stemware, glass bowl, sport watches
20	China	Platinum	Platter, soup tureen, bracelets
25	Silver	Silver	Coffee service, serving spoon, picture frame
30	Pearl	Diamond	
35	Coral	Jade	
40	Ruby	Ruby	
45	Sapphire	Sapphire	
50	Gold	Gold	
55	Emerald	Emerald	
60	Diamond	Diamond	

PRESENTS BY MAIL

A beautifully wrapped present lovingly sent by mail brings immeasurable pleasure to its lucky recipient. To make sure your package arrives in mint condition, review the handy checklist below.

▶ If the gift you're planning to mail is especially fragile, first wrap it in protective bubble paper available at packaging stores before you wrap it in paper. Place the gift in the gift box and fill all around the gift with protective loose fill or styrofoam peanuts, shredded tissue, or straw. Then wrap the box as desired.

▶ Make sure the box you're planning to use is sturdy and stable. The box should provide ample space all around the gift for a protective packing material.

▶ Fill the bottom of the box with the desired protective packing material.

▶ Overwrap the wrapped gift in a protective plastic bag. This keeps the packing material from becoming entangled in the bow or decorative adornment and allows the recipient to easily lift the gift from the box. In addition, the plastic covering protects the gift in case the box should become damaged by water while in transit. You can use a cooking bag for small packages; a small trash bag works well for large packages.

▶ Place the gift in the mailing box. Add additional packing material to secure the gift on all sides.

▶ Tape the box shut using box sealing tape suitable for mailing.

▶ Properly label the gift, double-checking names and addresses, and be sure to include the name and address inside the box in case the label gets damaged. Be sure to mark food gifts properly. Consult your local packaging store if you have questions regarding the best way to wrap and send a perishable gift.

▶ Recycling tip: Many local packaging stores recycle styrofoam peanuts and other plastic-based packaging. Ask at your local store before you discard this material in the trash.

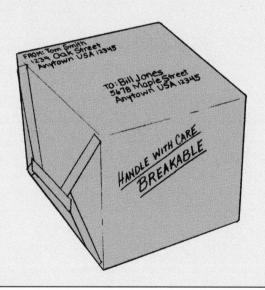

4. Fold the bottom triangle up toward the center of the box, pressing firmly and overlapping the top triangle. Fold down the top triangle ½ inch. Secure the folded triangle with double-sided tape. Repeat on the opposite end of the package. Turn the package right-side up.

Basic wrapping materials:

▶ A pair of scissors

▶ Double-sided tape or glue

▶ A sturdy ruler

▶ Extras: acrylic paints, brushes, sponges, markers, stencil patterns

Bow Basics

Once wrapped, one of the simplest ways to lend a finishing flourish is to top your gift with a brilliant, sumptuously tied bow. It may look difficult, but tying a beautiful bow is as easy as tying your shoe. It's a matter of building on the basics. Here's how it works.

To create an eye-catching double bow, first place an appropriate length (generally (2 × Box Width) + (2 × Box Height)) of the ribbon under the wrapped box with equal ends extending. Bring the ends together at the center and tie them into a single knot. Pass the end of a second length of ribbon (approximately 1 to 1½ yards) under the knot. Bring the ends together and tie them into a

MAKE YOUR OWN PAPER

There's absolutely no limit to the number of elegant packages you can create when you rely on store-bought wrapping papers. But presenting an extraordinary package wrapped in a pretty paper that you created yourself adds to the enjoyment of both giving and receiving. Whether it's a whimsically sponged, stamped, or stenciled paper for the kids or an elegantly drizzled and painted paper for that once-in-a-lifetime occasion, there's a fun and easy technique to suit your gift-giving needs. Check out your local craft, party, or stationery stores for a great selection of ready-to-use stamps, stencils, paints, and craft sponges.

Although ready-made craft sponges are available in a variety of shapes and sizes, you can easily create your own pleasing designs using the following tips:

1. Draw your design onto tracing paper or plain white paper. Cut out the design and place it on a dry sponge. (For best results, choose a sponge with tiny holes.)
2. Using a pen or felt-tip marker, trace the design onto the sponge.
3. Cut out the design with sharp scissors and you're set.

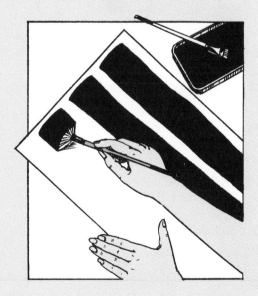

bow over the knot. To make a double bow, pass a second length (1 to 1½ yards) of ribbon under the first bow. Bring the ends together once again at the center and tie the second length into a bow over the knot of the first bow. To make a triple or a quadruple bow, simply repeat again using a third or fourth length of ribbon of the same length.

▶ Dress up a plainly wrapped package by spelling out the recipient's name or a greeting from letters cut from newspaper or magazine headlines.

▶ If your mother or father likes to cook, use an oven mitt as the wrapping for a small Mother's Day or Father's Day gift, especially if the practical mitt hides something exotic—like a piece of jewelry or a bottle of perfume or cologne.

Creative Gift-Wrapping

▶ Wrap a baby gift in a receiving blanket or diaper.

▶ Use a paper Christmas tablecloth to wrap an oversize Christmas gift. It is easier to handle than several sheets of ordinary wrapping paper.

▶ Pack gifts in practical baskets or decorative tins or containers. Your gift will be doubly useful, and you won't have to buy wrapping paper and ribbon.

▶ If a paint or wallpaper store will give you old wallpaper sample books, you can use the sample pages as gift-wrapping paper—elegance at no cost at all.

If you don't want to take the time to learn anything about your finances, hire someone to do it for you. Managing your money isn't a full-time job, but you do need some financial savvy in today's world to make the right decisions about how to plan a budget, buy or sell a home, and plan for your retirement. If you neglect this area of your life, it's highly likely that your family will suffer down the road. While it may seem that today's financial dealings are extremely complicated, they become much easier when you break them into segments and learn what you need to know as you go.

MANAGING YOUR MONEY

Setting up a budget and sticking to it, contributing to savings, buying the right insurance for your family's needs, and making sure you have a will that protects your family are key ingredients to a healthy financial picture. Earning more money or winning the lottery will only brighten your financial outlook if you know how to wisely spend and save your money.

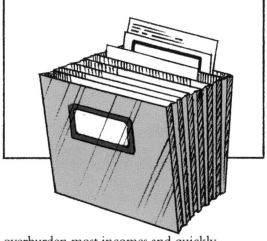

ESTABLISHING A FAMILY BUDGET

What you save depends on many factors— your current expenses, savings earmarked for other expenses (college education, house purchase, etc.), job stability, current income, and potential future earnings. A good rule of thumb to go by is to save 10 percent of your income.

▶ First and foremost, to live within a budget means avoiding credit-card debt. Spending money to pay interest on credit-card charges means that you are not living within a budget. Annual interest charges of 18 to 20 percent

overburden most incomes and quickly undercut savings plans. Also remember that interest paid on credit-card debt no longer can be deducted against other income on your federal tax return.

▶ If you have to borrow, borrow from a bank or credit union where you will pay reasonable interest rates. If your family is in serious credit-card debt, arrange to see a credit counselor; a budget may not be enough to get you out of a serious financial hole.

▶ If you currently lack a household budget or savings plan, consider establishing a plan or making some arrangement to save on a monthly basis. Many people find that credit union deductions or automatic savings deposits from their paychecks help them meet monthly savings goals. If you classify yourself as a "spender," rather than a "saver," find a way to defeat your spending tendencies. You may need to consult a professional for help.

▶ It's somewhat optimistic to assume you'll never dip into your savings. Unless you are an unusually disciplined saver, you should adjust your savings plan to account for some emergencies or contingencies. An emergency fund in your savings account should equal at least two months' income.

▶ Try to take advantage of tax-deferred savings plans. The benefits of tax-free and compound savings nearly always pay off, particularly for retirement savings.

▶ Think of your savings plan as a long-term commitment when considering strategies and instruments. Don't let a temporary setback disrupt your long-term goals.

▶ If you set a savings goal and discover there is no way for you to maintain your savings contribution, you need to make some major adjustments in your attitudes, spending habits, or future earning capacity. In some cases, it may pay to consult a professional financial counselor.

▶ Set both short-range and long-range goals in your budget. Goals might include a new car next year, a university education for 10 years down the road, and retirement for yourself in 25 years. Setting goals gives you the incentive to control your spending.

▶ Don't punish yourself or your family. Avoid setting goals that will overly tax your earning or savings abilities. Keep in mind that a budget is a lifetime plan, not a crash diet.

▶ A simple way to budget if there's more than one worker in your household is to use one of your paychecks each month to meet a big expense, such as an installment payment or the rent, and to use all other paychecks to cover the monthly expenses.

▶ Don't worry about tracing every expenditure down to the last penny. This wastes too much time and often causes family arguments. Instead, overlook the inevitable small items that you can't seem to track down. Most people have a few dollars' worth of such unaccountable expenses every month. Attempting to pinpoint them entails useless bookkeeping.

▶ If your cash flow is unmanageable because several large household payments fall due within a short time, arrange a more convenient payment time for some of them. For example, if taxes and an insurance premium are due the same month, contact the insurance company to see about rescheduling your premium due date.

▶ Establish when your regular bills—including credit-card accounts—are due each month, and work out the most convenient order in which to pay them over the course of the month. You will avoid service charges wherever possible and avoid being hit with a whole bunch of bills that have to be paid at the same time.

THE INVESTMENT TRIANGLE

There is no perfect investment. Even the "safest" investments provide little protection against inflation. Most financial professionals advise investors to diversify their investments to safeguard against risk.

If you visualize your investments as an upright triangle with a secure base, you can understand how diversification works:

▶ The base—and largest—tier at the bottom is constructed of income-oriented, secure investments, such as bank CDs, money market funds, and government securities. All of these investments carry little risk of loss of principal.

▶ Once this base is established, the investor can add tiers to the triangle. The second tier includes growth-oriented investments that carry a low risk of principal, such as life insurance, highly rated corporate and municipal bonds, and bond mutual funds. This tier generates some income and has some growth potential.

▶ Investors with larger amounts of capital can add additional tiers. The third tier includes growth-oriented investments, which carry a significant risk of loss of principal. The secure base of the first two tiers allows the investor to handle more risk at the triangle's higher levels.

▶ The fourth tier includes growth-oriented investments, such as real estate and capital appreciation stocks, which carry higher amounts of risk, but offer higher return potential.

▶ The top tier consists of investments that offer the greatest potential for appreciation and the greatest risk of loss. These include commodities, options, futures, and venture capital.

▶ Remember that safety comes first. Unless you establish a firm base, you cannot afford greater risk.

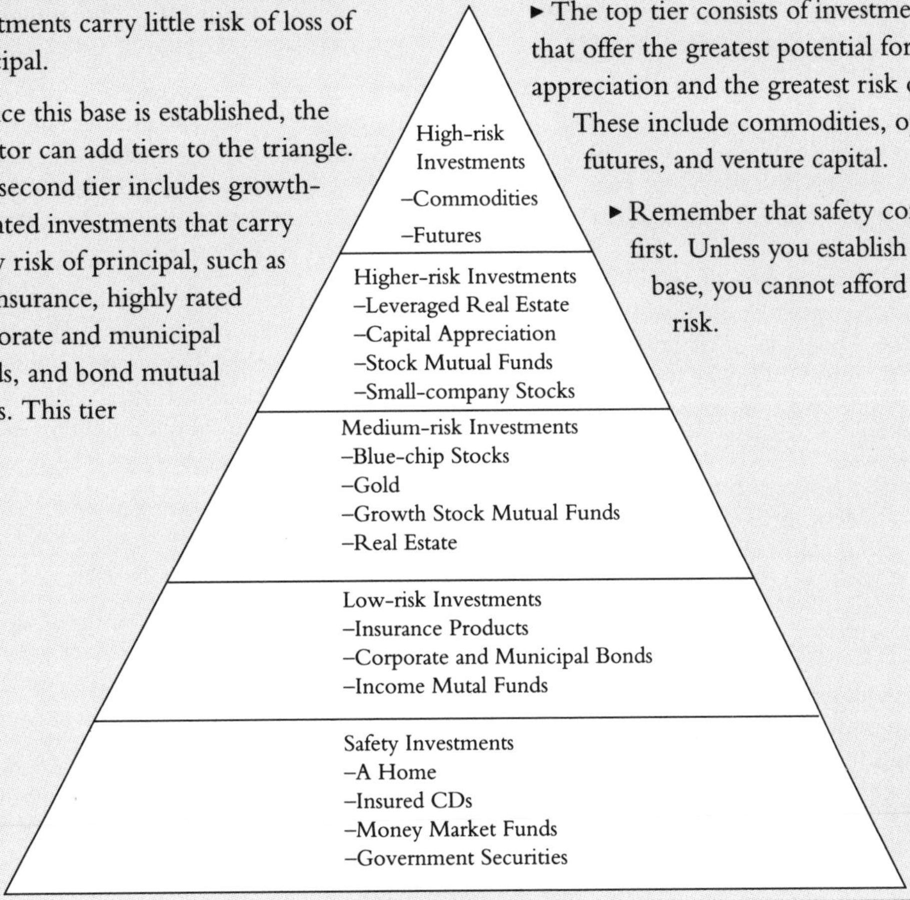

High-risk
Investments
–Commodities
–Futures

Higher-risk Investments
–Leveraged Real Estate
–Capital Appreciation
–Stock Mutual Funds
–Small-company Stocks

Medium-risk Investments
–Blue-chip Stocks
–Gold
–Growth Stock Mutual Funds
–Real Estate

Low-risk Investments
–Insurance Products
–Corporate and Municipal Bonds
–Income Mutal Funds

Safety Investments
–A Home
–Insured CDs
–Money Market Funds
–Government Securities

► To avoid having family expenditures occur simultaneously, stagger the medical and dental checkups of family members.

► When budgeting for clothes, plan to spend the most money on items you'll wear frequently. An expensive winter coat is a more sensible buy, for example, than a costly evening dress that you'll wear only occasionally.

SAVINGS STRATEGIES

If your household lives from paycheck to paycheck, the best thing you can do for yourself is learn how to save money, even if it's only $5 or $10 a week. Without savings, you cannot cope well with emergencies or invest for the future.

► Even after you've paid off a loan, continue paying out the same amount to your own savings account every month. You are used to making the payment, so you won't miss the amount so much.

► If you find it difficult to save money, force yourself to do so by purchasing United States savings bonds under a payroll savings plan where you're employed, or by means of a bond-a-month plan at your local bank. You can build sizable savings over the years by authorizing small, regular deductions from your paychecks. There may be shrewder ways to invest, but there are no better ways to save. When you've built up a nest egg, divide it among several sound investments.

► Consider further education to increase your salary potential. Many employers help out with tuition, and if your company does, take advantage of the program.

► Avoid wasting money on a service contract when you buy an expensive appliance. The contract price will typically be low for the first year when you can reasonably expect that nothing in the appliance is likely to go wrong. However, for each succeeding year, when things are more likely to go wrong, the contract may cost you more than it's worth paying.

► Cut down on your magazine subscription bills by trading magazines with your neighbors and friends.

► When a repair estimate is more than 15 percent of an appliance's replacement cost, seriously consider buying a new appliance.

► If you really don't need a second car, make do with only one car and rearrange your schedules and appointments accordingly. Not only will you save the price of the car, you'll save in insurance and maintenance costs, and state and local annual fees.

► To conserve money, pay cash for things you'll soon use up, such as food items and cleaning supplies. Use credit only for things you'll continue to use after you've finished paying for them, or for emergencies, such as medical bills.

► Make your own house-cleaning products, which offer substantial savings over commercial cleaning solutions.

► Save on supermarket costs by preparing shopping lists for a full week of planned menus. Always plan menus so you can make good use of store specials and leftovers.

► Avoid buying nonfood items for sale in supermarkets. Shop for such items at discount outlets that specialize in nonfood products, where you'll usually find these products priced lower.

▶ It pays to use "cents off" coupons when buying food, particularly if stores "double" coupons. Look for such coupons in your daily newspaper as well as in shopper "throwaways" and mailers, but avoid buying items—no matter what the savings—that you don't typically use.

▶ Trade your extra food discount coupons with neighbors and friends, or form a club in the neighborhood that meets at intervals to exchange coupons.

▶ When shopping for durable items, save on gasoline and wear and tear on your car by using mail-order catalogs.

▶ Take a calculator with you to the store. It makes it much easier to figure out price comparisons and make sure you're getting the best-priced item.

▶ Although it's convenient to buy sandwich fixings already sliced, you'll save money buying meats and cheeses in chunks and slicing them yourself.

▶ Don't automatically associate brand names and high prices with high-quality merchan-

dise. Some of the best bargains are lower priced or generic.

▶ Take advantage of storewide clearance sales after Christmas, Easter, and July 4th. You'll find bargains galore in linens, clothes, and scores of other items.

▶ The best time to buy back-to-school clothing for youngsters is at the *end* of September.

▶ When you purchase furniture it makes good financial sense to buy the best quality you can afford. Cheap furniture wears out or goes out of style quickly—necessitating the purchase of more cheap furniture. High-quality furniture generally remains in style longer and stays in good condition for many years.

▶ Buying clothes out of season allows you to save 50 percent or even more on in-season prices. Storewide clearance sales are usually held after Easter, July 4th, and Christmas and offer values on off-season garments.

▶ November is a good time to buy men's and women's overcoats at reduced prices; that's when merchants offer bargains to hype pre-Christmas business.

▸ Curtail hospital expenses by avoiding being admitted on a Friday. Friday admissions result in longer stays than admissions on another day. For the shortest length of stay, try to have yourself (or any family member) admitted on a Tuesday.

SAVINGS BONDS

The safety, low minimum investment, and ease of purchase of savings bonds have made

them popular investments with Americans since they were first issued. The interest rate accrued on the Series EE bonds is variable, but a minimum rate of 6 percent is guaranteed if they are held for five years. Note that this guaranteed rate can and has changed. Some bonds purchased before 1987 pay a guaranteed minimum rate of 7.5 percent.

All savings bonds are registered in the name(s) of the owner, and Series EE bonds can be bought at most commercial banks. The purchase price is one-half of their face value ($25, $50, $75, $100, $200, $500, $1,000, $5,000, and $10,000). The return on the investment is the difference between the purchase price and the value of the bond at maturity.

These are accrual-type securities. Interest earned on the bonds is *accrued;* it is not paid until the bonds are redeemed. After six months and before five years, Series EE bonds can be cashed in and the owner will receive the principal investment, not the face value, plus interest based on a fixed, graduated scale. No interest is paid on bonds bought and redeemed within the same calendar year.

Advantages of Savings Bonds

▸ They are direct obligations of the U.S. Treasury, making them very safe investments.

▸ Interest earned is exempt from state and local income taxes.

▸ Bonds are replaced without charge if lost.

▸ Series EE bonds can be bought for small amounts of money at any time through most

continued on page 430

TAX-DEFERRED SAVINGS

Think of tax-deferred savings as an interest-free loan from Uncle Sam. You are able to avoid paying taxes on your money, which allows your money to earn interest tax free.

▸ Take advantage of any tax-deferred savings plan offered by your employer, particularly if the employer matches all or a portion of your contributions.

▸ Find out if you are eligible for a tax-deferred IRA contribution of up to $2,000 annually.

▸ If you are self-employed, set up a Keough plan or a Simplified Employee Pension (SEP) plan. Your accountant can help you determine which is the best strategy based on the terms of your self-employment.

▸ Don't use a tax-deferred savings plan for any money that may be needed for emergencies. There is a hefty penalty for withdrawing money too early.

▸ Avoid high-risk investments with tax-deferred money, because you will not be able to deduct any losses against other income.

YOUR RIGHTS AS AN INVESTOR

▶ Any kind of advertising, including solicitation by phone, is expected to be honest. False or misleading advertising is subject to civil, criminal, or regulatory penalties. But that doesn't mean that advertising brochures will disclose all you need to know about a product. Avoid investing in anything on this basis alone.

▶ Make sure you are aware of all the factors that will affect the performance of an investment. Be sure to find out whether a firm selling an investment has had prior regulatory problems.

▶ Ask for all available literature about the investment. If there is a prospectus, read it before making an investment. Obtain annual reports about companies and any credit ratings by agencies.

▶ Ask for a written explanation of the risks of an investment, all costs, and any obligations on your part as an investor. You have the right to full disclosure of any costs that will be incurred. These could include sales charges, fees or commissions, and maintenance or service charges. Also, make sure you know whether you will have access to your funds or if they will be restricted, or if there will be a penalty for early withdrawal.

▶ Avoid high-pressure sales tactics. This is a sure sign of a risky investment. Most

reputable investment advisers will not push you into anything that will make you uncomfortable.

▶ As an investor, you have the right to "responsible" advice. In the securities industry, brokers are obliged to make sure investment advice is appropriate for the customer. Beware of someone who insists that an investment is right for you without knowing much about your financial picture.

▶ Keep track of your account. Learn how to read statements you receive regarding your investment. If something suggests that your account is being traded without your permission, contact the firm immediately.

▶ If you believe your account has been handled dishonestly or unfairly, you have the right to seek a remedy, either through arbitration, mediation, or court.

PUTTING YOUR BUDGET ON PAPER

This sample budget can be used in one of two ways. Either go through your bills and figure out how you've been spending your money, or budget where you want to spend your money, making sure that it accurately reflects those expenses over which you have no control, such as insurance premiums and rent or mortgage payment. If your expenses are larger than your income, use the following section on saving strategies to figure out where you can cut your costs to implement a reasonable budget for your family.

		Annual Expenses	Monthly Expenses	Monthly Income
Housing	Rent/house payment			
	Insurance			
	Property tax			
	Repairs			
	Improvements			
Transportation	Car payment			
	Car insurance			
	Commuting			
	Gas			
	Maintenance			
	Registry fees			
Food	Groceries			
	Dining out			
	School lunches			
	Work lunches			
Medical	Checkups			
	Dental visits			
	Insurance			
	Prescriptions			
	Other			
Utilities	Heat			
	Electricity			
	Phone			
	Water			

		Annual Expenses	Monthly Expenses	Monthly Income
Household	Allowances			
	Dues/fees			
	Cleaning supplies			
	Cleaning service			
	Clothing			
	Furnishings			
	Gifts			
	Haircuts			
	Life insurance			
	Newspapers/magazines			
	Paper supplies			
	Other			
Entertainment	Books			
	Concerts			
	Music			
	Sports			
	Vacations			
	Videos			
	Other			
Other	Credit card payments			
	Other loan payments			
	College loan			
	Other			
Savings	Charitable contributions			
	Credit union			
	Savings account			
	Tax-deferred savings			
	Education/tuition			
	Other			
	TOTALS			

continued from page 426

commercial banks and savings and loan associations. They pay a variable rate of interest, which can cushion your investment if interest rates rise.

▸ U.S. savings bonds cannot be called in by the Treasury.

Disadvantages of Savings Bonds

▸ There is a $30,000 annual limit on the face value of Series EE bonds that may be bought by an individual.

▸ They cannot be sold, given away, or used as collateral.

▸ Series EE bonds cashed in during the same calendar year in which they are bought earn no interest.

▸ Series EE bonds redeemed before five years from the issue date are not guaranteed a minimum rate.

▸ Series EE bonds cannot be redeemed in the first six months after they are purchased.

▸ Any bonds older than 40 years no longer accrue interest. Check the maturity dates of any old bonds you own and consider whether to keep them, exchange them for other bonds, or simply redeem them.

Using Savings Bonds for College Tuition

Beginning with bonds purchased in 1990, the interest earned on Series EE savings bonds may be excluded from federal income tax if they are redeemed to pay tuition and fees at colleges, universities, and qualified technical

schools and if your family meets income limitations.

Even if your family does not meet requirements for the Education Tax Benefit outlined below, you can reduce taxes paid on interest by purchasing the bonds in your child's name. When he or she redeems them, interest will be taxed at the child's tax bracket, not yours. Make sure that you do not co-own the bonds, but you can list yourself as the beneficiary.

Eligibility criteria for the Education Tax Benefit include:

▶ The bonds must be issued in 1990 or later and be in the name of a person who is at least 24 years old in the month before the bonds are purchased.

▶ If bonds are intended to benefit a dependent's children, they must be issued in either one or both parents' names; the child cannot be listed as the owner or co-owner, but can be registered as the beneficiary.

▶ The bonds must be redeemed in the year the bond owner pays qualified educational expenses to an eligible educational institution. Room, board, and books are not qualified educational expenses in this instance.

▶ Interest is excluded from federal income tax only if the qualifying tuition and fees paid during the year are equal to or more than the value of the redeemed bonds, including interest paid. For example, if you redeem $10,000 worth of bonds and pay $8,000 in tuition, 80 percent of the interest income would be excluded from federal income tax.

▶ Income limits cannot be exceeded and apply to the year of redemption of the bonds. To qualify for full exclusion of tax on the interest in 1992, a single parent could earn $44,150 or less to qualify; a married couple filing a joint return could earn $66,200 or less. Income is considered Modified Adjusted Gross Income, which includes the bond's interest before exclusion. Inflation levels are adjusted annually.

▶ The amount of interest that can be excluded is gradually reduced for higher incomes and phased out entirely for single persons with incomes above $59,150 and married couples filing jointly with income above $96,200.

Information regarding the current rates on Treasury Bonds is available by calling 1-800-US-BONDS. In Washington, D.C., call USA-8888.

BANKING AND CREDIT

▶ Avoid passbook savings accounts that compound money annually, rather than monthly or quarterly.

▶ If possible, never withdraw funds from a savings account before the stated interest payment date. If you do withdraw prematurely, you'll lose all the interest due for that particular interest period.

▶ When you receive a check, deposit it at once. First of all, you'll collect more money in an interest-bearing checking account; secondly, many banks won't honor checks that are two or three months old.

▶ Don't keep more money than is necessary in a checking account that doesn't pay interest, unless maintaining a minimum balance qualifies you for free checking or other benefits.

▶ Remember that endorsing a check and depositing it doesn't mean you have that cash to draw on immediately. When making the deposit, ask the teller how long the check will take to clear so that you'd know when you'll be able to write your own checks against it.

▶ It doesn't pay to postdate a check, because a bank may refuse to accept it or may hold it until its date is reached. The bank's caution is understandable: If the check is charged to your account before you expected it to be, it might cause other checks that you've written to bounce.

▶ It's smart to obtain maximum lines of credit well in advance of need. If a credit card grantor opens your account with several hundred dollars' worth of credit, request an increase after six months, even though you may not actually need it. Continue to pump up your credit availability until you achieve the maximum line. That way, it's there when and if you need it.

▶ If you're planning to move out of the area covered by your local credit bureau, you may have trouble reestablishing credit quickly. For fast action on new credit applications, keep several copies of your credit file from the bureau covering the area where you used to live.

▶ Maintain your credit standing if you're temporarily unable to make a payment on a debt. See your creditor and discuss rearranging the payment schedule with him or her. Most creditors are understanding about this. They're not understanding if you try to avoid them.

▶ To avoid being irritated by a collection notice that you know is due to a creditor's error (a not uncommon occurrence), pay the item in question if it's less than $25. Immediately forward your statement, with a complete explanation of the error, to the creditor. Your account should reflect a correction within 30 days.

▶ A good way to keep out of credit binds is to completely pay off a series of payments before committing yourself to a new series of payments for something else.

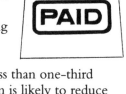

▶ Try not to put down less than a one-third cash payment when purchasing a car, or to let the financing extend more than 36 months. With less than one-third down, a car's depreciation is likely to reduce its market value faster than you can shrink the balance of the loan.

▶ Whatever you do, don't sign a credit contract that contains a "balloon" clause. A balloon clause stipulates a final payment that's much larger than any of the installments that precede it. If you discover such a clause too late, you may lose property after having paid a hefty part of its price, or be forced to refinance at disadvantageous terms.

▶ Offer the best security you can when taking out a loan. When you secure a loan with top-notch collateral, you usually get it at a cheaper rate than on your signature only.

▶ Always make sure that all collateralized loan balances are less than the collateral's value. For instance, auto loans that entail a lien on the car should be reduced more rapidly than the decline in the car's resale value.

▶ It's foolhardy to use emergency funds as collateral for a loan. If you default in payment and the funds are seized, you'll have painted yourself into a corner should any catastrophe occur.

▶ Avoid any loan that permits repossession of the property purchased without providing cancellation of the full amount of the debt at the time of repossession.

▶ To save on interest charges when borrowing money, make the largest down payment possible and repay the balance in the shortest time possible. (It's always expensive to make a small down payment and to extend the life of a loan excessively.)

▶ If you plan to take out a loan to finance a vacation, make certain you can pay it completely within one year. Otherwise, you may grudgingly be paying off this year's vacation when next year's vacation time rolls around.

▶ It seldom pays to borrow money from small loan companies, because their interest rates are often significantly higher than those of banks or established savings and loan associations.

▶ Avoid commercial debt poolers at all costs. They will charge you as much as 35 percent of your debts for lumping them all together and collecting one regular periodic payment from you.

CONTROLLING INSURANCE COSTS

The most important tool to reduce costs in buying insurance is to shop around for a policy. Compare the loss ratios of different companies. A loss ratio is the percentage of premiums that a company pays back to its policyholders in benefits. A high loss ratio means a good value for you. A company that returns 60 percent of its premiums to policyholders is a better value than one returning only 30 percent.

Unless you're totally satisfied, you're under no obligation to purchase an insurance policy. Keep in mind that the inflated price

sometimes quoted by one insurer over another is purportedly due to so-called "service." Never accept this as a valid reason for an extreme cost difference between two policies that are otherwise roughly identical. Make certain the price you pay is truly competitive,

CHECKING YOUR CREDIT AND MEDICAL RECORDS

Credit records are compiled by major credit bureaus, including Equifax, Trans Union, and TRW, whenever you apply for a loan, a mortgage, a credit card, and sometimes even a job. To make sure this report is accurate, get a copy (for a nominal fee) before you apply for credit. If you have been denied credit, this report is free.

▶ To correct any errors, explain the error in writing to the credit bureau. By law, it must reverify the information or remove it from the report.

▶ If there are problems with your credit, you can write a letter of explanation up to 100 words long that must be included with the report.

▶ Negative information can be kept for seven years; bankruptcy information can be kept for ten years.

▶ The Medical Information Bureau compiles both medical and nonmedical information used by insurance companies. Although the bureau helps protect insurance companies from fraud, this information can be obtained by prospective employers. Any records you or your family may have can be obtained for free. If you find an error, be sure to discuss it with your physician.

and find out whether you can save money by paying insurance premiums annually, rather than quarterly or twice a year.

▶ Make sure you can prove any insurance claims. One of the best ways is to take some photos or a videotape of the insured property—your car and every wall in every room—and store them somewhere outside the home for safekeeping, preferably in a safety deposit box. If a claim has to be made, these pictures will show exactly what the property looked like before it was damaged.

Car Insurance

▶ Maintain only the auto insurance coverage you need. You may wish to dispense with collision and comprehensive coverage on older cars if you can afford to pick up any possible losses yourself. You should, however, have liability insurance on every car you own.

▶ Buy substantial deductibles on auto insurance, if you want to save money on your comprehensive and collision coverage. This can reduce your premium anywhere from 45 to 56 percent.

▶ If you are 65 years or older, the auto insurance rates in many states are substantially lower.

Health Insurance

▶ If your employer offers several different packages of insurance, compare them carefully, even if opting for one plan means that your family will have to switch physicians.

▶ If your employer does not offer health insurance, check out group insurance plans available through professional organizations. These plans offer substantial savings over individual plans, even when the cost of dues is considered.

▶ If you are over 65, make sure you understand the basic provisions of Medicare coverage so that you do not pay for additional health insurance that merely parallels it. Neither Medicare nor most "medigap" policies cover long-term nursing care.

▶ If you lose your job, you may be able to extend your health insurance through your former employer under COBRA (Consolidated Omnibus Budget Reconciliation Act) provisions for a certain length of time. While you will have to pay for

WHAT TO KEEP IN A SAFETY DEPOSIT BOX

▶ A copy of your will—not the original

▶ Stock certificates, bond certificates, and bank savings certificates—not passbooks

▶ Insurance policies—not life insurance policies

▶ Property records, such as mortgages, deeds, and titles—not burial plot deeds

▶ Birth certificates, marriage licenses, divorce papers, military discharge papers, passports, and other personal documents

▶ List of valuable items with costs, purchase dates, and photos

this coverage, it is usually much less expensive than individual health insurance policies.

▶ If you are retiring at 65 and are thus eligible for Medicare but your spouse is not, see if you are able to extend coverage from your employer under the COBRA provisions.

▶ Some insurance products provide for long-term nursing home care, but they are very expensive. The fees could be warranted, however, if your family has a history of chronic mental disease.

Home Insurance

▶ The ideal insurance policy should protect the homeowner against all of the hazards itemized in the basic HO-1 (homeowner's) policy, plus $100,000 or more of personal liability, plus any perils that frequently occur in the area, such as snow damage or floods.

▶ The policy should provide living expenses in case the home is damaged by fire or other disaster, and it should cover the full replacement cost of personal property that might be stolen or damaged.

▶ As the value of your home increases, make sure your insurance company provides an "inflation rider" in its policy. An inflation rider automatically increases coverage as the value of your home increases.

Life Insurance

▶ Determine your insurance needs before trying to figure out what kind of policy to buy. If your primary need is to protect your family in the event of your death, make sure you know exactly what the policy will pay.

▶ If you have small children, consider the cost of future child care and/or the loss of income from either spouse.

▶ Don't make the mistake of buying life insurance for your children, when you should be buying life insurance on yourself to protect your children.

▶ Compare policies by determining how much it costs to own a company's policy over a fixed period of time, such as five or ten years.

▶ Always work with an adviser or agent who has access to several insurance products, rather than an agent who works for only one company.

▶ Make sure agents use the same assumptions about how various policies work. For example, if one policy uses 12-percent interest rates and another uses 9-percent rates, you will not be able to adequately compare the policies in terms of future premiums.

▶ Make sure the projected rates of return are realistic, and ask for lower-than-current rates in projecting performance.

▶ Look for high-quality insurance companies with A or A-plus ratings.

▶ Avoid having too many different life-insurance policies. Consolidate your program into a few policies rather than buying a half-dozen different policies. Your premium will be considerably lower.

▶ If you're carrying more whole life insurance than you need, you can switch to a universal life policy for a better return on your money.

▶ Shop for term life insurance by comparing the cost of the policy over the time period that you expect to use the policy, not the first-year rate. Avoid riders covering accidental death, which are usually much more expensive than they are worth.

▶ Don't let potential tax savings dominate your considerations of a life-insurance policy. Some plans offer few investment choices, and the high fees must be weighed against any tax savings.

▶ Don't accept advertisements and brochures at face value. Make sure you understand how the policy works and what you're paying for.

ESTATE PLANNING

Financial professionals often find that people who don't have a will want to write one quickly when they discover the alternative—dying without a will may create problems for their heirs. Under current federal law, estates of up to $600,000, including taxable gifts made in your lifetime, are excluded from federal taxation. This is because everyone is entitled to a credit of $192,800 against federal estate taxes, which works out to the tax on a $600,000 estate. Whether you will want to write a simple will or include provisions for a trust will usually depend on the size of your estate, the management abilities of your beneficiary, and your wishes regarding the beneficiaries of your estate. Your financial situation, projected future needs, and other factors will all influence your decisions regarding estate planning.

If your will was written before 1981, you should write a new one as soon as possible. In general, it is a very good idea to periodically review your will and to keep it up to date. Not only can your life change—for example, when you retire, tax laws do, too.

If you move, make sure that your will conforms to the laws of your new state of residence. Remember that a will is administered according to the laws of the state of a person's legal residence at the time of death, not according to the laws of the state in which it was written.

Writing a Will

▶ For between $100 and $500, an attorney will write a simple will according to your specifications and keep a copy in his or her office so that it is immediately available. Higher fees are charged for wills involving the creation of trusts and/or other legal devices. But your will needn't be complicated, even if you have a relatively large estate.

▶ Never put your will in a safety deposit box. In the event of your death, the bank may order that the box be sealed until a court order is issued to open it. Your will should be immediately available at your death, particularly if it includes instructions for your burial or cremation.

▶ Make a complete list of your assets: cash, savings accounts, stocks, bonds, mutual fund shares, IRAs, house, furnishings, automobiles, etc. Be sure to include all your property and any debts, such as a home mortgage or credit card balances.

▶ Decide who will benefit after your death. If you are married, you and your spouse will want to discuss these items ahead of time. Although this step sounds fairly easy, many

married couples discover that when they sit down to talk about their wills they don't automatically agree about the disposition of their assets.

▶ Decide who will be named as trustees. Ask yourself if you or your spouse can handle investments and manage your estate. You may find that your spouse doesn't want to, and by establishing a cotrustee—a lawyer or friend— you can ease the burden.

▶ Decide on a guardian for small children. It's a good idea to get permission from the designated guardian, so that you don't have to rewrite your will if you later discover that he or she isn't interested in the job.

▶ Parents may also use a will to create a trust that takes effect only after their deaths (a testamentary trust). Under the terms of the trust, they can arrange for some of the estate to be set aside for college expenses, a home purchase, or any other purpose they choose. You can thus avoid the children receiving their entire inheritance at age 18 when they may not be able to handle a large sum of money.

▶ Choose an executor (sometimes called a personal representative). The executor or personal representative is not to be confused with a trustee. The executor makes sure the assets are distributed according to the will and takes care of all public announcements and filings to settle the estate. The job ends when the estate is settled; the trustee's job continues. Most married couples name each other as executor and choose a third party in the event

that they die at the same time. You may also want to name a coexecutor—such as another relative or an attorney—particularly if your spouse would be overwhelmed by the job. The larger your estate, the more complicated and time-consuming the job will be for the executor. There is a considerable amount of paperwork involved with even small estates, so you should make sure the named executor is comfortable with the role.

Creating a Trust

▶ Consider establishing a trust, which is a relatively simple vehicle to assist your heirs— either your spouse or your children—in managing their assets. A trust is a legal device in which a person places property that will ultimately belong to one or more beneficiaries. In the trust agreement, that person (called the grantor) stipulates the way in which property is to be disbursed.

▶ A trust that takes effect while you are alive is called a **living trust.** A trust that takes effect after you die is called a **testamentary trust,** because it is created entirely by the provisions of your will.

▶ People with small estates typically use a testamentary trust. Parents may use it to provide for their children or a married couple may use a testamentary trust to divide the estate to minimize or avoid estate taxes.

▶ With a **general power of appointment trust,** the surviving spouse has full control of the assets.

▶ With a **qualified terminable interest property (Q-TIP) trust,** the surviving spouse also controls the assets, but the beneficiaries are fixed. For example, you could leave your estate in a Q-TIP for your spouse with the designation that your children receive the estate at the spouse's death. A Q-TIP is particularly useful for couples with children from other marriages, because a spouse can provide income for the surviving spouse, while making sure his or her children are not disinherited.

▶ With a **life insurance trust,** the proceeds of insurance are placed into a trust. Designated heirs receive the principal at the death of the beneficiary of the trust.

▶ With a **charitable remainder trust,** you can receive income during your lifetime and stipulate that the trust passes to a charity at your death.

BUYING AND SELLING A HOME

For most people, buying or selling a home is the largest financial transaction they make in their lives. To do this without sound financial advice can lead to economic disaster. While the following should help guide you through the process, it's wise to consult professionals in the field to help you.

BUYING A HOME

Determining how much house you can afford is the first step to buying a new home. This helps narrow the search, as well as avoids disappointment that comes from finding your "dream" home only to discover that it is way beyond your means. Once you find your price range, you'll want to know how to look at prospective homes critically, how to make an offer, and the extent of your legal obligations both in buying and living in your home.

Affordability

Affordability hinges on several factors:

▶ **Down payment.** With conventional financing, you will need to have 20 percent of the purchase price to avoid Private Mortgage Insurance (PMI), which adds an additional monthly charge to your mortgage. Some government loans are available with a down payment of as little as 5 percent.

▶ **Closing costs.** These costs (survey fee, title insurance, etc.) average between 4 and 6 percent of the mortgage amount and must be paid at the closing.

▶ **Income.** Income is calculated as net income after taxes.

▶ **Expenses.** Along with the interest that you will be paying on the mortgage, any current payments to which you are obligated are considered. These include car and credit-card payments and legally ordered payments (alimony and/or child support). To qualify for a higher mortgage, pay off your debts.

▶ **Credit history.** A poor credit history, such as late payments or default on payments, can significantly affect a lender's willingness to grant you a mortgage.

▶ **Current interest rates on mortgages.** Because almost all of what you will be paying each month will go to paying interest on your loan, the interest rate offered by a lender is extremely important in determining whether you can afford a home. A difference of 1 percent in rates on a $100,000 mortgage represents $75 a month for payments on a 30-year mortgage.

▶ **Property tax.** Most lenders no longer allow buyers to pay property tax themselves. Instead, a portion of your monthly payment goes into an escrow account and the lender pays the tax directly to the municipality. This payment will be figured into what you can afford.

▶ **Lifestyle.** The rule of thumb traditionally maintains that a home purchase should be no more than 2½ times annual income. If your tastes run to expensive evenings out and costly vacations, you may want to consider mortgaging less than this amount.

Shopping for a Home

Most people want to find the home that meets their needs in the best neighborhood they can afford. To evaluate prospective homes, consider the following:

▶ Check out the neighborhood, such as schools, availability of transportation, parks, medical facilities, and recreational opportunities. You may want to list these types of criteria in order of importance to you. For example, public transportation might be more important to one family, while another family might consider top medical facilities its first priority.

▶ Bargain-priced homes in less desirable neighborhoods are often not bargains at all. And while you may do well to buy a neglected home in a good neighborhood, it's unlikely that you can expect to see an increase in

value if you buy a quality home in a neglected neighborhood or one that is next to a neglected property.

▶ Avoid areas in which zoning changes to less desirable uses or conversion of uses (usually residential to business or commercial) are being considered or approved.

▶ Make a list of your priorities in a home itself—two bathrooms, fireplace, garage, large lot, etc. It's highly unlikely that you will find a home that has everything you want, but you should know what is most important to you before you start your search.

PAYMENT TABLES

8.0 Percent Annual Percentage Rate

Amount Financed	Monthly Payments (Principal and Interest)	
	15 Years	30 Years
$30,000	$286.70	$220.13
40,000	382.26	293.51
50,000	477.83	366.88
60,000	573.39	440.26
70,000	668.96	513.64
80,000	764.52	587.01
90,000	860.09	660.39
100,000	955.65	733.76

9.0 Percent Annual Percentage Rate

Amount Financed	Monthly Payments (Principal and Interest)	
	15 Years	30 Years
$30,000	$304.28	$241.39
40,000	405.71	321.85
50,000	507.13	402.31
60,000	608.56	482.77
70,000	709.99	563.24
80,000	811.41	643.70
90,000	912.84	724.16
100,000	1014.20	804.62

▶ Unless you have hired a seller's agent, any real estate agent you are working with is working for the seller, who pays the commission. Never indicate to the agent that you will pay more than you are offering. Although the agent is obligated to disclose information about you to the seller or his or her agent, this does not mean that the agent can't help you locate the best home.

▶ Make sure you are comfortable working with an agent. If you distrust him or her, you will have trouble throughout the process.

▶ Check out newspaper ads for prices and go to open houses to get a feel for the market.

▶ Carefully inspect the condition of prospective homes. Forget the color of the carpet and the decorating. Concentrate on the size of the rooms, amount of storage space, age and condition of heating and plumbing facilities, and appliances that are being sold with the house. Unless you're an expert about the mechanical aspects of a home, you'll want to have a home inspection either before you make an offer or as a contingency on your offer. Paying attention to prospective problem areas will help you eliminate homes that look like trouble.

Obtaining Financing

The vast majority of homes are financed with money borrowed from a financial institution, commonly referred to as a mortgage. This obligates the buyer to pay back the lender and requires that the lender has a lien on the home.

A wide variety of available mortgages, along with other types of financing, are briefly explained below. Federal law requires that the lender provide you with detailed disclosures about the loan. Make sure that you

understand this material thoroughly before signing. When you apply for the loan, the lender must disclose all costs of the loan, including interest rate, which is stated as an annual percentage rate (APR). Additionally, the lender must disclose service charges, appraisal fees, survey fees, title insurance or escrow fees, and any attorney's fee.

▶ A fixed-rate mortgage has a fixed interest rate that will never fluctuate over the life of the loan. These are amortized mortgages, in which the loans are paid off over the life of the mortgage (30 years or 15 years) in equal monthly installments, which cover both interest on the loan and payment on the principal. The major advantage to a 15-year mortgage is that more principal is paid each month, lowering the interest costs over the life of the loan.

▶ An adjustable-rate mortgage (ARM) has an interest rate that floats with a specified index, such as the Treasury Bill Index. Typically, the interest rate on the first year of the loan is much lower than prevailing mortgage rates. After the first year, the rate is usually adjusted annually, and the payment will either increase or decrease depending on the index to which the rate is tied. With some ARMs, the monthly payment remains the same, and additional costs to cover a higher interest rate is added to the principal amount of the loan and the term for repayment may be extended.

Most ARMs have a 2 percent annual cap and a 6 percent lifetime cap. In other words, a 7 percent initial rate on an ARM cannot exceed 13 percent, despite the index.

▶ A convertible ARM offers some type of conversion to a fixed-rate mortgage, usually on the anniversary of the loan origination. Usually this involves a fee and is only available for a limited time period, typically within 5 years of the home purchase.

▶ A graduated-payment mortgage (GPM) is one in which the borrower's payments for the first few years are very low and then increased.

▶ FHA and VA loans are loans insured by the Federal Housing Administration and the Veterans Administration. Because these are insured, buyers are able to make lower down payments. If you are finding it difficult to save enough for a down payment, you should investigate whether you could qualify for these loans. Information should be readily available in your community.

▶ With a land contract, the seller, rather than a financial institution, provides the financing of the purchase. Typically, the purchaser makes a down payment in an amount agreed on between the seller and the purchaser and then makes periodic payments to the seller. Usually the contract specifies that the buyer pay the remainder of the purchase price, together with interest, over an agreed number of years.

SIGNS OF TROUBLE

Serious structural problems make for expensive repairs. Make sure you have an inspection by a qualified or accredited home inspector. Unless you can accurately estimate the cost of repairs, will receive a break on the price, and can afford to correct problems, steer clear of homes that evidence the following:

▶ Maximum number of roof layers or a roof that already exceeds the maximum number of layers according to municipal code. When the roof needs to be redone, the old roofing will have to be torn off, greatly increasing the expense.

▶ Any evidence that the roof has structural problems, including a swayback or depression.

▶ Foundation problems, including cracks or a water line in the basement or cellar indicating that the home has taken in water.

▶ Inadequate or old electrical wiring. Service should be 150 amp or better. This can be a very expensive item to correct.

▶ Stairs that have a lot of "give." Most people can live with squeaks, but a staircase that is in serious trouble will require serious, and expensive, work to repair.

▶ Septic systems in a neighborhood that has access to municipal water. Municipal code might forbid any repairs or replacement, and you would have to absorb the cost of connecting to city facilities.

▶ Pipes, boilers, furnaces, and air ducts wrapped in white cloth or cementlike material. This could be asbestos; removal and disposal costs are considerable.

▶ Any evidence of formaldehyde foam insulation. The cost of removal is considerable.

Sometimes, the land contract stipulates a "balloon" payment after a specified period of time. The buyer is expected to arrange alternate financing at the time.

▶ The mortgage market is very competitive, and it is important to shop for the best interest rate.

▶ Most mortgages will specify a monthly payment date and the charge for late payments. Make sure you know your payment date and avoid late payments.

Making an Offer

▶ Determine whether you are in a "buyer's market" or a "seller's market." If homes are being sold very quickly at or near asking prices, you are in a seller's market, and you may have to act quickly and be prepared to pay the best price. In a buyer's market, when sales are slow and homes are sold for 15 to 25 percent below asking price, you will have a lot more room for negotiation on the price.

▶ Before you make an offer, ask for recent sales of comparable homes in the neighborhood. This will be helpful in negotiating an offer.

▶ Try to determine when the owner bought the house and what was paid for the house. In some areas, this information is readily available.

▶ Be flexible. When making offers, it's easy to get caught up in the fever of the moment. Don't fall in love with a house, and don't let pride or tough negotiations prevent you from buying a house that you really want.

SELLING YOUR HOME

Preparing Your Home for Sale

▶ First impressions are crucial. Realtors call it "curb appeal," and prospective buyers may not even get out of the car if the exterior of the home looks shabby. Keep the lawn in good shape and well mowed, and plant flowers in shrub beds or in containers to brighten up the front of the house. Put children's toys, hoses, and garden tools out of sight.

▶ Make sure the exterior is in good condition. If the house needs painting, it's worth it to get the job done before you put the house up for sale. Repair or replace broken or cracked windows, gutters, and downspouts.

▶ Make sure everything is clean, including carpets, walls, and appliances. Buyers will remember grime and dirt, along with wet towels and dirty dishes, rather than the good qualities of your home.

▶ Keep tables and countertops free of clutter. Designate a drawer for everyday papers.

▶ Make the beds and keep the bathrooms tidy.

▶ Cluttered closets give the impression of too little storage. Put things away in boxes if you can't declutter them by better organization.

▶ Open up the drapes and curtains as much as possible unless the view is poor.

Working with an Agent

▶ Interview several agents from various local firms. You'll want to make sure you feel comfortable with the agent, as well as question him or her on how long they've been in the business, how familiar they are with the neighborhood, their recent sales, and their plans to sell your home. You will be

paying between 6 and 7 percent commission on the sales price of your home, and you should expect a quality job.

▶ Make sure you understand the terms of the listing contract and how long the contract will be in effect.

▶ If you intend to sell your house yourself and avoid paying commission, remember that you will be responsible for the following: costs of advertising, time to work with potential buyers, and the negotiations of the sale.

▶ In some states, the seller is obligated to disclose known material defects and nonfunctional items that would otherwise appear to be functioning, such as a furnace,

THE PURCHASE CONTRACT

The contract for a sale of real estate can be called a contract, bid, binder, offer to purchase, or a deposit receipt. Once signed, it is a legally binding contract. In most cases, you will want to have your attorney go over this document before you submit it or include an "attorney contingency rider" that allows your attorney to inspect the document. Minimally, the contract should include the following:

▶ Purchase price and how it is to be paid. This will cover the amount of the deposit, any planned financing, its cost, interest charges, and length of mortgage.

▶ Legal description of the property; sometimes a survey of the property is required.

▶ Provision that a good title will be furnished by the seller.

▶ Date when the transfer of possession will occur and a provision for payment to the buyer if possession does not occur.

▶ Proration of utility bills, property taxes, and similar expenses, along with a stipulation that the owner is responsible for risk of fire or other hazard before the property is transferred.

▶ List of everything to be included in the sale, including drapes, light fixtures, appliances, etc.

▶ The terms of any escrow agreement.

▶ A provision that the initial payment (earnest money or binder deposit) will be returned if the sale is not completed.

▶ Signature of the parties.

▶ A financing contingency clause that allows the buyer a certain amount of time to obtain financing.

▶ An inspection contingency clause that allows the buyer to have the home inspected within a specific period of time and the right to cancel the contract within a certain period of time if the inspection reveals faults with the home.

hot-water heater, etc. To avoid any future legal problems, it's best to be honest about any defects in your home, whether the law requires it or not.

TAX CONSEQUENCES OF HOME OWNERSHIP AND SALE

Mortgage Interest and Property Tax

Mortgage interest and property tax paid on a home that is a primary residence is fully deductible against income on your federal tax return. Check state tax codes for deductibility of these items on state tax returns.

Capital Gains Rollover

When you sell your home, any profit realized on the sale is generally taxable, but you can defer taxes if your home is a primary residence and you buy another primary residence.

▶ To qualify for a rollover of capital gains from one home to another, you must buy a new home within 24 months of the sale of your previous home. (Some military personnel and persons who have lived outside the United States may be eligible for a longer time period.)

▶ In most cases, the cost of the new home must exceed the selling price of the old home.

▶ You will have to file a form in the tax year the home was sold. On this form, list the "adjusted cost basis" of your home from the "adjusted sales price." The adjusted cost basis is determined by subtracting eligible items from the price of your home. These include certain selling expenses, such as the broker's commission, attorney's fees, and fix-up

expenses completed within 90 days of the sale and paid for within 30 days of the sale.

▶ The cost of capital improvements, not repairs, may also be deducted from the selling price to arrive at the adjusted sales price. For example, repairing a refrigerator is not an improvement, but adding a new room is an improvement. Also, while you may deduct the labor costs paid to a tradesperson (such as a contractor's fee for remodeling), you may not deduct any costs for your own labor. Be sure to keep all of your receipts for any costs you are deducting from the sale. The IRS will not allow unsubstantiated deductions.

▶ The difference between the adjusted cost basis and the adjusted sales price is considered the profit on which you owe tax. If there is no profit, you do not have to worry about deferring or paying taxes.

▶ If you do not buy a new home within 24 months, if the cost of your new home does not exceed the cost of your old home, or if you choose to pay the taxes, you will be taxed on the profits depending on your tax bracket.

Capital Gains Exclusion

The capital gains exclusion on the sale of a primary residence is allowed to homeowners age 55 and older. This allows homeowners to avoid paying capital gains tax (up to $125,000) on any profit from the sale of a principal residence.

▶ This exclusion is allowed only once to a homeowner and should be considered very carefully in making present and future home buying plans.

▶ You must live in the home as your primary residence for a minimum of 3 of the 5 years before sale to qualify for the exclusion. This means that you cannot rent out your home or fail to live there for more than 6 months or at least 3 of the 5 years preceding the sale.

▶ Be sure you carefully consider the rules to obtain the exclusion before selling your home. A widow and widower who are considering marriage, for example, may want to sell their

marriage, for example, may want to sell their homes before they marry to individually allow them to take advantage of this exclusion on any profits realized from the sale of their homes.

Vacation Homes

▶ Mortgage interest on second homes is fully deductible against other income.

▶ Deductible losses on rental, vacation, or second homes are capped at $25,000 for taxpayers with adjusted gross income under $100,000. This cap is reduced for taxpayers over this income limit. The limitation is reduced by 50 percent for the amount that adjusted gross income exceeds $100,000.

▶ To be eligible for deductible losses, you must not use the residence for more than 14 days in 1 year or 10 percent of the total number of days it is rented at fair market value. If you rent it for 150 days a year, you may use it yourself for 15 days annually.

▶ Eligibility for deductible losses also requires you to actively participate in rental operations. This means you must have a minimum of 10 percent ownership in the home and be involved in management decisions.

▶ If you qualify for deductible losses, buying a second or vacation home that you ultimately will move into at retirement may be a good investment. It would give you tax advantages now and allow you to begin paying for your future retirement home.

PLANNING FOR RETIREMENT

Whether you're just starting out or planning to retire very soon, what you save and how you invest your savings will largely determine your lifestyle in retirement. Saving and appropriate investing are critical to successful retirement planning, because few people want to rely solely on Social Security benefits in retirement. Many financial publications, along with professional financial planners, are available to assist you in developing savings and investing strategies.

The basic elements of retirement planning include setting your goals, understanding Social Security and any pension you may have, and developing a retirement savings plan.

SETTING YOUR GOALS

▶ Create a realistic projection of your future income sources after retirement. Include estimated Social Security benefits, pension benefits, tax-deferred savings, and other savings.

▶ Determine a realistic concept of your future expenses. Do you want to travel? Do you plan to move to a new home?

▶ Build an adequate nest egg to provide income to help meet retirement expenses.

▶ Develop successful retirement savings and investment strategies to create your nest egg.

▶ Establish a diversified portfolio of investments that will protect your savings from market downturns, as well as inflation.

▶ Ensure that you have sufficient medical and disability insurance to protect your savings, and sufficient life insurance for a spouse who would lose income at your death.

UNDERSTANDING SOCIAL SECURITY

Most people take Social Security for granted. The tax generated by the Federal Insurance Contribution Act (FICA) has become a fixture in our working lives. Most of us expect to redeem at least some of the Social Security taxes we pay in the form of benefits when we retire. But while nearly everyone counts on Social Security benefits, few investors know how they fit into the scope of financial planning. Because they have no idea of what disability and survivors' programs pay, they often pay too little or too much for insurance. And some investors count too much on Social Security covering their retirement expenses, because they incorrectly assume they will receive as much as their neighbor or parent.

Social Security regulations have changed often and may change in the future. When significant changes occur, it is important to reconsider your future plans if you are counting on benefits as a major portion of your retirement income. Make sure you are working with complete, up-to-date information about Social Security and eligibility requirements if you are considering applying for benefits.

Eligibility

▶ Rights to Social Security benefits depend on whether you paid into the system, are the spouse of someone who paid into the system,

or are the children or parent of a worker covered under Social Security.

▶ Full individual eligibility is attained when you have paid into the system for a minimum of 10 years, the time required to acquire 40 credits to have full benefits in the system. These work credits are accumulated throughout your life. If you have been paying Social Security or self-employment tax since your 20s or 30s and expect to continue paying until retirement, you will undoubtedly be eligible for full benefits.

▶ Fewer work credits are required for the disability and survivors' programs.

▶ Be sure to check on your Social Security work credit periodically to make sure it accurately reflects your work and tax record. You will need to fill out a form, "Request for Social Security Earnings Information" (Form SSA-7050). This information can be checked against your tax records; any discrepancies should be noted immediately.

Paying Into the System

▶ Both you and your employer each pay a percentage of your earnings into the system up to a limit (7.65 percent on earnings up to $55,500 in 1992). The deduction is usually labeled FICA on your pay slip.

▶ Self-employed persons pay the whole contribution as a percentage of earnings up to a maximum (15.3 percent on earnings up to $55,500 in 1992).

▶ Although your contribution to Social Security stops once you earn more than the specified limit, you must continue paying the Medicare portion of Social Security up to a higher limit ($130,200 in 1992). This tax is 1.45 percent each for employees and employers, and 2.9 percent for self-employed people.

Benefits

▶ Benefits in retirement are based on your average earnings during the time you are paying into the system until you retire. Generally, if you've been paying the maximum into the system, you will receive the maximum benefit. Only earnings on which you have paid Social Security tax as an employee or as a self-employed person are considered.

▶ For retirement planning purposes, it is fairly easy to estimate what you will receive from Social Security if you are now in your 60s. Younger workers may have to work with more of a "guess estimate" in predicting Social Security benefits.

▶ Social Security is subject to income tax if adjusted gross income, nontaxable interest income, and half of the annual Social Security benefits exceed a base amount.

▶ Benefits are also reduced if you exceed the limit on the annual earnings test or if you (or your spouse) are receiving benefits from a government pension plan.

▶ Benefits to widows can begin at age 60, or before, if the widow is caring for children under age 16. The benefits stop once the child reaches age 16 if the widow is under 60 years of age.

Early Retirement

▶ The penalty for retiring early is permanently reduced benefits. The reduction is between 20 and 30 percent depending on when you retire.

▶ The penalty for early retirement also affects the benefits of a spouse drawing on his/her or a spouse's work record.

▶ If personal health is not an issue, the decision to consider early retirement often gets down to basic finances. Make sure you understand exactly how much future money will be at risk before electing to retire early and collect Social Security.

▶ If you're considering working past retirement, benefits are increased ¼ of 1 percent for every month you work past retirement age until age 70 under the current plan. Basically, the benefit works out to an approximate 3 percent increase for every year retirement is delayed.

Survivors' Benefits

▶ The surviving spouse of a retiree eligible for Social Security can receive as much as 100 percent of the deceased spouse's benefits.

CHECK YOUR RETIREMENT AGE

The present retirement age of 65 is effective for those born before 1938. A graduated scale has been established to meet the criteria for full, not maximum, benefits for those born in 1938 and after, according to the following chart.

Year of Birth	Full Retirement Age (years and months)
1938	65/2
1939	65/4
1940	65/6
1941	65/8
1942	65/10
1943-1954	66/0
1955	66/2
1956	66/4
1957	66/6
1958	66/8
1959	66/10
1960 and after	67/0

▶ Benefits are reduced by 19/40 of 1 percent (or 19/4000) for each month before 65.

▶ A spouse is eligible for 75 percent of the spouse's benefit at any age if caring for a dependent or disabled child.

▶ A widow or widower must be 60 or older, or between 50 and 60 and seriously disabled, to be eligible for benefits for themselves. Survivors' benefits paid to younger widows or widowers are to care for children under 16.

▶ Children are eligible for survivor's benefits, up to 75 percent of the parent's benefit, if they are under age 18, or under 19 if in high school. If they became disabled before age 22, they may receive 75 percent of your benefit for life or until no longer disabled.

▶ A divorced spouse is entitled to the same benefit as a wife or husband, but must meet criteria for eligibility. They must be at least 62, married at least 10 years to a former spouse who is eligible for benefits, and single or not remarried until age 60.

▶ Parents can receive benefits if they are 62 or older and formerly received half of their support from their child.

Applying for Benefits

▶ To apply for benefits as a worker, you will need proof of age, Social Security number, and a copy of your W-2 form or tax return for the previous year.

▶ To apply for benefits as a spouse, you need proof of your age; proof of your marriage; Social Security number for yourself and your spouse; your spouse's W-2 and your W-2 for the previous year.

▶ To apply for benefits as a surviving spouse, you need all the items required of a spouse plus the death certificate or proof of death of your spouse and proof of your spouse's age.

▶ To apply for benefits as a divorced spouse or surviving divorced spouse, you need all of the items of a surviving spouse plus proof of divorce.

▶ To apply for benefits on behalf of a child, you need the child's birth certificate and the child's Social Security number.

Disability

▶ To receive Social Security, a disability must prevent you from taking part in any "substantial gainful activity," is expected to last or has already lasted for at least one year, or is a condition that could result in death. The only exception to this rule is for people who qualify under the Social Security definition of "blind."

▶ Benefits paid under disability are based on your average earnings up to the year the disability started. Fewer years of low earnings are disregarded in calculating disability benefits.

▶ Eligibility for disability benefits is based on your work credit record at the following ages:
Before age 24: Credit for 1½ years of work in the 3 years preceding the onset of the disability.
Between ages 24–30: Credits for half the time between your 21st birthday and the start of the disability with a minimum of 6 credits required.
Between ages 31–42: A minimum of 20

credits earned in the 10-year period before the disability began.

Ages 43 and older: 21-40 credits, depending on age, with 20 credits earned in the 10-year period before the start of the disability.

UNDERSTANDING YOUR PENSION PLAN

While most of us plan to save for retirement, many of us will rely on a company pension to supplement Social Security benefits. It is important to understand how your plan works whether you are just starting out or preparing to retire.

Pension Plans

Employers offer various types of pensions, and it is important to understand how your pension works and whether you can add voluntary payments into the system.

▶ A defined-benefit plan or pension provides a specified sum to be paid periodically (usually monthly) during retirement. Sometimes the retiree can elect a lump-sum payment at the time you retire. A defined-benefit plan usually relies on a formula based on years of service and salary.

▶ A defined-contribution plan does not provide a specific income or lump-sum payment at retirement. Instead, what you collect at retirement will be based on the amount of money your employer has contributed on your behalf, any of your own contributions, and the earnings on that money over time.

▶ A profit-sharing plan bases an employee contribution on the employee's salary and the profitability of the company. In good years, the employee may receive the maximum contribution, perhaps 5 to 20 percent of salary. In poor years, the plan may make no contributions. Profit-sharing plans are generally offered in addition to other employee compensation plans, although small, start-up companies may rely exclusively on this plan to provide retirement compensation.

▶ With an Employee Stock Ownership Plan (ESOP), the employer may contribute company stock to the employee, or the employee may be offered the purchase of company stock with a matching contribution from the employer. Like profit-sharing plans, these are generally offered in addition to other plans, but they may be the only retirement compensation offered. If this plan is the only retirement plan, it's particularly important to remember that both your current income and future retirement benefits are totally dependent on the profitability of the company.

▶ A multiple-employer pension, such as the union pensions originated under the federal Taft-Hartley Act, are more complex than most other pensions. Employee benefits are typically based on hours or days worked. These plans usually provide a fixed monthly benefit at retirement. The greatest complications arise in projecting the employee's retirement benefit. If you are covered under such a plan, you should consult with the plan's administrators, who are required by law to provide information on regulations and benefits.

Pension Benefits

You should start planning for your retirement early in your working life. The sad fact is that too many retirees discover too late that if they had clearly understood their entitlements and exercised their options, they could have improved their post-retirement income.

▶ Carefully evaluate the plan; make sure you understand what kind of plan it is and how it works. Often the employee has the choice (and assumes the risk) of how contributions are invested.

▶ To make sure you understand your entitlements, get a copy of your employer's brochure or pamphlet that outlines the provisions of the plan. If you don't understand the provisions or if it fails to answer your questions, make an appointment with your personnel office to explain any uncertainties.

▶ Understand your options. Many married employees automatically sign up for an option to pay survivor's benefits in the event of their death before age 55. This option can cost employees up to 20 percent of their benefit at retirement under some plans. In other words, you win only if you die before 55. Buying life insurance to protect a spouse during that time period may be less costly than the survivor's rights option.

▶ Make sure you are covered. Sometimes part-time workers assume they are covered by a plan for full-time employees.

▶ Make sure you understand how benefits are calculated. Typically, defined benefits are based on years of service, salary or wages, contributions, and other variables. Make sure you understand the variables, including years required for vesting, early retirement provisions, calculation of years of service, and how the final average salary is calculated.

▶ If Social Security payments are integrated into the benefit structure, there are legal restrictions that prevent an employer from exceeding a percentage of Social Security payments in calculating benefits. An increase in Social Security payments could decrease the pension payment.

▶ Find out if the plan has a cost-of-living provision and how it is calculated.

▶ Many plans call for drastic reductions in benefits if an employee retires before the specified retirement age. Others encourage employees to retire early by providing near-maximum benefits before age 65.

▶ Check whether medical benefits are available in the event of early retirement.

▶ Make sure you are entitled to full benefits at age 65, know what happens to your benefits if you die before retirement, and whether your spouse is covered by the plan. Not all plans include survivor's rights, and sometimes survivor's rights are optional.

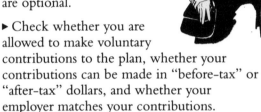

▶ Check whether you are allowed to make voluntary contributions to the plan, whether your contributions can be made in "before-tax" or "after-tax" dollars, and whether your employer matches your contributions.

▶ Make sure you understand how being fired or laid off would affect your rights in the system, as well as whether the plan addresses disability before retirement age.

▶ Make sure you keep track of rights to benefits under former employers. Don't assume that your former employer's book-keeping system is perfect. Companies change ownership, locations, and methods of personnel record-keeping. It's a good idea to write to former employers on a periodic basis to make sure your entitlements are secure.

▶ Be aware that many plans do not allow a widow or widower to collect survivor's rights to a pension until their spouse would have been eligible to retire, regardless of the widow or widower's age.

▶ If you're planning to retire in the near future, you may wish to make the effort to verify that your entitlements conform to legal requirements.

▶ The best defined-benefit pensions typically base the benefit on the average salary over three to five of your top-earning years. The least favorable pensions base the benefit on the average of your entire life with the employer, so that low-paying years cancel out high-paying years.

▶ Most defined-benefit plans are legally required to be insured with the Pension Benefit Guaranty Corporation. This insurance provides pensions if an insured company or its pension fund is unable to meet its obligations. This insurance, however, does not guarantee 100 percent of the expected benefit.

▶ Understand the rules for "vesting," which is the full and unconditional guarantee of your rights in the pension system. Most defined-benefit plans do not fully vest until the employee has worked at least five years.

▶ There are also a number of variables when it comes to payout. In some cases, the retiring employee takes his entire compensation with him, usually choosing to roll over the money into an IRA or annuity. Some plans restrict employees to an annuity payout; the amount of the annuity is usually based on the total value accumulated at retirement and the life expectancy of the employee.

▶ Employee tax-deferred contributions are limited to $7,000 annually, while the total amount contributed to the plan by an employee and employer cannot exceed $30,000 or 25 percent of the employee's compensation, whichever is less. Obviously, you would want to cut back your contribution rather than curtail your employer's contribution if the total combined contribution would exceed $30,000, or 25 percent of your income.

▶ As with IRAs, funds can be withdrawn from a defined-contribution plan before age 59½ in cases of financial hardship, but a 10-percent penalty on withdrawn funds is assessed. You will also have to pay taxes on the withdrawal according to your federal tax bracket.

▶ Despite the fact that you're locking up money, the advantages of tax-deferral and tax-free compounding in tax-deferred retirement plans nearly always pays off. If your employer offers a matching contribution, start taking advantage of it tomorrow.

DEVELOPING A RETIREMENT SAVINGS PLAN

Despite their best intentions, many individuals run into their first roadblock in planning for retirement, because they have no idea how much money they will need when they stop working and they have no idea what kind of nest egg is needed to produce an adequate income. To plan investment strategies and determine how to provide yourself with an adequate income when the paychecks stop, you first need a target income goal and a nest egg to provide the income.

Financial professionals have developed many ways to tackle this problem. Some use a "two-thirds target." They suggest aiming for an income that provides about two-thirds of your current living expenses. That works fine for some people, particularly those who are currently raising a family and know they will be able to reduce their future expenses and save more money when their children are on their own.

Other professionals suggest that many retirees don't want to live on less at retirement. They argue that many retirees expect to travel, have second homes, or have other expenses. For retirees who expect to maintain or increase their standard of living, they often suggest that the target retirement income be the same or very close to current income generated in the household.

To set a savings goal, it's much easier to think in current dollars and consider how your current income would suit you in retirement. Forget inflation for the moment, and concentrate on your current income and your current expenses. Most people find it easier to think in current dollars (the value of today's dollars), rather than to try to put a price tag on future costs.

Assessing Your Retirement Needs

The following steps should help you zero in on your financial needs at retirement:

▶ If you're currently devoting a large percentage of your income to house payments, children's education, business start-up costs, or some other major expense, you may want to reduce the income you will want at retirement. On the other hand, if you can handle your expenses now and manage to put away 10 to 15 percent of your income, you probably will want the same income in retirement.

▶ Take a look at your assets. Ignore the value of your home or automobile. Assets are any cash and/or the value of investments, including cash value of insurance, stock, bonds, paid-up value of investment real estate, mutual fund assets, government securities, certificates of deposit, savings bonds, etc. Remember, for the purposes of retirement planning, you won't want to include assets earmarked for other purposes, such as money saved for your children's college education or a down payment on a house.

▶ Estimate what income you can expect at retirement—Social Security eligibility, pension, a lump sum in deferred compensation, etc. If your employer sends you an annual pension statement, you may have the information at hand, even if it specifies future amounts in future dollars.

▶ A rule of thumb is that over 20 years, real savings will double in value. Unless your current savings are large, this income can be considered as a "hedge," to account for the 10 percent error factor and unexpected future expenses. Individuals who already have substantial sums saved may want to adjust their future savings to accommodate the projected earnings from their existing savings.

▶ Your annual savings should be adjusted upward each year to account for inflation. Changes in investment returns (either up or down) may also affect your savings schedule. You may want to update your savings schedule by going over your savings plan annually.

▶ If your household income doesn't keep up with inflation, you will have to devote a larger percentage of your income to savings to keep up with your retirement goals.

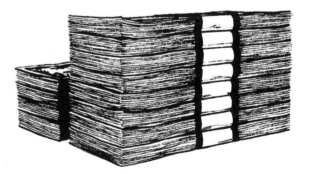

▶ Social Security benefits are expected to keep up with the inflation rate. Some people believe this is a dangerous assumption. Others believe recent changes in the system have secured benefits to at least 2050. If you are a skeptic, you will want to increase your nest egg substantially and decrease the estimate of projected Social Security income.

▶ Your pension is expected to keep up with inflation. If your pension is a defined percentage of your final salary, this assumption should be fairly accurate. If it is a pension that relies on contributions and performance of the pension fund, it may need to be

CHECKLIST FOR FINANCIALLY SUCCESSFUL RETIREMENT

Savings and proper investing, rather than income, are the crucial elements in successful retirement planning. Given your lifetime spending habits, you will need a predictable amount of money to support yourself in retirement. Deciding how to achieve this savings goal requires the following steps:

► A realistic projection of your future income sources after retirement, including Social Security benefits, pension benefits, tax-deferred savings, and others.

► A realistic concept of your future expenses.

► An adequate nest egg to provide income to help meet retirement expenses.

► Successful retirement savings and investment strategies to create and maintain your nest egg.

► A diversified mix of investments to achieve your goals and protect your savings from market downturns.

► Sufficient medical and disability insurance to protect your savings, and sufficient life insurance for a spouse who would lose income at your death.

► An estate plan that protects your family in the event of your death.

monitored to make sure it keeps up with inflation.

► Current and future savings are projected to earn a 3 percent real rate of return (the return on an investment after accounting for taxes and inflation). Over the past 60 years, the average real rate of return on investments was about 3 percent. Some investments are unlikely to produce a 3 percent real rate of return, while others should equal or better that return.

Adjusting Your Savings Plan

If in calculating your nest egg you find the savings goal too high, you should consider the following options:

► Adjust your expectations to meet current income.

► Reduce expectations, but also consider how to cut current expenses to save more money.

► Consider how to boost your future earning capacity.

► Consider taking the risk of trying for a better than 3 percent real rate of return on your investments. Remember, however, that the higher the rate of return, the riskier the investment.

Most diseases and disorders can be prevented with a healthy lifestyle. That includes eating nutritious meals, exercising regularly, controlling weight, getting adequate sleep and rest, avoiding hazardous substances and harmful habits, having regular physical examinations, and taking good care of ourselves when we have ailments. The following sections are designed to help you and your family pursue a healthy lifestyle, be an active participant in the responsibility for your health, and know what to do when accidents or illnesses pose emergencies.

HEALTH GUIDELINES

EATING FOR HEALTH AND FITNESS
Healthy Eating Habits

▶ Eat a variety of foods daily, selected from each of the four basic food groups: 1. fish, poultry, meat, legumes, nuts, and seeds; 2. vegetables and fruits; 3. breads and cereals; and 4. dairy products.

▶ Eating a nutritious breakfast every morning and avoiding snacks between meals are two ways to improve the family's eating habits.

▶ Take a positive approach to making healthy changes in your diet and lifestyle. Instead of bemoaning what you're giving up, concentrate on all the benefits you're getting from your improved diet.

▶ Read labels carefully. Many canned and frozen products contain high levels of sugar, salt, and fat—especially saturated fats. Avoid products with high levels of these ingredients.

▶ Along with all its other negative qualities, smoking destroys the body's supply of vitamin

C. If you haven't yet given up smoking, drink a glass of orange juice in the morning instead of lighting up a cigarette.

▶ Substitute raisins, nuts, apples, sunflower seeds, or crunchy vegetables for sugary or fatty snacks.

▶ Drink plenty of water daily. Water cleanses your system and promotes healthy skin.

▶ Cut down on sugar, which plays a role in the development of tooth decay, obesity, diabetes, and cardiovascular disease. And watch out for different forms of sugar, including corn syrup, honey, molasses, maltose, glucose, dextrose, and invert sugar. These are just other names for sugar that are often added to food products.

▶ Replace baked goods and fattening desserts with fresh fruits.

▶ Substitute fresh fruit juice or water for soft drinks and alcoholic beverages. Alcohol should be consumed only in moderation because it is associated with many serious diseases and is fattening.

▶ Cut down on salt painlessly by leaving it out of your cooking, by removing the salt shaker from the table, and by using salt substitutes if you really miss the taste.

▶ Substitute herbs, spices, and pepper for salt when seasoning foods, and use lemon and lime juices to flavor vegetables in place of salt.

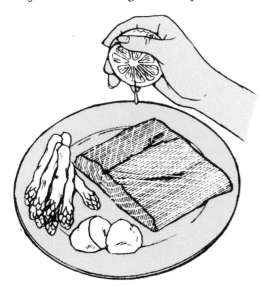

▶ Be aware that many commercial canned foods, especially canned soups, contain high levels of salt.

▶ Fats should comprise no more than 30 percent of calories daily. When buying meats, look for the leanest cuts. Trim off any visible fat before cooking, and whenever possible choose broiling over any other preparation method; broiling can reduce the fat content of meat by up to one-half.

▶ Although broiling is the best cooking method for meat if you're trying to avoid fat, you can also substantially reduce the fat and calorie content of meat by boiling or roasting it and skimming off the fat.

▶ Improve your family's diet by replacing some meat dishes with fish and poultry. You'll be eating less fat and fewer calories.

▶ Legumes, especially peas and beans, are an excellent source of protein and should be included in your weekly menus.

▶ Experiment with meatless meals to cut down on your fat intake. Meatless spaghetti sauce, chili, and vegetable soup can taste just as delicious as the meaty versions.

▶ Eat plenty of whole-grain bread, pasta, potatoes, rice, and other grains, which are good sources of protein, complex carbohydrates, fiber, and energy.

▶ Avoid eating too many preserved meats such as ham, hot dogs, and corned beef; most processed meats contain chemical additives.

▶ Scrub vegetables with a vegetable brush to remove any surface dirt before cooking, but don't remove the skins, because you'll also be throwing out most of the vitamins and minerals.

▶ Avoid overcooking vegetables, which quickly lose their vitamin C and mineral content.

▶ Get your children's taste buds used to nonsugared foods by preparing their breakfasts with sugarfree cereals. Sweeten with raw honey, sliced bananas, chopped apples, or raisins.

▶ Maintain a desirable weight. If you want to lose weight, cut down on portion size and exercise frequently.

Healthy Lunches and Snacks

▶ For more food value—and more energy— make lunchtime sandwiches from whole-grain breads and buns instead of white bread.

▶ Plan well-balanced box lunches. Include a protein-rich food, a crisp fruit or vegetable, and a beverage or soup. If you include a treat, make it a healthy treat.

▶ Good fillings for pita bread are grated cheese, cottage cheese mixed with tomatoes, onions, and cucumbers, or a spread made from chickpeas. Add plain yogurt and shredded lettuce just before serving.

▶ Cut down on calories at lunch (or at any other time) by eating hamburgers and sandwiches open-faced, with only one slice of bread or bun.

▶ Fill plastic sandwich bags with an assortment of fresh vegetable sticks for a light vegetarian lunch or snacks.

▶ A packet of powdered skim milk provides a quick, vitamin-packed, liquid lunch food. It's also a great source of protein, calcium, and vitamin B2.

▶ For a low-calorie lunch, freeze a carton of yogurt overnight and take it to work with you. The yogurt will be thawed but still cold by lunchtime the next day.

▶ If your workplace doesn't offer a place to keep your lunch refrigerated during hot weather, freeze sandwiches containing mayonnaise or salad dressing the night before. Although mayonnaise separates when frozen, the sandwiches will thaw by lunchtime without spoiling from the heat.

▶ Make extra servings of chili and stews to use in your lunch box. Pour them hot into vacuum containers for eating the next day, or freeze in serving-size portions for later.

▶ A 40-ounce plastic freezer container provides the perfect lunch box for carrying

STRIVING FOR HEALTHY WEIGHT

Weight charts have varied over the years, and health professionals are not in agreement about when a person is overweight or whether it is harmful to gain a little weight as you age.

The following chart is preferred by most health professionals. It is taken from a government booklet entitled "Nutrition and Your Health: Dietary Guidelines for Americans." It acknowledges that people over the age of 35 are likely to weigh more than people between the ages of 19 and 34.

Please note: The lower weight for each height applies to women; the higher weight to men. The weight range is in pounds, without shoes.

HEIGHT	AGE	
	19 to 34	35+
5'0"	97–128	108–138
5'1"	101–132	111–143
5'2"	104–137	115–148
5'3"	107–141	119–152
5'4"	111–146	122–157
5'5"	114–150	126–162
5'6"	118–155	130–167
5'7"	121–160	134–172
5'8"	125–164	138–178
5'9"	129–169	142–183
5'10"	132–174	146–188
5'11"	136–179	155–199
6'1"	144–189	159–205
6'2"	148–195	164–210
6'3"	152–200	168–216
6'4"	156–205	173–222
6'5"	160–211	177–228
6'6"	164–216	182–234

salad fixings to the office. If possible, keep it refrigerated. Add a low-calorie dressing of lemon juice and herbs just before eating your salad. If the salad is dressed ahead of time, it will be limp and unappetizing.

► Keep your lunch cool by putting several ice cubes into a plastic bag and sealing it with a twist tie. Just toss the bag into the lunch pail.

► Avoid that midafternoon slump that usually follows close on the heels of a heavy lunch by sticking to salads or light foods at lunchtime.

► In place of candy, potato chips, and pretzels, give your youngsters healthy snacks like sunflower seeds, raw almonds or cashews, roasted soy nuts, or fresh or dried fruits.

► Instead of taking a coffee and doughnut break, take an exercise break. Treat yourself to a handful of raw seeds or nuts afterward.

Hints for Weight Watchers

Gaining or losing weight is basically a matter of addition or subtraction. Each pound on your body is worth 3,500 calories. To lose one pound, you must cut back by 3,500 calories. To gain one pound you must increase your food intake by 3,500 calories.

► Despite extravagant claims by some advertisers and health clubs, vibrating machines, body massages, saunas, and steam baths won't really reduce your weight. You'll lose a lot of body fluid because of perspiration, but the fluid will return as soon as you drink liquids.

► Check the nutrition information printed on competing packaged products and choose the one with the lowest calorie and fat count. You'll save calories the same way a cost-conscious shopper saves money.

► If you're in the habit of eating while you're busy doing something else, such as watching TV or reading, make an effort to stop.

► Drink water when dieting. It will cut down on craving for food and improve digestion.

► Cutting down on alcohol can significantly reduce calories. For some people it's possible to lose weight simply by eliminating alcohol from the diet altogether.

► Don't expect to lose weight through exercise alone. Sensible dieting will help you lose weight, and exercise will help increase your metabolism and maintain firm, healthy muscles that burn fat.

► If you're on a diet, it may help to turn meal cleanup over to somebody else. You won't be tempted to munch on leftovers as you're putting them away.

► Keep a record of everything you eat, and it'll be easier to reinforce your goals for weight loss. The record will also be a reminder of how often you are straying from your diet.

► Eating meals with someone whose company you enjoy makes it easier to talk more and eat less.

► When you're severely tempted to have a second helping of some food, tell yourself you can have it in 5 minutes. Then do something else. Chances are, you won't "need" the second helping.

► Use smaller plates for diet-size meals. Smaller portions look more satisfying on a proportionately smaller plate, and you won't feel that you're on starvation rations. The same strategy applies to wine glasses and dessert dishes.

▶ When you're dieting, foods that take longer to eat can be more satisfying than easy-to-eat foods. For example, corn on the cob seems like more than the same amount of cut corn, and lobster in the shell will keep you busy longer than a boneless steak.

▶ When making stews and other dishes containing grease or fats, prepare them ahead and then store them in the refrigerator. The fat will rise to the surface, where you can easily lift it off before reheating and serving the dish.

▶ Substitute yogurt for whipped cream or artificial dessert toppings.

▶ Just because you're trying to lose weight doesn't mean you have to give up healthy snacks. There are many snacks that fall under 100 calories. Try 5 ounces of ginger ale over a peeled and sectioned orange. Add a bit of orange and lemon to tomato juice, then blend with ice cubes. Serve raw vegetables with one-third cup of plain yogurt splashed with herbs for dipping.

▶ Substitute club soda or mineral water for an evening cocktail.

▶ Dress your vegetables with lemon juice and herbs instead of butter.

▶ Dips made from packaged mixes pack a weighty wallop of calories, but it isn't the mix that makes them fattening, it's what they're mixed with. Most packaged mixes add only 50 calories, but the directions call for a base of sour cream (485 calories per cup) or cream

cheese (850 calories in an 8-ounce package). Cut calories dramatically by substituting plain, unsweetened yogurt—only 130 calories—for sour cream or the low-calorie, low-fat "imitation" cream cheese for the real thing.

▶ The lower the fat content in dairy products, the fewer calories they contain. For example, cottage cheese that's labeled 99 percent fat-free has only 160 to 180 calories a cup, while regular creamed cottage cheese has between 240 and 260 calories.

▶ It's best to look for specific calorie information on "dietetic" foods. A "dietetic" product doesn't always contain fewer calories; for example, some "dietetic" candies for diabetics have just as many calories as regular candy.

EXERCISING FOR HEALTH & FITNESS

Lifelong, consistent exercise has been linked to a host of health benefits—among them, fighting coronary heart disease, aiding in the treatment of high blood pressure, raising levels of "good" (high-density lipoprotein) cholesterol, strengthening bones, helping digestion, and possibly even combatting cancer. Exercise can also play a role in the treatment of coronary heart disease, respiratory disease, diabetes, and arthritis. And most impressive of all, an active lifestyle has actually been associated with longer life and slower aging.

Along with these health benefits, exercise boosts your energy and makes getting started in the morning easier. It improves muscle tone and flexibility. It can also help you feel better, calmer, and less stressed. Doctors are even "prescribing" exercise as a treatment for depression.

Getting Started with an Exercise Program

The only problem with exercise is that it only works if you do it. That means that you have to be committed. It is recommended that you consult your physician and go in for a

YOUR DIET WHEN YOU'RE PREGNANT

To control weight and nausea during pregnancy, ask your physician for a suggested diet during pregnancy and follow these tips:

▶ It's estimated that during pregnancy a woman needs 300 to 500 extra calories a day. These should be obtained from nutritious foods, not from high-calorie snacks that are low in food value. During pregnancy, a weight gain of at least 24 pounds is good for the mother and the growth of the baby.

▶ Cut down on sweets, but not on whole-grain bread and potatoes that you need for energy.

▶ To reduce feelings of nausea during pregnancy, try eating only cold foods.

▶ If you can't tolerate any other foods in the morning, at least eat bread or dry toast with milk.

▶ To control nausea, take small sips of cola or bites of bland food, such as custard, gelatin, or mashed potatoes, throughout the day.

▶ Nibbling on nuts, cheese, or other high-protein foods every 2 or 3 hours can help relieve feelings of nausea in early pregnancy. Substitute frequent nutritious snacks for three large heavy meals a day.

▶ To prevent constipation, eat fiber-rich foods such as whole-grain breads and lots of fresh fruits and vegetables.

checkup or physical exam before you begin an exercise routine, especially if you've been inactive up to now. If you are overweight, are over 45, or have any significant health problems, your doctor's OK is essential before you begin any exercise program. If you've been active, use the following principles to guide you through your exercise program:

▶ You should be able to hold a conversation with someone when you exercise. If you are too winded to talk, you can probably conclude that you're exercising too hard for your present fitness level.

▶ Exercising should be painless. If you experience a heaviness in your chest or any pain in your chest, jaw, neck, feet, legs, or back, you should slow down. If that doesn't stop the pain, see your doctor and describe what happened. Try to recall the circumstances under which the pain occurred.

▶ If you have pain in the middle of your chest that lasts more than 2 minutes, which may or may not be accompanied by pain in the arm, jaw, neck, or shoulders, get medical help immediately.

▶ If you seem excessively tired for an hour or more after exercising, it was too strenuous. You should feel exhilarated, not fatigued. If you experience a dizzy or lightheaded feeling, it's time to back off.

▶ If you feel like vomiting or are tired for at least a day after exercising, take it easy. You're pushing your body too hard.

▶ If you can't sleep at night or if your nerves seem shot, it means that you've been pushing too hard. The same is true if you seem to have lost your "zing" or can't catch your breath after a few minutes of exercising.

▶ If you have any questions about excessive fatigue, pain, or discomfort, see your physician.

Follow Your Heart

How do you know how much physical effort to exert? The answer is to follow your heart. Your heart rate can tell you when you're working hard enough to increase your aerobic fitness. Exercise physiologists have determined a heart rate range that is safe for most people during exercise. They call this your target heart rate range. This is between 60 and 90 percent of your maximum heart rate. The range tells you your optimum level of exertion. By exercising for 60 to 90 percent of your target heart rate range for at least 20 minutes, three or more days a week, you can safely and effectively increase your aerobic fitness. It is recommended that you work up to the target range gradually. The maximum heart rates shown are estimates obtained by subtracting age from 220. To find your precise maximum heart rate, you would need to take an exercise test.

1. Find your maximum heart rate, either by taking an exercise test or by subtracting your age from 220.
2. Multiply your maximum heart rate by .6 (60 percent) to find the lower limit of your target range.
3. Multiply your maximum heart rate by .9 (90 percent) to find the upper limit of your target range.

Checking Your Pulse

▶ To check your heart rate, you need a watch that measures seconds, not just minutes.

▶ Take your pulse either at the radial artery in your wrist (on the inner side of your wrist, below the heel of your hand) or the carotid artery in your neck (located on either side of your Adam's apple). Use the index and middle fingers of one hand to feel the pulse. If you use the artery in your neck, however, place

your fingers gently; putting too much pressure on this artery can actually slow down your pulse and give you a false reading.

▶ When you've found your pulse, count the number of beats for 10 seconds. Then multiply that number by six to find your heart rate in beats per minute.

▶ If you have trouble taking your pulse, you may want to purchase an inexpensive stethoscope that allows you to hear your heartbeat or use an automated pulse taker.

▶ Don't become a slave to your pulse, measuring it so often that it becomes a compulsion. Measure your pulse once a week for the first three months of exercising.

Warming Up and Cooling Down

The one exercise that will provide complete fitness for all parts of the body has not been devised. All exercises have their shortcomings. Most workouts do not promote flexibility, which is why it is important to warm up and cool down to prevent injuries.

▶ With any exercise program, each workout should start with a warm-up period and end with a cool-down period.

▶ After working out at your regular pace, end your workout with a five-minute slower

FINDING YOUR MAXIMUM HEART RATE RESERVE

Another way of finding your optimum level of exertion during exercise is to use your maximum heart rate reserve. Exercising at 50 to 85 percent of your maximum heart rate reserve will give you a healthy aerobic workout. This method is more precise than using a percent of your maximum heart rate (target heart rate range), but you'll need to do a little more calculating to figure it out. Use the following formula:

1. Measure your resting heart rate by counting your pulse for 10 seconds and multiplying by 6. (Be sure to do this while you're resting.)
2. Subtract your resting heart rate from your maximum heart rate. (You can find your maximum heart rate by taking an exercise test or by subtracting your age from 220.)
3. Multiply the result of Step 2 by .5 (50 percent) and add that to the result of Step 1 to find the lower limit of your maximum heart rate reserve target zone.
4. Multiply the result of Step 2 by .85 (85 percent) and add that to the result of Step 1 to find the upper limit of your maximum heart rate reserve target zone.

period, followed by another series of stretches to help maintain flexibility and prevent pain or injury.

▶ Warming up, cooling down, and stretching all become even more important if you gradually increase your workouts.

Stretching

To maintain flexibility and ward off injury, you need to stretch your muscles before you put them to work. Stretching, both before and after your workouts, is absolutely essential to any exercise program. Stretching is most effective when the muscles are already  warmed up. Therefore a morning jogger, for example, should stretch after a few minutes of easy jogging, and then again after the run. If you skip stretching to save time, you'll probably end up losing time in the end as you wait for your sore and injured muscles to heal.

▶ When you stretch, use a slow, smooth movement. Avoid bouncing, since this will cause the muscles to tighten.

THE TARGET HEART RATE RANGE

Age	Maximum Heart Rate (Beats per minute)	Target Heart Rate Range (Between 60% and 90 % of max. in beats per minute)
20	200	120 to 180
40	180	108 to 162
45	175	105 to 157
50	170	102 to 153
55	165	99 to 148
60	160	96 to 144
65	155	93 to 139
70	150	90 to 135

▶ Stretch as far as you can, but don't stretch to the point of pain.

▶ Hold a stretch for at least 15 seconds.

Exercises for Strength

Aerobic exercises, like walking and running, do not promote upper body strength. To round out an aerobic program, you can visit a local gym or health club and use weights or weight machines to strengthen muscles. You may also do exercises at home. The following are examples of the kinds of exercises that promote strength:

Regular Push-up

Lie facedown with your feet together and your hands palm-down beneath your shoulders. Keeping your body straight, push your entire body, except for your hands and feet, off the floor until your arms are straight. Return to the starting position to complete one repetition.

Right Angles

Lie on your back with weights in your hands and your arms on the ground at right angles to your body. Raise your arms so that they point straight up, pulling in your abdomen at the same time. Return to the starting position to complete one repetition.

Trunk Twister

Stand with your hands clasped behind your neck and your elbows drawn back. Raise your right knee as high as possible and turn your body to the right so that your left elbow briefly touches your right knee. When your right foot hits the floor, raise your left knee as high as possible and turn your body to the left so that your right elbow touches your left knee. This completes one repetition.

Head and Shoulder Curl

Lie on your back with your knees bent, your feet on the floor, and your arms crossed on your chest. Tighten your abdominal muscles and curl your head and shoulders up off the floor. Return to the starting position to complete one repetition.

Sit-up

Lie on your back with your knees bent and your arms across your chest. (If you prefer, you may place your arms at your sides, extend your arms over your head, or clasp your hands behind your head.) Curl your body up into a sitting position by first drawing your chin toward your chest, then lifting your upper body off the floor. Keep your back rounded throughout the movement. Sit up as far as possible, then return to the starting position to complete one repetition.

Single Leg Raises

Lie on your right side with your right arm extended above your head (palm against the floor) and your head resting on your extended arm. Place your left hand on the floor in front of you for stability. Raise your left leg to at least a 45-degree angle. Lower your leg to the starting position to complete one repetition. Do several repetitions, then turn over and do the exercise on your other side.

HEALTH HAZARDS

The nation's leading recreational drugs are alcohol, tobacco, cocaine, and marijuana. All are used by adults and minors, although only the first two are legal for adults. All are powerful substances that can be addictive to young and old alike and have the capacity to injure or destroy the body. It is important to note and remember that drug use is an area of our health over which we can exercise control. There are many sources of information about these subjects and how to stop abusing them. If you or someone you know needs help, consult a physician or counselor to get more information.

WALKING FOR FITNESS

Brisk walking is an aerobic exercise; it can help you train your heart, lungs, and muscles to work more efficiently. As they're conditioned, they'll require less oxygen to do the same amount of work. And that can translate into less strain on your heart and a lower risk of heart disease for you. Use the following tips for getting started with a walking program:

▶ Use a comfortable pair of well-constructed walking shoes that support and cushion your feet and prevent them from turning inward too much when they hit the ground.

▶ The secret to walking comfortably is to walk naturally—pretty much as you've been walking up to now.

▶ Keep your spine straight and hold your head high as you walk to avoid walking into trouble, such as cars or curbs.

▶ Keep your wrists, hips, knees, and ankles relaxed. Allow your arms to hang loosely at your sides. They will swing naturally in opposite action to your legs.

▶ As you walk, each foot should strike the ground at the heel. Transfer your weight forward from your heel, along the outer portion of your foot, to your toes. To complete the foot-strike pattern, push off with your toes. As you shift your weight from heel to toe, you should get a rolling motion.

▶ Avoid landing flat-footed or on the balls of your feet.

▶ Breathe naturally as you walk, using both your nose and your mouth. Remember that the faster you go the more air you'll need.

▶ Don't forget to warm up and stretch before you begin to walk.

Basic Starter Program:

Level	Time	Frequency
1	20 minutes a day	3-5 times a week
2	25 minutes a day	3-5 times a week
3	30 minutes a day	3-5 times a week
4	35 minutes a day	3-5 times a week
5	40 minutes a day	3-5 times a week
6	45 minutes a day	3-5 times a week

COLD-WEATHER EXERCISE CHECKLIST

▶ Wear dark-colored clothing to absorb the sun's rays.

▶ Dress in warm, loose-fitting layers to trap body heat, allow sweat to evaporate, and keep cold air out.

▶ If you're male, wear an extra pair of shorts to keep the groin area warm.

▶ Top off your layers of clothing with a breathable, waterproof windbreaker.

▶ Unzip or remove outermost layers as you begin to heat up.

▶ Wear a warm hat that covers your ears or wear earmuffs in addition to a hat.

▶ In cold, windy weather, cover all exposed skin to avoid frostbite. A ski mask or scarf can be used to protect the face.

▶ Wear mittens instead of gloves—or on top of gloves—to trap heat around fingers.

▶ Wear calf- or knee-length socks made of absorbent material like cotton or wool.

▶ Wear a waterproof sunscreen on all exposed skin.

▶ Don't wear jewelry, including earrings.

▶ Drink plenty of water before, during, and after outdoor exercise to avoid dehydration. Do not drink alcoholic beverages before or during exercise.

▶ Move your outdoor program indoors when the weather poses a threat of frostbite or hypothermia.

Alcohol

Alcohol is a central nervous system depressant. Short-term effects can disrupt mental and motor skills, resulting in poor judgment, poor coordination, and a tendency to have accidents. Consumed heavily on a regular basis, alcohol damages internal organs, especially the liver and heart, and decreases life expectancy. Alcoholism is a disorder in which a person repeatedly drinks excessive amounts of alcoholic beverages, with resulting harm to health, relations to other people, and work performance. If you or someone you know shows signs of alcoholism, or if you're just concerned that you're becoming too dependent on alcoholic beverages to relax, consult a physician for help.

Symptoms of alcoholism are:

▶ Frequent drunkenness.

▶ Tolerance to alcohol, in which the person must consume a great deal of alcohol before showing signs of intoxication.

▶ Physical dependence, resulting in withdrawal symptoms a day or more after stopping drinking, including tremors, physical pain, seizures, and hallucinations.

▶ Continued drinking even when it is harming the person's health, personal life, and financial situation.

▶ Poor job performance.

▶ Depression.

Drugs

Cocaine and its derivatives and marijuana are the most frequently used drugs today. Cocaine stimulates the central nervous system. At lower doses, it produces talkativeness, euphoria (a heightened sense of well-being), excitement, enormous self-confidence, and a deceptive sense of increased concentration. At higher doses, tremors, seizures, severe mental disorders, and even strokes and heart attacks can develop.

Usually, cocaine is used in one of four ways: nasal inhalation of the powdered form ("snorting"); intravenous injection; smoking the crystalline form ("crack"); and inhalation of the vapor ("free-basing"). The latter is extremely dangerous, both because it delivers high concentrations of cocaine into the central nervous system and because the equipment used to free-base can explode.

Marijuana or *cannabis* is the dried flower clusters, stems, and leaves of the Indian hemp plant. It looks like coarse tobacco and typically is smoked, although it can be cooked into foods and eaten. Marijuana raises the heart rate and lowers sex-hormone and fertility levels in both males and females. Other physical symptoms of marijuana use are reddened eyes, dry mouth and throat, dilated pupils, and lack of physical coordination. While marijuana appears to relax the body and mind, it alters depth perception, decreases reaction time, and reduces the ability to talk and think directly. Its effects are often followed by mood swings, panic, depression, and even hallucinations.

Although marijuana is not physically addictive like cocaine, if you or anyone you know is using these drugs, seek help from your physician or a qualified professional.

Smoking

Tobacco use typically begins as a social behavior and results in significant physical consequences, including addiction. Smoking cigarettes, pipes, and cigars, and chewing

HOT-WEATHER EXERCISE CHECKLIST

▶ Acclimatize yourself slowly to the heat and take rest periods in the shade during exercise.

▶ Drink plenty of cold water before, during, and after exercise.

▶ Wear as little clothing as possible.

▶ Choose loose-fitting clothing made of lightweight, breathable fabric. Cotton is a wise choice because it absorbs perspiration and promotes evaporation of sweat. Spread petroleum jelly on areas prone to chafing.

▶ Avoid walking outfits made of rubber, plastic, or other nonporous materials.

▶ Choose light-colored clothing to reflect the sun's rays.

▶ Cover your head with a lightweight, light-colored cap. Try soaking it in cold water before putting it on your head.

▶ Wear a waterproof sunscreen with a Sun Protection Factor (SPF) of 15 or more.

▶ Slow down your pace and decrease the intensity of your exercise especially when humidity is high.

▶ Exercise in a shaded area, such as a park or forest preserve.

▶ Avoid exercising in late morning or early afternoon when the sun's rays are strongest.

tobacco have been linked to oral cancer, lung cancer, circulatory disorders, respiratory diseases, heart diseases, and a shorter life span. Stopping smoking is beneficial to you and to those around you, even if you have no signs of disease. Despite the proven risks of tobacco use, however, many smokers who want to quit seem unable to break the habit. Help is available from many sources, including the American Cancer Society and the American Lung Association, as well as your physician.

HEALTH ISSUES FOR CHILDREN

Knowing When Your Child Is Ill

Parents rapidly become expert and accurate assessors of how their children feel. Any sudden or distinct change in your child's personality or demeanor can be a sign of illness. Don't be afraid to consult your pediatrician. Your pediatrician may suggest that you immediately bring your child in for a visit or that you should wait and see.

If you think your child is ill, check for signs of the following:

▶ Fever higher than 101°F for more than 24 hours, fever accompanied by extreme irritability, or the child is difficult to rouse.

▶ Sore throat for more than 3 days or accompanied by fever.

▶ Earache for more than 1 hour or accompanied by fever higher than 101°F.

▶ Persistent cough accompanied by wheezing or shortness of breath.

SECONDHAND SMOKE

Responsible parents should provide their children with a smokefree environment. Children can inhale smoke from their environment even if it's not directly blown in their faces. Many studies provide statistical proof that secondhand smoke affects the number of upper-respiratory infections and middle-ear infections in children. Children of smokers have more colds, ear infections, bronchitis, and pneumonia, and they show reduced pulmonary (lung) function. More recent research has indicated that the occurrence and severity of colic and coliclike conditions in babies are related to secondary smoke.

For many years, secondhand smoke has been a known factor in the severity of asthma in children. Studies investigating croup show tobacco smoke to be a contributing factor as well.

▶ Constant stomachache that persists for more than 2 hours or is accompanied by bloody stools or recurrent vomiting.

▶ Wetting a larger or smaller number of diapers than usual.

▶ Unusually loose and more frequent stools.

▶ Diarrhea that is bloody, lasts more than 1 day, or is accompanied by vomiting, fever, or absence of urination for eight hours.

▶ Vomiting accompanied by fever or blood, lasting more than 12 hours.

▶ Warm or moist skin.

▶ Pale or flushed appearance.

▶ Lethargic or withdrawn behavior.

▶ Clouded, glassy, or red rather than clear eyes.

▶ Blisters following a burn.

▶ Bulging or depression of the soft spot.

CHILDREN'S DISEASES AND AILMENTS

Today, most children are vaccinated against infectious diseases such as polio, mumps, measles, rubella, pertussis, tetanus, and diphtheria. Be sure that your child is immunized and keep a record of the immunizations. The most common infectious diseases today are influenza and chicken pox; more rare, and more dangerous, are diseases such as mononucleosis and meningitis.

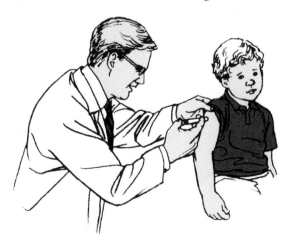

Consult your pediatrician or physician if you suspect that anyone has contracted an infectious disease.

For other childhood ailments, follow the guidelines for nursing a patient with an infectious disease, treating a cold, and knowing when to contact the pediatrician.

▶ **Bumps and bruises**—Most bumps are a normal part of childhood; however, a child who has sustained a blow to the head should be observed closely for the next 24 hours. If the child begins to vomit or becomes difficult to rouse, call your pediatrician at once and follow instructions. Don't try to keep your child awake after a head injury. If your child falls asleep, observe carefully and be sure that the level of consciousness is that of normal sleep. Check this every hour or two by giving your child a gentle nudge or by rolling him or her over; make sure the response is what you would expect during normal sleep. If it is not, or if your child begins to act abnormal in any way, call your pediatrician. This is another instance when you are better to be safe than sorry.

▶ **Ear infections**—Most ear infections are preceded by an upper respiratory infection (a cold). During a cold, the eustachian tube (which equalizes pressure between the middle ear and the nose) becomes blocked and malfunctions, resulting in an infection in the middle ear. In younger children, the eustachian tube is narrower and more crooked and is therefore easier to block. In older children, the tube enlarges, straightens, and is less likely to be obstructed when the child gets congested. Although ear infections can occur at any age, for these and other reasons, they are much less common after the age of 7 or 8. Consult a physician if the earache continues for more than 1 hour and pain is persistent.

▶ **Pinkeye**—Officially known as conjunctivitis, pinkeye is indicated by a redness or pinkness of the white portion of the eye that often accompanies a cold. The infection may be caused by the same virus that caused the cold or may be due to a secondary bacterial infection. Consult your pediatrician if you suspect your child has conjunctivitis.

HANDLING STRESS

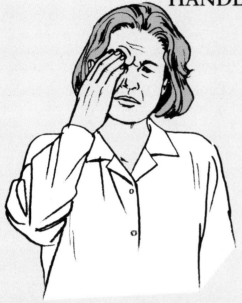

Without stress, our lives might be extremely boring; but too much stress—and particularly chronic, emotional tension—can be harmful to both our physical and mental well-being. There's no way to measure what is too much stress, because it is personalized. Rather, we need to understand how to cope with stress if it appears to be affecting our lives negatively.

The body's response to stress evolves through three stages: alarm, resistance, and exhaustion. When we are confronted with danger, our bodies respond by releasing hormones that allow us to react, sometimes in a life-saving manner. Once the danger passes, our bodies need time to repair damage caused by the alarm. When our bodies are exposed to prolonged stress and not allowed enough time to recover, we become exhausted, which can lead to other problems, such as migraine headaches and high blood pressure.

If you or another member of your family is undergoing stress, try some of the following techniques:

► Engage in physical activity. Many people find that exercise or physical activity relaxes them when they are nervous or angry.

► Share your problems with someone—a friend, relative, or counselor can often help you look at your problems in a different way. For serious problems, seek the help of a professional counselor.

► Know your limits. Learn to accept what you cannot change.

► Take care of yourself by getting enough rest and eating properly. Ask your doctor for help if stress is preventing you from sleeping well.

► Schedule time for fun to give you a break from a stressful routine.

► Make a list of your tasks and prioritize them if you feel overwhelmed.

► Try to cooperate instead of confronting people who seem to be upsetting you. This may reduce the strain and tension of a persistently negative situation.

► Feel free to cry if you need to. Sometimes crying brings healthy release, as does taking some deep breaths.

► Allow yourself some quiet time to think, read, listen to music, or just get away from a stressful situation.

► Avoid self-medications. If you feel you need medical help, consult your physician.

▶ **Ringworm**—This is a contagious fungal infection of the skin that causes red, scaly, itchy, ring-shaped lesions on the skin. Consult your physician if your child develops such symptoms.

▶ **Roseola**—This disease is marked by high fever that lasts 2 to 4 days and goes away. It is followed by the appearance of a transient, flat red rash. It occurs most commonly during the first 3 years. Always consult your physician if your child has a fever higher than 101°F.

IMPORTANT PHONE NUMBERS TO KEEP READILY ACCESSIBLE

Getting outside help immediately is critical in an emergency, but parents sometimes fail to understand that they may be confused in a crisis. To ensure your child's safety, post a list of appropriate phone numbers next to every phone in your house. Include phone numbers of the following on the list:

▶ Pediatrician

▶ Fire department

▶ Police department

▶ Poison control center

▶ Paramedics or ambulance service

▶ Nearest hospital emergency room, including explicit instructions regarding the fastest route to that hospital

▶ Nearest relative or friend

▶ Local taxi service

▶ Information about your child, including birth date, any allergies, and inoculations received

HOME NURSING

Giving Medications

▶ Follow the instructions for both over-the-counter and prescription medications. Use a measuring spoon to give the correct dose and keep track of when the medication is given and when the next dose is due.

▶ It is not wise to give any medication—especially prescription drugs—for any illness other than the one for which it was prescribed. For most illnesses that require an antibiotic, the amount prescribed is just enough to treat that illness so that there is none left over. Many antibiotics are outdated in a few weeks and should be discarded after that date.

▶ Never give your child any medication, including cathartics (drugs to make the bowels move) and over-the-counter medications, without first consulting your pediatrician.

▶ Use a medicine spoon tube or a dropper to give medicine to infants.

▶ A small child could choke on a large pill, so use liquid medication whenever possible. If a medication is not available in liquid form, mash the tablets and combine with juice or food (unless directed otherwise by your doctor).

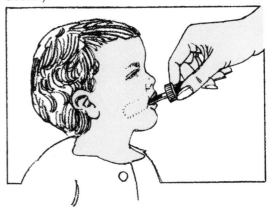

▶ If you use a medicine dropper to give your child liquid medicines by mouth, release the liquid slowly into a cheek; be careful not to point the dropper into the throat, which might force medicine down the windpipe.

IMPORTANT REASONS FOR CONTACTING YOUR PEDIATRICIAN

▶ Routine well-child examinations and immunizations

▶ Drastic changes in your child's behavior

▶ Severe pain

▶ Severe or worrisome injury

▶ Prolonged high fever

▶ Persistent cough

▶ Foul-smelling drainage from the nose, eyes, ears, or anywhere else

▶ Persistent vomiting

▶ Unexplained, persistent rash

▶ Prolonged diarrhea

▶ Blood in urine or stool

▶ Anytime you are really worried about your child's health or physical or emotional well-being

Handling Fevers

The temperature of the body is an indicator of health. When it varies from our normal temperature, it is an indication that the body is fighting infection. Normal body temperature varies between 97.8°F and 99°F. A slightly higher or lower temperature than 98.6°F does not necessarily indicate fever. Use the following as a guideline for handling fevers:

▶ A fever is only one symptom of illness, so be sure to pay attention to how a child or adult is feeling and acting.

▶ A thermometer can be used to take temperature orally, rectally, or under the arm.

You will need a rectal thermometer to take the temperature of an infant or very young child.

▶ By the age of 5 or 6, an oral temperature can usually be taken by placing an oral thermometer in your child's mouth and having it held under the tongue, lips closed, for 2 minutes. Make sure children are old enough to understand not to bite down on the thermometer.

▶ Remember that it's never necessary to take a temperature unless you think your child may be really ill.

RECOMMENDED IMMUNIZATION SCHEDULE FOR CHILDREN

Age	Immunization
2 months	DTP and oral polio
4 months	DTP and oral polio
6 months	DTP
12–15 months	Tuberculin test[1]
15 months	MMR
18 months	HiB
18 months[2]	DTP
18 months[3]	Oral polio
4–6 years	DTP and oral polio
14–16 years	Adult tetanus and diphtheria

DTP = Diphtheria, tetanus, and pertussis (whooping cough) vaccines given as single injection

MMR = Measles, mumps, and rubella vaccines given as single injection

HiB = Hemophilus influenza type b (meningitis) immunization

[1]May be repeated at yearly intervals; consult your physician

[2]Or 6 to 12 months after third dose

[3]Or anytime between 12 and 18 months

▶ If your baby is less than 6 months old and has a temperature above 100°F, call your pediatrician immediately.

▶ Treat an adult's fever with aspirin or aspirin substitute.

▶ Never give a child with a fever aspirin of any kind; this has been associated with Reye's syndrome, a rare illness that can be fatal. Consult your pediatrician for directions on how to treat a child's fever.

▶ Make sure an adult or child with a fever drinks plenty of liquids.

▶ Consult a physician if an adult's fever lasts more than 2 days or is accompanied by other symptoms, such as a sore neck or severe headache.

Nursing Patients with Infectious Disease

▶ Use aspirin substitutes to treat fevers.

▶ Keep the patient warm and comfortable.

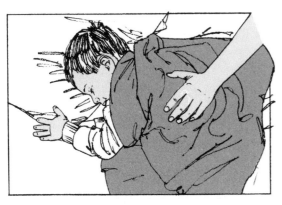

▶ Keep other people away from the patient, and wash your hands every time you come in contact with the patient.

▶ Treat sores, such as those from chicken pox, with calamine lotion.

▶ Provide lots of water and juice to the patient and encourage drinking liquids.

▶ Offer frequent small meals, rather than large meals.

▶ Consult your physician immediately if the patient's symptoms worsen, particularly if the patient's fever rises or is accompanied by other symptoms of illness.

Vomiting and Diarrhea

Both vomiting and diarrhea can be signs of relatively mild upsets in the body or symptoms of more serious disorders. Either ailment should be observed carefully, particularly among young children.

WHAT YOU NEED TO KNOW IN CASE AN ACCIDENT HAPPENS

All parents should be familiar with basic emergency procedures so that they can help their child before expert help arrives. Your local chapter of the Red Cross, the Heart Association, or other such organization, or your local hospital, health clinic, day-care center, or other such agency probably can help you to acquire essential training in first aid and cardiopulmonary resuscitation (CPR) for infants and toddlers. Even if you have had similar training before, taking an update or refresher course certainly wouldn't hurt. Note that providing first aid and CPR for a baby involves many considerations and techniques that are significantly different from those that are applicable to older children and adults. Choking, poisoning, head injuries, cuts, sprains, fractures, burns, etc., all need to be handled at least slightly differently with babies. If possible, responsibility for learning these first-aid and CPR procedures should not be relegated to just one parent. The more people who have this information—including close friends, relatives, and baby-sitters, as well as both parents—the more likely your child is to receive proper treatment.

▶ Offer tea, noncola beverages, and soup or broth to replenish liquids.

▶ Avoid solid foods until the vomiting or diarrhea subside; then offer bland crackers or toast before returning to a normal diet.

▶ After a bout of diarrhea, avoid eating irritating foods, such as bran, vegetables, fruit, fried foods, coffee, and alcohol, for a while.

▶ If vomiting occurs regularly or frequently, or if blood or red or dark brown spots are observed, consult your doctor immediately.

▶ If diarrhea lasts longer than 3 days in adults, there is blood in the stool, or it is a recurring problem, consult your physician, because it could be the sign of a more serious disease.

HEALTH AND FITNESS FOR THE ELDERLY
Nutrition

Good nutrition is essential to maintaining health as we age. Surveys show, however, that while older people believe that nutrition is

TAKING A TEMPERATURE RECTALLY

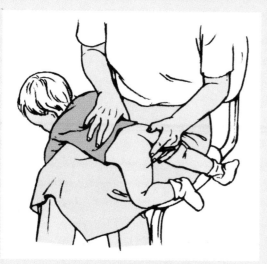

If you've never taken a child's temperature rectally before, ask for guidance when you are at your pediatrician's office. Select a rectal thermometer that has a short, round mercury bulb. (It's often helpful to have a spare on hand in case of breakage.) Learn to read it before you need it. To read the thermometer, roll it back and forth between your thumb and index finger until you can see the top of the mercury column.

Rub the bulb end of the thermometer with rubbing alcohol or soap and water, and rinse with clear, cool water. Shake the mercury column down so that it reads below 96°F. Do this by tightly gripping the end opposite to the bulb and snapping your wrist so that the mercury moves down toward the bulb. Place a small amount of lubricant on the bulb end of the thermometer. Vaseline, baby lotion, lubricating jelly, etc., are all acceptable.

Place the baby in a facedown position on a firm surface. With tiny babies, you can lay the baby facedown across your lap. Using the palm of your hand closest to the infant's head, apply firm pressure to the baby's back just above the buttocks. If the baby tries to roll over, increase the pressure. With your free hand, gently insert the lubricated end of the thermometer 1 to 1½ inches into the anal opening. Hold the thermometer between your second and third fingers and keep that hand cupped over the baby's bottom. Hold in place for 2 minutes. Remove and read.

important, they also admit to skipping meals and neglecting nutrition for a variety of reasons, including the following:

► They may be less interested in food, particularly if they are eating alone or their sense of smell has deteriorated.

► They may not feel like eating.

► Their appetites may be affected by medications they are taking.

► Illness or lack of stamina prevents them from preparing meals.

Poor nutrition is indicated by weight loss, light-headedness, disorientation, and lethargy. These also are symptoms of other illnesses, but many physicians quiz older patients about their eating habits. If you or an older person you know is showing symptoms of poor nutrition, consult a physician. There are also important steps to take to improve nutritional habits and intake:

► Social interaction can improve attitudes to meals. If you live alone, try to eat some meals with others. Invite friends and relatives to share meals or find out about a community group-dining program.

► The elderly may need more vitamins than younger people. Vitamins C and E and beta-carotene have been shown to benefit the body's immune system. These can be obtained from citrus fruits or green and yellow vegetables or can be taken as supplements.

COPING WITH COLIC

Colic means different things to different people. In general, colic refers to repeated episodes of inconsolable crying in a baby who previously was not especially fussy. The episodes of crying usually begin a few weeks after birth and occur during the day and at night. Nothing the parents do makes any difference. After what seems like forever (but is usually less than two hours), the baby calms down or sleeps. This pattern may be repeated several times daily. Most babies do not get colic, but those who do can try the patience of even the best parents.

If you have determined that your baby has colic, the following tips may help you cope. Remember that colic is a self-limiting set of symptoms that's usually tougher on the parents than on the baby.

►Try to console the baby with some kind of movement, such as rocking, walking, or a ride in an automobile.

►Do not overfeed a colicky baby, because an over-filled tummy can increase discomfort.

►Talk to your baby calmly, letting him or her know that you are concerned and available.

►If you feel you are losing your patience or perspective, get someone else to take care of the baby for a while until you feel better.

►If you are having trouble coping with the crying or it seems really excessive, consult your pediatrician and have the baby examined to make sure everything is normal.

THINGS TO DO AND NOT DO FOR A COLD

DO

▶ Offer fluids frequently and provide small nourishing meals.

▶ Pamper and offer sympathy.

▶ Encourage adequate rest and sleep.

▶ Treat fever (higher than 102°F) and discomfort with acetaminophen.

▶ Use disposable cups whenever possible to prevent spread of viruses.

▶ Teach your child to wash hands before and after meals and after using the bathroom.

▶ Use a cool-mist humidifier in the room of the person with a cold.

▶ Keep your child indoors if it is chilly outside.

▶ Watch for complications such as ear pain, severe cough, or a worsening of symptoms.

▶ Call your physician for advice if you think the illness is not following the expected course.

DO NOT

▶ Offer large, heavy meals.

▶ Criticize or show impatience.

▶ Allow a noisy or unpleasant environment.

▶ Give aspirin or aspirin products to children.

▶ Share eating or drinking utensils.

▶ Allow unwashed hands to handle food.

▶ Use hot-water vaporizers.

▶ Delay consulting with your physician or pediatrician about significant changes in someone's condition.

▶ If you're a recent widow or widower, pay particular attention to your nutrition. People who are just starting to live alone often skip meals and eat less. If someone you know tends to grow tired of cooking and eats less, encourage them to swap meals with friends. If they don't know how to cook, suggest taking a cooking class and purchasing a cookbook that concentrates on meals for one.

▶ Get help with the grocery shopping if you're avoiding cooking because you can't tote grocery bags.

▶ If you wear dentures and they don't fit well, make an appointment with your dentist.

Being unable to chew properly can affect both how often and what you eat.

▶ If your sense of smell has diminished, try using more herbs to enhance flavors and combining different foods to improve texture.

▶ Experiment with at least one new dish a week. You may not like it or you may find another meal to make your meals more varied.

Exercise

It can be depressing to think about the physical changes we consider to be a natural part of aging—including wasting away of muscle and bone, joint stiffening, and the tendency to get out of breath after only minor exertion. But it's possible that many of these changes are related more to inactivity, which older people too often fall into, than age per se. Many of these changes can occur at any age with extreme inactivity, such as bed rest.

The latest studies show that a combination of aerobic and strength-training exercises can promote good health in the aging. Several studies suggest that exercise improves cardiovascular fitness, reduces the risk of osteoporosis, reduces the risk of diabetes, and improves mental functioning. In fact, exercise may have a more powerful effect on improving the health of the elderly than it does on younger people.

Regular exercise should include both aerobic exercise, which improves the ability of the heart and lungs to pump blood through the body, and strength-training exercise to increase muscle mass. Both usually should be done three to four times a week for 20 to 30 minutes per day, beginning at 60 percent and progressing to 90 percent of the maximum heart rate. Consult your physician before beginning any exercise regimen.

▶ Take a brisk walk; in extremely hot summer weather or cold or icy winter weather, many elderly walkers can be found inside shopping malls. Some even have organized "mall-walking" routines that end with a social cup of coffee or tea and the opportunity to meet new people.

▶ If you golf, avoid taking a golf cart every time. Walk between holes.

▶ Recent studies show that muscle mass is crucial to good health. Join a gym and learn to lift weights or rent or buy a videotape that includes a weight-lifting segment.

▶ Find out if there are community groups or organizations that sponsor exercise outings or regular classes for seniors. These are designed for your age group, and you won't feel silly or awkward as you might with a group of young people.

▶ If you enjoy swimming, join a local community group that has a pool. Swimming is one of the best ways to combine aerobic exercise and muscle strengthening, and it puts very little stress on the bones and joints.

▶ Above all, don't think that you're too old to start exercising. A 91-year-old female runner who has completed 10 marathons didn't take up running until she was 70. And the success of people in their 80s and 90s who have increased their muscle mass through weight training proves that deterioration of the muscles is reversible.

RECOMMENDED DIET FOR OLDER AMERICANS

Like other age groups, older Americans should eat a variety of foods, maintain a desirable weight, avoid fried and fatty foods to reduce the intake of saturated fat and cholesterol, eat an adequate amount of fiber-rich foods, avoid too much sugar and starch, and drink alcohol only in moderation. Older women, especially those at risk for developing osteoporosis, should consume foods that are rich in calcium (milk, dark green vegetables, meats, etc.) and/or take calcium supplements.

For people age 51 and older, the Food and Nutrition Board of the National Research Council recommends the following daily diet:

▶ 2 to 3 servings (½ cup each) of milk, cheese, or yogurt for men; 4 servings for women.

▶ 6 or more servings of whole-grain breads or cereals.

▶ 2 to 4 servings (½ cup each) of fruit.

▶ 3 to 5 servings (½ cup each) of vegetables.

▶ 2 to 3 servings (5 to 7 ounces total) of protein from lean meat, poultry, fish, and alternates, such as eggs, nuts, dried beans, and peas.

Mental Fitness

Memory loss doesn't automatically indicate the presence of Alzheimer's disease. It can be caused by alcoholism, depression, vitamin B12 deficiency, thyroid problems, and even excessive medications. What researchers have learned about mental fitness is that good relationships, social involvement, physical fitness, and mental activity are key factors in sustained mental health. If you're concerned about your own mental abilities or those of an aging friend or relative, consult your physician to make sure that medications or illness are not responsible for mental lapses. The physician may also be able to suggest activities that can help exercise mental abilities. Additionally, look into activities geared for senior citizens run by local groups, communities, and churches.

MEDICAL ISSUES
Choosing a Physician

Whether your family chooses individual physicians for family members or a family practitioner who specializes in taking care of all members of the family, it is important to select a physician before there is an injury or emergency. County and state medical societies, the physician's referral service at a local hospital, and even friends and relatives can offer referrals. Additionally, some health insurance plans have lists of physicians who participate in their plans. Depending on your needs or the needs of your family, use the following questions to draw up a list of basic questions to ask a doctor you are considering:

▶ Will the doctor treat all family members?

▶ Does the doctor provide care during pregnancy and perform deliveries? Don't assume that all obstetricians perform deliveries.

▶ Does the doctor have staff privileges at a nearby accredited hospital?

▶ Does the doctor perform surgery? If so, what kind?

▶ Does the doctor encourage preventive medicine, such as routine checkups, immunizations, and follow-up tests?

▶ Does the doctor make emergency house calls for bedridden family members?

▶ Does the doctor have office hours that are convenient for your family, especially for those who work or attend school?

▶ What arrangement does the doctor have for a substitute when he or she is unavailable?

▶ What are the fees for various services?

▶ Is the doctor certified by the American Board of Family Practice (or a specialty board of another area)?

▶ Is the doctor willing to form a partnership with you and to take the time to discuss treatments and options?

Cutting the Costs of Health Care

With soaring medical costs, it's important for everyone, including those who are fully insured, to learn to cut costs for health care. This doesn't mean you have to go to cut-rate doctors or not get the care you need. It simply means you need to be a smart shopper. Take advantage of some of the following guidelines to help trim medical bills:

▶ Fees for medical services vary tremendously. Don't be afraid to discuss fees with your doctor and compare fees with relatives and friends. If you find that your doctor's fees are substantially higher for office visits and/or lab

tests, talk about the fees and/or consider switching physicians.

▶ If you change doctors for any reason, have your medical records sent to the new doctor so you don't have to undergo tests that have already been done.

▶ Ask your doctor about accepting the payment of the insurance company as full payment. If the answer is no, you may have to pay as much as 20 percent yourself for many services.

▶ Specialists are generally more expensive than other doctors. Make sure you're not going to a specialist for services that could be performed by a family practitioner, an internist, or a general practitioner.

▶ Buy generic drugs. Generic pills and capsules are equivalent to brand-name drugs, but cost a lot less. If your doctor insists on your choosing a brand-name drug, make sure you understand why.

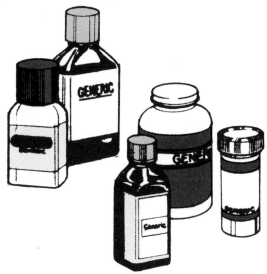

▶ Make sure you know how to take medications, and keep them from spoiling by storing them in a cool, but not cold, place. The bathroom is the worst place to store drugs, because of steam from the shower.

▶ Watch out for side effects. Make sure your doctor knows about other medications you are taking.

▶ Avoid unnecessary lab tests. Ask whether the tests your doctor is suggesting will affect the choice of treatment.

▶ Shop around for eyeglasses; prices vary widely.

▶ Always get a second opinion before having elective surgery. Have your doctor send your records so that you don't have to go through the same tests again.

▶ If you're hospitalized and the hospital loses or misplaces test results, make sure you're not paying for the second test. Insist that you not be billed for the hospital's mistake, whether or not your insurance company will pay for it.

▶ Avoid checking into the hospital on a weekend for elective surgery. Get tests done on an out-patient basis before the day of surgery.

▶ Read your hospital bill; make sure you are not being charged for services you did not have.

▶ If you're eligible for Medicare, make sure you understand how it works and what it pays for. If your doctor does not participate with Medicare, ask if the office "accepts assignment." If it doesn't, you will have to pay extra.

Second Opinions on Surgery

In some cases, particularly emergencies, surgery is unavoidable, but much of the surgery performed in the U.S. is considered "elective," in which patients choose to have

SAFE-PROOFING AN ELDER'S HOME

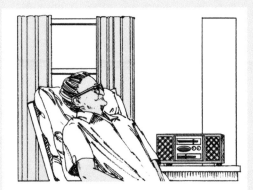

Elderly people who are temporarily or permanently disabled need to feel comfortable and secure in their environment. Take the following steps to avoid accidents and encourage the elderly to manage on their own:

▶ Arrange furniture so that the elderly person can maneuver easily.

▶ Install higher wattage bulbs if lighting is poor and add simple night-lights around the house so the elderly person can get to the bathroom or kitchen at night.

▶ Make sure that often-used items are stored conveniently in the kitchen and bathroom.

▶ Set the water heater at 120°F so there is no chance of the elderly scalding themselves.

▶ Remove all slip rugs or make sure they are firmly attached to the floor with carpet tape.

▶ Install handrails wherever a person may need them—in the tub or shower, next to the toilet, on stairways, in hall passages, and on porches.

▶ Use a nonslip mat in the tub or shower; if possible, install a shower seat to make bathing more comfortable.

▶ Make sure telephones are easily accessible and can be heard; consider purchasing a cordless phone and/or an amplifier for the ringer. Also make sure that an emergency list of phone numbers is next to all phones.

surgery to correct a medical problem. While physicians usually agree about when surgery is not warranted, they do not always agree that surgery is the best course of treatment. Today, many problems formerly treated with surgery are responding to new medical technologies. Before agreeing to any elective surgery, patients should know the range of choices available to them. The U.S. Department of Health and Human Services recommends that you should know the answers to the following:

▶ What does the doctor specifically say is the matter with you?

▶ Has the doctor performed all necessary tests to confirm the diagnosis?

▶ What surgery is being recommended?

▶ What are the likely benefits of the surgery?

▶ What are the risks of the surgery?

▶ How long is the recovery and what is involved?

▶ How much will surgery cost?

▶ What will happen if you don't have surgery?

▶ Are there alternative ways to treat your condition that could be tried before surgery?

Additionally, many insurance companies require a second opinion, and the U.S. Department of Health and Human Services recommends that anyone covered by Medicare obtain a second opinion whenever the surgery is not required for an emergency condition. Medicare will pay for a second opinion for people enrolled in Medicare Supplementary Medical Insurance (Part B) after the Part B deductible is met for the year.

GUIDE TO FIRST AID

Prevention is the best medicine when it comes to family emergencies. When a medical emergency does arise, however, you need to be prepared to act. Having information available is not enough. Particularly when young children are in the house, parents should be familiar with emergency procedures, know where to get their hands on such information immediately, and have a first-aid kit ready.

The following information about first aid is not intended to take the place of a family physician or emergency personnel, but it may help you care for your child or others who are injured until help arrives. Remember that seconds count in emergencies.

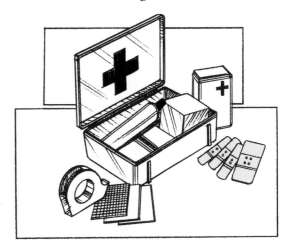

INTRODUCTION TO LIFE-SAVING PROCEDURES

In an emergency, the victim needs professional help. At the first opportunity, you must call an ambulance or emergency room. Additionally, basic skills in life-saving procedures should be followed when someone's life is in immediate danger. Cardiopulmonary resuscitation (CPR) is a life-saving technique used when a person is not breathing and when the heart may have stopped beating. The Heimlich maneuver is used when someone is choking. Neither procedure should be used when someone is not in distress. And if you are unsure what to do to a victim, DON'T DO ANYTHING. Remember, first do no harm. The exception to this rule is if you and the victim are in a life-threatening situation, such as a fire or an accident scene where an explosion might occur.

CPR must be learned through classroom instruction taught by qualified personnel. All parents should enroll in a CPR course. Remember, you must be trained in CPR to administer it to your child.

THE ABCs OF LIFE-SAVING

In an emergency, you should always follow the steps in a certain order. To remember these steps easily, think of them as the ABCs of life-saving:

▶ A = Airway: Clear the victim's airway.

▶ B = Breathing: Restore breathing.

▶ C = Circulation: Restore blood circulation.

WHEN SOMEONE IS UNCONSCIOUS

Among the many possible causes of unconsciousness are head injury, bleeding, diabetic coma, insulin shock, heatstroke, poisoning, choking, severe allergic reaction, and electric shock.

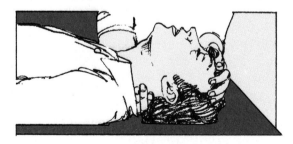

Signs and Symptoms

▶ Unresponsiveness

▶ Lack of awareness of surroundings

▶ Flushed, white, or blue face and gums

If you suspect someone is unconscious, do the following:

1. Pinch the victim's shoulder, and shout in his ear, "Are you OK?" Use the person's name if you know it. DO NOT shake the person violently, especially if it is possible that a head or neck injury has occurred.
2. If the victim does not respond, yell for help.
3. If a neck or back injury is possible, DO NOT move the victim unless absolutely necessary. If no neck or back injury is suspected, lay the person down on his or her back on the floor or ground.
   a. DO NOT let the victim's head strike the ground.
   b. DO NOT twist or bend the person's neck.
   c. DO NOT give the person anything to eat or drink.

Open the Airway

1. Use your finger with a hooking motion to clear the mouth of any foreign material.
2. If a neck injury is not suspected, tilt the head back by lifting the neck and pushing back on the forehead. If you suspect there might be a neck injury (if the victim was on a motorcycle, in an auto accident, or has fallen from a high place), do not move the neck.
3. Check for breathing for about 5 seconds. Lean over the victim's face, and listen and feel for breathing on your cheek. Check whether the chest is rising and falling.
4. If the victim is not breathing, check the pulse.
5. If you can readily see that the victim is breathing, do the following:

▶ Loosen clothing.

▶ Carefully turn the person onto his or her side to keep the airway open, to allow secretions to drain, and to prevent choking in case of vomiting.

▶ Look for possible causes of unconsciousness, such as bleeding, head injury, heatstroke, or poisoning. If you find evidence of such, seek a remedy, such as controlling the bleeding.

▶ Look for a bracelet, necklace, or wallet card that has medical information.

▶ Keep the victim warm but not hot.

▶ DO NOT give the person anything to eat or drink.

▶ DO NOT leave the person alone.

Check the Pulse

1. Check for a pulse by keeping one hand on the victim's forehead and putting your fingers on the Adam's apple on the front of the throat. Slide your fingers down into the neck groove and gently feel for a neck pulse for about 10 seconds.
2. If there is a pulse but no breathing, begin mouth-to-mouth resuscitation.

Mouth-to-Mouth Resuscitation

1. If the victim is not breathing, make sure he or she is on a hard surface and that the mouth is cleared of foreign material. Tilt the head back slightly.
2. Pinch the victim's nose with your thumb and index finger. Take a deep breath, cover the victim's mouth with your mouth, and give two quick, deep breaths; take your mouth away after each breath when the chest is expanding.

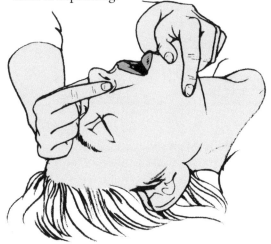

3. Turn your head toward the victim's chest so that your ear is over the victim's mouth and check to see whether air is being exhaled.
4. Continue giving a breath every 5 seconds

by blowing forcefully into the victim's mouth. Remember to take your mouth off the victim's mouth after each breath. Repeat every 5 seconds and check the pulse from time to time.
5. Continue breathing until the victim breathes on his or her own, medical assistance arrives, or there is no pulse, which means that CPR is indicated.

Cardiopulmonary Resuscitation

1. Only begin CPR if the victim does not have a pulse.
2. Yell for help. If someone else comes and you have been trained in CPR, send them to call an ambulance or rescue squad while you begin CPR.
3. Make sure the victim is on a flat surface and that the head is level or slightly lower than the rest of the body. Be sure to use the correct hand position so that you do not damage the ribs or internal organs.
   a. Kneel near the victim's chest.

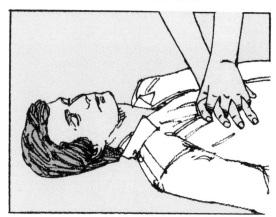

   b. Find the notch at the tip of the breastbone with the middle finger of the hand you used to feel the pulse.
   c. Measure up two finger widths.
   d. Place the heel of your other hand along the lower half of the breastbone, above your fingers.
   e. Place your other hand on top.
   f. Straighten your arms and lock your elbows, but be sure your fingers are not resting on the rib cage.
4. Use only the heel of your hand to press straight down to compress the chest $1\frac{1}{2}$ to

2 inches. Each compression should last ¾ second.

5. Push down on the chest 15 times but do not remove your hands from the chest. After every 15 compressions, remove your hands, open the airway, and give two quick, deep breaths to the victim.

6. Yell for help again.

7. If no one else comes, continue CPR for about 5 minutes, then call an ambulance or rescue squad.

 a. Tell them where you are and give them a phone number. Tell them the victim is unconscious and CPR is in progress.

8. Return immediately and continue CPR until the victim begins breathing and has a pulse or the ambulance arrives.

9. If the victim begins breathing and there is a pulse, keep the airway open.

WHEN SOMEONE IS CHOKING

Choking occurs when the airway is obstructed, resulting in an inability to breathe. A swallowed object is the most common cause. Young children are particularly susceptible to choking. When someone is choking, apply emergency treatment immediately. Seconds count.

Signs and Symptoms

▶ Inability to breathe.

▶ Inability to speak or cry out.

▶ If choking continues, the victim becomes blue, convulsive, limp, and unconscious.

Helping an Infant Who Is Choking

1. Observe breathing difficulties.

2. Lay the infant facedown on your forearm, with your hand on the bony portion of the infant's jaw to support the head. Keep the infant's head lower than the trunk and support your arm on your thigh.

3. Use your other hand to deliver four forceful back blows between the infant's shoulder blades.

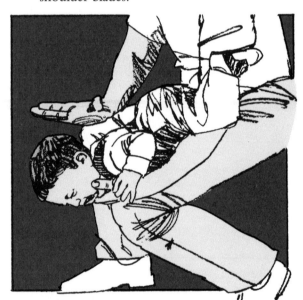

If Back Blows Fail to Dislodge Object

4. With infant still lying facedown on your forearm, lay your other forearm on the infant's back. Gently turn the infant over so that the infant now rests faceup on your other forearm. Be sure to support the infant's head with your hand and keep the infant's head lower than the trunk.

5. Use two or three fingers to deliver four thrusts to the middle of the breastbone between the infant's nipples.

6. Repeat steps 2 to 5 until the object is

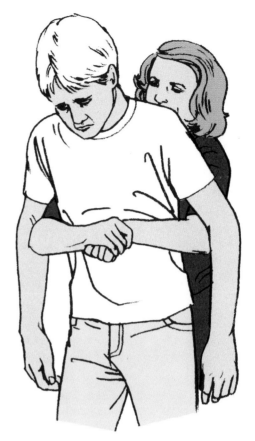

expelled or the infant becomes unconscious.

If the Infant Becomes Unconscious

7. Shout "Help!" Have someone call 911 or the operator.
8. Do the tongue-jaw lift.
    a. Place your thumb in the infant's mouthover the tongue.
    b. Wrap your fingers around the jaw and lift the tongue and jaw forward.
9. Use a hooking action with your finger to remove any visible foreign objects.
10. If breathing does not begin, attempt mouth-to-mouth resuscitation.
11. Repeat procedures until infant begins breathing.

Helping a Child or Adult Who Is Choking

1. Ask the child or person "Are you choking?" If the child or person can speak, or is coughing or breathing, do nothing.
2. If the choking person cannot speak, cough, or breath, perform the Heimlich maneuver:
    a. Stand behind the person and wrap your arms around his or her waist.
    b. Make a fist with one hand. Place the thumb-side of your fist against the person's stomach just above the navel and well below the lowest part of the breastbone.
    c. Grasp your fist with the other hand.
    d. Press into the person's stomach with quick upward thrusts.
3. Repeat thrusts, if necessary.

If Child or Adult Becomes Unconscious

4. Ease the child or person faceup, making sure the head does not strike the floor.
5. Shout "Help!" Have someone call 911 or the operator.
6. Proceed to open the airway and check for breathing.
7. Use a hooking action with your finger to remove any foreign objects from the mouth.
8. Attempt mouth-to mouth resuscitation.
9. Give abdominal thrusts.
    a. Straddle the person's thighs and place the heel of one hand on the stomach just above the navel and well below the lowest part of the breastbone. Place the other hand on top of that hand. Fingers of both hands should point toward the child or adult's heart.
    b. Give six to ten quick, upward thrusts.
10. Repeat procedures until object is dislodged and child or adult is breathing or until medical assistance arrives.

OTHER EMERGENCY PROCEDURES
Allergic Reactions

A severe allergic reaction known as anaphylaxis may occur when a person who is extremely sensitive to a particular substance comes in contact with that substance. Anaphylaxis can be triggered by an insect sting, such as from a bee or wasp; by an animal serum used in a vaccination; by a

ADMINISTERING MOUTH-TO-MOUTH RESUSCITATION ON A CHILD:

If a child stops breathing, BEGIN MOUTH-TO-MOUTH RESUSCITATION IMMEDIATELY.

1. Tap the child on the shoulder and shout "Are you OK?" If the child does not respond, yell "Help!"
2. Open airway: If no head, back, or neck injury is suspected, tilt the child's head back to open airway:
   a. Kneel by the child's side and place your hand on the child's forehead tilt it back.
   b. Place the fingers of your other hand on the bony part of the child's chin, not on the throat.
   c. Gently lift the chin straight up without closing the child's mouth.
   If head, back, or neck injury is suspected, open the child's airway using the jaw thrust:
   a. DO NOT tilt or reposition the child's head or torso.
   b. Place the tips of your index and middle fingers at the corners of the child's jaw (near ears) and your thumbs on the bony portion of the child's chin.
   c. Gently lift the jaw forward and open the child's mouth without moving the head.
3. Look, listen, and feel for breathing for 3 to 5 seconds by placing your cheek near the child's mouth and watching for the chest to rise and fall.
4. Give two breaths.
   a. Maintain the head-tilt position.
   b. Pinch the child's nose closed with your fingers and place your mouth over the child's mouth.
   c. Give two full, slow breaths, each lasting 1 to 1½ seconds.
   d. After each breath, pull your mouth away and allow the child's lungs to deflate.
   e. If there is no exchange of air, reposition the child's head and try again.
5. Check the child's breathing and pulse. To check the pulse:
   a. Keep the child's head tipped back by keeping your hand on the child's forehead.
   b. Place the fingertips of your other hand on the child's Adam's apple. Slide your fingers into the groove at either side of the Adam's apple.
6. Call 911 or the operator if no one else has done so.
7. If the victim remains unconscious and:
   a. There is a pulse but no breathing, continue giving one breath every 4 seconds for a child or one gentle puff every 3 seconds for an infant.
   b. There is no pulse and no breathing and you have not been trained in cardiopulmonary resuscitation (CPR), continue to give one breath every 4 seconds for a child or one gentle puff every 3 seconds for an infant. (There may be a very faint pulse that you did not feel.)

medication; or by ingesting a food or inhaling dust, pollens, or materials to which an individual is especially sensitive. Any of these can cause rapid and severe reaction. Without immediate medical treatment, the person may die. Signs and symptoms are:

► Swollen lips, tongue, or ears

► Uneasiness or agitation

► Red face

► Hives

► Prickling and itching sensations in the skin

► Throbbing or ringing in the ears

► Sneezing, coughing, and breathing difficulty

► Nausea or vomiting

► Dizziness

► Loss of bladder and bowel control

► Convulsions

► Weak, rapid pulse

► Cold, clammy, pale skin

► Unresponsiveness, loss of consciousness, cardiorespiratory collapse

Animal Bites

► Treat minor scratches with a disinfectant recommended by your doctor.

► Any animal bite that punctures the skin calls for medical assistance. For severe bleeding, call 911 or the operator. Do not attempt to clean a severely bleeding wound, but try to stop the bleeding. Observe the person for shock.

► For other wounds that have stopped bleeding, wash the wound with soap and water and rinse for 15 minutes. Apply a sterile dressing or a clean cloth and take the victim to a physician.

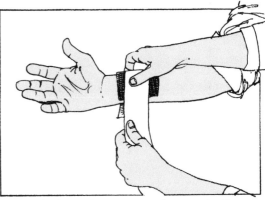

► Notify the police or animal control office so that the animal can be restrained and examined for rabies.

Back and Neck Injuries

Any severe blow, fall, or other accident involving the back or neck may result in injury to the neck, back, or spinal cord. It is critical that you follow instructions so that

---

EMERGENCY TREATMENT FOR SUSPECTED ALLERGIC REACTION

1. Seek medical assistance at the first sign of allergic reaction. Call 911 or the operator.
2. Check the victim's breathing. If breathing stops, begin mouth-to-mouth resuscitation.
3. If anaphylaxis kit containing epinephrine is available, follow instructions for use.

Until the Ambulance Arrives:
4. Have the person lie down; if shortness of breath occurs, have the person sit up.
5. Keep the victim's airway open.
6. Use a hooking action with your finger to clear foreign objects from the mouth.
7. Cover the victim with a blanket.

you do not worsen the injury. Signs and symptoms of back and neck injuries are:

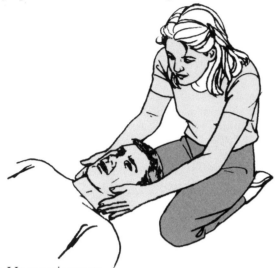

▶ Unconsciousness

▶ Breathing difficulty

▶ Pain

▶ Swelling

▶ Odd position of the head or neck

▶ Loss of sensation, weakness, inability to move

Bleeding

A wound is considered to be major if any of the following are present:

▶ Severe bleeding or gushing

▶ Cuts that are more than skin deep

▶ Cuts with ragged edges

▶ Cuts with deeply embedded dirt or objects

▶ Wounds made from impaled objects

▶ Amputations

For major wounds, seek medical attention immediately. Until help arrives, do the following:

▶ Control the bleeding by applying direct pressure to the wound: Cover the wound with a sterile dressing or a clean cloth and place your hand over the dressing; press firmly. Continue pressure until bleeding stops. Do not remove the dressing. If soaked through, add more material and continue pressure.

▶ Elevate the bleeding part higher than the level of the heart if no broken bone is suspected. DO NOT move the limb if it may be broken.

EMERGENCY TREATMENT FOR SUSPECTED BACK OR NECK INJURY

1. Seek medical assistance immediately. Call 911 or the operator.

Until the Ambulance Arrives:

2. DO NOT move the person unless absolutely necessary to save his or her life.

3. DO NOT bend or twist the neck or body. Careful handling is extremely important.

4. Check the victim's breathing. If breathing stops, use a jaw thrust to open the airway and attempt mouth-to-mouth resuscitation.

5. If the patient is breathing, maintain the position in which person was found and immobilize the head, neck, shoulders, and torso:

   a. Roll up towels, blankets, jackets, or clothing, and place around the head, neck, shoulders, and torso.

   b. If the person is lying on his or her back, slide a thin roll of cloth behind the neck WITHOUT MOVING THE HEAD OR NECK.

   c. Keep rolls of material in place by surrounding them with heavy books, rocks, or bricks.

6. Wait for medical professionals to transport the victim to a hospital.

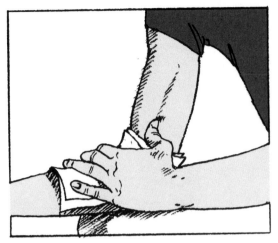

▶ If bleeding does not slow after 5 minutes of direct pressure, continue direct pressure on the wound as you push on the pressure point between the wound and the heart:

1. The most common pressure points are on the brachial point and the femoral point.
2. Brachial point: Use your fingers to apply pressure on the inner side of the upper arm in the groove between the muscles.
3. Femoral point: Use the heel of your hand to apply pressure at the middle of the crease where the thigh meets the groin.

▶ Release the pressure point as soon as the bleeding stops.

▶ Once bleeding is under control, secure the dressing with a bandage.

▶ Observe the victim for shock.

Eye Injuries

The first thing to remember about any possible eye injury is not to rub the eyes or allow someone with a suspected eye injury to rub the eye. Any injury to the eye is considered dangerous, and medical assistance should be sought immediately. Emergency treatment depends on the injury. Signs and symptoms of an eye injury are:

▶ Pain

▶ Redness

▶ Bleeding

▶ Tearing

▶ Sensitivity to light

▶ Swelling and discoloration of the area around the eye

Fainting

▶ If you or someone else feels faint, sit down and lean forward placing your head down between your knees. Take deep breaths.

▶ If someone collapses and is unconscious after feeling faint, put the person on his or her back and try to raise the legs above the level of the chest. Use pillows, wadded-up clothes,

TREATING MINOR WOUNDS

▶ Wash the wound with soap and water for 5 to 10 minutes.

▶ Control bleeding through direct pressure and elevation.

▶ Seek medical attention if signs of infection develop, such as swelling, redness, throbbing pain, sensation of heat, fever, pus, or red streaks.

a footstool, or chair to do this. Loosen clothing and make comfortable.

▶ If the person doesn't recover in a few seconds, check the breathing. Then begin procedures for treating an unconscious victim.

▶ Determine if there are other symptoms (chest pain, headache, palpitations, etc.). If so, or if recovery does not occur in a few minutes, transport patient to a hospital.

Fractures, Dislocations, Sprains, and Strains

Injuries can result when bones and muscles are stressed; in most cases, this type of injury is not life threatening, but medical attention is usually required. When muscles are strained, there may be pain, stiffness, and swelling. Pain in the joint area and tenderness to the touch, along with swelling and discoloration, are typical of sprains. More serious injuries, such as fractures and dislocations, are usually indicated by the following symptoms:

▶ A snapping sound as the bone breaks

▶ Bone protruding from the skin

▶ Detectable deformity of a bone

▶ Abnormal or unnatural movement of the bone

▶ Grating sensation during movement

▶ Pain and tenderness to the touch

▶ Difficulty in moving the affected part

▶ Swelling; discoloration

Heatstroke

If the victim's skin is red, very hot, and dry, even under the arms, the victim may be

suffering from heatstroke. The person's temperature can be 104°F or more, and he or she can be sweating or not. Call for help, move the victim to a cool area, cover him or her with sheets, soak with cold water, and fan to increase heat loss. Stop cooling measures when temperature is at 102°F. Check breathing and pulse from time to time.

TREATING A CHEMICAL BURN TO THE EYE

1. The eye must be flushed immediately, even before medical assistance is sought if you are alone with the victim.
2. Flood the affected area with clean, cool running water for at least 15 minutes.

   a. Hold the eyelid open and pour water slowly over the eyeball at the inner corner.
   b. Have the victim roll the eyeball as much as possible to wash the eye.
   c. Let the water run out of the eye as much as possible to wash the eye.
   d. DO NOT allow water to run into the unaffected eye.
3. DO NOT bandage the eye. Seek medical attention immediately.

Insect Bites and Stings

Signs and symptoms are:

▶ Stinger protruding from the skin

▶ Redness, inflammation

▶ Localized swelling and pain

▶ Burning and itching sensations

If no signs of allergic reaction appear, you can do the following:

▶ Remove the stinger by flicking it with your thumb or forefinger. DO NOT SQUEEZE A STINGER. Wash the area gently with soap and water, and apply an ice pack wrapped in a clean cloth to the area of swelling. Keep the stung area lower than the level of the heart.

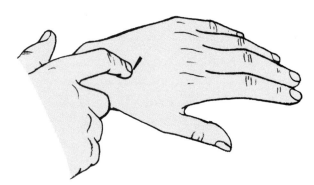

▶ Use ice packs and calamine lotion to soothe other bites and stings. Aspirin or antihistamine may relieve some of the discomfort.

Poisoning and Overdose

The most common sources of poisoning include analgesics; cleaning supplies; cosmetics; plants; medications; hydrocarbons, such as gasoline; and pesticides. Depending on the poison, signs and symptoms may include:

▶ Rapid breathing

▶ Ringing in the ears

▶ Nausea

▶ Overexcitement

▶ Convulsions

▶ Unconsciousness

▶ Burns on lips, mouth, and tongue

▶ Abdominal pain

▶ Vomiting

▶ Blood in vomit

Shock

Shock is a life-threatening condition in which the body's vital functions are threatened due to a lack of sufficient blood or oxygen

---

BURNS

Burns are skin and tissue injuries caused by contact with intense steam, sun, heat, chemicals, or electricity. Signs and symptoms are:

▶ Red skin

▶ Mild swelling and pain

▶ Blistered skin

▶ White or charred skin

▶ Destruction of skin layers

To apply treatment, you must first determine the degree of the burn:

▶ **First-degree burns** are indicated by red or discolored skin, mild swelling, or pain.

▶ **Second-degree burns** are deeper burns with red skin, tenderness, pain, and blistering.

▶ **Third-degree burns** are white or charred (black) skin; skin layers are destroyed, and sometimes the underlying tissue is also destroyed. Usually there is no pain because the nerves have been destroyed.

flow to the tissues. Shock can accompany injuries that cause loss of blood, body fluid, or nervous system control; severe infections; and heart problems. Signs and symptoms are:

▶ Pale or bluish skin, lips, and fingernails

▶ Moist, clammy skin

▶ Weakness

▶ Weak, rapid pulse (more than 100 beats per minute)

▶ Increased breathing rate

▶ Shallow or deep irregular breathing

▶ Restlessness

▶ Anxiety

▶ Thirst

▶ Vomiting

▶ Dull look in the eyes; dilated pupils

▶ Unresponsiveness

▶ Blotchy or streaked skin

▶ Possible unconsciousness in severe conditions

WHEN A STING IS AN EMERGENCY

Insect bites and stings can be extremely dangerous. Get medical help immediately by taking the victim to the hospital or calling for an ambulance if any of the following conditions are present:

▶ If the person who is bitten or stung has allergies.

▶ If the person begins to develop any symptoms of an allergic reaction. This may include sneezing; coughing, or breathing difficulty; weak, rapid pulse; cold, clammy, pale skin; dizziness; nausea or vomiting; swollen lips, tongue, or ears; hives, and others.

▶ If the person has multiple stings.

▶ If the victim is stung in the mouth or throat or is having any trouble breathing.

TREATING SPRAINS AND STRAINS

Signs and symptoms of sprains include pain in the joint, tenderness to the touch, swelling, and discoloration. Sprains cause pain, stiffness, and swelling.

▶ If you are not sure if the injury is a sprain or a fracture, treat it as a fracture and get medical assistance immediately.

▶ If the injury occurs during physical activity, stop immediately and rest. Apply a cold compress or ice pack wrapped in cloth to the affected area.

▶ Elevate the affected area.

▶ If pain and swelling continue for more than 2 days, consult a physician.

TREATMENT FOR FOREIGN OBJECTS IN THE EYE

▶ DO NOT attempt to remove the object. Seek medical attention immediately.

▶ Keep the victim lying down.

▶ Cover BOTH eyes with sterile or clean compresses and bandage lightly in place.

EMERGENCY TREATMENT FOR BURNS

1. DO NOT burst blisters. DO NOT use antiseptic sprays, ointments, butter, or other "home remedies." DO NOT put pressure on the burned area.

2. To treat a first- or second-degree burn:

   a. Immerse the burned area in cold (not ice) water and/or gently apply cold compresses until pain lessens.

   b. For a chemical burn, remove contaminated clothing and place person under a shower of cool water for at least 15 minutes.

   c. Blot dry gently with a clean cloth or gauze.

   d. Cover loosely with a clean bandage.

   e. Elevate the burned area higher than the heart.

   f. Seek medical attention for severe burns and if the burn begins to develop any sign of infection.

   To treat a third-degree burn:

   a. Seek medical assistance immediately. Call 911 or the operator.

   b. DO NOT remove shreds of skin or burst blisters.
   DO NOT apply water, antiseptic sprays, ointment, butter, or other "home remedies."

   DO NOT remove adhered particles of clothing, but be sure all clothing is extinguished.

   c. Watch for breathing difficulty. If breathing stops, begin mouth-to-mouth resuscitation.

   d. Cover burned area with sterile, nonadhesive dressing or clean, dry towel.

   e. Elevate burned area higher than the level of the heart. If face is burned, keep person or child sitting up.

   f. Observe for shock.

EMERGENCY TREATMENT FOR POISONING AND OVERDOSE

The first rule is to always keep poisons and medications out of the reach of children or people who do not know their dangers. This goes for many cleaning preparations, as well as medications. Above all, stay calm: Fewer than 20 percent of all suspected poisonings actually require hospital treatment.

Poisoning:

1. Look immediately for the poison's container, or look for signs of the poison itself (powder or liquid on the floor).
2. Determine what and how much a person swallowed and when.
3. Call the nearest Poison Control Center, hospital, or emergency room and tell them the following:

▶ Who and where you are

▶ A telephone number where you can be reached

▶ The name of the poison and the ingredients as they are described on the label of the container

▶ The amount of poison you think was swallowed
4. Follow the instructions that you are given by emergency personnel.
5. DO NOT give antidotes! Do not induce vomiting unless you are directed to do so by the Poison Control Center, hospital, or emergency room.
6. Do not give any (salt) solutions.

Drug Overdose:

1. Check breathing. If breathing stops, begin mouth-to-mouth resuscitation.
2. DO NOT give antidotes or induce vomiting unless you are specifically directed to do so by emergency personnel.

Until the Ambulance Arrives:

3. Place the person on his or her side.
4. If the person is awake and emergency personnel have instructed you to induce vomiting, give syrup of ipecac in the dose specified on the label. Then have the person drink 1 to 2 glasses of water.
5. If the person vomits, be sure the head is turned to the side. Clean the mouth afterward.
6. Check breathing.
7. Take drugs or the empty medication container with you to

the hospital or give it to ambulance attendants.

Reasons for Your Actions:

Poison swallowed

Your main objectives are to:

    a. find out exactly what was swallowed and

    b. call for help.

Since there are so many Poison Control Centers and emergency rooms throughout the country, you do not need to take any emergency measures without guidance. If you can find out exactly what poison was swallowed, you are well on your way toward getting that help.

The important thing is to call a Poison Control Center at once with the information you have obtained. Then do exactly what you are told.

Although inducing vomiting is the right measure in many cases, it is not necessarily so in all cases. For example, when acid, lye, or other corrosives or petroleum products such as lighter fluids are swallowed, vomiting could cause more harm than good. Also, some solutions that induce vomiting can be hazardous (for instance, salt).

Remember that diluting the poison by giving lots of milk or water may make things worse, since this increases the speed at which the poison is absorbed throughout the system.

This is a case where the cardinal rule applies in every instance: Do no harm. The main task is to identify the poison accurately and quickly and then call the PCC. Do exactly what the Poison Control Center tells you to do.

EMERGENCY TREATMENT FOR SHOCK

1. Make certain the airway is open. If breathing stops, begin mouth-to-mouth resuscitation.
2. Seek medical assistance. Call 911 or the operator.

Until the Ambulance Arrives:

3. If a back, neck, or head injury is suspected, DO NOT move the person.
4. If no head, back, or neck injury is suspected, lay the person faceup on a blanket and elevate feet 12 inches.
5. If the person has trouble breathing or has a head injury, slightly elevate the head and shoulders.
6. DO NOT place the victim in any position that is uncomfortable. Loosen clothing.
7. Look for injuries or bleeding. Control any bleeding.
8. Cover victim lightly with a blanket or jacket to conserve body heat.
9. Watch for changes in consciousness.
10. Keep victim calm. Do not ask unnecessary questions.
11. If the person vomits, turn his or her head to the side and clean out the mouth. Check breathing again.
12. DO NOT give victim anything to eat or drink.

HOME FIRST-AID KIT

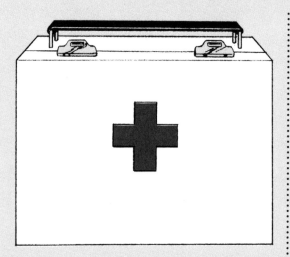

Keep the following supplies together in a clean, dry container. Place the container where it is easy for you to reach, but where small children will be unable to get at it. Use similar kits in cars, campers, and boats, along with other safety items, such as a blanket, flashlight, and flares.

► 1 roll adhesive tape, 1 inch wide

► Sterile gauze pads

► 2 rolls sterile gauze, 1 to 3 inches wide

► 1 roll absorbent cotton

► Adhesive bandages in assorted sizes

► 2 elastic bandages, 2 to 4 inches wide

► Butterfly bandages in assorted sizes

► Triangular bandage

► Ace bandage

► Cotton-tipped swabs (do not use in ears)

► Sterile eye wash

► Disposable moist towels for hand cleansing, sealed in airtight packages

► Tongue depressors

► Sharp scissors with rounded tips

► Rubber nose syringe with plastic tip for suctioning out mucus from baby's nose

► Thermometer, rectal for infants and small children, oral for older children

► Mild soap

► Antiseptic—rubbing alcohol

► Hydrogen peroxide

► Anti-itch lotion (e.g., Caladryl)

► Syrup of ipecac and activated charcoal (used for poisoning only when directed to do so by emergency personnel)

► Children's aspirin substitute, such as acetaminophen (used only under direction of physician)

► Ice pack and hot water bottle or heating pad

► Petroleum jelly

► Tweezers and fine sewing needle, for splinters

► Flashlight, for identifying medications

EMERGENCY TREATMENT FOR FRACTURES AND DISLOCATIONS

▶ If you suspect a back or neck injury, seek medical attention immediately and don't try to move the injured person. Check for shock, and if victim is unconscious, begin emergency procedures for unconsciousness.

▶ Immobilize other bones in the positions they are found. Use a board, straight stick, broom, piece of cardboard, or even a pillow to fabricate a makeshift splint. It should be long enough to extend beyond both joints where the bone is broken. Use towels or blankets to pad the area between the splint and the skin. Tie the splint in place with any suitable material, but don't tie it so tightly that circulation is impeded.

▶ DO NOT try to push a protruding bone back into the body, and do not touch the affected area.

▶ Control any bleeding through direct pressure, but DO NOT elevate the affected area.

▶ Observe for shock, and do not give the victim anything to eat or drink.

Filling Your Prescription

While you're having your prescription filled, you should make sure you understand what the drug is used for, your dosage schedule, how to store the medication properly, what kinds of precautions to take to prevent or reduce side effects, whether you should restrict your diet or drinking habits while taking the drug, which side effects are expected or unavoidable, and which side effects signal a need for a doctor's attention. Your first step in filling your prescription is reading what your doctor has written.

READING YOUR PRESCRIPTION

Prescriptions are not mysterious—they contain no secret messages. Many of the symbols and phrases doctors use on prescriptions are abbreviated Latin or Greek words; they are holdovers from the days when doctors actually wrote in Latin. For example, "gtt" comes from the Latin word *guttae,* which means drops, and "bid" is a shortened version of *bis in die,* which is Latin for twice a day.

You do not have to be a doctor, nurse, or pharmacist to read a prescription. You can (and should) learn how to read one yourself—after all, the prescription describes the drug you will be taking. You should understand what your doctor has written on the prescription blank to be sure that the label on the drug container you receive from your pharmacist coincides with your prescription.

The accompanying chart lists the most common prescription symbols and abbreviations.

Common Abbreviations and Symbols
Used in Writing Prescriptions

ABBREVIATION	MEANING	DERIVATION AND NOTES
aa	of each	*ana* (Greek)
ac	before meals	*ante cibum* (Latin)
AD	right ear	*auris dextra* (Latin)
AL	left ear	*auris laeva* (Latin)
AM	morning	*ante meridiem* (Latin)
AS	left ear	*auris sinistra* (Latin)
au	both ears	*auris* (Latin)
bid	twice a day	*bis in die* (Latin)
C	100	—
c	with	*cum* (Latin)
cap	capsule	—
cc or cm^3	cubic centimeter	30 cc equals one ounce
disp	dispense	—
dtd#	give this number	*dentur tales doses* (Latin)

ABBREVIATION	MEANING	DERIVATION AND NOTES
ea	each	—
ext	for external use	—
gtt	drops	*guttae* (Latin)
gt	drop	*gutta* (Latin)
h	hour	*hora* (Latin)
hs	at bedtime	*hora somni* (Latin)
M ft	make	*misce fiat* (Latin)
mitt#	give this number	*mitte* (Latin)
ml	milliliter (1 ml=1 cc)	30 ml equals one ounce
O	pint	*octarius* (Latin)
OD	right eye	*oculus dexter* (Latin)
OL	left eye	*oculus laevus* (Latin)
OS	left eye	*oculus sinister* (Latin)
OU	each eye	*oculus uterque* (Latin)
pc	after meals	*post cibum* (Latin)
PM	evening	*post meridiem* (Latin)
po	by mouth	*per os* (Latin)
prn	as needed	*pro re nata* (Latin)
q	every	*quaqua* (Latin)
qd	once a day; every day	*quaqua die* (Latin)
qid	four times a day	*quater in die* (Latin)
qod	every other day	—
s	without	*sine* (Latin)
sig	label as follows	*signa* (Latin)
sl	under the tongue	*sub lingua* (Latin)
SOB	shortness of breath	—
sol	solution	—
ss	half unit	*semis* (Latin)
stat	at once; first dose	*statim* (Latin)
susp	suspension	—
tab	tablet	—
tid	three times a day	*ter in die* (Latin)
top	apply topically	—
ung or ungt	ointment	*unguentum* (Latin)
UT	under the tongue	—
ut dict or UD	as directed	*ut dictum* (Latin)
x	times	—

Coping with Side Effects

Drugs have certain desirable effects—that's why they are taken. The desirable effects of a drug are known as the drug's activity or therapeutic effects. Drugs, however, have undesirable effects as well. Undesirable effects are called side effects, adverse reactions, or, in some cases, lethal effects. An adverse reaction is any undesirable effect of a drug. It can range from minor to toxic or lethal.

Even if you experience minor side effects, it is very important that you take your medication exactly as it was prescribed. You should take the full dose at the appropriate times throughout the day for the length of time prescribed by your doctor. Taking a lesser amount of medication to avoid side effects or because your condition appears to be improving is NOT appropriate. A smaller dose may not provide any benefit whatsoever; that is, half of the dose may not provide half of the therapeutic effects.

Some side effects are expected and unavoidable, but others may surprise the doctor as well as the patient. Unexpected reactions may be due to a person's individual response to the drug.

Side effects generally fall into one of two major groups—those that are obvious and those that cannot be detected without laboratory testing. Discussion between you and your doctor about your medication should not be restricted to easily recognized side effects; other, less obvious side effects may also be harmful.

If you know a particular side effect is expected from a particular drug, you can relax a little. Most expected side effects are temporary and need not cause alarm. You'll merely experience discomfort or inconvenience for a short time. For example, you may become drowsy after taking an antihistamine or develop a stuffy nose after taking reserpine or certain other drugs that lower blood pressure. Of course, if you find minor side effects especially bothersome, you should discuss them with your doctor, who may be able to prescribe another drug or at least assure you that the benefits of the drug far outweigh its side effects. Sometimes, side effects can be minimized or eliminated by changing your dosage schedule or taking the drug with meals. Be sure, however, to consult your doctor or pharmacist before making such a change.

Many side effects, however, signal a serious, perhaps dangerous, problem. If these side effects appear, you should consult your doctor immediately. The following discussion should help you determine whether your side effects require attention from your physician.

OBVIOUS SIDE EFFECTS

Some side effects are obvious to the patient; others can be discerned only through laboratory testing. We have divided our discussion according to the body parts affected by the side effects.

Ears

Although a few drugs may cause loss of hearing if taken in large quantities, hearing loss is uncommon. Drugs that are used to treat problems of the ear may cause dizziness, and many drugs produce tinnitus (a sensation of ringing, buzzing, thumping, or hollowness in the ears). Discuss with your doctor any persistent problem with your hearing or your ears.

Eyes

Blurred vision is a common side effect of many drugs. Medications such as digoxin may cause you to see a halo around a lighted object (a television screen or a traffic light), and other drugs may cause night blindness. Chlordiazepoxide and clidinium combination makes it difficult to judge distance accurately while driving and also makes the eyes sensitive to sunlight. While the effects on the eyes caused by digoxin are danger signs of toxicity, the effects caused by chlordiazepoxide and clidinium combination are to be expected. In any case, if any eye-related problems occur while you are taking medication, contact your physician.

Gastrointestinal System

The gastrointestinal system includes the mouth, esophagus, stomach, small and large intestines, and rectum. A side effect that affects the gastrointestinal system can be expected from almost any drug. Many drugs produce dry mouth, mouth sores, difficulty in swallowing, heartburn, nausea, vomiting, diarrhea, constipation, loss of appetite, or abnormal cramping. Other drugs cause bloating and gas, and some cause rectal itching.

Diarrhea can be expected after taking many drugs. Diarrhea caused by most drugs is temporary and self-limiting; that is, it should stop within three days. During this time, do not take any diarrhea remedy; drink liquids to replace the fluid you are losing. If the diarrhea lasts more than three days or is accompanied by fever, call your doctor.

Diarrhea sometimes signals a problem. For example, some antibiotics can cause severe diarrhea. When diarrhea is severe, the intestine may become ulcerated and begin to bleed. If you have severe diarrhea (diarrhea that lasts for several days, or stools that contain blood, pus, or mucus) while taking antibiotics, contact your doctor.

As a side effect of drug use, constipation is less serious and more common than diarrhea. It occurs when a drug slows down the activity of the bowel. Medications such as chlorpromazine and amitriptyline slow bowel activity. Constipation also occurs when drugs cause moisture to be absorbed from the bowel, resulting in a more solid stool. It may also occur if a drug acts on the nervous system to decrease nerve impulses to the intestine—an effect produced, for example, by methyldopa. Constipation produced by a drug can last several days. You may help relieve it by drinking eight to ten glasses of water a day, including more fiber in your diet, and getting plenty of exercise (unless your doctor directs you to do otherwise). Do not take laxatives unless your doctor directs you to do so. If constipation continues for more than three days, call your doctor.

Circulatory System

Drugs may speed up or slow down the heartbeat. If a drug slows the heartbeat, you may feel drowsy and tired or even dizzy. If a drug accelerates the heartbeat, you probably will experience palpitations (thumping in the chest). You may feel as though your heart is skipping a beat occasionally. For most people, none of these symptoms indicates a serious problem. However, if they occur frequently, consult your doctor, who may adjust your drug dosage or prescribe other medication.

Some drugs cause edema (fluid retention)—fluid from the blood collects outside the blood vessels. Ordinarily, edema is not serious. But if you are steadily gaining weight or have gained more than three pounds within a week, talk to your doctor.

Drugs may increase or decrease blood pressure. When blood pressure decreases, you may feel drowsy or tired; you may become dizzy, or even faint, especially when you rise suddenly from a sitting or reclining position. If a drug makes you dizzy or light-headed, sit or lie down for a while. To avoid light-headedness when you stand, contract and relax the muscles of your legs for a few moments before rising. Push one foot against the floor while raising the other foot slightly, alternating feet so that you are "pumping" your legs in a pedaling motion. Get up slowly, and be especially careful on stairs. When blood pressure increases, you may feel dizzy, have a headache or blurred vision, hear a ringing or buzzing in your ears, or experience frequent nosebleeds. If these symptoms occur, call your doctor.

Nervous System

Drugs that act on the nervous system may cause drowsiness or stimulation. If a drug causes drowsiness, you may become dizzy or your coordination may become impaired. If a drug causes stimulation, you may become nervous or have insomnia or tremors. Neither drowsiness nor stimulation is cause for concern for most people. When you are drowsy, however, you should be careful around machinery and should avoid driving. Some drugs cause throbbing headaches, and others produce tingling in the fingers or toes. If these symptoms don't disappear in a few days to a week, call your doctor.

Respiratory System

Side effects common to the respiratory system include stuffy nose, dry throat, shortness of breath, and slowed breathing. A stuffy nose and dry throat usually disappear several days after starting a medication. If these side effects are bothersome, you may use nose drops (consult your doctor first) or throat lozenges, or you may gargle with warm salt water to relieve them. Shortness of breath is a characteristic side effect of some drugs (for example, propranolol). If shortness of breath occurs frequently, check with your doctor. It may be a sign of a serious side effect, or you may simply be overexercising.

Skin

Skin reactions include rash, swelling, itching, and sweating. Itching, swelling, and rash frequently indicate a drug allergy. You should NOT continue to take a drug if you develop an allergy to it, but consult your doctor before stopping the drug.

Some drugs increase sweating; others decrease it. Drugs that decrease sweating may cause problems during exercise or hot weather when your body needs to sweat to reduce body temperature.

If you have a minor skin reaction not diagnosed as an allergy, ask your pharmacist for a soothing cream. Your pharmacist may also suggest that you take frequent baths or dust the sensitive area with a suitable powder.

Another type of skin reaction is photosensitivity (also called phototoxicity or sun toxicity)—that is, unusual sensitivity to the sun. Tetracyclines can cause photosensitivity. If, while taking such a drug, you are exposed to the sun for even a brief period of time (10 or 15 minutes), you may experience a severe sunburn. You do not have to stay indoors while taking these drugs, but you should be fully clothed while outside, and you should not remain in the sun too long. Furthermore, you should use a protective sunscreen while in the sun—ask your pharmacist to help you choose one. Since medications may remain in your bloodstream after you stop taking them, you should continue to follow these precautions for two days after treatment with these drugs has been completed.

SUBTLE SIDE EFFECTS

Some side effects are difficult to detect. You may not notice any symptoms at all, or you may notice only slight ones. Therefore, your doctor may want you to have periodic blood tests or eye examinations to ensure that no subtle damage is occurring to any of your organ systems while you are on certain medications.

Kidneys

If one of the side effects of a drug is to reduce the kidneys' ability to remove chemicals and other substances from the blood, these substances begin to accumulate in body tissues. Over a period of time, this accumulation may cause vague symptoms, such as swelling, fluid retention, nausea, headache, or weakness. Obvious symptoms, especially pain, are rare.

Liver

Drug-induced liver damage may result in fat accumulation within the liver. Since the liver is responsible for converting many drugs and body chemicals into compounds that can be eliminated by other organs of the body (kidneys, lungs, gastrointestinal tract), drug-induced liver damage can result in a buildup of these substances. Because liver damage may be quite advanced before it produces any symptoms, periodic blood tests of liver function are recommended during therapy with certain drugs.

Blood

A great many drugs affect the blood and the circulatory system but do not produce noticeable symptoms for some time. Some drugs decrease the number of red blood cells—the cells responsible for carrying oxygen and nutrients throughout the body. If you have too few red blood cells, you become anemic; you appear pale and feel tired, weak, dizzy, and perhaps hungry. Other drugs decrease the number of white blood cells—the cells responsible for combating infection. Having too few white blood cells increases susceptibility to infection and may prolong illness. If a sore throat or a fever begins after you start taking a drug and continues for a few days, you may have an infection and too few white blood cells to fight it. Call your doctor.

DRUG USE DURING PREGNANCY AND BREAST-FEEDING

Before taking ANY medication, it is very important to tell your doctor if you are pregnant (or planning to become pregnant) or are breast-feeding an infant. For most drugs, complete information on safety during pregnancy and while breast-feeding is lacking. This is not due to negligence or lack of concern on the part of regulatory agencies, but to the fact that it would be unethical to conduct drug experiments on pregnant and nursing women. With this in mind, you should discuss with your doctor the risks versus the benefits of taking any medications during pregnancy or while nursing an infant.

MANAGEMENT OF SIDE EFFECTS

Consult the drug profiles to determine whether the side effects you are experiencing are minor (relatively common and usually not serious) or major (symptoms that you should consult your doctor about). If your side effects are minor, you may be able to compensate for them (see the following table for suggestions). However, consult your doctor if you find minor side effects persistent or particularly bothersome.

If you experience any major side effects, contact your doctor immediately. Your dosage may need adjustment, or you may have developed a sensitivity to the drug. Your doctor may want you to switch to an alternative medication to treat your disorder. Never stop taking a prescribed medication unless you first discuss it with your doctor.

Common Minor Side Effects

SIDE EFFECT	MANAGEMENT
Constipation	Increase the amount of fiber in your diet; drink plenty of fluids*; exercise*
Decreased sweating	Avoid working or exercising in the sun or under warm conditions

SIDE EFFECT	MANAGEMENT
Diarrhea	Drink lots of water to replace lost fluids; if diarrhea lasts longer than three days, call your doctor
Dizziness	Avoid operating machinery or driving a car
Drowsiness	Avoid operating machinery or driving a car
Dry mouth	Suck on candy or ice chips, or chew sugarless gum
Dry nose and throat	Use a humidifier or vaporizer
Fluid retention (mild)	Avoid adding salt to foods; keep legs raised, if possible
Headache	Remain quiet; take aspirin* or acetaminophen*
Insomnia	Take the last dose of the drug earlier in the day*; drink a glass of warm milk at bedtime; ask your doctor about an exercise program
Itching	Take frequent baths or showers, or use wet soaks
Nasal congestion	If necessary, use nose drops*
Palpitations (mild)	Rest often; avoid tension; do not drink coffee, tea, or cola; stop smoking
Upset stomach	Take the drug with milk or food*

*Consult your doctor first

Moving a household is never easy, but it doesn't have to be traumatic for anyone. The easiest way to handle a move is to divide it into manageable chunks. With thoughtful preplanning and organization of tasks, you can minimize the work that remains to be accomplished on the day when you move from one home into another. Neglecting to take care of chores ahead of time, however, can turn a move into a nightmare.

GETTING THE MOVE ORGANIZED

To effectively organize your move, begin months ahead. Along with making arrangements, you'll want to tend to countless details that can overwhelm anyone if they're left to the last week before the move.

PLANNING THE MOVE

▶ Whether you're moving yourself or hiring a mover, don't move unnecessary items. A move is a good time to get rid of things that are no longer useful.

▶ Make a master checklist of everything that must be done in connection with the move. So that you don't fall behind, schedule a deadline for each task and check off each task when it is done. There's so much involved in a move that you may forget you've done something that's already been accomplished.

▶ Make reservations well in advance if you plan to rent a moving van or hire a mover.

▶ If you plan to ask friends for help, make sure they can make the commitment and ask

enough friends to make the job easier. Don't expect one or two people to move all your belongings.

▶ If you're planning on renting a truck, get a lesson or two in how to drive one, particularly if you have never driven a truck before or if you will be driving it for long distances.

▶ Get carpets and slipcovers cleaned before you move. They'll come back wrapped and ready to transport, and you won't have to spend time trying to do this at your new location.

▶ If you plan to travel by car over long distances, get your car checked out before you leave. Be sure to have a serviceable spare tire.

PACKING

▶ If you don't collect enough cartons, contact a local moving company to see if you can buy some.

▶ Take a few hours each day well before your move to begin packing items that you don't need on a day-to-day basis, such as your good china, stemware, books, out-of-season clothes, etc. Put these boxes in an out-of-the-way space until moving day.

▶ Save space by not packing the unbreakable contents of tightly loaded drawers. Simply tape the drawers in place with strips of wide masking tape. To minimize tape marks, remove the tape as soon as the furniture arrives at your new home.

▶ Get wardrobe boxes to pack clothes. By simply hanging clothes inside these boxes, you'll save time both packing and unpacking.

▶ Small linens such as towels, washcloths, and pillowcases can also serve as packing material.

▶ Alternate the spines of books when you pack them to save space.

▶ To prevent odors from developing in the refrigerator or freezer during the move, put several charcoal briquettes inside the unit to absorb the odors. Alternatively, fill the refrigerator or freezer with wadded-up newspapers. The paper will absorb any moisture and help prevent odors.

▶ Remove furniture casters ahead of time to prevent them from falling out during the

---

CHECKLIST FOR MOVING

TWO MONTHS BEFORE MOVE

Get estimates from movers

Collect cartons

Select mover and go over all details of
   the move

Begin packing unnecessary items

Go through your house to find
   unwanted items

Notify correspondents of move

Have a yard sale or donate items to a
   charity

Plan menus to use up food in the
   cupboards

Arrange air travel for family, if
   necessary

ONE MONTH BEFORE MOVE

Begin packing

Notify post office of change of address

Notify utility companies of change in
   account or disconnections

Notify newspaper of address change or
   stoppage

Collect important papers and medical
   records

Make any reservations for lodging

TWO WEEKS BEFORE MOVE

Check car; have any necessary repairs
   done

Renew or transfer prescriptions

THE WEEK OF THE MOVE

Transfer or close bank account if
   moving long distance

Obtain traveler's checks, if needed

Defrost refrigerator

Tag furniture to identify its location in
   the new home

Prepare "survival" package so the
   family can get along if the moving
   company is late

THE DAY OF THE MOVE

Strip beds

Disconnect all appliances

move. Tie them together with heavy twine, and tag them so you know which piece of furniture they fit.

▶ Pack similar items together. For example, if a box is nearly filled with items from the medicine cabinet, don't add kitchen items to completely fill it. It will just make unpacking more difficult.

▶ Plates are less likely to break if they are packed standing on edge. To minimize breakage of glass items, place the heavier ones on the bottom and the more delicate ones on top. Excelsior or pieces of crumpled newspaper make good packing material. If you have several days to pack before moving, dampen the excelsior so it will shape itself to the china and glassware.

▶ As you tape up each packed box, place a piece of string underneath the tape, leaving about an inch sticking out. When it's time to unpack, just pull on the string, which will slit right through the tape.

▶ Label each box with clear lettering as to its contents and where it should go. This will help when you go to unpack, because you will be able to quickly sort out the boxes that must be unpacked immediately and those that can wait.

HIRING A PROFESSIONAL MOVER

EVALUATING A MOVER

▶ For a local move, get references from friends and be sure to check with the Better Business Bureau about any moving company you are considering.

▶ On interstate moves, charges are based on the weight of the items to be moved, the distance to be moved, packing, and other services.

▶ Get two or three estimates well in advance of your move. A "nonbinding" estimate is just that. The final price is determined by the total charges for transportation and services. A "binding estimate" requires the mover to bill you for the specific services at a specific price. If you add additional services, however, you will void the binding estimate.

▶ Make sure the mover is aware of everything to be moved. The cost will increase if anything is added to the shipment that was not included in the estimate.

► Unless you pay the movers to pack your belongings, it's unlikely that they will be insured against breakage caused by improper packing.

► The mover will issue you a bill of lading, a legal contract between the customer and the mover. Be sure to hang on to it.

► Make sure that any contract you enter into covers rates and charges, the mover's liability for your possessions, dates for pickup and delivery, and claims protection.

► Instead of giving you an actual pickup and delivery date, the mover may give you a range of dates. The dates must be shown on the bill of lading.

► Interstate moves by moving companies are regulated by the Interstate Commerce Commission (ICC). The mover is obligated to give you a copy of a pamphlet prepared by the ICC titled "When You Move: Your Rights and Responsibilities." Make sure you read this pamphlet.

MANAGING A MOVING SALE

If you're holding a house or garage sale to dispose of unwanted items before moving, you'll not only make money, you'll save money by not having to pay for transporting unwanted possessions. Use the following hints to make your sale a success:

► Organize your sale by categorizing odds and ends in bins. For example, have one bin for kitchen gadgets, another for books, and another for records.

► To get the best prices at your moving sale, clean and shine the objects you're selling—and display them creatively.

► Be sure to post signs around the neighborhood in advance to let people know about the yard sale.

► If you have a lot of things to sell, take out an ad in the local paper.

► To display clothes, rig up a clothesline or rent a portable wardrobe hangar.

► Tag items individually with prices or put items together on a table with a sign of their price. Whether or not you want to negotiate the price further is up to

you, but it will save you the hassle of trying to come up with a price on the spot.

► Encourage your children to get rid of old toys and belongings by letting them keep the money from the sale of their possessions. If there are items you do not want sold, pack them away first.

► Make sure you have plenty of newspapers, old boxes, and grocery bags for packing up the items purchased.

▶ If you have the option to move between October and April, you may be able to receive a better price. If your move is scheduled between June and September, the busiest times for movers, be sure to call well in advance for estimates and to settle on a contract.

▶ Once your shipment is picked up, you may incur storage costs if you change the delivery date, so try to make sure you are able to move into your new home on the scheduled date.

HANDLING CLAIMS

▶ Movers are responsible for loss or damage to goods caused by the carrier. If anything is missing or if cartons are damaged, this should be noted when you check the inventory sheet at delivery.

▶ Liability on the part of the mover is usually limited to 60 cents per pound, per article, for any loss or damage claims filed. Some movers offer a lump-sum liability value, which usually requires the customer to pay an additional fee.

▶ It is not necessary to unpack all cartons, because any damages or losses discovered within 9 months of the delivery entitles you to file a claim. Don't throw away your inventory or any papers connected with the move until you have unpacked all cartons and/or the 9 months are up. Obviously, the earlier the claim is filed the better.

▶ An "inconvenience" or "delay" claim can be filed if the mover fails to pick up and/or deliver a shipment on the dated entered on the bill of lading. This claim must be based on expenses incurred because of the delay. If the

MOVING PLANTS

▶ If you are moving to another state, federal and state laws may be affected. In certain areas, plants may have to be quarantined or inspected to be certified that they are pest-free.

▶ Some states prohibit bringing any plants into the state. You will have to give them to friends, donate them to a willing institution, or sell them at a garage sale.

▶ Professional moving companies usually will move houseplants within the same state and within 150 miles. Do not expect moving personnel to water your plants during the move or to take special care of them.

▶ Most indoor houseplants cannot survive temperatures below 30° or higher than 100°F for more than an hour, particularly if they are not wrapped. If you are moving during the

winter over long distances, pack plants in cartons and try to make sure they are moved in a heated vehicle and not left in an unheated car or moving van overnight.

▶ Make sure plants are moist when they are packed for moving. They can usually survive for about 10 days without water.

▶ If you can't move your plants due to space limitations, consider taking cuttings from your favorite plants. Keep them in a plastic bag with damp vermiculite or peat moss.

mover refuses to honor the claim, he may be sued in Small Claims Court.

MANAGING THE MOVE

MOVING DAY

► To save time and eliminate confusion, draw a floor plan of your new home ahead of time. Sketch in and number your furnishings the way you want them arranged. Tag furniture pieces to correspond to the floor plan so the movers know where to put each piece.

► Be sure to be on hand during packing and pickup of your belongings. If you cannot be there, ask a friend or relative to be on hand. The mover will issue you an inventory of all items. Make sure the inventory is correct and legible before you sign it.

► If your friends are helping you move, have as much as possible packed ahead of time and ready to be loaded into a truck or van. Don't expect your friends to pack your belongings. Be sure to have plenty of soda and snacks, and send out for take-out food if the work goes into the lunch or dinner hour.

► Keep children and pets out of the way of the movers—whether they're your friends or professionals.

IN TRANSIT

► Keep important papers and documents with you, including birth certificates, marriage certificate, deeds, etc.

► Make sure you allow enough time to get to your destination before the movers.

► If you are moving over a long distance, keep in touch with the moving company so that they are able to notify you of any delays in delivery.

► If you drive to your new location and arrive late, spend the first night at a motel rather than trying to "settle in" when everyone's tired. Everything will seem much more manageable in the morning.

► Take a "survival" package along with the family so you can camp in your new home until the moving van arrives. Include instant coffee, cups, spoons, soap and towels, a can and bottle opener, some light bulbs, a flashlight, toilet paper, cleansing powder, and a first-aid kit. Also be sure that daily medications travel with you.

WHEN YOU ARRIVE

► If you have access to the new home a day or so before the van arrives, you could set off a bug bomb or spray. (Even if you don't see bugs, there may be some.) This way, you won't worry about your family, your pets, foods, or furnishings during the spraying.

► Make sure all goods are removed when you take possession of your new home. Otherwise you'll be stuck with disposing of old paint cans and junk.

GETTING THE WORD OUT

The more people you know and correspond with, the more work you'll have to do to let them know about your move. To save money on cards and stamps, type or use a computer to print a page giving your old address and new address. Make copies and then include this with any outgoing correspondence before you move. Going through your address book will help you to avoid leaving out friends and relatives that need notification.

The U.S. Post Office will forward mail under the following conditions:

▶ Free for one year for express mail, first-class, and priority mail

▶ Free for 60 days for second-class mail, including newspapers and magazines.

▶ Third-class mail, including circulars, books, catalogues, and advertising not forwarded unless requested by the sender

▶ Fourth-class mail, including packages weighing 16 ounces or more not mailed

as priority, forwarded locally for one year (Charges must be paid by you if you move outside the local area.)

The U.S. Post Office suggests that you notify the following people and institutions:

Present and future post offices
Associations
Banks
Book clubs
Catalog companies
Charge cards
Churches
Credit unions
Dentists
Department stores
Doctors
Electric company
Employers
Federal, state, and local government benefits payments
Gas company
Insurance companies
Internal Revenue Service
Journals
Lawyers
Libraries
Magazines
Motor Vehicle Department
Newsletters
Newspapers
Record clubs
Schools
Stockbrokers
Telephone company
Unions
Voter registration (both old and new jurisdictions)
Water company

▶ If you've hired a professional mover, make sure you have the payment ready for the mover when the truck arrives as specified in the contract. On interstate moves, if the charges exceed the written estimate, you are responsible for the estimate plus 10 percent of the balance when your goods are delivered. Any remaining amount is due the mover within 30 days.

▶ Check your list of contents against the list of what is delivered and inspect all cartons for damage.

▶ Unless you've hired the movers to help unpack, don't try to unpack everything at once. Sort your carefully labeled boxes so that you only have to unpack what is absolutely necessary. This gives you the time to organize your space as you go, instead of being forced to toss things randomly into cupboards and closets.

▶ If possible, hire a cleaning service to help you clean the house either before the movers arrive or after they've left.

MAKING THE TRANSITION TO YOUR NEW HOME

▶ If you're moving to an unfamiliar location, obtain local maps as soon as possible.

▶ Change your address on your driver's license or get a new license and get your car registered if you move to a new state. Make sure you're aware of local driving regulations and get your car a safety inspection sticker, if required.

▶ If your children are moving to a new school, try to find some time to volunteer for school activities. This will help you get to know the school and help you understand any problems your children experience as they get oriented to a new routine.

▶ If you're fortunate, your new neighbors will greet you. If they don't, spend some time outside so they have the opportunity to approach you. If all else fails, introduce yourself. Talk to the mail carrier and let him or her know where you're from and who are the members of your family. Mail carriers often will let your neighbors know.

▶ Make it a point to get to know your new community. Get library cards and find out about community-sponsored activities. Subscribe to the local paper so that you get a feel for how the community operates.

▶ If your children are having trouble with the move, give them extra attention and don't become impatient. Let them call their old friends, and, if possible, arrange for them to visit them.

▶ Make your pet feel at home by putting out its favorite toys, food dishes, blankets, etc. Don't allow your pet outdoors unleashed. The pet could easily become disoriented and be unable to find its way home.

MOVING WITH CHILDREN AND ADOLESCENTS

Whether you're moving out of state or around the block, children and adolescents rarely relish change. Your attitude about the move and your willingness to let your children share in the experience will influence their feelings about the move. Try the following to make the move as anxiety-free as possible:

▶ Talk to your children about the move, and encourage them to express their feelings. Acknowledge their feelings about losing a friend, and don't try to tell them that they will simply make new ones. It wouldn't work for you, and it won't work for them.

▶ Sending preschoolers to a sitter or relative during the move may make it easier for you, but it could produce anxiety for the children. Involve them in packing and make sure that some of their belongings are with them on the trip.

▶ When leaving your previous home, empty the children's rooms last, and restructure their rooms first when you've arrived at your new home. This helps them adjust psychologically.

▶ Try to learn as much as possible about a new neighborhood or school so that you can tell older children about them. You don't have to make them sound heavenly; matter-of-fact information will help ease their anxieties about fitting in.

▶ Encourage your children to look up facts on your new location at the library, and let them help you plot the most convenient route on a map. If you're moving only a short distance, let them examine the new house and neighborhood before the move.

▶ Don't think you have to postpone your move until summer vacation. Some experts believe that summer is the worst time to move children, because they have to wait until school starts again to get involved socially. Of course, if your children have learning problems or aren't doing well in school, it may be advisable to let them finish out the school year in familiar surroundings.

▶ Encourage children to exchange addresses and phone numbers with their friends. A few long-distance calls won't break the bank and will help your children make the transition easier.

▶ Involve children in the move itself so they feel part of the family.

MOVING WITH PETS

▶ Most states have laws regarding the entry of animals. Hawaii, for example, requires that cats and dogs be quarantined for 120 days. Although most states do no require quarantine, be sure to check on what you will need to move your pet if you are moving interstate.

▶ Border inspections of all animals being transported are conducted by some states, while others have random inspection. Be prepared to have health certificates for dogs and up-to-date rabies inoculations for dogs and cats.

▶ Pets cannot be shipped by professional movers. The best alternative is to have your pet travel with you to reduce anxiety. Be sure to have a leash with you, because your pet may react oddly to strange surroundings.

▶ If you are traveling by air, your pet will have to be in a carrier. Check with the airline whether the carrier can be kept in the cabin. Some airlines require that all carriers be stowed in luggage compartments; others allow small carriers to be kept in the cabin.

▶ Make sure your pet wears an identification tag with your name, the address of your destination, and the name and phone number of a friend or relative, in case the pet is lost during transit.

▶ Check ahead of time with the city clerk or county clerk about any local laws about pets before you move. Some communities restrict the number of pets per residence, and most expect pets to be licensed shortly after you move in.

Very few people don't have a poorly selected outfit lurking in their closet, or skin-care and makeup products that dried up waiting to be used. And who hasn't had a bad haircut? It takes experience and personal self-knowledge to make all the right decisions about personal grooming. But knowing how to select and use clothes, hair styles, skin-care products, and makeup can save you both time and money. Use the following tips and techniques to help you select and coordinate outfits, find the hairstyle best suited to your face, and pick the products that will help you look and feel your best.

CLOTHES AND ACCESSORIES

Clothing styles have become much more casual over the last 25 years. Children wear denims to school, women wear slacks to the office, men opt for blazers and slacks instead of suits, and most of the old "rules" about clothes have been cast aside. What's more important today is to select clothes that are appropriate to our figures and lifestyles. While the latter is easy, many people have difficulty attempting to suit their clothes to their figure. Use the following tips and hints to make it easier to select and wear apparel that's right for you.

CHOOSING APPROPRIATE APPAREL

Dressing to Suit Your Figure

▶ Dark colors tend to slim your figure and bright colors enlarge it.

▶ A vertically striped suit and a vest with waist points give the illusion of slimness and added height.

▶ If you're overweight, wearing undersized clothes will accentuate the fact. Wear looser clothing to give the illusion of a slimmer figure.

▶ If your legs are short, choose trousers that are straight, narrow, and uncuffed.

▶ To deemphasize a short, stocky figure, avoid horizontal stripes, large prints, plaids, and clingy fabrics.

▶ Extra-tall women find that longer jackets and tops and cuffed pants help minimize height. A ¾-length coat will also minimize height.

▶ Avoid oversized collars if you're broad-shouldered.

▶ The color of your belt can help to lengthen or shorten your torso. Match your belt to your shirt or sweater if you're short-waisted; match it to your skirt or slacks if you're long-waisted.

▶ To lengthen a short torso, wear belts loosely so they fall below your natural waistline. Avoid wide waistbands.

▶ To make your neck look longer, wear an open-collared shirt with a neck chain falling just below the collarbone. Open-collared shirts and sweaters with oval, square, or V necks will also help to elongate a short neck.

▶ Coats and suits with broad shoulder lines can help draw attention away from a too-plump stomach.

▶ Select shoes with heels in proportion to your height. Heels that are too high will make a person with short legs look awkward, not taller.

▶ Shoes with wide straps that cut across the instep of your foot can make your legs look heavy.

▶ Slingback shoes make your legs look longer.

▶ Dark stockings can help make your legs look more slender.

▶ Match the tone of your stocking color to your shoe color to create an unbroken line from your skirt hem to your feet. This gives a taller, slimmer impression.

▶ Nude stockings with an all-black outfit can make your legs look too stark against all that black. Choose a darker tone.

Dressing to Suit the Occasion

▶ Dress conservatively for a job interview. Your prospective employer is concerned with your qualifications—not your fashion sense.

▶ If you have trouble coordinating outfits or deciding what to wear, select your outfit for the next day the night before. You'll be better organized first thing in the morning and won't be surprised by missing buttons, stains, or ripped hemlines.

▶ Keep an all-purpose outfit, complete with belt and other accessories, up front in your closet as an emergency for rushed mornings.

▶ Always try on or at least check over a garment before you pack it for a trip. The morning of an important business meeting isn't the time to find that something needs cleaning or mending.

▶ Keep a sport coat and tie or scarf in the office closet, even if your normal attire is casual. This will ensure you're prepared for an unexpected luncheon or dinner invitation.

▶ Avoid heavy, chunky jewelry when wearing delicate fabrics.

▶ Generally, shoe color should be the same color as, or darker than, your outfit, particularly when you're dressing for the office.

▶ Wear neutral stockings with brightly colored evening shoes or slippers to allow attention to be focused on the shoe color.

▶ If you must wear black to a wedding, make sure you include another color in the outfit, particularly if it's a traditional wedding.

▶ In cold, windy weather, always wear a hat or scarf, because up to one-third of your body heat can escape through your head.

▶ Natural fibers such as wool and cotton are warmer in cold weather than synthetics. Because natural fabrics breathe, they allow body perspiration to evaporate so that you don't feel damp and chilled.

▶ White cotton is an ideal fabric for summer wear, because white reflects the sun's rays and keeps you cool and cotton lets your skin breathe.

▶ If you perspire heavily, include as many natural fiber garments as possible in your wardrobe, including cottons for summer. Remember that cotton blends will not wrinkle as easily as pure cotton fabrics.

SHOPPING FOR CLOTHES

▶ Factory outlets and fashion discount stores offer considerable savings on good-quality clothing. Some clothes offered at reduced prices as "seconds" have no visible flaws or have only minor flaws—a missing button or unraveled seam, for instance—that can be fixed easily without detracting from the overall appearance of the garment.

▶ When shopping for clothes, keep your eyes open for up-to-the-minute accessories—belts, scarves, earrings—that could give a fashion-conscious look to last year's basic dress or outfit. You may be able to put together a whole new look without buying a whole new outfit.

▶ Keep a "grocery list" of clothing needs inside your closet door. Then watch for sales and specials on the items you need.

▶ Avoid buying a garment with ornate or unusual buttons unless an extra button comes with the purchase. Otherwise you'll have to replace all the buttons if one is lost.

▶ Check the cleaning directions on any purchase you're considering. Some "Dry Clean Only" garments may cost you more in cleaning bills than you're willing to pay.

▶ Check the newspaper want ads and the yellow pages under "resale shops" to find stores that sell good used clothing. You may be able to pick up an as-new designer outfit for a fraction of the original cost.

▶ Before buying, test a stretch fabric garment by pulling it gently crosswise and lengthwise. If the material doesn't snap back into shape quickly you'll have trouble with bagging after wear.

▶ When buying permanent-press garments, remember that you may not be able to lengthen the hemline without leaving an unsightly crease.

▶ Never purchase a size smaller than you usually wear in the hope that you can alter the garment to fit. You can sometimes make a larger size smaller, but the reverse does not apply. Clothes that are too tight can actually make you feel tired.

▸ Keep receipts for clothing; some faults may not show up until you put the garment on at home.

▸ If possible, look at yourself in a three-way mirror when trying on a new outfit. See how the garment fits in front, on the side, and in the back. Also check to see how it looks when you move about and when you sit down.

▸ Fad fashions can be fun, but they aren't a good investment. Remember that you'll get only a few months' wear out of a fad fashion, so budget accordingly.

▸ If you're short but overweight, check out designers who make the same items in petite and regular-size clothes. You may be able to match roomier regular slacks with a petite jacket or vice versa.

▸ To get a good fit, shop for new shoes when you've been on your feet for a while. Shoes that feel fine first thing in the morning may be painfully tight after you've been walking around and your feet have swollen.

▸ Feet swell in the heat, so consider buying summer shoes a half-size larger for extra comfort.

▸ When buying shoes you'll be wearing a lot, consider choosing a pair made of leather or woven fabric. These materials breathe and are usually more comfortable than shoes made of synthetic materials.

▸ To see how a hose color will look on your legs, pull the stocking over your forearm, not the back of your hand. Your hand is likely to be more tanned and will therefore alter the color of the hose. Also keep in mind that hosiery will look different in natural light than in the fluorescent light of the store.

▸ Make sure your shoe wardrobe includes a pair of shoes in a neutral color that goes well with a wide range of clothing colors.

HAIR CARE

Designer clothing, perfectly applied makeup, and fine jewelry are all wasted if your hair looks greasy, dull, or messy. Fortunately, no one needs an expensive professional hair salon or expensive hair products to have hair that looks professionally cared for and styled. With the right techniques for shampooing, drying, and styling your hair, it can be one your most attractive features.

BASIC HAIR CARE
Healthy Hair Tips

▸ Since wet hair is vulnerable to stretching and breaking, make sure that your hair is thoroughly wet before applying shampoo. Use no more than a quarter-size dollop, and rub the shampoo between your palms first. Lather for no more than 30 seconds.

▶ After shampooing, rinse your hair with cool water to seal in the moisture in the hair shafts.

▶ To distribute the natural oils in your hair, bend over and brush your scalp and hair from back to front until the scalp tingles; then massage the scalp with your fingertips.

▶ Towel-dry your hair thoroughly before using a blow dryer. You'll save time and avoid damaging your hair with too much heat.

▶ To cut down on static electricity, dampen your hairbrush before brushing hair.

▶ Avoid using a brush on wet hair, because it is subject to breakage. Comb out snarls.

▶ If you suffer from a flaky scalp, try the following treatment every 2 weeks: Section your hair and rub the scalp with a cotton pad saturated with plain rubbing alcohol. Let the alcohol dry, then brush your hair and rinse thoroughly with warm water, but don't shampoo.

▶ To get a fuller look to your hairstyle, bend over so your hair falls forward and blow the underneath layers dry first.

▶ To perk up permed hair between shampoos, lightly mist your hair with fresh water and push the curls into place with your fingers.

▶ Dull, lifeless hair can be a sign of a poor diet. Try cutting down on cholesterol and fats.

▶ Wait at least 48 hours after coloring hair to shampoo it. Every time you wet hair you open the cuticle, so give hair time to seal in the color.

▶ When you're in the sun, use a spray-in sunscreen. This also protects color-treated hair from the sun's color-altering effects.

▶ Hair sprays, mousses, gels, and other styling aids tend to build up over time, despite judicious shampooing and rinsing. If you find this happening, buy a clarifier, which removes product buildup without stripping essential oils. Make your own by mixing one part vinegar with 20 parts water.

HAIRSTYLES

Choosing a Style That's Right for Your Facial Shape

There are two important factors to consider when selecting a hairstyle: facial shape and hair type. Personal preference is also important, but knowing what accentuates your best features and camouflages imperfections will help you fine-tune personal favorites.

The three primary types of facial shapes are oval, round, and square, with several subtypes. All of them can be positively or negatively affected by your hairstyle. For example, an extremely round face is "slimmed" if the eye is drawn upward to top layers. Conversely, a

ALL ABOUT CHILDREN'S CLOTHES

▶ If you offer your children a choice of outfits, they may be happier and more cooperative about getting dressed. Giving the child a choice of clothes is also a valuable introduction to decision making.

▶ Children will be more likely to hang up their clothes themselves if they can reach the hooks easily.

▶ Iron-on patches on the insides of the knees of new jeans will help the jeans last longer.

▶ When shopping for clothes for a toddler, look for zippers and front fasteners, which are easier than buttons.

▶ Shoelaces will stay tied if you dampen them before tying.

▶ Knots tied in the ends of your child's shoelaces will prevent the laces being pulled out altogether.

▶ If your child is outgrowing his or her winter jacket and you need to make it last the season, add knitted cuffs to the sleeves. (You can buy knitted cuffs at department store notion counters.) As a bonus, the cuffs will keep out cold air.

▶ Most youngsters have a tough time telling right from left, especially when putting on shoes. You can help by putting a distinctive mark (such as a square of red tape) on the right shoe.

▶ If your child seems to have trouble grasping the concept of matching the heel of his foot to the heel of his sock, take the easy way out—buy tube socks.

▶ If you cut two tiny parallel slits in the tongue of a child's shoe and pull the laces through the slots to tie as usual, the tongue won't slip down out of place.

▶ If you dip the ends of frayed shoelaces in clear fingernail polish, they'll be easier to poke through eyelets.

▶ If your toddler has figured out how to take off mitten clips, attach the mittens to a long string that goes across the back and down both coat sleeves.

▶ If you use elastic thread to sew buttons on the cuffs of your child's shirts, the child won't have to button and unbutton the cuffs continually. The elastic provides just enough stretch to allow the child to slip his or her hand through the cuff even when it's buttoned.

▶ If a crease remains after you've lengthened a child's dress, disguise it with a row of lace, braid, or ribbon. Try to use the same trim elsewhere on the garment as well, to give a well-put-together look.

▶ Extend the wear of your small daughter's pretty smock dresses that are too short by having her wear them as tops over jeans.

long chin is made to seem even longer by long, straight hair, because it "drags" the eye down.

▶ For the oval face, where facial features are in balanced proportion, almost any hairstyle can be appropriate, because there's nothing you're trying to "rebalance."

▶ An oblong face, an "elongated" oval, needs added width. Usually, the chin appears too long. A shorter cut with fullness at the sides will achieve this; long hair or a high, full top will do the opposite.

▶ The square face is wider than it is long and often features a strong, squared jawline. To create the illusion of more length and less width, hair that's somewhat longer than chin-length and full—not flat—on top works best. Layers soften the features of this strong facial shape even further. A blunt cut that's precisely jaw-length is least flattering for the square face and its two variations, the heart-shaped face and the pear-shaped face.

▶ The heart-shaped face has most width at the forehead, not the chin. Bangs, asymmetrical parts, and layers help conceal this imbalance. Hair that's slightly longer than chin-length and softly layered or curled also adds fullness at the narrower bottom.

▶ The pear-shaped face is too wide at the jawline and chin, but not at the forehead. It has the opposite problem of the heart shape. In the case of the pear-shaped face, exposing the forehead or eliminating bangs draws the eye away from the wide jaw.

▶ A round face needs to be slenderized because its proportions are excessively wide. The diamond-shaped face, which is too wide at the cheekbones, is a variation of the round face. Longer hair slenderizes the face, drawing the eye downward. Hair that covers the ears and moves onto the face also conceals some width, as does curl. A midlength layered cut works marvelously with the round face; a super-short cut or one with rounded, uniform layers is the least flattering. Solid bangs only emphasize wide cheeks and overall roundness. If you like bangs and have a round facial

shape, make them soft and feathery. As a rule of thumb, if a face is too round or full, think of drawing the eye upward; if it's too long, create volume and detail at the sides. Much of this can be done in finished styling.

Choosing a Style That's Right for Your Hair Texture

Hair can be anything from super straight to excessively curly. When selecting a cut based on hair texture, the rules of illusion apply, just as they do with facial shapes. A good cut can control unruly curls or make fine, straight hair look thicker. If hair is fine but there's lots of it, you have more latitude, but if the hair is fine and thin, only a shorter blunt cut will create the illusion of more hair. This is because the strong line of the short bob makes maximum use of what nature gave you. (Very fine hair that's left long often looks thin and scraggly.)

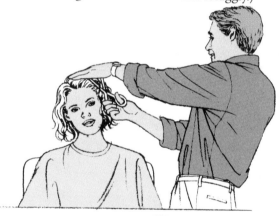

▶ Fine hair can be lightly "texturized" to add mobility, but if you layer fine hair, you're removing what there's very little of in the first place.

▶ Curly hair looks less uncontrollable when it's layered because you've removed excess curl at the ends and the hair "moves" in the direction it was cut. A blunt cut overemphasizes the ends and creates a pyramid shape—especially if there's no layering at all.

▶ A straight, blunt cut should be trimmed every 6 to 8 weeks to maintain its shape; layered hair can conceal a grown-out cut as

HOMEMADE HAIR-CARE AIDS

► For a homemade egg conditioner, separate the yolk from an egg and beat it until thick. Beat in 1 teaspoon of vegetable oil and ½ cup of water. Work this mixture into your hair after your shampoo. Leave it on for 1 to 2 minutes and rinse thoroughly.

► For a lemon rinse, blend ½ cup of strained lemon juice and 1 cup of distilled water in a bottle. Comb the liquid through your hair after each shampoo.

► For a quick, dry shampoo, rub baby powder into your hair and then brush it out thoroughly.

► Use flat beer as a setting lotion.

Cleaning Combs and Brushes

► Add shampoo to the water you use to remove hair oil trapped in the teeth or bristles of your combs and brushes.

► A baking soda solution cleans combs and hairbrushes effectively and inexpensively. Soak them for 10 minutes in a solution of 3 tablespoons of baking soda and 1 quart of warm water. The baking soda loosens oily deposits so they can be easily brushed away.

► Combs made of bone or hard rubber and hairbrushes with natural bristles can be sanitized with alcohol.

Making Your Hair Shine

Whether you have artificial hair color that needs refreshing, or you just want to enhance your own shade naturally, customized herbal rinses add highlights or depth and are gentle on your budget. If you want to experiment with customizing herbal rinses, there's no real risk because their effect is subtle. However, avoid acidic fruits and vegetable colors. Do not use lemons or beet juice, for example. These are very unpredictable over time and are greatly affected by sun exposure. Lemon juice and the sun might make you blonder the first time you try it, but after several treatments, your hair color will look like the rings of a tree trunk—in several shades.

Brighten a Blonde: Steep 2 tablespoons of dried chamomile and 2 tablespoons of dried marigold in 1 quart of boiled water for half an hour. Make certain the temperature is comfortable, then pour through wet hair.

Burnish a Brunette: Substitute sage and rosemary for the herbs above. For extra luster, add 1 tablespoon of cider vinegar.

Rev Up a Red: Mix one tablespoon of honey with 2 tablespoons of saffron and add a quart of boiled water. Allow to steep for half an hour, check the temperature, and pour slowly through wet hair as a final rinse.

long as 12 weeks. If you don't want to retrim regularly, a longer, layered cut "lasts" longer.

▶ While very dense hair is almost always an asset, it does take longer to cut and could end up looking too "bushy" if cut into a short, blunt cut.

Hints and Tips

▶ Use a pomade sparingly to remove static, control flyaway ends, and add a glossy sheen to either straight or curly hair. Apply a very small amount to one hand and liquefy it between your palms. Then run your hands through the hair. If braiding, apply before braiding and use it for small touch-ups.

▶ Use gel after a braid is finished to smooth down loose or uncontrolled hairs. Apply it to your fingertip or to the end of a hairpin, directing it on top of the stray hairs to encourage them back into the braided pattern.

▶ Use hair spray to hold the finished design in place or in spot areas as you work. Also, if you want a soft finish but need to control the hair, spray into the palm of your hand and then smooth over the surface of the hair to control flyaway strands.

▶ Use a coated rubber band to secure ponytails and the ends of a braid to reduce the stress on the hair.

▶ When selecting beads as ornaments, consider the color and weight of the beads and the amount of light they reflect. Glass beads reflect the most light; plastic and wooden beads weigh the least. Avoid putting heavy beads on fragile hair. Be imaginative and coordinate the color of the beads to eyes, wardrobe— even birthstone.

▶ Wrap a cord or ribbon in a spiral fashion around the pony tail or braid ends.

▶ Use gel to control hair when you want a "wet" affect. Apply gel sparingly to your hair once styled. To use for braiding, apply it to all of the hair before you braid, or, when you want a clean, off-the-face effect, you can apply it to the perimeter hairline where lengths tend to be shorter.

▶ Use gel after a braid is finished to smooth down loose or uncontrolled hairs. Apply it to your fingertip or to the end of a hairpin, directing it on top of the stray hairs to encourage them back into the braided pattern.

SKIN CARE

Your skin is a bellwether to your overall health. If you're not healthy, it will be reflected in your complexion. But that doesn't mean you should neglect your skin if you're feeling fine.

BASIC SKIN CARE

▶ Always wear a moisturized sunscreen when outdoors, winter and summer. The sun's rays can burn you even if the air feels cool, and sunlight reflected off water or the whiteness of snow can be particularly powerful.

▶ No matter what your skin type is, use a high-protection lotion the first time you are in the sun and don't expose your skin for more than 15 minutes. Use a total sunscreen on your face and the back of your hands, because these are constantly exposed to the sun's rays.

▶ Always remove your makeup before going to bed.

▶ If you usually wear makeup, give your skin a chance to breathe one day a week by going without.

▶ If your face tends to be puffy when you awake, keep skin freshener, astringent, and cotton pads for your eyelids in the refrigerator for a pickup.

▶ Rub moisturizing lotion on your legs before applying shaving cream for a smoother, softer finish when removing leg hair. Men who have

normal-to-dry skin can also benefit from this technique.

▶ Use a humidifier to lessen the drying effects of indoor heat on your skin in the winter.

▶ Take baths in the evening to avoid exposing your skin immediately to outdoor air.

CARING FOR YOUR HANDS AND NAILS

▶ When nails chip excessively, it may be caused by the use of nail polish remover. Leave your nails unpainted for a few days to see if the condition improves.

▶ When you're preparing anything with lemon and vegetable juices, which contain acids that are hard on your fingernails, rinse your hands often under cool running water.

▶ To break the habit of nail biting or cuticle chewing, carry a tube of cuticle cream with you. Whenever you start to nibble, put the cream on your cuticles instead. You'll promote healthy nails and possibly break yourself of a bad habit.

▶ To prevent nail polish from thickening, store it in the refrigerator.

▶ To rescue nail polish that has become hardened or gummy, place the bottle into a

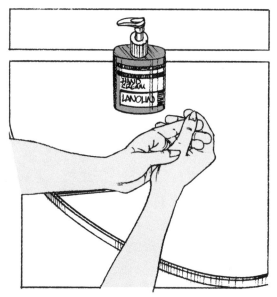

pan of boiling water for a few seconds to get the polish flowing smoothly again.

▶ In winter, cream your hands with lanolin before you go to bed. Once a week, moisturize your hands as usual and wear white cotton gloves while you sleep.

▶ Apply hand cream before putting on rubber gloves to prevent them from drying out.

▶ For an emergency treatment for dry, chapped hands, soak your hands in a bath of warm baby oil mixed with sesame oil.

▶ A light color nail polish gives your hands the illusion of being longer and more graceful.

▶ To soften cuticles, soak hands in a solution of 1 cup warm water and 1 teaspoon of dish-washing liquid.

▶ Use a diamond-dust nail file or an emery board. File nails in one direction only.

▶ To quick-dry nail polish, plunge your hands into a bowl of ice water while the polish is still wet.

▶ To prevent nail polish bottle tops from sticking, rub the inside of the cap and the

neck of the bottle with a thin layer of petroleum jelly.

Foundation and Blush

▶ Test the color of foundation by applying a drop to your face or neck, rather than the back of your hand. If possible, check the color in natural light by a door or window rather than under fluorescent lights in the store.

▶ In the winter, use oil-based, rather than water-based, makeup to protect your skin against dry, cold air. In the summer, switch to a water-based foundation to help moisturize your skin, but use waterproof makeup for lips, eyes, and lashes to prevent running and smearing in the heat.

▶ To apply foundation evenly, use a damp sea sponge, which allows the color to blend evenly and gives the most natural-looking coverage.

▶ To emphasize facial contours, select a foundation that's a shade lighter than your tan during summer months.

▶ Use a large makeup brush to dust translucent powder lightly over your face after you've applied makeup. Then further set the makeup with a light spray of mineral or ordinary water.

▶ To help your foundation last longer and give better coverage, mix it with an equal amount of skin freshener.

▶ To help camouflage a double chin, apply blush under the chin, then blend it upward to

HOMEMADE SKIN-CARE AIDS

▸ For an easy, weekly facial sauna that unclogs pores, add a few tablespoons of your favorite herbs to water and boil for several minutes. Remove the pot from the heat and use a bath towel as a tent while you let the steam rise to your face for 3 to 5 minutes. Then rinse your face with very cold water to close the pores.

▸ For a toning/cleansing mask for normal to oily skin, add 3 tablespoons of finely ground oatmeal to 3 tablespoons of witch hazel to form a paste. Apply to your face and allow to dry for 20 to 30 minutes, then rinse with warm water.

▸ For a drying facial mask for oily skin, slice a washed but unpeeled cucumber and purée the slices with a tablespoon of plain yogurt in a blender or food processor. Apply the mask to your face and allow to dry for 20 minutes. Wash off with warm water and finish with a cool rinse.

▸ For a toning mask for normal and oily skin, combine half a small papaya, 1 egg white, and ½ teaspoon lemon juice and mix in the blender until creamy. Leave the mask on your face for 20 minutes and then rinse with cold water.

▸ For a cleansing mask for dry skin, mix the yolk of an egg with 2 teaspoons of mayonnaise and ½ teaspoon of lemon juice. Apply to your face and allow to dry for 20 minutes. Wash off with warm water.

▸ For a skin-tightening mask for normal and oily skin, whip an egg white, apply to the face, and allow to dry. Rinse off after 20 minutes. Avoid this treatment on dry skin, where it may be too harsh.

▸ For an excellent astringent for oily skin, combine ½ cup witch hazel with ¼ cup lemon juice. Splash on your face and store in the refrigerator.

▸ To treat pimples and discourage blemishes, apply a mixture of calamine lotion and 1 percent phenol (available from a pharmacist).

▸ For a softener for rough areas, such as your feet, knees, and elbows, mix a paste of 1 tablespoon finely ground oatmeal and cold cream. Apply it several times a week and rub gently as you wash off the paste with warm water.

▸ For another softener for rough areas, mix ¼ cup table salt, ¼ cup Epsom salts, and ¼ cup vegetable oil. Stir constantly as you mix the ingredients. Massage the paste into rough skin for several minutes. Remove by bathing or showering.

the bone and across toward the outer edges of the jaw.

Gloss and Lipstick

▸ Always protect your lips with a thin coating of colorless lip balm whenever you aren't wearing lip gloss or lip color.

▸ For a long-lasting lipstick, apply a generous coat, then let it set for about 2 minutes. Blot with a tissue, puff on some powder, and then apply another generous coat of lipstick. Wait again and blot.

▸ Choose warm, tawny lip colors for office light.

▶ To make full lips appear slimmer, draw a lip line inside your natural lip line and fill in with a darker shade of lip color.

▶ To make thin lips appear fuller, draw a lip line outside your natural lip line and fill in with a lighter shade of lipstick.

▶ If your upper and lower lips are uneven, apply makeup foundation over your lips, then fashion a new lip line with a pencil a shade darker than your lip color.

Eye Makeup

▶ Use two shades of eyebrow pencil to make your brow color look more natural.

▶ To make the whites of your eyes appear whiter, line your lower lashes with a deep blue color stick.

▶ To bring out deep-set eyes, apply a light, frosted shadow on both your lids and brow bone, using a darker shade in the eyelid crease.

▶ Small eyes can be made to look larger by applying eye shadow under your lower lashes starting at the center of the eye and blending to the outer corner. Sweep the color along the brow bone out to the side of your eye.

▶ Prominent eyes will look deeper set if you apply dark color in the crease of the eyelid. Pale or frosted eye shadow will have the opposite effect.

▶ Avoid matching the color of your eye shadow to the exact shade of your eyes. The colors will cancel each other out, making your eyes look drab.

▶ Protect your eyelashes with a thin coat of waterproof mascara whenever you're outdoors.

▶ For thick-looking lashes, apply mascara and let it set for a few minutes. Then add a little more mascara to the tips. If you use an eyelash curler, curl the lashes before you add mascara to the tips.

▶ Applying fresh mascara over the old will make your lashes brittle. Be sure to use mascara remover to clean your lashes before

going to bed. If you like, put a little petroleum jelly on your lashes at night to condition and darken them.

▶ When your mascara begins to dry out, run hot water over the tube for a minute to soften the remaining mascara inside.

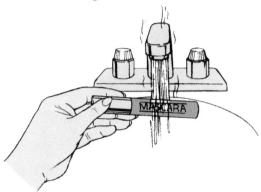

▶ Limit the use of eye drops during the summer, because overuse can prove harmful. Use mineral water instead.

QUICK PICK-ME-UPS FOR YOUR EYES

▶ For puffy eyes, cover them with cotton pads soaked in milk and relax for 10 minutes. Or dip 2 tea bags in boiling water for 2 minutes, then let the water cool slightly. Meanwhile, heat 1 teaspoon of olive oil until it's warm, not hot. Using an absorbent pad, carefully dab the oil around your eyes and on your eyelids. Lie down and cover each eye with a still-warm tea bag for 10 minutes. Remove the tea bags and gently wipe off the oil with tissue.

▶ Refresh tired eyes by laying cotton pads moistened with witch hazel over closed eyelids for a few minutes.

▶ To reduce swelling caused by overexposure to the sun, place thin, freshly cut slices of cucumber over closed eyelids for a few minutes.

▶ Apply perfume and cologne to your skin, rather than your clothes. Chemicals in the perfume may weaken fabric or change its color.

▶ For fragrance that lasts all day, saturate a cotton pad with your favorite perfume and tuck it into your bra.

▶ Dab petroleum on your pulse points, such as the throat, wrists, the insides of elbows, and the backs of knees, and then apply perfume directly to these areas.

▶ Apply perfumes and colognes before putting on your jewelry. The alcohol and oils in your favorite scent can cause a cloudy film on both real gold and costume jewelry.

▶ Don't stick to one fragrance all year-long, because temperatures affect the intensity of fragrance. Use heavy scents and oils in winter but lighter fragrances in smaller quantities during the summer.

FRESHENERS FOR THE BATH

▶ To revive tired muscles, add several handfuls of Epsom salts to your bath water.

▶ To save money on bath products, substitute 2 to 3 tablespoons of vegetable oil for bath oil.

▶ To soften skin, toss 2 to 3 teaspoons of baking soda into the tub.

▶ For a soothing and fragrant skin massage, mix equal parts of peanut oil, camphor oil, and castor oil and add to the tub as you draw the water.

▶ To get rid of flaky skin or the remnants of last summer's tan, add 1 cup of natural cider vinegar or the juice of 3 fresh lemons to your bath water. Slough off dead skin cells with a dry sponge or brush.

Miraculous
Baking Soda

ALL ABOUT JEWELRY

Buying

▶ The word "gold" refers to 24 carat (24K) gold, according to guidelines established by the Federal Trade Commission (FTC) and the jewelry industry. Gold is too soft to stand on its own, which is why it is mixed with other metals.

▶ The "karat" marking refers to the proportion of gold mixed with other metals to increase its hardness and durability. Thus 14K gold means that 14 parts of gold are mixed with 10 parts of base metal. The higher the karat rating, the higher proportion of gold. In the U.S., 10K gold is the lowest grade that can be sold.

"Solid gold" refers to any karat gold in which the inside of the jewelry is not hollow. The terms "plated," "gold-filled," "gold overlay," and "rolled gold plate" refer to jewelry that has a layer of at least 10K gold bonded to a base metal.

▶ Under jewelry standards, jewelry labeled "silver" or "sterling silver" must contain 92.5 percent silver.

▶ Either weight or size is used to measure gemstones. A carat is equal to ⅕ of a gram; carats are divided into 100 units called points. Size is expressed in millimeters.

▶ Make sure you know what kind of stone you are buying. Stones used in jewelry can be natural stones, those found in nature; synthetic, those made in a laboratory and resembling natural stones in their hardness and brilliance;

and imitation, which means they only need to resemble a natural stone. Both synthetic and imitation stones cannot be sold without disclosing that they are not natural.

▶ When buying a watch, the terms water-resistant and shock-resistant can be applied only to watches that meet FTC standards.

▶ Natural gemstones can be enhanced. If so, find out whether the treatment is permanent and whether it requires special care. The enhancement may or may not affect the value, depending on the method of enhancement.

▶ Ask that any information the sales clerk told you about the piece of jewelry be written on the sales slip—weight and/or size of the stone, enhancement or lack thereof, well-matched pearls, etc.

▶ Ask about warranties when buying watches. Be sure to ask about length of the warranty, what parts and labor are covered if repairs are required, who pays for shipping to the manufacturer, and any conditions on the warranty.

▶ Be sure to compare pieces and prices, particularly when dealing with brand names.

Cleaning

▶ To restore luster to a dried-out emerald or jade, dip a toothpick in olive oil and gently rub it over the stone's surface. (Use this method only if the piece won't be resold, since the stone may darken.)

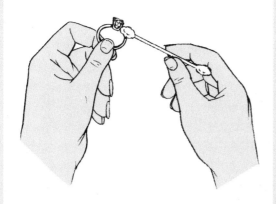

▶ To clean around the settings of precious stones, use a cotton swab dipped in alcohol.

▶ A piece of chalk in your jewelry box will prevent costume jewelry from tarnishing.

Storing

▶ Use cup hooks attached to the inside of your closet door to store bracelets and necklaces tangle-free.

▶ To prevent necklaces and fine chains from tangling together in your jewelry box, cut a plastic drinking straw in half and slip one end of the chain through the straw; fasten the clasp closed. Slip each chain through a separate straw.

▶ For an instant jewelry chest, line a small drawer with foam rubber; the foam will prevent jewelry from slipping around.

▶ Because post earrings are easy to lose when traveling, store them together on an index card.

▶ If you lose a post-type pierced earring, you can put its double to new use as a tie or scarf pin or as a pushpin for a bulletin board.

▶ To untangle a knot in a chain necklace, lay the chain on a piece of waxed paper and put a tiny drop of salad oil on the knot. Working with two straight pins, carefully loosen the knot.

▶ Storing jewelry in plastic bags will reduce tarnish by protecting it from dust, lint, and moisture. Don't store pearls this way, however, because they need to breathe.

▶ Protect pearls from dust, cosmetics, and perfume, all of which can dull them.

▶ Separate jewelry in a jewel box so that the harder stones won't scratch the softer stones and metals.

▶ Wear your silver jewelry frequently; it won't tarnish as quickly and your skin oils will eventually give the silver a protective satiny finish.

Savvy travelers have dozens, perhaps hundreds, of hints to help them avoid hassles during trips. Experience is probably the best teacher, because everyone has different styles of traveling and differing ideas of what they will need on a trip. While the tips below won't guarantee you a wonderful trip or vacation, they should help first-time as well as experienced travelers avoid problems and delays in reaching their destination and enjoying a vacation.

TRAVEL

PLANNING A TRIP

Packing

▶ Label luggage both inside and out with your name and address. Include your phone number on the inside identification; don't include it on the outside.

▶ Keep a notepad and pencil next to you while packing and jot down the items that go into the suitcase. When you're done, you'll have a list of your bag's contents, which will make it easier for your luggage to be found if lost and also help with any insurance claim if your bags are permanently lost.

▶ Take a few minutes to think ahead about what you will be doing on your trip. This will prevent you from packing items that you won't need or use. Avoid waiting to the last minute to pack; by giving yourself a few hours, or even a day for a long trip, you'll be better organized about what you pack and will avoid packing unnecessary items.

▶ Pack heavy items, such as shoes, at the "bottom" of a suitcase; given the various styles of luggage today, the bottom is defined as the area that will be at the bottom when the luggage is picked up.

▶ Stuff small items, such as rolled socks, into shoes and purses.

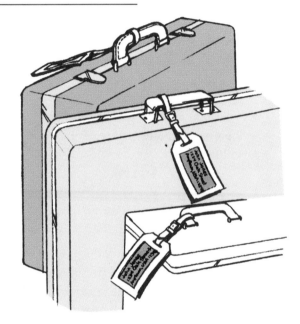

▶ Roll items, such as lingerie, socks, and underwear; they will take up less room and be easier to find.

▶ Layer large-size clothing, and then pack smaller items in between and in empty spaces.

▶ Pack anything that could spill or open in small plastic bags and toss a few extra into your luggage for anything that might need to be replaced.

▶ If you're going to be traveling by plane, pack a piece of night wear, change of underwear, toothbrush, paste, etc., in a carry-on, and make sure you're wearing something you can wear the next day, especially if you're on a business trip.

▶ Unless absolutely necessary, don't pack clothing that is prone to wrinkling, such as linen. Stick to clothes that fold easily and don't require ironing. If you're packing items that wrinkle easily, don't assume that a hotel will have an iron available. Call ahead to check or pack a travel iron.

▶ Wrapping wrinkle-prone materials in tissue paper or putting them in plastic bags inside a garment bag can help reduce wrinkles.

▶ Make sure that your bags are not too heavy for you to carry. Even if you intend to rely on porters and skycaps to carry your bags, you may end up having to carry them at some time.

▶ If you're planning to fly, make sure your carry-on bag conforms with airline regulations; otherwise, you will be forced to send it in the cargo compartment. Call the airline for regulations if you are unsure whether your bag will fit in the overhead compartment or underneath the seat.

Insurance Concerns

Many people assume that their insurance policies will protect them during a trip, but this isn't always the case. Medicare, for example, does not provide payment for hospitals or medical services outside the U.S. Make sure that your insurance covers you and your family while traveling by asking your insurance agent the following questions:

▶ Do I need additional life or car insurance for traveling abroad?

▶ Does my health insurance policy cover me in another state or overseas?

▶ How am I protected against baggage loss and/or cancellation of the trip?

▶ Is my car insurance adequate for an extensive road trip? What happens if my car breaks down?

▶ How does my car insurance policy cover me when I am renting a car?

Making Reservations

▶ Many hotel and motel chains have 800 telephone numbers you can use to call ahead and find out about rates, accommodations, facilities, availability, and specials. Use these if you're unsure about where to stay.

▶ Don't be afraid to ask for the price of a hotel room when you make a reservation. Many hotels have three room categories: economy, standard, and luxury. An economy room may provide all the comfort and amenities that you need.

▶ Make sure you understand the total cost of a room. The "European plan" in Europe usually includes breakfast; it does not include any meals in most U.S. hotels. "American plan" includes the room and three meals, usually with limited selections. "Modified American plan" usually includes two meals—breakfast and dinner.

▶ A confirmed hotel reservation is not the same as a guaranteed reservation. Typically, the hotel is not obligated to provide you with a room unless you arrive by a certain time with a confirmed reservation. Usually you must provide a credit card number or a deposit for a guaranteed reservation, and you will be charged if you do not use the reservation.

▶ Call well in advance to make airline reservations; not only will you have a better chance of traveling when you want to, you'll save money. Nearly all airlines offer discounts for advance reservations. You must pay for the tickets, however, when you make the reservation, and most discount reservations have penalties if you try to switch the time.

▶ A confirmed seat on an airplane does not obligate the airline to give you a seat. Most airlines overbook flights. Usually the airline will ask for volunteers to give up their seats in exchange for flight coupons or future discounts. If not enough people give up their seats, anyone can be bumped from the flight. Usually, the airline is obligated to provide compensation to someone who is bumped if they arrived before the check-in deadline.

▶ Make sure you know what happens if you decide to switch flights or change your schedule for a train trip.

▶ Once you receive a ticket or a hotel confirmation, check to make sure that all dates and times correspond with your schedule. Don't assume it is accurate; people taking reservations can and do make mistakes once in a while.

▶ Travel agents are paid by the airlines and hotels; there is no extra charge to you for this service. Ask friends and relatives for recommendations of good travel agents.

▶ If an agent seems rushed or doesn't want to answer your questions, find another agent. Good travel agents care about your satisfaction because they want to get repeat business.

WHEN YOU'RE AWAY FROM HOME

Safety Issues While Traveling

▶ Avoid carrying extra cash; use credit cards or traveler's checks.

▶ Don't carry your wallet in your hip pocket or coat pocket, where they are particularly vulnerable to theft. Women should carry shoulder bags and hold the strap; men should carry their wallets in a front pants pocket or wear a money belt.

▶ Keep your car doors locked at all times and keep the windows up. In hot weather, open the window only a crack, not enough for someone to put an arm into the car. Put your purse or wallet under the seat or in the trunk; it shouldn't be displayed prominently where someone could see it.

▶ Study traffic routes ahead of time and map out where you are going.

▶ Park in well-lighted areas, and carry your keys in your hand when returning to your car.

▶ If you don't know much about the area you're driving in, buy gas from stations with attendants, rather than self-service stations.

▶ Don't get out of your car if another car tries to block you or someone bumps your car. Honk your horn to get attention. If necessary, indicate to another driver that he or she can follow you to a police station.

► Avoid dangerous areas. If you don't know much about the area, ask at the front desk of your hotel about areas you might need to avoid whether walking or driving.

► Never travel alone after dark in unfamiliar areas.

► Be on the alert. If you look like a tourist lost in a fog, you're apt to be targeted by thieves.

► Don't take valuables with you; if you must, store them in a hotel safe.

► Always keep your hotel room door locked and use all locks when inside the room. Make sure anv hotel employee who wants to enter your room is wearing a uniform; ask for identification or call the front desk if you are suspicious about an employee.

► Be cautious if you are approached by a stranger, either in your hotel or on the street. If you are suspicious, walk away and look around for other people.

► Be careful with street peddlers.

WHAT-TO-TAKE CHECKLIST

Make sure a relative or friend has your complete itinerary and be sure to pack the following:

► Pack clothes appropriate for your destination. Check ahead for weather conditions; don't assume that the weather will be what it was the last time you visited.

► Renew all prescriptions and take them with you, along with an extra pair of eyeglasses or your eyeglass prescription; do not pack medications in luggage that could be lost.

► Always take comfortable shoes; you never know when you may have to be walking for a long time, including at the airport.

► Bring your own essential toiletries— toothpaste, toothbrush, floss, shampoo, deodorant or antiperspirant, cosmetics, sunscreen, shaver or razor, shaving cream, and soap. Add whatever else you require for your personal needs, such as cleaning solution for dentures or contact lenses. If you're a first-time traveler, make out a list ahead of time so you don't forget any items. If you travel

frequently for business purposes, buy extra items and keep them in your carry-on bag to avoid packing and unpacking them every time.

► Don't forget tickets, reservation slips, confirmations, itinerary, and directions to destinations.

► Bring along credit cards and driver's license.

► A traveling alarm clock, particularly if you are changing time zones or will need to make appointments, is a very good idea. Don't rely on a hotel clock or desk service to wake you up.

▶ If you're staying in a hotel or motel, check for the fire escape when you arrive. Instructions for emergencies are posted on the backs of most doors. Read them and make sure you know the location of the quickest exit.

Coping with Lost Luggage

There are three things that can go wrong with your baggage on a trip—it can be delayed, damaged, or lost. Regulations require certain obligations of both domestic and international carriers:

▶ Domestic carriers are not obligated to pay more than $1,250 for damage or loss of luggage. If your luggage and packed items are more valuable, you may want to consider buying additional insurance.

▶ International carriers, under the Warsaw Convention, are obligated to pay a certain amount per pound for lost or damaged luggage.

▶ If your bags are damaged, the carrier will usually pay for repairs or negotiate a settlement if the luggage cannot be repaired.

▶ If your luggage is delayed, don't assume it is lost. Report to the airline at once if your bags are not delivered to the proper baggage conveyor. They may have appeared at the airport earlier, especially if your flight was delayed, or they may be on another flight, in

which case the carrier will usually deliver them to you at no charge.

▶ Many carriers will pay reasonable expenses if your luggage is delayed for more than a day. Don't assume, however, that the airline will pay for everything you buy if your bags are delayed or lost. Keep all receipts and only buy what you absolutely need.

▶ A claim must be submitted if your bags are declared officially lost. Check with the airline to make sure you fulfill all your obligations if this happens. In negotiating a settlement, the airline will consider the depreciated value of your possessions, not the replacement costs.

TRAVELING ABROAD

Planning Ahead

▶ If you need a passport, make sure you apply well before you plan to travel. Allow several weeks for delivery of your passport. If you have a passport, make sure it is valid and will be valid throughout your trip. A passport is usually required to depart or enter the U.S. and most foreign countries.

▶ If you have a passport that you want to renew, you can apply by mail. A form to renew passports is available at many post offices and court-houses. You will need to fill in the form and send it with your old passport, new photos, and the fee to a 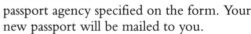 passport agency specified on the form. Your new passport will be mailed to you.

▶ Many countries require a visa, which is an official authorization stamped within the passport that permits travel within a country for a specified purpose and a limited time. To find out if you need a visa, contact the country's embassy or consulate. If you ask a travel agent, make sure he or she has the latest information on visa requirements.

▶ Make sure you have plenty of money in the form of traveler's checks; never travel with cash. Apply for traveler's checks at your bank and always record the serial number, denomination, date, and location of where they are purchased. Keep this record separate from the checks so replacements can be issued easily.

▶ If you plan to take more than $10,000 out of the U.S. with you, you will have to file a report ahead of time with the U.S. Customs Service.

▶ If international certificates of immunization are required by the country you are visiting, plan ahead to get the immunizations and be sure to take the certification of vaccination

TIPS ON TIPPING

Use the following guidelines to make tipping rules a little easier:

▶ Be sure to read the bill before you tip in a restaurant; in some restaurants, the tip is automatically included in the bill, particularly for large groups.

▶ For an easy way to calculate a 15 percent tip, figure out what 10 percent of the bill is by moving the decimal point one notch to the left (for a bill of $12.50, 10 percent would be $1.25). Then simply divide the number in half and add it to the 10 percent. (For a $12.50 bill, add one-half of $1.25—63 cents—to $1.25 and round off the number. The tip would be $2.)

If you have trouble with percentages, buy a tip card that makes it easier to figure out.

▶ If you are planning to be part of a tour, ask ahead for appropriate tipping procedures, particularly if you are traveling in foreign countries where tipping customs differ from American customs. Some travel agents will be happy to send you a suggested "tipping" list for your destination. Your tour guide may also have suggestions.

▶ In an expensive restaurant, tip the following people: server (15 percent) and captain (5 percent)—you don't need to figure this separately, just remember to tip 20 percent when the restaurant has a captain; host or maitre d' who seats you ($5 to $10); wine steward (15 percent of the wine bill—figure the meal and wine bill separately for tipping purposes); coat attendant ($1 per coat).

▶ In a hotel, tip the following people: bellboy ($1 to $2 per bag, depending on the hotel); chambermaid ($1 per day per person); door attendant ($1 for any service, such as calling a cab); pool attendant ($1 for service or 15 percent of meal bill if meals are served at the pool). You do not need to tip the concierge for recommendations or advice.

▶ For transportation: cab driver (15 percent of fare); skycap (50 cents to $1 per bag); rail porter (50 cents to $1 per bag). Bus drivers do not expect to be tipped.

▶ In a hair salon: barber or beautician (10 to 15 percent of bill); shampooer ($1); manicurist (15 percent of bill).

▶ On a cruise, tips are generally included in your bill at the end. Ask the cabin steward if you're unsure how to proceed or ask your travel agent before you go on the cruise.

with you. If you're unsure about whether immunizations are required, check with your local physician, the country's consulate, or the Centers for Disease Control in Atlanta, GA.

▶ If you plan to use credit cards, verify your available credit limit before you leave.

▶ Photocopy the page of your passport that describes you and keep it with a copy of all your credit card numbers and driver's license. If your wallet is lost overseas, this will help in replacing them.

▶ If you're traveling to any countries that may be politically unstable, check ahead with the Department of State's Citizens Emergency Center (202-647-5225) for 24-hour-a-day recordings of all current travel advisories.

▶ If you have any concerns about the country you're traveling in, register with the nearest U.S. embassy when you arrive.

▶ If you intend to drive while you're abroad, check with the country's embassy about whether you need an international driver's license.

What to Take Abroad

▶ If you are allergic to certain medications or insect bites, be sure to wear a medical alert tag.

▶ Pack an extra pair of eyeglasses and your lens prescription.

▶ If you suffer from any illness or disability, it's a good idea to take along a copy of your

medical records in case you need to see a physician.

▶ Renew all prescriptions that you need and carry them with you in their original containers. Don't pack them in luggage that could be lost. Ask your doctor for a certificate that indicates why you are carrying any prescription medications to prevent any hassles at customs.

▶ Take your camera, but leave it unloaded until you clear airport inspections. Many foreign officials insist on inspecting cameras. If your camera is new and foreign, fill out a customs form prior to departure or carry your original receipt. This will help avoid any aggravation at U.S. Customs when you reenter the country.

▶ You'll need an adaptor if you want to use electrical appliances, such as hair dryers, shavers, and curling irons.

▶ If you're unsure about the facilities where you are staying, pack along soap, washcloth, and small towel; some hotels don't offer these, particularly in shared-bath situations.

▶ A pocket calculator comes in handy when converting currencies, and a folding umbrella is essential, no matter what time of year you are traveling.

▶ Your planned activities overseas will dictate most of your wardrobe, but a lightweight raincoat, walking shoes, and sweater are essentials. It's a good idea for men to have a jacket and tie and for women to have a dress or skirt and jacket if you plan to dine in more formal restaurants.

During Your Overseas Trip

▶ When you exchange money or buy airline tickets or traveler's checks, only use authorized agents. Exchange rates vary, however, so shop around to make sure you are getting the most for your money.

▶ Notify the local police immediately if your passport, credit cards, or traveler's checks are lost. You will need to apply for a replacement passport at the nearest U.S. embassy or consulate as soon as possible. Contact the issuing company of the traveler's checks for replacements.

▶ Familiarize yourself with local laws and customs. Get some tour guides and travel books from your local library or bookstore before you leave and read about the countries

you're visiting. It goes without saying that you should not get involved with illegal drugs in any way. In addition, try to avoid offending people and be aware of local customs as to appropriate clothes, taking photographs, paying bills, etc. Remember, many countries do not have provisions for posting bail or jury trials, and any problems involving the police may lead to delays in departure.

▶ Keep all receipts for items you purchase overseas; this will avoid problems reentering the U.S.

▶ Never leave your luggage unattended in an airport, bus station, or train station.

▶ Don't expect hotels, restaurants, airlines, etc., to work the same as they do at home. You have a right to expect good service, but that doesn't mean it will be the same as it would be at a U.S. hotel or inn.

▶ If you intend to use overseas public transportation, get maps of the system when you arrive and familiarize yourself with routes before getting into a train or subway.

▶ Always remember that you are a guest in another country. Even if you don't speak the language, patience and kindness on your part will help to overcome barriers and make your trip more enjoyable.

WHAT YOU NEED TO GET A PASSPORT

If you've never had a passport, you must apply in person at a passport agency, or some post offices and courthouses. You will need the following:

▶ Proof of U.S. citizenship, such as a certified copy of a birth certificate or certificate of naturalization or citizenship

▶ Two 2 × 2-inch identical, recent, front-view photographs with a light background

▶ Proof of identity, such as a valid driver's license

▶ Passport fee

VACATIONS

TRAVELING WITH CHILDREN

▶ Select a vacation spot where children will be welcome and there will be activities they enjoy. Consider the personality of your children in making this choice. Don't assume that they will "love" a camping trip or a trip to a museum. Involve the children in your planning; they'll be much less inclined to be sullen or impatient if they help select some of your sites.

▶ If you're touring, keep your stops brief. Few children will enjoy spending more than an hour or two visiting even something they like, such as an aquarium.

▶ Don't try to cram too many activities into a day. Schedule rest periods and breaks.

▶ Make sure that any hotel has a casual dining room or nearby casual restaurants, so that you and your children aren't forced to spend time and money dining in restaurants that cater to adults interested in leisurely, expensive meals.

▶ If you're driving or traveling by train, be sure to have plenty of healthy snacks in the car and a cooler to bring along juices, skim milk, and water. If you're flying, take along a small cooler with a beverage and fruit. It may come in handy during delays or waiting at the airport.

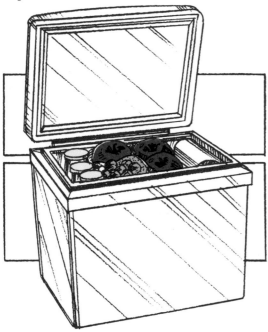

▶ If your trip is by car, limit your daily mileage to what your child can tolerate. End your driving in late afternoon, before you or your children are tired and cranky.

▶ Plan ahead for activities that will amuse your children on the road. Coloring books and portable desks are a good choice for children who like to draw. And don't expect your children to amuse themselves during the whole trip. Word games that the adults participate in can be fun and educational. Avoid taking hard or pointed objects that could become dangerous in a moving vehicle.

▶ If you have a tape deck in your car, bring some tapes the children will enjoy.

▶ If you're staying with friends or relatives who don't have children, talk to them ahead of time about the visit. Ask them about their rules for bedtime, pets, etc. Make sure your children know that they are guests in someone's house and that what is acceptable at home may not be acceptable elsewhere.

▶ Make sure your children know the address and phone number of any place at which the family is staying. Small children should have a paper with this information pinned inside their clothing, in case they are lost during the trip.

▶ Never allow small children to go into lavatories unattended or to be off on their own in strange surroundings; never leave children of any age in a hotel room alone.

▶ If you intend to fly with an infant, call the airline ahead of time to find out about regulations for carrying strollers, car seats, or other infant paraphernalia. Let the airline know that your infant is traveling with you and ask for an aisle seat. The airline may be able to seat you in the best place for a parent who will be holding an infant.

▶ Be sure to take your child's car seat to your destination if you expect to rent a car or travel with friends and relatives in a car. All 50 states require children to be in car seats, and these can be difficult and expensive to rent.

▶ If your child is not toilet trained or occasionally wets the bed, take along a rubber sheet.

▶ If your children are old enough, give them their own "spending money" for the trip. Tell them that this is their allowance for the trip and that they can use it to buy souvenirs, soft drinks, pennants, etc. This method will avoid constant discussions about spending money as well as teach your children to be responsible.

Vacationing on a Budget

▶ To save money on any trip, travel off season. You'll pay a lot less for a packaged European tour in October, rather than during the busy summer months. Wherever you go, off-season rates are likely to be cheaper.

▶ Check the travel section of the Sunday newspaper for bargains. For promotional purposes, many airlines and hotels advertise package-discount trips that can mean a lot of savings.

▶ Eat your main meal at lunch, rather than dinner, while traveling. Lunch is usually much less expensive.

▶ Stock your hotel room with sodas, juice, and alcoholic beverages purchased at local groceries, rather than using room service or machines. Keep snacks on hand, too.

▶ Avoid making telephone calls from your hotel room to avoid surcharges.

▶ Whenever possible, be flexible in your travel plans to get the best prices. Flying on Tuesdays and staying over weekends nearly always reduces the price of airline tickets purchased in advance.

▶ If you're planning to travel in your own car, make sure the car and tires are in good condition for a trip. Paying repair expenses on the road may be much more expensive than those at your local garage.

▶ If you're planning to rent a car, ask for the prices of various models, such as subcompact, compact, midsize. Don't pay for more car than you need. Inquire about discounts and rates if you keep the car over the weekend or for certain time periods. Also, check with your insurance agent to find out whether you need additional car insurance. You may be able to waive the fees for additional insurance if your policy covers you in a rental. It goes without saying that you'll save money by filling the tank before you return the car, rather than paying the higher prices for gas if the rental agency fills the tank.

▶ If you're going to a city with good public transportation, avoid the expense of renting a car and arrange your trip to take advantage of trains and buses.

▶ If you're over 62, check out discounts offered by airlines, free passes to national parks and discounts on camping fees, and restaurants that cater to senior citizens by offering lower prices at certain times.

VACATION HOMES
Buying a Vacation Home

▶ If you're considering buying a vacation home that you will convert to your primary residence when you retire, you'll want to consider climate, transportation, shopping, medical facilities, and other conditions that apply to retirement homes.

▶ Vacation homes are usually subject to more dramatic changes in value than primary residences, because they are a luxury. The value may be subject to a much sharper decline in recessionary times when people eliminate luxuries and there are fewer buyers.

▶ The best time to buy a vacation home is often during a recession, when the low supply of buyers reduces prices. Obviously the best time to sell is during general prosperity.

▶ Because the values of vacation homes react more directly to economic changes, loan qualifications are much stricter than for primary residences. Typically, a lender will expect a down payment of at least 25 percent on a second home, and interest rates may be $\frac{1}{2}$ to 1 percent higher than loans on first homes.

▶ Consider seller-financing on a vacation home. Sellers of vacation homes are less likely to need the cash than are sellers of primary residences. Often they are selling simply to reduce expenses and may be willing to finance buyers at attractive interest rates.

▶ Check out all aspects of any vacation home you are considering to avoid scams. Never buy property that you haven't personally inspected.

Tax Consequences

Most vacation homes are enjoyed by the owners themselves, not rented out. If you're interested in a vacation home for rental purposes, it is particularly important that you check with your accountant to find out the strict rules that apply to rental property and tax deductions. Vacation homes offer some advantages in tax deductions on interest and property tax expenses; any benefit from depreciation has been largely erased for most people considering a vacation property. Tax laws can change at any time, so be sure to consult an accountant for current information on tax deductions regarding housing. Generally, the following rules apply:

▶ Mortgage interest within certain limits and property taxes on a vacation or second home are deductible against other income on your federal tax return.

▶ Vacation homes offer the potential for appreciation, or an increase in the value of the property. If you're looking for appreciation, look for those in the best location, such as water-front property or property near a golf course. Remember, however, that most likely you will have to pay capital gains on the appreciation when you sell.

▶ If you live in your vacation home for less than 15 days a year and rent it out, you may be able to depreciate the property. However, any losses are subject to very strict rules because they are considered passive losses. Passive losses in real estate are usually losses created by depreciation, which is a decrease in the property value due to wear and tear. Under current tax law, any losses generated by depreciation can be deducted only against passive income, or income generated by other holdings. In other words, you cannot use losses generated by depreciation to offset income earned through salary, a business, or investments.

Time-Shares

Time-shares are interval ownership projects that allow a time-share owner to get exclusive possession of the property during an agreed time period each year. Typically, time-shares are resort-type properties. Before buying, consider the following:

▶ Time-shares make sense for people who want to lock in their future vacations to a set fee; this may include people who enjoy going to the same place at the same time every year. Remember, that when you buy a time-share, you need to make sure that you can dictate when you take vacations.

▶ Never buy a time-share in a place that you've never visited, no matter how inexpensive, or without thoroughly checking out the seller or agency involved in the sale.

▶ Time-share interest might be fee ownership that continues indefinitely, transferable by deed or inheritance, or a leasehold interest for a certain period of time, such as 50 years. At the end of the leasehold, all interest in the property reverts to the original owner. Make sure you know how your interest in the property is held and what are your rights and obligations.

▶ A time-share is not an investment. While a few very desirable developments have experienced an increase in value, most time-share resales have been for considerably less than the original sale price.

PET CARE

Peorle have various reasons for getting a pet. Pets are good company and may reduce the sense of isolation felt by many people, especially those who live alone. Taking responsibility for a pet also expands the owner's interest in the world. But like just about anything that's good for you, pets require commitment. Dogs and cats both have average 14-year life spans, and a parrot can easily outlive you. Humane societies are filled with pets whose owners didn't realize the care—and even cost—the pet would require. Food and veterinarian bills can add up; most dogs need to be exercised; and every pet requires attention, not to mention a sitter when you're out of town.

PET SELECTION GUIDELINES

If you've decided to make the commitment to a pet, keep the following in mind:

▶ Never give a young child a kitten or puppy (or any small animal) as a pet. The child may not understand that rough handling can cause the animal serious injury.

▶ Never give a pet to any child without getting parental approval.

▶ Monkeys don't make good pets. They tend to be destructive, ill-tempered, and apt to bite, because a solitary monkey is always unhappy. Simians crave the company of their own kind.

▶ Never try to raise wild animals as pets. They usually can't be tamed, their behavior is unpredictable, and it's cruel to keep a wild animal in captivity unless you have all the resources and facilities—and knowledge—necessary for its care.

▶ Don't buy a pet from any establishment that appears dirty or where the animals seem

listless. Unsanitary conditions breed unhealthy animals.

▶ Don't buy from a pet owner who is reluctant to answer your questions.

▶ Check out the reputation of an establishment you're considering. Your local veterinarian may be able to help you.

▶ Don't buy a puppy or kitten before it's 6 weeks old. The ideal age is 8 weeks.

▶ Don't buy a puppy or kitten from anyone who says that an animal under 4 months old has "had all its shots." It can't be true.

▶ Make sure that you get the necessary papers if you're buying a purebred pet.

▶ Spend time alone with the pet you're considering.

▶ If you want to get a pet from the Humane Society, ask the attendants about animals that interest you.

▶ Pet store owners are not necessarily reliable sources of information on animal nutrition or care. If you have questions about how to feed or take care of your new pet, see a veterinarian.

ALL ABOUT CATS

CHOOSING A CAT

Cats make delightful pets, even though they are very independent. Although they require far less care than dogs, ask yourself the following questions:

▶ Do you want a male or female cat? This is largely a matter of choice. Generally females are cautious, gentle, and quiet, but unless you have your cat neutered, you will have to contend with its heat cycles. Not only do female cats become very vocal, you will have to keep it away from males. Males are larger and more outgoing, and unneutered males tend to spray urine to mark their territory, roam, and are prone to fights with other cats.

▶ Do you want a long- or shorthaired cat? Long-haired cats are glamorous, but it will be someone's job to keep it that way. Long-haired cats also shed a great deal and tend to get hairballs more frequently.

▶ Do you want a purebred or mixed-breed cat? Although the difference is largely in cost, indiscriminate or inbreeding has produced cats that are not representative of the breed. If you want a purebred cat, make sure you buy it only from a reputable breeding establishment and know what you're looking for before you actually buy.

▶ Do you want a kitten or a cat? Kittens are cute, but they require more time and patience. Older cats require more socialization, but generally are easier to care for.

▶ Do you want a purebred cat? Make sure you're aware of any hereditary defects to which the breed is susceptible.

BATHING CATS

▶ Cats normally don't require bathing, but if your cat does need a bath, get a friend to assist. If you don't have help, place a small washable rug or Turkish towel over the side of the basin or tub for the cat to cling to. A cat gets panicky on a slippery surface where it can't get a foothold. Hold the cat with one hand and lather quickly with the other.

▶ A double kitchen sink is best for giving cats baths—one side for soaping, the other for rinsing. Two plastic dishpans will also work.

▶ Before bathing a cat, put a drop of mineral oil in each eye to prevent irritation from the soap.

▶ Make certain the water temperature is roughly 100°F. Warmer or cooler water will cause your cat distress and may make it difficult to handle.

▶ Wash the head, ears, and neck first. If you don't, any fleas that are on the animal will take refuge there while you clean the rest of its body. Be careful not to get shampoo in the eyes.

▶ To avoid colds, keep your cat inside for several hours after a bath.

▶ If washing your cat leaves you soaked with suds, make yourself a coverall apron by cutting holes for your head and arms in a large plastic trash bag.

▶ After bathing your cat, rinse it with water and add a little vinegar to the second rinse. Blot the fur with a towel, then let the cat finish the drying process by licking its fur.

▶ It's better to towel-dry a cat after a bath than to use a hair dryer. The noise of a hair dryer can terrify a cat.

FEEDING CATS

▶ Don't be misled into buying high-priced packaged food because it looks appetizingly red, like hamburger. Animals can't discern the difference between red and gray or brown. It's what's in the food that counts, not what it looks like.

▶ A teaspoon or so of oil mixed into your cat's food every day will make its coat glossy and stop dry-skin scratching. If the oil gives the animal diarrhea, however, withdraw the oil from the diet. If dry skin continues to be a problem, consult a veterinarian.

▶ Never offer your cat pork chop bones, chicken bones, or fish bones. These can splinter into sharp pieces and catch in your pet's throat. Make sure, too, not to leave these bones in the garbage where an enterprising pet can get at them.

▶ If moist pet food is not eaten within two hours, refrigerate it. Dry food and biscuits are the only foods that can be left out for any length of time.

▶ Never offer your cat any food that's spoiled or moldy. Food that's unsafe for humans is also unsafe for pets.

▶ If your dog steals the cat's food, put it on platforms out of the dog's reach or behind a barrier the dog can't squeeze its nose through.

▶ Do not feed dog food to a cat.

▶ If you have more than one cat, give each one its own food bowl. Separate the bowls by at least a foot at feeding time.

▶ If you're going to change your pet's diet, do it gradually. A too-sudden change may be a shock to the animal's system.

▶ Don't worry if your cat eats grass; many animals actually graze.

▶ On a hot day, be vigilant about a cat's water supply. Fill your pet's bowl with cold tap water and freshen it often.

GENERAL CARE

▶ When petting your cat, always stroke in the direction in which the fur lies. Being stroked the wrong way irritates rather than soothes your pet.

▶ Discourage your cat from leaping onto your stove, particularly if it's a smooth-top electric stove. Cats are heat-seekers by nature and could burn themselves severely by getting too near to one of the active elements.

▶ It is not unkind to keep your cat indoors, particularly if it has the companionship of another cat. Cats that are allowed to roam can get into fights with other cats, be attacked by dogs, or get hit by cars.

▶ If your cat spends time outdoors, make sure it wears a collar with an ID tag carrying your pet's name and your phone number. A cat collar should have an elastic insert so that if the collar gets caught on a branch or fence, the cat can slip its head right out of the collar and avoid choking. Attach a bell to its collar as a warning to birds.

GROOMING AND EXERCISE

▶ When your cat starts to shed hair, usually after the cold-weather months, massage its coat with your hands, then stroke the animal from head to tail with your palms. You'll have less all over the house.

▶ If you encounter matted or tangled fur when combing a long-haired cat, use your fingers, not the comb, to separate the tangles.

▶ When brushing shorthaired cats, be sure to brush between the shoulders where the cat can't reach to groom itself.

▶ Your cat's ears should be cleaned monthly. Clean only that part of the ear canal that you can see, using a cotton swab soaked in mineral oil or alcohol.

▶ Your cat's claws will be easier to trim if you press the paw to expose the nails. Use special clippers from the pet supply store—never use human nail clippers on a cat. Cut the nail well clear of the quick—the pink line you can see running through the nail.

▶ When you clip your cat's nails, don't forget the dewclaws, which are equivalent to the nails on the human thumb.

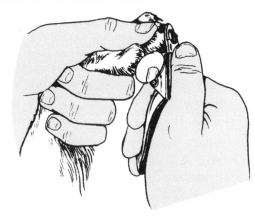

▶ Use your own comfort level as a guide to how weather is likely to affect your pet. If it's too cold or hot for you to be outdoors, your pet shouldn't be out either.

▶ Don't leave your cat in a car in hot weather, even if the windows are open. Heat builds up very quickly in a car and can cause collapse or even death.

▶ It's not necessary to buy an expensive pillow for a cat's sleeping basket. Two or three old towels will do just as well. Carpet scraps make a perfect lining for a pet's bed or basket.

HEALTH ISSUES FOR CATS

▶ Worming medications are dangerous if used incorrectly. Never worm your cat with any medication not prescribed by your vet.

▶ If a cat is too sick to clean itself, keep it brushed and rubbed down. Wipe runny eyes often.

▶ If you give your cat vegetable oil for constipation, never put the oil directly into your pet's mouth. It may trickle into the breathing tubes and lungs. Instead, mix the oil with food.

▶ Cats are prone to diabetes. If your cat is diabetic, have your vet show you how to give the required insulin injections. If you do this faithfully, diabetes will not shorten your cat's life.

▶ To give a cat a pill, hold the animal firmly on your lap or between your knees. Grasp the head on either side of the jaw so that the cat has to open its mouth. Place the pill as far back in the throat as possible. Close the cat's mouth and rub its throat gently to stimulate swallowing.

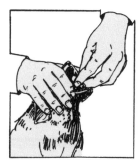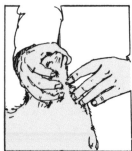

▶ If your cat has a fever, don't give aspirin without a veterinarian's recommendation. Your cat will have trouble detoxifying and excreting it.

▶ If a cat appears malnourished even though well fed, has frequent loose stools, a lackluster coat, and a bloated stomach, you should suspect worms. Consult a veterinarian.

▶ Ear mites are a common problem with cats. If you notice black, brown, or gray waxy material in the ear instead of the usual clean pink surface, the cat may have mites. You'll need to consult the vet for medicine. If you have more than one cat and one gets ear mites, chances are the others will, too.

▶ If a cat's membranous eyelids half-cover its eyes, it's usually a sign of an intestinal illness that should be treated immediately.

▶ Constant discharge from your cat's eye can be a symptom of either local infection or systemic disease that should be treated.

▶ If a kitten dies suddenly with no outward sign of illness, it probably had feline distemper. Your other cats should be vaccinated immediately.

▶ Cats keep themselves clean by licking their fur, and sometimes the hairs collect in the stomach and form hairballs. The easiest way to treat hairballs is to give the cat a preparation that will coat the stomach and combine with the hair so that it can be passed in the stool. White petroleum jelly is an excellent coating agent. Put a teaspoonful or two on the cat's mouth and paws and let it lick it off.

▶ Cats, like people, can have dental problems. A little dry food in the cat's diet helps prevent tartar buildup, but doesn't replace an annual dental checkup by the vet. If your cat will cooperate, clean its teeth once a week with a child's toothbrush or a cotton ball dipped in warm water.

▶ Cats love to play with yarn or string, but such games can be fatal. If your cat has swallowed yarn or string, give white petroleum jelly to ease the passage of the material through the system.

▶ Keep cats away from the poisonous houseplant dieffenbachia, mistletoe berries, and poinsettia.

ALL ABOUT DOGS

CHOOSING A DOG

All dogs require food, shelter, and medical care, including vaccinations. They also require leashes, grooming equipment, and will possibly incur kennel costs if you travel. Once you've made the commitment to buy a dog, consider what kind of dog is going to fit into your life most satisfactorily. Ask yourself the following questions:

▶ What size dog will fit into your home? Make sure you know the ultimate size of any puppy you are buying, because large dogs require space.

▶ Who's going to exercise the dog and take care of cleaning up after it? If your space and/or energy is limited, choose a dog that's a natural stay-at-home, not an outdoors lover.

▶ How much dog can you feed? The cost of dog food for large dogs can overstretch an already tight budget.

▶ What's the temperament of the breed? This is unrelated to size. If you have children, make sure you get a dog that does well with children.

▶ How much grooming will the dog require and who will handle it?

▶ How much do you travel? Some breeds don't mind the kennel, but others do. And costs rise with larger dogs.

▶ Do you want a male or female? Unless you plan to breed a female, it will have to be spayed, and many pet owners neuter male dogs as well.

▶ Do you want a purebred or a mutt? You'll know better what you're getting with a purebred, but the cost is much higher.

▶ Do you want a puppy or an adult? Puppies demand a great deal of time, attention, patience, and training, but they typically adjust more easily to your household than adult dogs. Before buying a puppy, try to check out its parents. The parents should be friendly and outgoing. If they're vicious or shy, the puppy will probably be the same. Don't choose the runt of the litter, even if you feel sorry for it, because runts are unlikely to grow into healthy adult dogs. Don't accept a puppy that has diarrhea. It may be a sign of parasites.

FEEDING DOGS

▶ Don't be misled into buying high-priced packaged food for dogs because it looks appetizingly red, like hamburger. Animals can't discern the difference between red and gray or brown. It's what's in the food that counts, not what it looks like.

▶ In general, "dry" dog food is more nutritious than "wet" dog food. This also applies to cat food. Any time you get a new pet, however, check with your veterinarian for dietary recommendations.

▶ A teaspoon or so of oil mixed into your dog's food every day will make its coat glossy and stop dry-skin scratching. If the oil gives the animal diarrhea, however, withdraw the oil from the diet. If dry skin continues to be a problem, consult a veterinarian.

▶ Never offer your dog pork chop bones, chicken bones, or fish bones. These can splinter into sharp pieces and catch in your pet's throat. Make sure, too, not to leave these bones in the garbage where an enterprising pet can get at them.

▶ Don't feed your dog immediately before or after exercising the animal.

▶ If you must give your dog a bone, give only marrow or knuckle bones that have first been boiled to remove fat and grease that might cause diarrhea. Take the bone away as soon as it starts to splinter.

▶ If moist pet food is not eaten within two hours, refrigerate it. Dry food and biscuits are the only foods that can be left out for any length of time.

▶ Never offer your dog moldy or spoiled food. If it's unsafe for humans, it's unsafe for dogs.

▶ If your pet dog has an outdoor water dish and always knocks it over, substitute an angel food cake pan for the dish. Put a sturdy stake through the pan's center hole and into the ground, and even a frisky dog won't be able to knock it over.

▶ Do not feed cat food to a dog; the two animals have entirely different dietary needs.

▶ If you're going to change your pet's diet, do it gradually. A too-sudden change may be a shock to the animal's system. Dogs—just like their wild ancestors—don't usually object to a monotonous diet.

▶ Don't feed a dog milk. It will probably give it diarrhea.

▶ Don't worry if your dog drinks from the toilet (and most do). Water in a flushed toilet bowl won't harm your pet in any way. But don't let a pet drink from a toilet that has a cleaner or freshener in the tank or bowl—the chemicals are toxic. Keep the lid down any time there are chemicals in the bowl.

▶ Don't worry if your dog eats grass; many animals actually graze.

▶ On a hot day, be vigilant about an animal's water supply. Fill your pet's bowl with cold tap water and freshen it often.

BATHING YOUR DOG

▶ Comb out a long-haired dog before a bath. Then you won't have to untangle wet hair.

▶ Make certain the water temperature is roughly 100°F. Warmer or cooler water will cause your pet distress and may make it difficult to handle.

▶ Wash the head, ears, and neck first. If you don't, any fleas that are on the animal will take refuge there while you clean the rest of it. Be careful not to get shampoo in the eyes.

▶ To avoid colds, keep your dog inside for several hours after a bath.

▶ When washing your dog in the bathtub, prevent clogged drains by placing a piece of nylon netting over the drain to collect hairs.

▶ If your dog smells bad but there's no time to give it a bath, rub baking soda into its coat and brush it off.

▶ If a skunk sprays your dog, it will help to wash the dog with tomato juice, then with shampoo and water.

GROOMING AND EXERCISE

▶ Groom shorthaired dogs once or twice a week with a grooming comb. Long-haired coats need bristle or wire brushes and pet combs with rounded teeth.

▶ Burrs will be easier to comb from your dog's coat if you first crush them with a pair of pliers.

▶ When your dog starts to shed hair, usually after the cold-weather months, massage its coat with your hands, then stroke the animal from head to tail with your palms. Get rid of loose hair this way and you'll have less all over the house.

▶ If it handles the noise, vacuum your dog's coat when it starts shedding in spring.

▶ Clean your dog's ears monthly. Clean only that part of the ear canal that you can see, using a cotton swab soaked in mineral oil or

alcohol. Wax protects the ear canal, so a small amount is beneficial.

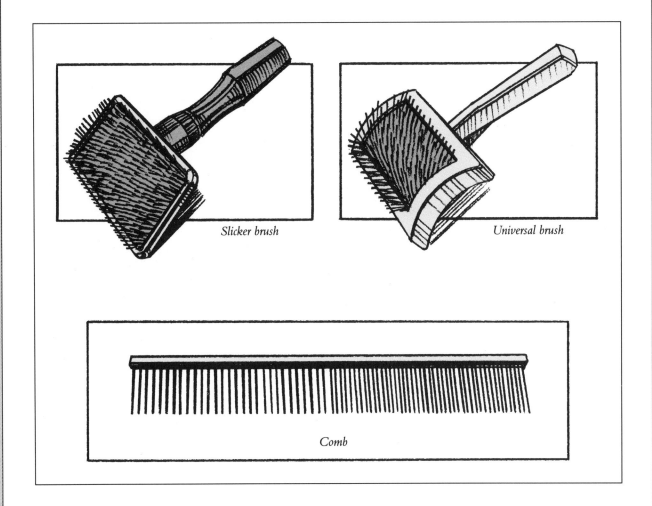

Slicker brush

Universal brush

Comb

▶ It's important to wash off your dog's feet in the winter, because it will probably pick up salt and chemicals from the street and these substances can injure its feet, especially if the pads are cracked. If the pads of your dog's feet become dry or cracked, rub a little petroleum jelly into them.

▶ If your dog has just been clipped, make sure you don't walk it in strong sun; it could get sunburned.

▶ To wipe away the rheum that gathers at the corners of your dog's eyes, use a dab of cotton dipped in a boric acid solution.

▶ If it's too cold for you outside, it's also too cold for your dog.

▶ Don't leave your dog in a car in hot weather, even if the windows are open. Heat builds up very quickly in a car and can cause collapse or even death.

▶ Remove the leash from your dog when in the car. A leash can get caught in door handles or other projections and cause injury to your pet. But put the leash on before you let the dog out of the car.

▶ In hot weather, it's best to exercise your dog early in the morning and late at night. Midday heat could be dangerous.

HEALTH ISSUES FOR DOGS

▶ Worming medications are dangerous if used incorrectly. Never worm your dog with any medication not prescribed by your vet.

▶ If you have to give a dog liquid medication and you know it's going to put up a fight, have it stand on a towel or bath mat in the tub. You'll have it in a confined space so it'll be easier to control, and any medication that gets spilled will go in the tub and not on your carpet. Pull out the dog's lower lip at the corner to make a pouch, and use a dropper or a syringe to place the medication in the pouch, a little at a time. Rub its throat to stimulate swallowing.

▶ To give a dog a pill, grasp its muzzle in one hand, then gently press the dog's lips over the upper teeth with your thumb on one side and your fingers on the other. Firm pressure will force the dog to open its mouth so that you can place the pill as far back in the mouth as possible with your free hand. Hold the dog's mouth closed and rub its throat to stimulate swallowing.

▶ If your dog won't take a pill readily, try disguising it in a piece of cream cheese, which most dogs will eat without complaint.

▶ If you need an outdoor stool sample from your dog, try not to include any soil in the sample. Dirt can contain harmless soil worms that may hamper the diagnosis.

▶ Don't worry about a young puppy's "garlic breath." This is normal and shows the presence of "good" bacteria in its mouth. The odor will disappear in a few months.

▶ Don't be alarmed if your dog twitches or jerks spasmodically when asleep. It isn't having convulsions, it's just dreaming.

▶ When walking a puppy, keep it away from the droppings of other dogs. A disease known as *parvovirus* kills 75 percent of the young dogs under 5 months of age who contract it. (Older dogs are more or less immune.) Most puppies contract it through contact with infected feces.

TRAINING YOUR PUPPY OR DOG

▶ Whenever you give a command to your dog, first establish eye contact. Eye contact tells the animal that you mean business.

▶ When disciplining an animal, never call its name and then administer a punishment. Calling its name should be reserved for positive acts.

▶ Never discipline a dog after the event. An animal cannot connect your present displeasure with a past misdemeanor.

▶ It's best to begin training a puppy at seven weeks old, but don't let the family get in on the act. Only one person should do the training, and it should be someone with patience who will also be spending a lot of time with the animal.

▶ In training a dog, use one-word commands because they're clear and easy to understand. Don't expect a dog to understand complicated language structure.

▶ If you want to keep dogs off the furniture, tuck mothballs in under the cushions.

OTHER PETS

CHOOSING A BIRD

▶ While small birds, such as parakeets and canaries, require minimal care, large birds, such as parrots, cockatoos, and cockateels, can require a great deal of care and demand a lot of affection. Make sure you know about the requirements of the bird you're considering.

▶ If you want a truly affectionate budgerigar, pick a male. They're friendlier than females.

▶ Avoid buying a canary between July and October, which is the canary's molting season. A sudden environmental change during that period may send it into shock.

▶ Before buying a parrot, be prepared for a lifetime relationship—it may live longer than you do. Never sell it to someone else because it will probably die of heartbreak if you do. Parrots become extremely attached to their owners.

▶ If you're buying a parrot, buy one born and raised in this country rather than one that's been imported—and possibly smuggled. Domestic birds are likely to be healthier, and you will know that your pet was not illegally removed from the wild.

▶ If you want a parrot whose imitative speech most closely resembles that of a human, purchase the rather drab-looking African Grey.

CARING FOR BIRDS

▶ When holding a pet bird, be very gentle. Bird bones are so fragile that even the slightest pressure on the wrong spot can cause a fracture.

▶ You won't be doing a pet bird a favor by putting it outside in its cage to enjoy fresh air. Wild birds will flutter around, attracted by the food in the cage, and your pet bird may pick up some of the parasites and diseases they carry.

▶ Never let a pet bird loose in the kitchen. It may land on a hot pan or burner. And don't let a bird loose in a room where an electric fan is operating. Many birds fly into whirling fans and damage or destroy themselves.

▶ If a pet bird breathes through its open mouth, you know it's sick. Buy a bird antibiotic at the pet store, pulverize it, and add it to your bird's drinking water. If this doesn't help, get it to the vet.

▶ If a parakeet's beak becomes soft, add a few drops of cod-liver oil to its diet.

▶ If you have a pet canary, protect it from drafts and from direct sunlight.

▶ Not every bird of the same species relishes the same type of food. For example, some parrots love spinach leaves and apple slices. Others prefer eggs, cheese, or tiny chunks of meat.

▶ It's easier for a girl or woman to train a budgerigar to speak because higher-pitched female voices are more like the budgie's than male voices.

▶ Should a budgerigar regurgitate, don't worry about it. It's normal for healthy adult birds to do it periodically, since this is the way they feed their young. The habit is programmed into them.

▶ Should your budgerigar escape from its cage and be difficult to catch, wait until dark. It can't see in the dusk as well as you can, and will make no attempt to avoid you.

CHOOSING AND CARING FOR OTHER PETS

▶ When you buy a goldfish at a pet shop and bring it home in a small plastic bag partially

filled with water, float the bag in your home aquarium for 30 minutes before releasing the fish. This helps the fish adjust to the tank's water temperature.

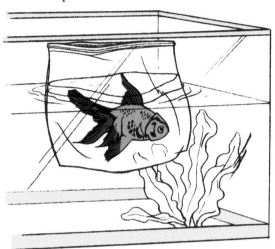

▶ If you have a pet reptile, such as a lizard or snake, and need to clean its terrarium home, have a duplicate (empty) terrarium handy in which you can place your pet while touching up its quarters. Otherwise it may escape.

▶ Handle a pet salamander or newt with wet hands. The rough texture of dry skin may injure it.

▶ If you have an adult land tortoise as a pet, you needn't confine it in an enclosure. Give it the run of your house or apartment. It will discover cozy places to sleep in and warm places to sun itself.

▶ Feed an adult land tortoise slices of ripe fruit and pieces of leafy vegetables, and provide it with a nontippable pan of water.

▶ If you keep aquatic turtles in a smartly appointed tank, feed them in another tank that you can empty with a minimum of fuss—they're very messy eaters.

▶ Be careful about moving a small animal's cage from one location to another. An animal has a strong sense of territory and may be seriously upset by relocation.

▶ Avoid sudden gestures when handling small mammals. They're easily frightened and may bite you in fear.

▶ If you have a pet rabbit (and no cat or dog), don't be afraid to let it loose in the house. It can be trained to use a litter pan filled with paper shreds. Keep an eye on it, however, to be sure it doesn't nibble on the furniture legs.

▶ Don't be surprised if a pet rabbit eats some of its own droppings. The droppings contain B vitamins necessary for the rabbit's health.

▶ Don't keep two male rabbits together in the same cage or hutch. They'll probably fight like gladiators.

▶ Never lift a rabbit by its ears. Doing so may damage the musculature around the head and make the ears floppy.

▶ When picking up a pet mouse, lift it by the root of its tail, not the tip. The skin at the tip of the tail is likely to slide right off.

▶ Make sure pet mice have a piece of unpainted hardwood to gnaw on. If they don't gnaw on something hard, their front teeth will grow so long that they'll have difficulty eating.

▶ It's best not to expose a hamster to direct sunlight for a prolonged period. If you do, it may die of heatstroke. Hamsters are nocturnal animals and prefer subdued light.

▶ If you have an exotic pet that gets sick or acts strangely, call the nearest zoo or nature center. Their trained personnel can tell you what to do.

HANDLING EMERGENCIES AND INJURIES

▶ Vomiting is nature's way of allowing your pet to get rid of an undesirable substance in the stomach, such as spoiled food. Withhold food and water for 12 hours from a pet that is vomiting, and then give your pet water, a little at a time. Consult your vet if your pet continues to vomit over a 24-hour period.

▶ Many pets get diarrhea, but the vet should be consulted if it continues more than 24 hours or if it is tinged with blood.

▶ Lethargy, loss of appetite, or change in your pet's personality are symptoms of disease, ranging from a cold to fatal illnesses. Watch your pet carefully, and be prepared to go to the vet if symptoms accelerate or continue after 24 hours.

▶ When approaching any injured animal, speak in a calm, soothing tone. Don't shout or cry out, which will only upset the animal more. Move closely to the animal without touching it and stoop down to its level. If the animal continues to growl or hiss, back away; you or someone else will have to restrain the animal.

▶ If a pet shows the signs of shock after being injured or involved in an accident, keep it warm and don't change its position too suddenly. Sudden movement can cause shock to move to the irreversible stage. Shock is an emergency condition; an animal in shock needs to be kept warm with blankets and hot water bottles and transported promptly to the veterinarian.

▶ In case of small heat burns to your pet, apply cold water or an ice pack to the affected area immediately. Never put grease or butter on a burn—it can make it worse.

PEST CONTROL

▶ Never use a flea collar at the same time as flea powder or flea sprays. This constitutes a harmful overdose.

▶ Fleas spend more time off your pets than on them. If you see evidence of fleas, vacuum weekly (especially in dark corners and crevices) and then throw out the vacuum cleaner bag. Spray commercial insecticide around the house periodically for a few months.

▶ It's particularly important to keep your cat or dog free of fleas if you have children, who can get tapeworms from swallowing infected fleas. Fleas sometimes carry tapeworm eggs in their stomachs.

▶ Check carefully for fleas when brushing or combing your pet, especially around the ears, face, and tail.

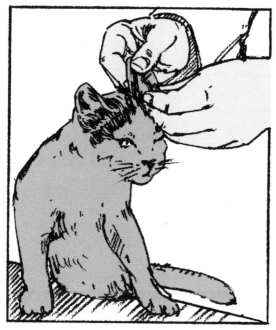

▶ Always air out a flea collar for several days before putting it on your pet; otherwise the chemicals may irritate its skin. Keep the collar away from both people and pets while it airs.

▶ Avoid applying excessive amounts of flea powder to your pet's coat and brush off all excess within 30 minutes of application. If your pet tries to lick off the flea powder it may get sick, so watch it while you're waiting to brush off the powder.

▶ A handful of naphthalene flakes in the vacuum cleaner bag will kill fleas vacuumed out of the carpet. Be sure to throw out the vacuum cleaner bag afterward.

▶ Ticks can be pulled out with a tweezers. If you try to burn them out with a match, you could burn your pet.

▶ Try not to let your cat hunt. Wild animals are often flea-infested and the fleas carry tapeworms. Empty the cat's litter pans

frequently, and wash them periodically with a disinfectant.

▶ Scatter fresh pine needles under your dog's sleeping pad to repel fleas. If your dog sleeps in a doghouse, wash it out periodically with salt water, which also repels fleas.

TRAVELING WITH PETS

▶ If you want to take your cat on a car trip, first take it for short rides; increase the time on each subsequent trip so it gets used to the car.

▶ If your pet is traveling in a carrier, put some of its favorite toys inside to make it feel more secure. Or line the traveling container with an old sweater of yours—the familiar smell will comfort the animal.

▶ Don't feed your pet for six hours before a car trip. If it has a tendency to car sickness, try to avoid giving even water for two hours before you leave home.

▶ When you travel with your pet in a car, bring along a plastic freezer container of frozen water. As you travel, the water will thaw, and your pet will have a fresh drink ready.

▶ If possible, carry water from home for your pet. The different mineral content of water in a new location could give it diarrhea.

▶ When traveling with a dog, make sure it's on a leash before you get out of the car at your destination. Otherwise it may get overexcited and jump out of the car—and, possibly, get hit by another vehicle.

▶ If you're traveling with a cat, keep the carrier firmly closed and don't release the cat until you get indoors. If the cat panics and jumps out of the car in a strange place, you'll have little chance of finding it again.

▶ Before traveling with a pet, let the animal get used to the pet carrier. Leave the carrier out where the animal can smell it, explore it, and sleep in it.

A PET-OWNER'S CHECKLIST OF HOME HEALTH CARE AND FIRST-AID SUPPLIES

☐ Adhesive tape, 1-inch and 2-inch rolls

☐ Antibacterial skin ointment, such as Bacitracin

☐ Boric acid eye wash

☐ Cotton-tipped swabs (for cleaning the ears)

☐ Gauze bandage, 1-inch and 2-inch rolls

☐ Ice bags or chemical ice pack (for use in case of burns or heat prostration)

☐ Kaopectate (for treatment of diarrhea, if recommended by veterinarian)

☐ K-Y or petroleum jelly (for treatment of hairballs)

☐ Mineral oil and eye dropper (for use at bath time)

☐ Pepto-Bismol (for treatment of vomiting, if recommended by veterinarian)

☐ Rectal thermometer (for taking temperature, if recommended by veterinarian)

☐ Plastic or nylon eye dropper or dose syringe

☐ Scissors

☐ Sterile gauze pads

☐ Styptic powder (to stop bleeding from a nail)

☐ Triangular bandage and safety pins (for holding dressings in place)

☐ Tweezers

☐ Wooden paint mixing sticks and cotton batting (for splints)

☐ Wooden rule or tongue depressor (for use with a tourniquet)

▶ If you have cats, add cat nail clippers, slicker brush, and cat comb for grooming.

▶ If you have dogs, add dog nail clippers, slicker brush, dog comb for grooming, and a nylon rope (4 to 5 feet of one-quarter or three-eighths inch) for restraint.

WHAT TO DO WHEN YOUR DOG OR CAT GIVES BIRTH

Most of the time cats and dogs give birth without any assistance. During delivery, keep an eye on the procedure and call the veterinarian immediately if any of the following problems develop:

▶ Failure to deliver within 3 hours of intermittent labor

▶ Failure to deliver within 30 minutes of continuous hard labor

▶ Heavy, bright red bleeding during labor

▶ Brown or foul-smelling discharge during labor

▶ General weakness of the mother

▶ Failure to deliver by the 65th day of pregnancy

▶ Presentation of the first water sac with no delivery after 1 hour

If the kitten or puppy is stuck in the birth canal:

1. If the kitten or puppy is stuck in the birth canal with half of its body exposed, grasp the animal with a clean towel.
2. Applying steady traction, gently pull the kitten or puppy at a slight downward angle.
3. Continue pulling gently and steadily until the animal is delivered.
4. If you are unable to remove the kitten or puppy or if the mother is not cooperative, contact the veterinarian immediately.

If the newborn is not cleaned immediately by the mother:

1. Put the baby, covered in the fetal membrane, into a clean towel.
2. Peel the membrane off its face.
3. Continue to pull the membrane from its body. The membrane will collect around the umbilical cord. Do not pull on the umbilical cord.
4. Wipe any fluid off the nostrils and mouth and rub the animal's body with a towel to stimulate breathing.
5. If there is heavy mucus in the mouth and nose, clean out what you can with a finger.
6. If the kitten or puppy is still having trouble breathing, place the animal in a towel on the palm of your hand and cradle its head.
7. Using your other hand to secure the animal, lift your hands to head level and swing down toward the floor.
8. Vigorously rub the animal again with the towel. Stop when the kitten or puppy is actively moving.
9. Tie a thread around the umbilical cord about 1 inch above the abdomen.
10. Leaving that tied portion attached to the animal, cut off the rest of the umbilical cord and fetal membrane.
11. Place the kitten or puppy with its mother, who will take care of it.
12. If she does not take care of the kittens or puppies or if any other problems develop, contact the veterinarian as soon as possible.

INDEX